Introduction
to Abstract Data
Types Using Ada

Introduction to Abstract Data Types Using Ada

Bruce Hillam

California State Polytechnic University, Pomona

PRENTICE HALL, Englewood Cliffs, New Jersey 07632

Library of Congress Cataloging-in-Publication Data

Hillam, Bruce P.
    Introduction to abstract data types using ADA / Bruce P. Hillam.
        p. cm.
    Includes bibliographical references and index.
    ISBN 0-13-045949-6
    1. Abstract data types (Computer science) 2. Ada (Computer
program language) I. Title.
QA76.9.A23H54 1994
005.7 '3—dc20   93-2187
                    CIP

Acquisitions editor: Bill Zobrist

Production editor: Irwin Zucker

Production coordinator: Linda Behrens

Supplements editor: Alice Dworkin

Cover illustration: Portion of Charles Babbage's
    difference engine; photo from the Granger Collection

Cover design: Design Solutions

Editorial assistant: Phyllis Morgan

© 1994 by Prentice-Hall, Inc.
A Paramount Communications Company
Englewoods Cliffs, New Jersey 07632

The author and publisher of this book have used their best efforts in preparing this book. These efforts include the development, research, and testing of the theories and programs to determine their effectiveness. The author and publisher make no warranty of any kind, expressed or implied, with regard to these programs or the documentation contained in this book. The author and publisher shall not be liable in any event for incidental or consequential damages in connection with, or arising out of, the furnishing, performance, or use of these programs.

Ada ia a registered trademark of the U.S. government, Ada Joint Program Office.
OpenAda is a registered trademark of Meridian Software Systems, Inc. DEC and VAX are registered trademarks of the Digital Equipment Corporation.

Printed in the United States of America

10 9 8 7 6 5 4 3 2 1

ISBN   0-13-045949-6

Prentice-Hall International (UK) Limited, London
Prentice-Hall of Australia Pty. Limited, Sydney
Prentice-Hall Canada Inc., Toronto
Prentice-Hall Hispanoamericana, S.A., Mexico
Prentice-Hall of India Private Limited, New Delhi
Prentice-Hall of Japan, Inc., Tokyo
Simon & Schuster Asia Pte. Ltd., Singapore
Editora Prentice-Hall do Brasil, Ltda., Rio de Janeiro

To my parents Bruce and Harriet, and to my wife Wai-Wah

Contents

Preface

To the Student

On the first day of class there is always a student who asks the instructor why they must take this particular class. For some classes the answer is evident. For other classes the answer is not so evident. Computer programming is the fundamental discipline of computer science. In this technological age computer programming and use are an integral part of all scientific and engineering projects. Programs intertwine basic algorithms and abstract data types, often called ADTs. There can be no continued success in programming without the mastery of these basic ADTs. This book provides a systematic study of the basic ADTs. The fundamental ADTs are fully developed as reusable Ada components. The use of abstract data types supports the object oriented development method of writing computer programs.

What is a data type? A data type is a way of representing data, commonly called a data structure, and the allowable operations defined on that structure. The material in early textbooks focused almost entirely on the data structure. Operations on the data structure were viewed as applications. The focus of this book is on both the basic data structure and the manipulation of that data structure. Everything within the computer must be represented in some fashion. This is true of everything programmed. You cannot study graphics or databases or numerical analysis without understanding their data representation. The representation of an object, no matter how elegant, is useless unless the object can be manipulated.

Consider the integer type. The representation of integers within a computer is a binary representation. The representation has several elegant features. If an integer isn't too large, it can be represented exactly. Real numbers cannot be represented exactly. The difference between any two consecutive integers is always 1. The difference between two successive floats depends on the exponent of the float. The sign of an integer can be changed by taking its complement. None of these features, except possibly the last one, makes the integer type useful. What does make integer types useful is what can be done with them. Integers can be added together, subtracted from one another, multiplied together, divided, raised to a power, mod'ed, and so on. The point is that both the integer data representation and the operations on it are important. They must be studied together. Study of the data type combines the data structure or data representation and the operations on that representation.

Programming is a creative and constructive activity. "Creative and constructive" does not mean "redundant." After mastering a concept, it should never have to be learned again. Mastery of the basic ADTs (abstract data types) provides the programmer with the tools needed to ensure future success. The foundation of programming is an understanding of the basic algorithms, a knowledge and mastery of the basic ADTs, and the ability to combine these concepts into useful programs.

Programs are "living" things. Students beginning a study of computer science often have the impression that assigned programs are completed and then forgotten. In reality, they grow, mature, and evolve, and sometimes they die. For ten years I worked for a large defense contractor doing software engineering. My primary duty was to provide software support for a group of engineers doing test analysis. This involved the maintenance and modification of a group of moderate-sized programs geared toward data reduction and data acquisition. ("Moderate sized" means 5000 to 20,000 lines of FORTRAN code.) Most of these programs had their birth ten years before the start of my employment. A friend still working at the contractor recently commented that the same basic programs are still being used. Another point must be made here. I was not the user of the programs. The users were a group of engineers, many trained in the days of the slide rule. They viewed these programs as a tool. Like all tools, the expectation was that these programs were forgiving, reliable, and consistently accurate. Programming is not the end of the process. The process continues long after the initial coding terminates.

The economics of programming and computing has undergone a radical metamorphosis. In the early days of computing, the machine was king. The computer had its own room. An ever-present army of operators, technicians, and system gurus protected the computer from its users. Programming was viewed as an art. Those with the knack often were viewed as different. Now everyone has a computer on his or her desk. Programming is now a discipline. A discipline can be taught. The exceptional software engineer has discipline, insight, and the knack, but first there is always discipline.

The prerequisite for learning the discipline of programming is the ability to think logically. The next step is knowledge of the syntax of the target programming language. In this book that language is Ada. Most programming languages explicitly provide only a handful of data types from which to build a program. Ada, as well as many other programming languages, provides the tools to develop user-defined and user-specific data types. These basic data types must be made to fit the particular application. The presentation is done in a systematic abstract manner. "Abstract" does not mean that the material cannot be understood or used, nor does it mean that the material has no pratical use. Here "abstract" means that the presentation is on a fundamental level, with no initial application in mind.

Every introductory computer science textbook attempts to support the discipline of software engineering, and this book is no exception. Most students in introductory courses get an assignment, code, and then repeatedly correct and patch the program until it minimally meets the problem specification. This undisciplined effort is not programming. It is hacking. The requirement to think first, then program, is emphasized implicitly and repeatedly. Every ADT in this book begins with a basic documentation of what it is and what it does. The ADT is implemented as a generic package. Proper instantiation of the package allows widespread application of the ADT. This use of existing packages aids productivity and reliability, two of the major goals of the software engineer. Finally, ADTs are planned with every end user in mind. The package has built-in exceptions to signal the user when something unplanned has happened. If the user wishes, the project can be designed to handle these extreme conditions.

This section opened with the question: Why study ADTs? The follow-up question, usually asked silently, is: What knowledge will be gained after successful completion of this course in ADTs? The most important accomplishment is an understanding and an exposure to the basic abstract data types that form part of the foundation of programming. The second attainment is an advance in Ada programming skill. Third, there will be a heightened level of software engineering maturity and programming discipline. Fourth, there will be a basic exposure to fundamental applications whose implementation is based on various ADTs. And finally, depending on the depth of study and which exercises were assigned and completed, students should have the beginnings of a small library of reusable software components. These components are the basic ADTs, which can be applied to solve future problems. Although computer science is rapidly changing, it is my hope that this book can serve as a reference for any serious Ada programmer.

To the Instructor

This book is the result of the need for a suitable data structures text at the California State Polytechnic University at Pomona. Recently, the instructional environment in the Computer Science Department changed from a Pascal-based environment to an Ada-based environment. The one hole in the literature was a strong Ada-based text that used basic software engineering principles to teach Ada programming concepts while teaching abstract data types. This book aims to retify that deficiency.

The data structures class at Cal Poly is a two-quarter sequence. The orientation of the course sequence is somewhere between the old CS-2 and the old CS-7 course. This book has more material than is covered in a basic CS-2 course. In many situations it could serve as the primary text of a CS-7 text. The book has several features that prepare the student for more advanced computer science classes. The stress is on developing ADTs that are both useful and applicable. Some of these features are:

1. This book emphasizes the data type, not just the data structure. The Ada generic package allows implementation of the data type. The data structure and the operations on that data structure are presented as a single entity, the data type.

2. Basic Ada programming style requires that the implementation of all ADTs be reusable generic packages that use private types. This book achieves this goal. A systematic attempt has been made to separate the study of the abstract data type from the applications of the data type. Each chapter presents one or more variations of an abstract type. Each chapter ends with applications. Most chapters end with a semicomplete case study. In all cases the stress is on data abstraction, reusability, and program application.

3. This book tries to foster good programming discipline. The typical student completes programming project in the following manner.

```
Get Assignment;
Immediately make first pass at the programming project;
repeat
```

```
       check code;
       patch code;
       correct code;
    until project is done;
```

The missing link is the initial planning stage. Inexperienced students do not plan first, then program. They program first and then they correct, and correct, and . . . . Before the start of coding for any abstract data type, a design specification is prepared. This specification describes what the particular ADT does, what objects the user must supply, a description of the operations of the ADT, and a description of the exceptional conditions that the operations may pass back to the program.

4. Every ADT is developed in four parts. The first is a design documentation that describes what the ADT does and its limitations. Second, a reusable Ada generic package specification is developed with the operations in the public part and the supporting data structures in the private part. Third, package body implements the operations of every abstract data type described in the design documentation and specified in the package specification. Fourth, the ADT is tested and validated. The testing and validation is usually left to the student.

5. This book introduces the student to various software engineering principles. All the developed ADTs are reusable generic software components. This supports the object-oriented development philosophy of programming. Most new students believe that programs are assigned, completed, and never used again. The reality is that most large software projects exist as entities in a continuous maintenance and modification phase. The presentation of the abstract data type as a software component should dispel that notion. In addition, several applications in one chapter use ADTs developed in earlier chapters.

6. Some students have the misconception that there is just one way to do something, or that there is always a best way. Most ADTs are developed in several versions. These might include a bounded or discrete version and one or more unbounded versions. The trade-offs are discussed. The "big O" notation allows the listing of the operational and space overhead of all operations and data structures at the end of each chapter.

7. Every chapter ends with a variety of exercises and project suggestions. Many exercises complete the implementation of particular ADTs studied earlier in the chapter. At the end of the course students should have a basic collection of generic Ada ADTs available for their future use.

8. Answers to selected exercises are included. An instructor's manual and a diskette of programs, ADTs, and exercises is available to instructors. Because the ADTs are implemented as generic packages, Ada programs that test many abstract data types are included. Problems and packages have been compiled and tested on both the Meridan Open Ada and DEC VAX Ada compilers.

Murphy's law applied to technical textbooks states that "No book is error free." I will be happy to supply any user with a current list of known errors via email. I would appreciate being informed of any errors found. My email address is bphillam@csupomona.edu.

The book is organized into 18 chapters.

• In the Introduction we look at the goals of a beginning course in data types.

- In Chapter 1 we review some basic features of the the built-in Ada types. This chapter reviews arrays, array attributes, records, variant records, and exceptions. It may be skipped by students who are already familiar with this material.

- Chapter 2 provides an introduction to the access type. This chapter introduces the linear dynamic structure in the form of the linear linked list. Nonlinear dynamic structures in the form of a binary tree are also introduced. Exceptions based on access types are reviewed. The idea of a data structure and its generalization the data type are discussed. This chapter can be used as an introduction to the access type.

- In Chapter 3 we review the concept of generic packages and limited private and private types. The object-oriented development process is defined and its relationship to object-oriented programming is further explored. All ADTs in this book are developed as reusable generic packages, so it is important that this material be understood.

- In Chapter 4 we introduce "big O" notation, the concepts of time, space, and parameter overhead, and the programming concept of recursion. All of these concepts are used repeatedly throughout the book.

- Chapter 5 begins with a brief introduction of software engineering principles and goals. Reusability is discussed and then the concept of the abstract data type used in this book is fully illustrated and defined. To illustrate the ADT concept, the LIST type is developed in both a bounded and an unbounded implementation.

- In Chapter 6 we introduce several stack-based ADTs, including a bounded version implemented with a variant record type. A full case study that uses both a list and a stack data type to evaluate infix expressions is developed.

- In Chapter 7 the queue ADT and several of its variations, including the deque and the balking queue, are introduced. In this chapter we also study the priority queue implemented as a queue. The more efficient tree-based implementation is covered as a tree application in Chapter 8. The concept of a priority queue is important to the development of sparse matrices and unbounded graphs. The representation is integral to the representation of a sparse matrix, studied in Chapter 16, or unbounded graph, studied in Chapter 10. Both are developed as an interlocking grid of four priority queues. The background of this chapter is necessary to the understanding of these advanced ADTs. A case study that implements a basic discrete simulation is developed.

- In Chapter 9 we look at several types of tree ADTs. Bounded and unbounded binary search trees are fully developed. The unbounded version is developed in a balanced version. B-trees and lexicographic tries are also studied. A case study that combines the unbounded tree and the unbounded queue to build a subject index closes the chapter.

- Chapter 9 begins with an overview of basic set theory. Then both bounded and unbounded set ADTs are introduced and applied.

- In Chapter 10 we develop both the bounded and unbounded versions of the graph. A variety of applications are studied. These applications include both the breadth-first and depth-first searches, finding the shortest path, determining if two nodes are reachable, network flow, and PERT analysis. The transition graph is also introduced.

- In Chapter 11 we introduce sorting. Basic internal sorting algorithms are implemented as generic procedures. The concept of an external sort is introduced but not developed.

- In Chapter 12 ADTs that support searching are introduced. Array- and link list–based hashing are covered. Both open and closed hashing are fully developed. The chapter closes with a case study devoted to the control of the inventory at a video rental store.
- In Chapter 13 we look at dynamic strings. The string type in Ada is a static string. Strings are used as a device to study several pattern-matching schemes, including the Boyer–Moore and the Rabin–Karp method. The chapter closes with a case study that examines simple cryptographic schemes.
- In Chapter 14 we discuss rings. This ring is the only doubly linked list studied and the only circularly linked structure included in the book. The ring is used to implement arbitrary precision arithmetic operations.
- In Chapter 15 a matrix-vector ADT is developed by overloading the basic binary operators and implementing elementary matrix operations. This ADT gives Ada a simple APL language capability. The chapter includes a case study devoted to the iterative solution of a linear system of equations.
- In Chapter 16 we look at several representations of a sparse matrix or vector and then builds a basic type in the spirit of Chapter 15.
- In Chapter 17 we summarize what has been learned and outline how specialized ADTs can be developed.

Courses at this level typically contain introductory material related to sorting and searching. Chapter 11 covers the sorting of array components. The treatment stresses generality by developing generic sort procedures that will stand alone after instantiation. Searching methods stress the concept of the key-data pair. Data is accessed, inserted, updated, and deleted based on the key. Topics related to searching are included in material that is developed in the study of sets, priority queues, search trees, and hashing as well as an introduction to pattern matching.

The ADTs developed in this book have more features than might be used by any one application. There are several reasons for this. The design of ADTs stresses their use as reusable generic components applicable to a wide range of programs. One application might use few features of a particular abstract data type, while another application might use other features. More operations for an ADT translate into more exercises at the end of the chapter. And more implemented operations should increase understanding of a particular abstract data type. Nothing prevents the definition of a package of a partial subset of ADT features.

This book contains more material than can be covered in a standard semester course on data types. This allows for flexibility by instructors in both the selection of topics and the depth of coverage of any particular topic. The basic underlying assumption is that students already have a miminum Ada background. The assumed background is the equivalent of a one-semester course in Ada that covers access types, packages, exceptions, and generics. The material presented in Chapters 1 and 2 is a quick review of this material.

A minimum one-semester course in abstract data types would include an introduction to lists, stacks, queues, sorting, binary search trees, binary search tables, hash tables, sets, and graphs. The following portions of this book cover these basic abstract data types.

SECTIONS	TOPICS	ADTS DEVELOPED
1.–1.5	Review. Skip if not needed.	
2.–2.9	Access types. Skip if not needed.	

SECTIONS	TOPICS	ADTS DEVELOPED
3.1–3.4	Packages, generics, private types	Complex
4.1–4.3	"Big O," recursion	
5.1–5.6	Software engineering principles reusability, separate compilation, developing ADTs	Lists
6.1–6.4, 6.6	Stacks, eliminating recursion	Stack
6.7	Infix expressions	
7.1–7.7	Queues, balking queues, and priority queue	Queue Balking queue Priority queue
8.2–8.4, 8.7	Binary search trees, balanced trees, bounded tree representation, Applications	Binary search trees, Balanced binary tree
9.1–9.3	Sets	Set
10.1–12.3, 10.5	Graphs and digraphs, weighted digraphs, breadth first search, depth-first search, paths and shortest path, topological search, PERT	Digraph Weighted digraph
11.1, 11.3	Internal sorting, sorting linked lists	
12.1–12.6	Searching, including sequential open and closed hashing	Binary search Closed hashing open hashing

Most data types are developed in a bounded or array-based version, and a dynamic version that uses access types. When different data representations are considered, the foregoing list includes over 20 abstract data types. All, except COMPLEX, are implemented as reusable generic packages in both bounded and unbounded versions. Several case studies are developed in depth. These usually use several data types and often illustrate real-life problems. At least three should be studied in depth. Programming projects are an integral part of any course at this level. Projects of suitable diversity and difficulty must be assigned. There is enough material not covered to allow the instructor to present other topics as time permits. Topics from other chapters can be studied as time permits.

Special Features of This Book

1. This is the first Ada text that develops ADTs systematically as generic packages. These ADTs combine both the data structures and the operations on these structures. This is a basic Ada style requirement as specified in the Software Productivity Consortium's publication *Ada Quality and Style: Guidelines for Professional Programmers*.

2. All ADTs are developed systematically using an innovative pedagogical approach. Every ADT is first motivated. A formal specification presents a description of what the

ADT does, what the user must supply to the generic package, a description of each operation in the ADT, and the exceptions that the operations can export back to the application. Figures and graphic descriptions are provided to increase understanding. All ADTs are formally listed as a generic package specification that conforms to the ADT specification. Finally, some ADT operations contained in the package body are fully implemented.

3. The principles and practice of software engineering are used throughout the book. Repeatedly, the student is exposed to a discipline that says think first, plan ahead, implement, and then test. The principles of reusability are stressed. Good programming habits should be learned early. There is no need to reinvent the wheel, or the queue as the case may be, for every new project. After developing an ADT package, that ADT is used throughout the book instead of being redone on a case-by-case basis. The idea of software as a reusable component is reinforced repeatedly. The stress is on writing self-contained packages where no manipulation of the data structure outside the package is allowed. The private and limited private types are rigorously used throughout the book.

4. Basic material not normally covered in a course at this level is presented. An ADT that manipulates vectors and matrices in a natural format is fully developed. Sparse matrices and their operations are also covered. In addition, bounded, or array-based data structures, and unbounded, or link-based structures, are developed for most ADTs.

5. The concept of the "big O" is developed early. Every chapter ends with a section devoted to the time constraints and space constraints listed using the "big O" notation.

6. Each chapter ends with an extensive set of exercises. Answers to selected exercises are provided at the end of the book. A more complete list is available on an optional floppy disk. This allows students to build up a working library of basic ADTs implemented as generic Ada packages. This library is referenced repeatedly throughout the book. The library is developed in sufficient generality and students will find it useful in future course work. An instructor's manual and instructor's disk are also available. Most ADTs are included with the disk as well as all programming examples used throughout the book. Also included are several test programs that can be used to evaluate ADTs developed by students.

7. The pedagogical approach allows ADTs to be developed and implemented separately from any later application. This supports the object-oriented development process. All ADTs are used in applications. Some chapters end with a significant case study that combines several ADTs in the solution of a typical problem. These case studies illustrate proper use of the ADT concept, various ADT packages, and applications. Performance trade-offs are noted throughout the book.

8. Several appendices are included that contain information and other procedures that are used in the book but not developed.

Preparing a textbook is a team effort. I would like to thank my students in the summer 1992, fall 1992, and spring 1993 quarters for suffering through class testing of portions of this manuscript, as well as Professor Malcolm Bruce and his fall 1992 data structures class at Cypress Junior College for independent testing of the manuscript. I also want to thank my colleagues, especially Professors Chung Lee and Mandym Srinivas, for their continued encouragement. I am grateful to the reviewers—Malcolm Bruce of Cypress Junior College,

Ronald Carlisle of Oglethorpe Universisty, Dennis Falconer of the California State University at Fullerton, Bill Hightwoer of Elon College, William Kraynek of Florida International University, Peter Maher of the University of Missouri at St Louis, Brian Malloy of Clemson University, Rich Pattis of the University of Washington, Charles Petersen of Mississippi State University, and Dennis Volper of the California State University at Long Beach—for their comments, which improved and strengthened the book. I also want to thank Gerry Johnson, Alan Apt, and especially Danielle Robinson and my editor at Prentice Hall, Bill Zobrist, for their help and encouragement in getting the manuscript into publishable form, and Irwin Zucker, the production editor. Finally, and certainly not last, I want to thank my wife for her patience, tolerance, encouragement, and love.

B. P. Hillam

Introduction to Abstract Data Types Using Ada

Introduction

In the infancy of computer science, any program that worked was a good program. The problems of programming in machine language made programming more of an art than a discipline. Donald Knuth [27–29] as much as acknowledged this situation when he named his classic series of reference works *The Art of Computer Programming*. During this period—to use an old cliché—the wheel was constantly being reinvented. Certain structures, such as stacks, queues, trees, and graphs, were constantly reimplemented from the ground up. These structures were thought of as unique. The prevailing view was that every programmer needed to know these programming techniques.

Later the data representation or data structure was viewed as a basic building block in the programmer's toolbox. The programmer knew how to set up a linked list and all the tricks of manipulating the list. One group of manipulations made the linked list into a stack, another into a queue, and a third set into a sparse vector. The record structure allowed for easy creation and manipulation, but the data structure was still the basic building block.

From the late 1970s to the mid-1980s the evolving concept was that the structure and the operations needed to be studied together. Texts and reference works talked about the *abstract data type* (ADT). The study of these types did not combine the implementation of the structure and the operations on that structure. Until the advent of languages such as Ada, which support generics and object-oriented development, or languages that support object-oriented programming, there was a separation between the study of ADTs and their use. The programming environment did not support the total use of abstract data types.

Formally, a type is a data representation, called the *data structure,* along with the operations defined on that data structure. Ada has six built-in types: the integer type, the float type, the character type, the string type, the boolean type, and the enumerated type. Each has its own built-in operations. Some of these operations even have the same name. Looking at the addition operator "+" without examining the context, it cannot be determined if it is the integer addition operator or the float addition operator. The boolean binary operator "and" is a uniquely boolean operator. However, these six built-in types are insufficient for building the basic programming tools of computer science. There are many other structures with associated operations that need to be understood by every programmer.

Consider the need to mimic the behavior of a checkout line at the market. Customers go to the rear of the line and wait their turn. The next person to be served is the person at the front of the line. This behavior appears again in the implementation of a print queue. Files to be printed are put at the end of the queue. The file that has been on the queue, just a word for a line with the rule that "first come is first served," the longest is the next file printed. This "queue behavior" forms the operations on the objects that compose the queue. Examples of operations on a queue include putting items on the queue, taking items off the queue, and counting the number of items on the queue. The new *object-oriented development* philosophy now allows the programmer to build a general-purpose data type with the ability to insert specific programmer-defined objects into the type's structure. The encapsulation of the programmer-defined objects does not force rebuilding of the general-purpose queue. The operations on the new programmer-defined queue remain valid provided that they were valid to begin with. Program correctness and programmer productivity go up when this programming philosophy is applied rigorously.

Other computer languages, such as Pascal, allow the programmer to create natural data representations. These representations, the data structures, mimic the form of the objects they represent. Operations on these programmer-defined structures can occur in a random haphazard way. Wirth [51] titled a text

Algorithms + Data Structures = Programs

This definition assumes discipline by the programmer. It implies that the operations on the data structures are part of the study of algorithms. One does not study integers or strings without considering the operations on them. Splitting the study of abstract data types into a study of the data structures and the study of the associated operations on those data structures is unnatural. It is a major weakness of this definition.

The concept of an abstract data type combines a study of the data structure and the operations on that data structure. Both need to be developed and studied simultaneously. The operations on a data structure and the data structure itself cannot be separated. Wirth's definition must now be reformulated as

Algorithms + Abstract Data Types = Programs

This definition separates the representation from the problem. The previous definition made the operations on the structure part of the algorithm. The reformulation combines the structure with the operations on the structure. An algorithm to find the shortest shipping route between two cities is no longer dependent on the representation of a road map. The road map can be represented in several ways, none of which alter the basic algorithm.

Most computer languages cannot combine or encapsulate the data structure and the operations on that structure. The cornerstone of object-oriented development is this ability to encapsulate programmer-defined objects into general data types. In low-level assembly languages, the programmer must exercise total discipline as data structures are defined, built, and operated upon. The assembly language programmer can use any programming trick to redefine the structure or take any shortcut while manipulating the structure. The result can be a program that performs one function well but whose workings cannot be understood by anyone other than the original programmer. The low-level language programmer continually reinvents the wheel.

High-level languages such as Pascal allow the programmer to define specific data structures that remain fixed. The structure remains fixed for the project, but the operations can still be applied in a haphazard fashion. Nothing prevents the programmer from taking programming shortcuts any time in any way while manipulating the structure. These structures are still specific to the problem at hand. It is not possible to write very basic structures that will work for all similar programming needs. The concept of an abstract data type may be well understood but the language does not support their full implementation. Proper programming discipline is not enforced. The proper use of the abstract data type is at the mercy of the discipline of the programmer. Even then, particular applications must still be reimplemented.

Ada has four features that overcome the shortcomings mentioned above: the package, the private part, the use of generics, and separate compilation. The *package* allows the grouping of various programming units into a single entity. Programmer-defined data structures and operations on these structures can be grouped together in a package. Unfortunately, objects defined in a package can still be manipulated outside the package. To prevent this undisciplined behavior, Ada allows *private* types. Types defined in a package as private types can be declared outside the package. However, they can be manipulated only by functions and procedures contained in the package. This first step toward abstraction separates the objects of a type from the operations on those objects. This allows types to be built up, but they are still specific to each application. The concept of *generics* overcomes this shortcoming. A generic package with a private part allows a specific programmer-defined object to be embedded into a general type. This general type can be manipulated only by the operations defined in the package. The entire generic package becomes the abstract type. The embedding of the specific object or data structure into the abstract data type contained in a generic package, called *instantiation,* alleviates the need to reimplement various minor versions for each new application. The final Ada feature, *separate compilation,* allows a generic package to be added to the programmer's program library and thus become immediately accessible to any particular application.

The Ada language style guide requires that generic packages implement all abstract data types. This is not surprising. Ada was designed to support object-oriented development. In this book each abstract data type is presented as a generic package. This concept has even been accepted by compiler vendors. The Meridian Ada compiler, for example, comes with a standard group of ADTs.

The phrase "uses the principles of software engineering" has become one of the holy grails of programming and programming texts. The design, implementation, and use of reusable software components is one of these principles. As stated above, this book presents abstract data types as reusable components in the form of generic packages. Once documented, specified, implemented, and validated, these abstract data types can be assumed to be error free. This increases programmer productivity by allowing the programmer to concentrate on the details of the specific application and not the specific details of the implementation of that application.

In this book specific forms of some basic abstract data types are motivated, developed, implemented, and applied, but not all possible variations of any of the abstract data types are developed completely. The reader should concentrate on the definition of the particular type, especially the implementation of the operations on the abstract structure. Many basic algorithms of computer science are implemented using these abstract data types. These basic algorithms, and the abstract data types covered, form part of the software engineer's basic toolbox.

1

Review

In this chapter we review the basic types: the array type, the record type, and the exception type. The useful Ada concept of type attributes is also reviewed. Throughout the book it is assumed that the reader is familiar with this material. The purpose of this chapter is to review the Ada foundation needed for the study of data types. Readers with a strong background in Ada may scan the chapter. Readers with only an introductory background should review the chapter in detail. In Ada, types have specific essential qualities called *attributes,* a basic knowledge of which is assumed throughout the book. A summary of attributes is provided in Appendix A. Generalized applications use attributes.

The central idea motivating the book is that data types can be viewed at an abstract or conceptual level. Properly implemented, these abstract structures become reusable components. At this conceptual level, all nonessential details can be ignored so that the focus of attention can be the underlying idea. We begin the chapter by looking at the basic scalar types. Scalar types are the basic building blocks of abstraction. Then the composite types, such as arrays and records, are studied. The types in the first two chapters are the basic building blocks of the abstract data types to come.

1.1 BASIC TYPES

Scalar types are characterized as those that can be assigned a single value. Ada has four predefined scalar types (integer, float, character, and boolean) and one class of user-defined scalar types, the enumerated types. A type is composed of two things, the values an object can assume and the operations that can be performed on those objects. Intuitively, integers are whole numbers; floats are numbers with a decimal, or radix, point; character is a structure whose values are a single character; and boolean types have one of two possible values, true and false. Integers represent things that cannot be divided, such as the number of coins in your pocket. Floats represent things that can be divided, such as the exact amount of gasoline, expressed in liters, in the tank of an automobile. Figure 1.1.1 lists these four basic scalar types, their operations, and some of their more common attributes. These basic types are referred to as the standard types in the Ada LRM [1].

Type	Operations	Attributes
integer	+, −, *, /, ** rem, mod, abs	integer ' first integer ' last
float	+, −, *, /, ** abs	float ' digits float ' small float ' large
character		character ' pos character ' val
boolean	and, or, not, xor, and then, or else	

Figure 1.1.1 Scalar types, their operations, and their attributes.

A type's attributes are the qualities associated with that type. The integer attribute integer'first is the most negative integer that a particular Ada implementation can handle, and integer'last is the most positive integer. Seldom does integer'first equal a negative integer'last. In a computer where integers are represented as 16-bit words, integer'first might equal −32,764 and integer'last might equal 32,763. They should be treated as program constants. Integer division is the quotient without any remainder. Ada defines the division of one integer, A, by a second integer, B, as an integer that satisfies the expression

$$A = (A/B)*B + (A \text{ rem } B)$$

The mod operation must satisfy the relation

$$A = B*N + (A \text{ mod } B)$$

for some integer N. The integer operations rem and mod are equivalent for numbers of the same sign but different for numbers of opposite sign. The operation (A rem B) has the same sign as A, while (A mod B) has the same sign as B. The result has absolute value strictly less than the absolute value of B (see Figure 1.1.2).

$$
\begin{array}{llll}
5 \text{ rem } 3 = 2 & \text{because} & 5 = (5/3)*3 & + 2 \\
-5 \text{ rem } 3 = -2 & \text{because} & -5 = (-5/3)*3 & - 2 \\
5 \text{ rem } -3 = 2 & \text{because} & 5 = (5/-3)*(-3) & + 2 \\
-5 \text{ rem } -3 = -2 & \text{because} & -5 = (-5/-3)(-3) & - 2 \\
5 \text{ mod } 3 = 2 & \text{because} & 5 = 3(1) & + 2 \\
-5 \text{ mod } 3 = 1 & \text{because} & -5 = 3(-2) & + 1 \\
5 \text{ mod } -3 = -2 & \text{because} & 5 = -3(1) & - 2 \\
-5 \text{ mod } -3 = -2 & \text{because} & -5 = -3(1) & - 2 \\
\end{array}
$$

Figure 1.1.2

The unary operator "abs" returns the positive magnitude of any nonzero number. It does not require that parentheses bracket the literal; that is, abs 5 and abs (5) are the same.

The float type represents numbers with decimal points. float'large is the largest positive number handled by the particular implementation, and float'small is the smallest positive number the computer can handle. As far as the computer is concerned, there is no positive number between zero and float'small. Float'digits is the number of significant digits carried by the computer.

The exponentiation operator ** must have an integer as its second argument. The first argument may be a float or an integer. The exponentiation operator cannot handle expressions like A**N**2. Ada doesn't know if A**N**2 = (A**N)**2 or A**N**2 = A**(N**2). The user must supply the parentheses.

The character attributes are useful when manipulating characters. An example is the need, in a word processor, to decide if a letter is uppercase or lowercase, and to change the case if needed. The attribute character'pos('A') returns an integer that is the position of the character A (not the position of the lowercase character a!) in the enumerated defining set. The attribute character'val(n) returns the character located at position n in the defining character set. For example, if the variable CHAR of type character contains a capital letter in the range A..Z, the character expression

```
CHAR := character'val(32 + character'pos(CHAR))
```

changes char to its equivalent lowercase letter. This function works because the ASCII character set is organized so that the corresponding lowercase letter is located exactly 32 positions after the corresponding uppercase letter in the ASCII character set.

The boolean operators and, or, and xor are defined in Figure 1.1.3. The two operators "and then" and "or else" yield the same result as "and" and "or," respectively. The difference is that if the first argument determines the value of the expression, the second is not evaluated. Clearly, the expression "false and then P" is always false independently of the value of P. Similarly, "true or else P" is always true regardless of the value of P.

A	B	A and B	A or B	A xor B
true	true	true	true	false
true	false	false	true	true
false	true	false	true	true
false	false	false	false	false

Figure 1.1.3   Boolean operators.

Characters and booleans are specific cases of enumerated types. An enumeration is a list of identifiers or values that are specified one after another. Strictly speaking, the character type is an enumerated type because it is defined by the ASCII enumeration of the character set. The boolean type is also an enumerated type. The only values that an enumerated type can assume are just those listed. The listed values can be compared. The comparison is based on the objects' place in the list. For example,

```
type SUIT is (CLUBS, DIAMONDS, HEARTS, SPADES);
```

defines an enumerated type SUIT by listing the four values that an object of type SUIT can take. All enumerated types are defined in this way. The values that a particular enumerated type can assume are only those listed. The list says that the value CLUBS is less than the value DIAMONDS, DIAMONDS is less than HEARTS, and HEARTS is less than SPADES. Some attributes of an enumerated type are T'first, T'last, T'pred(value), and T'succ(Value), and T is the name of the enumerated type. T'first is the first item in the enumeration (SUIT'first equals CLUBS). T'last is the last item in the enumeration (SUIT'last equals SPADES). T'pred(value) is the item in the enumeration that appears before the value in the enumeration [SUIT'pred(HEARTS) equals DIAMONDS but SUIT'pred(CLUB) causes a run-time error because there is no value before CLUBS in the enumeration of the type SUIT]. Finally, T'succ(value) is the item that immediately follows value in the enumeration [SUIT'succ(HEARTS) equals SPADES but SUIT'succ(SPADES) is undefined and also causes a run-time error because there is no value after SPADES in the enumeration of the type SUIT]. The use of enumerated types increases program readability.

An enumerated type defines a new type by listing the valid objects. Ada allows types to be declared in other ways. Two methods are illustrated below.

```
type INSTRUMENT_PRECISION is digits 6;
type WHOLE_NUMBER is range integer'first..integer'last;
```

Any new type that is defined using "digits" is derived from the "float" type, but it is a new type. Ada is strongly typed. This means that expressions with mixed types are not allowed. A variable of float type cannot be added to a variable of INSTRUMENT_PRECISION type because float type and INSTRUMENT_PRECISION are distinct types. The variables of the new type INSTRUMENT_PRECISION, which all have float operations and attributes, have six significant digits. The type WHOLE_NUMBER looks like the type integer, but isn't. Variables of type integer and WHOLE_NUMBER cannot be mixed.

The general pattern for using digits and range is

```
type TYPE_NAME is digits POSITIVE_VALUE;
type TYPE_NAME is range MIN_VALUE..MAX_VALUE;
```

In summary, derived types are new types. Derived types are distinct from their parent type. They cannot be mixed with their parent types.

The following examples illustrate the three methods of declaring types discussed previously.

```
type WEEK is (MON, TUE, WED, THU, FRI, SAT, SUN);
type LINE_NUMBER is range 1..54;
type COLUMN_NUMBER is range 10..70;
type TEMPERATURE is range -476.0..5000.0;
type VELOCITY is digits 12;
type MASS is digits 4 range 0.0 .. float'large;
```

Ada also allows the declaration of a subtype using one of the forms

```
subtype SUBTYPE_NAME is TYPE_NAME;
subtype SUBTYPE_NAME is TYPE_NAME range MIN_VALUE..MAX_VALUE;
```

Creating a subtype does not create a new type, it merely puts restrictions, usually on the allowable range, on the parent type. Subtypes are not distinct from their parent type. Examples of subtype declarations, using the types declared previously, are

```
subtype WORK_WEEK is WEEK range MON..FRI;
subtype NEW_INTEGER is type integer;
subtype COMFORTABLE_TEMPERATURE is temperature range 65.0..80.0
```

Subtypes are so useful that the Ada package Standard has several "standard" subtypes, including

```
subtype natural is integer range 0..integer'last;
subtype positive is integer range 1..integer'last;
```

Variables of type integer and subtypes natural and positive can be mixed in any expression. However, the only values that can be assigned to natural or positive variables are values in the appropriate range for that type.

The scalar types are the enumerated type, the integer type, and the float types. If T is the name of some scalar type or subtype, the attributes T'first and T'last always exist. Other specialized attributes also exist. See the Ada LRM [1] or Appendix A for a more complete list. The relational operators =, /=, <, <=, >, and >= exist for all scalar types and return a boolean. The operator & is used to *catenate,* the Ada term for *concatenation,* strings, discussed in the next section. The operators "in" and "not in" are relational operators used with ranges.

Expressions without parentheses need to be evaluated uniformly. Since 3+4*5 can be evaluated as either (3+4)*5 = 35 or 3 + (4*5) = 23, many results are possible. The precedence of operators solves this problem. Evaluation of an expression without parentheses is left to right using the precedence in Figure 1.1.4. Operators on the same line in Figure 1.1.4 have the same precedence. Operators in a line have precedence over all operators in lines below their line. Operators with the same precedence are evaluated left to right as they appear.

```
**   abs  not
*   /  mod  not
(unary operators +  -)
&  (binary operators +  -)
=  /=  <  <=  >  >=  in  not in
and  or  xor  and then  or else
```

Figure 1.1.4 Operator precedence.

Because many of the boolean operators have the same operator precedence, care must be taken. It should be common practice to use parentheses for boolean expressions such as

A and B or C

if only for the sake of clarity.

The operators above are predefined for certain standard types. Ada allows most of these operators to be user defined, or overloaded, for user-defined types. An overloaded operator has the same names as built-in Ada operators. All operators but "/=," "in," "not in," "and then," and "or else" can be overloaded. Actually, overloading the equality operator = implicitly overloads the inequality operator /= too. In defining the overloaded operator, the operator name is listed as a string between quotes. Figure 1.1.5 illustrates how the binary addition operator and the less-than relational operator are overloaded and referenced for some type NEW_TYPE.

```
function "+"( LEFT, RIGHT : NEW_TYPE ) return NEW_TYPE is
  ANS : NEW_TYPE;
begin
  ANS := --expression to get answer
  return ANS;
end "+";

function "<"( LEFT, RIGHT : new_type ) return boolean is
  ANS : boolean;
begin
  ANS := --expression to get answer
  return ANS;
end "<";

A := A + B;
A := "+"(A,B);
A := "+"(RIGHT => B, LEFT => C);
if A < B then
```

Figure 1.1.5. Overloading operators and their use.

Type and subtypes have many uses. They allow good representation of reality. If the width of the paper is 80 columns, any value outside the range 1..80 is an error that can be caught immediately. This can be of significant help in tracing logic errors.

By creating a numeric type, a set of conversion functions is also created. If type_name is the name of a numeric type, and if expression is a valid Ada numeric expression of some other type, type_name(expression) is a value of converted value of type type_name. For example, if temperature_expression is a numeric expression of type temperature, float(temperature_expression) is a float value. Since Ada does not normally allow mixed type expressions, conversions must be done explicitly by the programmer. The programmer can overload operators that result in Ada allowing mixed expressions.

The conversion function for integer types rounds and does not truncate. Thus integer(2.0)*integer(2.3) =4 but integer(2.0*2.3) =5. Declaring variables as constants follows the pattern.

```
A                     : constant integer :=90;
PI                    : constant float := 3.14;
MAXIMUM_LINES_PER_PAGE : constant integer := 66;
```

For the numeric types only, it is possible to omit the type name. Again, use of properly named constants increases the readability and maintainability of a program.

1.2 ARRAY TYPE

An *array* is an indexed list of similar components. The individual components all share the same name and type. The index can be any discrete type, discrete type range, or enumerated type. Examples of array type declarations include

```
type HOURS is array (MON..SUN) of float;
type GRADE is array (1..33) of integer;
type SET is array ('a'..'z') of boolean;
```

Objects or variables of the array type hours might be used in computing a paycheck, an array of type GRADE might be used to store the results of a test, and an array of type SET might be used to keep track of which characters have been used in the children's game Hangman.

The array types HOURS, GRADE, and SET are all constrained array types. A constrained array type specifies the numbering of the index, the range of the index, and the type of components. All variables that are of type GRADE have 33 components, the range is between 1 and 33, and each component is an integer. Array indices must be a discrete type such as an integer range, character range, boolean, or other enumerated type. Other examples of constrained arrays are

```
N : constant := 200;
type COLOR is (RED, GREEN, BLUE);
type LINE_NUMBER is range 1..60;
type COLUMN_NUMBER is range 1..80;
type LINE is array (COLUMN_NUMBER) of character;
type PAGE is array (LINE_NUMBER) of LINE;
type RASTER_LINE is array (natural range 0..639) of COLOR;
type LIST is array (integer range -100..100) of integer;
type VECTOR is array (1..N) of character;
```

The discrete types LINE_NUMBER and COLUMN_NUMBER are known, so the array types LINE and PAGE are constrained type. A constrained type definition may contain a constant that is unknown until compile time, so the array type VECTOR is a constrained array type. The index type of the array types LINE, PAGE, and RASTER_LINE are specifically of type positive, so any array of type LINE, PAGE, or RASTER_LINE can be indexed by any positive value as long as it is within the index range. This positive value can be any positive, natural, or integer variable or expression. The array type PAGE is itself an array of arrays. Whenever the component type of an array is an array type, it must be a constrained array type. It is always good practice to declare the index of array types using the form

```
"discrete_type range min_value..max_value".
```

The indexed array component A(N) of an array A is accessed by setting N to be a value, variable, or expression of the index type that is within the index constraint range. If P is an array of type PAGE, P(I) is the Ith component of P, which is an array line. P(I)(J) is the Jth character on the Ith line of P.

An unconstrained array type specifies only the type of the index range; the range of the index is not fixed. The index type is an unconstrained range. formal parameters in procedures often contain unconstrained array types. The symbol <> denotes the index's unspecified limits. The general form of an unconstrained array is

```
type TYPE_NAME is array (index_type range<>) of COMPONENT_NAME;
```

Following are examples of unconstrained arrays and variables declared using an unconstrained array type.

```
type VECTOR is array (integer range <>) of float;
type MY_INDEX_TYPE is range 1..1000;
type MY_LIST_TYPE is array (MY_INDEX_TYPE <>) of integer;
type WEEK_DAY is (SUN,MON,TUE,WED,THU,FRI,SAT);
```

```
type WEEK is array (WEEK_DAY RANGE <>) of natural;
type CHARACTER_COUNT is array (character range <>) of natural;
type SET is array (integer range <>) of boolean;
V1 : VECTOR(1..10);
V2 : VECTOR( 22..31);
V3 : VECTOR(-9..10);
WORK_WEEK : WEEK(MON..FRI);
MONTH : SET(1..12);
```

Unlike a variable declared as a constrained type array, a variable declared from an unconstrained array type must have the range of its index specified at declaration. Note that at declaration, the variables V1, V2, V3, WORK_WEEK, and MONTH all have their index ranges specified. All declared arrays are constrained. Only array types can be unconstrained. The attributes of arrays are examined in the next section.

A second point to be emphasized is that all arrays declared as vectors are the same type, no matter what their range is. Thus V1, V2, and V3 are all of type VECTOR even though the ranges and the number of elements in the range are different. Values can be assigned to arrays in a variety of ways. Individual assignment

```
V1(3) := 5.0;
```

is possible. The entire array can be assigned at once in an aggregate by explicitly listing the values of each component in index order. The

```
V1 := (2.0,4.0,2.1,5.3,7.0,9.0,1.0,2.0,5.0,10.0);
```

enumeration of the values of V1 has exactly 10 components. One array can be set equal to another array,

```
V2 := V1;
```

as long as both arrays are of the same type and they have the same length. The index range may be different. The values are copied element by element: the first element to the first, the second to the second, and so on. The entire array can be set to a default value

```
WORK_WEEK := (others => 0)
```

as was done in WORK_WEEK, or a range can be set to a common value:

```
MONTH := (1..6 => true, others => false);
```

Any combination of these methods is acceptable as long as the default operator "others" appears last.

Array components can be specified using slices. A *slice* is a range of indices. The third through the eighth element of V3 is specified by V3(3. .8). Slices of array types have the same array type, so expressions like

```
V3(-2..7) := V3(0..9);
```

are valid as well as expressions like

```
V1(2..5) := V2(22..25);
```

Arrays can also be *catenated,* or adjoined together. Expressions like

```
V1 := 2.0 & V2(23..31);
V3 := V1 & V2;
V1 := V1(2..10) & V1(1);
```

are valid. The third expression is called a *circular shift.* The assignment goes element by element. The expressions above are equivalent to

```
V1(1) := 2.0;
V1(2..10) := V2(23..31);
V3(-9..0) := V1;
V3(1..10) := V2;
```

Two arrays can be compared for equality "=" and inequality "/=" if they have the same component type. Two arrays are equal if they have the same length and the corresponding components are equal. It is possible for an array V1 to equal an array V2 even though they don't have the same index range. V1 and V2 must have the same number of components. V1 and V3 can also be compared for equality if they don't have the same number of components but the answer is always false.

Two arrays can be compared for <, <=, >, and >= if the component types are discrete types (integers or enumerated types). Suppose that

```
MINE, YOURS : MY_LIST_TYPE(1..10);
```

so that MINE and YOURS are two variables whose components happen to be integers; then the expression

```
if MINE < YOURS then .......
```

is well defined. Comparison goes on element by element. If the first elements of MINE and YOURS satisfy the relation, the result is true. If the first elements are not equal and don't satisfy the logical operator, the result is false. If the first elements are equal, the test goes on to the second element. The comparison is modeled after the lexicographic ordering in a dictionary.

The type string is defined in the LRM in the Ada package Standard as an unconstrained array of characters with positive range. That is,

```
type string is array (positive range <>) of character;
```

Since any variable of type string has discrete components (character is an enumerated type), the rules of arrays apply. All array assignment operations, slices, and comparisons work for string types. In fact, thinking of string types is an excellent memory device for remembering what operations can be performed on arrays.

Consider an array of boolean defined as

```
type BOOLEAN_ARRAY is array (integer range <>) of boolean;
```

and suppose that A and B are two variables of type BOOLEAN_ARRAY with the same number of components. The boolean array expressions "not A," "A and B," "A or B," and "A xor

B" are defined. The result is an array of BOOLEAN_TYPE with the same number of components and with each boolean operation being done on a component-by-component basis.

The arrays considered so far have been single-dimensioned arrays because they have only one index. Arrays with more than one index are called multidimensional arrays. Multidimensional arrays can be either constrained or unconstrained. Since both the index range and the component type are specified, the following type declarations specify constrained arrays.

```
type SCHOOL is (CAL_POLY, UCLA, CALTECH, MIT, HARVARD);
type SPORT is (FOOTBALL, BASEBALL, TRACK, DONKEY_KONG);
type TEAM_SPORT is array (SCHOOL, SPORT) of boolean;
type TABLE_ARRAY is array (integer range 1..10,
                           integer range 1..10) of float;
type X_RAY_DOSE is array (integer range 1..3) of float;
type GRAD is array (positive range 1..100,
                    positive range 100..300,
                    positive range 1..250) of float;
```

The following multidimensional arrays have their components specified but not the exact ranges of the indices; thus the array type declarations are unconstrained.

```
type MATRIX is array (integer range < >,
                      integer range <>) of integer;
type TEAM_PLAYER_ARRAY is array (SCHOOL range< >,
                                 integer range <>) of float;
type DATA_ARRAY is array (natural range < >,
                          positive range < >,
                          integer range <> ) of boolean;
```

Note in both cases above that all the array indices were of discrete type, but some array declarations defined types where the indices were not of the same type. The indices of multidimensional arrays do not need to be the same type.

All operations except assignment on multidimensional arrays must be done on a component-by-component basis unless the programmer has overloaded the particular binary operator. Boolean operations on multidimensional arrays are not defined. Ada stores two-dimensional arrays in row major form (i.e., row by row). A two-dimensional array is implemented as a one-dimensional array of rows. This fact is important when initializing arrays and when using specialized subroutine libraries written in other languages, such as Fortran, but calling them from inside Ada routines. Suppose that

```
M1 : MATRIX (1..3, -2..3);
```

then initializing M1 with an aggregate can be done in any of the following four basic ways:

```
M1 := ( (0, 0, 0, 0, 0, 0),
        (0, 0, 0, 0, 0, 0),
        (0, 0, 0, 0, 0, 0));

M1 := ( 1 => (0, 0, 0, 0, 0, 0),
        2 => (0, 0, 0, 0, 0, 0),
        3 => (0, 0, 0, 0, 0, 0));

M1 := ( (others => 0),
```

```
                    (others => 0),
                    (others => 0) );

        M1 := ( others => (others => 0));
```

Note that in each case the array is initialized row by row. The methods can be mixed and matched. If the first and third rows must be initialized to 0, then

```
        M1 := ( 2 => (1, 2, 3, 4, 5, 6),
                others => (0, 0, 0, 0, 0, 0));
```

There are some picky details that occasionally trip up new Ada programmers, including the anonymous type. The variable declarations

```
        A : array (integer range 1..10) of integer;
        B : array (integer range 1..10) of integer;
```

are interpreted by Ada as

```
        type TYPE_1 is array (integer range 1..10) of integer;
        type TYPE_2 is array (integer range 1..10) of integer;
        A : TYPE_1;
        B : TYPE_2;
```

It is possible to make the assignment

```
        A(1) := B(1);
```

but the assignment statement

```
        A := B;
```

raises a compile error. Ada considers A and B to be variables of different types that cannot be mixed.

1.3 ARRAY ABSTRACTION THROUGH ATTRIBUTES

Just as the basic types have attributes, which were listed in Figure 1.1.1, arrays have attributes. Any declared array variable as well as any constrained array type have the same attributes. The four array attributes are T'first, T'last, T'range, and T'length, where T is either the name of an array object or the name of a constrained array type. Consider the declaration sequence

```
        type VECTOR is array (integer range <>) of integer;
        type HOURS is array (Mon..Fri ) of float;
        A    : VECTOR(2..10);
        B    : VECTOR(-3..5);
        C, D : VECTOR(1..20);
        MIKE : HOURS;
```

Then the array attributes of A, C, and the constrained array type HOURS are

```
    A'first = 2          C'first = 1             HOURS'first = Mon
```

```
A'last = 10            C'last = 20            HOURS'last = Fri
A'range = 2..10        C'range = 1..20        HOURS 'range = Mon..Fri
A'length = 9           C'length = 20          HOURS'length = 5
```

Don't underestimate the importance of array attributes. The attributes of any array are always available and they are passed to procedures and functions along with the value of the array components. Consider the array declaration

```
type VECTOR is array (positive range <>) of integer;
V : VECTOR (1..10);
```

There are three different procedures listed in Figure 1.3.1 to sum up the components of a vector. The first version works only for the particular vector V above. The second and third versions work for any object of type VECTOR, but the third version has two fewer parameters because of its use of array attributes. All three will function properly for the vector V defined above, but only SUM_VECTOR_2 and SUM_VECTOR_3 will return the sum of the components on any properly defined array of type VECTOR.

```
function SUM_VECTOR_1 (V : VECTOR) return integer is
  SUM : integer := 0;
begin
  for INDEX IN positive range 1..10 loop
    Sum := Sum + V (INDEX);
  end loop;
  return SUM;
end SUM_VECTOR_1;


   function SUM_VECTOR_2 (V : VECTOR;
                             FIRST, LAST : positive) return integer is
     SUM : integer := 0;
begin
  for INDEX in FIRST..LAST loop
    SUM := SUM + V (INDEX);
  end loop;
  return SUM;
end SUM_VECTOR_2


function SUM_VECTOR_3 (V : VECTOR) return integer is
  SUM : integer := 0;
begin
  for INDEX in V'range loop
    SUM := SUM + V (INDEX);
  end loop;
  return SUM;
end SUM_VECTOR_3;
```

Figure 1.3.1 Summing an unconstrained array with and without attributes.

By using attributes, a very general procedure capable of working on many vectors has been written. The last version of SUM_VECTOR listed in Figure 1.3.1 returns the correct answer regardless of what the parameter V's index range is. The third version of SUM_

VECTOR correctly handles slices of variables of type VECTOR. Consider SUM_VEC-TOR(V(2..6)). The slice V(2..6) is of type VECTOR, so the attributes of the slice are defined and passed to the function SUM_VECTOR. Whenever possible, attributes should be used. Proper use of attributes yields more general program code that is usable in a wider variety of applications.

Consider the problem of adding two matrices where

```
type MATRIX is array (integer range <>, integer range <>) of float;
```

Each index in the type MATRIX has it own attributes. If A is of type matrix, the ith index counting from the left has four attributes: A'first(i), A'last(i), A'range(i), and A'length(i), where A is an appropriate array variable. By convention, matrices are added element by element. Two matrices cannot be added together unless they have the same row and column index. Nothing in the definition of the type MATRIX requires that variables of type MATRIX satisfy this requirement. If two arrays of type MATRIX are properly defined, a second problem is how to return a properly dimensioned and defined array. Attributes allow all of these problems to be handled elegantly. The function in Figure 1.3.2 overloads the standard addition operator as it computes the sum of two arrays of type MATRIX. If the actual parameters to the function do not have the same row index and column index, a constraint_error exception is raised. Exceptions and constraint_errors are reviewed in Section 1.5. Again, the use of attributes allows a general solution without requiring that the attributes be passed explicitly. The exercises at the end of the chapter illustrate other uses of array attributes.

```
function "+" ( LEFT, RIGHT : MATRIX ) return MATRIX is
  ANS : MATRIX (LEFT'range(1), LEFT'range(2));
begin
  If LEFT'first(1) /= RIGHT 'first(1)
    or else LEFT'length(1) /= RIGHT'length(1)
    or else LEFT'first(2) /= RIGHT 'first(2)
    or else LEFT'length(2) /= RIGHT'length(2) then
      raise constraint_error;
  else
    for ROW in LEFT'range(1) loop
      for COLUMN in LEFT'range(2) loop
        ANS(ROW, COLUMN) := LEFT(ROW, COLUMN) + RIGHT(ROW, COLUMN);
      end loop;
    end loop;
    return ANS;
  end if:
end "+";
```

Figure 1.3.2 Overloading "+" to define matrix addition.

1.4 RECORD TYPE

So far, the basic types have been reviewed and a new array structure of basic types has been defined. The basic types (integers, floats, character, string, boolean, and enumerated), together with the array type, make up the supply of building blocks used by programmers for defining data structures. There is a need to combine these basic types together. Suppose that there was a need to form a phone directory of 100 people and store it in the computer's memory for instant access. This directory would consist of three strings: one for the last name, one for the first name, and one for the telephone number. One solution, outlined in Figure 1.4.1, would be to use three arrays: LAST, FIRST, and PHONE, where

```
type NAME      is array (1..100) of string(1..15);
type LISTING   is array (1..100) of string(1..7);
LAST, FIRST    : NAME;
PHONE          : LISTING;
```

Figure 1.4.1 Array-based data structure.

To find the phone number of a particular person, the array LAST would be searched and the index of the person with that particular last name is determined. If the search is successful, the array FIRST would be checked at the given index because there might be several people with the same last name. If both those checks were successful, the proper value at the index of the array PHONE would be returned. Logically, there ought to be a way of combining all the information about a person, and this is what the record type does. The general form of the declaration is listed in Figure 1.4.2.

```
type RECORD_NAME is
  record
    FIRST_COMPONENT : FIRST_COMPONENT_TYPE;
        . . . . . . . . . . . .
    LAST_COMPONENT : LAST_COMPONENT_TYPE;
  end record;
```

Figure 1.4.2 Record type declaration pattern.

Any type, including a previously declared record, can be used as a component of a new record type definition. Since a record type is a component pype, it is possible to have an array of records. Thus the directory above could be defined as shown in Figure 1.4.3. Note that all of the information about one person has been combined into one component of the array PHONE.PHONE(I) references the Ith person. The Ith person's FIRST, LAST, and PHONE are PHONE(I).FIRST, PHONE(I).LAST, and PHONE(I).PHONE, respectively.

```
type PERSON is
  record
    LAST,
    FIRST : string(1..15);
    PHONE : string(1..7);
  end record;
type DIRECTORY is array (1..100) of PERSON;
PHONE : DIRECTORY;
```

Figure 1.4.3 Pattern for an array of records.

Every record type has two basic operations: assignment and comparison for equality. Remember, the relational operator = automatically defines the relational operator /=. The allowable operations on the subfields of a record are the same as the allowable operations on their parent types. This allows operations to be defined as needed by looking at the subcomponents of a record. For example, if

```
type PHONE_LISTING is
record
LAST,
FIRST  : string(1..15);
STREET : String(1..30);
CITY   : String(1..15);
NUMBER : string(1..7);
end record;
```

the only operators defined on PHONE_LISTING are :=, = , and /=. The relational operator less than, <, can be defined by overloading < (see Figure 1.4.4) and using the definitions of the relative operators on the fields of the record.

```
function "<" (LEFT, RIGHT : PHONE_LISTING) return boolean is
begin
  if LEFT.LAST /= RIGHT.LAST then
    return LEFT.LAST < RIGHT.LAST;
  elsif LEFT.FIRST /= RIGHT.FIRST then
    return LEFT.FIRST < RIGHT.FIRST;
  else
    return LEFT.CITY < RIGHT.CITY;
  end if
end "<";
```

Figure 1.4.4 Example of overloading "<" for a record type.

Occasionally, the record type must be specified so that it can take different forms. This type of record is called a discriminant record with a variant part. Suppose that an airline has a reservation system that allows the passenger to preorder their meal based on class ticket purchased. A variant record type for this situation might be

```
type TICKET_CLASS is (ECONOMY, REGULAR, BUSINESS, FIRST);
type FIRST_CLASS_MEAL IS (FILET_STEAK, LOBSTER, VEGETARIAN);
type BUSINESS_CLASS_MEAL is (SIRLOIN_STEAK, CHICKEN_WINE, FISH);
type REGULAR_CLASS_MEAL is (CHOPPED_STEAK, BAKED_CHICKEN, FRUIT);
type ECONOMY_CLASS_MEAL is (HAMBURGER, CHEESE_SANDWICH, HOT_DOG);
type TICKET (CLASS : TICKET_CLASS) is
  record
    NAME : string(1..30);
    AREA_CODE : string(1..3);
    PHONE : string(1..7);
    FLIGHT : FLIGHT_TYPE;
    DATE : DATE_TYPE;
    DESTINATION : CITY_TYPE;
    case CLASS is
      when ECONOMY =>
             MEAL : ECONOMY_CLASS_MEAL;
```

```
                    when REGULAR =>
                        MEAL : REGULAR_CLASS_MEAL;
                    when BUSINESS =>
                        MEAL : BUSINESS_CLASS_MEAL;
                    when FIRST =>
                        MEAL : FIRST_CLASS_MEAL;
                end case;
            end record;
```

When objects are declared, the variant part must be specified. There are two ways of doing this, one by specifying the variant and the other by making subtypes.

```
        NEXT_FIRST : TICKET(FIRST);

        subtype FIRST_TYPE is TICKET (CLASS =>FIRST);
        NEXT_FIRST : FIRST_TYPE;
```

The variable can be assigned, but the variant part must be specified:

```
    NEXT_FIRST :=(FIRST, "George W. Bush
                "202", "5551212",
                (United, 567,"Gate 5",7,pm), (Mar, 23, 89), LAX
                Lobster);
```

Note that the variant value, which is called the *discriminant,* must be listed first. One goal throughout this book is to achieve both generality and abstractness. Variant records are useful when creating tables. It is not desirable to create several different table types whose only difference is the size of the table, a type definition similar to

```
        type TABLE_TYPE is array ( positive range <> ) of ENTRY_TYPE:
        type MY_TABLE (SIZE : positive ) is
          record
          IN_USE : natural := 0;
          TABLE : TABLE_TYPE(1..SIZE);
          end record;
```

When needed, variant types will be reviewed with respect to the application. The size parameter of any variable of type MY_TABLE is referenced in the same manner as any other record field. The example above illustrates one other point about the record type. Individual record components can be initialized to a default value. The component IN_USE has a default value of 0 at declaration.

1.5 EXCEPTION

In this section we outline the Ada facilities for dealing with errors or other exceptional situations that occur during program execution. These situations are called *exceptions.* To raise an exception is to cause the normal execution of the program to halt by calling attention to the exceptional situation. Executing some action in response to the raised exception is called *handling* the exception. It is not necessary to handle an exception, but any exception not handled will cause program termination. It is possible for a program to resume normal execution, depending on the handling of the exception. The words *raise* and *exception* are reserved words.

Ada has certain predefined exceptions. Figure 1.5.1 lists some of these exceptions and how they are raised. Other commonly used packages, such as Text_io, use exceptions defined in a predefined package IO_exception. Some of these are listed in Figure 1.5.2.

Exception Name	Exception Causes
constraint_error	1. The violation of a range constraint for some type or subtype.
	2. A reference to a value outside the index of some variable of array type.
	3. A reference to a value outside the allowable range of a variant records discriminant.
	4. An attempt to reference a variable not defined for the current discriminant of a variant record.
	5. An attempt to reference any part of a record pointed to by an access variable if the access variable has a null value.
numeric_error	1. The execution of a predefined operation that cannot deliver a valid result.
program_error	1. An attempt to call a subprogram whose body has not been elaborated.
	2. An attempt to call an instantiated generic procedure whose generic package body has not been elaborated.
	3. Reaching the end of a function without finding an end statement.
storage_error	1. The storage allocated to a task is exceeded.
	2. An attempt to create storage for a record referenced by an access type using the "new" operation if there is not enough storage left to hold the record.
	3. During a subroutine call.

Figure 1.5.1 Ada predefined exceptions and their causes.

Exception Name	Exception Causes
end_error 1.	1. Attempt to read past or skip past an end-of-file marker.
data_error 1.	1. An attempt to have the procedure READ get a value where the data is not of the required type.
	2. An attempt to have the procedure GET read a sequence of characters that fails to satisfy the expected SYNTAX.

Figure 1.5.2 Exceptions declared in the package Text_io.

The constraint_error and the data_error are two of the most often occurring predefined exceptions. Data_error, for example, occurs when a decimal point or other nonnumeric character is present in a sequence that is supposed to represent an integer. An illegal index value of an array or trying to get an undefined record value are two ways of raising a constraint_error.

User-defined exceptions must first be declared. Declaring an exception is like declaring any other variable. The statements

```
LINKED_LIST_EMPTY : exception;
UNDERFLOW, OVERFLOW : exception
```

define three new exceptions. User-defined exceptions must be explicitly raised by the programmer. The optimal exception handler must appear after the last executable statement in the function, procedure, or block (more about blocks later). For example, Figure 1.5.3 lists a recursive function with an exception handler. A numeric_error could be raised if the machine is not capable of holding a large enough value. This function handles its own numeric_error exception. Here the attribute float'large, the largest positive float value, is returned. Note that execution continues although an incorrect value was returned. Only the numeric_error exception is handled. this function might raise a storage_error exception by its repeated calls to itself. This exception would have to be handled elsewhere or program termination would result.

```
function n_FACTORIAL( N : positive) return float is
begin
  if N = 1 then
    return 1.0;
  else
    return float(N) * N_FACTORIAL(N - 1);
  end if;
exception
  when numeric_error => return float'large;
end N_Factorial;
```

Figure 1.5.3 Function with built-in exception handler.

Where are exceptions handled? Raising an exception inside the body of a procedure or function causes normal execution to halt. If there is an exception handler in that function or procedure, control is transferred to the exception handler. If the specific exception is not handled in the handler or if there is no exception handler, control passes back to the line after the procedure call in the calling subroutine. Execution, which is suspended in the calling subroutine, is transferred to its exception handler, if present, or to the calling subroutines call. This process continues until either the main program is encountered and execution terminates, or an exception handler is found.

Some functions or procedures have variables declared with default values. Sometimes an exception is raised in the declaration section when attempting to initialize one of these variables. In this case, execution halts and control returns to the exception handler in the calling procedure.

Ada has a block statement that allows exceptions to be localized. The block is implemented with the form listed in Figure 1.5.4.

```
Block_label:     --optional user-defined block label
declare          --optional user-defined declarations
  --optional declarations here, scope of declarations
  --is restricted to the body of the block
begin --required
  --executable statements in block
exception --optional exception handler
  when .....
end Block_label; --if no block_label, just 'end;'
```

Figure 1.5.4 Form for defining a block.

Blocks have many uses. In some sense every function and procedure is a block. Nothing prevents blocks from being nested. One application of blocks is to build user-friendly input/output routines. Figure 1.5.5 lists an unnamed block that prompts the user for an integer until

```
with text_io;use text_io;
package INTEGER_TEXT_IO is new integer_io(integer);
use INTEGER_TEXT_IO;
I : integer;
FINISHED : boolean := false;
  .................
  put_line("Enter an integer:");
  while not FINISHED loop
    begin -- start of block;
      get(I);
      FINISHED := true;
      exception
        when data error =>
        put_line("You blew it, please try again.");
  end; --end of block
end loop;
  .............
```

Figure 1.5.5 Example of I/O routine using a block structure.

a correct value is entered. The initial prompt is output. As the loop is entered, the beginning of the block is encountered. The block acts like a single statement. After inputting a valid integer value, the "get" procedure is executed successfully, and the boolean variable FINISHED is set to true. The exception handler is skipped and the block is exited. The loop test now fails and program control passes to the next statement after the "end loop." If an improper sequence of letters was entered instead, a data_error is raised and program control passes to the exception handler without changing the value of the boolean variable FINISHED. The exception is cleared by outputting the new prompt. The end loop is encountered and the loop is again executed.

Packages are discussed in Chapter 3. Most of the packages in this book are logical groupings of data structures and the operations on these structures. By supplying exceptions in these packages, exceptional situations can be signaled to the outside user, who can handle these as needed.

EXERCISES

Section 1.1 Basic Types

1.1.1 For your particular computer installation, determine the value of the following attributes.
   a. integer'first
   b. integer'last
   c. float'digits
   d. float'small
   e. float'large
   f. boolean'first
   g. boolean'last

1.1.2 Write a function that changes all characters in 'a'..'z' to uppercase. All other characters are return unchanged.

1.1.3 Consider

```
type SUIT is (CLUBS, DIAMONDS, HEARTS, SPADES);
```

Write a function called NEXT that returns the successor of any variable of type SUIT where the successor of SPADES is defined to be CLUBS.

1.1.4 Suppose that

```
I : integer;
X : float;
```

Some languages, such as Pascal, define I+X, X+I, I*X, X*I, and so on, for any arithmetic expression involving floats and integers. Write a set of 10 overloaded arithmetic operators that would allow any arithmetic expression involving floats and integers to be defined in Ada.

Section 1.2 ARRAY Type

1.2.1 **a.** What is the difference between a constrained and an unconstrained array?
b. Write three examples of constrained array types and three examples of unconstrained arrays. our examples should use distant index type.

1.2.2 **a.** What is the difference between a constrained and an unconstrained multidimensional array?
b. Write three examples of constrained multidimensional array types and three examples of unconstrained multidimensional arrays.

Section 1.3 Array Abstraction through Attributes

1.3.1 **a.** List the array attributes of each of the constrained array types in Exercise 1.2.1b.
b. List the array attributes of each of the constrained multidimensional array types in Exercise 1.2.2b.

Exercises 1.3.2 through 1.3.5 use the following type definitions.

```
type VECTOR is array (positive range <>) of integer;
type GRID is array   (natural range<>,
                      character range <>) of integer;
```

1.3.2 Write a function that finds the largest integer in any array of type VECTOR.

1.3.3 Write a function that finds the location of the smallest integer in any array of type VECTOR.

1.3.4 Write a function that finds the smallest integer in any array of type GRID.

1.3.5 Write a procedure that returns the indices of the largest integer in any array of type GRID.

Section 1.4 Record Type

1.4.1 Write a function to find the telephone number of a person using the data structure outlined in Figure 1.4.1.

1.4.2 Write a function to find the telephone number of a person using the data structure outlined in Figure 1.4.3.

1.4.3 **a.** Convert the record in Figure 1.4.3 into a variant record where SIZE is the number of entries in the directory.
b. Write a function to find the telephone number of a person using the data structure defined in Figure 1.4.3.

1.4.4 a. Define a record type that defines a check. Include the date the check was written, the amount of the check, and to whom it was written.

   b. Suppose that during the preceding year, you write 312 checks starting with check number 537. Define a suitable array.

PROGRAMMING PROJECTS

P1.1 Write a program that balances your checking account and then prints out a summary, including the running balance. Minimum input includes the beginning balance, the check numbers of the first and last checks, and basic information for each check. See Exercise 1.4.4.

P1.2 Modify the program in Project P1.1 so that the check summary is printed out in sorted order using the name or organization that the check was payable to as the key.

P1.3 Write a program to deal cards randomly from a deck of cards. (A random number generator is supplied in Appendix C.) The program must keep track of cards already dealt. Minimum input is the number of cards to be dealt and whether or not the deck is to be reshuffled. Assume that the deck will be reshuffled automatically if there is not enough undealt cards in the deck to deal the number of requested cards.

P1.4 Write a program that reads a text file and counts how many times a letter or numeral appears in the file. The case of letters is ignored. All other characters, such as punctuation, are ignored. The output is how many times each letter or numeral appears in the file. Such programs are useful in cryptography.

P1.5 Consider

```
type COEFFICIENT_ARRAY is array (natural range <>) of float;
```

A polynomial of degree n is defined by

$$p(x) = A(n)*x**n + A(n-1) + \ldots + A(1)*x + A(0)$$

where A is an array of type COEFFICIENT_ARRAY. Write and test a program to add, subtract, multiply, and evaluate polynomials.

NOTES AND REFERENCES

There are several references that can be used for review. Volper and Katz [48] and Savitch and Petersen [43] are both excellent introductory texts. Barnes [5] is a more advanced text that assumes a moderate level of past programming experience. Some additional material is included in the appendices. The *Ada Language Reference Manual* [1], or ADA LRM, is "the" Ada reference. The third edition of Barnes includes the LRM.

2

A Basic Building Block: The Access Type

In this chapter we review the access type. Even though access types are not as familiar as integers, floats, or booleans, they are at least as important as the more familiar types. The value stored by an access type is an address. The variable literally accesses an object or value at that address. The object stored at that address can be any Ada type, including another access type.

2.1 ACCESS TYPE

At times the terminology of computer science is very precise and at times it is not so precise. Consider the declaration

```
A : integer := 5;
```

The symbol A has three meanings. The context tells what the true meaning is. The first meaning is that A is an integer variable name. The phrase "add 3 to A" is meaningless if we restrict the meaning of A to be a name. This phrase really means "add 3 to the value represented by A," so the second meaning of A is as an integer value. The expression "A := B + C;" means to add the value represented by B to the value represented by C and store this value in the location called A. In other words, the third meaning of A is a storage location called A where the value represented by the name A exists.

The access type defines a fourth meaning. An access type is a memory location that contains the address of an object. The object can be any valid Ada type. Consider the following declarations:

```
type APPLE is access integer;
type ORANGE is access character;
type PERSON is
  record
    FIRST,
    MIDDLE,
    LAST : string (1 .. 10);
  end record;
type PERSON_ACCESS is access PERSON;
```

```
MACINTOSH, GOLDEN_DELICIOUS, GRANNY_SMITH : APPLE;
VALENCIA, NAVEL : ORANGE;
P1, P2 : PERSON_ACCESS;
```

All seven variables above are addresses to objects. The three variables of APPLE type can access, or address, only integers. VALENCIA and NAVEL can only access characters. P1 and P2 can only contain the addresses of a record of type person. All uninitialized access types, including the seven above, have an initial value of null. Both *access* and *null* are reserved Ada words. An access variable with value null does not reference any address of its object type.

To initialize an access type, a memory address must be found. The Ada allocator operator now performs this function. The word *new* is also a reserved Ada word. The "new" operator causes the operating system to allocate enough memory from the system available memory, called the *heap,* to hold whatever data type is indicated and then to assign that address to the access variable. The programmer cannot address the heap directly. Consider

```
MACINTOSH := new integer;
GOLDEN_DELICIOUS := new integer'(5);
P1 := new PERSON;
P2 := new PERSON' ("Ronald    ","none       ","McDonald ");
```

MACINTOSH and P1 are now defined, but the address they reference has not been initialized. GOLDEN_DELICIOUS and P2 are defined and the addresses they point to have been initialized. Note the apostrophe. The expression

```
P1 := P2;
```

assigns to P1 the same address that P2 references. Any change to the record at that address affects both variables since both reference the same object. The assignment statement

```
GOLDEN_DELICIOUS := null;
```

is also valid. No arithmetic operations are permitted on variables defined as access type. Comparison for equality is permitted. The statement

```
if P1 = P2 then
```

is valid. The statement "if P1 /= P2 then" is not legal, but the statement "if not (P1 = P2) then" is valid. What is being compared is the address that each variable references, not the value that each references. For example, if

```
GOLDEN_DELICIOUS := new integer' (5);
    MACINTOSH := new integer' (5);
```

then the comparison in the statement

```
if GOLDEN_DELICIOUS = MACINTOSH then
```

would be false even though both addresses contain the same value. That common value is stored in two distinct locations. Finally, the comparison

```
if VALCENCIA /= MACINTOSH then
```

is illegal. It is true that both VALENCIA and MACINTOSH are access types, but the strong typing of Ada still holds. VALENCIA is of ORANGE type, and MACINTOSH is of APPLE type. An APPLE and an ORANGE cannot be compared.

It is easy to reference the objects pointed to by an access type. To assign a value to the memory addressed by an access type requires the use of ".all". The assignment expression

```
MACINTOSH.all := 5 + 2 * GOLDEN_DELICIOUS.all;
```

does not change the value of MACINTOSH, but it does alter the contents of the memory location that MACINTOSH references.

Record types that are accessed by access types have two methods of reference. Using ".all" it is possible to reference an individual record field by

```
P1.all.FIRST := "Ron
```

but the alternative representation

```
P1.FIRST := "Ron
```

is also correct. The assignment statement

```
P1.all := P2.all;
```

copies the complete record pointed to by P2 into the address referenced by P1. Clearly, the boolean expression "P1.all = p2.all" is true, but this fact does not imply that the boolean expression "P1 = P2" is also true.

Array types referenced by access types are handled in a similar manner. Consider

```
type VECTOR is array (positive range 1 .. 10) of integer;
type VECTOR_ACCESS is access VECTOR;
V1 : VECTOR_ACCESS;
```

The statement

```
V1 := new VECTOR' (others => 0);
```

would allocate memory for a vector and initialize each vector component. Individual vector components can be addressed in one of two ways. One form uses the ".all" mode: for example,

```
V1.all(3):= 7;
```

and the other form references the component directly:

```
V1(3) := 7;
```

The dereferencing is automatic and the two forms are equivalent.

The use of access types with variant records requires some care. Depending on the discriminant record's variant, varying amounts of memory would have to allocated by the "new" operator. Consider

```
type VECTOR is array (positive range <>) of integer;
type TABLE (SIZE : positive) is
  record
```

```
            IN_USE : natural := 0;
              T : VECTOR (1 . . SIZE);
           end record;
         type TABLE_ACCESS is access TABLE;
         T1 : TABLE_ACCESS;
```

The "new" operator cannot be applied directly to T1. "New" needs more information. "New" needs to know how much memory to allocate when creating a table. The statement

```
         T1 := new TABLE(20);
```

creates a TABLE of size 20. Note that there is no apostrophe. This form of variant record will be used throughout the book for reasons that will become apparent. If it is necessary to allocate memory for a variant record and to initialize it, the assignment statement

```
         T1 := new TABLE' (SIZE =>30, IN_USE = >0, T =>(others => 0));
```

suffices. The interested reader is referred to Section 4.8 of the Ada LRM.

A compiler is not required to reclaim storage when an access type is reassigned. Consider the case for T1 above when

```
              T1 := null;
```

is executed. What happens to the memory allocated to the TABLE of SIZE 20? This memory is no longer accessible. There are several methods that can be used if it is necessary to ensure that inaccessible memory is reclaimed. The pragma CONTROLLED will cause memory to be reclaimed at the end of the block, subprogram body, or task body that encloses the access type declaration (see Ada LRM Sections 4.8.10 and 13.1). An alternative is to deallocate memory explicitly by calling a procedure that is obtained by instantiation of a predefined library procedure UNCHECKED_DEALLOCATION (see Ada LRM Sections 4.8.12 and 13.10).

Many modern languages have some form of access type built into the language. In Pascal, access types are called *pointer* types. Other names, such as *references* have also been used.

2.2 PASSING BY REFERENCE

Consider the procedure SWAP below whose sole purpose is to exchange two values.

```
         procedure SWAP (A, B : in out integer) is
           TEMP : integer := A;
         begin
           A := B;
           B := TEMP;
         end SWAP;
```

Ada passes the values to the formal parameters A and B by copying their value at the invocation of the procedure, performing the procedure, and then copying the updated results back to the calling statement. If the mode had been mode in, neither of the identifiers A or B can appear on the left-hand side of the assignment operator and the updated result would not be copied back. Similarly, if the mode had been mode out, neither A nor B can appear on the right side of the assignment operator. The updated results would have been copied back, but the initial values would not have been copied in at the invocation. Ada uses this copy mechanism for all scalars and access types.

The situation is not as strict if the formal parameters in SWAP were records or arrays instead of integers. The compiler writer has the option of passing by reference instead. When an array or record is passed by reference, the address or reference (an access variable) of the array or record is copied to the procedure, not the actual array or record. This use of access types reduces system overhead. If the formal parameter is a large array, a considerable amount of system overhead and memory is used if the actual parameter is copied into the formal parameter. If the formal parameter is an access type to the array, only one access value and some attributes are copied.

Suppose that a programmer explicitly uses access types to pass an array to a function. In effect, the programmer is forcing the vector to be passed by reference. Consider the example in Figure 2.2.1.

```
type VECTOR is array (positive range < >) of integer;
type VECTOR_ACCESS is access VECTOR;

function MINIMUM_VECTOR_VALUE (V : VECTOR_ACCESS) return integer is
   MIN : integer := V (V'first);
begin
   for INDEX in V.first + 1 . . V'last loop
      if V(INDEX) < MIN then
         MIN := V (INDEX);
      end if;
   end loop;
   return MIN;
end MIN_VECTOR_VALUE;
```

Figure 2.2.1 Correctly implemented function to find the minimum value of a vector component.

However, nothing stops the undisciplined programmer from doing sneaky things. The formal function parameter of V is the mode "in." V is an access type, so no statement in the function MIN_VECTOR_VALUE can alter the value of V, but does this apply to what V accesses? The function MIN_VECTOR_VALUE_OOOPS in Figure 2.2.2 returns the correct value and then redefines the components of the vector being accessed.

```
function MINIMUM_VECTOR_VALUE_OOOPS( V : VECTOR_ACCESS) return integer is
   -- The value of V_TEMP, and whatever it references, can be changed
   V_TEMP : VECTOR_ACCESS := V;
   MIN : integer := V (V'first);
begin
   for INDEX in V'first + 1 . . V'last loop
      if V(INDEX) < MIN then
         MIN := V (INDEX);
      end if;
   end loop;
```

Figure 2.2.2 Incorrectly implemented function to find the minimum value. Continues on page 31.

```
    V_TEMP.all := (others = > MIN);
    return MIN;
  end MIN_VECTOR_VALUE_OOOPS;
```

Figure 2.2.2 Concluded.

The address of the formal parameter is not modified, but the vector it references is modified. All the Ada compilers with which the author is familiar pass arrays and records by reference. If the programmer is not careful, subtle programming errors can be introduced. It is the programmer's responsibility to be aware of this possible complication (see Ada LRM Section 6.2.1–7).

2.3 DYNAMIC STRUCTURES USING ACCESS TYPES

Data structures can be classified in several ways. One convention is by the amount of memory that a particular structure uses. This convention classifies data structures as either static or dynamic. The following types define static structures.

```
type VECTOR is array (positive range 1 . . 10) of integer;
type CAR is (FORD, DODGE, BUICK);
type CUSTOMER is
  record
    FIRST,
    LAST : string (1 . . 15);
    INVOICE_NUMBER : string(1 . . 4);
  end record;
type CUSTOMER_LINE is array (natural range 1 . . 10) of CUSTOMER;
type SERVICE_QUEUE is
  record
    NUMBER_OF_CUSTOMERS : natural := 0;
    QUEUE : CUSTOMER_LINE;
  end record;
Q1, Q2 : SERVICE_QUEUE;
V1, V2 : VECTOR;
MY_CAR : CAR;
CEO : PERSON;
I1, I2 : integer;
```

Once the variable is declared, the amount of memory that variable uses is fixed. The vectors V1 and V2 both use the same amount of memory, never more, never less. Any other object of type vector, no matter what the values of the individual components, uses the same fixed amount of memory as V1.

Static structures have their advantages and their disadvantages. Static structures are often implemented using arrays or records, so they are easy to visualize, to use, and to understand. The disadvantage is that the maximum size needed must be known in advance. Static structures cannot grow or contract in size. Suppose that a program must simulate people waiting in line to have their car serviced. The variable Q1 can be used to keep track of up to 10 customers. If there are never more than five customers in line, half the memory in the array has been wasted. If one busy day 20 customers show up, Q1 can only keep track of half the customers.

A dynamic structure is one that can grow or contract as needed. Its size is not fixed. Dynamic structures are implemented using access types. The following declaration defines a line of customers dynamically.

```
type CUSTOMER;
type SERVICE_QUEUE is access CUSTOMER;
type CUSTOMER is
  record
    FIRST,
    LAST : string (1..15);
    INVOICE_NUMBER : string (1..4);
    NEXT_CUSTOMER : SERVICE_QUEUE;
  end record;
LINE : SERVICE_QUEUE;
```

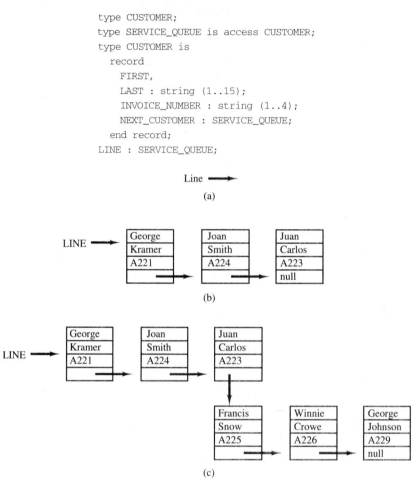

Line ──────▶

(a)

(b)

(c)

Figure 2.3.1 (a) An empty linked list. Note that LINE accesses nothing. (b)LINE with three customers waiting. (c)LINE with six customers waiting.

Consider Figure 2.3.1. Part (a) shows an empty line, part (b) shows a line with three customers, and part (c) shows a line with six customers. Each box represents an object of type customer. The access type variable LINE references, or points to, the first customer. Each customer references the customer that follows. The only thing that limits the number of customers in line is the amount of memory available at a particular installation.

The dynamic declaration above illustrates both a problem with dynamic structures and the Ada solution to that problem. Before an access type can be defined, the object that it accesses must be defined. In this case SERVICE_QUEUE cannot be defined until CUSTOMER is known. In a dynamic structure, the object accessed, CUSTOMER, also has a component of the access type; that is, NEXT_CUSTOMER is a SERVICE_QUEUE. The problem is circular. Which comes first, the CUSTOMER or the SERVICE_QUEUE? Ada solves this problem by means of the *incomplete type definition*. The first statement above,

```
type CUSTOMER;
```

signals the Ada compiler that a type called CUSTOMER will be defined later. Ada now allows the access type SERVICE_QUEUE to be defined. Once SERVICE_QUEUE is defined, the full definition of the type CUSTOMER can be listed. The component NEXT_CUSTOMER is called a *recursive access type*.

Recall that a data type is both the data structure and the operations on that structure. Throughout this book most data types will be implemented in a variety of ways. Data types will be implemented using both a static or array type–based data structure and a dynamic or access type–based data structure.

2.4 SINGLY LINKED LINEAR LIST

A list is a sequence of zero or more items where a strict linear ordering is maintained and where items can be added or removed from any position. A linear ordering is where items are lined up one after another. The items in the list can be made up of any valid Ada type. A list that contains no items is a null or empty list. The first item in a nonnull list is the head of the list. The tail of a list is itself a list whose head is the second item on the list. The tail of a nonnull list may be null.

Figure 2.4.1. Singly linked list of INTEGER_NODE.

The simplest dynamic structure is a linear linked list. Linear lists represent lines of objects. The line of customers in the preceding section was an example of a singly linked linear list. In a singly linked list, every object references the object that follows it but does not know what object references it. It follows that every object in the list, except the first, is referenced by exactly one object, and every object, except the last, references one object. The first object in any nonempty list is referenced by an access variable. The examples in the remainder of this section will manipulate a singly linked linear list of integers defined by

```
type INTEGER_NODE;
type LIST is access INTEGER_NODE;
type INTEGER_NODE is
   record
      DATA : integer;
      NEXT : LIST;
   end record;
```

A singly linked linear list of integers is illustrated in Figure 2.4.1. The concepts illustrated here apply to any singly linked list, no matter what the nodes of that list are composed of. The procedure below creates a node with a given integer and adds it to the front of the list. Figure 2.4.2 illustrates the list before and after the integer 5 is added.

```
procedure ADD_TO_FRONT (L : in out LIST; ITEM : in integer) is
begin
    L := new INTEGER_NODE' (ITEM, L);
end ADD_TO_FRONT;
```

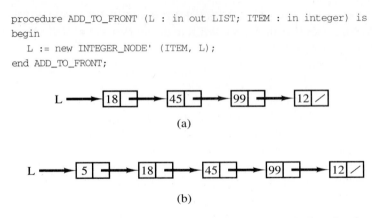

(a)

(b)

Figure 2.4.2 (a) List of four INTER_NODEs before insertion. (b) Same list after the creation of an INTEGER_NODE containing 5 is added to the front of the list.

In the procedure ADD_TO_FRONT, the head of a list L and integer are passed to the procedure. It is not necessary to know anything about the list, such as whether it is empty or how long it is, in order to add a new node. A new INTEGER_NODE is created that points to the original list, and the access value L of type LIST is set to point to the new node. The next function returns the number of nodes in a list L. Note that nothing can be assumed about the list except that its length is finite.

```
function LIST_LENGTH (L : list) return natural is
    -- TEMP_NODE allows function to traverse the list node by node
    TEMP_NODE : LIST := L;
    LENGTH : natural := 0;
begin
    -- Start traversing the list node by node
    while TEMP_NODE /= null loop
        -- For each node found, add 1 to the LENGTH
        LENGTH := LENGTH + 1;
        -- Change the reference of TEMP_NODE to the next node
        TEMP_NODE := TEMP_NODE.NEXT;
    end loop;
    return LENGTH;
end LIST_LENGTH;
```

The variable TEMP_NODE of type LIST is required because the list must be traversed. Since LIST_LENGTH is a function, the variable L is mode in and can only be referenced. The next function returns the sum of all the integers in the list.

```
function SUM_UP_THE_LIST (L : LIST) return integer is
    TEMP_NODE : LIST := L;
    SUM : integer := 0;
begin
    while TEMP_NODE /= null loop
    SUM := SUM + TEMP_NODE.DATA;
```

```
        TEMP_NODE := TEMP_NODE.NEXT;
      end loop;
      return SUM;
    end SUM_UP_THE_LIST;
```

The two functions LIST_LENGTH and SUM_UP_THE_LIST are similar in concept. A list must be traversed. No new INTEGER_NODEs are going to be inserted or deleted from the list. Nodes are processed, and perhaps updated, but there is no insertion or deletion. In cases like this a loop is used to traverse the list. The boolean expression "TEMP_NODE /= null" says to continue processing as long as TEMP_NODE references a node. Stop when you reach the end of the list, that is, when TEMP_NODE no longer references a node.

A different strategy must be used when a node is to be added or deleted from a list. Consider the procedure ADD_TO_REAR_OF_LIST. This procedure creates an INTEGER NODE with a given integer and then adds it to the rear of the list (see Figure 2.4.3).

```
    procedure ADD_TO_REAR_OF_LIST (L    : in out LIST;
                                   ITEM : in integer) is
      TEMP_NODE : LIST := L;
    begin
      if L = null then
        -- The list L is empty, so the new node will be first and rear
        L := new INTEGER_NODE' (ITEM, null);
      else
        -- Traverse the list until TEMP_NODE reference the last node
        while TEMP_NODE.NEXT /= null loop
          TEMP_NODE := TEMP_NODE.NEXT;
        end loop;
        -- TEMP_NODE now references the rear node
        -- because TEMP_NODE.NEXT is null
        TEMP_NODE.NEXT := new INTEGER_NODE' (ITEM, null);
      end if;
    end ADD_TO_REAR_OF_LIST;
```

(a)

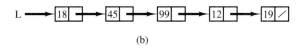

(b)

Figure 2.4.3 (a) Singly linked list before insertion. (b) The list from part (a) after creation of an INTEGER_NODE containing 19 was added to the rear.

Before a new INTEGER_NODE can be added to the end of the list, it must be determined if the list is empty. If the list is not empty, the list must be traversed so that the temporary access variable references the last INTEGER_NODE of the list. The NEXT component of the last INTEGER_NODE will always be null, so the list is traversed as long as

```
    TEMP NODE.NEXT /= null;
```

If an INTEGER_NODE is to be added or deleted from the list, the traversal will use this construct. Suppose that the integers in all the INTEGER_NODE of the list L are in ascending order. Consider a procedure that adds a value ITEM to the list while maintaining the order in the list. The same method can be applied.

```
procedure ADD_INORDER_TO_LIST (L : in out LIST;
                               ITEM : in integer) is
  TEMP_NODE : LIST := L;
begin
  if L = null then
    -- L is an empty list, so just add the node
    L := new INTEGER_NODE' (ITEM, null);
  elsif ITEM < L.DATA then
    -- ITEM is less, in value, than the value in the first
    -- integer_node, so create a node and put it first in the list
    L := new INTEGER_NODE' (ITEM, L);
  else
    -- Check the list node by node
    while TEMP_NODE.NEXT /= null loop
      if ITEM < = TEMP_NODE.NEXT.DATA then
        -- The value goes between the node referenced by TEMP_NODE
        -- and the node referenced by TEMP_NODE.NEXT
        TEMP_NODE.NEXT := new INTEGER_NODE' (ITEM, TEMP_NODE.NEXT);
        -- Now that the node has been placed, leave the procedure
        return;
      end if;
      -- Go on to the next node
      TEMP_NODE := TEMP_NODE.NEXT;
    end loop;
    -- What if ITEM is larger than the value in every node
    -- TEMP_NODE references the last node, add a node after it
    TEMP_NODE.NEXT := new INTEGER_NODE' (ITEM, null);
  end if;
end ADD_INORDER_TO_LIST;
```

There are actually four cases that must be considered. The order of consideration is critical. The first case is if the list is empty, the second case is if the new integer is less than the first integer in the list, the third case is if the new integer is greater than or equal to the first but strictly less than the last integer in the list, and the final case is if the integer is greater than or equal to the last integer in the list. Note the "return" statement. This causes execution of the procedure to terminate immediately.

In summary, there are two basic methods for traversing a list. In both cases, the first thing that must be done is to get a temporary variable to store the current place in the list. This is often done in the declaration section of a function or procedure in a manner similar to

```
TEMP_NODE : LIST := L;
```

The first method is a simple traversal of a list. This method is used when a list is being searched, counted, or processed node by node. It is not used when inserting a node into a particular location or when deleting a particular node. The general form is

```
loop
  exit when TEMP_NODE = null;
  if (action needed at this node) then
    do_the_action_to_this_node;
  end if;
  TEMP_NODE := TEMP_NODE.NEXT;
end loop;
```

This method is used when there is no need to alter a node's position in the list or to add or delete nodes from the list. This method is characterized by the variable TEMP_NODE referencing the node of interest. The procedure COPY is a final example that illustrates the power of this method.

```
procedure COPY (FROM : in LIST; TO : out LIST) is
  -- Makes a distinct copy of FROM and returns it as TO.
  TEMP_FROM : LIST := FROM;
  TEMP_TO : LIST;
begin
  If TEMP_FROM = null then
    -- List is empty, nothing to copy
    To := null;
  else
    -- List is not empty, copy the value in the first node
    TEMP_TO := new INTEGER_NODE' (TEMP.DATA, null);
    -- The parameter TO must reference the first node in the list
    TO := TEMP TO;
    -- TEMP_FROM must reference the next node
    TEMP_FROM := TEMP_FROM.NEXT;
    -- Continue copying the list FROM node by node
    loop
      exit when TEMP_FROM = null;
      -- More to copy, so add the next node to list TO. Note that
      -- TEMP TO references the last node, so TEMP_TO.NEXT will
      -- reference the next node that is added
      TEMP_TO.NEXT := new INTEGER_NODE' (TEMP.DATA, null);
      -- Update TEMP_TO and TEMP_FROM to the next node
      TEMP_TO := TEMP_TO.NEXT;
      TEMP_FROM := TEMP_FROM.NEXT;
    end loop;
  end if;
end COPY;
```

When two lists are catenated, the second list is either adjoined or copied to the end of the first list. The following procedure copies the second list onto the end of the first list.

```
procedure CATENATE (L1 : in out LIST; ONTO_L1 : in LIST) is
  -- Adjoins a distinct copy ONTO_L1 onto the end of L1
  L1_TEMP : LIST := L1;
begin
  If L1 = null then
    COPY (ONTO_L1, L1);
```

```
    else
      -- Find the end of the list
      loop
        exit when L1_TEMP.NEXT = null;
        L1_TEMP := L1_TEMP.NEXT;
      end loop;
      COPY (ONTO_L1, L1_TEMP.NEXT);
    end if;
  end CATENATE;
```

The second method of operating on a list is characterized by the variable TEMP pointing to the node before the node of interest. The node of interest is not the node referenced by TEMP but the node to which TEMP.NEXT points. Typical tasks involve the insertion or deletion of a node at a particular place. Some care must be taken with this method. Two or three exceptional cases must always be examined. It must be determined if the list is empty, if the action takes place before the first node on the list, or if the action takes place after the last node in the list. The general form is

```
if TEMP = null then
  -- List empty, what are you going to do?
  ACTION_FOR_EMPTY_LIST;
elsif (Action must be done at, to, or before the first node) then
  DO_REQUIRED_ACTION;
else
-- Go through the list node by node
loop
  exit when TEMP.NEXT = null;
  if (Next Node is where the action is at) then
    DO_IT_NOW;
    -- Action completed, leave the loop now. Note TEMP.NEXT /= null.
    exit;
  end if;
  TEMP := TEMP.NEXT;
end loop;
-- Check to see if the action was done or loop was left normally
if TEMP.NEXT = null then
  -- action must be done after last node in list
  DO_IT_NOW;
  end if;
end if;
```

The procedure ADD_INORDER_TO_LIST used a variation of this second method. In Chapter 4 the concept of recursion is introduced. Many dynamic structures have almost trivial implementations that involve the use of recursion. For now the use of recursion should be avoided in order to gain insight and skill in manipulation of dynamic structures.

2.5 DOUBLY LINKED LINEAR LIST

A doubly linked linear list is illustrated in Figure 2.5.1. Note that every node, except the last node, references its successor node, and every node, except the first node, also references its predecessor node. Consider the following basic data structure for a doubly linked list of integer nodes.

```
type INTEGER_NODE;
type DOUBLE_LINKED_LIST is access INTEGER_NODE;
type INTEGER_NODE is
  record
    DATA        : INTEGER;
    PREVIOUS,
    NEXT        : DOUBLE_LINKED_LIST;
  end record;
```

Exactly the same method can be used in doubly linked lists as in singly linked lists provided that no node is being inserted, deleted, or moved. Since a node in a doubly linked list can access both its successor and its predecessor, the insertion, deletion, or moving of a node requires twice as much bookkeeping. Compare the implementation of ADD_TO_FRONT below with the singly linked list version.

```
procedure ADD_TO_FRONT(L     : in out DOUBLE_LINKED_LIST;
                       ITEM : in integer ) is
begin
  if L= null then
    -- List is empty
  L := new INTEGER_NODE' (ITEM, null, null);
  else
    -- List has one or more nodes in it
    L := new INTEGER_NODE' (ITEM, L, null);
    -- The PREVIOUS pointer on the second node does not reference the
    -- first node
    L.NEXT.PREVIOUS := L;
  end if;
end ADD_TO_FRONT;
```

(a)

(b)

Figure 2.5.1 (a) Doubly linked list before insertion of an INTEGER_NODE at the front. (b) List from part (a) after creation of an INTEGER_NODE is added to the front.

If the list is not empty, the old first node must have its previous value changed from null to now reference its just created predecessor. Assume that a doubly linked list has at least k

nodes. The procedure DELETE_NODE_K must check three cases: the deletion of the first node, the deletion of an interior node, and the deletion of the last node.

```
procedure DELETE_NODE_K (L : in out DOUBLE_LINKED_LIST;
                         (K : in        positive) is
    TEMP_NODE : DOUBLY_LINKED_LIST := L;
begin
   if K = 1 then
     -- Must delete the first node
     if L.NEXT /= null then
       -- If L has 2 or more nodes, delete previous reference of the
       -- second node to the first node
       L.NEXT.PREVIOUS := null;
     end if;
     -- Reset the value of point L to the second node
     L := L.NEXT;
   else
     -- Traverse the list until Temp references the k-1 node
     for J in 1..K-1 loop
       TEMP := TEMP.NEXT;
     end loop;
     -- TEMP references the node to be deleted. Set the next node
     -- reference of the preceding node to the next node.
     TEMP.PREVIOUS.NEXT := TEMP.NEXT;
     if TEMP.NEXT /= null then
       -- If there are more than K nodes, rest to next node's
       -- previous pointer
       TEMP.NEXT.PREVIOUS := TEMP.PREVIOUS;
     end if;
   end if;
end DELETE_NODE_K;
```

(a)

(b)

Figure 2.5.2 (a) Doubly linked list from Figure 2.5.1 (b) before deletion of the third node. (b) List from part (a) after deletion of the third INTEGER_NODE.

The situation for *k* equal to 3 encountered in the procedure DELETE_NODE_K is shown in Figure 2.5.2. Sometimes the last node in a list is made to reference the first node. This makes the list circular (see Figure 2.5.3). Circular linked lists are sometimes called rings, which are the subject of Chapter 14.

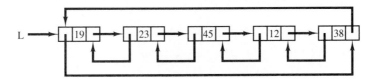

Figure 2.5.3 Circular doubly linked list, sometimes called a ring.

2.6. TREES: NONLINEAR ACCESS DATA STRUCTURE

The lists in Sections 2.4 and 2.5 were linear structures where the nodes reference at most one successor. A tree is a hierarchical data structure where each node can be referenced by at most one node but each node can reference more than one node. Consider the fictional family tree shown in Figure 2.6.1. The relationship is birth. A person is picked at random to start the tree. They are directly related, by birth, to two people who are the biological mother and father. Each parent, in turn, is related by birth to their parents, or the grandparents of the person at the head of the chart.

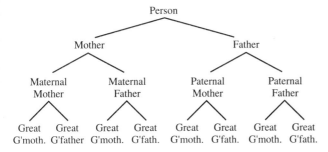

Figure 2.6.1 Hierarchical structure TREE used to represent a family tree.

Trees will be studied in depth in a later chapter. For now consider the data structure of a binary tree. A tree is called a *binary tree* if each tree node can reference at most two other tree nodes.

```
type TREE_NODE;
type TREE is access TREE_NODE;
type TREE_NODE is
   record
   DATA : integer;
   LEFT,
   RIGHT : TREE;
end record;
```

Figure 2.6.2 shows a TREE that uses a data structure similar to the one above with one additional convention. Pick any node. The integer in that node is greater than or equal to any successor node on its left side and less than any successor node on its right side. The procedure ADD_NODE_TO_TREE adds a new node to the tree while preserving the convention.

```
procedure ADD_NODE_TO_TREE ( ROOT : in out TREE;
                             ITEM : in integer) is
   TEMP : TREE := ROOT;
```

```
begin
   if ROOT = null then
      -- Nothing in the tree
      ROOT := new TREE_NODE' (ITEM, null, null);
   else
      loop
if ITEM <= TEMP.DATA then
  -- Value less than the current node, so go left
  if TEMP.LEFT = null then
     -- only add where it's null, we have arrived
     TEMP.LEFT := new TREE_NODE' (ITEM, null, null);
     -- Value added, get out of the loop
     exit;
  else
     -- Go left
     TEMP := TEMP.LEFT;
  end if;
else
  -- VALUE is greater than value in node, go right
  if TEMP.RIGHT = null then
     -- Only add where it's null, we have arrived
     TEMP.RIGHT := new TREE_NODE' (ITEM, null, null);
     -- Value added, get out of the loop
     exit;
  else
     -- Go right
     TEMP := TEMP.RIGHT;
  end if;
```

Figure 2.6.2   TREE organized so that all values accessible from the left are less than the value in the node, which is less than all values on the right. Note that each TREE_NODE is referenced by only one other TREE_NODE, but each TREE_NODE references zero or two other TREE_NODES. Not shown is the case where a TREE_NODE references just one other TREE_NODE.

```
            end if;
          end loop;
      end ADD_NODE_TO_TREE;
```

Note how the variable TEMP descends along the branches of the tree until it finds the proper place to insert the node. Once the node is inserted, the loop is exited, and the procedure terminates.

There are many possible operations on a tree, but even the simplest are much easier to implement using recursion, the subject of Chapter 4. Even the simplest task, such as counting the number of nodes in a tree, cannot be done without recursion unless the programmer has knowledge of the abstract data type called a stack. Stacks are studied in more detail in Chapter 6.

2.7 EXCEPTIONS AND ACCESS TYPES

There are two Ada-defined exceptions that are associated with access types. Access types can raise both a storage_error and a constraint_error. Suppose that L is a singly linked list as defined in Section 2.4, that is,

```
            type INTEGER_NODE;
            type LIST is access INTEGER_NODE;
            type INTEGER_NODE is
              record
                DATA : integer;
                NEXT : LIST;
              end record;
            L : LIST;
```

Suppose further that the boolean expression "L = null" is true. L references an empty list. If L did not reference an empty list, both L.DATA and L.NEXT would be defined. However, this is not the assumption. Under this scenario, either expression raises a constraint_error. A reference to the array component V(0) raises a constraint_error for a VECTOR V when V is defined by

```
            type VECTOR is array (positive range < >) of integer;
            V : VECTOR (1..10);
```

The reason is that there exists no component of the VECTOR V with index = 0. Similarly, a reference to either L.DATA or L.NEXT when L= null raises a constraint_error because L.DATA and L.NEXT are not defined.

A storage_error will be raised when there is not enough memory to create a new node. Recall that the allocator operator "new" allocates enough memory to create whatever structure. The structure depends on the access type. The procedure ADD_TO_FRONT can be modified to print a message if desired.

```
            procedure ADD_TO_FRONT(L : in out LIST; ITEM : in integer) is
            begin
              L := INTEGER_NODE' (ITEM, L);
            exception
```

```
    when storage_error =_>
      put_line ("Storage_error raised during attempt to add a node.");
  end ADD_TO_FRONT;
```

A more common practice is to declare exceptions that more closely describe the actual happening. Consider two programmer-defined exceptions:

```
OVERFLOW : exception;
LIST_EMPTY : exception;
```

Suppose that a function or procedure involving list raises the exception overflow when no memory is available to create a new integer_node. The exception LIST_EMPTY is raised when some function or procedure references an empty list even though the operation requires a nonempty list. This sounds confusing, but consider two examples. The first example is a function that returns the integer in the first node of the list. Obviously, this procedure cannot return anything if the list is empty. Below are two equivalent methods of raising the exception LIST_EMPTY.

```
function HEAD_OF_LIST ( L : LIST) return integer is
begin
  if L = null then
    raise LIST_EMPTY;
  else
    return L.DATA;
  end if;
end HEAD_OF_LIST;

function HEAD_OF_LIST (L : LIST) return integer is
begin
  return L.DATA;
exception
  when constraint error =>
    raise LIST_EMPTY;
end HEAD_OF_LIST;
```

The procedure REVERSE_LIST_ORDER returns a second list, REVERSE, that references a list of nodes that contain the same integers as the list L, but the order is exactly reversed. If there is insufficient memory to finish making the list REVERSE, the exception OVERFLOW is raised.

```
procedure REVERSE_LIST_ORDER (L        : in     LIST;
                              REVERSE :    out LIST) is
  TEMP : LIST := L;
  TEMP_R : LIST;
begin
  loop
    exit when TEMP = null;
    TEMP_R := new INTEGER_NODE' (TEMP.DATA, TEMP_R);
    TEMP   := TEMP.NEXT;
  end loop;
  REVERSE := TEMP_R;
```

```
exception
   when storage_error =>
      raise OVERFLOW;
 end REVERSE_LIST_ORDER;
```

The exception handler can handle more than one type of exception. Consider the procedure ADD_TO_END_OF_LIST below. When the exception is raised in the declaration section of a procedure or function, the exception is not handled by that procedure or function's
exception handler. If a storage_error occurs while trying to initialize the variable TEMP_
NODE, execution returns immediately to the statement after the calling procedure where the
exception is raised, and perhaps handled. If the formal parameter L is null, TEMP_LIST.NEXT
is undefined and a constraint_error is raised. Then a message is printed, the item is not added
to the list, and normal execution again begins at the statement following the procedure call.
Any other exception is handled by the "others" clause and normal execution continues at the
statement following the procedure call. The "others" clause must always be the last case in the
exception handler.

```
procedure ADD_TO_END_OF_LIST( ITEM : in integer;
                              L    : in out LIST) is
   TEMP_NODE : LIST := new INTEGER_NODE' (ITEM, null);
   TEMP_LIST : LIST := L;
   --Warning! This procedure cannot handle an empty list or L = null
begin
   loop
      exit when TEMP_LIST.NEXT = null;
      TEMP_LIST := TEMP_LIST.NEXT;
   end loop;
   TEMP_LIST.NEXT := TEMP_NODE;
exception
   when constraint_error =>
      put("Constraint_error in ADD_TO_END_OF_LIST.");
   when others =>
      put ("Non-constraint_error in ADD_TO_END_OF_LIST.");
 end ADD_TO_END_OF_LIST;
```

It is dangerous to use an "others" clause in an exception handler. Something unplanned
and catastrophic might occur with unforeseen future consequences. The "others" clause delays
the final catastrophe and masks its cause.

The proper signaling of exceptional cases is fundamental to good programming practice.
In this book we concentrate on building self-contained packages of abstract data types. These
packages must be robust. A robust procedure is one that is designed to handle the exceptional
situation when it arises. All packages developed in this book will signal exceptional situations
robustly as they arise.

2.8 BUILDING THE GENERALIZED DATA STRUCTURE

Recall that a data structure is a method of representing data. Often, there are many equivalent
representations of the same structure. Computers represent integers using a binary representa-

tion involving the binary operation complement, while humankind uses a sign-magnitude base 10 representation. The two systems are, in the general sense, equivalent. The binary representation is more natural to the computer because of the way the computer stores data. The use of complements to represent negative quantities arose when some sharp engineer figured out that

```
A - B = A + TWO_COMP(B)
```

where TWO_COMP denotes adding one to the basic word bit-complement operation. This allows the computer's CPU to be designed without circuitry to perform subtraction because complements are a basic electronic digital operation. Humanity probably got stuck with base 10 because we all have 10 digits on our hands. The author once heard a lecture by the Nobel laureate physicist Richard Feynman, who claimed that human beings made a big mistake by not starting with binary. He argued that we can only count from 0 to 10 using our fingers in the sign-magnitude representation. If we used the binary representation, we could count from 0 to 1023 on our fingers.

Integers, floats, characters, and booleans all have different internal representations within the computer. These representations are fixed and cannot be modified by the programmer. All of the built-in structures might be called *built-in data structures*. Arrays of components are accessed as a contiguous sequence of components. Each component takes up a certain amount of memory. The known beginning of the array structure and the known size of each component make the accessing of a particular component a simple task (see Figure 2.8.1). Even the record type, which the programmer designs, is just a convenient grouping of components. The grouping creates a new object, whether it is a phone listing, a videotape listing, a customer profile at the video store, or the complete inventory of the store. These data structures might be called *programmer-defined data structures*.

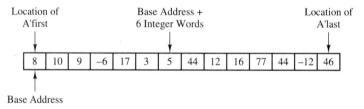

Figure 2.8.1   Array as a programmer-defined data structure. Each component of the array, here integers, has the same size and its location is easily computed with reference to the first component.

The generalized data structures typically involve some representation of the programmer-defined data structures. Consider how you might maintain a service line (see Figure 2.8.2). An object is placed in the line based on some priority scheme and then that object's position in line is maintained. As you check out of the store with your purchases, you get in line at the checkout register. As customers in front of you are served, you move closer to the front of the line. New customers go to the end of the line. Finally, it is your turn, the bill is computed, you pay, gather your purchases, and then leave. A job runs on a large computer generating one or more files to be printed. When the file is closed, it is placed on a print queue to wait its turn to be printed. The line, or queue, is a generalized data structure that will be studied further in Chapter 7. It makes no difference what the queue is composed of—it is still a queue.

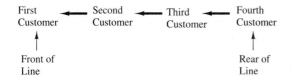

First Customer ← Second Customer ← Third Customer ← Fourth Customer

Front of Line   Rear of Line

Figure 2.8.2 Line of customers waiting to be served. This could also represent a line of text files waiting to be printed.

Now consider how the family tree might be represented. There would be a hierarchy of parents first over children. Since every parent is somebody's child, the structure looks like a pyramid. The file structure on a computer is a similar structure. Each directory contains files. Every directory but one, usually called the root, may contain subdirectories [see Figure 2.8.3(b)]. A typical university has this same organization. The president is on top. Reporting to the president are various deans. Reporting to the deans are the department chairs of the college [see Figure 2.8.3(c)]. These three specialized data structures are really three specific examples of the same hierarchical structure, called a tree. Trees are the subject of Chapter 9.

In this book we introduce the reader to a variety of these basic generalized structures. The reader should realize that it often happens that some previously used generalized data

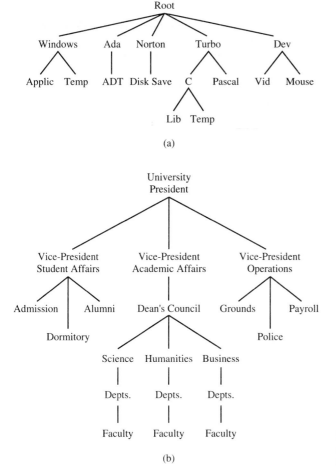

Figure 2.8.3   (a)Hierarchical file structure of a typical PC. (b) Hierarchical university administrative structure.

structure with a different encapsulated programmer-defined structure will solve some particular problem. Experience and practice will reinforce this maxim. If it looks like a queue, and acts like a queue, it probably *is* a queue.

2.9 DATA TYPE

A data type is a data structure plus the operations on that data structure. Data types can also be defined as a set of values and the operations on those values. The definitions are the same. An abstract data type is a data structure containing a programmer-defined object or data structure in it and the allowable operations on the abstract data structure. Programming is the implementation of algorithms using appropriate abstract data types.

Figure 1.1.1 lists the basic data structures plus their operations. Arrays and their operations were studied in Sections 1.2 and 1.3, while the record types and their operations were examined in Section 1.4. In the preceding section two generalized data structures, the queue and the tree, were mentioned briefly. The operations on the queue are based on the need to insert, delete, peek at, or count items on the queue. The operations on the tree are grounded on the need to insert, delete, traverse, and search the items on the tree. It is important to realize that there are two things involved in implementing a data type, defining first, the data structure, and second, the operations on that data structure.

The idea of the abstract data type is introduced in Sections 5.3 and 5.4. Intuitively, the abstract data type is a data type with a programmer-defined data structure embedded inside a generalized data structure along with the operations on the generalized structure. Properly done Ada implementations of abstract data types become reusable software components. These are the subject of Section 5.2. They are used in the same manner that an engineer would use off-the-shelf parts when designing and building a new product. Properly used ADTs (abstract data types) increase programmer productivity while making it easier to verify program correctness. When studying the material in this book, the reader should keep in mind that the components being developed might be harder to understand at first. Once mastered, components will make the future job of programming easier.

Building abstract data types is a bootstrap process. The foundations of any abstract data type are the basic data types, the array, the record, and the access type. These are the building blocks of data structures. The structure that encases the abstract data type is the generic package. This is the subject of Chapter 3.

EXERCISES

Section 2.1 Access Type

2.1.1 Consider the following data structure:

```
type PHONE is
  record
    LAST, FIRST : string(1..10);
    EXTENSION : string(1..7);
  end record;
```

```
type PHONE_ARRAY is array (integer range 1..100) of PHONE;
type PHONE_DIRECTORY is access PHONE_ARRAY;
COMPANY_DIRECTORY : PHONE_DIRECTORY;
```

a. Write a procedure that initializes all the components of each array component to blanks.

b. Write a boolean-valued function to search COMPANY_DIRECTORY for a particular last name. Assume that entries are in random order and that the procedure in part a has been applied to the COMPANY_DIRECTORY to initialize it.

c. Write a function to find a person's telephone number.

Section 2.4 Singly Linked Linear List

Exercises 2.4.1 through 2.4.6 all use the following data structure:

```
type ELEMENT;
type NEXT_ELEMENT is access ELEMENT;
type ELEMENT is
  record
    DATA : integer;
    NEXT : NEXT_ELEMENT;
end record;
```

2.4.1 Write an operation called PUSH that has two parameters, one an integer and one of type NEXT_ELEMENT. Push makes a new element containing the passed integer and adds this element to the front of the list.

2.4.2 Write an operation called POP that has two parameters: one of type NEXT_ELEMENT and mode in, and the second of type integer and mode out. POP takes a nonempty list of elements and returns the integer in the first element and the tail of the list.

2.4.3 Write a boolean-valued operation LIST_EQUAL that returns true if two lists are equal, and false otherwise. Two lists are equal if both have the same length and they contain the same elements in the same order.

2.4.4 Write a boolean-valued operation LIST_EQUAL that returns true if two lists have the same number of elements in them and every element that is in the first is in the second, and vice versa, without regard to order.

2.4.5 Write an operation called ENQUEUE that has two parameters, one an integer and one of type NEXT_ELEMENT. ENQUEUE makes a new element containing the passed integer and adds this element to the end of a possibly empty list.

2.4.6 Write an operation called LIST_AVERAGE that returns a float equal to the average value of the integers in the list. Assume that 0.0 is the average value of an empty list.

2.4.7 Write a procedure that returns a given list with its entries in ascending order. (*Hint:* It is easy to remove the elements from one list and add them to a second list.)

Section 2.5 Doubly Linked Linear List

Exercises 2.5.1 through 2.5.4 all use the following data structure for a doubly linked list:

```
type ELEMENT;
type NEXT_ELEMENT is access ELEMENT;
type ELEMENT is
record
  DATA : float;
```

```
                    PREVIOUS,
                    NEXT : NEXT_ELEMENT;
               end record;
```

2.5.1 Write a procedure that removes a particular element at a given place from the list. Assume that the list is long enough.

2.5.2 Write a procedure that doubles the value in every element on a given list.

2.5.3 Write a procedure that removes all elements that contain a given value from a list. If no element has the given value, the list is not modified. The list may be empty.

2.5.4 Write a function that returns a list that contains the elements in the passed list but in reverse order. The passed list is not modified in any way.

Section 2.6 Trees: a Nonlinear Access Data Structure

2.6.1 Using the tree structure defined in Section 2.6, write a boolean-valued function that returns true if a particular integer is in a list.

2.6.2 Write a function that returns the smallest value in the tree under the assumption that the tree is not empty.

2.6.3 Write a function that returns the largest value in the tree under the assumption that the tree is not empty.

Section 2.7 Exceptions and Access Types

2.7.1 Redo Exercise 2.4.2 so that it raises a predefined exception LIST IS EMPTY if it attempts to POP an empty list.

2.7.2 Redo Exercise 2.5.2 so that it raises a predefined exception TREE_IS_EMPTY if the tree is empty.

PROGRAMMING PROJECTS

P2.1 Write a program for Joe's Jiffy Oil Change. Joe has no idea how many customers are waiting in line at any one time. He has decided that a linked list is a suitable answer to this problem. Each node contains the make of the car, its year, its current mileage, and the owner's name and phone number. When a customer arrives, this information is recorded. The program can add a new customer to the end of the line, tell Joe how many customers are in line, and which car is the next one to be served.

P2.2 Project P2.1, Joe realizes that he made a mistake. A valued customer just phoned up and asked when his car would be ready. Add an option that lists the cars yet to be serviced in the order in which they will be serviced.

P2.3 In Project P2.2, Joe now has decided to add "express service." For an extra fee, customers go to the front of the line. Add this feature. (Joe said to make sure that if there are already express customers waiting, the new express customer is served after all the express customers who arrived before.)

P2.4 Joe is doing so much business now that some customers get tired of waiting. They tell Joe that they will come back some other day. Upgrade Joe's program so that customers who leave are no longer in the service queue.

NOTES AND REFERENCES

There are many treatments of access types at an elementary or introductory level, including Volper and Katz [48] and Barnes [5]. A more advanced look can be found in Bryan and Mendal [11].

3

Packages and Generic Packages

In this chapter we provide an introduction to the concepts of the package and its Ada abstraction, the generic package. In this book, generic or abstract data types are developed using reusable generic packages. The programmer-defined data type is constructed by encapsulating a suitable programmer defined data structure into a particular abstract data type. In this book the emphasis is on developing fully self-contained generic packages that encapsulate one or more programmer-defined structures. Generic packages, with their own built-in exception handlers, use a special Ada construct called a private type. The use of these private types helps prevent corruption of the programmer-defined data type. The twin concepts of reusability and robustness are stressed. Reusability allows already developed software to be used in other applications. Robustness is a description of how forgiving the software is when inadvertent errors are committed. A basic understanding of the ideas contained in this chapter is assumed throughout the book.

3.1 PACKAGES

A package is a logical grouping of related objects. Examples of these groupings include a package that contained the program constants and type definitions. Another example package could be a group of related functions, such as the trigonometric functions. A package that implements an abstract data type is another use. Such a package might build, maintain, and access a search structure. Packages contain a required part, called the *specification,* and an optional part, called the *body.* The form for a package is

```
package name is
   --declaration part
   ...............
[private
   declarations (optional)]
end name;
[package body name is
   declarations and procedures
   ..........................
[begin
```

```
                    statements (optional)]
              end name; (optional)]
```

The specification must always be compiled first. The specification part is sometimes called the *visible* part. The optional private section in the specification is discussed later. When an optional statement section in the package body exists, the statements it contains are executed exactly once, when the package is originally elaborated. The statement section often is used to initialize package global variables. These variables are global to the procedures and functions in the package body but not available outside the package body. After compiling the specification, either the package body or any program that references the package can be compiled. Naturally, all parts of the program must be compiled and the program linked before program execution.

An example of a package without a body is shown in Figure 3.1.1.

```
package DISTANCE is
  FEET_TO_INCHES : constant := 12.0;
  YARDS_TO_FEET  : constant := 3.0;
  MILES_TO_FEET  : constant := 5280.0;
end DISTANCE;
```

Figure 3.1.1   Example of a package without a body.

Once compiled, the package can be accessed by any program using a "with" clause on the first line of the compilation unit. For example, if the clause

```
with DISTANCE;
```

were referenced at the beginning of the program unit named P_1, the compilation unit DISTANCE becomes accessible to P_1.

To reference the objects within the packages, one of two things must be done. One method is to insert the clause

```
use DISTANCE;
```

after the "with" clause. It may be either inside or outside the procedure or program unit. For example, if the "use" clause is inserted outside the unit, as in Figure 3.1.2(a), all the declarations in the package DISTANCE can be referenced directly inside procedure P_1 and all procedures that it contains. By placing the "use" clause inside the declaration section, as in Figure 3.1.2(b), the declarations are available only in the body of P_1.

```
with DISTANCE;                          with DISTANCE;
use DISTANCE;                           procedure P_1 is
procedure P_1 is                          --declarations, including
  --declarations, including               --other procedures
  --other procedures                    use DISTANCE;
begin                                   begin
  --body                                  --body
end P_1;                                end P_1
  (a)                                     (b)
```

Figure 3.1.2

Serious side effects can occur when a programmer invokes the "use" clause. Suppose that two distinct packages are written by two different programmers. Imagine what would happen if both packages used the same name to define a type, procedure, or function. This situation could cause a compile-time syntax error. Programmers must be able to tell the compiler which name definition to use.

If the procedure did not invoke the "use" clause, the items contained inside the package must be fully referenced, for example:

```
A := DISTANCE.MILES_TO_FEET * B;
```

When the package name (here DISTANCE) appears before a variable name (here MILES_TO_FEET) defined in a package and separated by a period, the compiler knows which name to use. A second problem with the "use" clause can occur with generic packages. Multiple uses of the same generic package can lead to several distinct types with the same name. This problem is illustrated in Section 3.2.

The next example package (Figure 3.1.3) contains a body. This package also reveals implementation of the COMPLEX data type. The type declaration for the record COMPLEX_NUMBER is the data structure. The functions in the package, many of them overloaded, are the operations on this type.

```
package COMPLEX is
  type COMPLEX_NUMBER is
    record
      REAL,
      IMAGINARY : float := 0.0;
    end record;
  function "+" (LEFT, RIGHT : COMPLEX_NUMBER ) return COMPLEX_NUMBER;
  function "-" (LEFT, RIGHT : COMPLEX_NUMBER ) return COMPLEX_NUMBER;
  function "*" (LEFT, RIGHT : COMPLEX_NUMBER ) return COMPLEX_NUMBER;
  function "/" (LEFT, RIGHT : COMPLEX_NUMBER ) return COMPLEX_NUMBER;
  function REAL_PART ( Z : COMPLEX_NUMBER ) return float;
  function IMAGINARY_PART ( Z : COMPLEX_NUMBER ) return float;
  function SET_Z ( REAL_PART, IMAGINARY_PART : float ) return COMPLEX_NUMBER;
  function COMPLEX ( X : Float ) return COMPLEX_NUMBER;
  function "abs" ( Z : COMPLEX_NUMBER ) return float;
end COMPLEX;
package body Complex is
  function "+" (LEFT, RIGHT : COMPLEX_NUMBER ) return Complex_number is
  --Returns LEFT + RIGHT
  begin
  return (LEFT.REAL + RIGHT.REAL, LEFT.imaginary + RIGHT.imaginary);
  end "+";
  function "-" (LEFT, RIGHT : COMPLEX_NUMBER ) return COMPLEX_NUMBER is
  . . . .
end COMPLEX;
```

Figure 3.1.3 Package COMPLEX without private type.

Full implementation of the package body is left as an exercise. Note the form of the function declarations in the specification part of the package. The function declaration ends in a semicolon.

The package COMPLEX has a serious flaw. When implementing the data type COMPLEX, the implementation should completely encapsulate the data structure, the type COMPLEX_NUMBER. Good programming practice requires that programmer be restricted from accessing the data structure directly. The goal is correct code and high programmer productivity. This is the reason for the two kinds of private types. Proper use of private types restricts the manipulation of variables of a data type to the valid operations defined by the procedures and functions within the package. As the package specification now stands, the code segment shown in Figure 3.1.4 will compile.

```
with COMPLEX;
use COMPLEX;
procedure EXAMPLE_3 is
  Z : COMPLEX_NUMBER;
begin
  Z.REAL := 25.0;
  Z.IMAG := -17.8;
end EXAMPLE_3;
```

Figure 3.1.4

Ada has two mechanisms for preventing this. Types can be declared as either private or limited private. A type within a package declaration can be made private. A variable of private type allows only three operations outside the package: "=," "/=," and ":=." A type declaration in a package can be further restricted by making it limited private. Limited private types can only be referenced outside the package. Assignment and comparison of limited private types are illegal outside the package. Both private and limited private types can be fully manipulated inside the package by the functions or procedures in the package that use them in their formal parameter list. Types declared as private or limited private in the specification of the package must be fully defined in a special private section. The form of the package specification is shown in Figure 3.1.5.

```
package PACKAGE_NAME is
  --private or limited private type declarations;
  --other declarations;
  ...............
  package functions and procedure specifications
  ...............
private --sets apart the private section
        --definitions of the private or limited private types;
end PACKAGE_NAME;
```

Figure 3.1.5 Package specification form.

The visible part of the specification is the declaration section. The invisible part, even though it is there, is between the reserved word *private* and the end of the package specification. This private section is needed by the Ada compiler because types may be defined as private or limited private in the visible part of the package. In this case the compiler needs more information to support separate compilation. It may contain type declarations not hinted at in the public section. Variables declared as private or limited private types in the visible section must be defined in the package's private section. The package COMPLEX can be redefined as shown in Figure 3.1.6.

```
package COMPLEX is
        type COMPLEX_NUMBER is private;
        function "+" (LEFT, RIGHT : COMPLEX_NUMBER ) return COMPLEX_NUMBER;
        function "-" (LEFT, RIGHT : COMPLEX_NUMBER ) return COMPLEX_NUMBER;
        function "*" (LEFT, RIGHT : COMPLEX_NUMBER ) return COMPLEX_NUMBER;
        function "/" (LEFT, RIGHT : COMPLEX_NUMBER ) return COMPLEX_NUMBER;
        function REAL_PART ( Z : COMPLEX_NUMBER ) return float;
        function IMAGINARY_PART ( Z : COMPLEX_NUMBER ) return float;
        function SET_Z (REAL_PART, IMAGINARY_PART : float)return COMPLEX_NUMBER;
        function COMPLEX (X : Float ) return COMPLEX_NUMBER;
        function "abs" ( Z : COMPLEX_NUMBER ) return float;
private
    type COMPLEX_NUMBER is
      record
        REAL,
        IMAGINARY : float := 0.0;
      end record;
end COMPLEX;
```

Figure 3.1.6   Package COMPLEX with private type.

Note that the type COMPLEX_NUMBER is declared to be private in the public section of the COMPLEX package specification and then fully defined later in the private section. With this implementation the procedure in Figure 3.1.4 cannot be compiled. The only possible operations outside the package are assignment, comparison for equality, and comparison for inequality. The manipulation outside the package body of the record's individual components is not allowed. It may appear that all the arithmetic operators are defined for COMPLEX_NUMBER. They are. This does not violate the private type because the only allowed manipulation is by a procedure or function in the package with variables of COMPLEX_NUMBER type in the formal parameter list.

After developing and compiling the package, COMPLEX becomes a programmer data type. The package is fixed; nothing can be changed or modified. Many applications have a built-in abstract structure. As an example, things of array type are essentially indexed vectors. The manipulation of the components of an array depends only on the array's indices, not on the array's components. Arrays of integers and arrays of strings are all indexed in a similar manner. Arrays can be thought of as abstract data structures. They become programmer data structures when the index range and the element type are supplied. In this sense the array type is generic. In the abstract sense, array types can be thought of as a general pattern. Ada extends this idea of abstractness to procedures and packages.

As a final example, a package that implements a STACK is developed. A STACK is a data type where items, in this case integers, are put in a list and then removed from the list by a rule which says that the most recently added integer is the first to be removed. A stack of trays in a cafeteria provides a good example. Customers remove trays from the top of the stack. Trays placed on top of the stack were the most recently cleaned. The operation PUSH places a new integer on the TOP of the stack. The operation POP removes the integer from the top of the stack and returns this value to the program (Figure 3.1.7).

```
package STACK is
    procedure PUSH (X : in integer);
  procedure POP (X : out integer);
end STACK;
package body STACK is
    BOUNDED_STACK : array (1..50) of integer;
    TOP : integer range 0 .. 50;

    procedure PUSH (X : in integer ) is
      --Adds X to the top of a stack
    begin
      TOP := TOP + 1;
      BOUNDED_STACK(TOP) := X;
    end PUSH;
    procedure POP (X: out integer ) is
    --Removes X from the Top of a nonempty stack
    begin
    X := BOUNDED_STACK (TOP);
    TOP := TOP - 1;
    end Pop;

    begin
    TOP := 0;
end STACK;
```

Figure 3.1.7   Package STACK.

This package has several interesting features. The reserved word "begin" in the package body denotes a statement section where TOP is initialized. Statements that appear in this section are executed exactly once at the beginning of a program that uses the properly instantiated package. This gives the package "memory." Even after studying the package specification the user of the package does not need to know how the programmer built the structure. The package body hides these details. The array BOUNDED_STACK can only be accessed through the two operations in the specification. BOUNDED_STACK is inaccessible to the program from outside the body. This package also has several severe limitations. It generates only one stack, and this is a stack of integers. In Section 3.5 we illustrate how this fixed data type can easily be rewritten as an abstract data type.

3.2 GENERIC SUBPROGRAMS

The sorting algorithm appears throughout computer science. The idea of sorting does not depend on the type of the items being sorted. The concept behind an algorithm to sort an array of integers is the same concept behind the algorithm that sorts an array of any Ada type. The algorithm is fundamental, not the type being sorted. Ada allows generic subprograms that become patterns for a particular application. To make the generic subprogram into a usable subprogram a programmer-defined data type or function must first be inserted or "instantiated" into the generic unit.

Generic units have four main uses. First, they are the building blocks that should reduce future programming effort. The wheel is not continuously being reinvented. Second, they allow for more manageable programs. Generic library units should be error free and their use should reduce the effort to verify that a program is error free. Third, generics increase portability. The specification for text_IO is the same for all Ada compilers, but its body is different. Fourth, they provide the perfect vehicle to build abstract data types, the subject of this book. The guide *Ada Quality and Style: Guidelines for Professional Programmers* [24] stresses that all abstract data types should be implemented using generic packages.

Consider a generic procedure that exchanges two objects of type ITEM_TYPE.

```
generic
  type ITEM_TYPE is private;
procedure SWAP (X, Y : in out ITEM_TYPE);
procedure SWAP (X, Y : in out ITEM_TYPE) is
  TEMP : ITEM_TYPE := X;
begin
  X := Y;
  Y := TEMP;
end SWAP;
```

Figure 3.2.1 Generic procedure SWAP.

The generic procedure SWAP (Figure 3.2.1) interchanges two things of type ITEM_TYPE. ITEM_TYPE is a formal generic parameter inside the subprogram. Formal generic parameters are the mechanism for inserting generality into a generic package. The actual types swapped are the types supplied to the procedure at instantiation. Declaring it as private does not limit the actual parameter outside the generic unit. Declaring a parameter as private limits the operations inside the package to assignment, equality, and inequality. Whatever the item, this basic pattern will work. It makes no difference if integers are swapped or if some complex programmer defined record is swapped. To use this pattern, it must be instantiated in the declaration section. For example:

```
procedure INTEGER_SWAP is new SWAP (integer);
procedure BOOLEAN_SWAP is new SWAP (boolean);
```

creates two new procedures, one for interchanging integers and the other for interchanging boolean. Since SWAP is a generic template, it can never be called.

The patterns for generic subprograms are shown in Figure 3.2.2.

```
generic
  --generic formal parameters
function NAME (formal parameter list) return ... ;
function NAME (formal parameter list) return ... is
  --function declarations
begin
```

Figure 3.2.2 Generic subprogram patterns. Continues on page 58.

```
        --generic function body
      end NAME;


      generic
        --generic formal parameters
      procedure NAME (formal parameter list);
      procedure NAME (formal parameter list) is
        --procedure declarations
      begin
        --generic procedure body
      end NAME;
```

Figure 3.2.2 Concluded.

Examples of the kinds of formal parameters that may be used in generic units are listed in Figure 3.2.3. Instantiation supplies all parameter attributes.

```
type INTEGER_ITEM is range < >;    --matches any integer type
                                   --all integer operations allowed
type FIXED_ITEM is delta < >;      --matches any fixed point type
                                   --all fixed operations allowed
type FLOAT_ITEM is digits< >;      --matches any floating point type
                                   --all float operations allowed
type DISCRETE_TYPE is ( < > );     --matches any discrete type such
                                   --as integer or enumerated types
                                   --operations allowed =. /=, :=, <,
                                   --< =, >, > =, pred, succ, first,
                                   --last
type LINK is access OBJECT;        --matches any access type as long
                                   --as it designates the same object
type CONSTRAINED_ARRAY is array (INDEX) of ITEM;
                                   --matches any constrained array.
                                   --Index and Item can be generic
type UNCONSTRAINED_ARRAY is array ( INDEX RANGE < > ) of ITEM;
                                   --matches unconstrained array
type ITEM is private;              --only assignment and comparison
                                   --are defined in the generic unit
                                   --operations allowed =, /=, :=
type ITEM is limited private;
```

Figure 3.2.3 Generic formal parameters.

A word of warning is in order. Private types and limited private types have additional restrictions when used as formal parameters in generic units. In a generic subprogram, as in a generic package, any formal generic parameter declared as private may be assigned or compared for equality within the generic subprogram or generic package. Its exact appearance is known only outside the generic subprogram or generic package. Inside the package the private type's exact appearance is not known, nor is it relevant. If a type is declared as limited private, assignment and comparison inside the package are not allowed. Outside the generic subprogram or generic package, a limited private type may have no restrictions at all. Like the private type, a limited private type's outside appearance is unknown inside the package. It could be anything from an integer, or an array, or a record, and the generic unit would operate on it in the same mechanical fashion.

To clarify the distinction between private and limited private further, consider the two sets of rules for private and limited private types. First, there are the rules for formal parameters that are private or limited private. This case was discussed above. Then there are the rules for a type being declared as private or limited private inside a package's private part. The first set of rules affect access inside the package. The latter set affects access outside the package.

One special case deserves attention. In Figure 3.2.1, SWAP has a formal generic type parameter ITEM_TYPE that is private. If the actual parameter were limited private, the instantiation would fail because of the assignment operations inside the procedure. A type declared as limited private can be manipulated only by procedures or functions outside the package.

Consider the generic subprogram that finds the succeeding value of a discrete type. Recall Exercise 1.1.3. The attributes T'first, T'last, and T'succ are defined at instantiation for all discrete types. The one possible undefined case for this function is the last value of the actual discrete type. In this case the generic procedure returns the first value (Figure 3.2.4).

```
generic
  type DISCRETE_TYPE is (< >);
function NEXT (X : DISCRETE_TYPE ) return DISCRETE_TYPE;
function NEXT (X : DISCRETE_TYPE ) return DISCRETE_TYPE is
  --Extends the definition of the succ attribute
begin
  if X = DISCRETE_TYPE'last then
    return DISCRETE_TYPE'first;
  else
    return DISCRETE_TYPE'succ (X);
  end if;
end NEXT;
```

Figure 3.2.4   Discrete generic formal parameter.

Suppose that the following statements appeared in a program:

```
subtype OCTAL_DIGIT is integer range 0..7;
type RGB_COLOR is (RED, GREEN, BLUE);
function NEXT_OCTAL_DIGIT is new NEXT (OCTAL_DIGIT);
function NEXT_RGB_COLOR is new NEXT (RGB_COLOR);
```

Both are discrete type. NEXT_OCTAL_DIGIT(7) will return 0 because OCTAL_DIGIT ' last = 7 and OCTAL_DIGIT ' first = 0. Clearly, NEXT_RGB_COLOR(RED) equals GREEN.

The next example (Figure 3.2.5) is a generic procedure that sums up the values of any vector or single-dimensioned array of arbitrary float types. This example has several interesting features. In arrays the index of the array often depends on a previously declared discrete type. Again, note that all array attributes are available for use. Array attributes must be used because the subprogram was written before instantiation. The generic procedure did not fix the indices of the vector to be summed. This procedure sets the precision.

```
generic
  type ARRAY_INDEX is (< >);
  type PRECISION is digits < >;
  type PRECISION_ARRAY is array ( ARRAY_INDEX < > ) of PRECISION;
function VECTOR_SUM (VECTOR : PRECISION_ARRAY) return PRECISION;
function VECTOR_SUM (VECTOR : PRECISION_ARRAY) return PRECISION is
  --Returns the sum of the elements of an array
  SUM : PRECISION := 0.0;
begin
  for INDEX in VECTOR'range loop
    SUM := SUM + VECTOR(INDEX);
  end loop;
  return SUM;
end VECTOR_SUM;
```

Figure 3.2.5 Function to sum the elements of a vector.

Note that PRECISON_ARRAY is constrained because ARRAY_INDEX is fixed at instantiation.

Generic subprograms can also have generic default values. Note here that values are being specified, not types.

```
generic
   START : integer := 10;
   COST  : float    := 28.0;
procedure ESTIMATE ( SQ_FT : in    float;
                     CHARGE :   out  float);
procedure ESTIMATE ( SQ_FT : in    float;
                     CHARGE :   out  float) is
begin
   ..........
end ESTIMATE;
```

The following three instantiations show an instantiation that uses the default values, an instantiation that supplies values, and an instantiation that uses named parameters, respectively.

```
procedure EST_1 is new ESTIMATE;
procedure EST_2 is new ESTIMATE ( 27, -18.2);
procedure EST_3 is new ESTIMATE ( COST  = > 55.0,
                                  START = > 0.0 );
```

Functions can be passed to generic packages. The next example (Figure 3.2.6) searches a vector to find the largest object of some type with respect to a supplied boolean operator.

```
generic
  type ITEM_TYPE is private;
  type ITEM_ARRAY is array (integer range < >) of ITEM_TYPE;
  with function "<" (LEFT, RIGHT : ITEM_TYPE) return boolean;
function MAX (VECTOR : ITEM_ARRAY) return ITEM_TYPE;
```

Figure 3.2.6 Function to find the maximum value in a vector. Continues on page 61.

```
function MAX (VECTOR : ITEM_ARRAY) return ITEM_TYPE is
  --Returns the maximum item as defined by "<"
  BIG : ITEM_TYPE := VECTOR (VECTOR'first);
begin
  for INDEX in VECTOR' first + 1 . . VECTOR' last loop
    if BIG < VECTOR(INDEX) then
      BIG := VECTOR(INDEX);
    end if;
  end loop;
  return BIG;
end MAX;
```

Figure 3.2.6 Concluded.

Since ITEM_TYPE is declared as private, no assumptions about the existence of an operator "<" can be made. In the three instantiations shown in Figure 3.2.7, the first creates a function that returns the largest integer in an array, while the second returns a function that returns the smallest integer. The third example creates a function that finds the ITEM_TYPE with the largest zip code.

```
type INTEGER_ARRAY is array ( integer range < > ) of integer;
function MAX_INTEGER is new MAX (integer, INTEGER_ARRAY, "<");
function MIN_INTEGER is new MAX (integer, INTEGER_ARRAY, ">");
type LISTING is
  record
    NAME              : string (1..40);
    STREET_ADDRESS    : string (1..50);
    CITY              : string (1..20);
    STATE             : string (1..2);
    ZIPCODE           : string (1..5);
  end record;
type LISTING_ARRAY is array ( integer range < > ) of LISTING;
function "<" (LEFT, RIGHT : Listing ) return boolean is
begin
  return LEFT.ZIPCODE < RIGHT.ZIPCODE;
end "<";
function HIGH_ZIP_LISTING is new MAX ( LISTING, LISTING_ARRAY, "<");
```

Figure 3.2.7 Three instantiations of Figure 3.2.6.

No functions to define the relational operators < and > listed in lines 2 and 3 were defined, so how does Ada instantiate these two functions? In the instantiation, if no function is supplied for a function formal generic parameter, Ada searches for any previously defined operator of the same name that matches the types. The Ada-defined integer functions are used.

If the third line of the package MAX in Figure 3.2.6 were

```
with function "<" (LEFT, RIGHT : ITEM) return boolean is < >;
```

the token "is < >" would signal the possible use of the default function. If no operator is supplied, the Ada compiler searches for a match. This can occur if ITEM is an integer, float, or character. Here the instantiation

```
          type INTEGER_ARRAY is array ( integer range < > ) of integer;
          function MAX_INTEGER is new MAX (integer, INTEGER_ARRAY);
```

would have used the normal "<" function for integers if no function was declared at instance.

Generic units can be used when a function must be passed as a formal parameter. A simple case occurs in numerical integration. For a standard numerical algorithm to work, the programmer needs to supply three parameters: the left endpoint of integration, the right endpoint of integration, and the function to be integrated. The following example has a single formal generic parameter, the function to be integrated. The endpoints are formal parameters of the integration process. The method illustrated breaks the region of integration into N subregions and approximates the integral over each region by the area of the trapezoid that uses the height of the graph of the function at the endpoints (see Figures 3.2.8 and 3.2.9).

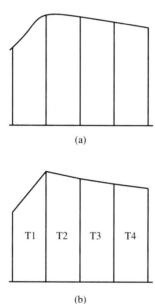

(a)

T1 T2 T3 T4

(b)

Figure 3.2.8 Trapezoid rule for $n = 4$. (a) Curve to be integrated using the trapezoid rule. (b) Four trapezoids whose area approximates the above integral in part (a).

```
generic
  with function F (X : float) return float;
function TRAPEZOID_RULE (LEFT,
                         RIGHT                 : float;
                         NUMBER_INTERVALS      : positive) return float;
function TRAPEZOID_RULE (LEFT,
                         RIGHT                 : float;
                         NUMBER_INTERVALS      : positive) return float is
   --Uses the trapezoid rule to estimate the area under a given
   --curve F and between the LEFT and RIGHT interval endpoints
   H : float := (RIGHT - LEFT)/float(NUMBER_INTERVALS);
   SUM : float := (F(LEFT) + F(RIGHT)) / 2.0;
   X : float := LEFT;
begin
```

Figure 3.2.9 Generic function that integrates using the trapezoid rule. Continues on page 63.

```
   for I in positive range 1 .. NUMBER_INTERVALS - 1 loop
     X :=X + H;
     SUM := SUM + F(X);
   end loop;
   return SUM * H;
end TRAPEZOID_RULE;
```

Figure 3.2.9   Concluded.

We finish this section by building a generic function that can determine if two vectors of arbitrary generic type are equal (Figure 3.2.10). It illustrates how to pass a parameter as limited private type so as to promote abstractness. Note that since normal assignment and comparison operations are not available, these operations must be supplied if needed.

```
generic
  type ITEM_TYPE is limited private;
  type ITEM_ARRAY is array (integer range < >) of ITEM_TYPE;
  with function "=" (LEFT, RIGHT : ITEM_TYPE) return boolean is < >;
function EQUAL (LEFT, RIGHT : ITEM_ARRAY) return boolean;
function EQUAL (LEFT, RIGHT : ITEM_ARRAY) return boolean is
  --Extends the equality operator to arbitrary arrays
begin
  if LEFT'length /= RIGHT'length then
    return false;
  end if;
  for INDEX in LEFT'range loop
    if LEFT(INDEX) /= RIGHT(INDEX + RIGHT'first - LEFT'first) then
      return false;
    end if;
  end loop;
  return true;
end EQUAL;
```

Figure 3.2.10   Function to determine if two arbitrary arrays of arbitrary ITEMS are equal.

In Figure 3.2.10 it appears that two variables of limited private type are being compared. This comparison appears to violate the definition of a limited private type. However, the comparison is not being done inside the procedure. The values being compared are being passed back to the generic "=" as actual parameters. This results in the comparison being done outside the package by the function instantiated as the third formal generic parameter.

3.3 GENERIC PACKAGES

Generic packages combine the features of a package and a generic subprogram. In Ada generic packages supply the mechanism to build abstract data types as reusable software components. This form combines the package form and the generic subprogram form (Figure 3.3.1).

```
generic
  --formal generic parameter section
  ............
package GENERIC_PACKAGE_NAME is
  --generic package specification
  ............

end GENERIC_PACKAGE_NAME;
package body GENERIC_PACKAGE_NAME is
--generic package body
............
end GENERIC_PACKAGE_NAME;
```

Figure 3.3.1 Concluded.

Implementing abstract data types in Ada requires the instantiation of actual parameters into the formal generic parameters of a particular generic package. This package contains the defined operations on that data structure. A linked list implements a stack where programmer-defined items are added or deleted from the front of the list. The operations PUSH and POP were described at the end of Section 3.1. A simple generic package for stack is given in Figure 3.3.2.

```
generic
  type ITEM_TYPE is private;
package GENERIC_STACK is
  type STACK is limited private;
  procedure PUSH ( ONTO : in out STACK;
                   ITEM : in      ITEM_TYPE);
  procedure POP  ( FROM : in out STACK;
                   ITEM :     out ITEM_TYPE);
private
  type STACK_NODE;
  type STACK is access STACK_NODE;
end GENERIC_STACK;
package body GENERIC_STACK is
  type STACK_NODE is
    record
        ITEM : ITEM_TYPE;
        NEXT : STACK;
    end record;

  procedure PUSH ( ONTO : in out STACK;
                   ITEM : in      ITEM_TYPE) is
  --Adds ITEM to the top of the stack ONTO
  begin
  ONTO := new STACK_NODE' (ITEM, ONTO);
  end PUSH;
  procedure POP  ( FROM : in out STACK;
                   ITEM :     out ITEM_TYPE) is
  --Returns the Top ITEM of a stack FROM,
```

Figure 3.3.2 Simple abstract data type. Continues on page 65.

Packages and Generic Packages   Chap. 3

```
         --and removes it from FROM
    begin
        ITEM := FROM.ITEM;
        FROM := FROM.NEXT;
    end POP;


end GENERIC_STACK;
```

Figure 3.3.2   Concluded.

This simple generic package has several limitations; for example, there is no protection from trying to POP an empty stack. However, the example does illustrate several points. First note that formal generic parameter STACK_NODE is referenced in the private section declaration but not in the visible section of the specification. STACK must be defined in the private section because it is referenced in the visible section of the package. STACK_NODE is referenced in the private section but never in the visible section. It can be defined in either the private section or in the package body itself. The programmer does not need to know how the stack is implemented when using the package. Consider the following three instantiations.

```
type STUDENT_NAME is
  record
    S_NAME : string (1..20);
    MAJOR  : string (1..10);
    PIN    : string (1..6);
  end record;
package INT_STACK is new package GENERIC_STACK (integer);
package FLT_STACK is new package GENERIC_STACK (float);
package STU_STACK is new package GENERIC_STACK (Student_name);
INT_STACK_EXAMPLE : INT_STACK.STACK;
FLT_STACK_EXAMPLE : FLT_STACK.STACK;
STU_STACK_EXAMPLE : STU_STACK.STACK;
```

There are three distinct instantiations of the package GENERIC_STACK above. Without a "use" clause, the operations in each new package must be fully referenced. There are three pop operations: INT_STACK.POP, FLT_STACK.POP, and STU_STACK.POP. When referenced in this manner, Ada, and the programmer, has no problem determining which operation in the respective package is being called. A compile-time error results if the four statements

```
        use INT_STACK;
        use FLT_STACK;
        use STU_STACK;
        MY_STACK : STACK;
```

are added to the previous declarations. The type stack has three distinct definitions. This example illustrates the possibility of multiple instantiations of the same generic package. It also illustrates why the "use" clause can lead to trouble when distinct packages have variables, procedures, or functions with common names. In contrast, the simple package STACK in Figure 3.1.7 only defined a bounded stack for integers.

The second point the example above illustrates is the power of abstraction. The generic package concept forces the programmer to concentrate on the outside view of the abstraction, that is, its interface. Details of implementation are deferred to the package body. The operations are, in the abstract sense, the same. The only differences are the programmer-defined data structures upon which the packages operate. The operations in the package can be verified and validated by using a simple type such as integers, but any valid type can be supplied at instantiation.

The third thing to note is the declaration of STACK as limited private. STACK defines a class of objects and the limited private type allows the declaration of multiple objects of the same type. The package GENERIC_STACK exports this single type declaration. The limited private type is the mechanism Ada provides to build encapsulated types. The declaration of STACK as a limited private type completely limits the operations on STACK to the functions and procedures in the package that have STACK as a formal parameter. The specification provides the two operations PUSH or POP. Why not define STACK as private? The answer is that the abstraction could not be fully enforced. The assignment operator could be used to redefine any variable of type STACK. For example, two variables of type STACK could be assigned or compared. The type STACK in Figure 3.3.2 is implemented using linked lists and access types. It is possible to have two lists that contain the same objects in the same order fail the test for equality.

There are times when the variables exported by a package must be of private type instead of limited private type. If one package is built of objects defined as limited private in another package, assignment is illegal and the objects cannot be manipulated. This situation will become clear in later chapters as applications and examples are developed.

Finally, consider the situation in Figure 3.3.3.

```
generic
   type ITEM_1 is private;
   type ITEM_2 is limited private;
package FIG_3_3_3 is
   type ITEM_3 is private;
   type ITEM_4 is limited private;
......--other declarations, procedures and functions
private
   ......
end FIG_3_3_3;
```

Figure 3.3.3 Use of private and limited private types.

ITEM_1 and ITEM_2 are formal generic parameters. Inside package FIG_3_3_3 ITEM_1 acts like a private type and ITEM_2 acts like a limited private type. At instantiation the declaring of the formal generic parameters does not put any restrictions on the actual parameters. If the actual instantiated parameter ITEM_1 is limited private, an error results. This error occurs because inside the package assignment might occur where outside it is forbidden. ITEM_3 and ITEM_4 must be fully defined in the private section. Variables outside the package declared as type ITEM_3 can only be assigned or tested for equality or tested for inequality outside the package. Inside the package there are no restrictions. Variables outside the package declared as type ITEM_4 can only be referenced outside the package by functions and procedures defined inside the package. Inside the package there are no restrictions. It is very important to keep the limitations of the private types in mind when designing generic packages.

This section finishes with the package COMPLEX_NUMBER generalized to accept floating-point numbers of arbitrary precision. This package is the same as the previous non-generic version when instantiated with the value float'digits. It could just as easily be instantiated with any other suitable value. If later it is determined that more precision is needed, a simple change in the generic parameter at instantiation and a recompiling of the program will gain that precision.

```
generic
   type REAL is digits < >;
package GENERIC_COMPLEX is
   type COMPLEX_NUMBER is private;
   function "+" (LEFT, RIGHT : COMPLEX_NUMBER ) return COMPLEX_NUMBER;
   function "-" (LEFT, RIGHT : COMPLEX_NUMBER ) return COMPLEX_NUMBER;
   function "*" (LEFT, RIGHT : COMPLEX_NUMBER ) return COMPLEX_NUMBER;
   function "/" (LEFT, RIGHT : COMPLEX_NUMBER ) return COMPLEX_NUMBER;
   function REAL_PART ( Z : COMPLEX_NUMBER ) return REAL;
   function IMAGINARY_PART ( Z : COMPLEX_NUMBER ) return REAL;
   function SET_Z ( REAL_PART, IMAGINARY_PART : REAL ) return COMPLEX_NUMBER;
   function COMPLEX (X : Real ) return COMPLEX_NUMBER;
   function "abs" ( Z : Complex_number ) return REAL;
private
   type COMPLEX_NUMBER is
     record
     REAL,
     IMAGINARY : REAL :"= 0.0;
   end record;
end GENERIC_COMPLEX;
```

Figure 3.3.4   Generic package COMPLEX.

Implementation of the package body is left as an exercise.

3.4 PRIVATE TYPE VERSUS LIMITED PRIVATE TYPE

In this section we examine the way that Ada can restrict a type within a package. Ada has three ways of specifying a type within a package. The following discussion applies to both packages and generic packages, but for simplicity, the discussion is limited to packages. The discussion is further restricted to the use of a type outside the package where declaration occurred. Inside the package there are no restrictions. The three ways of declaring a type within a package are without any restrictions, declaring the type to be private, and declaring the type to be limited private. Each has its uses, and the use of each has its consequences.

Figure 3.1.3 specified the package COMPLEX. The definition of the data structure for COMPLEX_NUMBER did not cause any restrictions on its use outside the package. The lack of restrictions allows programmer-defined operations on the type that might violate the accepted mathematical operations on this type. The solution to this problem was to redefine the type COMPLEX_NUMBER as private, which occurred in the package COMPLEX specified in Figure 3.1.6. This restriction allowed equations of variables of type COMPLEX_NUMBER to be written in a natural way, such as

$$A := (B + C) / (A - D);$$

while preventing programmer abuse of the type. The next-higher level of restriction, limited private, is not appropriate for this application. Limited private types cannot be assigned or compared for equality outside the package where they are defined. If COMPLEX_NUMBER is limited private, the expression above would be illegal outside the package. To perform simple mathematical operations, the operation ASSIGN, listed in Figure 3.4.1, would have to be added to

```
procedure ASSIGN (TO LEFT HAND SIDE :   out COMPLEX NUMBER;
                       RIGHT_HAND_SIDE : in    COMPLEX_NUMBER ) is
   --Allows assignment TO_LEFT_HAND_SIDE := RIGHT_HAND_SIDE
   --in the case that COMPLEX_NUMBER is limited private.
begin
   TO_LEFT_HAND_SIDE := RIGHT_HAND_SIDE;
end ASSIGN;
```

Figure 3.4.1 Complex operation ASSIGN.

the package COMPLEX in Figure 2.1.6. The natural expression

```
A := (B + C)/(A - D);
```

would have to be replaced by

```
Assign(A, (B + C)/(A - D));
```

A second boolean-valued operation to check for equality also would have to be added to the package COMPLEX. Making the type COMPLEX_NUMBER limited private causes an unnatural expression for formulas and expressions of type COMPLEX_NUMBER.

A set is a collection of objects. The three sets

$$\{a, b, c\} \qquad \{ b, c, a\} \qquad \{c, a, b\}$$

are all equal because they contain the same group of objects. The same group of students makes up the set of students enrolled in a particular class. It makes no difference where they sit in class, the order in which their names appear on the roll, or who signed up for the class first. They are either in the class or not. Sets will be studied further in Chapter 9. Suppose that the simple linked list data structure below represents a set.

```
type ELEMENT;
type SET is access ELEMENT;
type ELEMENT is
   record
   X : OBJECT_TYPE;
   NEXT : SET;
end record;
```

Figure 3.4.2(a) represents a simple set of characters. This representation needs to be either private or limited private. The programmer must not be allowed direct access to the structure. Several problems can occur if the set type is private. Figure 3.4.2 (b) illustrates the situation where the assignment statement

```
S2 := S1;
```

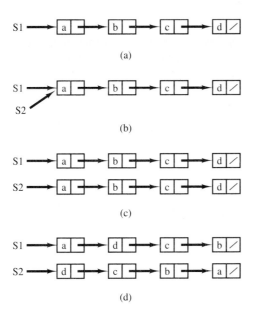

(a)

(b)

(c)

(d)

Figure 3.4.2 Set types as private and limited private types. (a) Set as a linked list. (b) Set as a private type after S1 := S2; for S1 as in part (a). (c) Set in part (a) after a call to COPY_SET. Result is two distinct sets. (d) Two distinct but equal sets implemented as linked lists.

replaces the set operation COPY_SET shown in Figure 3.4.2(c). If the element "b" is removed from the S1 in Figure 3.4.2 (b), it is also removed from S2. This behavior does not occur in Figure 3.4.2(c). Finally, Figure 3.4.2(d) pictures two distinct but equal sets S1 and S2. Unfortunately, the comparison

```
if S1 = S2 then . . . . .
```

would yield the wrong result, because the access values S1 and S2 are distinct. The values S1 and S2 access different sets that have the same elements. The sets in Figure 3.4.2(d) are the same but the linked lists that represent them are distinct. These examples clearly justify the requirement that the type set be limited private. In this way the comparison for equality operator can be overloaded inside the package and properly defined. The unfortunate side effect is that the programmer of this package cannot have programer-defined functions or procedures that have sets as mode "out" or mode "in out" parameters.

There are no inflexible rules for when a type should be unrestricted, private, or limited private. Sometimes, as in the case of the types COMPLEX_NUMBER and SET, the answer is self-evident after a bit of consideration. There are cases where the intended use forces a choice. Section 7.4 of the Ada LRM lists several restrictions on private and limited private types. For example, Section 7.4.4(4) implies that a subprogram formal parameter that is a limited private type can be mode "out" only if the subprogram specification is in the visible part of the package specification where the limited private type was declared. This means that programmer-defined subprograms cannot have a limited private formal parameter that is either mode "out" or mode "in out." If there is a need to pass types as formal parameters of programmer-defined subprograms, the type cannot be limited private; it must be private.

What if a composite type such as a record or an array is to contain a private type? If a composite type has components that are of private type (not limited private) and the definition of the composite type is outside the package, the composite type, even though its definition occurs outside the package, acts almost as if it were private. Assignment and comparison for equality are allowed, but all other operations that involve the subcomponent of private type must reference some operation within the package. Consider the COMPLEX_NUMBER type as defined in Figure 3.1.6. Note that the type COMPLEX_NUMBER is private. The definition

```
type COMPLEX_ARRAY is array (integer range < >) of COMPLEX_NUMBER;
```

is legal but any operations on things of type COMPLEX_ARRAY must reference the operations of the package COMPLEX. Another rule is then that a type must be private instead of limited private if the limited private type is a part of a programmer-defined composite structure.

A final rule is that a type must be private instead of limited private if it is going to be instantiated into a formal generic parameter that is private. Consider the generic package

```
generic
   type ITEM_TYPE is private;
package THIS_EXAMPLE is
   ...........
end THIS_EXAMPLE;
```

and the instantiation

```
package MY_NEW_EXAMPLE is new THIS_EXAMPLE (MY_TYPE);
```

The type MY_TYPE cannot be limited private. It must be either unrestricted or private. Often, objects of one type are composed into another type defined by a package. If the original declaration of the type within the package was limited private, the whole package specification and body must be recompiled after redefining the type as private. This must occur before the instantiation. This situation will occur in several case studies that appear throughout the book. When it does, it will be noted.

3.5 OBJECT-ORIENTED PROGRAMMING

The phrase *object-oriented programming* (OOP) is a programming methodology that is becoming increasingly common. The languages C++, Smalltalk, and recent versions of Pascal all support the concepts of OOP. While Ada's generic packages support some of the concepts of OOP, Ada is not yet a true object-oriented language. The first revision of the specifications of Ada, called Ada 9X, are due out in December 1993. That revision will make Ada an object-oriented language.

What is an object-oriented language, and how can programming with Ada support the concepts of OOP? The major cornerstones of OOP are encapsulation, inheritance, and polymorphism. Encapsulation allows combining a data structure with the operations on that data structure. Inheritance requires that a hierarchy of objects inherit the operations from their predecessor. An operation is polymorphic if the operation is shared within the hierarchy. The concept of polymorphism requires that the implementation of each operation be specific for each object in the hierarchy.

Consider the generic package specification shown in Figure 3.5.1, which allows us to compare Ada concepts with the OOP philosophy. The package is called LINE. It has three operations, one to put an object on the end of the line, one to return the object from the front of the line and then return the object, and one to determine if the line is empty.

```
generic
   type OBJECT_TYPE is private;
package GENERIC_LINE is
   type LINE is limited private;
   procedure ADD_OBJECT_TO_LINE      (L : in out LINE;
                                       X : in OBJECT_TYPE);
   procedure REMOVE_OBJECT_FROM_LINE( L : in out LINE;
                                       X : out OBJECT_TYPE);
   function LINE_EMPTY (L : LINE) return boolean;
private
   .................
end GENERIC_LINE;
```

Figure 3.5.1 Simple Ada package.

Encapsulation is fully supported. Any programmer-defined object is fully encapsulated at instantiation. Once instantiated, a line of those objects is created along with the operations on that line. Unlike languages such as standard Pascal, the encapsulation is strictly enforced by the use of private and limited private types.

Inheritance is also supported. The package GENERIC_LINE is the parent or predecessor of every instantiation. It can be used to define a line of student records, a line of calls to be answered in the order received by an automated switchboard, and a line of computer programs waiting to be executed. Inheritance requires that the three operations in the parent generic package be available to each line of objects instantiated, which they are.

With work, generic packages can be polymorphic when needed. Suppose that a line of objects must be created with the additional requirement that the objects must be added to the line based on some priority. This can be accomplished by defining a new generic package that passes along a priority operator "<" as a generic parameter (see Figure 3.5.2).

```
generic
   type OBJECT_TYPE is private;
   with function "<" ( LEFT, RIGHT : OBJECT_TYPE) return boolean;
package GENERIC_LINE is
   type LINE is limited private;
   procedure ADD_OBJECT_TO_LINE      ( L : in out LINE;
                                        X : in OBJECT_TYPE);
   procedure REMOVE_OBJECT_FROM_LINE  ( L : in out LINE;
                                        X : out OBJECT_TYPE);
   function LINE_EMPTY (L : LINE) return boolean;
private
   .................
end Generic_LINE;
```

Figure 3.5.2 Modified Ada package that illustrates polymorphism.

The operator "<" can be used to add objects to the line subject to some priority. Other examples of polymorphism are easy to generate. Consider a generic package of matrix vector operations of objects. These objects could conceivably be integer, float, complex, or boolean types. The particular operations for "+", "/", "−", and "*" would have to be supplied along with the objects themselves.

In the true sense, Ada is not yet an object-oriented language, but Ada does support an object-oriented development process. The use of generic packages allows the creation of classes of objects along with the operations on these classes. The major mechanism lacking from Ada and available in a true object-oriented language such as Smalltalk is full inheritance. Ada has what has been described by Booch as "static" inheritance. It is possible to build a type of dynamic inheritance into Ada, but the price is the loss of full encapsulation. The objects cannot be private or limited private, which removes the protection and safety provided by Ada's strong typing mechanism. Booch has written prolifically about Ada and the object-oriented development process. See, in particular, Booch [7,8].

All the abstract data types studied in this book will be implemented as reusable generic packages that encapsulate programmer-supplied data types, functions, or values. The concepts and rules illustrated in this chapter will become clearer as more examples are fashioned.

EXERCISES

Section 3.1 Packages

3.1.1 Create a package specification that contains the constants for unit conversion. It should include constants of float type for INCH_TO_CM, CM_TO_INCH, INCH_TO_FEET, and so on. See Figure 3.1.1.

3.1.2 a. Implement the function − in Figure 3.1.3.
  b. Implement the function * in Figure 3.1.3.
  c. Implement the function / in Figure 3.1.3.
  d. Implement the function REAL_PART in Figure 3.1.3.
  e. Implement the function IMAGINARY_PART in Figure 3.1.3.
  f. Implement the function SET_Z in Figure 3.1.3.
  g. Implement the function COMPLEX in Figure 3.1.3.
  h. Implement the function abs in Figure 3.1.3.
  i. Gather parts a through i into a package body for the type COMPLEX as in Figure 3.1.3.

3.1.3 a. Implement the function "+" in Figure 3.1.6.
  b. Implement the function "−" in Figure 3.1.6.
  c. Implement the function "*" in Figure 3.1.6.
  d. Implement the function "/" in Figure 3.1.6.
  e. Implement the function REAL_PART in Figure 3.1.6.
  f. Implement the function IMAGINARY_PART in Figure 3.1.6.
  g. Implement the function SET_Z in Figure 3.1.6.
  h. Implement the function COMPLEX in Figure 3.1.6.
  i. Implement the function "abs" in Figure 3.1.6.
  j. Gather parts a through i into a package body for the type COMPLEX as in Figure 3.1.6.

3.1.4 a. The unary "−" operator changes the sign of the real and imaginary parts of a complex number. Add a unary minus and a unary plus operator to the specification of Figure 3.1.6 and its body as defined in Exercise 3.1.3j.
  b. The complex exponential operator is defined by

$$z**n = (z.\text{real}**n)*(\cos(n*z.\text{imag}) + i*\sin(n*z.\text{imag}))$$

where cos and sin are trigonometric functions. Add the exponential operator to the complex package specification in Figure 3.1.6 and to the package body as defined in Figure 3.1.6.

3.1.5 a. Write a package specification that computes the areas and volumes of regular figures and solids such as squares, cubes, rectangles, and spheres.

b. Write a body for the package specified in part a.

3.1.6 After consulting any basic freshman analytic geometry and calculus text, write the specification for the package TWO_D that performs simple two-dimensional operations on points in the plane. The package must include a record defining a point and procedures to translate the point, rotate a point, and skew the point. Implement the body of this package. The type point must be a private type.

3.1.7 After consulting any basic freshman physics or calculus book, write the specification for a three-dimensional vector package. The type VECTOR must be private. The package should include operations to add two vectors, subtract two vectors, multiply a vector by a float, find the scalar or dot product, compute the vector or cross product, and find the length of the vector. Implement the package that you specify.

3.1.8 A rational number is the quotient of an integer divided by a positive number, where the integer, commonly called the *numerator*, and the positive, commonly called the *denominator*, have no common factors. Another name for rational numbers is *fractions*. They can be defined as

```
type RATIONAL is
record
  NUMERATOR : integer := 0;
  DENOMINATOR : positive := 1;
end record;
```

a. Euclid's algorithm to find the greatest common divisor of two positive numbers M and N is recursively defined as

$$GCD(N, M) = N \qquad\qquad \text{if } M = 0$$
$$= GCD(M, N \text{ rem } M) \quad \text{otherwise}$$

Implement Euclid's algorithm.

b. Specify a package that does rational number arithmetic.
Use Figure 2.1.6 as a pattern.

c. Write a body for the specification in part b.

Section 3.2 Generic Subprograms

3.2.1 Write a generic function FIND_LOCATION that returns the index of a given element in a given array. The index of the array should be any discrete type.

3.2.2 Write a generic selection sort procedure that sorts an array of things of type item. The formal generic parameter list should look as follows:

```
type ITEM_TYPE is private;
type INDEX is (<>);
type ITEM_ARRAY is array ( Index ) of ITEM_TYPE;
with function "<" (Left, Right : ITEM_TYPE) return boolean;
```

Selection sort finds the location of the maximum item and then it exchanges the maximum item with the last entry in the array. The process is repeated on the array between INDEX'first and INDEX'pred(INDEX'last) until there is only one item left to sort.

Exercises

3.2.3 Write a generic function to integrate a function over a closed interval [A, B] using Simpson's rule. If N=number of intervals is even, Simpson's rule is defined by

```
H = (B-A)/N
X(I) = A + I*H  I = 0, 1, 2, ..., N
INTEGRAL = H*(F(X(0)) + 4*F(X(1)) + 2*F (X(2) +4*F (X(3))
     + . . .  2*F(X(N-2)) + 4*F (X(N-1))+ F(X(N)))/3.0
```

3.2.4 Write a generic function to find the root of a function in the interval $[A , B]$ using the method of bisection. The method of bisection requires that $f(A) *f (B) < 0$; that is, the sign of f differs at the endpoints. Then:
   a. Set $X = (A+B)/2$.
   b. Compute $F(X)*F(A)$.
   c. If $F(X)*F(A) < 0$ then
        replace B with x
        else
        replace A with x
        end if.
   d. Repeat steps a, b, and c until (B–A) is "small enough."

3.2.5 Write a generic function "*" for multiplying two arbitrary matrices of type ITEM_TYPE. The formal generic parameter list would be similar to

```
type ITEM_TYPE is private;
type INDEX is (<>);
type ITEM_MATRIX is array (INDEX range <>, INDEX range <>) of ITEM_TYPE;
with function "+" (LEFT, RIGHT : ITEM_TYPE) return ITEM_TYPE;
with function "*" (LEFT, RIGHT : ITEM_TYPE) return ITEM_TYPE;
```

Section 3.3 Generic Packages

3.3.1 Rewrite package VECTOR defined in Exercise 2.1.7 with the goal of making it a generic package with one formal generic that sets the precision.

3.3.2 A queue is an abstract data type in the form of a linear list. Items are added at the end of the list by an operation called ENQUEUE. Items are removed from the front by an operation called DEQUEUE. Write a simple generic package that includes ENQUEUE and DEQUEUE, and include a third operation called QUEUE_EMPTY (see Figure E3.3.2). Use the generic package in Figure 3.3.2 as a pattern.

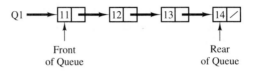

Front
of Queue

Rear
of Queue

Figure E3.3.2

3.3.3 Write a generic package POLY that defines a polynomial as an array of float coefficients. The formal generic parameter list should include the maximum degree n, and the package must include the basic minimum polynomial operations of addition, subtraction, and evaluation.

3.3.4 Redo Exercise 3.3.3 by using a discriminant record to hold the coefficient array.

3.3.5 a. Implement Figure 3.3.4.

b. Compare part a with Exercise 3.1.3. Which is more general? Which is harder to implement?

NOTES AND REFERENCES

The concept of object-oriented development closely parallels that in Booch [8]. For a general discussion of the concepts of object-oriented programming, see Meyer [37]. Meyer has an excellent discussion concerning object-oriented techniques in other environments, including a chapter devoted to object-oriented programming in Ada and a chapter devoted to genericity versus inheritance. The first major revision of the Ada Standard, called Ada 9X, will make Ada into a true object-oriented language.

4

Recursion and Performance Evaluation

4.1 "BIG O"

It is said that "There are liars, damned liars, and statisticians." Part of the problem lies in making sure that everyone understands the terms being used. Benchmarking is a perfect illustration of this problem. Two cars can be benchmarked for speed by going to the local drag strip and seeing which car finishes first. This benchmarks acceleration. A different test would be needed to benchmark the miles-per-gallon value of each vehicle. Indeed, the author is fond of saying that there are "lies, damned lies, and benchmarks." It is hard to benchmark computers. One obviously cannot compare the running time of different programs running on different computers using different data sets. What criteria can be used to compare the running time of the same program with the same data set on different computers? Even this is not as straightforward as it sounds. Measuring the running time of the same program on two different computers can be biased by how efficiently each program is compiled. There is a way of reducing the arguments to a common level. In this section we present the mathematical concept of the "big O" as a way of measuring performance. Although there are other measures of program performance, these measures are not as basic. This performance measure can be used to describe the time an algorithm takes to execute, the space required for it to execute, the number of times that a particular operation is performed, or the overhead associated with parameter passing. The "big O" measure is not an exact measure but a proportional measure.

Consider a procedure with two integer parameters called

```
DO_IT (I, J);
```

and suppose that this procedure takes the same amount of time to execute regardless of the integer values of the arguments. This procedure executes in constant time. Executing in constant time does not mean that it takes the same amount of time to execute on any computer from a small microcomputer to a large supercomputer. Nor does it say that if there is a second procedure,

```
DO_AGAIN (I,J,K);
```

which also executes in constant time, then both procedures execute in the same time on the same computer. Some programs take longer than others to execute. All it means is that anytime the procedure executes, it will take approximately the same time regardless of the arguments passed: faster perhaps on a supercomputer than a PC, but about the same time on a given machine.

Suppose now that one of the procedures above is placed inside a loop, that is,

```
for INDEX in integer range 1..N loop
   DO_IT(INDEX, J);
end loop;
```

The procedure will be executed N times, so the time to execute the loop is dependent on the time it takes to execute the procedure DO_IT multiplied by the length of the loop N. This code segment executes in time that is proportional to the length of the loop. If the procedure were placed inside a second nested loop,

```
for OUTER in integer range 1..N loop
   for INNER in integer range 1..N loop
      DO_IT(OUTER, INNER);
   end loop;
end loop;
```

the execution time is now proportional to $N**2$, the number of executions of DO_IT. Doubling the value of N increases the execution time by a factor of 4. The discussion above does not answer the question of how fast a particular code segment will execute. It does provide a basis for comparison.

Definition.   A process that uses a resource proportional to $f(n)$ is said to be $O(f(n))$ in that resource.

Note the word *proportional* in the definition above. $O(f(n))$ is read "big O of $f(n)$." In other words, if something is $O(f(n))$, there is a constant C and a fixed integer N, where the absolute value of the "something" is less than $C*abs(f(n))$, usually for $n >= N$. DO_IT by itself is $O(1)$. The process that nests DO_IT in a single loop is $O(n)$ or "big O of n." The process that nests DO_IT within a double loop is $O(n**2)$, or "big O of $n**2$."

Consider a game where the computer generates a random number between 1 and n and the player must guess the number. The player must continue guessing until the correct answer is found. If the computer only answers yes or no for your guess, it will take an average of $n/2$ guesses. The game is at best $O(n)$. It is $O(n)$ even if sometime you guess correctly on the first guess. It is an average. Note that $O(n)=O(n/2)$. Remember, something is $O(n)$ if there is a constant k such that the process uses approximately $k*n$ of a resource. Suppose that the computer were programmed to return one of three answers: "too high" if the guess is high, "too low" if the guess is low, and "right on" if the guess is correct. This extra information allows a strategy that is $O(\log_2(n))$. At each step the information "too high" is used to restrict all guesses to guesses less than the one that got the response "too high."

The algorithm shown in Figure 4.1.1 outlines the new optimal strategy. Each iteration cuts the number of possibilities in half. If the range is n, the first guess reduces the number of possibilities to $n/2$, $n/4$ after the second guess, and so on. An answer must be reached after at most $[\log_2(n)]$ guesses where the notation $[x]$ means the first integer equal to or larger than x. Why must the answer be reached in at most $[\log_2(n)]$ guesses? Each guess reduces the number of possibilities by half. After k guesses, the number of possibilities is at most $n/2**k$. This continues until $n/2** k<=1$ or until $k=[\log_2(n)]$.

```
LOW := 1;
HIGH := N
loop
  NEXT_GUESS := (LOW+HIGH)/2;
  If ANSWER="TOO HIGH" then
    HIGH := NEXT_GUESS;
  elsif ANSWER="TOO LOW" then
    LOW :=NEXT_GUESS;
  else
    exit; —finished, NEXT_GUESS is the answer;
  end if;
end loop;
```

Figure 4.1.1   Strategy to guess number.

How does the "big O" notation answer the question about algorithm efficiency? Consider Figure 4.1.2. The column farthest to the left lists various values of n. Each column to the right is some function evaluated at that n.

	$\log_2(n)$	n	$n*\log_2(n)$	$n**2$	$n**3$	$2** n$	$n!$
1	0	1	0	1	1	2	1
2	1	2	2	4	8	4	2
4	2	4	8	16	64	16	24
8	3	8	24	64	512	256	40320
16	4	16	64	256	4096	2**16	
32	5	32	160	1024	32768	2**32	
64	6	64	384	4096	2**18	2**64	
128	7	128	896	2**14	2**21		
256	8	256	2048	2**16	2**24		
512	9	512	3618	2**18	2**27		
1024	10	1024	10**2**10	2**20	2**30		
65536	16	2**16	16*2**16	2**32	2**48		
1048576	20	2**20	20*2**20	2**40	2**60		

Figure 4.1.2   Relationship of $O(f(n))$.

What does this table show? Avoid processes that require resources such as processing time or storage located to the right of the table if possible.

Suppose that a programmer had a choice between two sorting methods, one that executes in $O(n**2)$ with constant 5 and one that is $O(n*\log_2(n))$ with constant 10. Figure 4.1.3 shows that the difference is not worth noting for "small" n. If, however, $n = 1024$, the $O(n**2)$ process will take considerably more of the resource than the $O(n*\log_2(n))$ process.

n	$10*n*\log_2(n)$	$5*n**2$
2	20	20
4	80	80
8	240	320
16	640	1280
32	1600	5120
64	3840	20480
128	8960	81920
256	20480	327680
512	36180	1310720
1024	102400	5242880
65536	10485760	21474836480

Figure 4.1.3 Comparison of execution time for two sorting methods.

Remember, there is no guarantee that the constant for the $O(n**2)$ method is the same as the constant for the $O(n*\log_2(n))$ method.

As a final example consider the following code segment, which multiplies two $N \times N$ square matrices together and stores the result in a third $N \times N$ matrix.

```
for ROW in integer range 1..N loop
  for COLUMN in integer range 1..N loop
    C(ROW, COLUMN) := 0.0;
    for INDEX in integer range 1..N loop
      C(ROW, COLUMN) := C(ROW,COLUMN);
        + A(ROW, INDEX) * B(INDEX, COLUMN);
    end loop;
  end loop;
end loop;
```

This code segment is $O(N**2)$ for memory because each array requires $N**2$ words. This code segment executes in time proportional to $O(N**3)$ because of the three nested loops. Doubling N increases the memory by a factor of 4 while increasing the execution time by a factor of 8.

Are there any rules in combining $O(f(n))*O(g(n))$ and $O(f(n)) + O(g(n))$? The rules below follow directly from the definition of $O(f(n))$.

Rule 1.   For any constant k, $k* O(f(n)) = O(f(n))$. The reason behind this rule is that $O(f(n))$ requires that there be a constant C such that $C*f(n) = O(f(n))$. $k*c$ is also a constant, so $(k*c)* f(n) = O(f(n))$.

Rule 2.   If $f(n) = O(g(n))$ and, $g(n) = O(h(n))$, then $f(n) = O(h(n))$. The statement $f(n) = O(g(n))$ requires the existence of a constant k where $abs(f(n)) < k*abs(g(n))$, and $g(n) = O(g(n))$ requires that $abs(g(n)) > C*abs(h(n))$, which combined yields $abs(f(n)) < k*C*abs(h(n))$ or $f(n) = O(h(n))$.

Rule 3. $f(n) + g(n) = O(\max\{f(n), g(n)\})$.

Rule 4. If $f_1(n) = O(g_1(n))$ and $f_2(n) = O(g_2(n))$, then $f_1(n)*f_2(n) = O(g_1(n)*(g_2(n))$.

Consider the case where there are two loops. One loop executes in $O(f(n))$ time and the second executes in $O(g(n))$ time. If the two loops are not nested one inside the other, Rule 3 says that together they will execute in $O(\max\{f(n), g(n)\})$ time. If the loops are nested one inside the other, Rule 4 says that they will execute in $O(f(n)*g(n))$ time.

This section began with the quote, "There are liars, damned liars, and statisticians." Suppose that process 1 executes at the rate of $O(f(n))$ and process 2 also executes at the rate of $O(f(n))$. Does this mean that the two processes execute in the same time? Absolutely not. Process 1 could execute at $5*f(n)$ while process 2 could execute at $5000*f(n)$. If a process is $O(2**n)$, the relative difference of $5*2**n$ and $5000*2** n$ is small for large n.

4.2 ALGORITHM TIME AND SPACE CONSTRAINTS

One objective in computer science is the minimizing of the computer resources needed to solve a problem. Two basic resources are the CPU time and the memory required to do the job. If the memory needed to store a computer program and the data it requires together exceed the memory available, the program is useless. The concept of memory requires some clarification. Many databases cannot run in main memory. They require secondary memory or disk memory. In some applications memory means both main and secondary memory. Conversely, a program is useless if it isn't feasible to solve the problem in a reasonable period of time on a given computer. Just because something works or is correct does not make it feasible.

Economists have long dreamed of developing a computer model of a nation. If they attempted to model every consumer's behavior and predict the effect of that behavior on the economy, their effort would be doomed to failure. Even if the data describing each individual consumer's preferences could be collected, storing these statistics would not be feasible. If the storage problem could be solved, the computational task of summing individual consumer interactions and determining long-range trends would be beyond the computational capabilities of a network of supercomputers. The Internal Revenue Service has a hard enough task just collecting and organizing the data needed to determine if individual taxpayers are filling out their income tax returns correctly.

Consider a much simpler problem. An arbitrary 40-digit integer is to be divided by another arbitrary 10-digit integer. A program is to be written that determines the remainder after dividing the 40-digit integer by the 10-digit integer. Assume that both integers are positive. The answer will be some natural number strictly less than the 10-digit number. The following algorithm is correct, but is it feasible?

```
N := FORTY_DIGIT_INTEGER;
while TEN_DIGIT_INTEGER< N loop
  N := N-TEN_DIGIT_INTEGER;
end loop;
put(N);
```

Suppose that this algorithm is implemented on a computer that can iterate through the loop 10 billion=10**10 times per second. The loop must execute 10**30 times. The computer would take

$$10**30 \text{ seconds} = 1.6667 \times 10**28 \text{ minutes}$$
$$= 2.7777 \times 10**26 \text{ hours}$$
$$= 1.1577 \times 10**25 \text{ days}$$
$$= 3.1709 \times 10**22 \text{ years}$$
$$= 3.1709 \times 10**20 \text{ centuries}$$

This is clearly not feasible. It still requires almost 1000 years to find the remainder if N is reduced from 40 digits initially to 20 digits initially. Yet this problem can be quickly solved on a microcomputer using a different approach. This problem can even be solved long-hand in under an hour using pencil and paper by any careful student who knows the multiplication tables.

Just because something is correct, elegant, and clearly understood does not make it feasible. What makes something feasible? Feasibility is not an absolute. The speed of computers is increasing while their cost, as a function of their capability, is decreasing. Something not feasible on a microcomputer, such as computing the energy bond of a simple chemical molecule, is a trivial task on a supercomputer. Inverting an $n \times n$ square matrix might not be feasible for some value of n on a microcomputer but easily feasible for a much larger value of n on a supercomputer. In the 1950s, the statistical average time between component failure on a "large" computer was measured in minutes. Computers used vacuum tubes in their hardware. A large computer might have several thousand tubes. If you turned on a bank of 10,000 incandescent light bulbs, how long would it be until the first bulb failed? There are computers that exist now, for use in space probes to other planets or to regulate artificial hearts, where the mean time between failure is measured in years. Certain problems are not attempted because it is known that the computer will either never finish within a reasonable period or the computer would crash before it found the problem's solution.

In this book, data structures will be developed together with the basic operations on those data structures. Most chapters will include a summary section of the time and space constraints for the data types developed in that chapter. There are three constraints of interest. First, what are the execution times of the operations on the particular structure? Second, how much space does it take to store the abstract data structure? Third, what is the parameter passing overhead for a particular implementation? The "big O" notation is perfect for the job. It can be used to describe the space a structure occupies, the time a particular operation takes to execute, and the overhead associated parameter passing.

The ideal is the use of algorithms where the resources needed for a particular operation are $O(1)$. These algorithms are not affected by the size of the data structure or the complexity of the task. Algorithms where the resources needed are either $O(n)$ or $O(n*\log_2 (n))$ are generally agreed to be feasible. Those problems that are $O(n**p)$ are workable for small values of p if n is less than a certain size. Problems that are $O(2**n)$ or $O(\exp(n))$ or $O(n!)$ are not feasible except for small values of n.

4.3 RECURSION

A *recursive* process is one that is defined in terms of itself. There are many very natural recursive processes. The mathematical function $n!$, read n factorial, can be defined as shown in Figure 4.3.1.

```
n! := n*( n-)! if n > 1
   := 1   if n = 0
```

Figure 4.3.1   Recursive definition of *n*!.

Recursive definitions are not circular definitions. A circular definition defines an object in terms of itself. Recursion reduces the problem to a simpler expression in terms of itself. Eventually, the problem is reduced to a base case. In Figure 4.3.1, *n*! is not defined in terms of *n*!; *n*! is defined in terms of (*n*–1)!.

N factorial has the simple recursive Ada implementation shown in Figure 4.3.2.

```
function NFACTORIAL ( N : natural ) return positive is
  -- Computes N!
begin
  if N<=1 then
    return 1;
  else
    return N * NFACTORIAL (N-1);
  end if;
end NFACTORIAL;
```

Figure 4.3.2.   Recursive Ada function for *n*!.

This nine-line function illustrates several features of a recursively implemented function. The first is that it is easy to prove the correctness of the algorithm. Second, it follows directly from the definition, so it is quick to program. Third, the recursive call in the seventh line has reduced or simplified the problem. Fourth, there is a point where the algorithm is not defined in terms of itself. In NFACTORIAL this occurs in line 5.

Figure 4.3.3 illustrates how NFACTORIAL is computed for 5!. Note that the problem reduces itself to a base case and then rebuilds itself while computing the final solution.

$$5!=5*4!$$
$$=5*4*3!$$
$$=5*4*3*2!$$
$$=5*4*3*2*1!$$
$$=5*4*3*2*1$$
$$=5*4*3*2$$
$$=5*4*6$$
$$=5*24$$
$$=120$$

Figure 4.3.3.   Model of the computation of 5! based on recursion.

In developing a recursive algorithm, the base cases must be identified and solved. Then the rules to reduce the harder cases to the simpler and the base cases must be stated. The first two rules of writing a procedure that use recursion are:

1. There must be at least one base case that can be solved without the use of recursion.
2. For any case that is solved recursively, the recursion must move the solution toward a base case.

In the factorial example above, the "N<= 1" case is the base case that illustrates rule 1. In the NFACTORIAL example, rule 2 is illustrated by the "else" case, where the problem of computing n! is reduced to the problem of computing (N-1)!. Rule 2 says you must make progress toward the base cases. If you don't make progress, the process would go on forever and never terminate. There are two warnings when programming recursively.

1. Don't worry about how the compiler implements recursion.
2. Never duplicate by solving the same case of the problem in separate recursive calls.

Ada supports recursion. Assume that the compiler writer knew his or her business. If your problem was correctly defined recursively, let the compiler implement the call correctly. Warning 1 says to work at the language level. Warning 2 says to beware of cases where the work increases exponentially. Each call to the function NFACTORIAL is $O(1)$, but the process that computes $n!$ is $O(n)$ in time, space, and overhead because n calls are made. Later several simple examples are developed that violate warning 2, with the computation being $O(2^{**} n)$.

One constraint that is often ignored is the overhead associated with parameter passing. A procedure has constant parameter overhead of $O(1)$ for each call to itself. It follows that a recursive procedure that calls itself n times will be $O(n)$. Ada passes scalar parameters in one of three modes. They are mode "in," mode "out," and mode "in out." Nonscalar parameters are usually passed by reference in order to reduce overhead. When an array is passed by reference, its base address, an access type, and some attribute information are passed. If each call to a recursive procedure requires k words of memory to pass the parameters, then n calls will ultimately require $k*n$ words. This says that the parameter overhead is $O(n)$, where n is the number of calls.

Recall the singly linked linear list introduced in Chapter 2 with data structure

```
type INTEGER_NODE;
type LIST in access INTEGER_NODE;
type INTEGER_NODE is
  record
    DATA : integer;
    NEXT : LIST;
  end record;
L1, L2 : LIST;
```

Consider now a boolean-valued function LIST_EQUAL that returns true if two lists are equal. Two lists are equal if both lists are equal in length and if the kth node of each list contains the same object. Both the recursive and nonrecursive versions are given below.

```
function LIST_EQUAL (L1, L2 : LIST) return boolean is
  --recursive version of LIST_EQUAL
begin
  if L1=null and L2=null then
    --Empty lists are always equal
    return true;
  elsif L1=null xor L2=null then
    --If one list is empty and the other isn't....
    return false;
```

```
        else
          -- If the first nodes are equal, then two lists are equal if
          -- the lists starting at the second node are equal
          return L1.DATA=L2.DATA and then LIST_EQUAL(L1.NEXT, L2.NEXT);
        end if;
    end LIST_EQUAL;


    function LIST_EQUAL(L1, L2 : list) return boolean is
        --nonrecursive version of LIST_EQUAL
        TEMP_L1 : LIST := L1;
        TEMP_L2 : LIST := L2;
    begin
        -- Check both lists node by node
        while TEMP_L1 /= null and then TEMP_L2 /= null loop
          exit when TEMP_L1.DATA /= TEMP_L2.DATA;
          TEMP_L1 := TEMP_L1.NEXT;
          TEMP_L2 := TEMP_L2.NEXT;
        end loop;
        --If the end of both lists were reached, they must be equal
        return TEMP_L1=null and TEMP_L2=null;
    end LIST_EQUAL;
```

Both versions of LIST_EQUAL are correct. The recursive version is simple to understand. The two base cases are when two empty lists are compared, which returns true, or when
an empty and a nonempty list are compared, which returns false. The nonbase case says return
true if both the first integer_nodes in each list contain the same integer and if the tails of each
list (the tail of a list is a list whose first INTEGER_NODE is the second INTEGER_NODE of
the original list) are equal. For two equal lists of length n, both functions execute in $O(n)$. Each
call to the recursive version executes in $O(1)$, but it must call itself n times. In the nonrecursive version the loop must execute n times. A similar argument implies that the parameter overhead is of the recursive version is $O(n)$ because it is called a total of n times. The nonrecursive
version is called once, so its parameter overhead is $O(1)$.

The recursive pattern above is quite common. Do the simple case at the node at the beginning and apply the procedure or function recursively to the remainder of the structure. The
procedure COPY has a simple recursive implementation using this strategy. Copy the first
node and then copy the tail of the list to the end of the INTEGER_NODE.

```
        procedure COPY ( FROM : in  LIST; TO :  out LIST ) is
          --Make an exact copy of list FROM and return it as TO
          TEMP : LIST;
        begin
          if FROM = null then
            --Empty list, done
            TO := null;
          else
            --FROM not empty, copy the next INTEGER_ NODE
            TEMP := new INTEGER_NODE'(FROM.DATA, null);
            COPY (FROM.NEXT, TEMP.NEXT);
            TO := TEMP;
```

```
      end if;
   end COPY;
```

Let a VECTOR type again be defined as an unconstrained array of integers, that is,

```
   type VECTOR is array (integer range <>) of integer;
```

and consider the following two functions to sum up the integer components of a VECTOR.

```
function SUM_VECTOR_1 (V: VECTOR ) return integer is
   --recursive implementation to add up the components of V
begin
  if V'length=1 then
     -- V has one component, sum is trivial
     return V (V'first));
  else
     -- V has more than one component, return sum of first+rest
     return V (V'first))+SUM_VECTOR (V(V'first+1..V'LAST');
  end if;
end SUM_VECTOR_1;

function SUM_VECTOR_2 (V : VECTOR) return integer is
   --nonrecursive implementation to add up the components of V
   SUM : integer := 0;
begin
  for INDEX in V'range loop;
     Sum := Sum+V(INDEX);
  end loop;
  return Sum;
end SUM_VECTOR_2;
```

Like the function LIST_EQUAL, both execute in $O(n)$ for a vector with n components, while the parameter overhead is $O(n)$ for the recursive version and $O(1)$ for the nonrecursive version. To use or not to use recursion, that is the question. There is no answer. More accurately, the answer depends on who you ask. It is the author's position that the use of recursion in applications is justified, particularly when it makes implementation easier to understand. The author also believes that when writing reusable components, especially when writing generic packages, all unnecessary overhead should be avoided, so recursion should be avoided in this case.

A procedure uses tail recursion when it is implemented if the last executed statement is a recursive call to itself. NFACTORIAL, LIST_EQUAL, COPY, and SUM_VECTOR_1 are all examples of tail recursion. Any procedure or function that uses tail recursion can be implemented using iteration or a loop. Some compilers are smart enough to recognize tail recursion and then generate the code nonrecursively.

The same pattern works in nonlinear dynamic structures. Consider the tree defined in Section 2.6. The tree data structure is given by

```
      type TREE_NODE;
      type TREE is access TREE_NODE;
      type TREE_NODE is
```

```
record
    DATA : integer;
    LEFT,
    RIGHT : TREE;
end record;
```

Tail recursion even has a nonlinear counterpart. The current node is processed, then the left and right "subtrees" are processed recursively. The function TREE_NODE_COUNT returns the number of nodes in the tree.

```
function TREE_NODE_COUNT (T : TREE ) return natural is
   -- Counts the number of TREE_NODES in a tree
begin
  if T = null then
    -- The TREE is empty, so it has no nodes
    return 0;
  else
    -- TREE not empty, the number of nodes is 1 + number of
    -- nodes in left subtree+number of nodes in the right subtree
    return 1 + TREE_NODE_COUNT (T.LEFT)+TREE_NODE_COUNT(T.RIGHT);
  end if;
end TREE_NODE_COUNT;
```

This same recursive process can be used to write simple, easy-to-understand procedures and functions to process trees. Inserting nodes into a tree and summing up the integers in all the nodes in a tree are other simple-to-implement recursive procedures and functions.

Many things other than numerical functions have recursive definitions in computer science. For example, one method of defining the syntax of a language is by using BNF (Backus–Naur form) notation, which can be expressed symbolically or graphically. The BNF definition of an expression is as shown in Figure 4.3.4.

expression = [optional sign] term |term + term|
term – term
term = factor |term * factor| term / factor
factor = variable name |constant value| (expression)

Figure 4.3.4   BNF for expressions involving +, –, *, and /.

Each line has multiple choices, with each choice separated by |, read "or." A choice must be made. The BNF definition shown in Figure 4.3.4 is recursive in "expression" and in "term." The base cases for this recursive definition are "variable name" and "constant." These values terminate a derivation. Constants are expressions through the logic outlined in Figure 4.3.5.

expression => term
=> factor
=> constant value
=> 8

Figure 4.3.5   BNF evaluation of constant function.

An expression is derivable if it can be computed from its BNF definition. Simple algebraic expressions such as $-5*x+3$ are derivable (Figure 4.3.6).

expression => –term
=> –term + term
=> –term * factor + term
=> –factor * factor + term
=> –constant value * factor + term
=> –5 * factor + term
=> –5 * variable name + term
=> –5 * x + term
=> –5 * x + factor
=> –5 * x + constant value
=> –5 * x + 3

Figure 4.3.6 BNF evaluation of a linear function.

Algebraic expressions involving parentheses, such as $(x+3)*(x * x+x)$, are also derivable (Figure 4.3.7).

expression => term
=> term * factor
=> factor * factor
=> (expression) * factor
=> (term+term) * factor
=> (variable name + term) * factor
=> (x+term) * factor
=> (x+constant value) * factor
=> (x+3) * factor
=> (x+3) * (expression)
=> (x+3) * (term + term)
=> (x+3) * (term * factor + term)
=> (x+3) * (factor * factor+term)
=> (x+3) * (variable name * factor + term)
=> (x+3) * (x * factor + term)
=> (x+3) * (x * variable name + term)
=> (x+3) * (x * x + term)
=> (x+3) * (x * x + factor)
=> (x+3) * (x * x + variable name)
=> (x+3) * (x * x + x)

Figure 4.3.7 BNF evaluation of product of two linear functions.

A compiler verifies the syntax of a program in a similar manner. The recursive definition is needed because the variety of possible expressions cannot be anticipated.

The backtracking strategy is another application of recursion. Many problems systematically search for a solution using recursive definitions. The backtracking strategy can be outlined as shown in Figure 4.3.8.

1. Divide the problem into smaller problems. This can typically be done as a result of the recursive definitions.

2. At the next step of the solution, make a systematic guess until the solution is found. Since the guess is systematic, all possible solutions will be examined until a solution is found.

3. For each guess, determine which condition applies.
   a. Record the guess.
   b. Is it a solution? If yes, we are done.
   c. Is the guess a dead end? Stop and backtrack one step.
   d. If not done and not stuck, go on to the next step.

Figure 4.3.8. Strategy for implementing backtracking using recursion.

There is a famous chess problem called the eight queens problem that can be solved easily using the backtracking strategy. The object is to place eight queens on a standard chessboard in a way that no queen can capture any other queen. A queen threatens another chess piece if they are both on the same row or the same column or on the same diagonal. Clearly, there can only be one queen in any row or column, so the first assumption is that each queen will be placed in a fixed column. The strategy is to keep placing queens on the board and backtrack when a problem occurs.

1. For a particular column, put a queen in row 1.
2. For all rows:
   a. If the placed queen is OK with respect to queens placed previously, place the queen.
   b. If this queen in column 8, exit.
   else
   Place queen in next column (recursive step)
   If no placement possible, remove guess, and move to next row
   c. If the queen does not interfere, move to next row.

Figure 4.3.9 Backtracking strategy for the eight queens problem.

The procedures outlined in Figure 4.3.9 implement the eight queens problem. The printing of the solution is left to the student.

```
procedure EIGHT_QUEENS is
type CHESS_BOARD is array ( integer range 1..8,
                            integer range 1..8 ) of boolean;
BOARD : CHESS_BOARD := (others=> (others => false));
DONE : boolean := false;

procedure PRINT_BOARD (BOARD : in CHESS_BOARD) is
begin
  --left to the student
  null;
end PRINT_BOARD;

function NEXT_QUEEN_OK (ROW, COL : integer;
                        BOARD : in BOARD_TYPE ) return boolean is
begin
```

Figure 4.3.10. Eight queens Ada program. Continues on page 89.

```
                --left to student
              null;
          end NEXT_QUEEN_OK;
          procedure PLACE_NEXT_QUEEN (COLUMN   : in integer;
                                      BOARD    : in out CHESS_BOARD;
                                      FINISHED : in out boolean ) is
            ROW : integer := 1;
          begin
            loop
              if NEXT_QUEEN_OK (ROW, COLUMN, BOARD) then
                --Mark chess board as holding a queen
                BOARD (ROW, COLUMN) := true;
                if COLUMN=8 then
                    --All queens placed
                    FINISHED := true;
                    exit;
                else
                    --Place next queen in the next column
                    PLACE_NEXT_QUEEN (COLUMN+1, BOARD, FINISHED);
                    --Exit when queen ok in columns 1 to COLUMNS+1
                    exit when FINISHED;
                    -- Queen is not ok, set board position as empty
                    BOARD (ROW, COLUMN) := false;
                    --Put the queen in the next row
                    ROW := ROW+1;
                    -- Only eight rows on a chess board
                    exit when ROW > 8;
                  end if;
              else -
                  -- Current position is not ok,
                  if ROW=8 then
                      -- new Queen can't be placed in any row, backtrack
                      exit;
                  else
                      -- try the next row
                      ROW := ROW+1;
                  end if;
                end if;
              end loop;
            end PLACE_NEXT_QUEEN;
          begin - Main
            PLACE_NEXT_QUEEN (1, BOARD, DONE );
            PRINT_BOARD (BOARD);
          end EIGHT_QUEENS;
```

Figure 4.3.10. Concluded.

The student should satisfy himself or herself that the procedure not only works but fits the backtracking mode.

The power of recursion should not be underestimated. There are computer languages with no loop structure that are incredibly powerful. LISP is an example.

There are many reasons to use recursion. Proper use of recursion makes algorithms easier to describe, easier to understand, easier to verify, and often shorter in length. The programmer focuses on the details, while the compiler and the operating system string the pieces together. Often, recursive solutions are not limited by the size or complexity of the problem. The eight queens problem could be redone as the twenty queens problem with little effort. Recursive algorithms often require less development time, less programming work, less debugging effort, and less time to verify correctness. The result can be very cost-effective from a labor point of view. Finally, certain algorithmic approaches, such as backtracking, cannot be implemented easily without using recursion.

Recursion behaves like the "good news, bad news" joke. The good news was contained in the preceding paragraph. The bad news is that like all good things, there can be hidden costs. The hidden costs of recursion can be unacceptably high system overhead. As an example, the recursive implementation of the Fibonacci sequence illustrates another hidden problem with recursion. The Fibonacci sequence starts with two 1's. From that point on, any term is the sum of the two preceding terms:

$$1, 1, 2, 3, 5, 8, 13, 21, 34, 55, 89, 144, 233, \ldots \ldots$$

which implies the recursive definition outlined in Figure 4.3.11.

$$f_0 = f_1 = 1$$
$$f_{n+1} = f_n + f_{n-1}$$

Figure 4.3.11 Definition of Fibonacci Sequence.

The recursive call to compute the nth Fibonacci number has both a recursive (Figure 4.3.12) and a nonrecursive (Figure 4.3.13) implementation. This is not surprising since the recursive version uses what might be called double-tail recursion.

```
function FIBONACCI ( N: natural ) return natural is
  --recursive implementation
begin
  if N = 0 or N = 1 then
    -- Base cases
    return 1;
  else
    return FIBONACCI (N - 1) + FIBONACCI (N - 2);
  end if;
end FIBONACCI;
```

Figure 4.3.12. Recursively implemented Ada function to generate the nth Fibonacci number.

```
function FIBONACCI ( n : natural) return natural is
  -- Nonrecursive implementation
  ANSWER, TEMP1, TEMP2 : natural := 1;
begin
  if N = 0 or N = 1 then
```

Figure 4.3.13. Nonrecursively implemented Ada function to generate the nth Fibonacci number.
Continues on page 91.

```
            return 1;
        else
            for COUNT in 2..N loop
                -- Compute the current Fibonacci number and keep track
                -- track of the last two Fibonacci numbers
                ANSWER := TEMP2 + TEMP1;
                TEMP1 := TEMP2;
                TEMP2 := ANSWER
            end loop;
            return ANSWER;
        end if;
    end FIBONACCI;
```

Figure 4.3.13. Concluded.

The recursive version violates warning 2. Note that the reduced case repeatedly solves the same case. The situation is so out of control that a student using a hand calculator could find the thirtieth Fibonacci number faster than any but the fastest workstations. System overhead associated with the recursive call overwhelms the calculation. To calculate FIBONACCI(6), two recursive calls must be made, one to FIBONACCI(5) and one to FIBONACCI(4). A call to FIBONACCI(5) requires two additional calls, one to FIBONACCI(4) and one to FIBONACCI(3). The pyramid structure shown in Figure 4.3.14(a) hints at the problem. Figure 4.3.14(b) points out the gross violation of rule 2. Work is being duplicated needlessly. A total of 25 calls to Fibonacci were made to find FIBONACCI(6). FIBONACCI(7) requires 41. Later a table will be developed that shows the number of calls required to compute by recursion the first n Fibonacci numbers.

The computational effort increases by an order of magnitude when the Fibonacci number index increases by 5. The effort associated with a single function call is minimal, but the

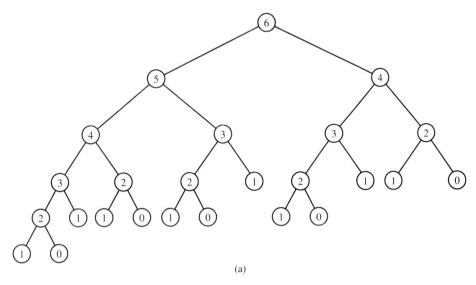

(a)

Figure 4.3.14. Overhead of a recursive Fibonacci function. (a) Diagram of recursive function calls to compute FIBONACCI (6). Part b is on page 92.

| | Number of Calls |
n	to FIBONACCI(n)
5	1
4	2
3	3
2	5
1	8
0	5

(b)

Figure 4.3.14. (b) Summary of the 24 calls to FIBONACCI(*n*) needed to compute FIBONACCI (6).

total effort can be overwhelming. A short Ada program using Meridian Ada on a 20-MHz 80386-based machine took about 30 seconds to compute the first 20 Fibonacci numbers and about 90 seconds just to compute the twenty-fifty number. The nonrecursive version executed almost instantly. The price for this clear short program is too high.

As a final example of bad recursion, consider the recursive implementation of a function to find the maximum integer value in an array of integers that is listed in Figure 4.3.15.

```
function MAX_ARRAY_VALUE ( V : VECTOR ) return integer is
  --Recursive function to find the largest component in V
begin
  if V'length = 1 then
    --V only has one component, the maximum
    return V (V'first);
  elsif V(V'first) > MAX_ARRAY_VALUE (V(V'first+1..V'last)) then
    --V has more than one component, if the first is largest ...
    return V (V'first);
  else
    -- V has more than one component and the first is not the largest
    return MAX_ARRAY_VALUE(V (V'first+1..V'last));
  end if;
end MAX_ARRAY_VALUE;
```

Figure 4.3.15. Recursive function to find maximum value in an array.

It appears that the only problem with the function MAX_ARRAY_VALUE is that it might call itself twice with the same parameter list. This behavior makes the potential number of recursive calls of order $O(2**n)$, where *n* is the length of the array. Consider an array of length *n* and range 1. . *n*, with the last element the largest. The following behavior occurs. The evaluation of MAX_ARRAY_VALUE(V(1. .n)) requires two evaluations of MAX_AR-RAY_VALUE(V(2. .n)). But each evaluation of MAX_ARRAY_VALUE(V(2. .n)) also requires two additional evaluations of MAX_ARRAY_VALUE (V(3. . n); and so on. The conclusion is that the amount of work performed as system overhead can double when the length of the array is incremented by 1. This function suffers from the same problems as the Fibonacci function. If V is a vector whose integer components are in strict descending order, MAX_AR-

RAY_VALUE is $O(n)$. For this reason, whenever the time or space constraints of an operation or algorithm are listed, the worst case will be listed unless otherwise noted. This example also illustrates the importance of proper testing. If a test vector with elements in strictly descending order is used as the test case, the programmer might feel that the function is $O(n)$ when it is $O(2**n)$ for any vector with its maximum element located in its last position.

This section closes with an example of how recursion can speed up algorithm development. A permutation is a grouping of objects where the ordering is important. The set of three objects {1,2,3} is just one group but there are six permutations. These permutations are {1,2,3}, {1,3,2}, {3,1,2}, {2,1,3}, {2,3,1}, and {3,2,1}. A group of n distinct objects has $n!$ permutations. Once the permutations of {1,2,3} are known, it is a simple matter to generate the permutations of {1,2,3,4}. Each of the six permutations of {1,2,3} generates four permutations of {1,2,3,4}. This is accomplished by inserting a 4 into the first, the second, the third, and the fourth places in each permutation of {1,2,3}. This observation is exactly how permutations can be recursively implemented.

A list containing zero or one objects cannot be permuted further. To get all the permutations of the ordered list {1,2,. . . , n} of n objects, generate n permutations of the reduced list of $n-1$ objects {1,2,. . . , $i-1$, $i+1$. .n} by placing the ith object into each of n positions. The group of $n-1$ objects is permuted in the same fashion. Define:

```
type PERMUTE_ARRAY is array (natural range <>) of natural;
```

and let P be of type PERMUTE_ARRAY. If $n = 4$, then $P = (3\ 4\ 1\ 2\ 0)$ represents the permutation {3,2,1,4}. $P(0) = 3$ contains the first object and says that the second object is in location 3. $P(3) = 2$ contains the second object and the location of the third object. $P(2) = 1$ is the third object and the location of the fourth object. When $P(i) = 0$, the next permutation has been generated and it is time to place the ith object into the next position. The following procedure will list the permutations stored with this convention.

```
procedure LIST_PERMUTATION (P : in         PERMUTE_ARRAY) is
  NEXT : natural := 0;
begin
  while P (NEXT) /= 0 loop
    put (P(NEXT));
    NEXT := P (NEXT);
  end loop;
  new_line;
end LIST_PERMUTATION;
```

If PROCESS_PERMUTATION represents a procedure that does something with the permutation, Figure 4.3.16 outlines a procedure that generates and processes all permutations.

```
procedure GENERATE_ALL_PERMUTATIONS (K : in      natural;
                                     P : in out PERMUTE_ARRAY) is
begin
  for each index in P loop
    insert K into that index;
    if K = P'last then
      PROCESS_PERMUTATION(P);
```

Figure 4.3.16 Pseudocode to generate permutations of a set. Continues on page 94.

```
      else
         GENERATE_ALL_PERMUTATIONS(K+1, P);
      end if;
      Remove K from index
   end loop;
end GENERATE_ALL_PERMUTATIONS;
```

Figure 4.3.16   Concluded.

When K = P'last, the list of n objects has been generated. If K / = P'last, the list is only K objects long and the result of it must be appended, which is what the recursive call does. Figure 4.3.17 is the full Ada implementation.

```
procedure GENERATE_ALL_PERMUTATIONS ( K : in      natural;
                                      P : in out PERMUTE_ARRAY) is
   PLACE : natural := 0
begin
   loop
      -- Insert K after position PLACE in PERMUTE_ARRAY
      P(K) := P(PLACE);
      P(PLACE) := K;
      if K =P'last then
         PROCESS_PERMUTATION(P);
      else
         GENERATE_ALL_PERMUTATIONS(K + 1, P);
      end if;
      P(PLACE) := P(K);
      PLACE := P(PLACE);
      -- 0 denotes the end of the list in P
      exit when PLACE = 0;
   end loop;
end GENERATE_ALL_PERMUTATIONS;
```

Figure 4.3.17   Ada code to generate permutations of a set.

A generic procedure for a next permutation is listed in Appendix C. If it is called, it returns the next permutation of n discrete objects. The procedure shown in Figure 4.3.17 generates and processes all permutations whenever the procedure call

```
GENERATE_ALL_PERMUTATIONS(0, P);
```

is made where P := (1, 2, 3, . . . , n, 0). This procedure makes n! recursive calls to itself because there are n! permutations of a set of n objects.

When should recursion be used? If the goal is simple-to-understand code that can be written easily, tested quickly, and rapidly corrected, a recursive algorithm should be considered provided that the storage and time constraints can be held within bounds. The goal of this book is to develop data types. Data types combine data structures with efficiently implemented operations on these data structures. Tail recursion should be removed if space considerations are important. In all cases, simple tail recursion should replaced by a loop if there is no loss in the clarity of the algorithm. In all cases recursive procedures or iterative procedures using stacks can accomplish exactly the same task. This subject is reviewed in Chapter 6. Recursion can always be translated into iteration. Unfortunately, the result often obscures the algorithm. In such cases, extra attention must be paid to documentation.

4.4 CASE STUDY: RECURSION OVERHEAD

Recursion can have several drawbacks. In this section we examine the time overhead of a poorly implemented recursive function. In this case study we study the number of recursive calls for the computation of the Fibonacci function while displaying the time it takes to compute each value. This illustrates the reason for warning 2 given near the beginning of Section 4.3:

Never duplicate by solving the same case of the problem in separate recursive calls.

To illustrate this point, a global variable count has been added to the function FIBONACCI in CASE_STUDY_3 to keep track of the number of recursive calls. Figure 4.4.1 contains CASE STUDY_3 as run on a 20-MHz 80386 PC using the Meridian Ada compiler.

```
with text_io;        use text_io;
with calendar;       use calendar;
procedure CASE_STUDY_3 is

Package NAT_IO is new integer_io (long_integer); use nat_io;
package MY_FLT_IO is new float_io(float); use MY_FLT_IO;

COUNT : long_integer := 0;
N : long_integer := 0;
TIME_START : float;

function FIBONACCI (N : long_integer) return long_integer is
begin
  -- Keep track of calls to FIBONACCI
  COUNT := COUNT + 1;
  if N=0 or N=1 then
    return 1;
  else
    return FIBONACCI (N-1)+FIBONACCI (N-2);
  end if;
end FIBONACCI;

begin --main
  for INDEX in long_integer range 1..35 loop
    -- Compute Nth Fibonacci number
    N := N + 1;
    -- Set number of calls to FIBONACCI to 0 at start
    COUNT := 0;
    -- Get the current system time using package calendar
```

Figure 4.4.1 CASE_STUDY_3. Continues on page 96.

```
TIME_START := float (SECONDS(CLOCK));
put ("N = "); put (N,1); put (" FIB(N) = "); put (FIB(N),1);
    put (" COUNT = "); put (COUNT,1); put ("ELAPSED TIME = ");
    put (float (SECONDS(CLOCK))-TIME_START); new_line;
end loop;
end CASE_STUDY_3;
```

Figure 4.4.1 Concluded.

Figure 4.4.2 was generated by the output of CASE_STUDY_3. The times were recorded from the system clock using the Ada Standard package calendar (see Ada LRM Section 9.6). The times listed in the third column are the times needed to compute the *n*th Fibonacci number. The number of recursive function calls is 2*FIBONACCI(n)-1. It took over 7 minutes just to compute the single value of FIBONACCI(35). The author was able to do the same computation using a hand calculator in less than 5 minutes. This case study illustrates one of the bad sides of recursion. Usually, the good (program readability or programmer productivity) outweighs the bad (program execution time).

n	FIBONACCI(n)	Number of Calls	Elapsed Time (seconds) to Compute the *n*th Fibonacci Number (approximately)
5	8	15	0.00
10	89	177	0.06
15	987	1973	0.00
20	10,946	21,891	0.33
25	121,393	242,785	3.51
30	1,346,269	2,692,537	38.61
31	2,178,301	4,356,617	62.51
32	3,524,578	7,049,155	101.11
33	5,702,887	11,405,773	163.57
34	9,227,465	18,454,929	264.62
35	14,930,352	29,860,703	428.26

Figure 4.4.2 Data from CASE_STUDY_3.

EXERCISES

Section 4.1 "Big O"

4.1.1 One $O(n)$ procedure has constant 100, and a second procedure that is $O(n**2)$ has constant 10. This implies that for values of n between 1 and 10, the second procedure will execute faster. Is this true? Why? Usually, procedures that are $O(n)$ are preferred over those that are $O(n**2)$. What about this case?

Recursion and Performance Evaluation   Chap. 4

Section 4.2 Algorithm Time and Space Constraints

4.2.1 Determine the execution time and the parameter overhead using the "big O" notation for the following functions.
   a. The function + in Figure 1.3.2
   b. The function < in Figure 1.4.4
   c. The function MINIMUM_VECTOR_VALUE in Figure 2.2.1
   d. The function ADD_TO_FRONT in Section 2.4
   e. The function ADD_INORDER_TO_LIST in Section 2.4
   f. The function ADD_TO_REAR in Section 2.4

Section 4.3 Recursion

4.3.1 Finish implementing the eight queens problem in Figure 4.3.10.

4.3.2 Implement the eight queens problem using the procedure GENERATE_ALL_PERMUTATIONS.

4.3.3 Put a global variable inside the function MAX_ARRAY_VALUE in Figure 4.3.15 to keep count of the number of times the function is called for a vector of length 10.
   a. The vector contains distinct elements in ascending order.
   b. The vector contains distinct elements in descending order.
   c. Every element of the vector is the same.
   d. The vector contains distinct elements in random order.

4.3.4 The binomial coefficient $B(n, k)$ can be defined as either

$$n!/(k!*(n-k)!)$$

or recursively as

$B(n, 0) = 1 \ \ n >= 0$
$B(n, n) = 1 \ \ n >= 0$
$B(n, k) = B(n - 1, k) + B(n - 1, k - 1) \ \ n > k > 0$

Implement both versions and complete the following two tables for each version.

Values for B(n,k) for n=2, ..., 10

n/k	1	2	3	4	5	6	7	8	9	10
2		×	×	×	×	×	×	×	×	×
3			×	×	×	×	×	×	×	×
4				×	×	×	×	×	×	×
5					×	×	×	×	×	×
6						×	×	×	×	×
7							×	×	×	×
8								×	×	×
9									×	×
10										×

Number of Recursive Calls to Compute $B(n,k)$ for $n=2, ..., 10$

n/k	1	2	3	4	5	6	7	8	9	10
2		×	×	×	×	×	×	×	×	×
3			×	×	×	×	×	×	×	×
4				×	×	×	×	×	×	×
5					×	×	×	×	×	×
6						×	×	×	×	×
7							×	×	×	×
8								×	×	×
9									×	×
10										×

4.3.5 Ackermann's function is a standard benchmark for determining how well recursion has been implemented by a particular compiler. Ackermann's function is defined as follows:

$$A(0, n) = n + 1 \qquad\qquad n >= 0$$
$$A(m, 0) = A(m - 1, 1) \qquad\qquad m > 0$$
$$A(m, n) = a(m - 1, A(m, n -1)) \qquad m > 0 \text{ and } n > 0$$

a. Write a recursive implementation that includes a global variable that counts the number of recursive calls.

b. Complete the following table.

	Value	Number of Calls
$A(0,0)$		
$A(0,4)$		
$A(0,6)$		
$A(0,8)$		
$A(2,2)$		
$A(2,1)$		
$A(2,0)$		
$A(4,3)$		
$A(3,3)$		
$A(3,2)$		
$A(3,1)$		

NOTES AND REFERENCES

There are other measures of software performance besides "big O." These include $\Omega(f(n))$ and $\Theta g(n)$. See any book on the design and analysis of algorithms, in particular Baase [4]. The use of permutations and combinations is important in many areas of computer science and modeling. The functions used here are similar to ones used by Peck and Schrack [40] and Kurtzberg [32].

5

Introduction to Abstract Data Types

Just like any trend or commodity, times and standards change. From the period just before World War II to the early 1950s, computer programming standards stressed efficient use of memory. Computers were very expensive. Large machines had minuscule memories by today's standards. All programming was done in machine or assembly language and any programming trick was acceptable. Today's hackers would have felt at home.

In the late 1950s the first two widely accepted high-level computer languages, Cobol and FORTRAN, appeared. In addition to increasing programmer productivity and increasing computer sales, these two languages changed standards of programming while opening up the ranks of programmers to people who were more user oriented than hardware oriented. The first single-user batch-oriented operating systems appeared. These simple operating systems allowed almost any engineer to use FORTRAN to help meet computational needs. As larger and more sophisticated computational problems were solved successfully, it became necessary to divide programming tasks. These initial attempts at program specification mark the infancy of that part of computer science now called *software engineering*.

5.1 SOFTWARE ENGINEERING

A wag once said that "Anything with science in its name isn't." All true sciences rely on the scientific method and the ability to replicate results. However, most things with engineering in their name do deal with engineering, although some things, such as the "sanitation engineer" who picks up the trash weekly, are not. Engineering has as its basis the application of scientific laws and principles. Electrical engineering would not be possible without Maxwell's laws, quantum mechanics, and modern mathematics. By this definition, software engineering is not a valid field of engineering. It is more of a craft or discipline.

Engineers also design, build, test, and maintain things. By this definition, software engineers are engineers. The products of a software engineer are not tangible things such as airplanes, bridges, or industrial plants that bottle soft drinks or manufacture home appliances. The software engineer's product is sequences of instructions that control a computer's operation. This control allows a single machine to perform many useful but varied tasks. These tasks range from preparing a manuscript with a program called a word processor to monitoring the launch of the Space Shuttle.

Professional engineers systematically apply their craft with rigor and discipline. Consider the design, testing, and production of an automobile. Two groups of people, a marketing group and a style group, come to a consensus regarding the qualities and appearance that a successful automobile should have. From this consensus comes a set of specifications for the car's appearance, performance, and cost. After examining all options, a final design is fixed. The final design is implemented, built as a prototype, and tested. After successful testing comes production, after which, hopefully, the public will buy and return profits to the manufacturer. New owners expect the manufacturer to provide a network of dealers and service centers to maintain and repair their purchases.

Software is developed using the same discipline. Suppose that a new word processor is going to be developed for sale to the public. Someone has an idea of what will sell and what will not sell. Specifications describing the new word processor's features are developed and approved. These specifications include the user interface, the minimum hardware configuration, the level of acceptable performance, and the cost. Software is developed, tested, refined, and validated. The new product is marketed, and later, if it is a success, new versions with unique features are released periodically.

A small company might employ a handful of engineers trying to solve one or two major problems. A large company or government agency might have thousands of engineers and scientists working on many projects. Sometimes these projects are independent, and sometimes they are coordinated. The same discipline, now called software engineering, applies to computer programming. The *software life cycle,* outlined in Figure 5.1.1, might better be called the *software product cycle.* The product of the software engineer is software. The goal is to produce reliable software.

Analysis	Understand the nature of the problem and prepare system specification.
Requirements	System specification is approved, and the detailed requirements of the software are determined. The result is an approved software specification.
Design	Detailed design developed for the software solution, which includes a definition of interfaces between the program units and the specification of program units.
Code	The individual program units are programmed and tested as individual units to see if they meet the design criteria.
Test	The program units are combined and tested to see if they meet the requirements. Testing and coding are usually conducted in tandem.
Release	The program is released.
Maintain	Errors that escaped detection in the design phase are corrected, updates are released, and new features are added.

Figure 5.1.1 Software life cycle.

A nursery fable divides people in two groups, those who know and those who don't know. Each of these two groups is further divided into two subgroups, those who think they know and those who know they know. The four cases are listed in Figure 5.1.2. The fable states further that those in the first group are fools, members of the second group are characterized as ignorant but capable of being educated, those in the third group lack confidence but can grow, while the fourth group consists of leaders and should be acknowledged. Ledgard [33]

1. Those who don't know, and think they do know
2. Those who don't know, and know they don't know
3. Those who know, but think that they don't know
4. Those who know, and know they know

Figure 5.1.2 People and knowledge.

feels that most people think there are two groups of paid programmers, professionals and amateurs. Ledgard argues that there is a third class, paid amateurs who are called professionals. There are four groups of amateurs who are called professional and their characteristics are listed in Figure 5.1.3. These groups correspond, in a rough sense, to the groupings listed in Figure 5.1.2.

1. Amateurs who think they are professionals (recent college graduates)
2. Amateurs learning to be professionals (journeyman transitioning to professional ranks)
3. Professionals who are really amateurs (amateurs promoted for reasons other than skill)
4. Professionals who are becoming amateurs (professionals who do not take the time to keep up)

Figure 5.1.3 Four types of amateur programmers.

What criteria can be used to distinguish a professional from an amateur? The nine characteristics of paid-amateur and paid-professional programmers, according to Ledgard, are listed in Figure 5.1.4. Two conclusions that can be made about these characteristics. Amateurs program first, then think and patch their work together. Professionals think first, then plan, and then program.

1. An amateur assumes that the user is like the programmer, but the professional never assumes user knowledge.
2. An amateur sees anomalies as a way of life, but the professional's design includes unusual cases.
3. An amateur considers review a nuisance, whereas the professional welcomes it.
4. The amateur is continually eliminating bugs, whereas the professional releases code with no known errors.
5. The amateur writes the documentation last; the professional writes documentation first.
6. The amateur works with incomplete specifications and does not fully understand the problem, whereas the professional has complete specifications and full understanding of the problem.
7. The amateur ignores the program life cycle, but the professional has well-defined phases and benchmarks.
8. The amateur gets on with the job, whereas the professional works with one eye on future enhancements and upgrades.
9. Amateurs write for the computer; professionals write for human beings.

Figure 5.1.4 Nine differences between amateur and professional programmers.

The second observation is that a professional has discipline, whose goal is a quality product. One of the beliefs of those who believe in software engineering is that this methodology and discipline can be studied and learned. Any professional in any profession is expected to have discipline.

Murphy's law states: "If something can go wrong, it will go wrong and at the worst possible moment." Amateurs validate Murphy's law continuously. This is not surprising. Anecdotal field experience suggests that a computer science–based corollary to Murphy's law is: "For every error corrected in a large program, two errors are introduced." The preceding paragraph suggests that

Professional software engineers plan first, then code.

Amateurs code first, then correct and correct and. . . .

Planning and understanding are an essential part of the software engineering discipline. Every abstract data type developed in this book will start with a documentation of its features.

5.2 SOFTWARE COMPONENTS AND REUSABILITY

Some lazy people get rich or famous by working smart, and some get rich or famous by hard work, but the really consistent success stories deal with those who both work hard and work smart. One characteristic of working smart is that the wheel is never reinvented unless it must be. A second characteristic of someone working smart is that lessons are learned once, and when a similar situation comes up, knowledge from the past is applied.

Consider the building of a house. The prospective owner discusses his or her needs, desires, limitations, and budget with an architect. The architect analyzes the problem, draws up a set of preliminary requirements and options, and gets these approved by the prospective owner. At this point the architect completes the design, prepares a set of blueprints and specifications, and submits the plans to the owner for approval. After approval, a contract is let and the building phase starts. The foundation is constructed from available materials according to the specification. Next, carpenters erect the frame of the structure according to the specification using standard component lengths and lumber and nails that come in standard sizes. The electrician installs standard component wiring and fixtures, as does the plumber. All the subcontractors do their part using standard components and materials according to the plans. After the houses passes inspection by the owner and the building department, the happy owner pays everyone and moves in. Periodically, the structure needs maintenance such as painting or replacement of burned-out lights.

Each phase of this house building project has an analogy to some part of the software life cycle. In addition, during the building phase, every craftsmen was skillfully using standard tools to perform the job at hand. The carpenter did not relearn how to use a hammer and a saw, nor did the electrician relearn how to string and splice wire. Each of these craftsmen reused their tools and knowledge. Why should a programmer start from scratch at the beginning of each project? Every programmer should have an available toolbox of reusable software tools and components. If a routine is needed to solve a system of equations, the programmer should have it in the toolbox. If the task at hand is to keep certain things in line, the programmer should have a tool or component in the toolbox that keeps things in line. These tools are called *software components.*

What is software engineering, and what does a software engineer do? Obviously, a software engineer writes quality software according to specification. Professional software engineers do not write "hacker code" or "spaghetti code." That is left to amateur programmers. What is quality software? Whole sections of libraries devoted to computer science are devoted to this issue. According to Booch [8], the goals of software engineering are that the software be capable of modification and enhancement, easy to understand, reliable, and efficient. These goals are often hard to measure. Most software engineers spend more time modifying and adding capabilities to code than they do completing a project that they started from scratch. The software, along with its supporting documentation, must be easily understood. Typically, someone other than the person who originally wrote the code will maintain and modify the code. Whoever wrote the code is usually not the person who uses the code, so it must be reliable and forgiving. Who would use any computer with an operating system that locks up and must be rebooted twice an hour? Finally, the code must be efficient. Time is money.

How are these lofty goals met? There are many software engineering principles, but seven of the more important principles are abstraction, information hiding, modularity, localization, uniformity, completeness, and verifiability. Object-oriented development is the application of this principle. Proper use of abstraction eliminates the unnecessary details so that only function and form are left. Developing abstract software that can act in a particular fashion is the goal of this book. Information hiding makes inaccessible to the programmer details regarding the implementation of operations on the data structure. Software components must be wholly self-contained and accessible only through the documented interface. Modularity implies breaking up tasks into easily understood subtasks. If it can be understood easily, it probably can be easily implemented and manipulated. *Localized code* is code in which similar things or manipulations are found in a common area. The opposite of localization is "spaghetti code," where it is almost impossible to find where things happen and what happens next. Writing code in a disciplined manner results in uniformity. A good coding style is one result of uniformity. Complete code works for all cases and ensures that all required elements are present. Finally, there must be some way that good code can be tested at all levels, from individual modules to the entire project.

How can the goals of software engineering be achieved? Part of the answer is the systematic use of abstract data types implemented as reusable generic software components. One of the design goals of Ada was to facilitate the creation and use of reusable parts to improve productivity. The Ada type system supports localization of data definitions so that consistent changes are easy to make. Generic units support the development of general-purpose adaptable code that can be instantiated to perform specific functions. The criteria that a reusable component must fulfill include:

1. Reusable components must be understandable.
2. Reusable components must be high-quality components.
3. Reusable components must be adaptable.
4. Reusable components must be independent

5. Reusable components must be easy to use.

6. Reusable components must be efficient.

7. Reusable components must be portable.

The first criterion follows from the observation that if the programmer cannot understand the component, the programmer will not use it. The second criterion might be call the confidence criterion. The programmer must feel that they cannot write a higher-quality component. The third and fourth criteria are somewhat related. It makes no sense to write a reusable component if there is only one specific use. Reusable components are not application specific. They must be independent so that if one application requires the use of one component in two different ways, the use of one will not affect the other. The fifth criterion follows from the observation that a programmer will create code for a specific application in the manner that requires the least effort. The reason for the sixth criterion is obvious. Finally, something that is reusable must not be specific to any machine, configuration, or installation.

The Ada mechanism for implementing reusable components is the generic package. Generic packages allow the component to meet the foregoing criteria. The use of private types within generic packages enforces independence.

5.3 PARTS OF AN ADA ABSTRACT DATA TYPE

A data type is composed of objects and operations on those objects. Some data types are standard. Those standard data types were reviewed in Chapter 1. In an abstract data type the programmer specifies and/or supplies the item types, which are called user-supplied or programmer-supplied data structures. An example of an abstract data type is a *queue*. A queue is simply a line of objects of type item where an object is put on the end of the queue, and the object at the front is the next object that can be removed. The operations on the queue maintain order and access to the objects on the queue. The queue itself is an abstract data type that encapsulates the programmer-supplied item types. The maximum size of the queue may be specified by the programmer. However, the structural definition of the objects of type item placed on the queue, and later manipulated by the queue operations must be supplied by the programmer. The structure of the queue is hidden in the package while the programmer-allowable operations on the queue are listed in the specification and described in the documentation.

A second example of an abstract data type is a *set*. A set is a collection of objects of type element. The objects that can be placed in a set, the size of the set, and the implementation details must be supplied by the programmer. The operations on sets include seeing if a particular object is in a set, and deciding what objects are common to two sets or unique to two sets.

An Ada *abstract data type* (ADT) is a reusable generic package that defines a set of generic objects that encapsulate a programmer-defined type along with the operations on the generic objects. Furthermore, an ADT is a documented and validated Ada software component that contains its own documentation, specification, and implementation. The documentation contains five sections. The first section contains a description of what the abstract type does. The second section contains a description of the necessary programmer-supplied specifications and/or types. The third section lists the operations and what they do. These operations are the names of the functions and procedures that appear in the specification. The fourth section is a list of exceptions and how they are raised, in the ADT itself. All exceptions raised in an ADT must be handled in the calling program. The final section is an optional warning section. The ADT specification is an Ada package, usually a generic package whose formal generic parameter list contains the programmer supplied specifications and/or data structures. Most of the time the functions and procedures within the specification are the only operations allowed on the abstract data structure. The implementation is the generic package body, which is implemented so that all details of the basic structure and access to the basic structure are hidden from the programmer. Since the abstract data structure is usually implemented using private types, it can only be operated on by using a function or procedure in the specification.

The last part of the ADT is the part most often ignored, the validation and verification. Does it do what the documentation says it is supposed to do? The first test is: Does it compile without errors and warnings? The second test is: Does it work on the basic cases? Many sort routines will work on randomized lists of more than one object, but these routines are not robustly written. They sometimes fail when the list has exactly one object in it or if the list is empty. Their behavior changes when the list is either already in sorted order or in reverse order. The third test is: Does it work on extreme cases? The final test is: How are exceptional cases handled? The measuring of performance and the validation and verification of software are major subject areas of software engineering. It is assumed for the rest of the book that all operations have been tested to a basic level. At a minimum all operations are expected to conform to the basic documentation.

5.4 BASIC ABSTRACT DATA TYPE

As noted above, an abstract data type (ADT) is a basic data structure composed of generic type that encapsulates a programmer-defined type ITEMS as well as the operations permitted on objects of the generic type. The only operations allowed on the basic abstract data structure are implemented as functions and procedures. The arguments of these functions and procedures are either the programmer-supplied types typically in the form of a data structure, or the abstract data structure, or both. These programmer-supplied types and occasionally, operations are supplied via the formal generic package parameter list at instantiation. The abstract data structure itself will usually be either a private or a limited private type defined within the package. All the allowable operations are listed in the generic package specification.

Ada has several features that aid in the building of abstract data types. The Ada programing environment allows outside packages to be added and referenced. Separate compilation allows incremental progress. The wide range of programmer-defined data structures allows very abstract generic packages to take on very programmer-specific forms at instantiation. The details of how the package works are hidden in the body of the instantiated generic package, a practice called *information hiding*. The representation and the implementation are separate.

Operators and subprograms can be overloaded, which allows for a natural representation of objects of type ITEM and operations on those objects. Implementation of the COMPLEX_NUMBER type in Chapter 3 is an example of this. The use of private types prevents the programmer from operating on the structure directly. This allows for ease in verifying program correctness while simultaneously improving programmer productivity. A correctly implemented ADT allows the programmer to concentrate on the big problem at hand, not the boring little distracting details. The defining of exceptions allows the ADT to respond to improper data or conditions by signaling the main program when an error occurs, where it occurred, and what it was.

A large library of ADTs implemented as reusable generic software components becomes a fundamental programmer resource. This basic store of reusable components can be customized for whatever application is at hand. Just as mechanical engineers have a warehouse of parts to use in the design and construction of the next doodad, software engineers have this library of program components to use as they design, implement, and validate the current programming project.

There are several requirements that must be satisfied when building an abstract data type. Since the ADT will be implemented as a reusable component, the seven criteria listed at the end of Section 5.2 must be satisfied. A naming convention must be adhered to. In this book the name of the ADT will be split into three parts. The first is the word *generic*. The second is an indicator of the size limitation of the ADT. This will typically be one of the words *bounded, discrete,* or *unbounded. Bounded* implies that a maximum fixed size must be set. *Discrete* implies that the formal generic parameter encapsulated by the ADT is a discrete type. All discrete types are bounded. The third part is a name descriptive of what the ADT does. Some examples are

```
GENERIC_UNBOUNDED_QUEUE
GENERIC_BOUNDED_DIGRAPH
GENERIC_BOUNDED_TRIE
GENERIC_DISCRETE_DIGRAPH
GENERIC_UNBOUNDED_SEARCH_TABLE
```

Generic packages have formal generic parameters that must be supplied by the programmer at instantiation. Many of these parameters are of the form

```
type ITEM_TYPE is private;
type ELEMENT_TYPE is private;
type KEY_TYPE is private;
type DATA_TYPE is private;
```

Many ADTs operate on items or elements. One can have a queue of things of type ITEM_TYPE but sets are composed of things of type ELEMENT_TYPE. ADTs that involve searching typically use key-data pairs. A key-data pair is inserted into a search-based ADT by key, but the data associated with a particular key may have a form different than that of its key. The key in a telephone book is a name; the data is a number. The use of private types allows generic packages to implement ADTs independent of their programmer-defined component type.

Exceptions are handled differently by ADTs implemented as generic packages. The usual situation is for a raised exception to be handled locally. If a procedure or function raises an exception, it should be handled by the procedure or function that raised it. Exceptions raised by an ADT operation are exported back to the programmer after doing any necessary cleanup. Variables and parameters should not be modified when raising an exception. The documentation for the ADT must alert the programmer to what can happen when invoking a particular ADT operation, and what exceptions might be exported back. It is the programmer's responsibility to handle these exceptions.

5.5 ADT LIST

In Section 2.4 a set of routines that set up a singly linked list of integers was constructed. The ADT list will be built up now. This ADT can build a list composed of any programmer-defined data structure or type (see Figure 5.5.1). The slash in the pointer component of the last list node in Figure 5.5.1 denotes a "null" value. Recall that a list is a sequence of one or more items where a strict ordering is maintained and items can be added or removed from any position in the list. The programmer-supplied data structure is a record type called ITEM_TYPE. Since the assignment of things of type ITEM_TYPE is needed in the ADT, but the manipulation of objects of type ITEM by the ADT must not be allowed, the ITEM type must become a formal generic parameter of private type.

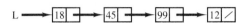

Figure 5.5.1 Singly linked list of nodes containing integers.

Since the abstract data type list will be embedded inside a package, a decision must be made on how strict the encapsulation of the type list must be. Recall that there are three choices: no restriction on the access to a list or anything that makes up the list; making things of type list private so that assignment, comparison for equality, and reference are all that is allowed; or making things of type list limited private so that referencing by operations defined in the package is the only option. The first choice violates the spirit of the abstract data type. This option allows programmer-defined list operations that use procedures and functions not in the package, so this option is rejected. Making the list limited private is too strict in this case. There is a list operation that is implemented as a function named TAIL_OF_LIST. TAIL_OF_LIST returns a list. If A_LIST is a list,

```
A_LIST :=  TAIL_OF_LIST (A_LIST);
```

is not allowed if list is made limited private. A procedure called ASSIGN, defined as

```
procedure ASSIGN (FROM : in LIST; to out LIST) is
begin
   TO :=  FROM;
end LIST;
```

must be added to the list package specification and body. The procedure ASSIGN then makes the assignment statement above equivalent to

```
ASSIGN (TAIL_OF_LIST (A_LIST), A_LIST);
```

The second problem with list being defined as limited private is the need to determine if two lists are equal. There are two possible definitions for equality and both are needed. One definition defines two possibly distinct lists as equal if both lists have the same length and they are equal element by element. The alternative definition says that both lists are equal if the access type references the same linked list. The compromise is to define the list as private. Assignment is allowed and the now-defined comparison for equality allows a check to be made that determines if two list variables point to the same list. Figure 5.5.2 illustrates the two scenarios for equality. The package documentation for this ADT is given in Figure 5.5.3.

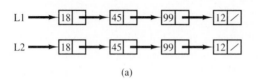

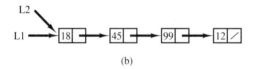

(b)

Figure 5.5.2 Two types of equality for lists. In (b) two access variables L1 and L2 that point to the same list. The comparison L1 = L2 is true.

GENERAL ADT SPECIFICATION FOR GENERIC_UNBOUNDED_LIST

Description

This ADT inserts an object of a programmer-supplied item into a list of objects. A list is a sequence of items where linear order is maintained and operations are provided so that items can be added or removed from any point in the list. Implementation uses access types so that lists of arbitrary lengths limited only by system memory limits can be maintained and manipulated. The head of the list is the first object on the list. The tail of a list is itself a list starting at the second object. Objects can be added to the end directly by creating a list of length one and adjoining it to the desired list. The list itself is implemented as a private type.

Programmer-Supplied Data Structures or Specifications

At instantiation the programmer must supply a single type name, generically denoted ITEM_TYPE. This programmer-supplied data structure defines the objects in the list.

Operations

NAME	DESCRIPTION
CLEAR	Deletes all objects from the list L.
COPY	Result is two distinct lists with the same items in the same order.
ADD_ITEM_TO_HEAD	Adds an object of type ITEM_TYPE to the front of the list.
ADD_ITEM_TO_REAR	Adds an object of type ITEM_TYPE to the end of the list.
CATENATE	Copys the second list onto the end of the first list.
SWAP_TAIL	Exchanges the tails of two lists.
EMPTY	Boolean-valued operation that returns true if the list is empty, otherwise returns false.
FULL	Boolean-valued function that returns true if the list is full, otherwise returns false.
TAIL_OF_LIST	Returns a list starting at the second object and going through the last object.
HEAD_OF_LIST	Returns the value of the first programmer-defined object of ITEM_TYPE in the first node of the list. This operation does not change the list.

Figure 5.5.3 Documentation for ADT list. Continues on page 109.

EQUAL	Boolean-valued function that returns true if both lists contain exactly the same sequence of items in exactly the same order.
LENGTH	Returns the number of items in the list.

Exceptions

There are two exceptions, implemented as LIST_IS_EMPTY and OVERFLOW. The raising of LIST_IS_EMPTY indicates that an operation requiring a nonempty list was attempted on an empty list. The operations raising this exception are TAIL_OF_LIST, HEAD_OF_LIST, and SWAP_TAIL. The exception OVERFLOW occurs when an object of type ITEM_TYPE cannot be added or copied. Boolean operations that raise this exception are ADD_ITEM_TO_HEAD, ADD_ITEM_TO_REAR, COPY, and CATENATE. Operations are provided by this ADT to test for error conditions that may raise these exceptions. No other exceptions are implemented by this ADT.

Warnings

Lists are implemented as private. Assignment and comparison for equality are available outside this package. Two distinctly equal lists can fail the test "L1 = L2" but pass the test EQUAL(L1, L2).

Figure 5.5.3 Concluded.

The generic package specification for the ADT list is given in Figure 5.5.4. Note that the specification of the ADT is a generic package whose operations were described in the documentation listed in Figure 5.5.3. These operations are the only functions and procedures contained in the generic package. The single formal generic parameter is a private type, so it cannot be modified inside the package. Things of type LIST are declared as private, so they can only be assigned or compared for equality outside the package unless a function or procedure listed in the specifications, the ADT's only allowed operations, is used.

```
generic
   type ITEM_TYPE is private;
package GENERIC_UNBOUNDED_LIST is
   type LIST is private;
   procedure CLEAR            (THIS_LIST :    out LIST);
   procedure COPY             (FROM : in    LIST
                              TO        :    out LIST);
   procedure ADD_ITEM_TO_HEAD (OF_LIST  : in out LIST;
                              ITEM      : in     ITEM_TYPE);
   procedure ADD_ITEM_TO_REAR (OF_LIST  : in out LIST;
                              ITEM      : in     ITEM_TYPE);
   procedure CATENATE         (THIS_LIST : in out LIST;
                              ONTO_LIST : in     LIST);
   procedure SWAP_TAIL        (LIST_1,
                              LIST_2    : in out LIST);
   function EMPTY             (THIS_LIST : LIST) return boolean;
   function FULL              (THIS_LIST : LIST) return boolean;
   function TAIL_OF_LIST      (THIS_LIST : LIST) return LIST;
   function HEAD_OF_LIST      (THIS_LIST : LIST) return ITEM_TYPE;
```

Figure 5.5.4. ADT specification for GENERIC_UNBOUNDED_LIST. Continues on page 110.

```
   function EQUAL              (LIST_1, LIST_2 : LIST) return boolean;
   function LENGTH             (OF_LIST   : LIST) return natural;
   OVERFLOW          : exception;
   LIST_IS_EMPTY     : exception;
 private
   type LIST_NODE;
   type LIST is access LIST_NODE;
   type LIST_NODE is
     record
        ITEM : ITEM_TYPE;
        NEXT : LIST;
     end record;
 end GENERIC_UNBOUNDED_LIST;
```

Figure 5.5.4 Concluded.

It is important to realize that the Ada generic package specification has three sections, with barriers separating the sections. The first section contains the formal generic package parameters. These are the package programmer-supplied types or data structures and the optional operations. These programmer-supplied types and operations are merged into the abstract data structure and the operations on the abstract data structure at instantiation. The second section, which the programmer cannot modify, contains the allowable operations on the abstract data part. These are the functions and procedures of the package. The only way to operate on the abstract structure is through these operations. The third section is the abstract structures themselves. These are placed in the private part of the generic package. These barriers between the programmer-supplied types and operations, the operations on the abstract structures, and the abstract structures themselves enhance the usability and generality of the abstract data type. These barriers also enforce a discipline on the programmer which promotes good programming practice, aids in programmer productivity, and helps in the writing of correct software. These barriers form the basis of object-oriented development.

The implementation details are similar to those covered in Section 2.4. Previously singly linked linear lists of integers had been developed. A list is an abstract singly linked linear list of objects of type ITEM_TYPE. Full implementation of this package body is given in Figure 5.5.5.

```
package body GENERIC_UNBOUNDED_LIST is

  procedure CLEAR   (THIS_LIST : out LIST) is
    -- Deletes all objects from the list L.
  begin
    THIS_LIST := null;
  end CLEAR;

  procedure COPY            (FROM : in     LIST;
                             TO   :    out LIST) is
    -- Returns an exact copy of FROM with same items in the same order
    -- Exception OVERFLOW raised if there is no storage left to
    --         copy the list.
```

Figure 5.5.5 Body of package GENERIC_UNBOUNDED_LIST. Continues on page 111.

```
  TEMP_TO : LIST;
  TEMP_FROM : LIST := FROM;
begin
  if FROM = null then
    TO := null;
  else
    TEMP_TO := new LIST_NODE'(TEMP_FROM.ITEM, null);
    TO := TEMP_TO;
    TEMP_FROM := TEMP_FROM.NEXT;
    while TEMP_FROM /= null loop
      TEMP_TO.NEXT := new LIST_NODE'(TEMP_FROM.ITEM, null);
      TEMP_FROM := TEMP_FROM.NEXT;
      TEMP_TO := TEMP_TO.NEXT;
    end loop;
  end if;
exception
  when storage_error =>
    raise OVERFLOW;
end COPY;

procedure ADD_ITEM_TO_HEAD (OF_LIST : in out LIST;
                            ITEM    : in      ITEM_TYPE) is
  -- Adds an ITEM to the front of the list
  -- Exception OVERFLOW raised if there is no storage left to
  --           add an item to the head of the list.
begin
  OF_LIST := new LIST_NODE'(ITEM, OF_LIST);
exception
  when storage_error =>
    raise OVERFLOW;
end ADD_ITEM_TO_HEAD;

procedure ADD_ITEM_TO_REAR (OF_LIST : in out LIST;
                            ITEM    : in      ITEM_TYPE) is
  -- Adds an Item to the end of the list.
  -- Exception OVERFLOW raised if there is no storage left to
  --           add an item to the tail of the list.
  TEMP : LIST := OF_LIST;
begin
  if OF_LIST = null then
    OF_LIST := new LIST_NODE' (ITEM, null);
  else
    -- Find the last node in the list
    loop
      exit when TEMP.NEXT = null;
      TEMP := TEMP.NEXT;
    end loop;
    -- TEMP references the last node, TEMP.NEXT = null, so ...
    TEMP.NEXT := new LIST_NODE'(ITEM, null);
```

Figure 5.5.5 Continues on page 112.

```
      end if;
exception
  when storage_error =>
    raise OVERFLOW;
end ADD_ITEM_TO_REAR;

  procedure CATENATE      (THIS_LIST : in out LIST;
                          ONTO_LIST : in      LIST) is
    -- Copys the list ONTO_LIST onto end of the list THIS_LIST
    -- Exception OVERFLOW raised if there is no storage left to
    --          copy of the list.
    TEMP : LIST := THIS_LIST;
  begin
    if THIS_LIST = null then
      -- THIS_LIST is null, so result is a simple copy
      COPY (ONTO_LIST, THIS_LIST);
    else
      -- Find last node in the list
      loop
      exit when TEMP.NEXT = null;
        TEMP := TEMP.NEXT;
      end loop;
      COPY (ONTO_LIST, TEMP.NEXT);
    end if;
  exception
    when OVERFLOW =>  --raised from COPY
      raise OVERFLOW;
  end CATENATE;

  procedure SWAP_TAIL  (LIST_1,  LIST_2 : in out LIST) is
    -- Exchanges the tails of two lists.
    -- Exception LIST_IS_EMPTY raised if one or the other list is empty.
    TEMP : LIST;
  begin
    if LIST_1 = null or else LIST_2 = null then
      raise LIST_IS_EMPTY;
    else
      TEMP := LIST_1.NEXT;
      LIST_1.NEXT := LIST_2.NEXT;
      LIST_2.NEXT := TEMP;
    end if;
  end SWAP_TAIL;

  function FULL (THIS_LIST : LIST) return boolean is
    -- Returns true if there is no storage left to add a node.
    TEMP : LIST;
  begin
    TEMP := new LIST_NODE;
```

Figure 5.5.5 Continues on page 113.

```
  return false;
exception
  when storage_error => return true;
end FULL;


function EMPTY (THIS_LIST : LIST) return boolean is
  -- Returns true if the list THIS_LIST is empty.
begin
  return THIS_LIST = null;
end EMPTY;


function TAIL_OF_LIST (THIS_LIST : LIST) return LIST is
  -- Returns a list starting at the second ITEM and going through the
  -- last ITEM.
  -- Exception LIST_IS_EMPTY raised if the list is empty.
begin
  if THIS_LIST = null then
    raise LIST_IS_EMPTY;
  else
    return THIS_LIST.NEXT;
  end if;
end TAIL_OF_LIST;


function HEAD_OF_LIST (THIS_LIST : LIST) return ITEM_TYPE is
  -- Returns the first programmer-defined ITEM in the first LIST_NODE.
  -- This operation does not change the list.
  -- Exception LIST_IS_EMPTY raised if the list is empty.
begin
  if THIS_LIST = null then
    raise LIST_IS_EMPTY;
  else
    return THIS_LIST.ITEM;
  end if;
end HEAD_OF_LIST;


function EQUAL (LIST_1, LIST_2, : LIST) return boolean is
  -- Returns true if both lists contain exactly the same sequence of
  -- ITEMS in exactly the same order.
  TEMP_L1 : LIST := LIST_1;
  TEMP_L2 : LIST := LIST_2;
begin
  loop
    exit when TEMP_L1 = null or else TEMP_L2 = null;
    if TEMP_L1.ITEM = TEMP_L2.ITEM then
      TEMP_L1 := TEMP_L1.NEXT;
      TEMP_L2 := TEMP_L2.NEXT;
    else
      return false;
```

Figure 5.5.5   Continues on page 114.

```
      end if;
    end loop;
    -- Check to see if lists are the same length
    return TEMP_L1 = null and TEMP_L2 = null;
  end EQUAL;

  function LENGTH (OF_LIST : LIST) return natural is
    -- Returns the number of LIST_NODES in the list.
    TEMP : LIST := OF_LIST;
    COUNT : NATURAL:= 0;
  begin
    -- traverse the entire list while counting nodes
    loop
      exit when TEMP = null;
      COUNT := COUNT + 1;
      TEMP := TEMP.NEXT;
    end loop;
    return COUNT;
  end LENGTH;

end GENERIC_UNBOUNDED_LIST;
```

Figure 5.5.5   Concluded.

Note that the integer list built up in Chapter 2 can easily be attained by

```
    package INTEGER_LIST is new package GENERIC_UNBOUNDED_LIST (integer);
```

while a string or list of characters would be instantiated as

```
    package CHARACTER_LIST is new package GENERIC_UNBOUNDED_LIST (character);
```

It is instructive to note that the programming difficulty involved in building the ADT in Figure 5.5.5 is only slightly more involved than doing the original integer list in Chapter 2. The difference is that the next time a list is needed, it doesn't have to be reinvented and reimplemented. It need only be reinstantiated using the appropriate programmer-supplied type for the formal generic parameter ITEM_TYPE.

Clearly, other implementations of lists are possible. For example, the private part in Figure 5.5.4 could be replaced by the structure shown in Figure 5.5.6

```
            type LIST_NODE;
            type LIST is access LIST_NODE;
            type LIST_NODE is
              record
                ITEM : ITEM_TYPE;
                PREVIOUS,
                NEXT : LIST;
              end LIST_NODE;
```

Figure 5.5.6   Doubly linked list structure.

Typical Double Linked List Node

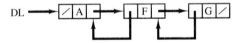

DL

Figure 5.5.7 Doubly linked list of nodes containing characters.

Figure 5.5.7 illustrates the structure in both Figures 5.5.4 and 5.5.6. The list structure used would make no difference to the programmer of the package GENERIC_UNBOU-NDED_LIST, because that part can only be manipulated by the operations in the package specification.

Even an array-based bounded version is possible. A slight modification of the documentation is required. A second programmer-supplied formal generic parameter SIZE is needed as well. Figure 5.5.8 contains the specification for the bounded form.

```
generic
  type ITEM_TYPE is private;
  SIZE : positive;
package GENERIC_BOUNDED_LIST is
  type LIST is private;
  procedure CLEAR              (THIS LIST :    out LIST);
  procedure COPY               (FROM      : in     LIST;
                               TO         :    out LIST);
  procedure ADD_ITEM_TO_HEAD   (OF_LIST   : in out LIST;
                               ITEM       : in     ITEM_TYPE);
  procedure ADD_ITEM_TO_REAR   (OF_LIST   : in out LIST;
                               ITEM       : in     ITEM_TYPE);
  procedure CATENATE           (THIS_LIST : in out LIST;
                               ONTO_LIST  : in LIST);
  procedure SWAP_TAIL          (LIST_1,
                               LIST_2     : in out LIST);
  function EMPTY               (THIS_LIST : LIST) return boolean;
  function FULL                (THIS_LIST : LIST) return boolean;
  function TAIL_OF_LIST        (THIS_LIST : LIST) return LIST;
  function HEAD_OF_LIST        (THIS_LIST : LIST) return ITEM_TYPE;
  function EQUAL               (LIST_1, LIST_2 : LIST) return boolean;
  function LENGTH              (OF_LIST : LIST) return natural;
  OVERFLOW      : exception;
  LIST_IS_EMPTY : exception;
private
  type LIST_ARRAY is array (positive range <>) of ITEM_TYPE;
  type LIST is
    record
      LAST_USED : natural := 0;
```

Figure 5.5.8 ADT specification for GENERIC_BOUNDED_LIST. Continues on page 116.

```
        L : LIST_ARRAY (1..SIZE);
      end record;
  end GENERIC_BOUNDED_LIST;
```

Figure 5.5.8 Concluded.

Figure 5.5.9 illustrates how an array might be used to implement a list. The head of the list is always at L(1).With this convention the operations ADD_ITEM_TO_HEAD and TAIL_OF_LIST are as follows:

L.L:=

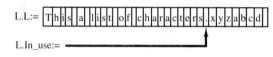

L.In_use:=

Figure 5.5.9 Bounded implementation of a list of characters.

```
procedure ADD_ITEM_TO_HEAD (OF_LIST : in out LIST;
                            ITEM    : in     ITEM_TYPE) is
  -- Adds an ITEM to the front of the list
  -- Exception OVERFLOW raised if the list is full.
begin
  if OF_LIST.LAST_USED = SIZE then
    raise OVERFLOW;
  elsif OF_LIST.LAST_USED /= 0 then
    OF_LIST.LAST_USED := OF_LIST.LAST_USED + 1;
    OF_LIST.L(2..OF_LIST.LAST_USED) := OF_LIST.L(1..OF_LIST.LAST_USED-1);
  else
    OF_LIST.LAST_USED := 1;
  end if;
  OF_LIST.L(1) := ITEM;
end ADD_ITEM_TO_HEAD;

function TAIL_OF_LIST (THIS_LIST : LIST) return LIST is
    -- Returns a list starting at the second ITEM and going through the
    -- last ITEM.
    -- Exception LIST_IS_EMPTY raised if the list is empty.
  TEMP : LIST;
begin
  if THIS_LIST.LAST_USED = 0 then
    raise LIST_IS_EMPTY;
  else
    TEMP.LAST_USED := THIS_LIST.LAST_USED - 1;
    TEMP.L(1..TEMP.LAST_USED) := THIS_LIST.L(2..THIS_LIST.LAST_USED);
    return TEMP;
  end if;
end TAIL_OF_LIST;
```

All versions of this basic ADT behave in the same way. All have the same operations and exceptions. There may be minor differences in the formal generic parameter list, but these do not affect the application. Significant differences in the private part are hidden from the programmer in reality.

This section ends by returning to the discussion of whether a list should be private or limited private. There is a great temptation to make a list fully encapsulated by making it limited private and overloading the equality operator using

```
function "=" (L1, L2:List) return boolean is
   --returns true if L1 and L2 access the same list
begin
   return L1 = L2;
end "=";
```

This innocent little operation will cause a hangup every time it is called. It violates both rules of recursion at the same time. Recall that every case of recursion must be reduced to a simpler case and there must be a base case. This function does neither. It doesn't look recursive, but it is.

Consider the simple statement

```
if L1 = L2 then
   Process(L1);
else
   . . . . . . . . . . . . . .
```

This simple code would be evaluated, using the function "=" above, by using

```
To Find if L1 = L2
   then Compute and return L1 = L2
   but to Compute L1 = L2 first Compute and return L1 = L2
   but to Compute L1 = L2 first Compute and return L1 = L2
   but to Compute L1 = L2 first Compute and return L1 = L2
   . . . . . . . . . . . . . .
```

The first rule of recursion says that each call to a recursively implemented procedure must move the problem closer to the base case. There is no base case. This is why the second rule of recursion is being violated. The same case is being reevaluated continually. This function never reduces the case, while again and again solving the same case. This example illustrates two points: care must be taken when implementing recursion, and care must be taken when overloading the comparison operating function "=" for equality.

5.6 TIME AND SPACE CONSTRAINTS

The time and space constraints for seven basic list operations of GENERIC_UNBOUN-DED__LIST as specified in Figure 5.5.3 are listed in Figure 5.6.1. It is assumed that all the operations were implemented without using recursion on a list of n objects of generic type ITEM_TYPE. Operations that perform one statement not embedded in a loop, such as CLEAR, ADD_ITEM_TO_HEAD, HEAD_OF_LIST, FULL, and EMPTY are $O(1)$ because they execute without regard to the length of LIST. Other operations that must traverse a loop, such as COPY, ADD_ITEM_TO_REAR, CATENATE, EQUAL, and LENGTH, are dependent on the length of the LIST. They execute in $O(n)$, where the list has n ITEMS in it.

	Total time overhead	Total space overhead
COPY	$O(n)$	$O(n)$
ADD_ITEM_TO_HEAD	$O(1)$	$O(n)$
ADD_ITEM_TO_REAR	$O(n)$	$O(n)$
ADD_ITEM_TO_REAR	$O(n)$	$O(n)$
CATENATE	$O(n)$	$O(n)$
EMPTY	$O(1)$	$O(n)$
EQUAL	$O(n)$	$O(n)$
LENGTH	$O(n)$	$O(n)$

Figure 5.6.1   Time and space constraints for Figure 5.5.3.

There are only minor differences in Figure 5.6.1 for the GENERIC_BOUNDED_LIST implementation specified in Figure 5.5.6, so it is left to the reader. The one big difference is that space is $O(\text{SIZE})$ no matter how many items are in the list. It is important that the concepts of this chapter be understood thoroughly. All the abstract data types studied in this book will be implemented as generic packages.

EXERCISES

Section 5.1 Software Engineering

5.1.1 What is the difference between software engineering, programming, and using a computer program?

5.1.2 How can a program be designed to be tested and validated?

Section 5.4 Basic Abstract Data Type

5.4.1 What is the difference between a data type and an abstract data type?

5.4.2 Describe the operations that an ADT called "LINE" would have. LINE would be designed for occasions where programmer-supplied data types must be kept in strict sequence.

5.4.3 Describe the operations that an ADT called "BASIC_GRAPHING" would have. This ADT would draw basic figures on a plotter of any specified size.

Section 5.5 ADT List

5.5.1 Consider the ADT GENERIC_UNBOUNDED_LIST specified in Figure 5.5.4. The operations LENGTH and ADD_ITEM_TO_REAR are $O(n)$, where n is the length of the list. If the private part of Figure 5.5.4 is replaced by

```
type LIST_NODE;
type LIST_ACCESS is access LIST_NODE;
type LIST_NODE is
```

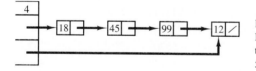

Figure E5.5.1   Linked list of LIST NODES instantiated with integers using the private type specified in Exercise 5.5.1.

```
record
    ITEM : ITEM_TYPE;
    NEXT : LIST_ACCESS;
end record;
type LIST is
record
    LENGTH : natural := 0;
    FRONT,
    REAR   : LIST_ACCESS;
end record;
```

where LENGTH is the length of the list, FRONT points to the head of a list and REAR points to the last item in the list (see Figure E5.5.1).

a. Implement the operation CLEAR.
b. Implement the operation EMPTY.
c. Implement the operation TAIL_OF_LIST.
d. Implement the operation HEAD_OF_LIST.
e. Implement the operation COPY.
f. Implement the operation EQUAL.
g. Implement the operation CATENATE.
h. Implement the operation LENGTH.
i. Implement the operation SWAP_TAIL.
j. Implement the operation ADD_ITEM_TO_HEAD.
k. Implement the operation ADD_ITEM_TO_REAR.
l. Implement the operation FULL.
m. Combine parts a through m into a package body for GENERIC_UNBOUNDED_LIST as specified for Figure 5.5.3.
n. Prepare a table of time and space constraints similar to Figure 5.6.1.

Your answers must follow the documentation in Figure 5.5.2.

5.5.2 Consider the ADT GENERIC_BOUNDED_LIST as specified in Figure 5.5.6.
a. Implement the operation CLEAR.
b. Implement the operation EMPTY.
c. Implement the operation HEAD_OF_LIST.
d. Implement the operation COPY.
e. Implement the operation EQUAL.
f. Implement the operation CATENATE.
g. Implement the operation LENGTH.
h. Implement the operation FULL
i. Implement the operation ADD_ITEM_TO_REAR.
j. Implement the operation SWAP_TAIL,
k. Combine parts a through j into a package body for GENERIC_UNBOUNDED_LIST as specified for Figure 5.5.3.
l. Prepare a table of time and space constraints similar to Figure 5.6.1.

Your answers must follow the documentation in Figure 5.5.2.

5.5.3 A stack is a list where items are all added or removed from the head of the list.
a. Implement the operation PUSH. PUSH adds an object to the head of the stack.
b. Implement the operation POP. POP returns the object at the head of the list and replaces the list by the tail of the list.

c. Implement the operation COUNT. COUNT returns the number of items on the list.

d. Implement the operation EMPTY. EMPTY returns the boolean value true if the list is empty, and false otherwise.

Stacks are studied in depth in Chapter 6.

5.5.4 A queue is a list where items are all removed from the head of the list and added to the list by concatenating the object onto the end of the list.

a. Implement the operation ENQUEUE. ENQUEUE adds an object to the end of the list.

b. Implement the operation DEQUEUE. DEQUEUE returns the object at the head of the list and replaces the list by the tail of the list.

c. Implement the operation COUNT. COUNT returns the number of items on the list.

d. Implement the operation EMPTY. EMPTY returns the boolean value true if the list is empty, and false otherwise. Queues are studied in depth in Chapter 7.

PROGRAMMING PROJECTS

P5.1 Write a program that makes up a list of mailing addresses for sending out Christmas cards to one's family and friends. Names and addresses must be able to be added to the list, deleted by name from the list, and printed out in label form. This program should use GENERIC_UNBOUNDED_LIST.

P5.2 Modify the program in Project P5.1 so that the address list is maintained in ascending order by name.

P5.3 Make a simple modification to Project P5.2 so that it uses the ADT GENERIC_BOUNDED_LIST. Assume that your Christmas card list will be smaller than 50 names.

NOTES AND REFERENCES

The discussion at the end of Section 5.2 concerning reusable components and the basic requirements for implementing an ADT in Ada using generic packages were taken from Chapter 8 of Johnson et al. [24]. The Waterfall software development model listed in Section 5.1 assumes a fairly large project. Other variations of the Waterfall model, such as the Whirlpool, incremental, and spiral models, are described in Degrace and Stahl [14] and Sommerville [46]. Dijkstra [18] was one of the first to call attention to programming practice in his classic monograph *A Discipline of Programming*. The material on the distinctions between a professional and an amateur programmer appeared on pages 5–12 of Ledgard [33]. Ledgard has written several small, humorous monographs on programming practice, including *Programming Proverbs* [34]. A humorous survey of the software development problem can be found in Degrace and Stahl [14].

6

Stacks

Lists were introduced in Chapter 5. By definition a *list* is a sequence of objects of some type where the objects can be inserted or deleted from any place in the sequence. Placing an object on the list fixes its place on the list. A *stack* is also a sequence of objects. In a stack, one end of the stack is designated as the TOP. Objects can be added or deleted only from the end designated TOP. The TOP acts like both the beginning and end of the line. Adding an object to the stack makes the object that was previously on top now second. The object added first becomes the last object in the stack. This behavior is called *last in, first out* (LIFO). By convention, stacks are drawn vertically. Figure 6.0.1 illustrates a simple stack. Figure 6.0.2 shows last in, first out.

This behavior of the stack's TOP acting as both the front and rear of the sequence is not as unusual as it might sound. When a dishwasher cleans a tray, the most recently cleaned and dried tray is placed on the top of the stack of clean trays. If the objects in Figure 6.0.2 were trays, that illustration shows the operations on a stack of trays. The next customer does not take the tray on the bottom, which has been on the stack the longest, but instead, takes the tray on top.

Consider the evaluation of the parenthesized expression

$$f(x) = 5 + (x**4 + (x**2 - 2*(x + 5 - \sin(x))**3 + 2\ x)*x + 7)*x$$

The first closing parenthesis matches with the last open parenthesis, here the argument of the function sin. Then the next closed parenthesis lines up with the third open parenthesis, and so on. Open parentheses are evaluated in the reverse order encountered; that is, they exhibit LIFO behavior.

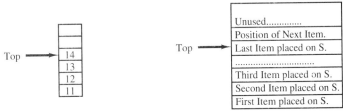

Figure 6.0.1   Basic stack. Item 14 is at the top, item 13 is second, and item 11 is on the bottom

Figure 6.0.2   LIFO behavior of a stack.

Now, consider a large program with many built-in procedures. When procedure A is invoked, the program transfers control to the first statement in the body of procedure A. After the last statement of procedure A is executed, procedure A returns control to the first statement following the original call statement in the calling procedure. This is the same behavior as that of a function with one pair of parenthesis. Think of the opening parenthesis as a call to a function or procedure and the closing parenthesis as the return from the function or procedure (see Figure 6.0.3). What about a more complicated situation? A procedure invokes procedure A, procedure A invokes procedure B, and procedure B invokes procedure C. After procedure C is finished, control returns to procedure B. When procedure B terminates, control returns to procedure A. Control always returns to the statement following the original call. This is last in, first out, or stack, behavior. Applications using stacks range from the correct evaluation of fully parenthesized expressions to the operating system handling of interrupts. A modern compiler could not be written without the use of stacks.

The basic stack operations all involve the addition of objects onto the stack or deletion of objects from the stack. Objects are added to the top of the stack by an operation called PUSH. The object previously on top of the stack is now second. These objects are removed from the top of the stack by an operation called POP. The depth of the stack is the number of objects on a stack. One can PEEK at the top element without removing that object from the stack, but elements below the top element remain hidden. At times it is necessary to CLEAR the stack or to COPY the stack. There are times when it is necessary to decide if a stack is empty or if the stack is full. At other times it might be necessary to decide if two stacks are equal.

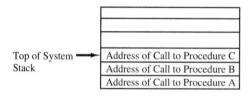

Top of System Stack →

| Address of Call to Procedure C |
| Address of Call to Procedure B |
| Address of Call to Procedure A |

Figure 6.0.3 Use of stack to keep track of procedure call return order.

6.1 ADT STACK

A stack is a linear sequence of objects that are added or deleted from one end of the sequence designated the TOP. The last in, first out mode of access characterizes the behavior of a stack. It must be stressed that in a stack there is no distinction between the front of the stack and the rear of the stack. Everything is added or deleted from the same location, called the TOP. Figure 6.1.1 lists the basic description of the ADT stack.

GENERAL ADT SPECIFICATION FOR STACK

Description

This ADT implements a stack that stores objects of a programmer-supplied type ITEM_TYPE. A stack is a linear sequence of objects of type ITEM_TYPE where the objects are added or deleted from one end of the sequence designated TOP. The last in, first out mode of access characterizes stack behavior. The objects most recently added to the stack is the first object removed. The object first added to the stack is the last object removed.

Figure 6.1.1 Documentation for STACK. Continues on page 123.

Programmer-Supplied Data Structures
or Specifications

The programmer must supply a single type, ITEM_TYPE, at instantiation. This programmer-supplied type defines the objects that are added or deleted from the stack. This supplied object is a private formal generic parameter. No stack operation modifies the programmer-supplied object in any way.

Operations

Name	Description
CLEAR	Removes all objects from the stack. The boolean function EMPTY is true after the execution of CLEAR.
COPY	Makes a copy of the current stack. The result is two stacks with the same number of objects in the same order. The function EQUAL returns true when the original is compared against the copy.
PUSH	Adds a new object to the top of the stack while preserving the LIFO order.
POP	Returns the top object on the stack and deletes that object from the top of the stack while preserving the LIFO order of the stack.
DEPTH	Returns a natural number equal to the number of objects on the stack.
FULL	Returns true if the stack has no room to add an object, and false otherwise.
EMPTY	Returns true if the stack is empty, and false otherwise.
EQUAL	Returns true if two stacks have the same depth and the two sequences are equal when compared object by object from their respective tops, and false otherwise.
PEEK	Returns the object at the top of the stack without removing that object from the stack.

Exceptions

Two exceptions are implemented, OVERFLOW and STACK_IS_EMPTY. An OVERFLOW is raised when there is no memory or room to PUSH an object onto the stack or to COPY two stacks. The exception STACK_IS_EMPTY occurs when an attempt has been made to POP or PEEK at an empty stack.

Warnings

No warnings.

Figure 6.1.1 Concluded.

Stacks will now be implemented in a variety of forms. With the exception of their private sections, the operations and specifications are similar.

6.2. BOUNDED IMPLEMENTATION

The bounded implementation uses a record with an array of components of a programmer-supplied type to implement the stack. The stack type must be implemented as a limited private type. This allows the declaration of multiple objects of the same type, and it prevents the manipulation of stacks outside the package. The generic package GENERIC_BOUNDED_ STACK requires two formal parameters. The first formal generic parameter is the type of components of which the stack is composed. The second parameter fixes the maximum size of the stack. The second generic parameter can be eliminated by using a variant record. The data structure for the bounded stack is a record type composed of two fields. The first field is a natural number used to keep track of TOP. The second field consists of an array of objects. The following generic package listed in Figure 6.2.1 fully specifies the abstract data type GENERIC_BOUNDED_STACK.

```
generic
  type ITEM_TYPE is private;
  SIZE : positive;
package GENERIC_BOUNDED_STACK is
  type STACK is limited private;
  procedure PUSH  (ITEM           : in      ITEM_TYPE;
                   ONTO_THE_STACK : in out  STACK);
  procedure POP   (ITEM           :     out ITEM_TYPE;
                   FROM_THE_STACK : in out  STACK);
  procedure COPY  (FROM_STACK     : in      STACK);
                   TO_STACK       :     out STACK);
  procedure CLEAR (STACK_TO_CLEAR : in out  STACK);
  function DEPTH  (STACK_TO_COUNT : STACK)  return natural;
  function EMPTY  (STACK_TO_CHECK : STACK)  return boolean;
  function FULL   (STACK_TO_CHECK : STACK)  return boolean;
  function PEEK   (AT_THE_STACK   : STACK)  return ITEM_TYPE;
  function EQUAL  (STACK1, STACK2 : STACK)  return boolean;
  STACK_IS_EMPTY  :exception;
  OVERFLOW        :exception;
private
  type ARRAY_OF_ITEM_TYPE is array (positive range <>) of ITEM_TYPE;
  type STACK is
    RECORD
      TOP : natural := 0;
      STACK : ARRAY_OF_ITEM_TYPE (1..SIZE);
    end RECORD;
end GENERIC_BOUNDED_STACK;
```

Figure 6.2.1 Package Specification for GENERIC_BOUNDED_STACK.

Implementing the body of the package is straightforward. Figure 6.2.2 illustrates the idea of GENERIC_BOUNDED_STACK. The value of TOP is the highest index of the array that contains a defined object. The next object that is pushed, or added, onto the stack goes into position TOP+1. An object that is popped, or removed, comes from the position at index TOP. Several functions or procedures are implemented with a single statement. To decide if a stack is empty can be done with a single statement:

```
return STACK_TO_CHECK.TOP = 0;
```

The depth of a stack is the value of TOP, the number of objects on the stack. Clearing a stack can be done with a single assignment statement,

```
                    STACK_TO_CLEAR.TOP := 0;
```

Two stacks are equal if their depth is equal and if the same objects appear on both stacks in the same order. It is not sufficient to use

```
                    return STACK1 = STACK2;
```

because the stacks may be equal but there could be previously popped items located beyond TOP that are different (see Figure 6.2.3). Thus EQUAL must be implemented as follows:

```
        function EQUAL (STACK1, STACK2 : STACK) return boolean is
          -- Returns true if two stacks have the same depth and the two
          -- sequences of items are equal when compared item by item starting
          -- at their respective tops.
        begin
          if STACK1.TOP = 0 THEN
            return STACK2.TOP = 0;
          else
            return STACK1.TOP = STACK2.TOP AND THEN
               STACK1.STACK(1..STACK1.TOP) = STACK2.STACK (1..STACK2.TOP);
          end if;
        end EQUAL;
```

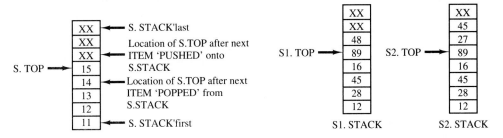

Figure 6.2.2 Bounded or array-based stack implementation.

Figure 6.2.3 Two equal stacks where S1.STACK /= S2.STACK.

The only problem that occurs with the operation PUSH appears if the stack is full. Similarly, the only problem that occurs when performing a POP or PEEK appears when the stack is empty.

```
        procedure PUSH (ITEM      : in       ITEM_TYPE;
                        ONTO_THE STACK :     in out      STACK) is
          -- Adds a new object to the top of the stack while preserving the
          -- LIFO order.
          -- Exception OVERFLOW is raised if there is not enough room left
                       to put the item onto the stack.
        begin
          if ONTO_THE_STACK.TOP = SIZE THEN
            raise OVERFLOW;
          else
            ONTO_THE_STACK.TOP := ONTO_THE_STACK.TOP + 1;
            ONTO_THE_STACK.STACK (ONTO_THE_STACK.TOP) := ITEM;
```

```
      end if;
    end PUSH;

    procedure POP (ITEM              :    out ITEM_TYPE;
                   FROM_THE_STACK : in out STACK) is
      -- Returns the top item on the stack and deletes that item from
      -- the stack while preserving the LIFO order of the stack.
      -- Exception STACK_IS EMPTY is raised if there is no item to pop
    begin
      if FROM_THE_STACK.TOP = 0 THEN
        raise STACK_IS_EMPTY;
      else
        ITEM := FROM_THE_STACK.STACK(FROM_THE_STACK.TOP);
        FROM_THE_STACK.TOP := FROM_THE_STACK.TOP - 1;
      end if;
    end POP;
```

The function PEEK is similar to POP but the value of TOP remains unchanged. COPY is just a simple assignment statement of the two formal parameters.

After adding the package specification and body of GENERIC_BOUNDED_STACK to the Ada program library, implementation of the abstract data type GENERIC_BOUN-DED_STACK is complete. The ADT data structure is an array of programmer-defined things of type ITEM_TYPE, where the ordering is the order in which objects were added to the stack. The only way the stack can be accessed or modified is through the legitimate operations, which are the functions and procedures of the instantiated generic package.

The bounded stack specified by the specification contained in Figure 6.2.1 has one major shortcoming. All of the stacks created must be the same size. By using a record with a variant, two outcomes are achieved. First, the stack can be of any size. Because the size is no longer the same for all stacks, it no longer needs to be specified at instantiation. The number of generic parameters is reduced to one. Figure 6.2.4 contains the resulting generic specification.

```
      generic
        type ITEM_TYPE is private;
      package GENERIC_BOUNDED_STACK is
        type STACK (SIZE : positive) is limited private;
        procedure PUSH          (ITEM              : in       ITEM_TYPE;
                                 ONTO_THE_STACK : in out STACK);
        procedure POP           (ITEM              :    out ITEM-TYPE;
                                 FROM_THE_STACK : in out STACK);
        procedure copy          (FROM_STACK      : in       STACK;
                                 TO_STACK          : in out STACK);
        procedure CLEAR         (STACK_TO_CLEAR : in out STACK);
        function DEPTH          (STACK_TO_COUNT : STACK) return natural;
        function EMPTY          (STACK_TO_CHECK : STACK) return boolean;
        function FULL           (STACK_TO_CHECK : STACK) return boolean;
        function PEEK           (AT_THE_STACK    : STACK) return ITEM_TYPE;
        function EQUAL          (STACK1, STACK2 : STACK) return boolean;
        STACK_IS_EMPTY : exception;
```

Figure 6.2.4 Alternative package specification for GENERIC_BOUNDED_STACK. Continues on page 127.

Stacks   Chap. 6

```
           OVERFLOW -       : exception;
        private
          type ARRAY_OF_ITEM_TYPE is array (positive range <>) of ITEM_TYPE;
          type STACK (SIZE : positive) is
            RECORD
              TOP : natural := 0;
              STACK : ARRAY_OF_ITEM_TYPE (1..SIZE);
            end RECORD;
        end GENERIC_BOUNDED_STACK;
```

Figure 6.2.4   Concluded.

An integer stack of size = 25 using the ADT as specified in Figure 6.2.4 can be defined
by

```
        with GENERIC_BOUNDED_STACK;
        INT_STACK is new package GENERIC_BOUNDED_STACK (integer);
        MY_STACK : INT_STACK.STACK(25);
```

The major differences between the two versions of GENERIC_BOUNDED_STACK are in the
COPY and EQUAL operations. It is possible that a stack is being copied onto another stack of
different size. It is necessary to see if it is physically possible to make the copy.

```
     procedure COPY             (FROM_STACK    : in      STACK;
                                 TO_STACK      : in out STACK) is
        -- Makes an exact copy of the FROM_STACK and returns it as TO_STACK.
        -- The result is two stacks with same items in the same order.
        -- Exception OVERFLOW raised if TO_STACK is not large enough to
        --           hold FROM_STACK.
     begin
        -- Check to see if data in FROM_STACK will fit in TO_STACK
        if FROM_STACK.TOP > TO_STACK.SIZE then
          raise OVERFLOW;
        else
          TO_STACK.TOP := FROM_STACK.TOP;
          TO_STACK.STACK(1..TO_STACK.TOP) :=
                          FROM_STACK.STACK(1..FROM_STACK.TOP);
        end if;
     end COPY;
```

A minor difference is that the formal parameter TO_STACK must be mode "in out." If not, the
value of TO_STACK.SIZE cannot be determined. Full implementation of this variation is left
to the exercises.

6.3 UNBOUNDED IMPLEMENTATION

Suppose that it is not known in advance what the maximum number of items in a stack might
be needed. This can be a major problem. All bounded forms suffer from this deficiency. The
maximum size of the structure, here the stack, must be determined in advance so that the
generic parameter SIZE can be set.

The unbounded implementation, which uses access types, does not suffer from this limitation. The package specification, listed in Figure 6.3.1, has the same operations as those of the bounded implementation in Figure 6.2.4.

```
generic
  type ITEM_TYPE is private;
package GENERIC_UNBOUNDED_STACK is
  type STACK is limited private;
  procedure PUSH        (ITEM             :  in      ITEM_TYPE;
                         ONTO_THE_STACK   :  in out  STACK);
  procedure POP         (ITEM             :      out ITEM_TYPE;
                         FROM_THE_STACK   :  in out  STACK);
  procedure COPY        (FROM_STACK       :  in      STACK;
                         To_STACK         :      out STACK);
  procedure CLEAR       (STACK_TO_CLEAR   :  in out  STACK);
  function DEPTH        (STACK_TO_COUNT   :  STACK) return natural;
  function FULL         (STACK_TO_CHECK   :  STACK) return boolean;
  function EMPTY        (STACK_TO_CHECK   :  STACK) return boolean;
  function PEEK         (AT_THE_STACK     :  STACK) return ITEM_TYPE;
  function EQUAL        (STACK1, STACK2   :  STACK) return boolean;
  STACK_IS_EMPTY : exception;
  OVERFLOW : exception;
private
  type STACK_NODE;
  type STACK_NEXT is access STACK_NODE;
  type STACK_NODE is
    record
      ITEM : ITEM TYPE;
      NEXT : STACK_NEXT;
    end record;
  type STACK is
    record
      DEPTH : natural := 0;
      TOP : STACK_NEXT;
    end record;
end GENERIC_UNBOUNDED STACK;
```

Figure 6.3.1 Package specification for GENERIC_UNBOUNDED_STACK.

The result is that all operations on the stack can only be performed using functions and procedures in the package. Figure 6.3.2 shows how various stack operations are performed. The stack is a record whose first component, DEPTH, keeps a running tally of the number of objects on the stack, and whose other component, TOP, is the top of a singly linked linear list where objects are both added and deleted from the front of the list. The body starts with a definition of the data structure STACK_NODE.

Many functions and procedures of GENERIC_UNBOUNDED_STACK are exact analogs of their list counterparts in GENERIC_UNBOUNDED_LIST. To peek at a stack, one returns the object field at the top of the stack.

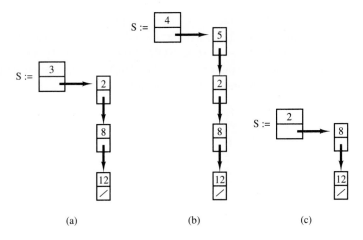

Figure 6.3.2 Operations on a stack S using linked implementation. (a) Original stack. (b) Stack in part (a) after "5" is "Pushed." (c) Stack in part (a) after "Pop."

```
function PEEK ( AT_THE_STACK : STACK ) return ITEM_TYPE is
  -- Returns the item at the top of the stack without removing that
  -- item from the stack.
  -- Exception STACK_IS_EMPTY is raised if there is no item to peek at.
begin
  if AT_THE_STACK.DEPTH = 0 then
    raise STACK_IS_EMPTY;
  else
    return AT_THE_STACK.TOP.ITEM;
  end if;
end PEEK;
```

The remaining functions and procedures are simple linked list operations that all operate on the first object in the stack, because in a stack the front and the rear are the same. The operation PUSH illustrates this principle.

```
procedure PUSH ( ITEM           : in      ITEM_TYPE;
                 ONTO_THE_STACK : in out STACK) is
  -- Adds a new object to the top of the stack while preserving the
  -- LIFO order.
  -- Exception OVERFLOW is raised if there is not enough memory left
  --           to put the item onto the stack.
begin
  ONTO_THE_STACK.TOP := new STACK_NODE' (ITEM, ONTO_THE_STACK.TOP);
  ONTO_THE_STACK.DEPTH := ONTO_THE_STACK.DEPTH + 1;
exception
  when storage_error =>
    raise OVERFLOW;
end PUSH;
```

Note that the depth of the stack is incremented after a node is added to the top of the stack. This results in the depth having the right value in the case that an OVERFLOW exception is raised by the "new STACK_NODE" statement. POP pulls objects from the front of the list, the only way in or out of a stack. Note that POP does not have to worry about re-setting pointers to null if the initial stack has depth 1.

```
procedure POP    ( ITEM              :    out ITEM_TYPE;
                    FROM_THE_STACK : in out STACK) is
  -- Returns the top item on the stack and deletes that item from
  -- the stack while preserving the LIFO order of the stack.
  -- Exception STACK_IS_EMPTY is raised if there is no item to pop.
begin
  if FROM_THE_STACK.DEPTH = 0 then
    raise STACK_is_EMPTY;
  else
    ITEM := FROM_THE_STACK.TOP.ITEM;
    FROM_THE_STACK.TOP := FROM_THE_STACK.TOP.NEXT;
    FROM_THE_STACK.DEPTH := FROM_THE_STACK.DEPTH - 1;
  end if;
end POP;
```

The procedure COPY is a simple assignment statement. It is not necessary to make a distinct exact copy of a stack, as Figure 6.3.3 suggests. Note that as objects are pushed and popped from the stack, the common "tail" is not affected. The only problem that might occur is if the user could directly modify an object in the common tail. Since stacks are limited private types, the only access to any stack is by the operations specified in the generic package specification. These do not allow modification. The remainder of the functions and procedures are left as exercises.

It is also possible to build the ADT STACK on top of the LIST ADT. Many list operations correspond to stack operations. For example, the private section of Figure 6.3.1 could be replaced by that shown in Figure 6.3.4.

```
package LIST_AS_STACK is new GENERIC_UNBOUNDED_LIST (ITEM_TYPE);
use LIST_AS_STACK;
type STACK is
  record
    STACK : LIST;
  end record;
```

Figure 6.3.4   Private section of Figure 6.3.1 when implementing a stack using the package GENERIC_UNBOUNDED_LIST.

All the stack operations in the body must be defined in terms of their list counterparts. For example, the operations POP and STACK are implemented by invoking the list operations HEAD_OF_LIST, TAIL_OF_LIST, and CLEAR.

```
procedure POP  (ITEM              :    out ITEM_TYPE
                FROM_THE_STACK  :  in out STACK) is
  -- Returns the top item on the stack and deletes that item from
  -- the stack while preserving the LIFO order of the stack.
```

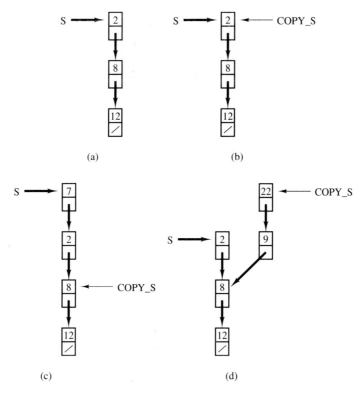

Figure 6.3.3 A simple assignment of pointers is sufficient when copying a stack implemented as a linked list. Note that pushing or popping items onto one stack does not affect the contents of the other. (a) Original stack. (b) Result of part (a) after a simple copy by assignment. (c) Result after PUSH(6.S) and POP(X.COPY_S). (d) Stack states after S is popped once and two items are pushed on COPY_S.

```
  -- Exception STACK_IS_EMPTY is raised if there is no item to pop.
begin
  if EMPTY (FROM_THE_STACK.STACK) then
    raise STACK IS EMPTY;
  else
    ITEM:= HEAD_OF_LIST (FROM_THE_STACK.STACK);
    FROM_THE_STACK.STACK := TAIL_OF_LIST (FROM_THE_STACK.STACK);
  end if;
end POP;

Procedure CLEAR (STACK_TO_CLEAR : in out STACK) is
  -- Removes all ITEMS from the stack.
begin
  CLEAR (STACK_TO_CLEAR.STACK);
end CLEAR;
```

Whether the stack ADT is built on its own structure or the list structure is transparent to the programmer, the instantiation is the same and the operations in the package are identical.

6.4 ELIMINATING RECURSION

Any recursively defined function or procedure can be implemented without recursion by using a stack. The definition of the function n factorial is

$$n! = n*(n-1)*...*1$$

or

$$n! = n*(n-1)! \quad \text{if } n >= 1$$
$$= 1 \qquad\qquad \text{if } n = 0$$

A recursively implemented function is

```
function NFACTORIAL ( N : natural ) return natural is
begin
  if N = 0 or N = 1 then
    return 1;
  else
    return N * NFACTORIAL ( N - 1 );
  end if;
end NFACTORIAL;
```

Ignore, for now, the fact that the function NFACTORIAL uses tail recursion and the fact that every recursive procedure that uses tail recursion can be implemented without recursion by using a loop. A stack also can be used to eliminate recursion. Consider the following computation of 5!. The left-hand column shows how the function NFACTORIAL computes 5!, and the column on the right shows how a stack can be used to do the computation.

$5! = 5 * 4!$	Push 5, try to compute 4!
$= 5 * 4 * 3!$	Push 4, try to compute 3!
$= 5 * 4 * 3 * 2!$	Push 3, try to compute 2!
$= 5 * 4 * 3 * 2 * 1!$	Push 2, try to compute 1!
$= 5 * 4 * 3 * 2 * 1$	$1! = 1$, by definition
$= 5 * 4 * 3 * 2$	Pop 2, multiply $2 * 1$ and save
$= 5 * 4 * 6$	Pop 3, multiply $3 * 2$ and save
$= 5 * 24$	Pop 4, multiply $4 * 6$ and save
$= 120$	Pop 5, multiply $5 * 24$ and save
	Stack empty, finished

All of the values are pushed onto the stack until the tail vanishes. When the tail vanishes, the base case is found. Once the tail vanishes the values are popped and the operation performed until the stack is empty. The nonrecursive definition below uses stacks in this manner.

```
with GENERIC_UNBOUNDED_STACK;
package N_STACK is new GENERIC_UNBOUNDED_STACK (integer);
function NFACTORIAL ( N : natural ) return natural is
  use N_STACK;
  STK : STACK;
  COUNT_DOWN : natural := N;
  PRODUCT : natural := 1;
begin
  if N <= 0 then
    return 1;
```

```
              else
                loop
                  PUSH (COUNT_DOWN, STK);
                  COUNT_DOWN :=  COUNT_DOWN - 1;
                  exit when COUNT_DOWN = 0;
                end loop;
                loop
                  POP (COUNT_DOWN, STK);
                  PRODUCT :=  PRODUCT * COUNT_DOWN;
                  exit when EMPTY (STK);
                end loop;
                return PRODUCT;
              end if;
          end NFACTORIAL;
```

A second example of classic tail recursion involves summing the elements of an unconstrained array. Suppose that

```
          type VECTOR is array (integer range <>) of integer;
          ..........
          function SUM_VECTOR(V : VECTOR) return integer is
          begin
            if V'length = 1 then
              return V(V'first);
            else
              return V(V'first) +  SUM_VECTOR (V(V'first+1..V''last));
            end if;
          end SUM_VECTOR;
```

SUM_VECTOR is another obvious example of tail recursion, and there is an equally obvious nonrecursive implementation involving a loop. Recursion could also be eliminated by the following use of a stack.

```
          type VECTOR is array (integer range <>) of integer;
          .........
          with GENERIC_UNBOUNDED_STACK;
          Package N_STACK is new GENERIC_UNBOUNDED_STACK (integer);
          function SUM_VECTOR (V: VECTOR) return integer is
            use N_STACK;
            STK : STACK;
            SUM : integer;
            NEXT_TERM : integer;
          begin
            --push entire tail onto the stack
            for INDEX in V'range loop
              PUSH(V(INDEX), STK);
            end loop;
            -- get the base case
          POP(SUM, STK);
            -- get next value from the top of the stack and perform
            -- the indicated operation until the tail is gone
```

```
loop
   exit when EMPTY(STK);
   POP (NEXT_TERM, STK);
   SUM := SUM + NEXT_TERM;
end loop;
--when tail is gone, return the answer
return SUM;
end SUM_VECTOR;
```

Using stacks to eliminate recursion often has a price. Many functions and procedures have simple and natural recursive definitions. Eliminating recursion sacrifices this natural expression while often increasing the coding complexity. The Fibonacci function in Figure 6.4.1 is a perfect function example.

```
FIBONACCI (N: natural) return natural is
begin
   if N <= 1 then
      return 1;
   else
      return FIBONACCI(N-1) + FIBONACCI(N-2);
   end if;
end FIBONACCI;
```

Figure 6.4.1   Recursive implementation to compute Fibonacci numbers.

To compute the nth Fibonacci number, a snapshot of the state of the function must be taken. The following record type serves this purpose.

```
type SNAPSHOT is
   record
      N : natural;
      FIB_N_MINUS_1 : natural := 0;
      FIB_N_MINUS_2 : natural := 0;
   end record;
```

The field N denotes which term of the Fibonacci sequence is being computed. If either FIB_N_MINUS_1 or FIB_N_MINUS_2 is zero, the intermediate terms have not been computed. The snapshot is pushed onto the stack and manipulated until the stack is empty. Figure 6.4.2 lists one nonrecursive version. The program shown in the figure has a very complicated logic. What is the probability of writing correctly on the first try a procedure similar to the one shown in Figure 6.4.2? The simplicity of the recursive Fibonacci implementation listed in Figure 6.4.1 was lost with the nonrecursive stack-based implementation. The original recursive procedure could usually be implemented error free on the first try.

```
function FIBONACCI (N : natural) return natural is
   type SNAPSHOT is
      record
         N : natural;
         FIB_N_MINUS_1 : natural := 0;
         FIB_N_MINUS_2 : natural := 0;
      end record;
```

Figure 6.4.2   Nonrecursive stack-based implementation of the function Fibonacci. Continues on page 135.

```
           package FIB_STACK is new GENERIC_UNBOUNDED_STACK (SNAPSHOT);
           use FIB_STACK;
           STK : STACK;
           TEMP1, TEMP2 : SNAPSHOT;
       begin
         if N <= 1 then
           return 1;
         else
           -- Push initial snapshot on the stack
           PUSH ((N,0,0), STK);
           loop
             TEMP1 := PEEK(STK);
             if TEMP1.FIB_N_MINUS_1 = 0 then
               -- First term has not been computed
               if TEMP1.N = 2 then
                 POP(TEMP1, STK);
                 -- first base case found, stop recursion
                 PUSH((2,1,1), STK);
               else
                 --Compute first term, FIBONACCI(N-1)
                 PUSH((TEMP1.N-1, 0, 0), STK);
               end if;
             elsif TEMP1.FIB_N_MINUS_2 = 0 then
               -- First term computed, now compute second term
               if TEMP1.N = 3 then
                 -- Second base case encountered, stop recursion
                 POP(TEMP1, STK);
                 PUSH((3,2,1), STK);
               else
                 -- Compute second term, FIBBONACCI(N-2)
                 PUSH((TEMP1.N-2, 0, 0), STK);
               end if;
             else
               -- Fib_n_minus-1, Fib_n_minus_2 both defined,
               -- FIBBONACI (N) = Fib_n_minus_1 + Fib_n_minus_2
               POP(TEMP1, STK);
               if not EMPTY(STK) then
                 -- Get Snapshot to put answer in
                 POP (TEMP2, STK);
                 if TEMP2.FIB_N_MINUS_1 = 0 then
                   TEMP2.FIB_N_MINUS_1 := TEMP1.FIB_N_MINUS_1
                                               + TEMP1.FIB_N_MINUS_2;
                   PUSH(TEMP2, STK);
                 else
                   TEMP2.FIB_N_MINUS_2 := TEMP1.FIB_N_MINUS_1
                                               + TEMP1.FIB_N_MINUS_2;
                   PUSH(TEMP2, STK);
                 end if;
               end if;
```

Figure 6.4.2 Continues on page 136.

```
            end if;
            exit when EMPTY (STK);
         end loop;
         return TEMP1.FIB_N_MINUS_1 + TEMP1.FIB_N_MINUS_2;
      end if;
   end FIBONACCI;
```

Figure 6.4.2 Concluded.

As a last nontrivial example of eliminating recursion, consider the basic nonlinear tree structure introduced in Section 2.6. Chapter 2 covers trees in depth. Figure 6.4.3(a) shows the record structure of a tree. Figure 6.4.3(b) illustrates a basic tree. Note that the top node, called the root, is not referenced by any other node. Every other node is referenced by a node one level above it. A traversal of a tree is a scheme where every node is visited once and only once. Figure 6.4.3(c) shows a recursive traversal procedure that prints the integer in each node. This traversal recursively lists every integer in the left subtree of a node, then the integer in the current node, and then it recursively lists every node in the right subtree. Every integer in every node is listed. A node is either the root node, or it is in the left subtree, or it is in the right subtree. Figure 6.4.3(d) lists the traversal of the tree in Figure 6.4.3(b) by the procedure in Figure 6.4.3(c).

```
            type TREE_NODE;
            type TREE is access TREE_NODE;
            type TREE_NODE is
               record
                  X : integer;
                  LEFT,
                     RIGHT : tree;
               end record;
            ROOT : TREE;
```

(a)

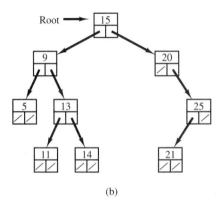

ITEM

LEFT | RIGHT

Node structure of a typical tree node

(b)

Figure 6.4.3 (a) Tree data structure. (b) Typical binary search tree with integer nodes. (c) Recursive tree traversal procedure. (d) Traversal order of tree in part (b) using procedure traversal in part (c).

```
procedure INORDER_TRAVERSAL (T : in    Tree) is
begin
   if T /= null then
      TRAVERSAL(T.LEFT);
      put(T.X); --output integer field in node
      TRAVERSAL(T.RIGHT);
   end if;
end INORDER_TRAVERSAL;
```

(c)

5–9–11–13–14–15–20–21–25

(d)

Again, a snapshot of the procedure state must be kept. Any snapshot must tell whether the left side of the tree has or has not been traversed. The solution in Figure 6.4.4 puts on the full left descent of a side whenever on the stack it puts the side on. The result is that the node on top of the stack will be the next node to be printed. After it is printed the full left side of the right subtree and the right subtrees root must be pushed onto the stack. Figure 6.4.4 lists one nonrecursive version of the procedure INORDER_TRAVERSAL. Note again that the top of the stack always contains the next node that will be printed in the traversal.

```
procedure INORDER_TRAVERSAL(T : in    Tree) is
   package TREE_STACK is new GENERIC_UNBOUNDED_STACK(TREE);
   use TREE_STACK;
   STK : STACK;
   TEMP : TREE;
begin
   -- Put the root or first node on the stack
   PUSH(T, STK);
   -- Put the full left subtree on the stack
   loop
      exit when PEEK(STK).LEFT = null;
      PUSH(PEEK(STK).LEFT, STK);
   end loop;
   loop
      exit when EMPTY(STK);
      -- Get and print the current node on top of the stack
      POP(TEMP, STK);
      -- print node field X
      put(TEMP.X);
      -- put the node on the right and its left subtree on the stack
      if TEMP.RIGHT /= null then
         PUSH(TEMP.RIGHT, STK);
         loop
            exit when PEEK(STK).LEFT = null;
            PUSH(PEEK(STK).LEFT, STK);
         end loop;
      end if;
   end loop;
end INORDER_TRAVERSAL;
```

Figure 6.4.4   Nonrecursive implementation of the procedure INORDER_TRAVERSAL.

Nonrecursive versions often execute faster than the recursive versions. This is often due to the time it takes to do the system overhead of a recursive call. When the work is the same, the simplicity and clarity of recursion are desirable. Other times, as in the case of the Fibonacci function that does not store intermediate values, recursion must be avoided. Every person who has implemented a recursively defined function using assembly language or any other language that does not support recursion is familiar with the programming techniques outlined above.

6.5 APPLICATIONS

One useful fact about stack behavior is that items come off a stack in the reverse order in which they were added. The following simple procedure reverses the items in a list and returns a list with the items in reverse. The procedure REVERSE_LIST can handle an empty list.

```
package MY_STACK is new GENERIC_UNBOUNDED_STACK (MY_ITEM);
package MY_LIST is new GENERIC_UNBOUNDED_LIST (MY_ITEM);
    ..................
procedure REVERSE_LIST (L : in LIST; REVERSE_L : out LIST) is
  Use MY_STACK;
  Use MY_LIST;
  S : STACK;
  TEMP_R, TEMP_L : LIST;
  X : MY_ITEM;
begin
  COPY(L, TEMP_L);
  loop
    exit when EMPTY (TEMP_L);
    push (HEAD_OF_LIST( TEMP_L ), S);
    TEMP_L := TAIL_OF_LIST (TEMP_L);
  end loop;
  loop
    exit when EMPTY (S);
    CLEAR(TEMP_L);
    POP (X, S);
    ADD_ITEM_TO_HEAD(TEMP_L, X);
    CATENATE(TEMP_R, TEMP_L);
  end loop;
  COPY(TEMP_R, REVERSE_L);
end REVERSE_LIST;
```

An application that uses this fact involves determining if a given string is a palindrome. A palindrome is a string that equals the reverse of itself. For example, the names "Bob," "Otto," and "Anna" are all palindromes. The following simple boolean-valued function determines whether a string is a palindrome if the function reverse is defined for strings.

```
function PALINDROME ( S : string ) return boolean is
begin
  return S = REVERSE(S);
end if;
```

The details are left to an exercise.

Another application of a stack is the *depth-first search* of a maze. This problem will be solved completely in Chapter 10, but for now an outline of the problem and its solution is given. A maze is a puzzle that can be visualized as a series of N rooms. Suppose that each room is assigned a unique integer between 1 and N (see Figure 6.5.1). Each room may have doors leading to adjacent rooms, but a room may also be a closet with no way out but the way in. The goal is to start in room 1 and to find a path to the exit in room N. Any successful path from the start to the exit will never visit a room more than once. If a path visits a room twice, the path is literally going around in circles. Paths with circles are eliminated by a simply mechanism. Any room visited is marked as visited. A simple way to mark a room as visited is to use a boolean array where the ith component has the value true if the ith room has been visited and false otherwise. What is needed is a way of backtracking when a path is found to lead back to a room already visited or to get out of a closet. The stack, with its last in, first out behavior, supplies the perfect mechanism to meet this need.

A brief description of the maze algorithm, which is a depth-first search, follows. To start, mark room 1 as visited and push the number 1 onto the stack. Now choose any path out of room 1 and into an adjacent room, say room k. Mark room k as visited and push the number k onto the stack. Continue moving from room to room using the following rules. A room is never visited twice, because any room visited is immediatley marked. As soon as a room is visited, the room number is pushed onto the stack. If a room is entered where there is either no way out or no way out without visiting an already visited room, pop the last room number off the stack and go back to that room number. That room is clearly an adjacent room. Eventually, one of two things will happen. One possibility is that the stack is empty, which means that there is no path from the start to the finish. The other possibility is eventually to enter room N. To display the path back to start, just pop the stack until it is empty.

Occasionally, human interest stories appear in the media announcing that someone has computed the value of π to an additional million significant digits, or that a new super-computer undegoing testing has just broken the record for the largest known prime number. The current record for a known prime number is an integer approaching 1 million digits in

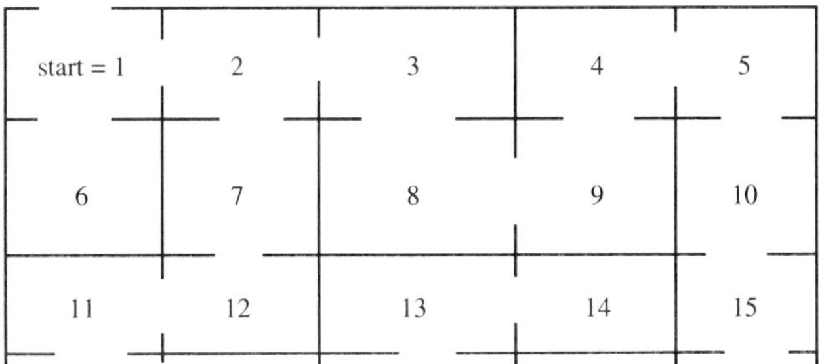

Figure 6.5.1 Typical maze.

length. Obviously, these are not normal integers with normal integer operations. Using the following list representation makes for a natural representation of long_number.

```
subtype DIGIT is integer range 0..9;
package LONG_NUMBER_LIST is new GENERIC_UNBOUNDED_LIST(DIGIT);
use LONG_NUMBER_LIST;
LONG_NUMBER : LIST;
```

LONG_NUMBERS are lists of digits. The most significant digit is at the head of the list and the least significant digit is at the end of the tail of the list. It is assumed that the head of the list never contains the digit zero. Figure 6.5.2(a) shows a 10-digit integer and Figure 6.5.2(b) illustrates the list representation.

```
Long_number = 2576578904
```

(a)

```
Long_number  ->2->5->7->6->5->7->8->9->0->4
```

(b)

Figure 6.5.2 (a)   Ten-digit LONG_NUMBER. (b)   LONG_NUMBER_LIST representation of number in part (a).

Since lists are private and not limited private, lists can be passed as parameters of all functions and procedures. This allows the addition operator to be overloaded. The two lists to be added are first pushed onto their respective stacks of digits. This puts the least significant digits on the top of the stack. Remember, numbers are read left to right, but numbers are added right to left.

```
function "+" (LEFT, RIGHT : LONG_NUMBER_LIST.LIST)
                        return LONG_NUMBER_LIST.LIST is
   package DIGIT_STACK is new GENERIC_UNBOUNDED_STACK(DIGIT);
   use DIGIT_STACK;
   LEFT_STACK, RIGHT_STACK : STACK;
   TEMP_LEFT, TEMP_RIGHT, ANSWER : LIST;
   CARRY : natural := 0;
   TEMP_DIGIT, TEMP_DIGIT_1, TEMP_DIGIT_2 : DIGIT;
begin
   COPY (LEFT, TEMP_LEFT);
   COPY (RIGHT, TEMP_RIGHT);
   -- Reverse both left and right so least significant digit on top
   loop
      exit when EMPTY(TEMP_LEFT);
      TEMP_DIGIT := HEAD_OF_LIST(TEMP_LEFT);
      TEMP_LEFT := TAIL_OF_LIST(TEMP_LEFT);
      PUSH(TEMP_DIGIT, LEFT_STACK);
   end loop;
   loop
      exit when EMPTY(TEMP_RIGHT);
      TEMP_DIGIT := HEAD_OF_LIST(TEMP_RIGHT);
      TEMP_RIGHT := TAIL_OF_LIST(TEMP_RIGHT);
```

```
           PUSH(TEMP_DIGIT, RIGHT_STACK);
     end loop;
     -- Add, digit by digit ....
     loop
        exit when EMPTY(LEFT_STACK) or else EMPTY (RIGHT_STACK);
        -- Get the next digits to add
        POP(TEMP_DIGIT_1, LEFT_STACK);
        POP(TEMP_DIGIT_2, RIGHT_STACK);
        -- Add and determine if there is a carry
        CARRY := CARRY + TEMP_DIGIT_1 + TEMP_DIGIT_2;
        if CARRY >= 10 then
           TEMP_DIGIT_1 := CARRY - 10;
           CARRY := 1;
        else
           TEMP_DIGIT_1 := CARRY;
           CARRY := 0;
        end if;
        -- Put the digit on answer list and continue
        ADD_ITEM_TO_HEAD(ANSWER, TEMP_DIGIT_1);
     end loop;
     --one or both stacks empty, must finish up
     loop
         exit when EMPTY (LEFT_STACK);
         POP(TEMP_DIGIT_1, LEFT_STACK);
         CARRY := CARRY + TEMP_DIGIT_1;
         if CARRY >= 10 then
            TEMP_DIGIT_1 := CARRY - 10;
            CARRY := 1;
         else
            TEMP_DIGIT_1 := CARRY;
            CARRY := 0;
         end if;
         ADD_ITEM_TO_HEAD (ANSWER, TEMP_DIGIT_1);
     end loop;
     loop
        exit when EMPTY (RIGHT_STACK);
        POP(TEMP_DIGIT_1, RIGHT_STACK);
        CARRY := CARRY + TEMP_DIGIT_1;
        if CARRY >= 10 then
           TEMP_DIGIT_1 := CARRY - 10;
           CARRY := 1;
        else
           TEMP_DIGIT_1 := CARRY;
           CARRY := 0;
        end if;
        ADD_ITEM_TO_HEAD(ANSWER, TEMP_DIGIT_1);
     end loop;
     -- Allow for nonzero carry digit
     IF CARRY /= 0 THEN
        ADD_ITEM_TO_HEAD(ANSWER, 1);
```

```
        end if;
      return ANSWER;
    end "+";
```

A more efficient method of doing arbitrary integer arithmetic is developed in Chapter 14. Until then the other arithmetic operators can be implemented similarly.

6.6 TIME AND SPACE CONSTRAINTS

Stack operations are time efficient. The reason for this efficiency is that stack operations all operate on the top or front of the stack. The amount of memory used is proportional to either the number of elements on the stack in the unbounded case, or the maximum stack size in the bounded case. There are some overhead differences if the bounded stack is implemented as in Figure 6.2.1 or 6.2.2.

In Figure 6.6.1, the first column denotes the overhead due to time to compute the stack operations while the second column is the space by the bounded stack.

	Operation Overhead	Space Overhead
PUSH	$O(1)$	$O(\text{SIZE})$
POP	$O(1)$	$O(\text{SIZE})$
COPY	$O(N)$	$O(\text{SIZE})$
EQUAL	$O(N)$	$O(\text{SIZE})$
DEPTH	$O(1)$	$O(\text{SIZE})$

Figure 6.6.1 Time and space overhead for ADT stack GENERIC_BOUNDED_STACK in Figure 6.2.1.

PUSH and POP are essentially two assignment statements no matter what the size of the STACK. Thus PUSH and POP are $O(1)$. COPY and EQUAL require the assignment and comparison, respectively, of two array slices of length N, where N is the number of elements in the STACK, so these two operations are $O(N)$. The unbounded case is similar to the time and space constraints of GENERIC_UNBOUNDED_LIST and so is left to the exercises.

6.7 CASE STUDY: EVALUATION OF INFIX EXPRESSIONS

This first case study examines the problem of evaluating simple infix expressions. It uses two abstract data types, GENERIC_UNBOUNDED_LIST and GENERIC_UNBOUN-DED_STACK. An infix expression is one in which every binary operator is in order. This means that every binary operator is surrounded by numbers. For example, $5 + 3$ or $8 - 7$ or $3 + 4 + 5 * 7$ are all simple infix expressions, but $3+$ or $3 + 5*$ or $3 \ 4+$ are not. To evaluate even these simple expressions requires several rules. First, does

$$2 + 3 * 5 = (2 + 3) * 5 = 30$$

or does

$$2 + 3 * 5 = 2 + (3 * 5) = 17$$

The precedence of arithmetic operators in Ada, which will be adopted, requires the second interpretation. Second, how are parentheses to be handled? Logically, the expression inside the parentheses is a unique number to that part of the expression outside the parentheses. That is,

$$5 + (2 + 3 * 5) + 7 = 5 + 17 + 7$$

Evaluating infix expressions directly is a tedious task. It is easier to convert these expressions to an intermediate form called a *postfix expression* and then evaluate the postfix expression. Postfix expressions, often called *RPN* (reverse Polish notation) *expressions,* are popular because they do not use parentheses. It is called *postfix* because the operators immediately follow the numbers on which they operate. For example, the expressions listed in Figure 6.7.1 are all valid postfix expressions. The evaluation of postfix expressions is simple. Scan the postfix expression, starting from the left, until the first binary operator is found. This operator operates on the two numbers that immediately precede it. Let "op" denote any binary operation. The rule is that X Y op is evaluated like the infix expression X op Y. As an example, the postfix expression in Figure 6.7.2 is evaluated in sequence. The parenthesis in Figure 6.7.2 are not part of the postfix expression. They are there to show which part of the postfix expression is being evaluated.

$$5 \ \ 3 + = 8$$
$$5 \ \ 6 - 4 + = 3$$
$$2 \ \ 3 \ \ 4 + * = 14$$

Figure 6.7.1 Examples of valid RPN expressions.

	$3 \ 9 \ 5 \ 4 + - \ 2 * 6 + + \ 3 \ / \ 2 +$
Step 1	$3 \ 9(5 \ 4 +) - 2 * 6 + + 3 \ / \ 2 +$
Step 2	$3(9 \ 9 -)2 * 6 + + 3 \ / \ 2 +$
Step 3	$3(0 \ 2 *)6 + + 3 \ / \ 2 +$
Step 4	$3(0 \ 6 +)+ 3 \ / \ 2 +$
Step 5	$(3 \ 6 +)3 \ / \ 2 +$
Step 6	$(9 \ 3 /)2 +$
Step 7	$(3 \ 2 +)$
Answer	5

Figure 6.7.2 Evaluation of simple integer postfix expression.

To evaluate infix expressions some intermediate data type must be used. A GENERIC__UNBOUNDED_LIST of character will serve. The converted postfix expression will be handled similarly. Expressions composed of simple expressions can be handled similarly. To simplify the programming, it is assumed that all variables in the infix expression are lowercase letters. This allows the variables, single-letter identifiers, to be stored in a list of characters. The input and output will be handled through a terminal. A sample session would look as shown in Figure 6.7.3.

```
INFIX EXPRESSION EVALUATOR
ALL VARIABLES ARE LOWERCASE
FIRST ENTER ALL VARIABLES FOLLOWED BY THE VALUE
USE THE FORM  a:=5.7
```

Figure 6.7.3 I-O for GET_INFIX_EXPRESSION and MORE_TO_DO. Continues on page 144.

```
DO NOT USE BLANKS IN ANY EXPRESSION
THEN ENTER THE INFIX EXPRESSION
$ a:=5.0
$ b:=6.0
$ c:=3.0
$ (a+b) / (b-c)

INFIX: (a+b) / (b-c)
EQUIVALENT POSTFIX EXPRESSION
ab+bc-/
VALUE = 3.667

DO YOU HAVE MORE TO DO? ENTER Y/ES FOR YES.
N
```

Figure 6.7.3   Concluded.

Figure 6.7.4 lists the outline for CASE_STUDY_6.

```
with text_io;                       use text_io;
with FLOAT_TEXT_IO;                 use FLOAT_TEXT_IO;
with GENERIC_UNBOUNDED_LIST;
with GENERIC_UNBOUNDED_STACK;

procedure CASE_STUDY_6 is

   type VECTOR is array('a'..'z') of float;
   package EXP_LIST is new GENERIC_UNBOUNDED_LIST (character);
   use EXP_LIST;
   ALL DONE : boolean := false;
   VALUE : VECTOR := (others => 0.0);
   INFIX,
   POSTFIX : LIST;
   ILL-FORMED : exception; --signals invalid expression

   function OPERAND (C : character) return boolean is
     --signals whether next term in an expression is an
     --operator or an operand
   begin
     return C in 'a'..'z';
   end OPERAND;

   Procedure PRINT_EXPRESSION (L : in List) is separate;
    --prints a list character by character
    --left as an exercise

   procedure GET_INFIX_EXPRESSION is separate;
     --reads infix expression from keyboard and stores it in the
     --variable INFIX. See sample in Figure 6.7.3
     --see Figure 6.7.8
```

Figure 6.7.4   Outline for CASE_STUDY_6. Continues on page 145.

```
procedure NO_MORE_TO_DO (FLAG :   out boolean) is separate;
  --sets flag = false if another expression is to be evaluated
  --left to exercises

function EVALUATE_POSTFIX (EXP : LIST) return float is separate;
  --evaluates a given postfix equation using values
  --stored in the vector value
  --see Figure 6.7.7

procedure CONVERT_INFIX_TO_RPN (INFIX : in     LIST;
                                RPN   :    out LIST) is separate;
  --see Figure 6.7.6

begin --CASE_STUDY_6
  loop
    -- start of block where exception ill_formed handle
    begin
     GET_INFIX_EXPRESSION;
     CONVERT_INFIX_TO_RPN (INFIX, POSTFIX);
     put_line ("EQUIVALENT POSTFIX EXPRESSION");
     PRINT_EXPRESSION (POSTFIX);
     put ("VALUE = ");
     put (EVALUATE_POSTFIX(POSTFIX),1,4,0);
     CLEAR (INFIX);
     new_line;
     VALUE := (others => 0.0);
     NO_MORE_TO_DO (ALL_DONE);
     exit when ALL_DONE;
     exception
        when ILL_FORMED =>
        put_line(" ERROR! Ill formed Expression, Try Again!");
        skip_line;
        CLEAR (INFIX)
        CLEAR (POSTFIX)
    end; --end of block that handles exception ill_formed
  end loop;
end CASE_STUDY_6;
```

Figure 6.7.4 Concluded.

Note that the exception ILL_FORMED is raised whenever the infix string was input improperly and cannot be converted to a postfix string, or the postfix string cannot be evaluated. All other exceptions, including those in GENERIC_UNBOUNDED_STACK and GENERIC_UNBOUNDED_LIST, either trigger ILL_FORMED or they are ignored.

The procedure CONVERT_INFIX_RPN requires the use of two stacks, one to store the operands and one to store the operators and the left parentheses. First, consider the simple case of infix expressions without parentheses. Any conversion must obey the rules of precedence. These rules mandate that expressions are evaluated left to right with $*$ and $/$ having the same precedence, + and – having the same precedence, but $*$ and $/$ having higher precedence than + and –. Thus the conversion algorithm must know that A+B$*$C = A+(B$*$C). The four cases listed in Figure 6.7.5 must be satisfied. These cases illustrate the four possibilities when comparing adjacent operators precedence. If op1 denotes the left operator and op2 denotes the right operator, cases 1, 3, and 4 convert, with op1 appearing before op2 in the postfix expression. In these three cases the priority of op1 was greater than or equal to the priority of op2. In case 2

Infix Expression	Equivalent Postfix Expression
op1 op2	
1. A + B + C	AB+C+
2. A + B * C	ABC*+
3. A * B + C	AB*C+
4. A * B * C	AB*C*

Figure 6.7.5   Four cases of operator precedence.

the priority of op2 is greater than the priority of op1. This example shows that the conversion procedure must keep track of the two most recent operators. The function priority handles the problem of precedence.

The conversion procedure uses a stack to keep track of the most recent operators encountered but not yet appended to the end of the postfix list. Operators are added to the stack until a new operator of equal or lower precedence appears. At that time the stack is popped and the popped operator is added to the expression, while the new operator is added to the stack. After scanning, the infix expression stops, the stack is emptied, and the contents of the stack are copied onto the postfix expression.

Now the case of the fully parenthesized infix expression can be considered. This case involves two extra requirements. The first requirement is to allow for an unlimited number of parentheses. The second requirement takes the form of an obvious observation. Any parenthesized expression is, in reality, a single term or expression. GENERIC_UNBOUNDED_STACK can store an unlimited number of operators and parentheses. The left parenthesis is considered a "term operator." After encountering the left parenthesis, it is put on the stack. After encountering the matching right parenthesis, the characters on the stack are popped and added to the end of the postfix list until the matching left parenthesis is popped. The popped left parenthesis is discarded. Figure 6.7.6 lists the procedure CONVERT_INFIX TO_RPN. This implementation does not handle exponentiation or the unary operators. These details are left to the exercises.

```
separate (CASE_STUDY_6)
procedure CONVERT_INFIX_TO_RPN (INFIX : in     LIST;
                                RPN   :   out LIST) is

   package CHAR_STACK is new GENERIC_UNBOUNDED_STACK (character);
   use CHAR_STACK;

   TEMP_RPN,
   TEMP_INFIX : LIST;
   OP_STACK : STACK;
```

Figure 6.7.6   Procedure CONVERT_INFIX_TO_RPN. Continues on page 147.

```
CHAR, CHAR_1 : character;

function PRIORITY (OPERATOR : character) return natural is
begin
  case OPERATOR IS
    when '+' | '-' => return 1;
    when '*' | '/' => return 2;
    when others    => return 0;
  end case;
end PRIORITY;

begin
 TEMP_INFIX := INFIX;
 loop
   exit when EMPTY (TEMP_INFIX);
   CHAR := HEAD_OF_LIST (TEMP_INFIX);
   TEMP_INFIX := TAIL_OF_LIST (TEMP_INFIX);
   if OPERAND (CHAR) then
     ADD_ITEM_TO_END_OF_LIST (TEMP_RPN, CHAR);
   elsif EMPTY (OP_STACK) then
     PUSH (CHAR, OP_STACK);
   elsif CHAR = '(' then
     PUSH ("(", OP_STACK);
   elsif CHAR = ')' then
     --pop until finding '('
     loop
       exit when PEEK (OP_STACK) = '(';
       POP (CHAR, OP_STACK);
       ADD_ITEM_TO_END_OF_LIST(TEMP_RPN, CHAR);
     end loop;
     POP (CHAR, OP_STACK);
   else
     while not EMPTY (OP_STACK)) and then
           PRIORITY (CHAR) <= PRIORITY (PEEK (OP_STACK)) loop
       POP (CHAR_1, OP_STACK);
       ADD_ITEM_TO_END_OF_LIST (TEMP_RPN, CHAR_1);
     end loop;
     PUSH (CHAR, OP_STACK);
   end if;
 end loop;
 loop
     exit when EMPTY (OP_STACK);
     POP (CHAR, OP_STACK);
     ADD_ITEM_TO_END_OF_LIST (Temp_RPN, Char);
   end loop;
   COPY (TEMP_RPN, RPN);
   exception
     when STACK_IS_EMPTY => raise ILL_FORMED;
end CONVERT_INFIX_TO RPN;
```

Figure 6.7.6   Concluded.

The function EVALUATE_POSTFIX also needs a stack to hold the values of the operands. The postfix expression is scanned from left to right. If the next character is an operand, its value is pushed onto a stack of values. If the next character is an operator, the top two values on the stack are popped off, the operation is performed, and the result is pushed back onto the stack. After completely scanning the postfix list, there should be one value left on the stack. This value is returned. Figure 6.7.7 lists the implementation of EVALUATE_POSTFIX.

```
separate (CASE_STUDY_6)
function EVALUATE_POSTFIX (EXP : LIST) return float is
  --evaluates a given postfix equation using values
  --stored in the vector value

  package FLOAT_STACK is new GENERIC_UNBOUNDED_STACK (FLOAT);
  use FLOAT_STACK;

  VALUE_STACK : STACK;
  TEMP_EXP : LIST;
  TEMP1,
  TEMP2 ; float;
  CHAR : character;
begin
  if EMPTY (EXP) then
      -- null expression
      return 0.0;
    else
      TEMP_EXP := EXP;
      loop
        exit when EMPTY (TEMP_EXP);
        CHAR := HEAD_OF_LIST (TEMP_EXP);
        TEMP_EXP := TAIL_OF_LIST (TEMP_EXP);
        if OPERAND (CHAR) then
          -- It's a value, push onto stack
          PUSH (VALUE(CHAR), VALUE_STACK);
        else
          -- It's an operator, pop off last two and perform operation
          POP (TEMP2, VALUE_STACK);
          POP (TEMP1, VALUE_STACK);
          case CHAR is
            when '+'     => PUSH (TEMP1 + TEMP2, VALUE_STACK);
            when '-'     => PUSH (TEMP1 - TEMP2, VALUE_STACK);
            when '*'     => PUSH (TEMP1 * TEMP2, VALUE_STACK);
            when '/'     => PUSH (TEMP1 / TEMP2, VALUE_STACK);
            when others => null;
          end case;
        end if;
      end loop;
      POP (TEMP1, VALUE_STACK);
```

Figure 6.7.7   Function EVALUATE_POSTFIX. Continues on page 149.

```
       if EMPTY (VALUE_STACK) then
         return TEMP1:
       else
         raise ILL_FORMED;
       end if;
     end if;
  end EVALUATE_POSTFIX;
```

Figure 6.7.7   Concluded.

The last procedure, GET_INFIX_EXPRESSION, is easy once a form of the GET procedure in FLOAT_TEXT_IO is understood. (FLOAT_TEXT_IO is just the instantiation of the float type by the generic package float_io.) This form reads from a string and converts it to a float. It is not necessary to write a conversion procedure that converts a character string of digits to a floating-point value. The procedure GET_INFIX_EXPRESSION (Figure 6.7.8) prompts the user, gets the values of the variables, inputs the infix expression as a string of characters, and puts the infix expression onto a list.

```
     separate (CASE_STUDY_6)
     procedure GET_INFIX_EXPRESSION is
       --reads infix expression from keyboard and stores it in the
       --variable INFIX. See sample in Figure 6.7.3.
       LENGTH,
       LAST : natural := 10;
       LINE : String(1..80);
     begin
       new_line; put_line("INFIX EXPRESSION EVALUATOR");
       put_line("ALL VARIABLES ARE LOWERCASE");
       put_line("FIRST ENTER ALL VARIABLES FOLLOWED BY THE VALUE.:);
       put_line("USE THE FORM a:= 5.7");
       put_line("DO NOT USE BLANKS IN ANY EXPRESSION");
       put_line("THEN ENTER THE INFIX EXPRESSION");
       loop
         -- Mark the beginning of the command line
         put("S ");
         get_line (LINE, LENGTH);
         if LENGTH = 1 then
           --single identifier, no operator
           put("Infix: ");
           put_line(line(1..Length);
           put("Postfix: ");
           put_line(line(1..Length);
           put("Value = ");
           put(value(line(1)),1,4,0);
           new_line;
           exit;
         elsif LINE(2..3) = ':=' then
           --assignmnent statement, must be an operand value
```

Figure 6.7.8   Procedure GET_INFIX_EXPRESSION. Continues on page 150.

Sec 6.7   Case Study: Evaluation of Infix Expressions

```
            get (LINE(4..LENGTH), VALUE(LINE(1)), LAST);
        else
          -- must be the infix expression
          for I in 1..LENGTH loop
            ADD_TO_END_OF_LIST (INFIX, LINE(I));
          end loop;

        end if;
      end loop;
   end GET_INFIX_EXPRESSION;
```

Figure 6.7.8   Concluded.

The remainder of the case study is left to the exercises.

EXERCISES

Section 6.2 Bounded Implementation

6.2.1 Consider the ADT GENERIC_BOUNDED_STACK whose specification is listed in Figure 6.2.1.
   a. Implement the operation COPY.
   b. Implement the operation DEPTH.
   c. Implement the operation FULL.
   d. Implement the operation PEEK.
   e. Implement the operation EQUAL.
   f. Combine parts a through e with the operations implemented in the text to complete the body of the package GENERIC_BOUNDED_STACK. This fully implements this ADT.

6.2.2 Consider the ADT GENERIC_BOUNDED_STACK whose specification is listed in Figure 6.2.4.
   a. Implement the operation COPY.
   b. Implement the operation DEPTH.
   c. Implement the operation FULL.
   d. Implement the operation PEEK.
   e. Implement the operation PUSH.
   f. Implement the operation POP.
   g. Implement the operation CLEAR.
   h. Implement the operation EMPTY.
   i. Implement the operation EQUAL.
   j. Combine parts a through i to complete the body of this version of the package GENERIC_BOUNDED_STACK. This fully implements this version of this ADT.

6.2.3 Suppose that the private section of the ADT GENERIC_BOUNDED_STACK in Figure 6.2.4 is replaced by

```
private
   type ARRAY_OF_ITEM_TYPE is array (positive range <>) of ITEM_TYPE;
   type STACK_NODE (SIZE : positive ) is
     RECORD
       TOP : natural := 0;
       STACK : ARRAY_OF_ITEM_TYPE (1..SIZE);
     end RECORD;
   type STACK is access STACK_NODE;
```

a. Since STACK is now an access type, define an extra exception STACK_NOT_DEFINED whenever a stack has value null. Define and implement a new operation CREATE that creates a stack of a specified size.

b. Implement the operation COPY.

c. Implement the operation DEPTH.

d. Implement the operation FULL.

e. Implement the operation PEEK.

f. Implement the operation PUSH.

g. Implement the operation POP.

h. Implement the operation CLEAR.

i. Implement the operation EMPTY.

j. Implement the operation EQUAL.

k. Combine parts a through j to complete the body of this verison of the package GENERIC__BOUNDED_STACK. This fully implements this version of this ADT.

l. What are the advantages or disadvantages of this implementation as contrasted with the one in Figure 6.2.4?

6.2.4 Sometimes there is an attempt to save space by having two stacks use the same array. One stack pushes and pops from the left to the right while the second stack pushes and pops from right to left. The data structure is similar to

```
type ITEM_STACK_TYPE is array(positive range <>) of ITEM_TYPE;
subtype TOP_TYPE is integer range 0..MAXIMUM_STACK_SIZE+1;
type STACK is
  record
    TOP_LEFT_STACK : TOP_TYPE := 0;
    TOP_RIGHT_STACK : TOP_TYPE := MAXIMUM_STACK_SIZE + 1;
    STK : ITEM_STACK_TYPE(1..MAXIMUM_STACK_SIZE);
  end record;
```

a. Specify a package GENERIC_BOUNDED_2_STACK that does this. Most functions and procedures, such as PUSH and POP, will need an additional argument saying whether the left or right stack is being manipulated.

b. Implement the body of the abstract data type GENERIC_BOUNDED_2_STACK.

Section 6.3 Unbounded Implementation

6.3.1 Consider the ADT GENERIC_UNBOUNDED_STACK whose specification is listed in Figure 6.3.1.

a. Implement the operation CLEAR.

b. Implement the operation DEPTH.

c. Implement the operation EMPTY.

d. Implement the operation EQUAL.

e. Implement the operation COPY.

f. Combine parts a through e with the operations implemented in the text to complete the body of the package GENERIC_UNBOUNDED_STACK. This fully implements this ADT.

6.3.2 Implement GENERIC_UNBOUNDED_STACK by instantiating the package GENERIC_UNBOUNDED_LIST and defining a STACK as a new list type. (*Hint:* See Figure 6.3.4.)

Section 6.4 Eliminating Recursion

6.4.1 The quicksort algorithm sorts the elements on an array by manipulating the array so that some fixed element at location SPLIT has the property that every element to its left is less than it and every element to its right is greater than it. In fact, the element at the *k*th position is in its final place. A recursive version of the QUICK_SORT algorithm is listed in Section 11.1. Use a stack to eliminate recursion. (*Hint:* QUICK_SORT sorts "in place." Use a stack to keep track of the endpoints of the vector after the call to split.)

Section 6.5 Applications

6.5.1 Write a program that tests whether a given string is a palindrome.

6.5.2 Write a program that inputs an arbitrary string and outputs all substrings contained within the given string that are palindromes. Programs similar to this have applications to DNA research.

6.5.3 Write a program that accepts as input a string composed entirely of {a,b} and outputs the word "equal" if the number of occurrences of the letter a equals the number of occurrences of the letter b, and "not equal" otherwise. Your program is not allowed to count directly.

6.5.4 Write a procedure that keeps track of the window boundaries on a screen. Such a procedure would be useful in an environment where the programmer can start new tasks and each task has its own viewing area on the screen. When a task is terminated by the programmer, the programmer would return to the preceding task. Assume that the screen can be divided in 480 rows and 640 columns with the origin in the upper left-hand corner.

Section 6.6 Time and Space Constraints

6.6.1 What are the time and space constraints for the ADT in Exercise 6.2.2?

6.6.2 What are the time and space constraints for the ADT in Exercise 6.2.3?

Section 6.7 Case Study: Evaluation of Infix Expressions

6.7.1 Fully implement CASE_STUDY_6 as outlined in Figure 6.7.3.

6.7.2 Modify the program in Exercise 6.7.1 so that the infix expression can handle the exponentiation operator.

6.7.3 Modify the program in Exercise 6.7.1 so that the infix expression can handle the unary plus and minus, that is, expressions of the form +a–b and –a∗b.

PROGRAMMING PROJECTS

P6.1 Implement a program to train your memory. A string of random lowercase characters and numerals is entered from the keyboard to the computer. The string entered is displayed on the terminal screen. After the user signals they are ready to be tested by pressing down a key, the screen is cleared and the player enters the answer in reverse order. The computer then answers whether or not the answer is correct and prompts to see if the player is up to another game.

P6.2 Modify the program in Project P6.1 to generate fixed-length random strings of characters of lowercase characters and numerals. (*Hint:* A random number generator is listed in Appendix C.)

P6.3 Modify the program in Project P6.2 to wait a fixed time after displaying the random string before clearing the screen (*Hint:* the package CALENDAR described in Ada LRM Section 9.6 can generate timing.)

Notes and References

Knuth [27] classic series *The Art of Computer Programming* is "the" resource for most basic operations on elementary data types, including stacks. It will be cited repeatedly.

7

Queues

A queue is a strictly ordered linear sequence of objects of some component type where one end of the sequence is designated as the front of the queue and the other end of the sequence is designated as the rear of the queue. Objects can be added to the queue only at its rear, and they can be removed only from the front. The queue's characterizing behavior is its FIFO (first in, first out) operation. In this chapter we implement two major forms of the ADT queue as well as the balking queue, deque, and priority queue variations of these two forms.

Queues mimic the behavior of standing in line. Just as the courteous customer at the checkout line at the cash register goes to the rear of the line and moves to the front, queues also have a front and a rear (see Figure 7.0.1). All objects in a queue are maintained in a strict linear order where one object follows another. This classifies a queue as a linear type. Second, an object's position in line must be preserved by the first in, first out rule. The longer that an object has been in the queue, the closer that object must be to the front of the queue. The objects in the queue can be of any component type. This means that the data structure for this abstract type is composed of components ranging from access types to integer types to record types. Queue applications range from determining which file to print next on the printer, to keeping track of a traversal through a graph. The operations for the abstract data type QUEUE must preserve the order of insertion into the queue (see Figure 7.0.2).

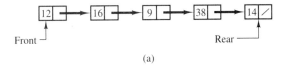

(a)

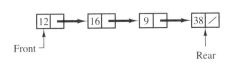

Figure 7.0.1   Basic queue.

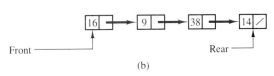

(b)

Figure 7.0.2   Two basic queue operations. (a) Queue from Figure 7.0.1 after adding item 14 to the rear. (b) Result of dequeue of the first item from the queue in part (a).

7.1 ADT QUEUE

Queue operations maintain and update queues while preserving first in, first out (FIFO) behavior. Objects are removed from a queue in the same order in which they are added. In contrast, objects are removed from a stack in the reverse order in which they were added. There are several names of operations that are unique to queues. To ENQUEUE an object is to add it to the rear of a queue. To DEQUEUE an object is to remove that object from the front of the queue and then to return the object to the program for processing. To POP a queue is to take the front object off the queue and then to discard that object. Figure 7.1.1 lists the full documentation for the ADT queue.

GENERAL ADT SPECIFICATION FOR QUEUE

Description

A queue is a strictly ordered linear sequence of objects of some component type ITEM_TYPE. One end of the queue is fixed as the front of the queue and the other end of the queue is fixed as the rear. Objects can only be removed, or dequeued, from the front. Objects can only be added, or enqueued, at the rear. Adding an object to the queue makes the added object into the new rear object. The old rear object is now second from the rear. An object can be dequeued only if it is the front object. A dequeued object is removed from the front and the object that was second in the queue is now the front object. After placing an object on the queue, its place on the queue, relative to the object that precedes it and the object that follows it, cannot be changed. FIFO or (first in, first out) ordering characterizes the queue's behavior.

Programmer-Supplied Data Structures or Specifications

The programmer must supply a component type ITEM_TYPE that makes up the objects on the queue. The component type ITEM_TYPE is private within the package.

Operations

NAME	DESCRIPTION
ENQUEUE	Adds an item of type ITEM_TYPE after the last item on the rear of the queue while preserving FIFO behavior. The previous rear object on the queue is now the next-to-last object.
DEQUEUE	Removes the first item from the front of the queue while preserving FIFO behavior. The second object is now the new front object. The first item is returned for processing.
COPY	Makes an exact copy of a queue that preserves FIFO behavior. The operation EQUAL returns true when the original queue and its copy are compared.
APPEND	Takes all the items from the front of the first queue and adds them to the rear of the second queue without modifying the order of the first queue. The result is equivalent to copying the first queue to a tempo-

Figure 7.1.1. Documentation for queue. Continues on page 155.

rary queue, then dequeuing each object from the temporary queue and immediately adding that object to the second queue until the temporary queue is empty.

CLEAR	Removes all items from the queue without processing any item.
POP	Removes the front item from the queue and discards that item without further processing.
LENGTH	Returns a natural number equal to the number of items on the queue.
EMPTY	Boolean-valued operation that returns true if the queue is empty, and false otherwise.
FULL	Boolean-valued operation that returns true if no more items can be added to the queue, and false otherwise.
FRONT_OBJECT	Returns the front item on the queue without removing it from the queue. The queue is not modified by this operation.
REAR_OBJECT	Returns the last item on the queue without removing it from the queue. The queue is not modified by this operation.
EQUAL	Boolean-valued operation that returns true when two queues have the same length and both queues are made up of the same items in the same order, and false otherwise.

Exceptions

Two exceptions can occur, OVERFLOW and Q_IS EMPTY. The OVERFLOW exception is raised when the queue cannot grow any larger. Any attempt made to ENQUEUE an ITEM, COPY two queues, or APPEND two queues will raise the exception OVERFLOW if no memory is left. The exception Q_IS_EMPTY is raised with the operations DEQUEUE, POP, FRONT_OBJECT, and REAR_OBJECT when an item is to be removed or referenced and the queue is empty.

Warnings

All warnings are implementation dependent.

Figure 7.1.1   Concluded.

The documentation does not include an iterator. Some applications require the traversal, or listing, or all the objects in a queue without modifying the queue. This is not a true queue in the sense that an object other than the front object is visible. One solution would be to add two more operations to the ADT queue. One possible description for the two iterator-based operations to be added to Figure 7.1.1 is shown in Figure 7.1.2.

NEXT_Q_OBJECT	Returns the next item on the queue without modifying the queue. If an item is enqueued or dequeued, the listing begins again at the queue's front. Once the queue's rear is reached, the next item listed will be the first item. If the queue is empty, the exception Q_IS_EMPTY is raised.
SET_NEXT_ITEM	Causes the next item listed from the queue to be the first item in the queue.

Figure 7.1.2   Documentation for queue iterator.

The basic documentation is now complete. The queue packages developed in the next two sections do not include the iterators described in Figure 7.1.2. In Section 7.4 two major queue variations, the balking queue and the deque, are studied. In that section the queue specification is partially rewritten.

7.2 BOUNDED FORM

A record type that contains an array of objects of type ITEMS implements the bounded form. As Figure 7.2.1 shows, the array stores the objects sequentially. The programmer must supply two formal generic parameters before the generic package can be instantiated. The first parameter is the maximum size of the queue. The component type is the second parameter that must be supplied.

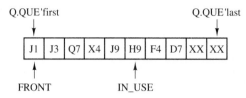

Figure 7.2.1 Array-based bounded queue as specified in Figure 7.2.3. The variable IN_USE is used in place of REAR. FRONT is always located at Q.QUE'first.

The type queue defined in the generic package (Figure 7.2.3) is a limited private type. Declaring the queue as a limited private type separates different queues of different type objects while preserving the commonality of the operations. Before the generic package specification for the package of bounded queues can be fully developed, a decision must be made. Every queue has a front and a rear. What strategy will be used to keep track of the front and the rear of the queue? There are a variety of methods for doing this.

One easy way to visualize strategy places the front of the queue in the first index in the array. This strategy uses just one parameter, IN_USE, to keep track of the number of objects in the queue. The rear of the queue can be identified as the variable IN_USE. If the queue is not empty, the value of IN_USE is not zero. The last element in the list, called the rear, has index IN_USE. The next object inserted would be placed at array location IN_USE+1 provided

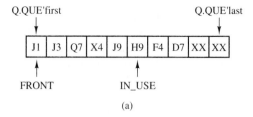

(a)

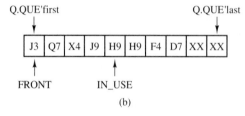

(b)

Figure 7.2.2 GENERIC_BOUNDED_QUEUE as specified in Figure 7.2.3 before and after a DEQUEUE operation. (a) Array-based queue holding six items. (b) Queue from part (a) after the front item has been removed and Q.Que(2..6) shifted to Q.Que(1..5) with IN USE set to 5.

that the queue is not full. This situation is illustrated in Figure 7.2.1. This strategy's simplicity comes with a price. The DEQUEUE operation causes excessive overhead. To maintain the front of the queue at the first location, every DEQUEUE operation will require that objects in locations 2 through IN_USE be shifted to positions 1 through IN_USE-1 (see Figure 7.2.2). Strategies for avoiding this unnecessary overhead will be developed later.

The data structure for our queue is

```
type ARRAY_OF_ITEM_TYPE is array (positive range <>) of ITEM_TYPE;
type QUEUE is
  record
    IN_USE : natural := 0;
    QUE : ARRAY_OF_ITEM_TYPE (1..MAXIMUM_Q_SIZE);
  end record;
```

Combining this abstract data structure with the functions and procedures needed to manipulate the structure creates the abstract data type GENERIC_BOUNDED_QUEUE. QUEUE is limited private. It can only be manipulated by functions or procedures in the generic specification that have type QUEUE arguments in their formal parameter list. The generic package encapsulates this ADT (see Figure 7.2.3).

```
generic
  type ITEM_TYPE is private;
  MAXIMUM_Q_SIZE : positive;
package GENERIC_BOUNDED_QUEUE is
  type QUEUE is private;
  procedure ENQUEUE      (ITEM       : in     ITEM_TYPE;
                          TO_THE_Q   : in out QUEUE);
  procedure DEQUEUE      (ITEM       : out    ITEM_TYPE;
                          FROM_THE_Q : in out QUEUE);
  procedure COPY         (FROM_Q     : in     QUEUE;
                          TO_Q       :    out QUEUE);
  procedure APPEND       (FROM_Q     : in     QUEUE;
                          ONTO_Q     : in out QUEUE);
  procedure CLEAR        (Q_TO_CLEAR : in out QUEUE);
  procedure POP          (FROM_THE_Q : in out QUEUE);
  function LENGTH        (Q_TO_COUNT : QUEUE) return natural;
  function EMPTY         (Q_TO_CHECK : QUEUE) return boolean;
  function FULL          (Q_TO_CHECK : QUEUE) return boolean;
  function FRONT_ITEM    (FROM_THE_Q : QUEUE) return ITEM_TYPE;
  function REAR_ITEM     (FROM_THE_Q : QUEUE) return ITEM_TYPE;
  function EQUAL         (Q1, Q2     : QUEUE) return boolean;
  Q_IS_EMPTY : exception;
  OVERFLOW   : exception;
private
  type ARRAY_OF_ITEM_TYPE is array (positive range <>) of ITEM_TYPE;
  type QUEUE is
    record
      IN_USE : natural := 0;
```

Figure 7.2.3 Package GENERIC_BOUNDED_QUEUE specification. Continues on page 158.

```
          QUE : ARRAY_OF_ITEM_TYPE (1..MAXIMUM_Q_SIZE);
      end record;
  end GENERIC_BOUNDED_QUEUE;
```

Figure 7.2.3 Concluded.

The implementation of the package body for GENERIC_BOUNDED_QUEUE is straightforward. The generic package focuses on the essence of the abstract case and not the details of the particular case. To reemphasize another benefit, abstractness makes it easier to prove correctness. If a queue is written specifically for a particular application, the programmer must verify that the queue operations are correct as well as the details of the particular queue.

The manner in which Ada handles arrays and records makes the implementation of most of the functions in the package GENERIC_BOUNDED_QUEUE almost trivial. An example follows.

```
procedure CLEAR ( Q_TO_CLEAR : in out QUEUE) is
  -- Removes all objects from the queue without
  -- processing any object.
begin
  Q_TO_CLEAR.IN_USE := 0;
end CLEAR;


procedure POP ( FROM_THE_Q : in out QUEUE) is
  -- Removes and discards the front ITEM from the queue.
  -- Exception Q_IS_EMPTY raised if there is no item to pop.
  TEMP : ITEM_TYPE;
begin
  if FROM_THE_Q.IN_USE = 0 then
    raise Q_IS_EMPTY;
  else
    FROM_THE_Q.IN_USE := FROM_THE_Q.IN_USE - 1;
    FROM_THE_Q.QUE (1..FROM_THE_Q.IN_USE) :=
          FROM_THE_Q.QUE (2..FROM_THE_Q.IN_USE + 1);
  end if;
end POP;


function LENGTH (Q_TO_COUNT : QUEUE) return natural is
  -- Returns a natural number equal to the number of ITEMs on the queue
begin
  return Q_TO_COUNT.IN_USE;
end LENGTH;


function  EMPTY (Q_TO_CHECK : QUEUE) return boolean is
  -- Returns true if the length of the queue is 0.
begin
  return Q_TO_CHECK.IN_USE = 0;
end EMPTY;


function  FULL  (Q_TO_CHECK : QUEUE) return boolean is
  -- Returns true if there is no room left to add ITEMs to the queue.
```

```
begin
  return Q_TO_CHECK.IN_USE = MAXIMUM_Q_SIZE;
end FULL;

function  EQUAL  (Q1, Q2 : QUEUE) return boolean is
  -- Returns true when two queues have the same length, and when
  -- both queues are made up of the same ITEMs in the same order.
begin
  if Q1.IN_USE = 0 then
    return Q2.IN_USE = 0;
  else
    return Q1.IN_USE = Q2.IN_USE and then
          Q1.QUE(1..Q1.IN_USE) = Q2.QUE(1..Q2.IN_USE);
  end if;
end EQUAL;
```

Some operations require that the queue not be empty.

```
function  FRONT_ITEM (FROM_THE_Q : QUEUE) return ITEM_TYPE is
  -- Returns the front ITEM on the queue without removing it from
  -- the queue.  The queue is not modified.
  -- Exception Q_IS_EMPTY raised if there is no item to return
begin
  if FROM_THE_Q.IN_USE = 0 then
    raise Q_IS_EMPTY;
  else
    return FROM_THE_Q.QUE(1);
  end if;
end FRONT_ITEM;

function  REAR_ITEM (FROM_THE_Q : QUEUE) return ITEM_TYPE is
  -- Returns the last ITEM added to the queue without modifying
  -- the queue.
  -- Exception Q_IS_EMPTY raised if there is no ITEM to return
begin
  if FROM_THE_Q.IN_USE = 0 then
    raise Q_IS_EMPTY;
  else
    return FROM_THE_Q.QUE(FROM_THE_Q.IN_USE);
  end if;
end REAR_ITEM;
```

The remaining six procedures in GENERIC_BOUNDED_QUEUE follow.

```
procedure ENQUEUE ( ITEM        : in ITEM_TYPE;
                    TO_THE_Q : in out QUEUE) is
  -- Add ITEM after the last object at the rear of TO_THE_Q
  -- preserving the FIFO behavior.  The previous rear object
  -- the queue is now the next-to-last object.
  -- Exception OVERFLOW raised if there is no space left to add an ITEM to
  --           the queue.
```

```
begin
  if TO_THE_Q.IN_USE = MAXIMUM_Q_SIZE then
    raise OVERFLOW;
  else
    TO_THE_Q.IN_USE := TO_THE_Q.IN_USE + 1;
    TO_THE_Q.QUE(TO_THE_Q.IN_USE) := ITEM;
  end if;
end ENQUEUE;


procedure DEQUEUE ( ITEM         :    out ITEM_TYPE;
                    FROM_THE_Q : in out QUEUE) is
  -- Returns the first ITEM from the front of the queue and then
  -- deletes that ITEM from the queue while preserving FIFO
  -- behavior.
  -- Exception Q_IS_EMPTY raised if there is no ITEM to return
begin
  if FROM_THE_Q.IN_USE = 0 then
    raise Q_IS_EMPTY;
  else
    FROM_THE_Q.IN_USE := FROM_THE_Q.IN_USE - 1;
    ITEM := FROM_THE_Q.QUE(1);
    if FROM_THE_Q.IN_USE /= 0 then
      FROM_THE_Q.QUE(1..FROM_THE_Q.IN_USE) :=
                      FROM_THE_Q.QUE(2..FROM_THE_Q.IN_USE + 1);
    end if;
  end if;
end DEQUEUE;


procedure COPY ( FROM_Q       : in    QUEUE;
                 TO_Q         :    out QUEUE) is
  -- Makes an exact copy of the queue FROM_Q
  -- Exception OVERFLOW raised if there is no space left to add
  --           an ITEM to the queue.
begin
  TO_Q := FROM_Q;
end COPY;


procedure APPEND ( FROM_Q     : in    QUEUE;
                   ONTO_Q     : in out QUEUE) is
  -- Takes all the objects from the queue FROM_Q and copies
  -- the queue onto the end of ONTO_Q.  FROM_Q is not modified.
  -- Exception OVERFLOW raised if there is no space left to add an ITEM to
  --           the queue.
begin
  if FROM_Q.IN_USE + ONTO_Q.IN_USE > MAXIMUM_Q_SIZE then
    raise OVERFLOW;
  elsif FROM_Q.IN_USE /= 0 then
    ONTO_Q.QUE(ONTO_Q.IN_USE+1..ONTO_Q.IN_USE + FROM_Q.IN_USE)
      :=  FROM_Q.QUE(1..FROM_Q.IN_USE);
```

```
        ONTO_Q.IN_USE := ONTO_Q.IN_USE + FROM_Q.IN_USE;
    end if;
end APPEND;
```

The two advantages of this implementation are its simplicity and its ease of coding. The price paid for this simplicity and ease of programming is in the procedure DEQUEUE. The code segment contains CPU overhead.

```
if FROM_THE_Q.IN_USE /= 0 then
    FROM_THE_Q.QUE(1..FROM_THE_Q.IN_USE) :=
            FROM_THE_Q.QUE(2..FROM_THE_Q.IN_USE + 1);
end if;
```

Every time that an object is popped or dequeued, the entire array must be shifted. For large arrays this overhead can be considerable. Can this overhead be avoided?

Several approaches avoid the overhead that the shift causes. One option is to delay the shift. The private section of the package GENERIC_BOUNDED_QUEUE, where the data structure is defined, is replaced by

```
private
    type ARRAY_OF_ITEM_TYPE is array (positive range <>) of ITEM_TYPE;
    type QUEUE is
      record
          FRONT, REAR : natural := 0;
          QUE : ARRAY_OF_ITEM_TYPE (1..MAXIMUM_Q_SIZE);
      end record;
```

Here an empty queue is defined as one where FRONT = 0, and a full queue as one where FRONT = 1 and REAR = MAXIMUM_Q_SIZE. If REAR=MAXIMUM_Q_SIZE is encountered during a call to ENQUEUE, a shift is attempted. With this convention, the procedure DEQUEUE becomes

```
procedure DEQUEUE ( ITEM        : out ITEM_TYPE;
                    FROM_THE_Q : in out QUEUE) is
-- Returns the first ITEM from the front of the queue and then
-- deletes that ITEM from the queue while preserving FIFO
-- behavior.
-- Exception Q_IS_EMPTY raised if there is no item to return
begin
    if FROM_THE_Q.FRONT = 0 THEN
      raise Q_IS_EMPTY;
    else
      ITEM := FROM_THE_Q.QUE(FROM_THE_Q.FRONT);
      if FROM_THE_Q.FRONT = FROM_THE_Q.REAR then
        FROM_THE_Q.FRONT := 0;
      else
        FROM_THE_Q.FRONT := FROM_THE_Q.FRONT + 1;
      end if;
    end if;
end DEQUEUE;
```

On the surface it appears that this implementation removed the overhead. Unfortunately, the overhead was transferred to ENQUEUE. Nothing can be added to the queue if REAR = MAXIMUM_Q_SIZE. ENQUEUE becomes

```
procedure ENQUEUE ( ITEM        : in ITEM_TYPE;
                    TO_THE_Q : in out QUEUE) is
  -- Add ITEM after the last object at the rear of TO_THE_Q
  -- preserving the FIFO behavior.  The previous rear object
  -- the queue is now the next-to-last object.
  -- Exception OVERFLOW raised if there is no space left to add
  an ITEM TO the queue.
begin
  if TO_THE_Q.FRONT = 1 and then TO_THE_Q.REAR = MAXIMUM_Q_SIZE then
    raise OVERFLOW;
  else
    if TO_THE_Q.REAR = MAXIMUM_Q_SIZE then
      TO_THE_Q.QUE(1..MAXIMUM_Q_SIZE + 1-TO_THE_Q.FRONT)
             := TO_THE_Q.QUE(TO_THE_QUE.FRONT..MAXIMUM_Q_SIZE);
      TO_THE_Q.REAR := MAXIMUM_Q_SIZE + 1 - TO_THE_Q.FRONT
      TO_THE_Q.FRONT := 1;
    end if;
    TO_THE_Q.REAR := TO_THE_Q.REAR + 1;
    TO_THE_Q.QUE(TO_THE_Q.REAR) := ITEM;
  end if;
end ENQUEUE;
```

Figure 7.2.4 illustrates the situation. If there is room at the end of the queue, objects are added. If there is no room at the rear, the shift is made. As more items are added and deleted, a nearly full queue would require shifting more often than would a nearly empty queue.

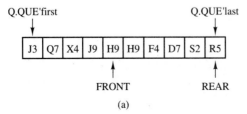

(a)

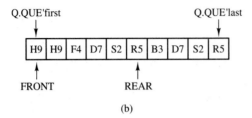

(b)

Figure 7.2.4 Alternative version of GENERIC_BOUNDED_QUEUE. (a) Rear is now at Q.Que'last. Room must be made to add the next item. Note that Q.Que(1..4) are not in use. (b) Result after shifting Q.Que in part (a) four places to the left and then enqueuing the item R5. Front and rear adjusted.

Completely avoiding DEQUEUE's built-in shift solves this dilemma. One solution uses two parameters to keep track of the location of the front of the queue and the length of the queue. The data structure located in the private section of the package becomes

```
private
   type ARRAY_OF_ITEM_TYPE is array (positive range <>) of ITEM_TYPE;
   type QUEUE is
     record
       FRONT,
       IN_USE : natural := 0;
       QUE : ARRAY_OF_ITEM_TYPE (1..MAXIMUM_Q_SIZE);
     end record;
```

FRONT and IN_USE, respectfully, will be used for these purposes. Front will be the position in the array of the first element in the queue. IN_USE will be the current length of the queue. The following formula computes the queue's rear:

```
REAR := 1 + (FRONT + IN_USE - 2) rem MAXIMUM_Q_SIZE;
```

This strategy wraps the objects on the queue around the end of the array. The use of the rem function cleverly implements this strategy. For example, Figure 7.2.5 illustrates the case where MAXIMUM_Q_SIZE = 10, FRONT = 5, IN_USE = 4; the formula yields the correct value of REAR = 8. If one additional object is enqueued, then IN_USE = 5 and REAR = 9. If an additional object is enqueued, IN_USE = 6 and REAR = 10. This technique avoids the need to shift all the data after each ENQUEUE operation, resulting in increased efficiency. Clearly, the bodies of other procedures also need to be modified.

Using a variant record, whose discriminant is the maximum queue length, is also possible. Two examples of this were given in Chapter 6. The same discussion there applies to

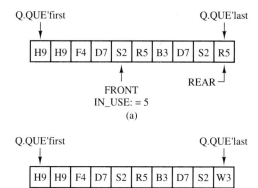

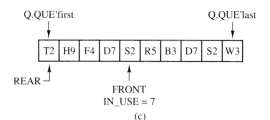

Figure 7.2.5 GENERIC_BOUNDED_QUEUE using a wraparound FRONT and REAR. (a) Initial state of a BOUNDED_QUEUE of size = 10. (b) State of queue in part (a) after enqueue of item W3. (c) State of queue in part (b) after enqueue of item T2.

queues. The bounded implementation using variant records removes one parameter from the formal generic parameter list. This form is also covered in the exercises.

Once the package specification and body for GENERIC_BOUNDED_QUEUE are added to the Ada program library, the abstract data type GENERIC_BOUNDED_QUEUE will be fully implemented and available for use. Counting the variant implementations alluded to previously, four different data structures for the bounded queue have been described. At the program level, no difference between three of the four approaches can be detected. Each data type builds an ordered list of things of type object. The ordering remains the order in which objects were added to the queue. The only way the queue can be accessed or modified remains through the legitimate operations that are the functions and procedures of the instantiated generic package.

7.3 UNBOUNDED IMPLEMENTATION

The package GENERIC_BOUNDED_QUEUE has limitations. MAXIMUM_Q_SIZE must be set large enough to handle the largest anticipated use, but not too large. Inefficient memory usage results if too large a value of MAXIMUM_Q_SIZE is chosen. Implementing the queue as a linked list eliminates both the size limitation and possible inefficient memory utilization. A linked list implementation uses only the number of nodes required (see Figure 7.3.1). As Figure 7.3.2 indicates, the queue has two pointers front and rear implemented as access types. These point to the first and last elements on the list. Each element in the queue points only to the element following it. The queue expands or contracts as items are added or deleted. The third component of the queue type is the length of the queue. This reduces the operation LENGTH from $O(n)$ to $O(1)$. The length of an empty queue is zero.

FRONT   REAR

Figure 7.3.1 GENERIC_UNBOUNDED_QUEUE implementation using linked lists.

Implementation of the package GENERIC_UNBOUNDED_QUEUE uses access types to overcome all the shortcomings based on queue size limitations. The specification for the generic package GENERIC_UNBOUNDED_QUEUE is given in Figure 7.3.2.

```
generic
  type ITEM_TYPE is private;
package GENERIC_UNBOUNDED_QUEUE is
  type QUEUE is limited private;
  procedure ENQUEUE      ( ITEM       : in     ITEM_TYPE;
                           TO_THE_Q   : in out QUEUE);
  procedure DEQUEUE      ( ITEM       :    out ITEM_TYPE;
                           FROM_THE_Q : in out QUEUE);
  procedure COPY         ( FROM_Q     : in     QUEUE;
                           TO_Q       :    out QUEUE);
  procedure APPEND       ( FROM_Q     : in     QUEUE;
                           ONTO_Q     : in out QUEUE);
```

Figure 7.3.2 Package GENERIC_UNBOUNDED_QUEUE specification. Continues on page 165.

```
procedure CLEAR        ( Q_TO_CLEAR   :    out QUEUE);
procedure POP          ( FROM_THE_Q  : in out QUEUE);
function LENGTH        ( Q_TO_COUNT   :        QUEUE) return natural;
function EMPTY         ( Q_TO_CHECK   :        QUEUE) return boolean;
function FULL          ( Q_TO_CHECK   :        QUEUE) return boolean;
function FRONT_ITEM    ( FROM_THE_Q   :        QUEUE) return ITEM_TYPE;
function REAR_ITEM     ( FROM_THE_Q   :        QUEUE) return ITEM_TYPE;
function EQUAL         ( Q1, Q2       :        QUEUE) return boolean;
OVERFLOW   : exception;
Q_IS_EMPTY : exception;
private
  type QUEUE_NODE;
  type Q_PTR is access QUEUE_NODE;
  type QUEUE is
    record
      COUNT  : natural := 0;
      FRONT,
      REAR   : Q_PTR;
    end record;
end GENERIC_UNBOUNDED_QUEUE;
```

Figure 7.3.2 Concluded.

The type QUEUE is implemented as limited private. It can only be referenced, not manipulated, outside the package. This fully encapsulates the abstract data type.

Note that the things going onto the queue, the things of type ITEM_TYPE, are not part of the package specification. The package body hides the full definition of QUEUE. The first detail in the package body describes the record type QUEUE_NODE (see Figure 7.3.3). After that follow the bodies of the individual functions and procedures that compose the package body.

```
package BODY GENERIC_UNBOUNDED_QUEUE is

  type QUEUE_NODE is
    record
      ITEM : ITEM_TYPE;
      NEXT : Q_PTR;
    end record;
    ............
end GENERIC_UNBOUNDED_QUEUE;
```

Figure 7.3.3 Package body GENERIC_UNBOUNDED_QUEUE.

The function EMPTY simply returns the boolean value of "COUNT = 0". The bodies of FRONT_OBJECT and REAR_OBJECT are almost exactly the same. For example:

```
function FRONT_ITEM ( FROM_THE_Q : QUEUE) return ITEM_TYPE is
  -- Returns the front ITEM on the queue without removing it from
  -- the queue.  The queue is not modified.
  -- Exception Q_IS_EMPTY raised if there is no item to return.
  begin
```

```
          if FROM_THE_Q.COUNT = 0 then
            raise Q_IS_EMPTY;
          else
            return FROM_THE_Q.FRONT.ITEM;
          end if;
        end FRONT_ITEM;
```

To implement the function EQUAL, both queues are traversed until one of four things occurs. Both queues are fully traversed with all elements equal, both queues are traversed to a point where the first is finished but the second still has more to go, or vice versa, or while traversing the queues an object on one does not equal an object on the other.

```
        function EQUAL ( Q1, Q2 : QUEUE) return boolean is
          -- Returns true when two queues have the same length, and when
          -- both queues are made up of the same ITEMs in the same order.
          TEMP1 : Q_PTR : Q1.FRONT;
          TEMP2 : Q_PTR : Q2.FRONT;
        begin
          if Q1.COUNT = 0 AND Q2.COUNT = 0 then
            return true;
          elsif Q1.COUNT /= Q2.COUNT then
            return false;
          else
            for I in 1..Q1.COUNT loop
              if TEMP1.ITEM = ITEMP2.ITEM then
                TEMP1 := TEMP1.NEXT;
                TEMP2 := TEMP2.NEXT;
              else
                return false;
              end if;
            end loop;
            return true;
          end if;
        end EQUAL;
```

The contents of the procedure bodies in the package body of GENERIC_UN-BOUNDED_QUEUE range from the obvious to the not so obvious. To clear the queue, CLEAR sets COUNT to zero and then sets the front and rear pointers to null. Recall that in Ada, the memory for a node created by the "new" operation by any access type is reclaimed at the end of the current block by the operating system when it no longer can be referenced. Since the null front node of a cleared queue no longer references the front object, the front node can be reclaimed. At this point the second node is not referenced. There are two possible cases when adding an object to a queue. The queue is either empty or not empty.

```
      procedure ENQUEUE ( ITEM        : in     ITEM_TYPE;
                          TO_THE_Q   : in out QUEUE) is
        -- Add ITEM after the last object at the rear of TO_THE_Q
        -- preserving the FIFO behavior.  The previous rear object of
        -- the queue is now the next-to-last object.
        -- Exception OVERFLOW raised if there is no space left to add an ITEM to
```

```
    --            the queue.
begin
  if TO_THE_Q.COUNT = 0 then
    TO_THE_Q.FRONT := new QUEUE_NODE'(ITEM, null);
    TO_THE_Q.REAR := TO_THE_Q.FRONT;
  else
    TO_THE_Q.REAR.NEXT := new QUEUE_NODE'(ITEM,null);
    TO_THE_Q.REAR := TO_THE_Q.REAR.NEXT;
  end if;
  TO_THE_Q.COUNT := TO_THE_Q.COUNT + 1;
exception
  when storage_error =>
    raise OVERFLOW;
end ENQUEUE;
```

The procedure to delete an object from the queue, DEQUEUE, has three possible cases to consider. The first case is that the queue might be empty, which raises an exception. The second possibility is that the queue contains exactly one node. This forces setting the front and rear pointers to null once the object has been removed. The third and last case occurs when the queue has two or more objects in it.

```
procedure DEQUEUE ( ITEM          :    out ITEM_TYPE;
                    FROM_THE_Q : in   out QUEUE) is
  -- Returns the first ITEM from the front of the queue and then
  -- deletes that ITEM from the queue while preserving FIFO
  -- behavior.
  -- Exception Q_IS_EMPTY raised if there is no item to return.
begin
  if FROM_THE_Q.COUNT = 0 then
    raise Q_IS_EMPTY;
  elsif FROM_THE_Q.FRONT = FROM_THE_Q.REAR then
    ITEM := FROM_THE_Q.FRONT.ITEM;
    FROM_THE_Q := (0, null, null);
  else
    ITEM := FROM_THE_Q.FRONT.ITEM;
    FROM_THE_Q.FRONT := FROM_THE_Q.FRONT.NEXT;
    FROM_THE_Q.COUNT := FROM_THE_Q.COUNT - 1;
  end if;
end DEQUEUE;
```

Consider the queue Q_OLD as in Figure 7.3.4(a). If a copy of Q_OLD is made by copying the front and rear pointers to the queue Q_COPY, a situation arises similar to the one illustrated in Figure 7.3.4(b). This situation will yield correct results as long as objects are added to only one queue. If an object is added to Q_OLD, the situation in Figure 7.3.4(c) follows and chaos results. If this is followed by an attempt to add an object to Q_COPY, the situation in Figure 7.3.4(d) arises and leaves the rear of Q_OLD isolated and unreferenced by the queue. The following solution makes a distinct copy by traversing the queue.

```
procedure COPY ( FROM_Q          : in    QUEUE;
                 TO_Q            :    out QUEUE) is
```

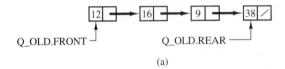

(a)

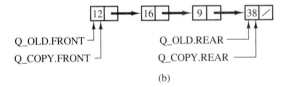

(b)

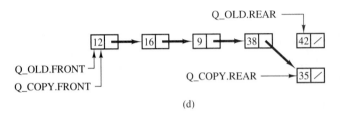

(c)

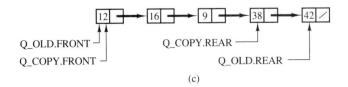

(d)

Figure 7.3.4 COPY of two queues cannot be done by assignment. (a) Original queue to be copied. (b) Copying Q_OLD by making second set of reference to front and rear. (c) Queue Q_OLD after enqueue of item 42. (d) Queue Q_COPY after enqueue of item 35. Note that Queue Q_OLD is now isolated.

```
-- Makes an exact copy of the queue FROM_Q
-- Exception OVERFLOW raised if there is no space left to add
--           an ITEM to the queue.
TEMP_FROM   : Q_PTR := FROM_Q.FRONT;
TEMP_TO : QUEUE;
begin
  if FROM_Q.COUNT = 0 then
     TO_Q := (0, null, null);
  else
    TEMP_TO.FRONT := new QUEUE_NODE'(TEMP_FROM.ITEM,null);
    -- Needed in case FROM_Q has length 1
    TEMP_TO.REAR := TEMP_TO.FRONT;
    TEMP_TO.COUNT := FROM_Q.COUNT;
    TEMP_FROM := TEMP_FROM.NEXT;
    for INDEX in 2..FROM_Q.COUNT loop
      TEMP_TO.REAR.NEXT := new QUEUE_NODE'(TEMP_FROM.ITEM, null);
      TEMP_TO.REAR := TEMP_TO.REAR.NEXT;
      TEMP_FROM := TEMP_FROM.NEXT;
    end loop;
    TO_Q := TEMP_TO;
  end if;
exception
```

```
      when storage_error =>
         raise OVERFLOW;
   end COPY;
```

Now with operation COPY implemented, the operation APPEND is easy to implement. The first statement copies the queue to be appended to a temporary queue. The second and third statements splice the temporary queue to the end of the resulting queue.

```
procedure APPEND ( FROM_Q :      in      QUEUE;
                   ONTO_Q :      in out QUEUE) is
  -- Takes all the objects from the queue FROM_Q and copies
  -- the queue onto the end of ONTO_Q.  FROM_Q is not modified.
  -- Exception OVERFLOW raised if there is no space left to add an ITEM to
  --          the queue.
  TEMP_Q : QUEUE;
begin
  COPY(FROM_Q, TEMP_Q);
  ONTO_Q.REAR.NEXT := TEMP_Q.FRONT;
  ONTO_Q.REAR := TEMP_Q.REAR;
  ONTO_Q.COUNT := ONTO_Q.COUNT + TEMP_Q.COUNT;
exception
  when OVERFLOW => raise OVERFLOW;
end APPEND;
```

The remaining two procedures to implement, CLEAR and POP_Q, are clear-cut. Setting the front and rear to null clears a queue. The procedure POP is similar to DEQUEUE except that it does not return an object.

```
procedure CLEAR (Q_TO_CLEAR :     out QUEUE) is
  -- Removes all objects from the queue without
  -- processing any object.
begin
  Q_TO_CLEAR := (0, null, null);
end CLEAR;

procedure POP ( FROM_THE_Q : in out QUEUE) is
  -- Removes and discards the front ITEM from the queue.
  -- Exception Q_IS_EMPTY raised if there is no item to pop.
begin
  if FROM_THE_Q.COUNT = 0 then
    raise Q_IS_EMPTY;
  elsif FROM_THE_Q.FRONT = FROM_THE_Q.REAR then
    FROM_THE_Q := (0, null, null);
  else
    FROM_THE_Q.FRONT := FROM_THE_Q.FRONT.NEXT;
    FROM_THE_Q.COUNT := FROM_THE_Q.COUNT - 1;
  end if;
end POP;
```

The package specification for GENERIC_UNBOUNDED_QUEUE has several other possible implementations.

7.4 VARIATIONS: THE BALKING QUEUE AND THE DEQUE

The addition of objects to the rear of the queue and their removal from the front characterize a queue. This behavior is too restrictive for many applications. Consider the print queue on a large mainframe computer. Files to be printed are usually added at the end and printed on a first come, first served basis. A job runs that produces a large file and it becomes apparent that this file contains garbage. Unfortunately, the file has been added to the print queue. The operator saves the day by locating the file's place in the queue and then removes the file from the print queue. This is the idea behind the balking queue.

The print queue can also be used to illustrate the deque. The deque allows objects to be added at either the front or the rear. Suppose that the operating system adds very short files to the front of the print queue and adds longer files to the rear of the print queue. This would keep the number of files on the print queue to a minimum because all the "small stuff" would be cleared between the printing of longer files.

The ENQUEUE operation in a deque can add an element at either the front or the rear of the DEQUEUE. Only the documentation for the operation ENQUEUE in Figure 7.1.1 must be altered. The new documentation for ENQUEUE is

> ENQUEUE   A third parameter PLACE with two values IN_FRONT and IN_REAR determines where an ITEM is to be added. If IN_REAR is specified, then the ITEM is added after the last object of a queue while preserving the FIFO behavior. If IN_FRONT is specified, then the ITEM becomes the new front while the old front ITEM is now the second ITEM. The order of all other ITEMs is preserved.

Figure 7.4.1 illustrates a DEQUE. The DEQUE has both bounded and unbounded forms.

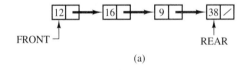

FRONT   REAR

(a)

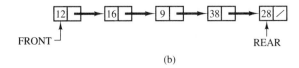

FRONT   REAR

(b)

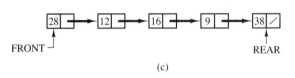

FRONT   REAR

(c)

Figure 7.4.1   ENQUEUE operation on GENERIC_UNBOUNDED_DEQUE. (a) Original deque. (b) Deque in part (a) after a call to Enqueue(28. In_Rear.Q). (c) Deque in part (a) after a call to Enqueue(28. In_Front.Q).

To implement the abstract data type DEQUE, a slight change in the procedure ENQUEUE allows ENQUEUE to add an object to either the front or the rear of the deque. An enumerated type handles this detail. Everything else remains the same as in

GENERIC_UNBOUNDED_QUEUE. The package specification DEQUE is shown in Figure 7.4.2. The implementation is left as an exercise.

```
generic
  type ITEM_TYPE is private;
package GENERIC_UNBOUNDED_DEQUE is
  type DEQUE is limited private;
  type PLACE_TO_ADD is (IN_FRONT, IN_REAR);
  procedure ENQUEUE      (ITEM        : in      ITEM_TYPE;
                          WHERE       : in      PLACE_TO_ADD;
                          TO_THE_Q    : in out DEQUE);
  procedure DEQUEUE      (ITEM        :     out ITEM_TYPE;
                          FROM_THE_Q  : in out DEQUE);
  procedure COPY         (FROM_Q      : in      DEQUE;
                          TO_Q        :     out DEQUE);
  procedure APPEND       (FROM_Q      : in      DEQUE;
                          ONTO_Q      : in out DEQUE);
  procedure CLEAR        (Q_TO_CLEAR  :     out DEQUE);
  procedure POP          (FROM_THE_Q  : in out DEQUE);
  function LENGTH        (Q_TO_COUNT  : DEQUE) return natural;
  function EMPTY         (Q_TO_CHECK  : DEQUE) return boolean;
  function FULL          (Q_TO_CHECK  : DEQUE) return boolean;
  function FRONT_ITEM    (FROM_THE_Q  : DEQUE) return ITEM_TYPE;
  function REAR_ITEM     (FROM_THE_Q  : DEQUE) return ITEM_TYPE;
  function EQUAL         (Q1, Q2      : DEQUE) return boolean;
  OVERFLOW   : exception;
  Q_IS_EMPTY : exception;
private
  type Q_NODE;
  type Q_PTR is ACCESS Q_NODE;
  type DEQUE is
    record
       LENGTH : natural := 0;
       FRONT,
       REAR   : Q_PTR;
    end record;
end GENERIC_UNBOUNDED_DEQUE;
```

Figure 7.4.2 Package GENERIC_UNBOUNDED_DEQUE specification.

The only change needed for either the bounded or unbounded queue to become a deque is the ENQUEUE operation. These modifications are left to the exercises.

The earlier print queue example can be used to illustrate some of the problems encountered in the design of a balking queue. First the balking queue is a search queue. Search structures typically have a key-data pair. The operator located the file to be deleted in the print queue by its job-id and then deleted the file from the queue. This implies a search of the print queue followed by deleting an object on the queue. How is a queue searched? Queues are linear sequential structures that must be searched sequentially key by key. This implies that a key-data pair should replace the single item type in the formal generic parameter list. Another way of saying this is that the component type object is just a pair of objects, one a key and the other a data type, that is,

```
type ITEM_TYPE is
   record
      KEY  : KEY_TYPE;
      DATA : DATA_TYPE;
   end record;
```

For the balking queue the programmer-supplied generic parameters will include two types, a KEY_TYPE and a DATA_TYPE. Both types are declared as a private types. This allows checking for equality of key types and for assignment. The result is a more natural program interface.

Consider the case where a queue is to be searched. The queue is searched for a particular key. The data associated with a particular key is ignored by the search. This emphasizes the searching of the queue and the extraction of information or the deletion of a key-data pair. Suppose that a small company installs the company's telephone directory as a balking queue where the programmer-supplied type is

```
type EMPLOYEE is
   record
      NAME           : string(1..25);
      MAIL_ZONE      : string(1..10);
      CLASSIFICATION : string(1..20);
      PHONE_EXT      : string(1..4);
   end record;
```

When making a call to the information operator, the list is searched by the key, the name. It is the other information that is being sought. No one phones the operator when they have all the information. Another reason relates to the instantiation of the package. If a key-data pair is not used, a search function must be supplied. If a key-data pair is used, a special search function is not required because the key type is private, not limited private. Private types allow for comparison for equality.

Now that the problem of searching is solved, how is the key-data pair to be deleted from the queue? One method would be to start searching the queue from the front and to delete the first key-data pair where the key matches the pattern. A second method is to specify a position and then to delete the element at that position without regard to the key-data pair that is at that location. There are applications where each is advantageous, so both types of delete operations will be supplied.

To implement the balking queue, a key type and a data type replace the formal generic function parameter. Two functions must be made into procedures, and two procedures and four functions must be added to the package. The two functions FRONT_ITEM and REAR_ITEM must be made into the respective procedures FRONT_PAIR and REAR_PAIR. The first returns the key-data pair of the front node and the latter returns the key-data pair of the rear node. A function called KEY_POSITION_ON_Q returns the position of a given key on the queue. If an object with a given key is not present, the function returns zero. A second function called RETURN_DATA_WITH_KEY_ON_Q returns the data associated with the first occurrence of that key on the queue. The third function, KEY_AT_POSITION_ON_Q key, returns the key of the key-data pair at a given position on a given queue. The fourth and last new function, DATA_AT_POSITION_ON_Q, returns the data of the key-data pair at a given position. Two procedures, REMOVE_KEY_DATA_BY_KEY and REMOVE_KEY_DATA_BY_LOC, remove a given node containing a key-data pair from the queue. One version removes the key-data pair of the first node where the passed key matches. The other version removes whatever node is at a given position.

Consider the case where either the first node or the last node on the queue must be removed. Implementing this would change the value of the front or rear pointer or both. This illustrates the reason that REMOVE_KEY_DATA_BY_KEY must be a procedure. An extra exception must be added to allow for the possibility of trying to find the location of a key not on the queue. There also could be problems if the program attempts to remove a pair from the list where the length of the list is less than the position specified. Full documentation for the balking queue is left to the exercises. Most of the implementation effort was done in the package for GENERIC_UNBOUNDED_QUEUE. The package specification for balking queue is given in Figure 7.4.3.

```
generic
  type KEY_TYPE is private;
  type DATA_TYPE is private;
package GENERIC_UNBOUNDED_BALKING_QUEUE is
  type QUEUE is limited private;
  procedure ENQUEUE               (KEY         : in     KEY_TYPE;
                                   DATA        : in     DATA_TYPE;
                                   TO_THE_Q    : in out QUEUE);
  procedure DEQUEUE               (KEY         :    out KEY_TYPE;
                                   DATA        :    out DATA_TYPE;
                                   FROM_THE_Q  : in out QUEUE);
  procedure COPY                  (FROM_Q      : in     QUEUE;
                                   TO_Q        :    out QUEUE);
  procedure APPEND                (FROM_Q      : in     QUEUE;
                                   ONTO_Q      : in out QUEUE);
  procedure CLEAR                 (Q_TO_CLEAR  :    out QUEUE);
  procedure POP                   (FROM_THE_Q  : in out QUEUE);
  procedure REMOVE_KEY_DATA_FROM_Q (FROM_Q     : in out QUEUE;
                                   KEY         : in     KEY_TYPE);
  procedure REMOVE_KEY_DATA_FROM_Q (FROM_Q     : in out QUEUE;
                                   AT_LOCATION : in     positive);
  procedure FRONT_PAIR            (FROM_THE_Q  : in     QUEUE;
                                   KEY         :    out KEY_TYPE;
                                   DATA        :    out DATA_TYPE);
  procedure REAR_PAIR             (FROM_THE_Q  : in     QUEUE;
                                   KEY         :    out KEY_TYPE;
                                   DATA        :    out DATA_TYPE);
  function KEY_POSITION_ON_Q      (KEY_TO_FIND : KEY_TYPE;
                                   ON_Q        : QUEUE) return natural;
  function RETURN_DATA_WITH_KEY_ON_Q (KEY      : KEY_TYPE;
                                   ON_Q        : QUEUE) return DATA_TYPE;
```

Figure 7.4.3 Package UNBOUNDED_BALKING_QUEUE specification. Continues on page 174.

```
function KEY_AT_POSITION_ON_Q      (AT_LOCATION : positive;
                                     ON_Q        : QUEUE) return KEY_TYPE;
function DATA_AT_POSITION_ON_Q     (AT_LOCATION : positive;
                                     ON_Q        : QUEUE) return DATA_TYPE;
function Q_LENGTH                  (Q_TO_COUNT  : QUEUE) return natural;
function Q_EMPTY                   (Q_TO_CHECK  : QUEUE) return boolean;
function Q_FULL                    (Q_TO_CHECK  : QUEUE) return boolean;
function Q_EQUAL                   (Q1, Q2      : QUEUE) return boolean;
OVERFLOW        : exception;
Q_IS_EMPTY      : exception;
POSITION_ERROR  : exception;
KEY_NOT_FOUND   : exception;
private
  type Q_NODE;
  type Q_PTR is ACCESS Q_NODE;
  type QUEUE is
    record
      LENGTH: natural := 0;
      FRONT:Q_PTR;
      REAR:Q_PTR;
    end record;
end GENERIC_UNBOUNDED_BALKING_QUEUE;
```

Figure 7.4.3   Concluded.

The package body has the full definition of Q_NODE. One suitable form is given in Figure 7.4.4.

```
package body GENERIC_UNBOUNDED_BALKING_QUEUE is
  type Q_NODE is
    record
      KEY  : KEY_TYPE;
      DATA : DATA_TYPE;
      NEXT : Q_PTR;
    end record;
    ............
end GENERIC_UNBOUNDED_BALKING_QUEUE;
```

Figure 7.4.4   Package GENERIC_UNBOUNDED_BALKING_QUEUE body detail.

The function KEY_POSITION_ON_Q requires a simple sequential search. The only problem that might occur is if the key is not in the queue, but this case always returns zero. This operation serves double duty. It can be raised to determine if a given key is in the queue.

```
function KEY_POSITION_ON_Q (KEY_TO_FIND : KEY_TYPE;
                            ON_Q        : QUEUE) return natural is
  -- Returns the position of the first key-data pair on the queue.
  -- If no key-data pair has the key, then 0 is returned.
  TEMP_Q : Q_PTR := ON_Q.FRONT;
begin
  for PLACE in 1..ON_Q.LENGTH loop
    if TEMP_Q.KEY = KEY_TO_FIND then
```

```
          return PLACE;
        else
          TEMP_Q := TEMP_Q.NEXT;
        end if;
      end loop;
      return 0;
    end KEY_POSITION_ON_Q;
```

The procedure REMOVE_KEY_DATA_FROM_Q starts by moving to the specified position and then joining the pointer from the previous object to the following object. The pointers to the front or the rear or both are adjusted as necessary. An exception is raised if the position specified exceeds the length of the queue. The second version searches for the first appearance of a specified key, which is deleted when found. If the key is not in the queue, an exception is raised.

```
procedure REMOVE_KEY_DATA_FROM_Q ( FROM_Q      : in out QUEUE;
                                   KEY         : in      KEY_TYPE) is
  -- Deletes the first key-data pair that matches the specified KEY
  -- Exception KEY_NOT_FOUND if no key-data pair has the specified key.
  -- Exception Q_IS_EMPTY raised when the queue is empty
  TEMP_NEXT : Q_PTR;
begin
  if FROM_Q.LENGTH = 0 then
    raise Q_IS_EMPTY;
  elsif FROM_Q.FRONT.KEY = K then
    if FROM_Q.LENGTH = 1 then
      FROM_Q := (0, null, null);
    else
      FROM_Q.FRONT := FROM_Q.FRONT.NEXT;
      FROM_Q.LENGTH := FROM_Q.LENGTH - 1;
    end if;
  else
    TEMP_NEXT := FROM_Q.FRONT;
    loop
      if TEMP_NEXT.NEXT.KEY = K then
        if TEMP_NEXT.NEXT = FROM_Q.REAR then
          FROM_Q.REAR := TEMP_NEXT;
          TEMP_NEXT.NEXT := null;
        else
          TEMP_NEXT.NEXT := TEMP_NEXT.NEXT.NEXT;
        end if;
        FROM_Q.LENGTH := FROM_Q.LENGTH - 1;
        EXIT;
      else
        TEMP_NEXT := TEMP_NEXT.NEXT;
      end if;
      if TEMP_NEXT.NEXT = null then
        raise KEY_NOT_FOUND;
      end if;
    end loop;
```

```
    end if;
    end REMOVE_KEY_DATA_FROM_Q;

    procedure REMOVE_KEY_DATA_FROM_Q ( FROM_Q        : in out QUEUE;
                                       AT_LOCATION : in      positive) is
      -- Deletes the key-data pair at a specified location
      -- Exception Q_IS_EMPTY raised if FROM_Q has length 0.
      -- Exception POSITION_ERROR raised if location not on the queue
      TEMP_NEXT : Q_PTR := FROM_Q.FRONT;
    begin
      if FROM_Q.LENGTH = 0 then
        raise Q_IS_EMPTY;
      elsif FROM_Q.LENGTH < AT_LOCATION then
        raise POSITION_ERROR;
      elsif AT_LOCATION = 1 then
        if FROM_Q.FRONT = FROM_Q.REAR then
          FROM_Q. := (0, null, null);
        else
          FROM_Q.FRONT := FROM_Q.FRONT.NEXT;
          FROM_Q.LENGTH := FROM_Q.LENGTH - 1;
        end if;
      else
        for I in 1..AT_LOCATION - 1 loop
          TEMP_NEXT := TEMP_NEXT.NEXT;
        end loop;
        -- TEMP_NEXT.NEXT is THE NODE TO BE REMOVED
        if FROM_Q.LENGTH = AT_LOCATION then
          FROM_Q.REAR := TEMP_NEXT;
          TEMP_NEXT.NEXT := null;
        else
          TEMP_NEXT := TEMP_NEXT.NEXT;
        end if;
        FROM_Q.LENGTH := FROM_Q.LENGTH - 1;
      end if;
    end REMOVE_KEY_DATA_FROM_Q;
```

Both the complete formal documentation and the full implementation are left to the exercises for the ADT GENERIC_UNBOUNDED_BALKING_QUEUE .

7.5 PRIORITY QUEUE AND ITS VARIATIONS

In earlier sections of this chapter, we discussed the basic queue and some of its variations. In this section, we examine the priority queue, a major variation of the queue. Like all queues, the priority queue removes an item from its front, but the insertion of an item is subject to some priority relationship. An item with high priority is put near the front of the queue. An item with low priority is added toward the rear of the queue. If an item to be added has the same priority as an item that is already on the queue, the added item is placed after the item already on the queue. All items on a priority queue have a higher or equal priority than that of the items that follow them.

Priority queues are often implemented as binary search trees because the tree ADT searches, inserts, and deletes more efficiently. Priority queues can be used to implement queues, stacks, and deques and have applications in all fields. Many universities offer certain groups of students, such as athletes, graduating seniors, members of the band, and the students with disabilities, priority in registering for the next term. In a mainframe batch environment, certain users willing to pay extra fees can have their computer jobs given priority. In a timeshare environment, tasks are often assigned a priority based on an estimate of how long they will take to complete. Users doing file editing have priority over users compiling programs, who have priority over users running long jobs. In Chapter 16 other data structures that represent sparse vectors, and in Chapter 10 unbounded graphs, will be implemented using priority queues. The study and understanding of priority queues yields insights about the structure of all basic linear abstract data types.

The situation is illustrated in Figure 7.5.1. An item with priority 4 needs to be put onto the priority queue. Since the item in the node at the head of the queue has priority 6 and the node with the second item has priority 3, a node containing this new item will be inserted between the first and second nodes. With two exceptions, the operations on the priority queue are the same as the operations on a queue operations. Normally, an object is added, or enqueued, at the end of the queue. In a priority queue objects are placed in the queue based on their priority. Since an item's final location on the queue is not known beforehand, the queue must be sequentially searched from the front of the queue to the queue's rear until the proper location is found. There is no need to keep track of the rear of the queue with a separate access type.

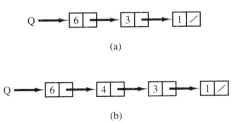

(a)

(b)

Figure 7.5.1 Insertion on a priority queue implemented as a linked list. (a) Q. a priority queue, before 4 is inserted. (b) Q from part (a) after Insertion of 4.

The second difference is that the append operation does not work. If one priority queue is appended to the rear of a second priority queue, the result is not necessarily a priority queue (see Figure 7.5.2). Instead of appending two queues, two priority queues are merged in order to preserve the priority on the resulting queue. The merge operation is illustrated in Figure 7.5.3. When two queues are merged, objects are dequeued from their respective fronts and added to the rear of the resulting queue. The resulting queue must be a priority queue.

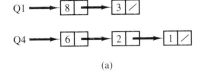

(a)

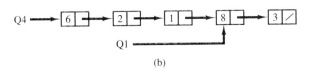

(b)

Figure 7.5.2 Appending two priority queues does not result in a priority queue. (a) Two priority queues before Q1 is appended to the end of Q4. (b) Result of Q1 from part (a) being appended to the end of Q4. Note: Q4 is no longer a priority queue.

Merge_Q

Figure 7.5.3 Merging two priority queues results in a priority queue.

When implementing the abstract data type priority queue, the programmer must supply some method to determine which of two objects has the higher priority. Two Ada features aid the programmer. First, Ada allows the relational operators, including >, to be overloaded. Second, functions can be formal parameters in generic packages. These features of generic packages were reviewed in Section 3.3.

Combining the comments above with the documentation for the ADT queue results in the documentation for the ADT PRIORITY_QUEUE in Figure 7.5.4. Note that priority is based solely on the programmer-supplied boolean operator > that operates on two items of type ITEM_TYPE.

GENERAL ADT SPECIFICATIONS FOR PRIORITY_QUEUE

Description

A priority queue is a strictly ordered linear sequence of objects of ITEM_TYPE. One end of the queue is fixed as the front of the queue. Items can be added at any place on the queue. ITEMs with higher priority are added nearer the front. If an ITEM to be added has the same priority as an ITEM already on the queue, the added ITEM appears after all ITEMS on the queue with equal or higher priority. ITEMs can only be removed, or dequeued, from the front. Once an ITEM is dequeued it is removed and the ITEM that was second in the queue is now the first ITEM. Once an ITEM is placed on a queue, its place in the queue, relative to the ITEMs that precede it and the items that follow it, cannot be changed unless an ITEM with suitable priority is added to the queue.

Programmer-Supplied Data Structures
or Specifications

The programmer must supply two parameters. The first parameter is the ITEM_TYPE that makes up the priority queue. This type is private within the package. The second formal parameter is an overloaded boolean function ">" that determines the priority of two things of type ITEM_TYPE.

Operations

NAME	DESCRIPTION
ADD_TO_Q	Adds an ITEM of type ITEM_TYPE to the queue subject to the priority determined by the programmer-supplied function ">". All objects of type ITEM_TYPE are placed on the priority queue with objects of higher priority nearer the front of the queue than objects of lower priority. If an object to be added has priority equal to objects already on the queue, the object to be inserted is added after all objects of equal priority.
DEQUEUE	Removes an first ITEM from the front of the queue. The second ITEM on the queue is now the front ITEM. ITEM is returned for further processing.
COPY	Makes an exact copy of a queue. The operator EQUAL returns true when the original queue and its copy are compared.

Figure 7.5.4 Documentation for PRIORITY_QUEUE. Continues on page 179.

MERGE	Takes all the ITEMs from the first queue and all the ITEMs from the second queue and merges them into a third queue. The third queue is a priority queue.
CLEAR	Removes all ITEMs from the queue.
POP	Removes the front ITEM from the queue and discards it without further processing.
LENGTH	Returns a natural number equal to the number of ITEMS on the queue.
EMPTY	Boolean-valued operator that returns true if the queue is empty, or false otherwise.
FULL	Boolean-valued operator that returns true if there is no storage left, or false otherwise.
FRONT_ITEM	Returns the front ITEM on the queue without removing it from the queue. The queue is not modified by this operation.
REAR_ITEM	Returns the last ITEM on the queue without removing it from the queue. The queue is not modified by this operation.
EQUAL	Boolean-valued operator that returns true when two queues have the same length and the same objects in the same order make up both queues, or false otherwise.

Exceptions

Two exceptions can occur, OVERFLOW or Q_IS_EMPTY. The OVERFLOW exception is raised when the queue cannot grow any larger when an attempt is made to ENQUEUE an ITEM or COPY, and no room is left. The exception Q_IS_EMPTY occurs in DEQUEUE, POP, FRONT_ITEM, or REAR_ITEM when an ITEM is to be removed or referenced and there is nothing on the queue.

Warnings

All other warnings are implementation dependent.

Figure 7.5.4 Concluded.

The specification for GENERIC_UNBOUNDED_PRIORITY_QUEUE is listed in Figure 7.5.5. The bounded case is deferred to the exercises. There are three differences to this specification when it is compared to Figure 7.3.2. First a boolean-valued function > has been added as a generic parameter. Second, the APPEND operation has been replaced by the MERGE operation in the package body. Third, the priority queue structure in the private part has been modified because it is no longer necessary to keep track of the rear of the queue. It is worth repeating that everything is the same as before except the criteria for adding objects to the queue and the merging of queues. Figure 7.5.5 contains the package specification.

```
generic
   type ITEM_TYPE is private;
   with function ">" (LEFT, RIGHT : ITEM_TYPE) return boolean;
package GENERIC_UNBOUNDED_PRIORITY_QUEUE is
   type PRIORITY_QUEUE is limited private;
   procedure ADD_TO_Q  ( ITEM        : in      ITEM_TYPE;
```

Figure 7.5.5 Package specification for GENERIC_UNBOUNDED_PRIORITY_QUEUE.
Continues on page 180.

```
                               TO_THE_Q    : in out PRIORITY_QUEUE);
     procedure DEQUEUE    ( ITEM        :    out ITEM_TYPE;
                            FROM_THE_Q  : in out PRIORITY_QUEUE);
     procedure COPY       ( FROM_Q      : in     PRIORITY_QUEUE;
                            TO_Q        :    out PRIORITY_QUEUE);
     procedure MERGE      ( FROM_Q1,
                            FROM_Q2     : in     PRIORITY_QUEUE;
                            ONTO_Q      :    out PRIORITY_QUEUE);
     procedure CLEAR      ( Q_TO_CLEAR  :    out PRIORITY_QUEUE);
     procedure POP        ( FROM_THE_Q  : in out PRIORITY_QUEUE);
     function  LENGTH     ( Q_TO_COUNT  : PRIORITY_QUEUE) return natural;
     function  FULL       ( Q_TO_CHECK  : PRIORITY_QUEUE) return boolean;
     function  EMPTY      ( Q_TO_CHECK  : PRIORITY_QUEUE) return boolean;
     function  REAR_ITEM(FROM_THE_Q   : PRIORITY_QUEUE) return ITEM_TYPE;
     function  FRONT_ITEM(FROM_THE_Q  : PRIORITY_QUEUE) return ITEM_TYPE;
     function  EQUAL      ( Q1, Q2     : PRIORITY_QUEUE) return boolean;
     OVERFLOW   : exception;
     Q_IS_EMPTY : exception;
  private
     type Q_NODE;
     type Q_PTR is ACCESS Q_NODE;
     type PRIORITY_QUEUE is
        record
          LENGTH : natural := 0;
          FRONT : Q_PTR;
        end record;
  end GENERIC_UNBOUNDED_PRIORITY_QUEUE;
```

Figure 7.5.5 Concluded.

All that remains to be done is to develop the ENQUEUE and the MERGE operations. ADD_TO_Q has three cases to consider. The first case is the trivial case; that is, the queue is empty. Insertion is straightforward. The second case is where the item to be inserted has higher priority than the item in the first node on a nonempty queue. The inserted node becomes the new first node. The last case is where the object to be inserted goes somewhere after the first object.

```
procedure ADD_TO_Q (   ITEM         : in      ITEM_TYPE;
                       TO_THE_Q  : in out PRIORITY_QUEUE) is
  -- Adds ITEM so that it precedes all items with lower priority and
  -- follows all ITEMs with higher or equal priority.
  -- Exception OVERFLOW raised if there is no space left to add an ITEM to
  --          the queue.
  TEMP_NODE : Q_PTR := TO_THE_Q.FRONT;
begin
  if TO_THE_Q.LENGTH = 0 then
    -- Queue empty, so ITEM will be first on the queue
    TO_THE_Q := (1, new Q_NODE'(ITEM, null));
  elsif ITEM > TO_THE_Q.FRONT_ITEM then
    -- New ITEM has higher priority than first item
    TO_THE_Q.FRONT := new Q_NODE'(ITEM, TO_THE_Q.FRONT);
```

```
      TO_THE_Q.LENGTH := TO_THE_Q.LENGTH + 1;
    else
      -- Find where ITEM belongs in the priority queue
      while TEMP_NODE.NEXT /= null loop
        exit when ITEM > TEMP_NODE.NEXT.ITEM;
        TEMP_NODE := TEMP_NODE.NEXT;
      end loop;
      -- ITEM belongs between the node pointed to by TEMP_NODE
      -- and the node pointed to be TEMP_NODE.NEXT
      TEMP_NODE.NEXT := new Q_NODE'(ITEM, TEMP_NODE.NEXT);
      TO_THE_Q.LENGTH := TO_THE_Q.LENGTH + 1;
    end if;
  exception
    when storage_error => raise OVERFLOW;
  end ADD_TO_Q;
```

For a queue of length n, ADD_TO_Q is timewise $O(n)$ instead of $O(1)$ for a regular queue. The reason for this is that any object, on average, will be inserted into the middle of the queue so that the loop is iterated $n/2$ times.

The MERGE operation is similar in concept to merge sorting that will be examined in Chapter 11. The basic idea, shown in Figure 7.5.6, is to compare the next item in each queue and then determine which has the higher priority. The item with the higher priority is copied onto the end of the answer queue and then deleted from its queue. This process continues until one queue is empty. Then the remaining items on the nonempty queue are copied onto the answer queue. A simple recursive implementation of merge is possible. The priority queue documentation, listed in Figure 7.5.4, requires that the merged queues not be altered. The full implementation of the ADT GENERIC_UNBOUNDED_PRIORITY_QUEUE is covered in the exercises.

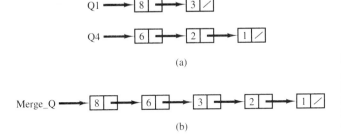

(a)

(b)

Figure 7.5.6 Operation MERGE in the ADT GENERIC_UNBOUNDED_PRIOR-ITY_QUEUE. (a) Two priority queues Q1 and Q4 before and after a call to MERGE(Q1, Q4, Merge_Q). (b) Result after merging Q1 and Q4 from part (a).

One variation of the priority queue is the priority search queue. Search structures involve key-data pairs instead of objects. The dictionary is a search structure. The key is the word and the data is the definition. In a priority search queue key-data pairs are added in priority order by key. The priority search queue has the features of a balking queue. Key-data pairs can be deleted by either position or key. The conventions used in Section 4 when describing balking queues are adopted except that instead of a queue of objects, the search queue is a queue of key-data pairs, and the priority is based on the key type. The documentation and the implementation are left to the exercises. Figure 7.5.7 provides a listing of the new specification of GENERIC_UNBOUNDED_PRIORITY_BALKING_QUEUE.

```
generic
  type KEY_TYPE is private;
  type DATA_TYPE is private;
  with function "<=" (LEFT, RIGHT : KEY_TYPE) return boolean;
package GENERIC_UNBOUNDED_PRIORITY_BALKING_QUEUE is
  type QUEUE is limited private;
  procedure ADD_TO_QUEUE              ( KEY          : in      KEY_TYPE;
                                        DATA         : in      DATA_TYPE;
                                        TO_THE_Q     : in out QUEUE);
  procedure DEQUEUE                   ( KEY          :    out KEY_TYPE;
                                        DATA         :    out DATA_TYPE;
                                        FROM_THE_Q   : in out QUEUE);
  procedure COPY                      ( FROM_Q       : in      QUEUE;
                                        TO_Q         :    out QUEUE);
  procedure MERGE                     ( FROM_Q1,
                                        FROM_Q2      : in      QUEUE;
                                        ONTO_Q       : in out QUEUE);
  procedure CLEAR                     ( Q_TO_CLEAR   :    out QUEUE);
  procedure POP                       ( FROM_THE_Q   : in out QUEUE);
  procedure REMOVE_KEY_DATA_BY_KEY    ( FROM_Q       : in out QUEUE;
                                        KEY          : in      KEY_TYPE);
  procedure REMOVE_KEY_DATA_BY_LOC    ( FROM_Q       : in out QUEUE;
                                        AT_LOCATION  : in      Positive);
  procedure FRONT_PAIR                ( FROM_THE_Q   : in      QUEUE;
                                        KEY          :    out KEY_TYPE;
                                        DATA         :    out DATA_TYPE);
  procedure REAR_PAIR                 ( FROM_THE_Q   : in      QUEUE;
                                        KEY          :    out KEY_TYPE;
                                        DATA         :    out DATA_TYPE);
  function KEY_POSITION_ON_Q          ( KEY_TO_FIND  : KEY_TYPE;
                                        ON_Q         : QUEUE) return natural;
  function RETURN_DATA_WITH_KEY_ON_Q(KEY            : KEY_TYPE;
                                        ON_Q         : QUEUE) return DATA_TYPE;
  function KEY_at_Position_on_Q       (AT_LOCATION  : positive;
                                        ON_Q         : QUEUE) return KEY_TYPE;
  function DATA_at_Position_on_Q      (AT_LOCATION  : positive;
                                        ON_Q         : QUEUE) return DATA_TYPE;
  function LENGTH        ( Q_TO_COUNT : QUEUE) return natural;
  function EMPTY         ( Q_TO_CHECK : QUEUE) return boolean;
  function EQUAL         ( Q1, Q2     : QUEUE) return boolean;
  OVERFLOW       : exception;
  Q_IS_EMPTY     : exception;
  POSITION_ERROR : exception;
private
  TYPE Q_ITEM;
  TYPE QUEUE is access Q_Item;
  type Q_ITEM is
    record
```

Figure 7.5.7 Specification of GENERIC_UNBOUNDED_PRIORITY_BALKING_QUEUE.
Continues on page 183.

```
      KEY : KEY_TYPE;
      DATA : DATA_TYPE;
      NEXT : QUEUE;
    end record;

end GENERIC_UNBOUNDED_PRIORITY_BALKING_QUEUE;
```

Figure 7.5.7   Concluded.

One word of caution is in order. Many operations of a priority search queue also can be implemented using other search abstract data types, such as hashing methods or binary search trees. These ADTs are the subjects of later chapters. Typically, the binary search tree is much more efficient than a version implemented using a queue. To the programmer the results are the same. Searching, insertion, and deletion can usually be reduced from $O(n)$ to $O(\log_2(n))$, where n is the number of objects in the queue or tree.

7.6 APPLICATIONS

A print queue is an operating system utility that controls the printer. In its simplest form the print queue prints the job that has been in the queue the longest. This is typical of most PCs. If a procedure PRINT_FILE exists, a task implementation of a print queue might look as follows:

```
with text_io, GENERIC_BOUNDED_QUEUE;
use text_io;
FILE_NAME : string(1..50);
package P_QUEUE is new GENERIC_BOUNDED_QUEUE (FILE_NAME,25);
P_QUE : P_QUEUE.QUEUE;

procedure PRINT_QUEUE (TO_PRINT : string) is
begin
  if PRINTER_BUSY then
    ENQUEUE(TO_PRINT,P_QUE);
  else
    PRINT_JOB(TO_PRINT);
  end if;
end PRINT_QUEUE;

procedure PRINT_JOB (TO_PRINT : string) is
  NEXT_FILE : string(1..50);
begin
  --open file and print
  if not EMPTY(P_QUE) then
    DEQUEUE(NEXT_FILE,P_QUE);
    PRINT_JOB(NEXT_FILE);
  end if;
end PRINT_JOB;
```

The procedures above can easily be modified to take care of the case where short files are put on the front of a DEQUE. Assume that FILE_LENGTH (FILE_NAME) is a procedure that returns the number of lines in a file; then the following print queue results.

```
with text_io, GENERIC_UNBOUNDED_DEQUE;
use text_io;
FILE_NAME : string(1..50);
package P_QUEUE is new GENERIC_UNBOUNDED_DEQUE(FILE_NAME);
P_QUE:P_QUEUE.QUEUE;

procedure PRINT_QUEUE (TO_PRINT : string) is
begin
  if PRINTER_BUSY then
    if FILE_LENGTH (FILE_NAME) < 500 then
      ENQUEUE(TO_PRINT, IN_FRONT, P_QUE);
    else
      ENQUEUE(TO_PRINT, IN_REAR, P_QUE);
    end if;
  else
    PRINT_JOB (TO_PRINT);
  end if;
end PRINT_QUEUE;

procedure PRINT_JOB (TO_PRINT : string) is
  NEXT_FILE : string(1..50);
begin
    --open file and print
  if not EMPTY(P_QUE) then
    DEQUEUE (NEXT_FILE, P_QUE);
    PRINT_JOB (NEXT_FILE);
  end if;
end PRINT_JOB;
```

A second application is simulation. This world is a world that believes in queues. People line up in queues to buy hamburgers at McDonald's. Airplanes, at least those not experiencing an emergency condition, land and take off from airports based on a queue model. Cars arrive and leave intersections in a queue. Persons seeking information over the phone often encounter an automatic phone-answering machine that plays back a message similar to this one: "You have reached the XYZ Corporation. All our service representatives are busy. Please stay on the line. Your call will be answered by the next available representative in the order received. Thank you." In other words, you have been placed on a queue. When waiting for service, most people consider waiting in a queue for service fair.

Actually, the XYZ Corporation probably did a simulation before they set up the service department. Psychologists have statistics that imply that a person will stay on hold for some maximum time before hanging up in frustration. Also, people don't want to keep calling and encountering a busy signal. The XYZ Corporation could supply some estimate as to the volume of calls to expect. This information would be used in setting up a simulation to determine how many incoming lines to have, to determine the optimum number of service representatives to hire, and how often they would allow people to wait too long or to get a busy signal.

The subject of the remainder of this section is the priority queue and its variations. In some sense it is a more abstract linear structure than either a stack or a queue. Both stacks and standard queues can be developed by properly instantiating the priority queue package.

In Figure 7.6.1 the priority operator for node types always returns true. This implies that the statement

```
KEY > Q.KEY
```

similar to one found in the ENQUEUE operation, returns true. Enqueue then assumes that key, the key of the key-data pair to be added, has a higher priority than the first object in the queue. This forces ENQUEUE to insert the key-data pair at the front of the queue. This is the last in, first out behavior that characterizes a stack.

```
type NODE is
  record
    . . . . . . . . . . .
  end record;
function ">" (LEFT, RIGHT : NODE) return boolean is
begin
  return true;
end ">";


package STACK is new GENERIC_UNBOUNDED_PRIORITY_QUEUE(NODE, ">");
```

Figure 7.6.1   GENERIC_UNBOUNDED_PRIORITY_QUEUE instantiated as a stack.

If the function ">" always returns false instead of true, the operation ENQUEUE places every key-data pair at the end of the queue. This is first in, first out behavior that characterizes the basic queue. Note that the merge procedure is affected by the instantiations in the discussion above. In the queue version, merge acts just like append. Just because a priority queue can be forced to act like a queue or a stack does not mean that it should be used in place of a stack or queue. To add an item to the end of a priority queue is a timewise $O(n)$ operation, but this same operation is $O(1)$ timewise in the regular queue package.

In many cases, selection of the object with the kth smallest key or priority is needed. For example, in statistics the median of a set of data is the object exactly in the middle of an ordered list of data. If the objects are on a priority balking queue, it is possible to get the median.

```
procedure FIND_MEDIAN_OF_Q (KEY    :    out Key_Type;
                            DATA   :    out Data_type;
                            Q      : in     Queue ) is
  PLACE := natural := LENGTH(Q)/2;
begin
  if PLACE = 0 then
    raise Q_IS_EMPTY;
  else
    KEY  := Key_at_Position_on_Q (PLACE, Q);
    DATA := Data_at_Position_on_Q (PLACE, Q);
  endif;
end FIND_MEDIAN_OF_Q;
```

Priority search queues can be used to store and manipulate polynomials in a natural way. Each term of a polynomial is composed of a coefficient, a value, and an exponent. For example,

$$p(x) = 10*x**5 + 3*x**3 - x$$

is a polynomial of degree 5 with three terms. Using the key to represent the exponent, and letting the data type be the coefficient, the instantiation

```
package POLYNOMIAL is new
        GENERIC_UNBOUNDED_PRIORITY_BALKING_QUEUE  (NATURAL,  float,  "<");
```

represents polynomials. Figure 7.6.2 shows how two polynomials represented as priority queues are added together. The following function adds to polynomials represented as balking priority queues together.

```
function "+" (LEFT, RIGHT : QUEUE) return QUEUE is
TEMP : QUEUE;
ANS  : QUEUE;
EXPONENT, PLACE : natural;
COEF : float;
begin
  COPY (RIGHT, TEMP);
  COPY (LEFT, ANS);
  loop
    exit when EMPTY(TEMP);
    -- Get next term to add
    DEQUEUE (EXPONENT, COEF, TEMP);
    -- See if a term with the same exponent is on the answer
    PLACE := KEY_POSITION_ON_Q(EXPONENT, ANS);
    if PLACE /= 0 then
       -- Term with same exponent already there.  Get and update.
      COEF := COEF + DATA_AT_POSITION_ON_Q(PLACE, ANS);
      REMOVE_KEY_DATA_BY_LOC(ANS, PLACE);
    end if;
    -- If the coefficient is 0, don't add.
    if COEF /= 0.0 then
       ADD_TO_QUEUE(EXPONENT, COEF, ANS);
```

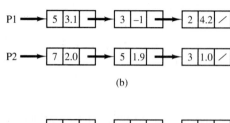

(a)

(b)

(c)

Figure 7.6.2 Polynomial operations where the polynomials are represented using priority-balking queues. (a) Diagram of a node in a priority balking queue used to represent a term in a polynomial. (b) Two polynomials represented as priority balking queues. (c) Sum of the two polynomials in part (b).

```
        end if;
      end loop;
    return ANS;
  end "+";
```

Since a number is in a real sense a polynomial with x-base, the function + above could also be used to add integers of arbitrary size. This method does not store any zero coefficients. For example,

$$10809 = 1*10**4 + 8*10**2 + 9*10**0$$

As a last application, priority search queues can be used to generate indexes. In the back of this book is an index of topics or key words followed by the page on which they appear. By scanning text page by page, a data structure based on a priority search queue of queues can be used to generate the index (see Figure 7.6.3).

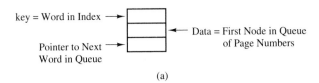

(a)

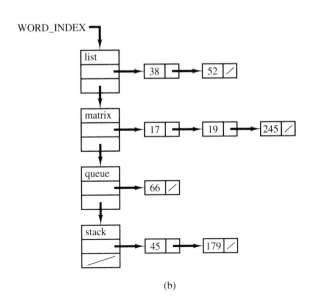

(b)

Figure 7.6.3   Word index built up as a prioroty balking queue of unbounded queues.(a) Priority balking queue node structure used to build a word index of page number queues.(b) Priority balking queue of queues used to make an index.

Each word will form the key of the node. The object associated with the word is a queue of page numbers. Thus

```
LAST_PAGE : integer constant := 546;
type PAGE_NUMBER is integer range 1..LAST_PAGE;
package PAGE_NUMBER_Q is new GENERIC_UNBOUNDED_QUEUE (PAGE_NUMBER);
subtype WORD is string(1..20);
type WORD_Q is
  record
```

```
    W : WORD;
    LIST : PAGE_NUMBER_Q.QUEUE;
  end record;


function "<" (LEFT, RIGHT : WORD_Q) return boolean is
begin
  return LEFT.W < RIGHT.W;
end "<";


package INDEX_Q is new
        UNBOUNDED_PRIORITY_BALKING_QUEUE (WORD,WORD_Q,"<",);
INDEX : INDEX_Q.QUEUE;
```

With the data type index, indexes can easily be built up. A word is scanned along with the current page number. The operator KEY_POSITION_ON_Q is used to determine if the word is in the index along with its position. Remember that this operator returns 0 if the key is not in the index. Next, a call to the operator RETURN_OBJECT_WITH_KEY_ON_Q returns the needed WORD_Q. Then enqueue procedure puts the current page number on WORD_Q.Q. Assuming that the index Q is global, the procedure update looks as shown in Figure 7.6.4. It is left as an exercise to print the index once it is built.

```
procedure UPDATE_INDEX (W  : in     WORD;
                P                 : in     PAGE_NUMBER is;
  PLACE : natural;
begin
  PLACE := KEY_POSITION_ON_Q (W, Q);
  if PLACE = 0 then
    --word W not in queue
    ENQUEUE(W, P, INDEX);
  else
    PAGE_NUMBER_Q.ENQUEUE (P,
              RETURN_OBJECT_WITH_KEY_ON_Q(W, Q).LIST);
  end if;
end UPDATE_INDEX;
```

Figure 7.6.4   Example of a queue of queues.

7.7 TIME AND SPACE CONSTRAINTS

Like the stack operations, queue operations are time efficient. Everything is added to the rear and removed from the front. The front and rear are directly accessed, so no traversal or searching is needed. The balking queue can access or remove objects at any place in the queue, so those operations will be considered separately. For the rest of the section n will denote the number of objects on the queue and SIZE will denote the maximum queue size in the bounded case. Operations that add or remove an item are $O(1)$. Those that copy the queue or compare two queues, that is, anything with a loop built into the operation, are $O(n)$. Figure 7.7.1 gives the time and space constraints for the GENERIC_BOUNDED_QUEUE specified in Figure 7.2.3.

	Operation Overhead	Space Overhead
ENQUEUE	$O(1)$	$O(SIZE)$
DEQUEUE	$O(1)$	$O(SIZE)$
COPY	$O(n)$	$O(SIZE)$
LENGTH	$O(1)$	$O(SIZE)$
EQUAL	$O(n)$	$O(SIZE)$

Figure 7.7.1 Constrains for GENERIC_BOUNDED_QUEUE in Figure 7.2.3.

The constraints for GENERIC_UNBOUNDED_QUEUE specified in Figure 7.3.2 and for GENERIC_UNBOUNDED_DEQUE in Figure 7.4.2 are contained in Figure 7.7.2. The constraints are similar to those for GENERIC_UNBOUNDED_LIST except for LENGTH. The LENGTH operation is updated whenever an item is added or deleted from the queue. It is not necessary to traverse and count the queue. This reduces LENGTH from $O(n)$ to $O(1)$.

	Operation Overhead	Space Overhead
ENQUEUE	$O(1)$	$O(n)$
DEQUEUE	$O(1)$	$O(n)$
COPY	$O(n)$	$O(n)$
LENGTH	$O(1)$	$O(n)$
EQUAL	$O(n)$	$O(n)$

Figure 7.7.2 Constrains for GENERIC_UNBOUNDED_QUEUE in Figure 7.3.2 and for GENERIC_UNBOUNDED_DEQUE in Figure 7.4.2.

The balking queue case is listed in Figure 7.7.3. The operations common to GENERIC_UNBOUNDED_QUEUE have the same constraints, but the operations to find or remove objects with a certain key or at a certain position require a traversal proportional to the length of the queue. Figure 7.7.3 lists the constraints.

	Operation Overhead	Space Overhead
ENQUEUE	$O(1)$	$O(n)$
DEQUEUE	$O(1)$	$O(n)$
COPY	$O(n)$	$O(n)$
LENGTH	$O(1)$	$O(n)$
EQUAL	$O(n)$	$O(n)$
KEY_POSITION_ON_Q	$O(n)$	$O(n)$
REMOVE_KEY_DATA_FROM_Q	$O(n)$	$O(n)$

Figure 7.7.3 Constrains for GENERIC_UNBOUNDED_BALKING_QUEUE in Figure 7.4.3.

7.8 CASE STUDY: DISCRETE SIMULATION

There are two basic types of simulation, discrete and continuous. Continuous simulations vary a quantity with time, and discrete simulations are event driven. An example of a continuous simulation is the modeling of the position of a rocket with respect to time. After launch, the acceleration of the rocket increases with time, although the thrust of the rocket motor is constant. Newton's second law of motion states that

$$
\begin{aligned}
\text{force} \quad &= \quad \text{thrust} \\
&= \quad (d/dt)(m*v) \\
&= \quad (dm/dt)*v + m*(dv/dt) \\
&= \quad (dm/dt)*v + m*a
\end{aligned}
$$

or

$$
a \quad = \quad (\text{thrust} - (dm/dt)*v)/m
$$

In the case of a rocket, the rate of change of the mass of the rocket is negative because the mass of the rocket decreases with respect to time as the rocket motor burns fuel. The expression for the acceleration is increasing. This simple example is the basis of a continuous simulation of a rocket's performance.

A discrete simulation is driven by an event. Random number generators usually generate the event. Consider trying to model the toss of a coin. Tossing a coin is an event. It happens a finite number of times, and this number is an integer. The method for modeling a coin toss is to use a uniformly distributed random number generator. A function that returns a uniform random number in the interval (0,1) is given in Appendix C. A random number is uniform if every value in the interval is uniformly likely. The computer can toss a coin in the following manner.

```
if UNIFORM_RANDOM_NUMBER <= 0.5 then
  return HEADS;
else
  return TAILS;
end if;
```

If a die is to be rolled, the event, then the outcome, can be determined by the following table.

```
X := UNIFORM_RANDOM_NUMBER;
if X < 0.166 then
  return 1;
elsif X < 0.332 then
  return 2;
elsif X < 0.5 then
  return 3;
elsif X < 0.667 then
  return 4;
elsif X < 0.833 then
  return 5;
else
  return 6;
end if;
```

The subject of this case study is the simulation of the queue of customers at a bank. Suppose that the Bank of Good Returns is thinking of remodeling. Before remodeling, the bank has four tellers. After remodeling, the number of tellers will be two. During remodeling, three electronic tellers will be installed. The architect has given the president of the bank two options. Option 1 is for each teller to have a customer line. When the customer who needs to see a teller enters the bank, he or she selects the shortest line. Option 2 is for the two tellers to share a line. A customer comes into the bank and goes to the end of the line. The customer at the front of the line goes to whichever teller is not busy.

The president of the Bank of Good Returns is wise. The president wants to pick the remodeling option that leads to the minimum customer frustration average. This crafty chief executive knows that two things frustrate customers. The first is coming into the bank and seeing long teller lines. He knows that if a customer sees a line longer than 15 customers, he or she will turn around and leave. The second thing that frustrates a customer is to wait in any line for an extended period.

The bank's president also knows that some people take longer to finish their business than others. Some customers are slow, some are meticulous, and some have more complicated business matters that must be completed. The time it takes for any teller to handle a customer transaction is a function of the customer's business with the bank. Two things must be recorded for any customer. The first quantity is the time the customer enters the bank. The second quantity is the time it will take to complete his or her business with the teller. With this insight the two-teller, two-queue option is illustrated in Figure 7.8.1(a) and the two-teller one-queue option is illustrated in Figure 7.8.1(b).

Before the model can be completed, several assumptions must be made. The first is the arrival times of the customers. This model will compute the cases for the arrival of 5 through 15 customers per hour at the bank. Using this assumption, the uniform random number distribution can be used to see if a customer arrives at any particular time. A customer will arrive at any point in time if the uniform random number generator is less than NUMBER_CUSTOMERS_PER_HOUR divided by the number of minutes in an hour.

Some method must be used to determine how long a customer will need to complete his or her business with the teller. After a meeting with the tellers, the president decides that there is no way to predict exact customer needs. An assumption is made that a customer needs between 1 and 10 minutes of a teller's time to conduct his or her business, and the distribution is uniform. The president of the Bank of Good Returns, who majored in computer science and minored in mathematics, now has enough information to write a simple program to do a discrete simulation. In this section only option 2, the case of two tellers with one line, will be considered. The bank is open from 9:00 A.M. to 4:00 P.M., so the simulation will go on for 420 minutes. At the end of the normal simulation, the process will continue until all customers in line at the close of business have been served. For each value of the number of customers expected per hour, the simulation will provide the following information.

The maximum length of the line

The average length of the line during business hours

The average number waiting in line

The time the line was empty

The number of customers served

The number of customers turned away

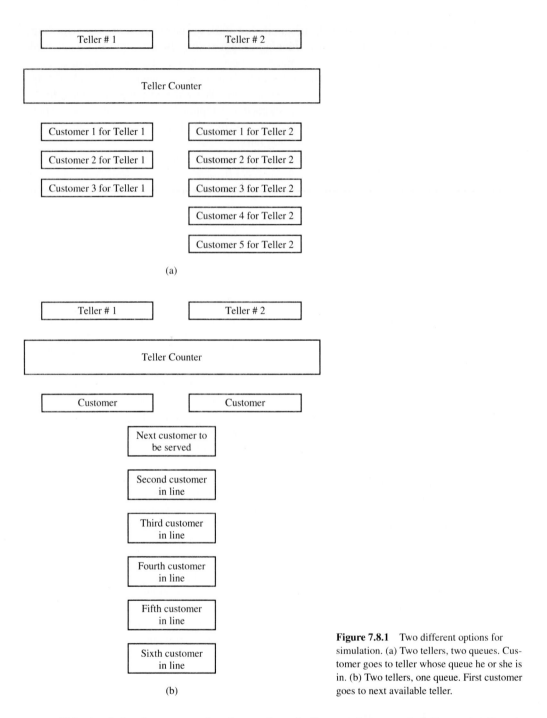

Figure 7.8.1 Two different options for simulation. (a) Two tellers, two queues. Customer goes to teller whose queue he or she is in. (b) Two tellers, one queue. First customer goes to next available teller.

This simulation is set up so that the number of tellers can be expanded. For each teller, there must be a boolean-valued variable to indicate whether or not the teller is busy. If the teller is busy, there must be a variable to indicate when the teller will finish with the current customer.

Figure 7.8.2 lists the full case study and Figure 7.8.3 lists some sample output. The ADT GENERIC_UNBOUNDED_QUEUE is perfect for simulation of the line of customers.

```
with text_io;                use text_io;
with GENERIC_UNBOUNDED_QUEUE;
with UNIFORM_RANDOM;

procedure CASE_STUDY_7 is

package MY_FLOAT_IO is new float_io(float);
   use MY FLOAT_IO;
package MY_INTEGER_IO is new integer_io(integer);
   use MY_INTEGER_IO;

   --get random number generator from Appendix C
package MY_RANDOM is new UNIFORM_RANDOM(131, 0.0, 1.0);
   use MY_RANDOM;

NUMBER_OF_TELLERS : constant := 2;
TELLER_BUSY : array ( positive range 1..Number_of_tellers)
                    of boolean := ( others => false);
TELLER_FREE : array ( positive range 1..Number_of_tellers)
                    of float := (others => 0.0);

type CUSTOMER is
   record
      TIME_GOT_IN_LINE          : float;
      TIME_NEEDED_FOR_BUSINESS : float;
   end record;

package CUSTOMER_QUEUE is new GENERIC_UNBOUNDED_QUEUE(CUSTOMER);
   use CUSTOMER_QUEUE;

   MAXIMUM_LINE_LENGTH : integer := 0;
   AVERAGE_LINE_LENGTH : float := 0.0;
   AVERAGE_WAITING_TIME: float := 0.0;
   TIME_LINE_EMPTY      : float:= 0.0;
   NUMBER_CUSTOMER      : integer := 0;
   NUMBER_TURNED_AWAY   : integer := 0;
   NUM_PER_HOUR         : positive := 1;
   TIME                 : float := 0.0;
   NEXT_CUSTOMER        : customer;
   TEMP_CUSTOMER        : customer;

   CUSTOMER_LINE : QUEUE;

   procedure PRINT_REPORT_HEADINGS is separate;
      --simple IO procedure, left to exercises
```

Figure 7.8.2 CASE_STUDY_7: bank frustration simulation. Continues on page 194.

```
      procedure PRINT_SIMULATION_RESULTS(CUST_HOUR: in    positive;
                                    MAX_LINE : in   integer;
                                    AVG_LINE : in   float;
                                    TIME_EMP : in   float;
                                    AVG_WAIT : in   float;
                                    NUM_AWAY : in   integer;
                                 NUM_CUST : in   integer) is separate;
         --left to the exercises

      procedure ADD_NEW_CUSTOMER( TIME_NOW : in     float) is

         TEMP_CUSTOMER        : CUSTOMER;

         function BUSY_TIME return float is
         -- Returns how long a particular customer will keep teller busy
         TEMP : float;
         begin
            TEMP:= 1.0 + 9.0*RANDOM;
            return TEMP;
         end BUSY_TIME;

         begin
         --new customer to be added
         TEMP_CUSTOMER.TIME_GOT_IN_LINE := TIME_NOW;
         TEMP_CUSTOMER.TIME_NEEDED_FOR_BUSINESS := BUSY_TIME;
         ENQUEUE(TEMP_CUSTOMER, CUSTOMER_LINE);
      end ADD_NEW_CUSTOMER;

begin --CASE_STUDY_7
   PRINT_REPORT_HEADINGS;
   for NUMBER_CUSTOMERS_PER_HOUR in positive range 5..20 loop
      NUM_PER_HOUR := NUMBER_CUSTOMERS_PER_HOUR;
      MAXIMUM_LINE_LENGTH := 0;
      AVERAGE_LINE_LENGTH := 0.0;
      AVERAGE_WAITING_TIME := 0.0;
      TIME_LINE_EMPTY := 0.0;
      NUMBER_TURNED_AWAY := 0;
      NUMBER_CUSTOMER := 0;
      TIME := 0.0;
      -- Banker's hours are 9-4 or 420 minutes
      -- When bank closes, must serve customers in line too!
      loop
         exit when TIME > 420.0) and then EMPTY(CUSTOMER_LINE));

         --update time in minutes
         TIME := TIME + 1.0;

         --See if a currently busy teller is finished
         for INDEX in positive range 1..NUMBER_OF_TELLERS loop
```

Figure 7.8.2   Continues on page 195.

Continues on page 195.

```
      if TELLER_BUSY (INDEX) and then TELLER_FREE(INDEX) <= TIME then
        TELLER_BUSY(INDEX) := false;
      end if;
  end loop;
  -- Average line length is taken over time
  AVERAGE_LINE_LENGTH := AVERAGE_LINE_LENGTH +
                            float (LENGTH(CUSTOMER_LINE));

  --See if a customer has come in the bank while bank open
  if TIME <= 420.0 and
    -- See if the next customer is coming through the door
    RANDOM <= float(NUM_PER_HOUR)/60.0 then
      --if line so long customers turn around and leave
      if LENGTH(CUSTOMER_LINE) >= 15 then
        NUMBER_TURNED_AWAY := NUMBER_TURNED_AWAY + 1;
      else
        ADD_NEW_CUSTOMER(TIME);
        NUMBER_CUSTOMER := NUMBER_CUSTOMER + 1;
      end if;
  end if;

  --update maximum line length
  if LENGTH (CUSTOMER_LINE) > MAXIMUM_LINE_LENGTH then
    MAXIMUM_LINE_LENGTH := Q_LENGTH(CUSTOMER_LINE);
  end if;

  --See if line is empty and update if necessary
  if EMPTY (CUSTOMER_LINE) then
    TIME_LINE_EMPTY := TIME_LINE_EMPTY + 1.0;
  end if;

  -- if teller is free, then serve the next customer
  for INDEX in positive range 1..NUMBER_OF_TELLERS loop
    if (not TELLER_BUSY(INDEX))
        and then (not EMPTY(CUSTOMER_LINE)) then
      -- A teller is free and there are customers waiting
      DEQUEUE(NEXT_CUSTOMER, CUSTOMER_LINE);
      TELLER_BUSY(INDEX) := true;
      TELLER_FREE(INDEX) := Time +
              NEXT_CUSTOMER.TIME_NEEDED_FOR_BUSINESS;
      AVERAGE_WAITING_TIME := AVERAGE_WAITING_TIME
              + TIME - NEXT_CUSTOMER.TIME_GOT_IN_LINE);
    end if;
  end loop;

end loop;

-- End of this case, initialize for next case
TELLER_BUSY := (others => false);
```

Figure 7.8.2 Continues on page 196.

```
        TELLER_FREE := (others => 0.0);
        --Compute averages, print results
        AVERAGE_LINE_LENGTH := AVERAGE_LINE_LENGTH/TIME;
        AVERAGE_WAITING_TIME := AVERAGE_WAITING_TIME/float(NUMBER_CUSTOMER);
        PRINT_SIMULATION_RESULTS(NUMBER_CUSTOMERS_PER_HOUR,
                MAXIMUM_LINE_LENGTH, AVERAGE_LINE_LENGTH,
                TIME_LINE_EMPTY, AVERAGE_WAITING_TIME,
                NUMBER_TURNED_AWAY, NUMBER_CUSTOMER);
    end loop;
end CASE_STUDY_7;
```

Figure 7.8.2   Concluded.

The results of running CASE_STUDY_7 are shown in Figure 7.8.3. The other option, one line for each teller, is left to the exercises.

SAMPLE SIMULATION RESULTS

Customers per hour	5	7	9	11	13	15	17	19
Maximum line length	1	2	2	3	2	4	6	8
Average line length	0.02	0.07	0.04	0.15	0.18	0.55	1.04	2.45
Time line empty	371	346	314	296	274	236	158	58
Average waiting time	0.16	0.58	0.28	0.83	0.85	2.53	3.80	7.80
Customers served	43	52	61	76	87	91	115	132
Customers not served	0	0	0	0	0	0	0	0

Figure 7.8.3   Sample output for CASE_STUDY_7.

The idea behind this simple simulation has wide applicability. Obviously, the model has several shortcomings. There are probably more customers at the bank during lunch hour or on payday than at other times. The queues that represented customer lines could just have easily been queues of cars at an intersection, queues of messages waiting to be processed on a network, or a queue of requests for disk access by an operating system. In this case study, 4 of the 11 operations of the ADT GENERIC_UNBOUNDED_QUEUE were used. Note that the ADT GENERIC_BOUNDED_QUEUE could also have been used if the size of the queue was made large enough.

EXERCISES

Section 7.2 Bounded Form

7.2.1 Implement the following operations in the ADT GENERIC_BOUNDED_QUEUE where the data structure

```
        type ITEM_TYPE is array (1..MAXIMUM_Q_SIZE) of ITEM_TYPE;
        type QUEUE is
          record
            FRONT,
```

```
        IN_USE : natural := 0;
        QUE    : ITEM_Q_TYPE;
    end record;
```

is put into the private part of Figure 7.2.3 and where the rear of the queue is defined by

```
        REAR := 1 + (FRONT + IN_USE - 2) MOD MAXIMUM_Q_SIZE;
```

  a. The operation ENQUEUE
  b. The operation DEQUEUE
  c. The operation COPY
  d. The operation APPEND
  e. The operation CLEAR
  f. The operation POP
  g. The operation LENGTH
  h. The operation EMPTY
  i. The operation FULL
  j. The operation FRONT_OBJECT
  k. The operation REAR_OBJECT
  l. The operation EQUAL
  m. Combine parts a through k into a new package body for GENERIC_BOUNDED_QUEUE.

7.2.2 Implement the following operations in the ADT GENERIC_BOUNDED_QUEUE where the data structure

```
        type ITEM_Q_TYPE is array (1..MAXIMUM_Q_SIZE) of ITEM_TYPE;
        type QUEUE is
          record
            FRONT, REAR : natural := 0;
            QUE : ITEM_Q_TYPE;
          end record;
```

is put into the private section of Figure 7.2.3.

  a. The operation ENQUEUE
  b. The operation DEQUEUE
  c. The operation COPY
  d. The operation APPEND
  e. The operation CLEAR
  f. The operation POP
  g. The operation LENGTH
  h. The operation EMPTY
  i. The operation FULL
  j. The operation FRONT_OBJECT
  k. The operation REAR_OBJECT
  l. The operation EQUAL
  m. Combine parts a through k into a new package body for GENERIC_BOUNDED_QUEUE.

7.2.3 Implement the following operations in the ADT GENERIC_BOUNDED_QUEUE where the data structure

```
        type ITEM_Q_TYPE is array (1..MAXIMUM_Q_SIZE) of ITEM_TYPE;
        type QUEUE_NODE is
          record
            FRONT, REAR : natural := 0;
```

```
              QUE : ITEM_Q_TYPE;
          end record;
      type QUEUE is access QUEUE_NODE;
```

is put into the private section of Figure 7.2.3.

  a. The operation ENQUEUE

  b. The operation DEQUEUE

  c. The operation COPY

  d. The operation APPEND

  e. The operation CLEAR

  f. The operation POP

  g. The operation LENGTH

  h. The operation EMPTY

  i. The operation FULL

  j. The operation FRONT_OBJECT

  k. The operation REAR_OBJECT

  l. The operation EQUAL

  m. Combine parts a through k into a new package body for GENERIC_BOUNDED_QUEUE. (*Note:* An object of type QUEUE could have a null value. Whenever this occurs, the object must be initialized.)

7.2.4 Implement the following operations in the ADT GENERIC_BOUNDED_QUEUE where the formal generic parameters and the definition of a queue is defined by

```
        generic
          type ITEM_TYPE is private;
        package GENERIC_BOUNDED_QUEUE is
        type QUEUE (SIZE : positive) is limited private;
```

and the data structure in the private section of Figure 7.2.3 is replaced by

```
      type ITEM_TYPE_ARRAY is array (positive range <>) of ITEM_TYPE;
      type QUEUE_NODE (SIZE: positive) is
        record
          FRONT, REAR : natural := 0;
          QUE : ITEM_TYPE_ARRAY (1..SIZE);
        end record;
      type QUEUE is access QUEUE_NODE;
```

  a. The operation ENQUEUE

  b. The operation DEQUEUE

  c. The operation COPY

  d. The operation APPEND

  e. The operation CLEAR

  f. The operation POP

  g. The operation LENGTH

  h. The operation EMPTY

  i. The operation FULL

  j. The operation FRONT_OBJECT

  k. The operation REAR_OBJECT

  l. The operation EQUAL

  m. Define and implement a procedure CREATE that initializes a QUEUE with a given SIZE.

n. Combine parts a through l into a new package body for GENERIC_BOUNDED_QUEUE. (*Hint:* Another exception QUEUE_NOT_DEFINED must be declared and allowed for.)

Section 7.3 Unbounded Implementation

7.3.1 Implement the following operations in the ADT GENERIC_UNBOUNDED_QUEUE where the data structure

```
type QUEUE_NODE;
type QUEUE is access QUEUE_NODE;
```

is put into the private section of Figure 7.3.2. Note that since REAR is not specified, the queue must be traversed to ENQUEUE.

a. The operation ENQUEUE
b. The operation DEQUEUE
c. The operation COPY
d. The operation APPEND
e. The operation CLEAR
f. The operation POP
g. The operation LENGTH
h. The operation EMPTY
i. The operation FULL
j. The operation FRONT_OBJECT
k. The operation REAR_OBJECT
l. The operation EQUAL
m. Combine parts a through k into a new package body for GENERIC_BOUNDED_QUEUE.

7.3.2 The procedure COPY and the functions LENGTH and EQUAL have simple recursive implementations. For example, two queues are equal if and only their first nodes are equal and the subqueues starting at their respective second nodes are equal. Implement these subprograms recursively for the queues defined above.

7.3.3 Add the two operations NEXT_Q_OBJECT and SET_NEXT_OBJECT defined in Figure 7.1.2 to the ADT GENERIC_UNBOUNDED_QUEUE specified in Figure 7.3.2.

Section 7.4 Variations: The Balking Queue and the Deque

In the following exercises, specify a package means to write the documentation in a manner similar to Figure 7.1.1 as well as writing the generic package specification.

7.4.1 **a.** For the abstract data type GENERIC_BOUNDED_DEQUE, specify a generic package.
b. Implement the package specified in Figure 7.4.1a.

7.4.2 **a.** For the abstract data type GENERIC_BOUNDED_BALKING_QUEUE, specify a generic package.
b. Implement the package specified in part a.

7.4.3 **a.** For the abstract data type GENERIC_UNBOUNDED_BALKING_QUEUE, specify a generic package.
b. Implement the package specified in part a.

7.4.4 **a.** For the abstract data type GENERIC_BOUNDED_BALKING_DEQUE, specify a generic package.
b. Implement the package specified in part a.

7.4.5 **a.** For the abstract data type GENERIC_UNBOUNDED_BALKING_DEQUE. Specify a generic package.
b. Implement the package specified in part a.

Section 7.5 Priority Queue and Its Variations

7.5.1 For GENERIC_UNBOUNDED_PRIORITY_BALKING_QUEUE as specified in Figure 7.5.7, implement the following operations.

  a. The operation ADD_TO_QUEUE
  b. The operation DEQUEUE
  c. The operation COPY
  d. The operation MERGE
  e. The operation CLEAR
  f. The operation POP
  g. The operation REMOVE_KEY_DATA_BY_KEY
  h. The operation REMOVE_KEY_DATA_BY_LOC
  i. The operation FRONT_PAIR
  j. The operation REAR_PAIR
  k. The operation KEY_POSITION_ON_Q
  l. The operation RETURN_DATA_WITH_KEY_ON_Q
  m. The operation KEY_AT_POSITION_ON_Q
  n. The operation DATA_AT_POSITION_ON_Q
  o. The operation LENGTH
  p. The operation EMPTY
  q. The operation EQUAL
  r. Fully implement GENERIC_UNBOUNDED_PRIORITY_BALKING_QUEUE, combining parts a through n.
  s. For all operations in GENERIC_UNBOUNDED_PRIORITY_BALKING_QUEUE, develop a table of time and space constraints

Section 7.6 Applications

7.6.1 Write a short program that might be used in a doctor's office to keep track of the next patient to be seen.

7.6.2 Modify the program in Exercise 4.5.1 so that the nurse can specify that a patient with a serious need is seen as soon as possible.

7.6.3 In a modern operating system, the computer must maintain a list of free memory. Suppose that a queue of records called FREE_MEMORY, defined as

```
type FREE_MEMORY is
  record
    First_loc,
    Last_loc   : integer;
  end record;
```

is used for this purpose.

  a. Instantiate an abstract data type for this purpose.
  b. Devise a procedure that searches the queue for a block large enough to meet a request and returns a block large enough to meet the request.
  c. Modify the procedure in part b so that only the amount of memory is needed is used and the rest put back on the queue.
  d. Devise a procedure that takes a recently freed block of memory and puts it back on the queue as available. Before the memory is put back on the queue, the queue is searched and contiguous blocks are combined before being put back on the queue.

Section 7.7 Time and Space Constraints

For each of the following problems, develop a time and space constraint table similar to the ones in Section 7.7.

7.7.1 For the ADT developed in Exercise 7.2.1.

7.7.2 For the ADT developed in Exercise 7.2.2.

7.7.3 For the ADT developed in Exercise 7.2.3.

7.7.4 For the ADT developed in Exercise 7.2.4.

7.7.5 For the ADT developed in Exercise 7.3.1.

7.7.6 For the ADT developed in Exercise 7.4.1.

7.7.7 For the ADT developed in Exercise 7.4.2.

7.7.8 For the ADT developed in Exercise 7.4.3.

7.7.9 For the ADT developed in Exercise 7.4.4.

7.7.10 For the ADT developed in Exercise 7.4.5.

Section 7.8 Case Study: Discrete Simulation

7.8.1 Finish implementing Figure 7.7.2 by completing the two IO based procedures.

7.8.2 Modify CASE_STUDY_7 to handle the case where each teller has a separate line. A customer coming into the bank goes to the shortest line.

7.8.3 Modify Exercise 7.7.2 so that there are three tellers, one of whom is a designated "express teller." Any customer whose business can be done in 3 minutes or less goes to the first teller and everyone else goes to either of the other tellers.

PROGRAMMING PROJECTS

P7.1 Specify, implement, and validate a package to do polynomial arithmetic that uses queues. Which type of queue would you use, and why? Your package must be able to handle polynomials of arbitrary degree.

P7.2 Using the ADT GENERIC_UNBOUNDED_PRIORITY_BALKING_QUEUE, redo Projects 2.8.1 to 2.8.4.

P7.3 The "Fly-by-the-Seat-of-Your-Pants" airline pilot school is expanding. They want to implement a class preregistration program on their first computer which was recently acquired at a swap meet. There are 30 classes offered every term, and each class has a maximum enrollment of 30. Students cannot drop until the first day of classes. After registration, a class list of registered students is printed in alphabetical order as well as a list of all students enrolled and the number of classes each is taking. Design and implement a simple class registration program.

NOTES AND REFERENCES

Knuth [27] surveys most of the linear linked representations, as does Booch [8].

8

Trees

In previous chapters, the linked structures were all linear. A linear, or line-like, structure can reference at most one node. In this chapter we introduce the simplest nonlinear structure, the tree. A tree node can be referenced by at most one node, but every tree node can reference many other tree nodes. In Chapter 10, we introduce graphs. A graph node can be referenced by any number of nodes and it can reference any number of nodes.

A *tree* is a collection of nodes where every node but one is referenced by exactly one node. No tree node may reference any predecessor node. Any node may reference any number of other nodes. The node that is not referenced by any other node is called the *root*. A node that does not reference any other nodes is called a *leaf*. A node that is referenced by one node and that references other nodes is called an *interior node*. The number of nodes referenced by a given node is the *degree of the node*. The degree of a tree equals the maximum of the degree of all the nodes in the tree. For any node in the tree, there is a unique path that is to the root. For any two nonroot nodes in the tree one of two situations always occurs. One possibility is that there is a path from one node to the second node that does not go through the root, or there is no path that joins the two nodes. A *null tree* is a tree without any nodes. Figure 8.0.1 illustrates these definitions for a tree of degree 3.

Another common way of describing a node is in family terms. A node is the *parent* of any node that it directly references. The nodes referenced by a particular node are its *children*. The node that directly references a particular node is called the *parent node*. For a particular node, its *descendents* are the set of nodes that can be reached by a path starting at that node. The *ancestors* of a node are all the nodes on the path that join that node to the root of the tree.

For a given node, a *subtree* is the tree formed by using that node as its root. Every node in a tree defines a subtree. The level or depth of a node is the length of the path joining it to the root. The root has depth zero. The height of a tree, subtree, or node is the length of the longest path from that node to any leaf that can be joined to the node (see Figure 8.0.2).

Most of the discussions in this chapter are restricted to binary trees, trees where the maximum degree of any node is 2. The children of a binary node are designated as the *left* and *right children*. This may seem restrictive but it is not. Figure 8.0.3 describes a tree of arbitrary order and its binary representation. The principle behind the conversion is rather simple. The binary tree's right node accesses to a node or sibling that is on the same level. The left node accesses to the leftmost child of the parent. With this convention any tree can be converted to

TREE_ROOT

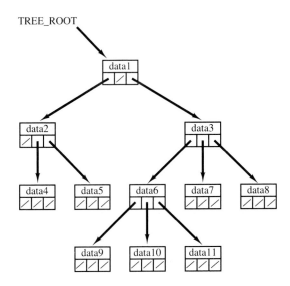

Figure 8.0.1 Tree of degree 3.

BINARY_TREE_ROOT

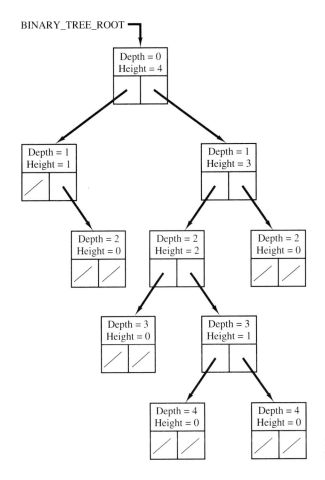

Figure 8.0.2 Height versus depth of a binary tree.

203

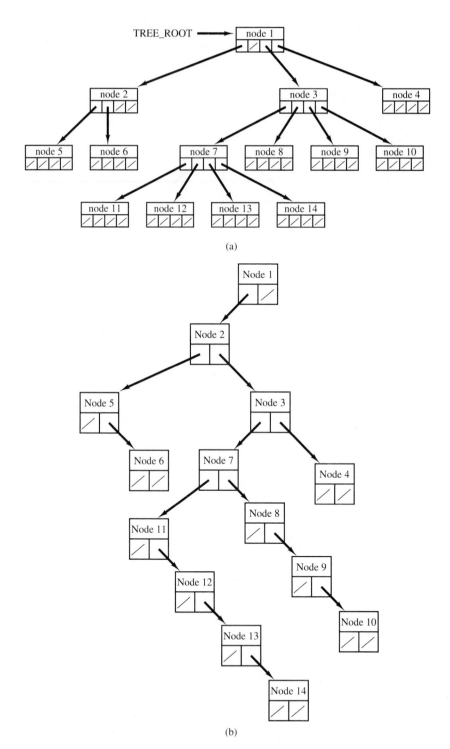

(a)

(b)

Figure 8.0.3 (a) Tree of degree 4. (b) Equivalent binary tree of the tree of order 4 in part (a).

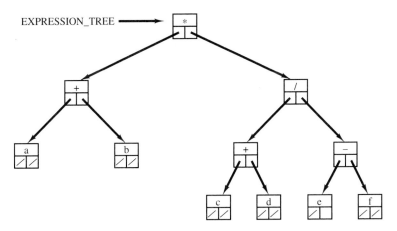

Figure 8.0.4   Binary tree whose inorder traversal yields an expression equivalent to $(a+b)^*\,(c+d)\,/\,(e-f)$.

an equivalent binary tree. Binary trees have a natural use for searching problems. If the item is not stored in a particular node, the nodes on the left subtree (the tree formed by using the left child as a root) have value less than that of the parent. The nodes on the right subtree are greater than the parent node. A traversal of a tree is a listing of the nodes of a tree where every node is visited exactly once. Figure 8.0.4 shows a tree whose inorder traversal yields a valid arithmetic expression. By definition, an inorder traversal is a traversal where the nodes of the left subtree are listed recursively inorder, then the current node is listed, and finally the nodes of the right subtree are recursively listed inorder. If the values in the left subtree all have value less than the value in the root, and if the value in the root is less than all values in the right subtree, an inorder traversal will list all the values in increasing order; that is, the listing is inorder.

Trees are among the most useful data types in computer science. Any application where there is a hierarchal relationship, such as a file system, or a necessity for fast search and access, such as a command interpreter, is a natural candidate for a tree structure. Applications where there is a relationship among three objects, such as the evaluation of a binary expression, are also candidates for a tree representation. These and other applications are explored after the basic data type for a tree is developed.

8.1 BINARY TREES AND THEIR OPERATIONS

The tree is useful only if it contains information. It is assumed that every node has fields that contain information, and possibly a key field for the information field. There is no requirement for the tree or any node to remain fixed or static. In many applications the information contained within nodes is updated. In other applications, nodes are constantly being added and deleted. It is assumed throughout this chapter that the children of the node can be differentiated. With this assumption, the designation of left child and right child is well defined. Binary trees can be built in two ways. One way, the subject of this section, is for the programmer explicitly to build and maintain the tree. The second option, the subject of the remainder of the chapter, is for the ADT to build and maintain the tree. Both have their place, but the second option is much more common.

The structure of all trees in this chapter will take one of four forms, illustrated in Figure 8.1.1. The structures illustrated are all single-link structures. This allows the parent always to reference a child, but not vice versa. A stack can be used if a child must directly access its parent.

```
type TREE_NODE;                     type TREE_NODE;
type TREE is access TREE_NODE;      type TREE is access TREE_NODE;
type TREE_NODE is                   type TREE_NODE is
  record                              record
    ITEM : ITEM_TYPE;                   KEY : KEY_TYPE;
    LEFT,                               ITEM : ITEM_TYPE;
    RIGHT : TREE;                       LEFT,
  end record;                           RIGHT : TREE;
                                      end record;
```

(a)

```
type INDEX_TYPE is                  type INDEX_TYPE is
  (positive range 1.,Size);           (positive range 1..Size);
type TREE_NODE is                   type TREE_NODE is
  ITEM : ITEM_TYPE;                   KEY : KEY_TYPE;
  LEFT,                              ITEM : ITEM_TYPE;
  RIGHT : INDEX_TYPE;               LEFT,
end record;                         RIGHT : INDEX_TYPE;
type TREE is array (INDEX_TYPE)    end record;
    of TREE_NODE;                    type TREE is array
                                              (INDEX_TYPE) of TREE_NODE;
```

(b)

Figure 8.1.1 (a)   Tree structures using access types. (b)   Trees implemented using array types.

Trees implementd using structures with access types are called unbounded and those using array types are called bounded. In all cases the operations that can be performed on trees are similar.

After the basic generic tree package is specified, the type TREE will be limited private. All operations on trees must be performed by the functions and procedures contained in the package. The basic operations performed on a tree are all performed at the root of the tree. This sounds extremely restrictive, but it is not. The nodes of a tree are all accessed though an access type. Any node is the root of some tree or subtree. This is true whether the node is a root node, an interior node, or a terminal node. All nodes are accessed by the type tree. Access to the child of a particular node is accomplished by designating a subtree with the particular child as a root of that subtree. The situation is illustrated in Figure 8.1.2.

What are the basic operations needed to acces and manipulate basic binary trees? Clearing a tree requires that the access value of the root of the tree to be set to null. Since nothing is accessing the root, the root and all its descendants will cease to exist. Copying a tree makes a new distinct tree with copies of the nodes while preserving the hierarchal relationships between the nodes. When a tree is copied, the result has no shared relationships.

There are at least five ways to build or add to a tree. The first is to add a new node that becomes a new root. The old tree becomes either the left or the right child or the new root,

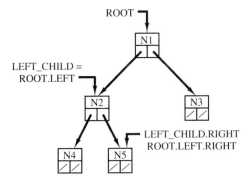

Figure 8.1.2 Access of a tree via identifiers of type tree. Node N1 is accessed via ROOT. Node N2 is accessed via ROOT.LEFT. Node N5 can be accessed either via LEFT_CHILD.RIGHT or by ROOT.LEFT.RIGHT which are the same.

whichever is specified. The second way to add to a tree is to add a node as either a left or right child of the root. The particular access value at the place to be added must be null or an exception results. You cannot place a new node where something already exists. The node that is added cannot have any children. This requires that the new node be a leaf. The third way to build a tree is to add a subtree as either the left or right child of the root. A subtree cannot be added where another nonempty subtree already exists or an exception results. Figure 8.1.3 illustrates each of these three cases. Fourth, it is sometimes necessary to reshape the tree by exchanging children. This procedure requires that two trees, nodes actually, be specified as well as which child of each is to be swapped. The fifth way to add to a tree is to create a node referenced by an access value. Figure 8.1.4 illustrates how adding a subtree to a tree can make the resulting structure that is not a tree. If a subtree is added to itself, a cycle results. It is the programmer's responsibility to avoid this case.

One way of avoiding the problems illustrated in Figure 8.1.4 is not to allow shared nodes. There are many applications where this would be troublesome. Suppose a tree were developed that give the phone numbers for all users whose last name began with A–M and a second similar tree had the numbers of all users whose names began with N–Z. Making up a new root with name Mzzzz and adding the subtrees as shown in Figure 8.1.5 is a simple way of generating a complete list while allowing the maintenance of the subtrees. The alternative is to add to new root for the second list and laboriously copy the first list to the subtree designated by the left child. This can often be wasteful and unneeded.

An operation that creates a node is needed. It returns the data item embedded in a childless node. This procedure is especially useful in adding terminal nodes to a tree. Inserting the created node as a nonterminal node requires the use of one of the procedures to add nodes or subtrees to a tree. Two boolean-valued procedures are needed. One determines whether a tree is null or empty. One use of such a procedure is to determine if a child of a particular node references anything. A second boolean function determines whether two trees are equal. Two trees are equal if and only if both trees have nodes with the same values in them and the hierarchal relationship between nodes is preserved.

Once the tree is built, there must be operations that extract the data from a node or update the data in specified node. Finally, a function is needed that returns the left or right child of a given node as a subtree. The documentation for the ADT UNBOUNDED_BINARY_TREE (Figure 8.1.6) summarizes this discussion.

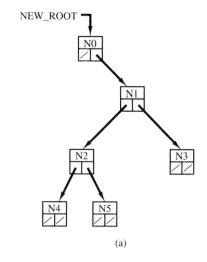

(a)

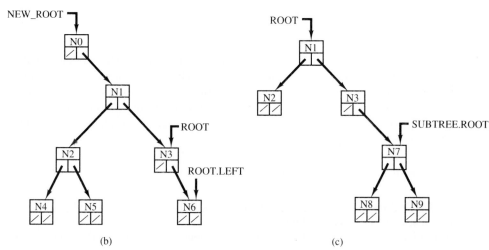

(b)   (c)

Figure 8.1.3(a)   New tree created by adding the tree in Figure 8.1.2 to the new root node NO. (b) By marking node N3 as the root in part (a), the node N6 can be added to the tree. (c) Subtree with nodes N7–N8–N9 is a root1 subtree. Root is added to node N3 of tree with nodes N1–N2–N3.

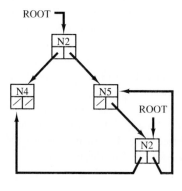

Figure 8.1.4   Subtree N2–N4–N5 accessed by identifier ROOT is added to the left side of node N5. The result is two circular references. The result is not a tree.

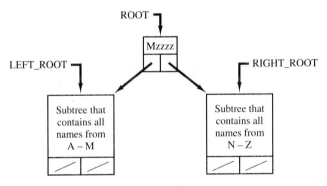

Figure 8.1.5 By adding two subtrees to a node with key = Mzzzz a tree with all nodes is made. The complete tree is accessed through the identifier ROOT, while LEFT_ROOT is used to maintain the subtree containing names beginning with A–M and RIGHT_ROOT is used to maintain the subtree containing names beginnig with N–Z.

GENERAL ADT SPECIFICATION FOR UNBOUNDED_BINARY_TREE

Description

This package implements the ADT UNBOUNDED_BINARY_TREE. A binary tree is a non-linear data structure that preserves a programmer-defined hierarchical relationship between nodes. All nodes but one, called the root, must be referenced by other nodes. Any tree may reference none, one, or two subtrees. If a node is referenced by a tree, it must be referenced as either the "left" or the "right" child. In the discussion that follows a node never has any children. The type tree is implemented as a limited private type and it can only be manipulated by the operations contained in the package.

Programmer-Supplied Data
Structures or Specifications

The programmer must supply a single type ITEM_TYPE which makes up the information contained in each node.

Operations

Name	Description
COPY	Makes exact copy of the given tree that preserves both the content of the given nodes and the hierarchal relationship between nodes.
CLEAR	Returns a tree that contains no nodes.
MAKE_NEW_ROOT	Takes a given tree and a previously defined node with either its left or right fields null and puts the tree as a specified left or right child of child and makes the new node the new root. If the access value of the node where the existing tree is to be placed is not null, an exception is raised.

Figure 8.1.6 Documentation for UNBOUNDED_BINARY_TREE. Continues on page 210.

ADD_CHILD_TO_ROOT	Adds a given node to become the specified child of the root node. If the specified root access value is not null or if the added node has any children, an exception is raised.
ADD_SUBTREE_TO_ROOT	Takes a given subtree to become the specified child of the root node. If the specified root access value is not null, an exception is raised.
SWAP_CHILDREN	Takes a specified child of a specific tree and exchanges it with a specific child of a possibly different second tree.
CREATE_NODE	Takes an object of item_type and returns a node with no children that contains the object.
EMPTY	Boolean-valued function that returns true if the specific tree is empty, or false otherwise.
EQUAL	Boolean-valued function that returns true if two trees are equal, or false otherwise. Two empty trees are equal, as are two trees with the same item in the root and left and right subtrees equal.
RETURN_ITEM	Function that returns the item contained in the root node of the specified tree.
RETURN_SUBTREE	For a specified tree, the specified subtree is returned.
UPDATE	Replaces the current item in the root of a specific tree.

Exceptions

Three exceptions can occur: OVERFLOW, TREE_NOT_NULL, and TREE_NULL. The exception OVERFLOW occurs when an attempt to copy a tree or create a node is made and a storage error is raised. The exception TREE_NOT_NULL occurs in MAKE_NEW_ROOT, ADD_CHILD_TO_ROOT, or ADD_SUBTREE_TO_ROOT when an attempt to insert a node or subtree to a nonnull access value is made or if a node has children. The exception TREE_NULL is raised by ADD_CHILD_TO_ROOT, ADD_SUBTREE_TO_ROOT, SWAP_CHILDREN, RETURN_ITEM, RETURN_SUBTREE, and UPDATE_ITEM when an attempt is made to access any child of a null tree or to return the item from a null root.

Warnings

This package allows shared trees and subtrees. It does not prevent a leaf of a subtree from referencing the root of a subtree creating a cycle. It is the user's responsibility to prevent this.

Figure 8.1.6   Concluded.

The specification of the package for this basic unbounded binary tree is listed in Figure 8.1.7. The TREE_NODE definition is not needed by the package specification, so it was placed in the package body. It could just as easily have been placed in the private part, but it is common practice to hide as much as possible from the package user.

```
generic
  type ITEM_TYPE is private;
package GENERIC_UNBOUNDED_BINARY_TREE is
```

Figure 8.1.7   Specification for GENERIC_UNBOUNDED_BINARY_TREE. Continues on page 211.

```
type TREE is limited private;
type CHILD_TYPE is (LEFT, RIGHT);
procedure CLEAR                  (STUMP      :    out TREE );
procedure COPY                   (FROM       : in      TREE;
                                  TO         : in out TREE );
procedure MAKE_NEW_ROOT          (NODE       : in      TREE;
                                  CHILD      : in      CHILD_TYPE;
                                  ROOT       : in out TREE );
procedure ADD_CHILD_TO_ROOT      (NODE       : in      TREE;
                                  CHILD      : in      CHILD_TYPE;
                                  ROOT       : in out TREE );
procedure ADD_SUBTREE_TO_ROOT (SUBTREE      : in      TREE;
                                  CHILD      : in      CHILD_TYPE;
                                  ROOT       : in out TREE );
procedure SWAP_CHILDREN          (TREE1      : in out TREE;
                                  CHILD_C1 : in      CHILD_TYPE;
                                  TREE2      : in out TREE;
                                  CHILD_C2 : in      CHILD_TYPE);
procedure CREATE_NODE            (ITEM       : in      ITEM_TYPE);
                                  NODE       :    out TREE );
function EMPTY                   (TREE_TO_CHECK : TREE ) return boolean;
function EQUAL                   (TREE_1, TREE_2 : TREE ) return boolean;
function RETURN_ITEM             (NODE : TREE ) return ITEM_TYPE;
function RETURN_SUBTREE          (TREE_ROOT : TREE; C : CHILD_TYPE)return TREE;
procedure UPDATE                 (ITEM       : in      ITEM_TYPE;
                                  NODE       : in out TREE );

  OVERFLOW      : exception;
  TREE_NOT_NULL : exception;
  TREE_NULL     : exception;
private
  type TREE_NODE;
  type TREE is access TREE_NODE;
end GENERIC_UNBOUNDED_BINARY_TREE;

package body GENERIC_UNBOUNDED_BINARY_TREE is

  type TREE_NODE is
    record
      ITEM    : ITEM_TYPE;
      LEFT,
      RIGHT   : TREE;
    end record;
....................
end GENERIC_UNBOUNDED_BINARY_TREE;
```

Figure 8.1.7 Concluded.

The binary guessing game can be used to motivate an application of a tree. Recall that a number must be guessed. All that is initially known is that the unknown number is in a certain interval. The optimum strategy is to guess the midpoint of the interval if it can later be determined that one of three things occurred: the guess was to high, it was too low, or it was correct. If the guess was too high, it follows that the unknown is bounded above by the mid-point, and your next guess should be the midpoint of the lower interval. A similar strategy follows for if the guess was too low.

How does this binary search problem relate to tree? Suppose that a tree is set up with items that can be ordered. Every item that is less than the item in the node is contained in the left subtree. Every item that is greater than the item is contained in the right subtree. Figure 8.1.8 illustrates this situation, where items are integers in the range 1 to 15. Trees such as this are called binary search trees, and they are the subject of the next section. How can such a tree be searched using the functions and procedures in the package GENERIC_UNBOUNDED_BINARY_TREE? Suppose that a program keeps track of the phone directory by using the record type listing defined as

```
type LISTING is
  record
    NAME : NAME_TYPE;
    EXTENSION : EXTENSION_TYPE;
  end record;
```

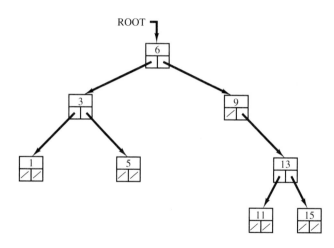

Figure 8.1.8   This binary search tree is a tree organized so that the value in any node of a left subtree is less than the value in the node, while the value in every node in the right subtree is greater than the value in the node.

and that LISTING is instantiated into the package GENERIC_UNBOUNDED_BINARY_TREE. Assuming that a listing with a given name is in the tree; how can the extension Ext be returned? If a tree called PHONE_DIR is set up as outlined above, how would the tree be searched for the extension associated with a given name? (See Figure 8.1.9.)

```
function FIND_EXTENSION (DIRECTORY : return EXTENSION_TYPE is TREE; NAME :
                         NAME_TYPE )
begin
  if RETURN_ITEM(DIRECTORY).NAME = NAME then
    return RETURN_ITEM(DIRECTORY).EXTENSION;
  elsif RETURN_ITEM(DIRECTORY).NAME < NAME then
    return FIND_EXTENSION (RETURN_SUBTREE (DIRECTORY, LEFT), NAME);
  else
```

Figure 8.1.9   Searching a tree. Continues on page 213.

```
        return FIND_EXTENSION (RETURN_SUBTREE (DIRECTORY, RIGHT), NAME);
    end if;
end FIND_EXTENSION;
```

Figure 8.1.9   Concluded.

There is the assumption in FIND_EXTENSION that the operator < is defined for things of NAME_TYPE. The implementation is given in Figure 8.1.10. The statement

```
    return FIND_EXTENSION (RETURN_SUBTREE (DIRECTORY, LEFT), NAME);
```

cannot be replaced by

```
        return FIND_EXTENSION (DIRECTORY.LEFT, NAME);
```

because the type TREE is limited private. The problem of inserting a new listing into PHONE_DIR is handled much the same way. New nodes can only be inserted as the child of a node that has a "null" access value. The tree is traversed recursively until its place is found, and a node is created and inserted. Figure 8.1.10(a) shows the implementation outline, and Figure 8.1.10(b) shows the full implementation.

```
    procedure INSERT_LISTING (DIRECTORY    : in out TREE;
                              NEW_LISTING : in     LISTING ) is
    begin
      if < tree DIRECTORY is null > then
        <insert node containing NEW_LISTING at root>
      elsif < name in NEW_LISTING < name in root node listing > then
        < recursively insert NEW_LISTING into left subtree>
      else
        < recursively insert NEW_LISTING into right subtree >
      end if;
    end INSERT_LISTING;
```
                                    (a)

```
  procedure INSERT_LISTING (DIRECTORY    : in out TREE;
                            NEW_LISTING : in     LISTING ) is
  begin
    if EMPTY (DIRECTORY) then
      CREATE_NODE (NEW_LISTING, DIRECTORY);
    elsif NEW_LISTING.NAME < RETURN_ITEM(DIRECTORY).NAME then
      INSERT_LISTING (RETURN_SUBTREE (DIRECTORY, LEFT), NEW_LISTING);
    else
      INSERT_LISTING (RETURN_SUBTREE (DIRECTORY, RIGHT), NEW_LISTING);
    end if;
  end INSERT_LISTING;
```
                                    (b)

Figure 8.1.10   (a) Implementation outline for INSERT_LISTING. (b) Implementation of INSERT_LISTING.

The functions and procedures in GENERIC_UNBOUNDED_BINARY_TREE are straight forward once the tree structure is understood. The procedures or functions CLEAR, EMPTY, CREATE, RETURN_ITEM, and UPDATE are simple to implement. The procedure

MAKE_NEW_ROOT takes a supplied node and adds the existing tree as a subtree to that node while changing the value of root accordingly.

```
procedure MAKE_NEW_ROOT (NODE      : in     TREE;
                         CHILD     : in     CHILD_TYPE;
                         ROOT      : in out TREE ) is
   -- Takes a given TREE and a previously defined node with either
   -- its left or right fields null and puts the TREE as the specified
   -- child of the ROOT. The new node becomes the new root.
   -- Exception TREE_NOT_NULL raised if the specified child of N is not
   --                         null.
   TEMP : TREE := NODE;
begin
   if CHILD = LEFT then
     if TEMP.LEFT := null then
       TEMP.LEFT   := ROOT;
     else
       raise TREE_NOT_NULL;
     end if;
   else
     if TEMP.RIGHT = null then
       TEMP.RIGHT := ROOT;
     else
       raise TREE_NOT_NULL;
     end if;
   end if;
   ROOT := NODE;
end MAKE_NEW_ROOT;
```

The procedures ADD_CHILD_TO_ROOT and ADD_SUBTREE_TO_ROOT (Figure 8.1.11) are exactly the same except for the conditions that can raise exceptions. Both place either a node or a subtree as a child of the root.

```
procedure ADD_CHILD_TO_ROOT  ( NODE     : in     TREE;
                               CHILD    : in     CHILD_TYPE;
                               ROOT     : in out TREE ) is
   -- Assigns a NODE to become the specified child of the root.
   -- Exception TREE_NOT_NULL raised if the specified child of N is not
   --                         null.
   -- Exception TREE_NULL raised if N is null.
begin
   if NODE = null then
     raise TREE_NULL;
   elsif NODE.LEFT /= null or NODE.RIGHT /= null then
     raise TREE_NOT_NULL;
   elsif CHILD = LEFT then
     if ROOT.LEFT = null then
       ROOT.LEFT := NODE;
```

Figure 8.1.11   Procedures ADD_NODE_TO_ROOT and ADD_SUBTREE_TO_ROOT. Continues on page 215.

```
      else
        raise TREE_NOT_NULL;
      end if;
    else
      if ROOT.RIGHT = null then
        ROOT.RIGHT := NODE;
      else
        raise TREE_NOT_NULL;
      end if;
    end if;
end ADD_CHILD_TO_ROOT;


procedure ADD_SUBTREE_TO_ROOT ( SUBTREE : in      TREE;
                                CHILD   : in      CHILD_TYPE;
                                ROOT    : in out TREE ) is
  -- Assigns a given subtree to be the specified child of the root
  -- Exception TREE_NOT_NULL raised if the specified child of N is not
  --                         null.
  -- Exception TREE_NULL raised if ROOT is null.
begin
  if ROOT = null then
    raise TREE_NULL;
  elsif CHILD = LEFT then
    if ROOT.LEFT = null then
      ROOT.LEFT := SUBTREE;
    else
      raise TREE_NOT_NULL;
    end if;
  else
    if ROOT.RIGHT = null then
      ROOT.RIGHT : = SUBTREE;
    else
      raise TREE_NOT_NULL;
    end if;
  end if;
end ADD_SUBTREE_TO_ROOT;
```

Figure 8.1.11   Concluded.

The procedure COPY and the function EQUAL have a similar implementation. Both operate on the node they are at and then they both recursively operate on the subtrees of the current node. In both cases the null cases are checked first. If T is null and a reference is made to T.LEFT, a constraint error exception will be raised.

```
function TREES_EQUAL (TREE1, TREE2 : TREE ) return boolean is
  -- Returns true if two trees are equal. Two empty trees are
  -- equal, as are two trees with the same items in their
  -- root and their left and right subtrees equal. Both the
  -- structure and the contents must be equal.
begin
```

```
      if TREE1 = null and TREE2 = null then
         return true;
      elsif TREE1 = null xor TREE2 = null then
         return false;
      elsif TREE1.ITEM /= TREE2.ITEM then
         return false;
      else
         return TREES_EQUAL(TREE1.LEFT, TREE2.LEFT) and then
                TREES_EQUAL(TREE1.RIGHT, TREE2.RIGHT);
      end if;
   end TREES_EQUAL;


   procedure COPY ( FROM : in      TREE;
                    TO   : in out TREE ) is
   -- Makes exact copy of the tree FROM that preserves both the
   -- content of the given nodes as well as the hierarchical relationship
   -- between the nodes
   -- Exception OVERFLOW raised if there is not enough memory to complete
   --                    the copy.
   begin
      if FROM = null then
         TO := null;
      else
         TO := new TREE_NODE' (FROM.ITEM, null, null);
         COPY (FROM.LEFT, TO.LEFT);
         COPY (FROM.RIGHT, TO.RIGHT);
      end if;
   end COPY;
```

The operations in the GENERIC_UNBOUNDED_BINARY_TREE are basic building blocks. In most applications the tree has specific behavior and a special abstract data type is created. The need to search and retrieve data efficiently is an application that is often encountered. The solution to this problem is a tree that has an efficient storage structure optimized for searching. This is the subject of the next two sections.

8.2 BINARY SEARCH TREES

The example in Section 8.1 illustrates one of the major applications of binary trees, the application to searching. If a list of the n items is enqueued on a search queue, the average number of compares before a match is found is $n/2$ and the number of compares before it can be determined that the item is not in that queue is n. Even when the n items are enqueued on a priority queue, the average number of compares before a match is found is $n/2$. The priority queue reduces the average number of compares before it can be determined if an item is in a tree to $n/2$. A binary search tree is a tree composed of nodes defined by

```
            type TREE_NODE is
               record
                  KEY      : KEY_TYPE;
```

```
DATA        : DATA_TYPE;
LEFT,
RIGHT       : TREE;
end record;
```

All the keys less than the root node's key appear in the left subtree and all the keys that are greater appear in the right subtree. If an optimal binary search tree is used, the number of possibilities is reduced by half for each compare. The maximum number of compares is the first integer k, where $n <= 2**k$, or $k <= \log_2(n)$ and the average number of compares until a match is found is less than $\log_2(n)$. The situation, using 15 random integers, is illustrated in Figure 8.2.1.

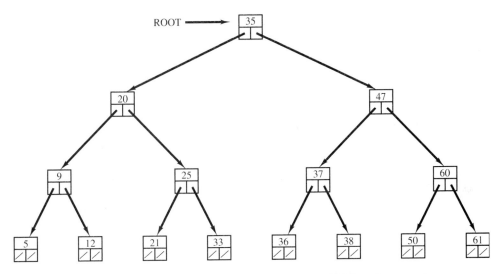

Figure 8.2.1   Binary search tree of random integers organized for optimum search.

The goal of a binary search tree is to minimize the search effort, data retrieval, and data update simultaneously. The underlying search strategy is to cut in half the number of possibilities after each step. This is done by comparing the key being considered with key at the current node. The three possibilities are that the key being considered is less than, equal to, or greater than the key at the current node. The binary search tree is organized in such a way that nodes containing keys that are less than the current node's key are all contained in the left subtree. Nodes containing keys greater than the keys in the current node are located in its right subtree [see Figure 8.2.1].

The functions and operations of a binary search tree assume both the binary structure of the nodes and the organization of the tree. As noted above, the tree is organized so that all keys less than the current node are in the left subtree and those nodes that are greater are in the right subtree. Since a binary search tree is a search structure, each node contains a key-data pair. The key could be a name and the data might be the address of the person whose name matches up the key. To maintain the tree, nodes containing a given key and its data must be available. The documentation for the ADT BINARY_SEARCH_TREE is given in Figure 8.2.2.

GENERAL ADT SPECIFICATION FOR UNBOUNDED_BINARY_ SEARCH_TREE

Description

This package implements the ADT UNBOUNDED_BINARY_SEARCH_TREE. A binary search tree is a binary tree that functions as a search structure. Every node contains a key field as well as a data field to hold data associated with a given key. Key-data pairs are inserted into the tree based on the key. All the keys that are less than the key in a node are in the left subtree of that node and all keys greater the node's key are in its right subtree. Duplicate keys are not allowed. Provisions to search for data based on key value, delete nodes based on key, update nodes based on key, as well as doing an inorder, preorder, and postorder traversal are included.

Programmer-Supplied Data Structures or Specifications

The programmer must supply three parameters: KEY_TYPE, which is used as the object that is searched for or the object on which insertion is based; a DATA_TYPE, which stores the information associated with the key in the node (both the KEY_TYPE and DATA_TYPE are private within the package); and a boolean-valued function <, which determines the ordering of the KEY_TYPE.

Operations

Name	Description
COPY	Makes an exact copy of a specified tree with no shared nodes.
CLEAR	Returns a tree with no nodes.
INSERT	Creates a node containing a given key-data pair and inserts the node into a specified tree while preserving the binary search structure. Automatically resets all the traversals to begin at the first node with respect to that traversal.
DELETE	Deletes a node with a given key from a specified tree while preserving the search structure. Automatically resets all the traversals to begin at the first node with respect to that traversal.
UPDATE	Searches for a node with a specified key in a specified tree and replaces the data field with a new value.
GET_DATA_FOR_KEY	Searches a specified tree for a node with a specified key and returns the associated data field.
COUNT	Natural valued function that returns the number of key-data pairs in the tree.
EMPTY	Boolean-valued function that returns true if a specified tree has no nodes, and false otherwise.

Figure 8.2.2   Documentation for GENERIC_UNBOUNDED_BINARY_SEARCH_TREE. Continues on page 219.

EQUAL	Boolean-valued function that returns true if both trees contain the same key-data pairs, and false otherwise. Trees may have different structures.
KEY_IN_TREE	Boolean-valued function that returns true if a specified tree contains a node with a specified key, and false otherwise.
NEXT_INORDER	Returns the key-data pair of the next node to be processed with an inorder traversal of a specific tree. When the traversal is finished it will start at the beginning. Any insertion or deletion of a node will cause the sequence to be reset to the first node to be processed.
NEXT_PREORDER	Returns the key-data pair of the next node to be processed with an preorder traversal of a specific tree. When the traversal is finished it will start at the beginning. Any insertion or deletion of a node will cause the sequence to be reset to the first node to be processed.
NEXT_POSTORDER	Returns the key-data pair of the next node to be processed with an postorder traversal of a specific tree. When the traversal is finished it will start at the beginning. Any insertion or deletion of a node will cause the sequence to be reset to the first node to be processed.
SET_PREORDER	Sets the traversal sequence to start at the first node normally processed for a preorder traversal.
SET_POSTORDER	Sets the traversal sequence to start at the first node normally processed for a postorder traversal.
SET_INORDER	Sets the traversal sequence to start at the first node normally processed for an inorder traversal.

Exceptions

Four exceptions can occur: OVERFLOW, KEY_NOT_IN_TREE, KEY_IS_IN_TREE, and TREE_IS_EMPTY. The exception OVERFLOW occurs when an attempt to copy a tree or to insert a node with a key-data pair is made and a storage_error is raised. The exception KEY_NOT_IN_TREE occurs in DELETE_NODE, UPDATE_NODE, and GET_DATA_FOR_KEY when a search is made for a node with a given key and the key is not found. The exception KEY_IS_IN_TREE occurs when an attempt is made to insert a node with the same key as a node already in the tree. The exception TREE_IS_EMPTY occurs when any search is made for a key in an empty tree. The three traversal functions NEXT_INORDER_KEY, NEXT_POSTORDER_KEY, and NEXT_PREORDER_TREE also raise TREE_IS_EMPTY when the tree is empty and there is no tree to traverse.

Warnings

All warnings are implementation dependent.

Figure 8.2.2   Concluded.

The data type for a binary search tree is specified in the package GENERIC_UNBOUNDED_BINARY_SEARCH_TREE, which is listed in Figure 8.2.3. Two private formal generic parameters, KEY_TYPE and DATA_TYPE, are programmer supplied at instantiation. Because KEY_TYPE might not be a scalar type, a compare procedure for "less than" must also be programmer supplied for use inside the package body. Since KEY_TYPE and DATA_TYPE are private and not limited private, comparison for equality between KEY_TYPES and DATA_TYPES is already defined inside the package. Note that the data structure for the node is defined inside the package body. The type TREE is limited private, so the only way to access or modify things or type TREE is through the operations in the package.

```
generic
   type KEY_TREE is private;
   type DATA_TYPE is private;
   with function "<" ( LEFT, RIGHT : KEY_TYPE ) return boolean;
package GENERIC_UNBOUNDED_BINARY_SEARCH_TREE is
   type TREE is limited private;
   procedure COPY            (FROM_TREE : in      TREE;
                              TO_TREE   :      out TREE);
   procedure CLEAR           (STUMP     :      out TREE );
   procedure INSERT          (KEY       : in      KEY_TYPE;
                              DATA      : in      DATA_TYPE;
                              INTO_TREE : in out TREE );
   procedure DELETE          (KEY       : in      KEY_TYPE;
                              FROM_TREE : in out TREE );
   procedure UPDATE          (KEY       : in      KEY_TYPE;
                              DATA      : in      DATA_TYPE;
                              IN_TREE   : in      TREE);
   procedure NEXT_INORDER    (KEY       :      out KEY_TYPE;
                              DATA      :      out DATA_TYPE;
                              IN_TREE   : in out TREE);
   procedure NEXT_PREORDER   (KEY       :      out KEY_TYPE;
                              DATA      :      out DATA_TYPE;
                              IN_TREE   : in out TREE);
   procedure NEXT_POSTORDER  (KEY       :      out KEY_TYPE;
                              DATA      :      out DATA_TYPE;
                              IN_TREE   : in out TREE);
   procedure SET_INORDER     (IN_TREE   : in out TREE);
   procedure SET_PREORDER    (IN_TREE   : in out TREE);
   procedure SET_POSTORDER   (IN_TREE   : in out TREE);
   function COUNT            (OF_TREE   : TREE ) return natural;
   function EMPTY            (IN_TREE   : TREE ) return boolean;
   function EQUAL            (T1, T2    : TREE ) return boolean;
   function KEY_IN_TREE      (KEY       : KEY_TYPE;
                              IN_TREE   : TREE ) return boolean;
   function GET_DATA_FOR_KEY (KEY       : KEY_TYPE;
                              FROM_TREE : TREE ) return DATA_TYPE;
   KEY_NOT_IN_TREE : exception;
   KEY_IS_IN_TREE  : exception;
```

Figure 8.2.3 Package GENERIC_UNBOUNDED_BINARY_SEARCH_TREE specification.
Continues on page 221.

```
        TREE_IS_EMPTY   : exception;
        OVERFLOW        : exception;
    private
      type NODE;
      type NEXT is access NODE;
      type TRAVERSAL;
      type NEXT_TRAVERSAL is access TRAVERSAL;
      type TREE is
        record
          ROOT       : NEXT;
          COUNT      : natural := 0;
          NEXT_PRE   : NEXT_TRAVERSAL; --used in NEXT_PREORDER
          NEXT_IN    : NEXT_TRAVERSAL; --used in NEXT_INORDER;
          NEXT_POST  : NEXT_TRAVERSAL; --used in NEXT_POSTERORDER
        end record;
    end GENERIC_UNBOUNDED_BINARY_SEARCH_TREE;


    package body GENERIC_UNBOUNDED_BINARY_SEARCH_TREE is

      type NODE is
        record
          KEY        : KEY_TYPE;
          DATA       : DATA_TYPE;
          LEFT,
          RIGHT      : NEXT;
        end record;

      type TRAVERSAL is
        record
          PROCESS    : NEXT;
          NEXT_PROC  : NEXT_TRAVERSAL;
        end record;
      ..............
    end GENERIC_UNBOUNDED_BINARY_SEARCH_TREE;
```

Figure 8.2.3 Concluded.

Most of the functions and procedures in the package are straightforward in their implementation. Many will be left to the exercises. The procedure INSERT_NODE traverses a tree while maintaining the binary search tree definition. The tree is traversed until a null tree access value is found. Then a node is created and inserted. Figure 8.2.4 lists a recursive and a non-recursive implementation for INSERT_NODE. Both procedures are $O(\log_2(n))$ when the tree is "treelike," but the constant associated with the recursive procedure is larger because it must cover the overhead of recursion. The algorithm is based on a traversal scheme. The access value to the current node is first checked to see if it is null or if its key value equals the passed key. If the access value is null, the new node is inserted. If the access value is not null, the new node must be inserted into either the left or the right subtree. COPY, EQUAL, UPDATE, KEY_IN_TREE, and GET_DATA_FOR_TREE are all implemented in the same manner as INSERT.

```
procedure INSERT    ( KEY      : in    KEY_TYPE;
                      DATA     : in    DATA_TYPE;
                      INTO_TREE : in out TREE ) is
  -- Creates a node containing a given key-data pair and inserts that
  -- node into the tree INTO_TREE while preserving the binary search structure
  -- All traversals are set to begin at the first key-data pair for the
  -- particular traversal
  -- Exception OVERFLOW raised if insufficient memory left to add a node
  -- Exception KEY_IS_IN_TREE raised if an attempt is made to insert a
  --           duplicate key

procedure INSERT    ( KEY      : in    KEY_TYPE;
                      DATA     : in    DATA_TYPE;
                      INTO_TREE : in out NEXT) is
  -- Recursive procedure to insert while preserving the binary search
  -- structure.
begin
  if INTO_TREE = null then
    INTO_TREE := new NODE' (KEY, DATA, null, null);
  elsif INTO_TREE.KEY = KEY then
    Raise KEY_IS_IN_TREE;
  elsif KEY < INTO_TREE.KEY then
    INSERT (KEY, DATA, INTO_TREE.LEFT);
  else
    INSERT (KEY, DATA, INTO_TREE.RIGHT);
  end if;
end INSERT;

begin
  if INTO_TREE.COUNT = 0 then
    INTO_TREE.ROOT :=  new NODE' (KEY, DATA, null, null);
  elsif INTO_TREE.ROOT.KEY = KEY then
    raise KEY_IS_IN_TREE;
  elsif KEY < INTO_TREE.ROOT.KEY then
    INSERT ( KEY, DATA, INTO_TREE.ROOT.LEFT);
  else
    INSERT (KEY, DATA, INTO_TREE.ROOT.RIGHT);
  end if;
  INTO_TREE.COUNT := INTO_TREE.COUNT + 1;
  INTO_TREE.NEXT_IN   := null;
  INTO_TREE.NEXT_PRE  := null;
  INTO_TREE.NEXT_POST := null;
exception
  when storage_error => raise overflow;
end INSERT;

procedure INSERT       ( KEY      : in    KEY_TYPE;
                         DATA     : in    DATA_TYPE;
                        INTO_TREE : in out TREE ) is
procedure Insert   ( KEY      : in    KEY_TYPE;
```

Figure 8.2.4 Listings for INSERT. Continues on page 223.

```
                    DATA       : in      DATA_TYPE;
                    INTO_TREE  : in out NEXT ) is
   TEMP : NEXT := INTO_TREE;
   TSAVE : NEXT;
begin
   if INTO_TREE = null then
      INTO_TREE := new NODE' (KEY, DATA, null, null);
   else
      loop
         exit when TEMP = null;
         If TEMP.KEY < KEY then
            TSAVE := TEMP;
            TEMP := TEMP.RIGHT;
         elsif KEY < TEMP.KEY then
            TSAVE := TEMP;
            TEMP := TEMP.LEFT;
         else
            -- TEMP.KEY= K
            Raise KEY_IS_IN_TREE;
         end if;
      end loop;
      If TSAVE.KEY < KEY then
         TSAVE.RIGHT := new NODE' (KEY, DATA, null, null);
      else
         TSAVE.LEFT := new NODE' (KEY, DATA, null, null);
      end if;
   end if;
end INSERT:

begin
   if INTO_TREE.ROOT = null then
      INTO_TREE.ROOT := new NODE' (KEY, DATA, null, null);
   elsif INTO_TREE.ROOT.KEY = KEY then
      raise KEY_IS_IN_TREE;
   elsif KEY < INTO_TREE.ROOT.KEY then
      INSERT (KEY, DATA, INTO_TREE.ROOT.LEFT);
   else
      Insert (KEY, DATA, INTO_TREE.ROOT.RIGHT);
   end if;
   INTO_TREE.NEXT_IN := null;        --reset traversal to first node
   INTO_TREE.NEXT_PRE := null;
   INTO_TREE.NEXT_POST := null;
   INTO_TREE.COUNT := INTO_TREE.COUNT + 1;
exception
   when storage_error => raise OVERFLOW;
end INSERT;
```

Figure 8.2.4 Concluded.

Whereas nodes can only be inserted as leaves, nodes can be deleted anywhere from a tree. When a node is deleted, the resulting tree must still maintain the hierarchy. In some cases it is easier to shift key-data pairs around. DELETE has four cases. If the node to be deleted is a terminal node, setting the access value to null deletes the node. There are two cases where the node to be deleted has a single child. By redefining the tree node access value of the node to be the access value of the nonnull child, the node is deleted. If the node

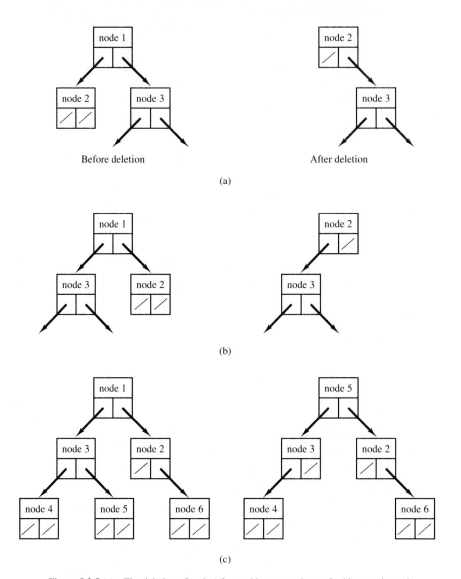

Figure 8.2.5 (a)   The deletion of node 1 from a binary search tree. In this case the node has a single left child. Its field is copied into the old node 1, and then it is deleted. (b) This case is similar to part (a) except that there is a right child with no children. (c) Deletion of a node (node 1) with both subtrees that are not leaves. Note that the rightmost node (node 5) replaces the node to be deleted. The rightmost node of the left subtree has the maximum value in that subtree.

has two children, the node in the left subtree with the largest key is copied into the position of the node to be deleted. The largest key is the one whose key exceeds every other key in the subtree. Figure 8.2.5 illustrates these three cases and Figure 8.2.6 has a recursive implementation of DELETE. The procedure DELETE_LARGEST_KEY deletes the terminal node of a tree with the largest key, and returns the key and the data of that node.

```
procedure DELETE      ( KEY          : in     KEY_TYPE;
                        FROM_TREE    : in out TREE ) is
   -- Deletes a node with a given key from a specified tree while
   -- preserving the search structure. All traversals are
   -- reset to start at the beginning of the particular traversal
   -- Exception KEY_NOT_IN_TREE raised if no node contains specified key.


procedure DELETE_LARGEST_KEY   ( FROM_NODE : in out NEXT;
                                 KEY       :    out KEY_TYPE;
                                 DATA      :    out DATA_TYPE) is
   -- Finds the node with the key, returns the key and data in that
   -- node, and deletes that node
begin
   if FROM_NODE .RIGHT = null then
     -- NODE with the largest key can never have a right subtree
     -- because all keys on the right would be larger
     KEY := FROM_NODE .KEY;
     DATA := FROM_NODE .DATA;
     -- NODE with largest KEY may have LEFT child with smaller keys
     FROM_NODE := FROM_NODE.LEFT;
   else
     -- Nonempty right subtree exists, continue the search
     DELETE_LARGEST_KEY (FROM_NODE.RIGHT, KEY, DATA);
   end if;
end DELETE_LARGEST_KEY;


procedure DELETE      (KEY        : in     KEY_TYPE;
                       FROM_NODE : in out NEXT ) is
   -- Recursive procedure that searches for a node with a
   -- given key and deletes it.
   -- Exception KEY_NOT_IN_TREE raised if key cannot be deleted.
begin
   If FROM_NODE = null then
     raise KEY_NOT_IN_TREE;
   elsif KEY < FROM_NODE.KEY then
     -- Node to be deleted must be in the left side
     DELETE (KEY, FROM_NODE.LEFT );
   elsif FROM_NODE.KEY < KEY then
     -- Node to be deleted must be on the right side
     DELETE (KEY, FROM_NODE.RIGHT);
```

Figure 8.2.6 Procedure DELETE. Continues on page 226.

```
    else
       -- FROM_NODE.KEY = KEY, Node with given key found
       if FROM_NODE.LEFT = null then
          -- no subtree or possibly just a right subtree, so delete
          -- node by changing parents reference. Note that FROM_NODE is
             mode "in out."
          FROM_NODE := FROM_NODE.RIGHT;
       elsif FROM_NODE.RIGHT = null then
          -- Node to delete has a left subtree
          FROM_NODE := FROM_NODE.LEFT;
       else
          -- Node to delete has both left and right subtrees. The deletion must
          -- preserve the search structure. The largest key in the left subtree
          -- will be less then every key in right subtree. Move its
          -- key-data pair to the present node and delete it.
          DELETE_LARGEST_KEY (FROM_NODE.LEFT, FROM_NODE.KEY, FROM_NODE.DATA);
       end if;
    end if;
 end DELETE;


 begin --  beginning of main
   If FROM_TREE.ROOT = null then
     raise KEY_NOT_IN_TREE;
   elsif KEY < FROM_TREE.ROOT.KEY then
     DELETE ( KEY, FROM_TREE.ROOT.LEFT );
   elsif FROM_TREE.ROOT.KEY < KEY then
     DELETE ( KEY, FROM_TREE.ROOT.RIGHT);
   else
      -- FROM_TREE.ROOT.KEY = KEY
      if FROM_TREE.ROOT.LEFT = null then
         -- no children or RIGHT child
         FROM_TREE.ROOT := FROM_TREE.ROOT.RIGHT;
      elsif FROM_TREE.ROOT.RIGHT = null then
         FROM_TREE.ROOT := FROM_TREE.ROOT.LEFT;
      else
         -- FROM_TREE has two non-empty subtrees
          DELETE_LARGEST_KEY
               (FROM_TREE.ROOT.LEFT, FROM_TREE.ROOT.KEY, FROM_TREE.ROOT.DATA);
      end if;
   end if;
   FROM_TREE.COUNT := FROM_TREE.COUNT - 1;
   -- Reset traversal to start at first node of that traversal
   FROM_TREE.NEXT_IN :   = null;
   FROM_TREE.NEXT_PRE :  = null;
   FROM_TREE.NEXT_POST : = null;
 exception
   when KEY_NOT_IN_TREE => raise KEY_NOT_IN_TREE;
 end DELETE_NODE;
```

Figure 8.2.6   Concluded.

This package can be used to build, maintain, and use the binary search tree. One of the common problems of binary trees is the traversal of the tree. A traversal is a visitation of every node in a tree in such a way that each node is visited exactly once. Traversals are defined recursively in terms of processing the current node, processing the node's left subtree, and processing the node's right subtree. There are six different orderings of these three processes, but for reasons lost in history only traversals where the left subtree is processed before the right subtree are considered. The traversals are called the preorder (process the current node, then recursively process its left subtreee, then recursively process its right subtree), the inorder (recursively process the left subtree, process the current node, then recursively process its right subtree), and postorder (recursively process its left subtree, then recursively process its right subtree, and finally process the current node). Figure 8.2.7 shows a simple tree and lists the three traversals of that tree. The three procedures NEXT_INORDER, NEXT_PREORDER, and NEXT_POSTORDER are essentially an incremental inorder, preorder, and postorder traversal.

By definition, the traversal starts at the root of the tree or subtree. If either NEXT_PRE, NEXT_IN, or NEXT_POST are null, the traversal will start at the root of the tree. Once the traversal has begun, it will continue unless it is reset to start again. To reset the traversal is a matter of setting the proper tree field to null. For the inorder traversal, this corresponds to

```
procedure SET_INORDER (IN_TREE : in out TREE) is
   -- Resets the traversal sequence to start at the first node normally
   -- processed for an inorder traversal.
begin
   IN_TREE.NEXT_IN := null;
end SET_INORDER;
```

The inorder traversal is recursively defined as follows:

1. Process the left subtree recursively.
2. Process the node.
3. Process the right subtree recursively.

The algorithm is simple to implement if the subtrees can be accessed. For ease of understanding, suppose that a tree is defined by

```
type TREE_NODE;
type NEXT is access TREE_NODE;
type TREE_NODE is
   X : NODE_DATA;
   LEFT,
   RIGHT : NEXT;
end record;
```

If the procedure PROCESS(T) processes the NODE_DATA in the root node of the tree or subtree, the recursively implemented inorder traversal is given by

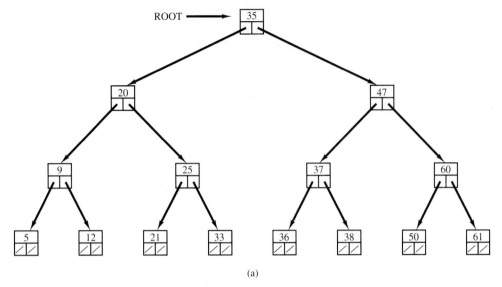

(a)

```
Preorder: Node- Process left subtree- Process Right subtree
35-20-9-5-12-25-21-33-47-37-36-38-60-50-61
Inorder: Process left subtree- Node- Process right subtree
5-9-12-20-21-25-33-35-36-37-38-47-50-60-61
Postorder: Process left subtree- Process Right subtree - Node
5-12-9-21-33-25-20-36-38-37-50-61-60-47-35
```

(b)

Figure 8.2.7   (a) Binary search tree from Figure 8.2.1. (b) Preorder, inorder, and postorder traversals of part (a).

```
Process INORDER_TRAVERSAL (THIS_TREE : in    TREE ) is
begin
   if THIS_TREE /= null then
      INORDER_TRAVERSAL (THIS_TREE.LEFT);
      PROCESS (THIS_TREE);
      INORDER_TRAVERSAL (THIS_TREE.RIGHT);
   end if;
end INORDER_TRAVERSAL;
```

In Chapter 5 it was shown how stacks can be used to eliminate recursion. A stack of trees and subtrees is needed. Define

```
type STACK_NODE;
type STACK is access STACK_NODE;
type STACK_NODE is
   record
      NEXT_TREE  : NEXT;
      STK        : STACK
   end record;
```

Remembering that items pushed on a stack come off the stack in a reverse order, the inorder traversal can be implemented without recursion by pushing the access value of the nodes onto a stack in a manner similar to that shown in Figure 5.4.4.

Since TREE is a limited private type, assignment outside the ADT is not defined. A variable of access type TREE is the only way to access a TREE_NODE. This prohibits a traversal algorithm that is defined outside the package because the nodes of the tree can only be accessed from the body of the package. The solution is to keep three stacks available that can be accessed from inside the package body. The fields NEXT_IN, NEXT_PRE, and NEXT_POST in TREE are stacks to keep track of the progress of the traversal. Instead of doing the entire traversal at once, the operation NEXT_INORDER returns the key-data pair of the next node traversed. This type of operation is called an *iterator*. Repeated calls to an iterator will eventual visit every node in the structure. The implementation of NEXT_INORDER can now be completed.

```
procedure NEXT_INORDER (KEY     :   out KEY_TYPE;
                        DATA    :   out DATA_TYPE;
                        IN_TREE : in out TREE) is
  -- Returns the key-data pair of the next node using an inorder traversal
  -- of IN_TREE. When the traversal has returned the last pair, it starts
  -- again. Any insertion or deletion of a key-data pair causes the traversal
  -- to start at the beginning. An inorder traversal recursively traverses
  -- the left subtree, the current node, then the right subtree.
  -- Exception TREE_IS_EMPTY raised if there is no key-data pair to return
  TEMP : NEXT;
begin
  if IN_TREE.COUNT = 0 then
    -- No key-data pairs to return
    raise TREE_IS_EMPTY;
  end if;
  -- IN_TREE.NEXT_IN is the top of a stack of node pointers. The top of the
  -- stack contains the next key-data pair to return.
  if IN_TREE.NEXT_IN = null then
    -- Stack is null, so must initialize the stack.
    -- The root is pushed onto the stack and all left nodes until a leaf
    -- is found. That leaf contains the first key-data pair.
    IN_TREE.NEXT_IN := new TRAVERSAL' (IN_TREE.ROOT, null);
    TEMP := IN_TREE.ROOT;
    if TEMP /= null then
      loop
        exit when TEMP.LEFT = null;
        IN_TREE.NEXT_IN := new TRAVERSAL' (TEMP.LEFT, IN_TREE.NEXT_IN);
        TEMP := TEMP.LEFT;
      end loop;
    end if;
  end if;
  -- Top of the stack references the node with the next key-data pair to
  -- return
  TEMP    := IN_TREE.NEXT_IN.PROCESS;
  KEY     := TEMP.KEY;
  DATA    := TEMP.DATA;
  -- node has been processed, so pop the stack
  IN_TREE.NEXT_IN := IN_TREE.NEXT_IN.NEXT_PROC;
  -- At this point the node's left subtree and the node have been processed
```

```
      -- so now process the node's right subtree. Stack must be updated
   if TEMP.RIGHT /= null then
      -- There is a right subtree, put its root on the stack.
      IN_TREE.NEXT_IN := new TRAVERSAL' (TEMP.RIGHT, IN_TREE.NEXT_IN);
      TEMP := TEMP.RIGHT;
      -- The leftmost node of the right subtree is the first to be processed
      if TEMP /= null then
         loop
            exit when TEMP.LEFT = null;
            IN_TREE.NEXT_IN := new TRAVERSAL' (TEMP.LEFT, IN_TREE.NEXT_IN);
            TEMP := TEMP.LEFT;
         end loop;
      end if;
   end if;
   -- Note IN_TREE.NEXT_IN points to next node to process, or it is null if the
   -- node returned was the last node in the traversal.
end NEXT_INORDER;
```

The implemenation of the rest of this ADT is left to the exercises.

Under optimal conditions a tree of n nodes will have about $\log_2(n)$ levels. This implies that searching for a node, inserting a node, and deleting a node ought to be $O(\log_2(n))$ also. This follows from the observation that only one compare is done on each level.

A binary search tree can be used to sort a queue. An inorder traversal of a binary tree gives an inorder listing of the key-data pairs in the tree with the ordering based on the key. Consider the following declarations.

```
type LISTING is
   record
      KEY_NAME : string(1..20);
      KEY_DATA : SOME_DATA_TYPE;
   end record;
MY_QUEUE is new package GENERIC_UNBOUNDED_QUEUE(LISTING);
USE MY_QUEUE;
MY_TREE is new package GENERIC_UNBOUNDED_BINARY_SEARCH_TREE
            (string (1..20), SOME_DATA_TYPE, "<" ):
use MY_TREE;
```

Suppose that My_Q is a queue of LISTING. Note that the "<" in the instantiation of MY_TREE is the built-in string operator. The following procedure will sort My_Q.

```
Procedure SORT_Q ( Q : in out Queue) is
   TEMP : TREE;
   T_LIST : LISTING;
   COUNT : natural := LENGTH(Q);
begin
   for INDEX in 1..COUNT loop
      DEQUEUE(T_LIST, Q);
      INSERT (T_LIST.KEY_NAME, T_LIST.KEY_DATA, TEMP);
   end loop;
   for INDEX in natural range 1..COUNT loop
```

```
        NEXT_INORDER(T_LIST.KEY_NAME, T_LIST.KEY_DATA, TEMP);
        ENQUEUE(T_LIST, Q);
    end loop;
end SORT_Q;
```

Another possible application of a binary search tree is the implementation of a command interpreter (Figure 8.2.8). Every operating system has commands such as list the directory, copy files, invoke the debugger, and so on. If the key field is the name of the command and the data field contains address of the desired procedure, a key search of a binary tree would return the address of the procedure to be executed. The exception KEY_NOT_IN_TREE would signal that there was no operating system command of that name in the tree and that the command should be evaluated as a user-defined executable.

```
procedure COMMAND_INTERPRETER (T       : in      TREE
                               COMMAND : in      KEY_TYPE) is
begin
  if KEY_IN_TREE (COMMAND, T) then
    --Get the address of the command and execute it.
    EXECUTE (GET_DATA_FOR_TREE(COMMAND, T));
  else
    Raise KEY_NOT_IN_TREE;
  end if;
end COMMAND_INTERPRETER;
```

Figure 8.2.8 Simple command interpreter.

The package GENERIC_UNBOUNDED_SEARCH_TREE has a possible serious shortcoming. In order to get $O(\log_2(n))$ search performance, the tree must be treelike. Figure 8.2.9(a) shows a treelike tree with 10 random integers as keys. Figure 8.2.9(b) shows what a binary search tree would look like if those same 10 integers were inserted in ascending order. Figure 8.2.9(b) is more queuelike than treelike and its search performance is $O(n)$. Making a tree more treelike is the subject of Section 8.3.

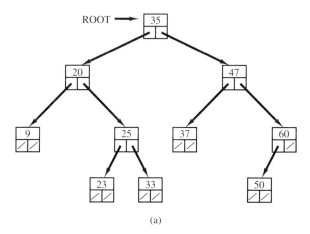

(a)

Figure 8.2.9 (a) Treelike binary search tree with 10 nodes.

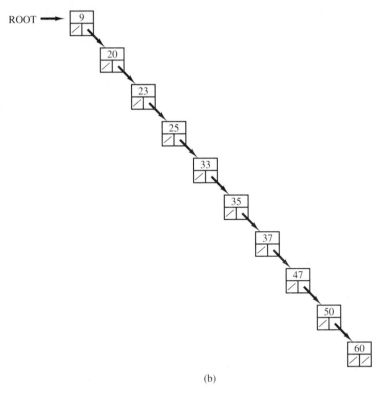

ROOT → 9

20

23

25

33

35

37

47

50

60

(b)

Figure 8.2.9 (b) Queuelike tree of 10 nodes. The inorder traversal of both trees is the same. The different order of node insertion results in a different tree shape. The nodes of this tree were inserted in ascending order.

8.3 BALANCED TREES

The depth of a node is the length of the path joining the root to the node. The root has depth 0 and the root's chlidren have depth 1. In general, the depth of a node is 1 plus the depth of the node's parents. The height of the node is the length of the longest path from that node to the root. Height and depth are different. Figure 8.0.2 illustrated this difference. The function in Figure 8.3.1 computes the height of the node provided that TREE is not a private or limited private type.

```
function HEIGHT (OF_TREE : TREE) return natural is
  HEIGHT_RIGHT, HEIGHT_LEFT : natural;
begin
  If OF_TREE.LEFT = null and OF_TREE.RIGHT = null then
    -- Tree has a single root node or its a leaf
    return 0;
  elsif OF_TREE.LEFT = null then
    -- No left side, so add the height of the right subtree
```

Figure 8.3.1 Function to compute the height of a node. Continues on page 233.

```
        return 1 + HEIGHT(OF_TREE.RIGHT);
   elsif OF_TREE.RIGHT = null phen
      -- No right side, so add the height of the left subtree
      return 1 + HEIGHT (OF_TREE.RIGHT);
   else
      -- Compute the height of the left and right subtrees
      HEIGHT_RIGHT := HEIGHT (OF_TREE.RIGHT);
      HEIGHT_LEFT := HEIGHT (OF_TREE.LEFT);
      -- return the maximum plus 1
      if HEIGHT_LEFT < HEIGHT_RIGHT then
        return 1 + HEIGHT_RIGHT;
      else
        return 1 + HEIGHT_LEFT;
      end if;
   end if;
 end HEIGHT;
```

Figure 8.3.1 Concluded.

A full binary tree of depth k is a tree where every node of depth k is a leaf and every node of depth less than k is a nonterminal node. A full binary tree of depth k is certainly treelike but it also contains exactly $2**(k+1) - 1$ nodes. Each level has a maximum of twice the number of nodes as the preceding level. Since the level containing the root has only one node, it follows that

$$\text{number of nodes} = 1 + 2 + 2**2 + 2**3 + \cdots + 2**k$$

which is a form of the geometric series

$$1 + x + x**2 + x**3 + \cdots + x**n = (x**(n+1) - 1) / (x-1)$$

where $x = 2$. The binary search tree in Figure 8.2.1 is full. Converting a binary search tree to a full binary is doomed to failure unless there are exactly $2**(k+1) - 1$ nodes for some natural number k. A less restrictive tree is a complete tree of level k. A tree of level k is complete if and only if it is either a full binary tree or it falls to be full because there are leaves at the right-hand end of level $k-1$. Complete trees appear to be heavy on the left, as in Figure 8.3.2. Converting a binary tree to a complete tree is still very restrictive. Both full and complete trees are treelike, and both by their shape minimize the search operation. There is still a less shape-restrictive tree that minimizes the search operation. To minimize searching requires that the number of compares be minimized. A nearly full or nearly complete tree will minimize the number of compares.

What is needed is a k-level tree that is full to level $k-2$ and "bushy" at the $k-1$ and k levels. This type of tree would still be "tree-like" so that efficient search is possible (see Figure 8.3.3). A tree is balanced if and only if every node is balanced. A node is balanced if and only if the heights of a node's subtrees differ by at most 1. The examples in Figure 8.2.9(b) do not represent a balanced tree. The definition of a balanced tree can be stated recursively.

A binary tree with 0 nodes is balanced.

A node with a single subtree is balanced if the subtree is a leaf.

A binary tree is balanced if and only if both the left and right subtrees are balanced and their heights differ by at most one.

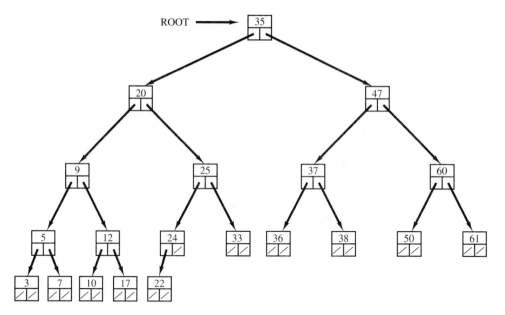

Figure 8.3.2 Complete binary search tree.

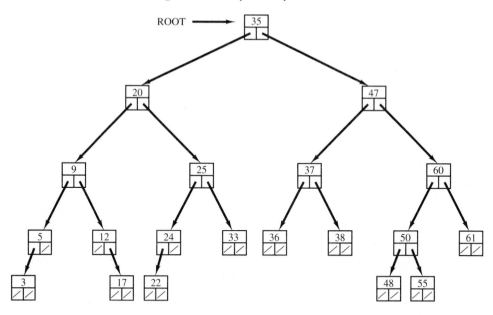

Figure 8.3.3 Balanced binary search tree that is neither full nor complete.

This type of binary search tree is called an AVL tree.

The public part of the package specification for GENERIC_UNBOUNDED_BI-NARY_SEARCH_TREE in Figure 8.2.3 is almost the same when a package GEN-ERIC_UNBOUNDED_BALANCED_BINARY_SEARCH_TREE is developed so that it op-erates like a search-optimized binary tree. Rebalancing the tree does not change the inorder traversal of the tree, but the preorder and postorder traversals are modified. For that reason, the NEXT_PREORDER, SET_PREORDER, NEXT_POSTORDER, and SET_POS-TORDER operations are deleted. The only other difference visible to the programmer in the two packages is that one package builds a balanced tree when items are inserted and maintains the balance when a node is deleted, and the other tree package does not. This requires the modification of the data structure for the node to indicate whether the node's left subtree has height less than, equal to, or greater than the height of the right subtree. A node is LEFT_HEAVY if the height of its left subtree is one higher than the height of the right subtree. A node is IN_BALANCE if the heights of the left and right subtrees are equal. Finally, a node is RIGHT_HEAVY if the right subtree is one higher then the height of the left subtree.

```
type BALANCE_TYPE is (LEFT_HEAVY, IN_BALANCE, RIGHT_HEAVY);

type TREE_NODE is
   record
      KEY      : KEY_TYPE;
      DATA     : DATA_TYPE;
      BALANCE  : BALANCE_TYPE;
      LEFT,
      RIGHT    : NEXT;
   end record;
```

The process of insertion of a node into a binary search tree consists of three steps:

1. Follow the search path until it is verified that the key is not in the tree.
2. Insert the new node and set its balance factor to IN_BALANCE.
3. Retreat along the search path and check the balance factor at each node, rebalancing if necessary.

The third step of the process is easily implemented by using recursion. All that is required is that a boolean variable be passed back to the calling procedure to indicate if the subtree height has been increased. If there has been no change in height of a subtree, the balance of the parent has not been altered. There are three possibilities (see Figure 8.3.4).

Case	Result If Node Inserted on the Left	Result if Node Inserted on the Right
RIGHT_HEAVY	Balance restored	Rebalancing necessary
IN_BALANCE	Balance now LEFT_HEAVY	Balance now RIGHT_HEAVY
LEFT_HEAVY	Rebalancing necessary	Now IN_BALANCE

Figure 8.3.4   Height rebalancing criteria for inserting nodes.

Each of the two rebalancing situations has two possibilities, so four cases must be considered. In the diagrams below, the nodes are represented by circles and balanced subtrees are represented by rectangles. The height of the rectangle represents the height of the subtree. Remember that a balanced subtree's root can be LEFT_HEAVY, RIGHT_HEAVY, or IN_BALANCE. A left rotation takes a left heavy subtree that has had a node added on its left and rotates it in a clockwise rotation to achieve balance. In the simplest case, the balanced node T is LEFT_HEAVY and then a node is inserted on T's balanced left subtree. This insertion causes the left subtree of T to become LEFT_HEAVY while forcing the subtree T to go out of balance [see Figure 8.3.5(a)]. After a SINGLE_LEFT_ROTATION, the subtree is balanced.

```
procedure SINGLE_LEFT_ROTATION (THIS_NODE : in out NEXT) is
   -- Situation as illustrated in Figure 8.3.5(a) where T = THIS_NODE,
   -- and T1 = TEMP_NODE
   TEMP_NODE : NEXT := THIS_NODE.LEFT;
begin
   THIS_NODE.LEFT := TEMP_NODE.RIGHT;
   THIS_NODE.BALANCE := IN_BALANCE;
   TEMP_NODE.RIGHT := THIS_NODE;
   THIS_NODE := TEMP_NODE;
   THIS_NODE.BALANCE := IN_BALANCE;
   -- Situation now as in Figure 8.3.5(b)
end SINGLE_LEFT_ROTATION;
```

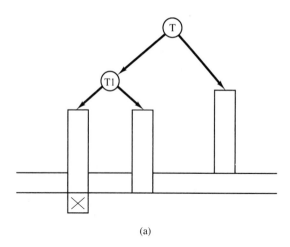

(a)

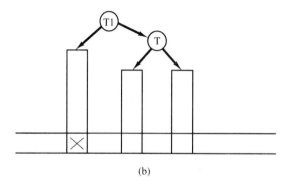

(b)

Figure 8.3.5 (a) Originally, node T was LEFT_HEAVY and node T1 was IN_BAL-ANCE. Adding a node to the left subtree of node T1 makes T1 LEFT_HEAVY and makes T out of balance. (b) Nodes T and T1 are both IN_BALANCE after a SINGLE_LEFT_ROTATION is applied to part (a).

The SINGLE_RIGHT_ROTATION is the mirror-image of the SINGLE_LEFT_RO-TATION case. Consider Figure 8.3.6(a). Before insertion the node T was RIGHT_HEAVY, while T's right subtree is IN_BALANCE. After insertion T's right subtree goes from IN_BALANCE to RIGHT_HEAVY. This throws T out of balance. The operation SINGLE_RIGHT_ROTATION restores the balance of both T and its right subtree T1. The result is shown in Figure 8.3.6.

```
procedure SINGLE_RIGHT_ROTATION (THIS_NODE : in out NEXT) is
   -- Situation as in Figure 8.3.6(a) where THIS_NODE = T and
   -- TEMP_NODE = T1.
   TEMP_NODE : NEXT := THIS_NODE.RIGHT
begin
   THIS_NODE.RIGHT := TEMP_NODE.LEFT;
   THIS_NODE.BALANCE := IN_BALANCE;
   TEMP_NODE.LEFT := THIS_NODE;
   THIS_NODE := TEMP_NODE;
   THIS_NODE.BALANCE := IN_BALANCE;
   -- Situation now as in Figure 8.3.6(b)
end SINGLE_RIGHT_ROTATION;
```

The third possibility is illustrated in Figure 8.3.7. Node T is LEFT_HEAVY and T1, T's left subtree, is IN_BALANCE. A node is added to T2, the right subtree of T1. T1 becomes

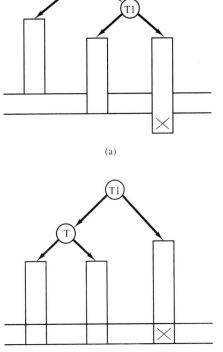

(a)

(b)

Figure 8.3.6 (a) Node T if RIGHT_HEAVY while node T1 is IN_BALANCE before a node is added to the right subtree of T1. The result is that node T1 is RIGHT_HEAVY and node T is out of balance. (b) After a SINGLE_RIGHT_ROTATION of part (a), both nodes T and T1 are IN_BALANCE.

LEFT_HEAVY, which makes T out of balance. See Figure 8.3.7(a) for one possiblity. (The other possiblity is if the node is added on T2's right subtree.) A right rotation is first performed on T1, the left subtree of T. The result is illustrated in Figure 8.3.7(b). This is followed by a single left rotation on node T, which results in Figure 8.3.7(c). This process is called a DOUBLE_LEFT_RIGHT_ROTATION.

```
procedure DOUBLE_LEFT_RIGHT_ROTATION (THIS_NODE : in out NEXT) is
  -- Situation as in Figure 8.3.7(a) with THIS_NODE = T,
  -- TEMP_NODE_1 = T1 and TEMP_NODE_2 = T2.
  TEMP_NODE_1 : NEXT := THIS_NODE.LEFT;
  TEMP_NODE_2 : NEXT := THIS_NODE.LEFT.RIGHT;
begin
  -- Do a right rotation on TEMP_NODE_1
  TEMP_NODE_1.RIGHT := TEMP_NODE_2.LEFT;
  TEMP_NODE_2.LEFT := TEMP_NODE_1;
  THIS_NODE.LEFT := TEMP_NODE_2;
  if TEMP_NODE_2.BALANCE = LEFT_HEAVY then
    -- as illustrated in Figure 8.3.7(a) with T2 LEFT_HEAVY
    TEMP_NODE_1.BALANCE := IN_BALANCE;
  else
    -- Other possibility not shown in Figure 8.3.7(a) is T2 RIGHT_HEAVY
    TEMP_NODE_1.BALANCE := LEFT_HEAVY;
  end if;
  -- Situation now as in Figure 8.3.7(b), do a left rotation on THIS_NODE.
  THIS_NODE.LEFT := TEMP_NODE_2.RIGHT;
  TEMP_NODE_2.RIGHT := THIS_NODE;
  TEMP_NODE_2.BALANCE := IN_BALANCE;
  if TEMP_NODE_1.BALANCE = IN_BALANCE then
    THIS_NODE.BALANCE := RIGHT_HEAVY;
  else
    THIS_NODE.BALANCE := IN_BALANCE;
  end if;
  TEMP_NODE_2.BALANCE := IN_BALANCE;
  -- Situation as in Figure 8.3.7(c).
  THIS_NODE := TEMP_NODE_2;
end DOUBLE LEFT_RIGHT_ROTATION;
```

The final case discussed is illustrated in Figure 8.3.8. Node T is RIGHT_HEAVY with a right subtree T1 that is balanced. The left subtree T2 of T1 is IN_BALANCE. A node is added to either the left or the right subtree of T2. This makes the subtree T2 either RIGHT_HEAVY or LEFT_HEAVY. The LEFT_HEAVY case is shown in Figure 8.3.8(a). Node T1 is now LEFT_HEAVY and node T is now out of balance. A single left rotation is applied to T1, resulting in Figure 8.3.8(b). After applying a right rotation to node T, balance is restored. The result, called a DOUBLE_RIGHT_LEFT_ROTATION, is shown in Figure 8.3.8(c).

```
procedure DOUBLE_RIGHT_LEFT_ROTATION (THIS_NODE : in out NEXT) is
  -- Situation illustrated in Figure 8.3.8 with THIS_NODE = T,
  -- TEMP_NODE_1 = T1, and TEMP_NODE_2 = T2
  TEMP_NODE_1 : NEXT := THIS_NODE.RIGHT;
```

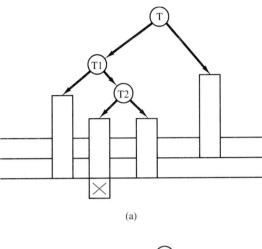

(a)

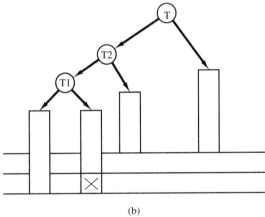

(b)

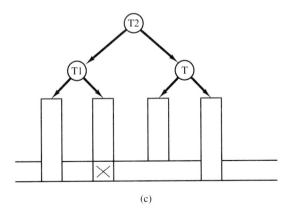

(c)

Figure 8.3.7 (a) Before insertion, nodes T1 and T2 are IN_BALANCE while node T is LEFT_HEAVY. After a new node is inserted on the left subtree of T2, node T2 is LEFT_HEAVY, node T1 is RIGHT_ HEAVY, and node T is out of balance. (b) The subtree T in part (a) is converted to an intermediate form by performing a SINGLE_RIGHT_ROTATION of node T1. Node T1 is IN_BALANCE but nodes T and T2 are out of balance. (c) The subtree T in part (b) is converted to a balanced form by performing a SINGLE_LEFT_ROTATION on node T. The result is called a DOUBLE_LEFT_RIGHT_ROTATION.

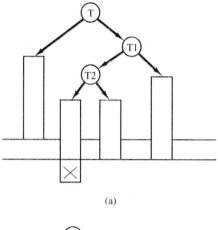

(a)

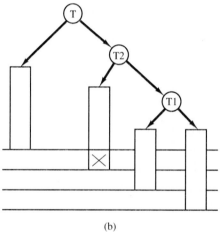

(b)

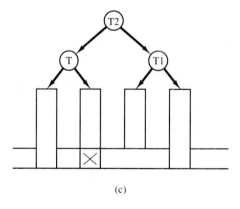

(c)

Figure 8.3.8 (a) Node is added to the left subtree of T2. The result is that nodes T1 and T2 are LEFT_HEAVY and node T is out of balance. (b) The result of part (a) after a SINGLE_LEFT_ROTATION on T1. Node T1 is LEFT_HEAVY but nodes T and T2 are out of balance (c) After performing a SINGLE_RIGHT_ROTATION on node T, balance is restored. Nodes T2 and T become IN_BALANCE while node T1 is RIGHT_HEAVY. The result is called a DOUBLE_RIGHT_LEFT_ROTATION.

```
      TEMP_NODE_2 : NEXT := THIS_NODE.RIGHT.LEFT;
   begin
      -- Start out with situation in Figure 8.3.8(a). Do a left rotation
      -- on TEMP_NODE_1
      TEMP_NODE_1.LEFT := TEMP_NODE_2.RIGHT;
      TEMP_NODE_2.RIGHT := TEMP_NODE_1;
      THIS_NODE.RIGHT := TEMP_NODE_2;
      if TEMP_NODE_2.BALANCE = LEFT_HEAVY then
        TEMP_NODE_1 := RIGHT_HEAVY;
      else
        TEMP_NODE_1 := IN_BALANCE;
      end if;
      -- Situation now as in Figure 8.3.8(b). Now do a Right rotation
      THIS_NODE.RIGHT := TEMP_NODE_2.LEFT;
      TEMP_NODE_2 := THIS_NODE;
      if TEMP_NODE_1.BALANCE then
         THIS_NODE.BALANCE := IN_BALANCE;
      else
         THIS_NODE_2.BALANCE := LEFT_HEAVY;
      end if;
      TEMP_NODE_2.BALANCE := IN_BALANCE;
      -- Situation now as in Figure 8.3.8(c).
      THIS_NODE := TEMP_NODE_2;
   end DOUBLE_RIGHT_LEFT_ROTATION;
```

The insert algorithm can now be outlined easily. The variable REBALANCE_FLAG in the inside procedure INSERT is a boolean variable that indicates whether the subtree's balance has been changed. It is used to signal to a node's parents that the height of a node has been changed and that rebalancing may be necessary.

The Insertion procedure uses recursion (Figure 8.3.9). After a leaf node has been inserted, the rebalance flag is set to true, indicating that its parent's balance must be changed. This process continues until either the root is reached or an intermediate node's balance is unchanged.

```
   procedure INSERT            (KEY       : in      KEY_type;
                               DATA      : in      DATA_type;
                               INTO_TREE : in out TREE) is
   -- Creates a node containing a given key-data pair and inserts that
   -- node into the tree T while preserving the binary search structure
   -- The inorder traversals is set to begin at the first key-data pair.
   -- After insertion, the tree is rebalanced if necessary.
   -- Exception OVERFLOW raised if insufficient memory left to add a node
   -- Exception KEY_IS_IN_TREE raised if an attempt is made to insert a
   --                           duplicate key

   REBALANCE_FLAG : boolean := false; -- Signals if node's balance has
                                      -- changed
```

Figure 8.3.9 Procedure INSERT in a GENERIC_UNBOUNDED_BINARY_SEARCH_TREE.
Continues on page 242.

```
      procedure INSERT (KEY              : in    KEY_TYPE;
                        DATA             : in    DATA_TYPE;
                        INTO_SUBTREE     : in out NEXT;
                        REBALANCING_FLAG : in out boolean) is
begin
  if INTO_SUBTREE = null then
    -- At the leaf, so insert an IN_BALANCE leaf.
    INTO_SUBTREE := new TREE_NODE' (KEY, DATA, IN_BALANCE, null, null);
    -- Height of the parent has been changed, set REBALANCE_FLAG
    REBALANCE_FLAG := true;
  elsif KEY < INTO_TREE.KEY then
    INSERT (KEY, DATA, INTO_SUBTREE.LEFT, REBALANCE_FLAG);
    if REBALANCE_FLAG then
      -- Subtree balance altered because the left subtree height increased
      case INTO_SUBTREE.BALANCE is
        when LEFT_HEAVY =>
          -- Current node was LEFT_HEAVY before insertion, situation now
          -- same as illustrated in Figure 8.3.5(a) or 8.3.7(a)
          if INTO_SUBTREE.LEFT.BALANCE = LEFT_HEAVY then
            -- The left child's left child is also left heavy, situation
            -- same as in Figure 8.3.5(a). Single left rotation needed
            SINGLE_LEFT_ROTATION (INTO_SUBTREE);
          else
            -- Left subtree is now right heavy, see Figure 8.3.7(a)
            DOUBLE_LEFT_RIGHT_ROTATION (INTO_SUBTREE);
          end if;
          -- Rebalancing now complete. Resulting node is IN_BALANCE
          -- No further rebalancing needed.
          REBALANCE_FLAG := false;
        when IN_BALANCE =>
          -- Present node was IN_BALANCE before insertion, its left subtree
          -- had its height increased. Balance is now LEFT_HEAVY.
          --  Rebalancing still necessary so REBALANCE_FLAG not changed.
          INTO_SUBTREE.BALANCE := LEFT_HEAVY;
        when RIGHT_HEAVY =>
          -- Present node was RIGHT_HEAVY, left subtree depth increased,
          -- Result is that node is IN_BALANCE, no further rebalancing
          -- is necessary as its depth has not been changed
          INTO_SUBTREE.BALANCE := IN_BALANCE;
          REBALANCE_FLAG := false;
      end case;
    end if;
  elsif INTO_SUBTREE.KEY < KEY then
    INSERT (KEY, DATA, INTO_SUBTREE.RIGHT, REBALANCE_FLAG);
    if REBALANCE_FLAG then
      case T.BALANCE is
```

Figure 8.3.9 Continues on page 243.

```
      when LEFT_HEAVY =>
        -- Present node was LEFT_HEAVY before insertion. Now that right
        -- subtree has had its height increased, node becomes balanced
        -- and no further rebalancing necessary
        INTO_SUBTREE.BALANCE := IN_BALANCE;
        REBALANCE_FLAG := false;
      when IN_BALANCE =>
        -- Present node was IN_BALANCE but its right subtree height
        -- increased, so node is now RIGHT_HEAVY, its height increased,
        -- so further rebalancing still necessary.
        INTO_SUBTREE.BALANCE := RIGHT_HEAVY;
      when RIGHT_HEAVY =>
        -- Present node was right heavy before insertion and now
        -- the right subtree height has increased. Situation same as
        -- illustrated in Figure 8.3.6(a) or 8.3.8.
        if INTO_SUBTREE.RIGHT.BALANCE = RIGHT_HEAVY then
          -- INTO_SUBTREE'S Right subtree is now RIGHT_HEAVY,
          -- see Figure 8.3.6(a). SINGLE_RIGHT_ROTATION NEEDED.
          SINGLE_RIGHT_ROTATION (INTO_SUBTREE);
        else
          -- The right subtree of INTO_SUBTREE left subtree height has
          -- increased, see Figure 8.3.8. DOUBLE_RIGHT_LEFT_ROTATION
          -- required. Result is a node IN_BALANCE without height of
          -- the subtree being changed. No further rebalancing needed
          DOUBLE_RIGHT_LEFT_ROTATION (INTO_SUBTREE);
        end if;
        REBALANCE_FLAG := false;
      end case;
    end if;
  else
    -- INTO_SUBTREE.KEY = KEY
    raise KEY_IS_IN_TREE;
  end if;
end INSERT;


begin -- main
  INSERT (KEY, DATA, INTO_TREE.ROOT, REBALANCE_FLAG);
  INTO_TREE.COUNT := INTO_TREE.COUNT + 1;
  INTO_TREE.NEXT_IN := null;
exception
  when KEY_IS_IN_TREE => raise KEY_IS_IN_TREE;
end INSERT;
```

Figure 8.3.9 Concluded.

The only other procedure affected by the balancing is DELETE. The deletion of a node is simple provided that the node has either no or one child. If it has two children the largest node in the left subtree is copied into the node to be deleted and then deleted.

The delete procedure is recursive. Just as in the case for inserting a node, a boolean variable is added to the delete procedure to indicate if the node's height has been reduced. This indicates that the parent node needs to be rebalanced after its child is itself rebalanced. If the flag is true, rebalancing must be considered. The flag is set to true if either a node is deleted or if rebalancing of a subtree has reduced the height of that subtree.

The procedure DELETE uses two procedures, BALANCE_RIGHT and BALANCE_LEFT (Figure 8.3.10). They are symmetric. By interchanging the words right and left, BALANCE_RIGHT becomes BALANCE_LEFT, and vice versa. BALANCE_RIGHT is applied to a node when the right subtree has had its height reduced.Similarly, BALANCE_LEFT is applied to a node when its left subtree has had its height reduced.

```
procedure DELETE  (KEY       : in     KEY_TYPE;
                   FROM_TREE : in out TREE ) is
-- Deletes a node with a given key from FROM_TREE while
-- preserving the search structure. The inorder traversal is
-- reset to start at the beginning. The tree is rebalanced if necessary
-- Exception KEY_NOT_IN_TREE raised if no node contains specified key.

REBALANCE_FLAG : boolean := false;

   Procedure Delete (KEY            :in KEY_TYPE;
                     FROM_SUBTREE   :in out NEXT;
                     REBALANCE_FLAG :in out boolean) is

   procedure DELETE_LARGEST_KEY ( FROM_SUBTREE   : in out NEXT;
                                  KEY            :     out KEY_TYPE;
                                  DATA           :     out DATA_TYPE;
                                  REBALANCE_FLAG : in out boolean) is
   -- Finds the node with the key, returns the key and data in that
   -- node, and deletes that node
   begin
     if FROM_SUBTREE.RIGHT = null then
       -- Node with the largest key can never have a right subtree
       -- because all keys on the right would be larger
       KEY := FROM_SUBTREE.KEY;
       DATA := FROM_SUBTREE.DATA;
       -- Node with largest key may have left child
       FROM_SUBTREE := FROM_SUBTREE.LEFT;
       -- Signal balance has changed because node deleted
       -- See Figure 8.3.12(a)
       REBALANCE_FLAG := true;
     else
       DELETE_LARGEST_KEY (FROM_SUBTREE.RIGHT, KEY, DATA, REBALANCE_FLAG);
       if REBALANCE_FLAG then
         BALANCE_RIGHT (FROM_SUBTREE, REBALANCE_FLAG);
       end if;
```

Figure 8.3.10   Procedure DELETE. Continues on page 245.

```
        end if;
      end DELETE_LARGEST_KEY;


  begin --  DELETE
    If FROM_SUBTREE = null then
      raise KEY_NOT_IN_TREE;
    elsif KEY < FROM_SUBTREE.KEY then
      DELETE (KEY, FROM_SUBTREE.LEFT, REBALANCE_FLAG);
      -- If balance of the left subtree has changed, must balance the left
      if REBALANCE_FLAG then
        BALANCE_LEFT (FROM_SUBTREE, REBALANCE_FLAG);
      end if;
    elsif FROM_SUBTREE.KEY < KEY then
      DELETE (KEY, FROM_SUBTREE.RIGHT, REBALANCE_FLAG);
      -- If balance of the right subtree has changed, must balance the right
      if REBALANCE_FLAG then
        BALANCE_RIGHT (FROM_SUBTREE, REBALANCE_FLAG);
      end if;
    else
      -- FROM_SUBTREE.KEY = KEY
      if FROM_SUBTREE.LEFT = null then
        -- Because FROM_SUBTREE is balanced,FROM_TREE either has no children
        -- or a single right child
        FROM_SUBTREE := FROM_SUBTREE.RIGHT;
        REBALANCE_FLAG := true;
      elsif FROM_SUBTREE.RIGHT = null then
        -- FROM_SUBTREE has a single left child
        FROM_SUBTREE := FROM_SUBTREE.LEFT;
        REBALANCE_FLAG := true;
          else
        -- T has two children
        DELETE_LARGEST_KEY (FROM_SUBTREE.LEFT,
                      FROM_SUBTREE.KEY, FROM_SUBTREE.DATA, REBALANCE_FLAG);
        -- The left subtree may have had its balance altered
        if REBALANCE_FLAG then
          BALANCE_LEFT (FROM_SUBTREE, REBALANCE_FLAG);
        end if;
      end if;
    end if;
  end DELETE;


begin --  DELETE_NODE
  DELETE (KEY, FROM_TREE.ROOT, REBALANCE_FLAG);
  FROM_TREE.COUNT := FROM_TREE.COUNT - 1;
  FROM_TREE.NEXT_IN := null;
exception
  when KEY_NOT_IN_TREE => raise KEY_NOT_IN_TREE;
end DELETE;
```

Figure 8.3.10 Concluded.

The only task that remains to be done is to develop BALANCE_LEFT and BAL-
ANCE_RIGHT. The situation is just the reverse of inserting a node. Now the balance is altered when a node is deleted from the tree. Figure 8.3.5 becomes Figure 8.3.11.

Case	Result if Node Deleted from the Left	Result if Node Deleted from the Right
RIGHT_HEAVY	Rebalancing necessary	Balance restored
IN_BALANCE	Balance now RIGHT_HEAVY	Balance now LEFT_HEAVY
LEFT_HEAVY	Balance restored	Rebalancing necessary

Figure 8.3.11   Height rebalancing criteria for deleted nodes.

BALANCE_LEFT is applied when the left branch has shrunk. If the left branch's right subtree was RIGHT_HEAVY, rebalancing is necessary. The situation in Figure 8.3.12(a) could
occur, in which case a SINGLE_RIGHT_ROTATION will put the tree back in balance as
in Figure 8.3.12(b). Or the situation could be as in Figure 8.3.12(c), which requires a
DOUBLE_RIGHT_LEFT_ROTATION to restore the balance. BALANCE_LEFT is listed in
Figure 8.3.13.

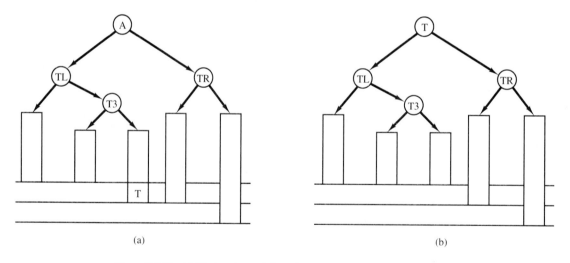

(a)   (b)

Figure 8.3.12   (a) The key-data pair in node A is to be deleted. Note that nodes A, TL, TR, and T3
are all RIGHT_HEAVY. To delete the key-data pair in node A, the right most node in node A's left
subtree (the key-data pair in node T) is copied into node A and the old node T is deleted. See the result in part (b). (b) To delete the key-data pair in node A, the key-data pair in node T is copied into
node T and the old node T replaces node A. Node T is now out of balance. The situation is the same
as in Figure 8.3.6(a). Node T is balanced by SINGLE_RIGHT_ROTATION.

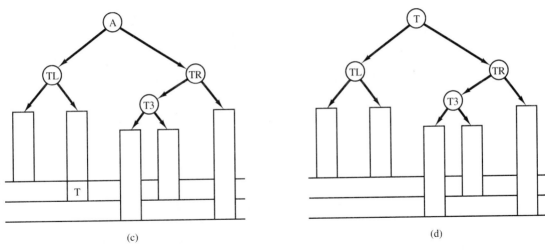

(c)   (d)

Figure 8.3.12 (c) Nodes A and TL are RIGHT_HEAVY, node TR is IN_BALANCE, and node
T3 is LEFT_HEAVY. When the key-data pair in node A is deleted, the key-data pair in T is copied
into node A and the old node T is deleted. The result is shown in part (d). (d) Node TL is now
IN_BALANCE and node T is out of balance. Noting that subtree TL is IN_BALANCE, the situation
is the same as in Figure 8.3.8(a). A DOUBLE_RIGHT_LEFT_ROTATION restores the balance.

```
procedure BALANCE_LEFT     (THIS_NODE  : in out NEXT;
                            BALANCE_FLAG:   out boolean ) is
  -- A node was deleted out of left subtree of T, and the height
  -- reduced. BALANCE_LEFT will rebalance.
  THIS_NODE_RIGHT : NEXT := THIS_NODE.RIGHT;
  THIS_NODE_LEFT : NEXT;
  SUBTREE_BALANCE : BALANCE_TYPE := THIS_NODE_RIGHT.BALANCE;

begin
  case THIS_NODE.BALANCE is
    when LEFT_HEAVY =>
      -- THIS_NODE was LEFT_HEAVY before the deletion, and left subtree
      -- has had its height reduced, so THIS_NODE must be in balance
      THIS_NODE.BALANCE := IN_BALANCE;
    when IN_BALANCE =>
      -- THIS_NODE was IN_BALANCE before the deletion, and left subtree
      -- has had its height reduced, so THIS_NODE is RIGHT_HEAVY and its
      -- height has not been changed.
      THIS_NODE.BALANCE := RIGHT_HEAVY;
      BALANCE_FLAG := false;
    when RIGHT_HEAVY =>
      -- THIS_NODE was RIGHT_HEAVY before deletion and the height of its
      -- left subtree has been reduced, so THIS_NODE is out of balance
      if SUBTREE_BALANCE /= LEFT_HEAVY then
        -- Right subtree is not LEFT_HEAVY, see Figure 8.3.12(b)
```

Figure 8.3.13 Procedure BALANCE_LEFT. Continues on page 248.

```
        -- where THIS_NODE = T, THIS_NODE_RIGHT = TR, A
        -- SINGLE_RIGHT_ROTATION on THIS_NODE restores balance
        -- SINGLE_RIGHT_ROTATION (THIS_NODE);
        THIS_NODE.RIGHT := THIS_NODE_RIGHT.LEFT;
        THIS_NODE_RIGHT.LEFT := THIS_NODE;
        if SUBTREE_BALANCE = IN_BALANCE then
            -- Right subtree still IN_BALANCE, THIS_NODE now RIGHT_HEAVY,
            -- and height of THIS_NODE not changed. No more rebalancing
            -- necessary
            THIS_NODE.BALANCE := RIGHT_HEAVY;
            THIS_NODE_RIGHT.BALANCE := LEFT_HEAVY;
            BALANCE_FLAG := false;
        else
            -- RIGHT subtree was RIGHT_HEAVY, THIS_NODE is now IN_BALANCE
            -- and its height has been reduced. More balancing needed.
            THIS_NODE.BALANCE := IN_BALANCE;
            THIS_NODE_RIGHT.BALANCE := IN_BALANCE;
        end if;
        THIS_NODE := THIS_NODE_RIGHT;
    else
        -- Situation similar to Figure 8.3.12(d) where THIS_NODE = T,
        -- THIS_NODE_RIGHT = TR. A DOUBLE_RIGHT_LEFT_ROTATION needed.
        THIS_NODE_LEFT := THIS_NODE_RIGHT.LEFT;
        SUBTREE_BALANCE := THIS_NODE_LEFT.BALANCE;
        -- THIS_NODE_LEFT now the same as T3 in Figure 8.3.12(d)
        THIS_NODE_RIGHT.LEFT := THIS_NODE_LEFT.RIGHT;
        THIS_NODE_LEFT.RIGHT := THIS_NODE_RIGHT;
        THIS_NODE.RIGHT := THIS_NODE_LEFT.LEFT;
        -- Single left done, do the right
        THIS_NODE_LEFT.LEFT := THIS_NODE;
        if SUBTREE_BALANCE = RIGHT_HEAVY then
            THIS_NODE.BALANCE := LEFT_HEAVY;
            THIS_NODE_RIGHT.BALANCE := IN_BALANCE;
        elsif SUBTREE_BALANCE = IN_BALANCE then
            THIS_NODE.BALANCE := IN_BALANCE;
            THIS_NODE_RIGHT.BALANCE := IN_BALANCE;
        else
            THIS_NODE.BALANCE := IN_BALANCE;
            THIS_NODE_RIGHT.BALANCE := RIGHT_HEAVY;
        end if;
        THIS_NODE := THIS_NODE_LEFT;
        THIS_NODE_LEFT.BALANCE := IN_BALANCE;
    end if;
  end case;
end BALANCE_LEFT;
```

Figure 8.3.13 Concluded.

A few comments are in order. Insertion may require the rotation of two or three nodes, but deletion may require the rotation of every node along the path from the root to the place occupied by the deleted node. Nodes are inserted as leaves but a key-data pair to be deleted can occupy any node in the tree. Surprisingly, empirical tests on random trees indicate that a single rotation occurs about 50 percent of the time during insertion and that one rotation is required, on average, for every five deletions. With these comments in mind, it is clear that insertion and deletion are still $O(\log_2(n))$ operations.

The random height-balanced tree is not optimal in one sense. Suppose that the reserved words of Ada were placed on a tree in such a way as to minimize the expected search time. Certain reserved words, such as *begin, end, is,* and *type,* appear in Ada programs much more often than other reserved words, such as *separate, generic,* and *exception.* The truly optimal true would be a height-balanced binary search tree that had the property that the most frequently referenced words would be close to the root. This problem is considered in Wirth [52].

8.4. BOUNDED TREES

A tree is bounded if the number is nodes cannot exceed a certain predetermined number. Bounded trees are typically used when the maximum number of key-data pairs is known beforehand or there is a desire to avoid the use of recursion. An additional parameter to specify the maximum number of nodes in the tree is required. This can be specified in one of two ways. One method is to specify the maximum number of nodes that a tree can have. The alternative method is to specify the maximum number of levels that a tree can have. Whichever method is chosen, an additional formal generic parameter must be added that specifies either the maximum number of nodes or the maximum number of levels. These two differences, the additional size parameter at instantiation and the additional boolean operation, are the only apparent differences between the bounded and unbounded versions that the programmer would see.

One approach would be to simulate the unbounded tree. Consider the new private part listed in Figure 8.4.1 for the unbounded tree package considered earlier. ROOT is the place in the TREE_ARRAY T where the root is placed. FREE is the head of a linked list of unused nodes. The tree must be initialized before it can be used. The initialization can be done by a call to CLEAR.

```
procedure Clear (T : in out Tree) is
   -- Initializes a tree and sets up the list of unused nodes
begin
  T.NODES_IN_USE := 0;
  T.FREE         := 1;
  for INDEX in positive range 1..(T.MAXIMUM_SIZE-1) loop
    T.T(INDEX).LEFT := INDEX + 1;
  end loop;
  T.NEXT_PRE.TOP  := 0;
  T.NEXT_POST.TOP := 0;
  T.NEXT_IN.TOP   := 0;
end begin;
```

After a tree has been initialized, the left pointer of each node references the next node. Figure 8.4.2 shows a simple tree and its storage using the structure in Figure 8.4.1. The advantage of this structure is that the program mimics the unbounded case. For example, whenever the operation "new TREE_NODE" appears in the program listing for INSERT in the unbounded case, the next node referenced by FREE must be accessed, FREE updated, and the accessed node referenced. When a key-data pair is removed by DELETE, the newly released node must be added to the free list. The implementation of this ADT closely parallels the unbounded version, so it is not presented.

```
type TREE_NODE is
    record
      KEY  : KEY_TYPE;
      DATA : DATA_TYPE;
      LEFT,
      RIGHT : natural := 0;
    end record;
type STACK is
    record
      TOP : natural := 0;
      STK : array (1..MAXIMUM_SIZE) of positive;
    end STACK;
type TREE_ARRAY is array (positive range <>) of TREE_NODE;
type TREE (MAXIMUM_SIZE : positive) is
    record
      NODES_IN_USE : natural := 0;
      FREE : positive;
      ROOT : positive;
      NEXT_PRE  : STACK -- used in NEXT_PREORDER
      NEXT_IN   : STACK -- used in NEXT_INORDER;
      NEXT_POST : STACK -- used in NEXT_POSTORDER
      T : TREE_ARRAY (1..MAXIMUM_SIZE);
    end record;
```

Figure 8.4.1 Package private part for GENERIC_BOUNDED_BINARY_SEARCH_TREE specification.

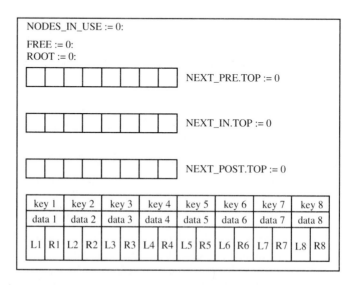

Figure 8.4.2 Data structure for a bounded binary search tree as specified in Figure 8.4.1.

Another possible bounded representation uses the structure first presented in heap sort or tree sort. The root always has index 1 in the TREE_ARRAY. If a node has index I, its left child will have index (2 * I) while its right child's index will be (2 * I + 1). Figure 8.4.3 shows a simple tree and its representation using this structure. This structure has a serious flaw. Suppose that T is a bounded tree of integer keys with 15 TREE_NODES. Let 1 be the first key added. This value becomes the key in the root node. The next value added, 2, goes in

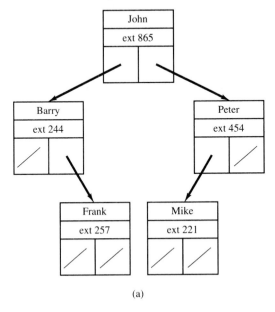

(a)

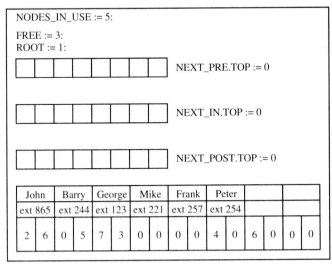

(b)

Figure 8.4.3 (a) Simple binary search tree of five nodes. (b) Bounded representation of the simple tree in part (a).

the right child of the root, or at index 3. The third value added, 3, goes in its right child, has index 7. The fourth value added, 4, ends up in the node with index 15. The tree has 11 unused nodes but no key whose value is greater than 4 can be added. In fact, there are no key values that can ever be placed in the left subtree of the node with key=2 in it. In this structure, the order of insertion is important unless some sort of balancing is done.

The bounded tree as described above is not balanced. The following implementation of a bounded tree is balanced. Because of the balance, the most used bounded tree operations, such as KEY_IN_TREE and GET_DATA_FOR_TREE, are minimized. The method outlined below forces the operations INSERT and DELETE to be $O(n)$, where n is the number of key-data pairs in the tree. Again, the data structure will be use an array of nodes. An access method that uses the same addressing convention as described above will be used. The root node will always be at the first index. If the index of a node is J, the left child of that node will have index $(2 * J)$ and the right child of that node will have index $(2 * J + 1)$. This convention allows access of a parent given the child's index. Anytime a node is added or deleted, the tree will be reshaped so that all of the nodes occupy the tree array slice from 1 to NODES_IN_USE. The nodes in the tree array slice from (NODES_IN_USE + 1) to MAXIMUM_NODES are not in use. The result is a complete tree of level k. Recall that a binary tree of level k is complete if and only if in a tree with k levels, every node of the first $k - 1$ levels is in use and the only nodes in level k not in use are bunched together at the right-hand end of level k. Trivially, every complete tree is balanced. Figure 8.4.4(a) shows a complete tree of level 3, and Figure 8.4.4(b) shows the table storage of such a tree. The formal generic parameters and the data structure in the private part have changed but the tree operations remain fixed. The specification for the unbounded balanced tree can be modified to get Figure 8.4.5.

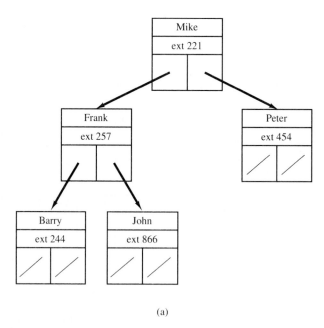

(a)

Figure 8.4.4 (a) Simple complete binary search tree of five nodes.

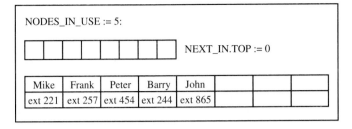

(b)

Figure 8.4.4 (b) Binary tree stored as a complete tree using a heap structure. The left child has twice the index of its parent, and the right child has twice the index plus one. The root is always stored at index 1.

```
generic
  NUMBER_OF_NODES : in positive;
  type KEY_TYPE is private;
  type DATA_TYPE is private;
  with function "<" ( LEFT, RIGHT : KEY_TYPE ) return boolean;
package GENERIC_BOUNDED_BALANCED_BINARY_SEARCH_TREE is
  type TREE is limited private;
  procedure COPY            ( FROM_TREE : in      TREE;
                              TO_TREE   :     out TREE);
  procedure CLEAR           ( T    :     out TREE );
  procedure INSERT          ( KEY  : in      KEY_TYPE;
                              DATA : in      DATA_TYPE;
                              T    : in out TREE );
  procedure DELETE          ( KEY  : in      KEY_TYPE;
                              T    : in out TREE );
  procedure UPDATE          ( KEY  : in      KEY_TYPE;
                              DATA : in      DATA_TYPE;
                              T    : in out TREE);
  procedure NEXT_INORDER    ( KEY  :     out KEY_TYPE;
                              DATA :     out DATA_TYPE;
                              T    : in out TREE);
  procedure SET_INORDER     ( T    : in out TREE);
  function EMPTY            ( T    : TREE ) return boolean;
  function FULL             ( T    : TREE ) return boolean;
  function COUNT            ( T    : TREE ) return natural;
  function EQUAL            ( T1, T2 : TREE ) return boolean;
  function KEY_IN_TREE      ( KEY  : KEY_TYPE; T : TREE) return boolean;
  function GET_DATA_FOR_TREE ( KEY  : KEY_TYPE; T : TREE) return DATA_TYPE;
  KEY_NOT_IN_TREE   : exception;
  KEY_IS IN_TREE    : exception;
  TREE_IS_EMPTY     : exception;
  OVERFLOW          : exception;
private
```

Figure 8.4.5 Package GENERIC_BOUNDED_BALANCED_BINARY_SEARCH_TREE specification.
Continues on page 254.

```
type TREE_NODE is
  record
    KEY  : KEY_TYPE;
    DATA : DATA_TYPE;
  end record;
type STACK_ARRAY is array ( positive range <> ) of positive;
type STACK is
  record
    TOP : natural := 0;
    Stk : Stack_array (1..NUMBER_OF_NODES);
  end record;
type TREE_TYPE is array (positive range <>) of TREE_NODE;
type TREE is
  record
    NODES_IN_USE : natural := 0;
    S : STACK; -- used in NEXT_inorder;
    T : TREE_TYPE (1..NUMBER_OF_NODES);
  end record;
end GENERIC_BOUNDED_BALANCED_BINARY_SEARCH_TREE;
```

Figure 8.4.5   Concluded.

The tree structure above is similar to the structure used in HEAP_SORT. A heap is an array representation of nodes where all the nodes are stored in a contiguous fashion. The boolean function KEY_IN_TREE illustrates how easy it is to access this structure.

```
function KEY_IN_TREE (KEY : KEY_TYPE; T : TREE) return boolean is
  -- Returns true if a specified Key is in T.
  INDEX: positive := 1;
begin
  while INDEX <= T.NODES_IN_USE loop
    if T.T(INDEX).KEY = KEY then
      return true;
    elsif KEY < T.T(INDEX).KEY then
      INDEX := 2 * INDEX;
    else
      INDEX := 2 * INDEX + 1;
    end if;
  end loop;
  return false;
end KEY_IN_TREE;
```

Before implementing INSERT and DELETE a utility operation REBUILD_TREE will be added to the package body. REBUILD_TREE takes an array of nodes with their keys in ascending order and places these nodes in a tree so that the resulting tree is complete and the inorder traversal is preserved. An inorder traversal is preserved if the inorder traversal lists the key-data pairs in ascending order after the tree is rebuilt. The INSERT and DELETE operations are similar in structure. Both build an array of nodes whose keys are in ascending order, and then let the utility procedure REBUILD_TREE finish the task. Assuming the existence of REBUILD_TREE, the operation INSERT becomes

```
procedure INSERT        ( KEY   : in     KEY_TYPE;
                          DATA  : in     DATA_TYPE;
                          T     : in out TREE ) is
-- Adds a node containing a given key-data pair and inserts that
-- node into the tree T while preserving the complete binary tree search
-- structure. The traversal are set to begin at the first key-data pair.
-- Exception OVERFLOW raised if insufficient space left to add a node
-- Exception KEY_IS_IN_TREE raised if an attempt is made to insert a
--                       duplicate key
  TEMP_ARRAY : TREE_TYPE (1..NUMBER_OF_NODES);
  COUNT : positive := 1;
begin
  if T.NODES_IN_USE = NUMBER_OF_NODES then
    raise OVERFLOW;
  elsif KEY_IN_TREE (KEY, T) then
    raise KEY_IS_IN_TREE;
  elsif T.NODES_IN_USE = 0 then
    T.T(1) := (KEY, DATA);
    T.NODES_IN_USE := 1;
    T.S.TOP := 0;
  else
    -- step 1 load into an array in order and insert new key-data
    --         pair in its proper place.
    SET_INORDER(T);
    for i in positive range 1..T.NODES_IN_USE loop
      NEXT_INORDER(TEMP_ARRAY(I) .KEY, TEMP_ARRAY(I) .DATA, T);
    end loop;
    while TEMP_ARRAY(COUNT).KEY < KEY and COUNT <= T.NODES_IN_USE loop
      COUNT := COUNT + 1;
    end loop;
    TEMP_ARRAY(COUNT+1..T.NODES_IN_USE+1) :=
                        TEMP_ARRAY(COUNT..T.NODES_IN_USE);
    TEMP_ARRAY(COUNT) := (KEY,DATA);
    T.NODES_IN_USE := T.NODES_IN_USE + 1;
    -- Step 2. Mimic an inorder traversal to insert elements back
    --              into the TREE so as to preserve inorder traversal
    REBUILD_TREE(TEMP_ARRAY, T);
    T.S.TOP := 0;
  end if;
end INSERT;
```

The idea behind REBUILD_TREE is deceptively simple. The nodes must form a binary search tree. An inorder traversal of a binary search tree will process all the nodes in ascending order by key. REBUILD_TREE uses the inorder traversal to place the nodes in the proper place in the tree structure. T_ARRAY is the name of an array of nodes with their keys in ascending order.

```
procedure REBUILD_TREE (T_ARRAY : in    TREE_TYPE;
                        T       : in out TREE ) is
  -- Auxiliary procedure used after the insertion or deletion of a
```

```
                -- key-data pair to rebuild the tree in a complete form.
        TEMP_STACK : STACK;
        TEMP_INDEX : positive := 1;
    begin
        -- The placement of nodes must preserve an inorder traversal
        -- a bounded stack is used to keep track of where things must
        -- be placed in the TREE. A "complete tree" is traversed to get the
        -- position of each key-data pair. As positions are determined, key-data
        -- pairs are placed into the tree in ascending order by key. Procedure
        -- NEXT_INORDER is the pattern.
        TEMP_STACK.TOP := 1;
        TEMP_STACK.STK(1) := 1;
        TEMP_INDEX := 1;
       while 2*TEMP_INDEX <= T.NODES_IN_USE loop
          -- get left child and push on stack
          TEMP_INDEX := 2*TEMP_INDEX;
          TEMP_STACK.TOP := TEMP_STACK.TOP + 1;
          TEMP_STACK.STK(TEMP_STACK.TOP) := TEMP_INDEX;
       end loop;
        -- Stack now set up for start of inorder traversal
        -- INDEX keeps track of the elements in the ordered temporary
        -- array while TEMP_INDEX is the elements location in the tree.
        for INDEX in 1..T.NODES_IN_USE loop
          TEMP_INDEX := TEMP_STACK.STK(TEMP_STACK.TOP);
          T.T(TEMP_INDEX) := T_ARRAY(INDEX);
          TEMP_STACK.TOP := TEMP_STACK.TOP - 1;
          -- Left child and node now done, so
          -- Load up left side of right subtree, if it exists
          if 2 * TEMP_INDEX + 1 <= T.NODES_IN_USE then
             -- Get index of the right node and push it onto the stack
             TEMP_INDEX := 2 * TEMP_INDEX + 1;
             TEMP_STACK.TOP := TEMP_STACK.TOP + 1;
             TEMP_STACK.STK(TEMP_STACK.TOP) := TEMP_INDEX;
             -- Put the node's left subtree on the stack
             while 2 * TEMP_INDEX <= T.NODES_IN_USE loop
               -- get left child and push on stack
               TEMP_INDEX := 2 * TEMP_INDEX;
               TEMP_STACK.TOP := TEMP_STACK.TOP + 1;
               TEMP_STACK.STK(TEMP_STACK.TOP) := TEMP_INDEX;
             end loop;
          end if;
        end loop;
    end REBUILD_TREE;
```

The procedure REBUILD_TREE is $O(n)$, where n is the number of nodes in the tree. This follows from the fact that REBUILD_TREE traverses all n node in the tree. Since both the operation INSERT and the operation DELETE call REBUILD_TREE, they are all $O(n)$. The extra work is the cost of maintaining a complete tree. The rest of the implementation of GENERIC_BOUNDED_BALANCED_BINARY_SEARCH_TREE is deferred to the exercises.

8.5 B-TREES

Only binary trees were considered in the first four sections. In the next two sections multiway search trees are examined. A search tree is of order m if each node has, at most, m children. A node with m children contains $m - 1$ keys. The keys are stored in ascending order. Inserting key-data pairs is based on a simple rule. If the key of the key-data pair is less than the first key, it is inserted in the first subtree. If the key of the key-data pair is greater than the $(i - 1)$st key but less than the ith key, the pair is inserted into the ith subtree. Finally, if the key of the key-data pair is greater than the $(m - 1)$st key, the key-data pair goes into the mth subtree. The root node in a tree of order m may have between 0 and m children, but internal nodes must have at least $m/2$ children. The insertion algorithm is modified accordingly. Figure 8.5.1 illustrates a tree of order 5.

When implementing an m-order tree, the insertion into a tree should be minimized if possible. An m-order tree will be balanced if three conditions hold. First, all leaves appear on one level. Second, no node above a leaf is an empty subtree. Third, every node that is not a leaf has a minimal number of children. One unwritten assumption about binary search trees is that the tree is small enough to fit in main memory. Suppose that the nodes of a tree are stored in a secondary storage device such as a hard disk with at least one node per disk block. A database with a million records set up as a tree with one record per block would require at least a million blocks of disk storage. Assuming a balanced tree, searches would require up to 20 disk accesses ($2**20$ records = 1 megablock).

There are two problems with this scenario. If a disk access takes 10 milliseconds, a successful search will require about 200 milliseconds = 20 accesses $*$ 10 milliseconds/access. This does not include the processing overhead associated with each access needed to determine the disk location of the next node. The second shortcoming is disk storage efficiency.

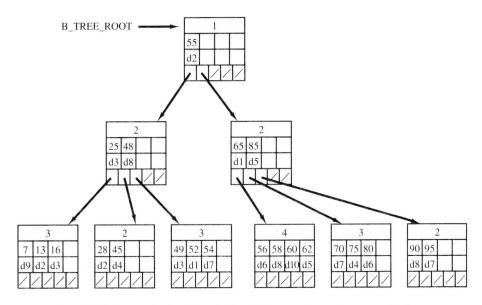

Figure 8.5.1 B-tree of order 5. Note that by adding nodes the maximum capacity of a B-tree of order 5 with three levels is 124 key-data pairs contained in 31 nodes.

The assumption that a node efficiently fills one disk block is probably not justified. The B-tree, first described by R. Bayer and E. M. McCreight, is designed to overcome both short-comings. By definition, a B-tree of order m is an m-way tree with the properties listed in Figure 8.5.2.

1. All leaves are on the same level.
2. All internal nodes, except possibly the root, have at least $\lceil m/2 \rceil$ nonempty children and at most m nonempty children.
3. The number of defined keys in a node is one less than the number of its children. The keys set up the tree as a search structure.
4. The root has at most m children, but may have as few as two children if it is not a leaf or no children if the root is a leaf.

Figure 8.5.2 Definition of m-way B_tree.

The motivation of a B-tree is to have both a large capacity and minimum access time. Access time here is defined as the number of nodes accessed, not the number of keys checked. Figure 8.5.3 lists the maximum capacity of B-trees with respect to order and depth. Recall that a full binary tree with five levels has 63 key-data pairs. This fact indicates how efficiently the B-tree maximizes capacity while minimizing node access. The ADT documentation for a B-tree is given in Figure 8.5.4.

B-Tree Order	Root Only	One Level	Two Levels	Three Levels	Four Levels	Five Levels
3	2	8	26	80	242	728
4	3	15	63	255	1021	4097
5	4	24	124	624	3124	15624
6	5	35	215	1295	7775	46655
7	6	48	342	2400	16806	117848
11	10	120	1330	14640	161050	1771561

Figure 8.5.3 Maximum B-tree capacity.

GENERAL ADT SPECIFICATION FOR M_WAY_B_TREE

Description

This package implements the ADT M_WAY_B_TREE as defined in Figure 8.5.3. A B-tree is an m-way balanced search tree structure defined to minimize access on an external storage device. The order of a B-tree m is the maximum number of children that a node may reference. Every node contains a field to indicate how many children a node has, an array of length $m - 1$ key-data pairs, and an array of length m to hold the location of a nonleaf's children. The tree is maintained in balance as a consequence of the definition of a B-tree. Duplicate keys are not allowed. Provisions to

Figure 8.5.4 Documentation for M_WAY_B_TREE. Continues on page 259.

insert key-data pairs, search for data based on key value, delete nodes based on key, update nodes based on key, and inorder traversals are included. The B-tree is limited private.

Programmer-Supplied Data Structures or Specifications

The programmer must supply four parameters. The first is a positive constant that corresponds to the order of the B-tree. The second and third parameters are a KEY_TYPE and DATA_TYPE that are private within the package. The fourth is an overloaded boolean function "<" used to determine the ascending order of objects of KEY_TYPE.

Operations

Name	Description
COPY	Makes a separate, exact copy of a specified tree.
CLEAR	Returns a tree with a root node that has only null pointers. No key-data pairs are in the root.
INSERT	Inserts a given key-data pair into a specified tree. Nodes are created as required. The tree search structure is preserved. The traversal will again start at the beginning if a key-data pair is inserted into the tree.
DELETE	Deletes a key-data pair with a specified key while maintaining the B-tree search structure. The traversal will again start at the beginning if a key-data pair is deleted from the tree.
UPDATE	Searches for a node with a specified key in the specified B-tree and replaces the data field with a new value. The traversal will again start at the beginning if an update occurs.
GET_DATA_FOR_KEY	Searches a specified B-tree for a node with a specified key-length pair and returns the associated data field.
EMPTY	Boolean-valued function that returns true if the root node that contains no key-data pairs, or false otherwise.
FULL	Boolean-valued function that returns true if there is not space to add additional nodes, or false otherwise.
COUNT	Returns the number of key-data pairs in the B_TREE.
EQUAL	Boolean-valued function that returns true if both B-trees contain the same key-data pairs, or false otherwise.
KEY_IN_B_TREE	Boolean-valued function that returns true if the key is in the tree, or false otherwise.
NEXT_INORDER	Returns the next key-data pair. The traversal will be in ascending order of key components. When the traversal is finished it will return to the beginning. Any insertion deletion or update of a key-data pair will cause the sequence to be reset to the first node to be processed.
SET_INORDER	Sets the traversal sequence to start at the key-data pair in a normal inorder traversal.

Figure 8.5.4 Continues on page 260.

Exceptions

Four exceptions can occur: OVERFLOW, KEY_NOT_IN_TREE, KEY_IS_IN_TREE, and TREE_EMPTY. The exception OVERFLOW occurs when making an attempt to copy a tree, to insert a key-data pair, or to traverse the tree using NEXT_INORDER and a storage_error is raised. The exception KEY_NOT_IN_TREE occurs in DELETE_KEY, UPDATE_KEY_DATA, and GET_DATA_FOR_KEY when a search is made for a given key and the key is not found. The exception KEY_IS_IN_TREE occurs when making attempt to insert a second key-data pair that contains a key that is already in the tree. The exception TREE_EMPTY occurs when attempting any operation requiring a key or a key-data pair on an empty tree. The traversal also raises TREE_EMPTY when there is either no tree to traverse or an empty tree to traverse.

Warnings

The order of the B-tree should be an odd positive greater than or equal to 5 for best results. B_TREE_FULL does not mean all nodes are full. All other warnings are implementation dependent.

Figure 8.5.4   Documentation for M_WAY_B_TREE. Concluded.

The specification is contained in Figure 8.5.5. Note that data structure for the B_TREE yields an unbounded tree.

```
generic
  B_TREE_ORDER : in positive := 5;
  type KEY_TYPE is private;
  type DATA_TYPE is private;
  with function "<" (LEFT, RIGHT : KEY_TYPE) return boolean;
package GENERIC_M_WAY_B_TREE is
  type B_TREE is limited private;
  procedure COPY             (FROM_TREE     : in     B_TREE;
                             TO_TREE       :    out B_TREE);
  procedure CLEAR            (THIS_TREE     : in out B_TREE );
  procedure INSERT           (KEY           : in     KEY_TYPE;
                             DATA          : in     DATA_TYPE;
                             INTO_TREE     : in out B_TREE );
  procedure DELETE           (KEY           : in     KEY_TYPE;
                             FROM_TREE     : in out B_TREE );
  procedure UPDATE           (KEY           : in     KEY_TYPE;
                             DATA          : in     DATA_TYPE;
                             IN_TREE       : in out B_TREE);
  procedure NEXT_INORDER     (KEY           :    out KEY_TYPE;
                             DATA          :    out DATA_TYPE;
                             IN_TREE       : in out B_TREE);
  procedure SET_INORDER      (IN_TREE       : in out B_TREE);
  function EMPTY             (TREE_TO_CHECK : B_TREE ) return boolean;
  function FULL              (TREE_TO_CHECK : B_TREE ) return boolean;
  function COUNT             (OF_TREE : B_TREE ) return natural;
  function EQUAL             (LEFT, RIGHT : B_TREE) return boolean;
  function KEY_IN_B_TREE     (KEY : KEY_TYPE; IN_TREE : B_TREE) return boolean;
```

Figure 8.5.5   Specification for GENERIC M WAY B TREE. Continues on page 261.

```
   function GET_DATA_FOR_B_TREE(KEY : KEY_TYPE; IN_TREE:B_TREE) return DATA_TYPE;
   KEY_NOT_IN_TREE    : exception;
   KEY_IS_IN_TREE     : exception;
   TREE_EMPTY         : exception;
   OVERFLOW           : exception;
private
   type TREE_NODE;
   type NEXT is access TREE_NODE;
   type STACK_NODE;
   type TREE_STACK is access STACK_NODE;
   type B_TREE is
     record
       ROOT : NEXT;
       COUNT    : natural := 0;
       NEXT_IN : TREE_STACK;      -- Used in traversal
     end record;
end GENERIC_M_WAY_B_TREE;

package body GENERIC_M_WAY_B_TREE is

   type NEXT_ARRAY is array (positive range 1..B_TREE_ORDER) of NEXT;
   type KEY_ARRAY is array (positive range 1..(B_TREE_ORDER-1)) of KEY_TYPE;
   type DATA_ARRAY is array (positive range 1..(B_TREE_ORDER-1)) of DATA_TYPE;
   type STACK_NODE is
     record
       KEY_NUMBER : positive;
       NEXT_NODE   : NEXT;
       NEXT_STACK : TREE_STACK;
     end record;
   type TREE_NODE is
     record
       IN_USE        : natural := 0; -- Number nonnull key-data pairs in node
       KEY           : KEY_ARRAY;
       DATA          : DATA_ARRAY;
       NEXT_NODE     : NEXT_ARRAY;
     end record;

   MAX_KEY_NUM, MIN_KEY_NUM : positive;
   ....................
end GENERIC_M_WAY_B_TREE;
```

Figure 8.5.5 Concluded.

Locating a key-data pair in a B_TREE is similar to a binary tree. Nodes are traversed until the proper node is found. The main difference is that a binary tree contains only one key-data pair, while an m-way tree contains up to $m - 1$ key-data pairs. One technique for searching a B_TREE is illustrated in the operation GET_DATA_FOR_B_TREE.

```
   function GET_DATA_FOR_B_TREE ( KEY : KEY_TYPE;
                                  IN_TREE : B_TREE ) return DATA_TYPE is
     -- Searches a specified B-tree for a node with a specified key-data
```

```
-- pair and returns the associated data field.
-- Exception KEY_NOT_IN_TREE raised if KEY not in T.

function FIND_DATA ( KEY : KEY_TYPE; THIS_NODE : NEXT) return DATA_TYPE is
begin
  if THIS_NODE.IN_USE = 0 then
    -- Node could be an empty root.
    raise KEY_NOT_IN_TREE;
  else
    for INDEX in positive range 1..THIS_NODE.IN_USE loop
      if KEY < THIS_NODE.KEY(INDEX) then
        if THIS_NODE.NEXT_NODE(INDEX) = null then
          -- THIS_NODE is a leaf
          raise KEY_NOT_IN_TREE;
        else
          return FIND_DATA (KEY, THIS_NODE.NEXT_NODE(INDEX));
        end if;
      elsif KEY = THIS_NODE.KEY(INDEX) then
        return THIS_NODE.DATA(INDEX);
      end if;
    end loop;
    if THIS_NODE.NEXT_NODE(THIS_NODE.IN_USE + 1) = null then
      raise KEY_NOT_IN_TREE;
    else
      return FIND_DATA (KEY, THIS_NODE.NEXT_NODE(THIS_NODE.IN_USE+1));
    end if;
  end if;
end FIND_DATA;

begin
  return FIND_DATA (KEY, IN_TREE.ROOT);
end GET_DATA_for_B_TREE;
```

If an operation to traverse a B_TREE had been included in the specification, a procedure to list key-data pairs in ascending order is needed. This is a simple modification of the inorder traversal of the binary tree. The procedure could be recursively implemented as

```
procedure INORDER_B_TREE_LISTING (OF_TREE : in B_TREE) is

procedure INORDER (NEXT_NODE :  in    NEXT) is
begin
  if NEXT_NODE /= null then
    for INDEX in positive range 1..NEXT_NODE.IN_USE loop
      INORDER (NEXT_NODE.NXT(INDEX));
      PROCESS (N.KEY(INDEX), N.DATA(INDEX));
    end loop;
    INORDER(NEXT_NODE.NXT(NEXT_NODE.IN_USE+1);
  end if;
end INORDER;
```

```
      begin
        if OF_TREE.ROOT.IN_USE = 0 then
          raise TREE_EMPTY;
        else
          INORDER(OF_TREE.ROOT);
        end if;
      end INORDER_B_TREE_LISTING;
```

   The procedure INORDER_B_TREE_LISTING cannot be implemented outside the
ADT package because B_TREE is limited private. It does provide a good pattern for how to
implement the operation NEXT_INORDER. The definition of the type B_TREE includes a
stack for use in eliminating the recursion in INORDER_B_TREE_LISTING. This technique
was exhibited earlier in this chapter.
   The insertion and deletion of key-data pairs can raise some tedious details. Issues relat-
ing to node splitting, key-data pair shifting, node combining, and tree rebalancing must be addressed. In the remainder of this section we address these issues.
   By definition, a B_TREE cannot grow at its leaves, it must grow at the root. If a level is
to be added, it must be added at the root. Consider the simple case illustrated in Figure 8.5.6(a).
The rightmost leafs are all full and a new leaf must be added as in Figure 8.5.6(b) and then
key-data pairs shifted so that the resulting structure is still a B-tree as in Figure 8.5.6(c). If the
tree were completely full, an entire new level 1 would need to be added. Consider the situation in Figure 8.5.6(d). To insert a new key-data pair into the tree, a new level must be added.
By definition all leaves are on the same level. The solution is to split the root into two nodes
and add a new root, as in Figure 8.5.6(e).

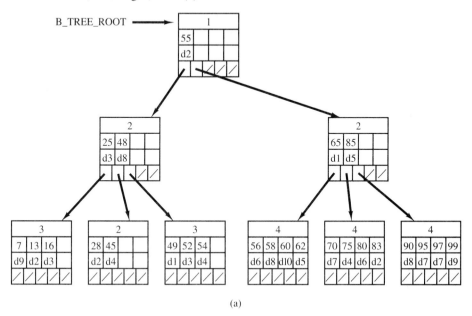

(a)

Figure 8.5.6 (a) B-tree of order 5 before the insertion of the key-data pair 61–d3. Note
that the node where this pair must go (third from the right) is full, so it must first be split.

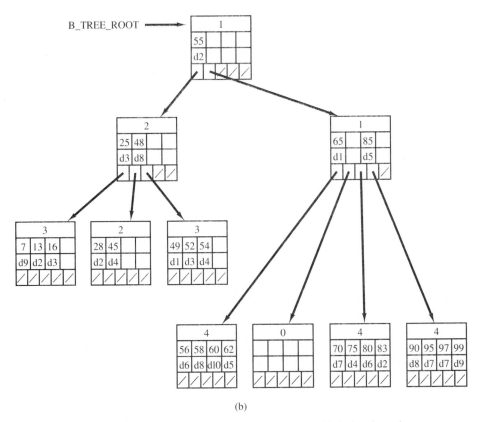

Figure 8.5.6 (b) A node has been added and the next step is to shift the key-data pairs around before adding the new key-data pair 61–d3. The median of the keys (56, 58, 60, 61, 62) will be shifted up to the parent and all fields updated.

The insertion procedure is easy to describe. A search is made for the key of the new key-data pair. If the search fails, the key-data pair is inserted into the leaf where the search failed provided that the leaf is not full. If the leaf is full, it is split into two leafs and the median key-data pair is inserted into the parent node if there is room. If the parent node is full, it is split. The process continues until reaching a root node. If the root is full, the root is split, a new node is created, the median key is placed in the new node, which becomes the new root, and the split root becomes the new level one. This process ensures that the B-tree is always balanced and that all leaves are on the same level.

If $m = 5$, every node must have between two and four key-data pairs. If a leaf where a key-data pair is to be inserted has two or three key-data pairs, the new pair is shifted into its proper place. If the leaf already has four key-data pairs, a new node is created. The two highest-order key pairs are placed in the new leaf, the two lowest-priority pairs are retained in the existing leaf, and the median key-data pair is inserted into its parent. Clearly, the insert operation must keep track of where it has been in the case a node is split and the median key-data pair moved up for insertion into the node's parent. Recursion is used for this purpose.

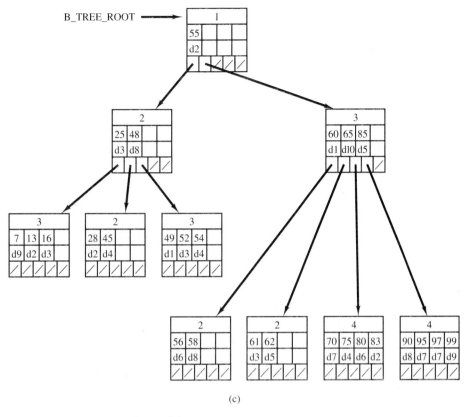

(c)

Figure 8.5.6. (c) Key-data pairs have now been moved and the result is a B-tree.

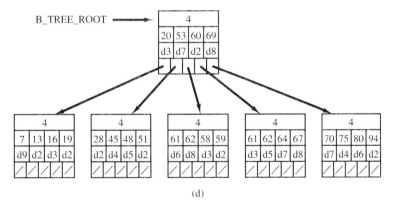

(d)

Figure 8.5.6 (d) B-tree of order 5 and level 2. This tree is full. To add the key data pair 55–d4 a new root must be added and the old root split.

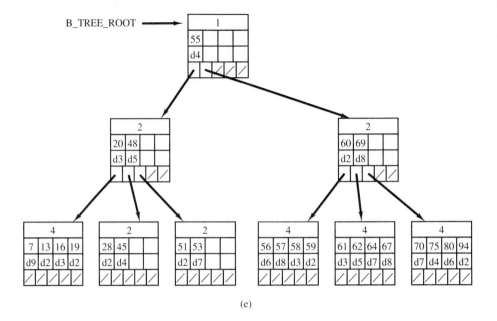

(e)

Figure 8.5.6 (e) To insert the key-data pair 55–d4 into part (d), a new root must be created and the old root split. The definition of a B-tree requires the creation of a new leaf
and the splitting of an old leaf.

```
procedure INSERT    ( KEY        : in      KEY_TYPE;
                      DATA       : in      DATA_TYPE;
                      INTO_TREE : in out B_TREE ) is
  -- Inserts a key-data pair into a given B_TREE. Nodes are
  -- created as required. Traversal reset to the beginning.
  -- Exception KEY_IS_IN_TREE raised if KEY already in IN_TREE.
  -- Exception OVERFLOW raised if there is not space to add a node.
  ADD_LEVEL: boolean;
  TEMP_KEY : KEY_TYPE;
  TEMP_DATA : DATA_TYPE;
  TEMP_RIGHT, TEMP_NEXT_NODE : NEXT;
begin
  INSERT ( KEY, DATA, INTO_TREE.ROOT, ADD_LEVEL,
                      TEMP_KEY, TEMP_DATA, TEMP_RIGHT);
  if ADD_LEVEL then
    -- Tree needs a new root
    TEMP_NEXT_NODE := new TREE_NODE;
    TEMP_NEXT_NODE.IN_USE := 1;
    TEMP_NEXT_NODE.KEY(1) := TEMP_KEY;
    TEMP_NEXT_NODE.DATA(1) := TEMP_DATA;
    TEMP_NEXT_NODE.NEXT_NODE(1) := INTO_TREE.ROOT;
    TEMP_NEXT_NODE.NEXT_NODE(2) := TEMP_RIGHT;
    INTO_TREE_ROOT := TEMP_NEXT_NODE;
  end if;
  INTO_TREE.COUNT := INTO_TREE.COUNT + 1;
```

```
             INTO_TREE.NEXT_IN := null;
        exception
           when storage_error => raise OVERFLOW;
        end INSERT;
```

All of the work needed to insert a key-data pair into a B_TREE is done in the procedure INSERT. INSERT takes a key-data pair and tries to insert it into some node of a B-tree with root T.ROOT Occasionally, the root must be split and a new level added. This is what the boolean flag LEVEL_ADDED signals. In that case the key-data pair for the new root are TEMP_KEY and TEMP_DATA, the value IN_TREE.ROOT becomes the left subtree and TEMP_RIGHT holds the access value that points to the right subtree.

The procedure INSERT recursively descends down the subtrees of the B-tree until it finds a leaf. If there is space in the leaf, the key-data pair is inserted. If there is no space, the boolean flag KEY_NOT_INSERTED is set to true and the procedure recursively returns to the level where it was called and tries to insert again.

```
procedure INSERT ( KEY                : in     KEY_TYPE;
                   DATA               : in     DATA_TYPE;
                   SUBTREE            : in     NEXT;
                   KEY_NOT_INSERTED   : in out boolean;
                   TEMP_KEY           : in out KEY_TYPE;
                   TEMP_DATA          : in out DATA_TYPE;
                   TEMP-R             : in out NEXT) is
   PLACE : positive;
   FOUND : boolean;
begin
   if SUBTREE = null then
      -- Tree searched and key not found. This is the base case for
      -- recursion. Insertion follows first return.
      KEY_NOT_INSERTED := true;
      TEMP_KEY := KEY;
      TEMP_DATA := DATA;
      TEMP_R := null;
   else
      SEARCH_THIS_NODE (KEY, SUBTREE, FOUND, PLACE);
      if FOUND then
         raise KEY_IS_IN_TREE;
      else
         -- INSERT called recursively until SUBTREE.NEXT_NODE(PLACE) = null
         INSERT(KEY, DATA, SUBTREE.NEXT_NODE(PLACE), KEY_NOT_INSERTED,
                                TEMP_KEY, TEMP_DATA, TEMP_R);
         -- Backtrack up the B_TREE until the key-data pair is inserted
         if KEY_NOT_INSERTED then
            if SUBTREE.IN_USE < MAX_KEY_NUM then
               KEY_NOT_INSERTED := false;
               ADD_KEY_PAIR_TO_NODE(TEMP_KEY,TEMP_DATA, TEMP_R,SUBTREE, PLACE);
            else
               KEY_NOT_INSERTED := true;
               SPLIT_NODE (TEMP_KEY, TEMP_DATA, TEMP_R, SUBTREE, PLACE,
                                       TEMP_KEY, TEMP_DATA, TEMP_R);
```

```
          end if;
        end if;
      end if;
    end if;
  end INSERT;
```

The procedure SEARCH_THIS_NODE does one of two things, depending on whether the returned boolean flag found is true or false. If the key is in the node, found is set to true and the positive value INDEX is the location of the key. If the key is not in the node, found is set false and the positive value INDEX is the subtree where the key will be found if it is present in the B_TREE. The procedure ADD_KEY_PAIR_TO_NODE does exactly what the name implies, provided that there is room in the node. The key-data pair and the subtree that they reference are inserted at the specified position. If there is not room in the current node, SPLIT_NODE does its job and returns the median key-data pair and two subtrees that are each half full.

```
  procedure SEARCH_THIS_NODE (KEY      : in     KEY_TYPE;
                              SUBTREE : in     NEXT;
                              FOUND    :    out boolean;
                              PLACE    :    out positive) is
    -- Searches a node for a given KEY. Signals if it is in
    -- the node and where. If not in node, signals which subtree.
    COUNT : positive := 1;
  begin
    loop
      if COUNT > SUBTREE.IN_USE then
        FOUND := false;
        return;
      elsif KEY < SUBTREE.KEY(COUNT) then
        FOUND := false;
        return;
      elsif KEY = SUBTREE.KEY(COUNT) then
        FOUND := true;
        return;
      else
        COUNT := COUNT + 1;
        PLACE := COUNT;
      end if;
    end loop;
  end SEARCH_THIS_NODE;

  procedure ADD_KEY_PAIR_TO_NODE(KEY      : in     KEY_TYPE;
                                 DATA     : in     DATA_TYPE;
                                 TEMP_R  : in     NEXT;
                                 SUBTREE : in     NEXT;
                                 PLACE    : in     positive) is
    -- Inserts a key-data pair at position PLACE in a node with room
  begin
    SUBTREE.KEY(PLACE + 1..SUBTREE.IN_USE + 1) :=
        SUBTREE.KEY(PLACE..SUBTREE.IN_USE);
    SUBTREE.DATA(PLACE + 1..SUBTREE.IN_USE + 1) :=
```

```
      SUBTREE.DATA(PLACE..SUBTREE.IN_USE);
    SUBTREE.NEXT_NODE(PLACE + 2..SUBTREE.IN_USE + 2) :=
      SUBTREE.NEXT_NODE(PLACE + 1..SUBTREE.IN_USE + 1);
    SUBTREE.KEY(PLACE) := KEY;
    SUBTREE.DATA(PLACE) := DATA;
    SUBTREE.NEXT_NODE(PLACE + 1) := TEMP_R;
    SUBTREE.IN_USE. := SUBTREE.IN_USE + 1
end ADD_KEY_PAIR_TO_NODE;


procedure SPLIT_NODE( KEY          : in      KEY_TYPE;
                      DATA         : in      DATA_TYPE;
                      TEMP_R       : in      NEXT;
                      PARENT       : in      NEXT;
                      PLACE        : in      positive;
                      MEDIAN_KEY :      out KEY_TYPE;
                      MEDIAN_DATA:      out DATA_TYPE;
                      MEDIAN_NEXT_NODE :     out NEXT) is
  -- Called from INSERT when a node where key-data pair belongs is full.
  -- Splits the full node PARENT before inserting a key-data-next
  -- triple. The two nodes have minimum entries and the extra
  -- key-data-next triple is passed back up the B_TREE
  -- TEMP_R is the access value that KEY_DATA references after insertion
  MEDIAN         : positive;
  TEMP_NEW_NODE : NEXT;
  TEMP_PARENT : NEXT := PARENT;
begin
  if PLACE <= MIN_KEY_NUM then
    -- New key-data will end up in the left node
    MEDIAN := MIN_KEY_NUM;
  else
    MEDIAN := MIN_KEY_NUM + 1;
  end if;
  -- Create the new "right" node and put right half of PARENT in it.
  TEMP_NEW_NODE := new TREE_NODE;
  TEMP_NEW_NODE.KEY(1..(MAX_KEY_NUM-MEDIAN)) :=
                              PARENT.KEY(MEDIAN + 1..MAX_KEY_NUM);
  TEMP_NEW_NODE.DATA(1..(MAX_KEY_NUM-MEDIAN)) :=
                              PARENT.DATA(MEDIAN + 1..MAX_KEY_NUM);
  TEMP_NEW_NODE.NEXT_NODE(1..(MAX_KEY_NUM-MEDIAN)) :=
                              PARENT.NEXT_NODE(MEDIAN + 2..B_TREE_ORDER);
  TEMP_NEW_NODE.IN_USE := MAX_KEY_NUM - MEDIAN;
  MEDIAN_NEXT_NODE := TEMP_NEW_NODE;
  TEMP_PARENT.IN_USE := MEDIAN;
  -- New node created, initialized. Parent adjusted.
  -- Now insert key-data-next triple and find median key-data-next triple
  if PLACE <= MIN_KEY_NUM then
    -- Add new key-data-next triple to PARENT
    ADD_KEY_PAIR_TO_NODE(KEY, DATA, TEMP_R, TEMP_PARENT, PLACE);
  else
    ADD_KEY_PAIR_TO_NODE(KEY, DATA, TEMP_R, TEMP_NEW_NODE, PLACE-MEDIAN);
```

```
        end if;
        MEDIAN_KEY := TEMP_PARENT.KEY(TEMP_PARENT.IN_USE);
        MEDIAN_DATA := TEMP_PARENT.DATA(TEMP_PARENT.IN_USE);
        TEMP_NEW_NODE.NEXT_NODE(1) :=
            TEMP_PARENT.NEXT_NODE(TEMP_PARENT.IN_USE + 1);
        TEMP_PARENT.IN_USE := TEMP_PARENT.IN_USE - 1;
    end SPLIT_NODE;
```

The procedure SPLIT_NODE splits the node pointed to by NEXT_NODE into two nodes (accessed by NEXT_NODE and MEDIAN_NEXT_NODE). The key-data pair and its associated subtree TEMP_RIGHT are inserted at the appropriate point and the median key-data pair and its relevant subtree are returned to be inserted into a higher node.

When examining INSERT_KEY it is important to realize that nodes can be added on any level where there is room, but never below the level of the leaves. A new node may be added at any level in such a way as to preserve balance provided that the parent node has room and a sibling is full. The procedure SPLIT_NODE takes the node in the first argument and splits it into two nodes. The passed key-pair combination is possibly inserted and the key-data pair in the median position is returned (see Figure 8.5.7).

Just as insertion splits nodes when they are full, the procedure DELETE_KEY will combine nodes if the number of children after deletion is less than MIN_KEY_NUM. For deletion a key-data pair will always be removed from a leaf. If the key is not in a leaf, either its prede-

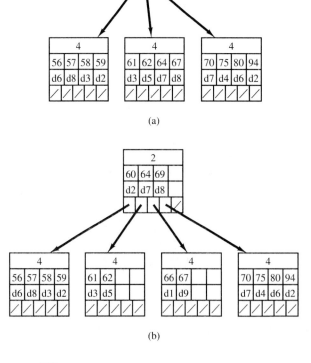

(a)

(b)

Figure 8.5.7 (a) Subtree of a B-tree of order 5 before insertion of the key-data pair 66–d1. There is no room in the leaf, and insertion in the parent requires the creation of a new leaf node. Inserting a new leaf requires the splitting of an existing node and the insertion of the median key-data pair into the parent and the readjustment of pointers. (b) The result after they key data pair 66–d1 is inserted into the B-tree segment. Note the splitting of the leaf node and the inserting of the median key-data pair into the parent node.

cessor or its successor is in a leaf in the natural inorder traversal. If there are more than MIN_KEY_NUM of keys in a leaf, one key can be deleted with no further action. If the leaf contains only MIN_KEY_NUM keys, one (if the leaf is on the end) or two leaves on either side are examined. If one of these leaves has more than MIN_NUM_NODES, a key pair can be rotated to the parent and one from the parent rotated to the leaf. If both nodes have min_key_num keys, these two leaves can be combined. If the parent ends up with fewer than MIN_KEY_NUM keys, the process propagates upward. The process is similar to the balancing of a height-balanced tree. Eventually, the ROOT can be eliminated and two level 1 nodes are combined to become the new ROOT (see Figure 8.5.8).

The procedure DELETE_KEY is similar to INSERT_KEY. Instead of pulling a key down from the parent during recursion, the recursive procedure will rebuild or combine nodes on its way up. The procedure DELETE is where most of the work is done. The exception is when the root has two children that must be combined. This last detail is handled in the procedure DELETE.

```
procedure DELETE      ( KEY       : in    KEY_TYPE;
                        FROM_TREE : in out B_TREE ) is
   -- DELETES a key-data pair with a specified from the B_TREE
   -- maintaining the B_tree structure. Traversal rest to beginning.
   -- Exception KEY_NOT_IN_TREE raised if KEY not in FROM_TREE.
begin
   DELETE (KEY, FROM_TREE.ROOT);
   if FROM_TREE.ROOT.IN_USE = 0 then
      -- The 2 subtrees of the root were combined, delete one level
      FROM_TREE.ROOT := FROM_TREE.ROOT.NEXT_NODE(1);
   end if;
   FROM_TREE.COUNT := FROM_TREE.COUNT - 1;
   FROM_TREE.NEXT_IN := null;
exception
   when KEY_NOT_IN_TREE => raise KEY_NOT_IN_TREE;
end DELETE;
```

The procedure DELETE must be able to handle the combining of nodes at the same level, the rotation of key-data pairs from the node through the parent to an adjacent node to keep the number of key-data pairs above the minimum per node, and the elimination of a level by combining the roots children to form a new root. The procedure is straightforward. A search is made for the node that contains the key pair to be deleted. If it is there and the node is not a leaf, the key's immediate inorder successor, which is in a leaf, is copied to key's position and deleted from the leaf. If the key to be deleted is in a leaf, the obvious takes place. If the key is not in the leaf, the recursive process continues.

```
procedure DELETE ( KEY      : in    KEY_TYPE;
                   THIS_NODE : in    NEXT ) is
   FOUND : boolean;
   PLACE : positive; -- Position of KEY in THIS_NODE or which subtree of
                     -- THIS_NODE if KEY not in THIS_NODE.
begin
   if THIS_NODE = null then
      raise KEY_NOT_IN_TREE;
   else
```

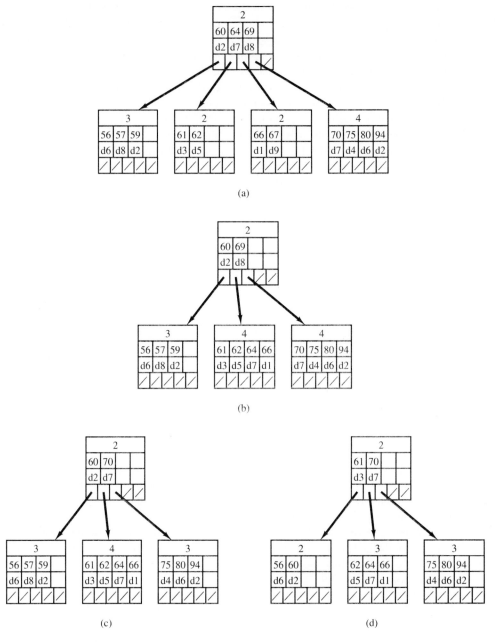

(a)

(b)

(c)   (d)

Figure 8.5.8 (a) Situation after deleting the key-data pair 58–d3 from the B-tree segment in Figure
8.5.7. (b) The deletion of the key-data pair 67–d9 forces the combining of two nodes because one
node has fewer than the minimum number of key-data pairs. (c) The key-data pair 69–d8 is deleted
next. Note the rotation of the key-data pair 70–d7 from the leaf. (d) After deleting the key-data pairs
57–d8 and 59–d2 from the same leaf, the number of key-data pairs is below the minimum. The adjacent nodes cannot be combined. Instead, the key-data pair 61–d3 is rotated from the leaf to its parent
and the pair 60–d2 is rotated from the parent to its leaf.

```
      SEARCH_THIS_NODE (KEY, THIS_NODE, FOUND, PLACE);
      if FOUND then
        if THIS_NODE.NEXT_NODE (PLACE) = null then
          -- THIS_NODE is a leaf, see Figure 8.5.7(a)
          REMOVE_KEY (THIS_NODE, PLACE);
        else
          -- Replace THIS_NODE.KEY(PLACE) with its successor, Figure 8.5.9(c)
          REPLACE_WITH_SUCCESSOR (THIS_NODE, PLACE);
          DELETE (THIS_NODE.KEY(PLACE), THIS_NODE.NEXT_NODE(PLACE));
        end if;
      else
        -- KEY is at least one level down
        DELETE (KEY, THIS_NODE.NEXT_NODE(PLACE));
      end if;
      -- Return here from recursive calls. Must make sure that all nodes have
      -- the minimum number of keys
      if THIS_NODE.NEXT_NODE(PLACE) /= null and then
          THIS_NODE.NEXT_NODE(PLACE).IN_USE < MIN_KEY_NUM then
        RESTORE_NODES (THIS_NODE, PLACE);
      end if;
    end if;
  end DELETE;
```

The DELETE procedure has three possibilities at each node. First, the key is found in a leaf node, then REMOVE_KEY removes the Kth key from the leaf. Second, if the key is found in a node that is not a leaf, it is replaced by its inorder successor, and then DELETE is called to delete the successor key from the subtree. Finally, the key is not in the current node, in which case the DELETE procedure is called using the appropriate subtree. The procedures REMOVE_KEY and REPLACE_WITH_SUCCESSOR are straightforward.

```
  procedure REMOVE_KEY      (THIS_NODE    : in     NEXT;
                   KEY_POSITION : in     positive) is
    TEMP : NEXT := THIS_NODE;
    -- Removes key-data pair at position key_position from a leaf
    --  Assumes KEY_POSITION <= THIS_NODES.IN_USE
  begin
    if KEY_POSITION < TEMP.IN_USE then
      TEMP.KEY(KEY_POSITION..TEMP.IN_USE-1) :=
              TEMP.KEY(KEY_POSITION+1..TEMP.IN_USE);
      TEMP.DATA(KEY_POSITION..TEMP.IN_USE-1) :=
               TEMP.DATA(KEY_POSITION+1..TEMP.IN_USE);
    end if;
    TEMP.NEXT_NODE(KEY_POSITION..TEMP.IN_USE) :=
             TEMP.NEXT_NODE(KEY_POSITION+1..TEMP.IN_USE+1);
    TEMP.IN_USE := TEMP.IN_USE - 1;
  end REMOVE_KEY;

  procedure REPLACE_WITH_SUCCESSOR    (THIS_NODE    : in     NEXT;
                                       KEY_POSITION : in     positive ) is
    -- Replaces key at KEY_POSITION key in node accessed by n with its
    -- successor. The bookkeeping is done in RESTORE_NODE
```

```
      TEMP : NEXT := THIS_NODE.NEXT_NODE (KEY_POSITION + 1);
      TEMP_THIS : NEXT := THIS_NODE;
   begin
     -- Find node with successor
     while TEMP.NEXT_NODE(1) /= null loop
       TEMP := TEMP.NEXT_NODE(1);
     end loop;
     TEMP_THIS.KEY(KEY_POSITION) := TEMP.KEY(1);
     TEMP_THIS.DATA(KEY_POSITION) := TEMP.DATA(1);
   end REPLACE_WITH_SUCCESSOR;
```

The key is now removed and the node must be restored. The leaf that the key or its successor was removed from might not have enough key-data pairs. Rebuilding nodes may cause other nodes to have too few key-data pairs. The procedure RESTORE_NODES deals with this problem. If a node needs restoring, there are three cases. First a key-data pair must be rotated right. A node has too few pairs, and its left adjacent node has at least one pair to spare. An excess key-data pair is moved from the left adjacent node to the parent, and a node in the parent is moved to the adjacent child with too few pairs. Case 2 is just the reverse of case 1. A key-data pair is moved from a node with a surplus of pairs to the parent and then to the left adjacent node. Finally, an adjacent node might not have a spare pair to balance out a deficient and adjacent node. In this case the two children are combined. The procedure RESTORE_NODE tackles all three cases.

```
      procedure RESTORE_NODES      (PARENT : in     NEXT;
                                    PLACE  : in     positive ) is
   begin
       if PLACE = 1 then
         if PARENT.NEXT_NODE(2).IN USE > MIN_KEY_NUM then
           -- Right node has extra key-data pair
           ROTATE_LEFT (PARENT, 2);
         else
           COMBINE (PARENT, 2);
         end if;
       elsif PLACE = PARENT.IN_USE then
         if PARENT.NEXT_NODE(PLACE-1).IN_USE > MIN_KEY_NUM then
           -- Left has extra key-data pair
           ROTATE_RIGHT (PARENT, PLACE-1);
         else
           COMBINE (PARENT, PLACE-1);
         end if;
       else
         -- Deficient child is an "interior" child
         if PARENT.NEXT_NODE(PLACE-1).IN_USE > MIN_KEY_NUM then
           ROTATE_RIGHT (PARENT, PLACE-1);
         elsif PARENT.NEXT_NODE(PLACE+1).IN_USE > MIN_KEY_NUM then
           ROTATE_LEFT (PARENT, PLACE+1);
         else
           COMBINE (PARENT, PLACE);
         end if;
       end if;
     end RESTORE_NODES;
```

The procedures ROTATE_RIGHT, ROTATE_LEFT, and COMBINE complete the implementation of the operation DELETE_KEY. Since ROTATE_LEFT is similar to ROTATE_RIGHT, it is not illustrated.

```
procedure ROTATE_RIGHT (PARENT : in      NEXT;
                        PLACE  : in      positive ) is
   -- Takes largest key-data in a given left child, puts it in
   -- the parent, and puts parent key-data pair in right child
   TEMP : NEXT := PARENT;
begin
   -- Make room in the right node
   TEMP.NEXT_NODE(PLACE+1).KEY(2..PARENT.NEXT_NODE(PLACE+1).IN_USE+1) :=
      TEMP.NEXT)NODE(PLACE+1).KEY(1..PARENT.NEXT_NODE(PLACE+1).IN_USE);
   TEMP.NEXT_NODE(PLACE).DATA(2..PARENT.NEXT_NODE(PLACE).IN_USE+1) :=
      TEMP.NEXT_NODE(PLACE+1).DATA(1..PARENT.NEXT_NODE(PLACE+1).IN_USE);
   TEMP.NEXT_NODE(PLACE).NEXT_NODE(2..PARENT.NEXT_NODE(PLACE).IN_USE+2) :=
      TEMP.NEXT_NODE(PLACE+1).NEXT_NODE(1..PARENT.NEXT_NODE(PLACE+1).IN_USE+1);
   --MOVE KEY-data from place in PARENT TO place+1 node NODE
   TEMP.NEXT_NODE(PLACE+1).KEY(1) := TEMP.KEY(PLACE);
   TEMP.NEXT_NODE(PLACE+1).DATA(1) := TEMP.DATA(PLACE)
   --Move last pair of place node to place in parent
   TEMP.KEY(PLACE) :=
      TEMP.NEXT_NODE(PLACE).KEY(TEMP.NEXT_NODE(PLACE).IN_USE);
   TEMP.DATA(PLACE) :=
      TEMP.NEXT_NODE(PLACE).DATA(TEMP.NEXT_NODE(PLACE).IN_USE);
   -- MOVE PLACE NEXT NODE to PLACE+1
   TEMP.NEXT_NODE(PLACE+1).NEXT_NODE(1) :=
      TEMP.NEXT_NODE(PLACE).NEXT_NODE(TEMP.NEXT_NODE(PLACE).IN_USE+1);
   --Adjust IN_USE for place, place+1 nodes
   TEMP.NEXT_NODE(PLACE).IN_USE := TEMP.NEXT_NODE(PLACE).IN_USE - 1;
   TEMP.NEXT_NODE(PLACE+1).IN_USE := TEMP.NEXT_NODE(PLACE+1).IN_USE + 1;
end ROTATE_RIGHT;

procedure COMBINE (PARENT : in      NEXT;
                   PLACE  : in      positive ) is
   TEMP : NEXT := PARENT;
   COUNT_NEXT, COUNT_THIS : positive;
   -- Combines the two subtrees at PLACE and PLACE+1
   -- Bookkeeping in RESTORE_NODE guarantees room
begin
   -- Puts key-data at PLACE in parent into child at place.
   TEMP.NEXT_NODE(PLACE).IN_USE := TEMP.NEXT_NODE(PLACE).IN_USE + 1;
   TEMP.NEXT_NODE(PLACE).KEY(TEMP.NEXT_NODE(PLACE).IN_USE) :=
   TEMP.KEY(PLACE);
   TEMP.NEXT_NODE(PLACE).DATA(TEMP.NEXT_NODE(PLACE).IN_USE) :=
      TEMP.DATA(PLACE);
   --Move all key data node triples from place + 1 to place
   COUNT.NEXT := TEMP.NEXT_NODE(PLACE+1).IN_USE;
   COUNT.THIS := TEMP.NEXT_NODE(PLACE).IN_USE;
   TEMP.NEXT_NODE(PLACE).KEY(COUNT_THIS+1..COUNT_NEXT+COUNT_THIS) :=
      TEMP.NEXT_NODE(PLACE+1).KEY(1..COUNT_NEXT);
```

```
TEMP.NEXT_NODE(PLACE).DATA(COUNT_THIS+1..COUNT_NEXT+COUNT_THIS) :=
    TEMP.NEXT_NODE(PLACE+1).DATA(1..COUNT_NEXT);
TEMP.NEXT_NODE(PLACE).NEXT_NODE(COUNT_THIS+1..COUNT_NEXT+COUNT_THIS+1) :=
    TEMP.NEXT_NODE(PLACE+1).NEXT_NODE(1..COUNT_NEXT+1);
TEMP.NEXT_NODE(PLACE).IN_USE := COUNT_NEXT + COUNT_THIS;
-- Shift out place in parent
if TEMP.IN_USE = PLACE then
  TEMP.NEXT_NODE(TEMP.IN_USE) := TEMP.NEXT_NODE(TEMP.IN_USE+1);
else
  TEMP.KEY(PLACE..TEMP.IN_USE-1) := TEMP.KEY(PLACE+1..TEMP.IN_USE);
  TEMP.DATA(PLACE..TEMP.IN_USE-1) := TEMP.DATA(PLACE+1..TEMP.IN_USE);
  TEMP.NEXT_NODE(PLACE+1..TEMP.IN_USE) :=
          TEMP.NEXT_NODE(PLACE+2..TEMP.IN_USE+1);
end if;
TEMP.IN_USE := TEMP.IN_USE - 1);
end COMBINE;
```

There is a modified B_TREE definition where key-data pairs appear only in leaves (Figure 8.5.9). This tree is called a B+ tree. One access is supposed to fill one disk sector. If the data definition is large, there are advantages to having key-data pairs only in the leaf nodes and

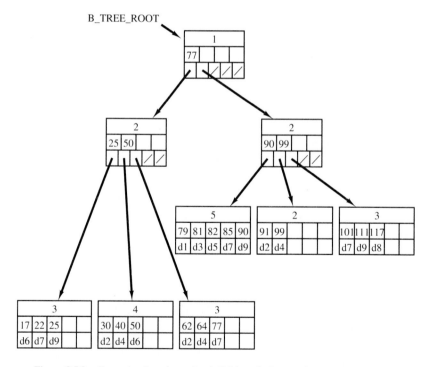

Figure 8.5.9. Example of an alternative definition of a B-tree of order 4. Note that the root and all interior nodes are composed of key-pointer pairs. The leaf nodes are made up of key-data pairs only.

key-access fields in the interior nodes. Figure 8.5.10 defines this B+ tree variation. The implementations are left to the exercises.

1. There are two types of nodes, ptr_nodes and data_nodes. All ptr_nodes contain only keys and access values. All data_nodes contain only keys and their associated data fields. All ptr_nodes are interior nodes and all data_nodes are leafs.
2. The root is either a leaf or it has between 2 and $m + 1$ children.
3. All interior nodes, except possibly the root, have between $\lfloor m/2 \rfloor$ and $n + 1$ children.
4. All leaves are on the same level. A leaf contains between $\lfloor m/2 \rfloor$ and $n+ 1$ key-data combinations.

Figure 8.5.10   Alternative definition of B-tree.

8.6 TRIES

In Section 8.5 multiway trees were introduced. In the binary case the key-data pair is placed in the left subtree of a node if the key is less than the key of the current node or the right subtree if it is greater. In the case of the B-tree, the key-data pair was placed in the ith subtree if the key was greater than the $(i − 1)$st key but less than the ith key. In a TRIE the key is a sequence of objects. All key-data pairs whose key has the same first object are in the same subtrie.

Consider the problem of looking up the word *cat* in a dictionary. The dictionary is not ordered like a hash table, where knowing the key you compute the page, column, and line of the word before turning the first page. The ordering is lexicographic. The first character, c, is used to find the section where all the words that begin with that letter are listed. Then the second letter, a, is used to find the subsection where all the words that begin with "ca" are listed. The letter "t" is used to find the sub-subsection where all the words that begin with "cat" are listed. Consequently, a TRIE is sometimes called a *lexicographic search tree*.

Before it can be determined how to operate on a TRIE, the node structure must be defined. The key is a sequence of objects, so one thing that must be specified is the length of the key. The objects that make up the key, such as lowercase letters or characters or digits, must also be specified. This must be done as a discrete type such as an enumeration. Third, there must be a way of telling whether the particular subsequence is valid. For example, in a trie-based spelling checker, the sequence "abb" is not a word but the sequence "abba" is. (At least the author's dictionary says that "abba" is a word.) The node "abb" must be in the trie even though "abb" is not a word. Some type of optional data field is also needed. A first definition of a node is

```
type TRIE_NODE;
type NEXT is access TREE_NODE;
type NEXT_ARRAY is array.(OBJECT_LIST) of NEXT;
type TRIE_NODE is
  KEY : OBJECT_LIST;
  IN_USE : boolean := false;
  DATA : DATA_TYPE;
  NXT   : NEXT_ARRAY;
end record;
```

Note that the entire key is not contained in a node, only a key object. Figure 8.6.1 illustrates the trie structure. The trie is a key-data table. Keys are integers with digits 1 to 4. The data associated with that key are common garden vegetables and herbs. The ADT trie that is documented in Figure 8.6.2 and specified in Figure 8.6.3 is based on a spelling dictionary.

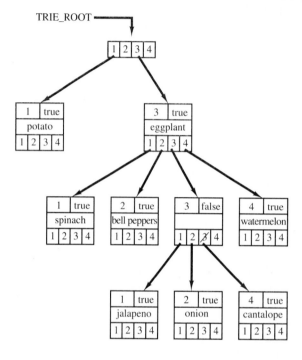

Figure 8.6.1   Partial diagram of a trie with KEY_COMPONENTS equal to in positive range 1..4. The keys represent identification numbers associated with common vegetables. There are no vegetables with id numbers beginning with 2 or 4, but other id numbers that begin with these digits are in the trie so these nodes must be present. The key "32" is bell peppers and the key "334" is cantalope. There is no key "33," so this node is marked false. No key has prefix "333," so the access value of the third field of node 33 is null.

GENERAL ADT SPECIFICATION FOR BOUNDED_SEARCH_TRIE

Description

This package implements the ADT BOUNDED_SEARCH_TRIE. A trie is a multiway search structure where the key has a maximum length. A node's placement depends on its individual components. The nodes on level 1 all have distinct first key components. The key of any node uses a single key component. All nodes on the kth level use the kth key component. A key of length k is in the trie if the search ends up on kth level with the node's key component flag field set to true. The data field is sometimes not used, particularly in dictionary-type applications. Every node contains a key component field, a boolean field to determine if the complete key is in the trie, an optional data field, and a multiway access array. Key-length-data triples are inserted into the tree based on the key's components. Duplicate keys are not allowed. Provisions to search for data based on key value, delete nodes based on key, update nodes based on key, as well as doing an inorder traversal are included. The key is an array of specified maximum length where only the key components 1 through length are used and the key components length+1 through maximum length are ignored. Key is not private but trie is limited private.

Figure 8.6.2   Documentation for BOUNDED_BINARY_SEARCH_TRIE. Continues on page 279.

Programmer-Supplied Data Structures
or Specifications

The programmer must supply three parameters. The first is a positive constant that corresponds to the maximum length of the key. The second is a discrete type that is used as the components of the key. The third is a DATA_TYPE that stores information associated with a key. The DATA_TYPE is private within the package.

Operations

Name	Description
COPY	Makes an exact copy of a specified trie with no shared nodes.
CLEAR	Returns a trie with a root node that has only null pointers. No key component is in the root.
INSERT	Inserts a given key-data pair into a specified trie. Nodes are created as required. The trie search structure is preserved. Automatically resets the traversal pointers to the beginning of the trie.
DELETE	Changes the IN_USE boolean field of any key to false in a specified trie while preserving the trie search structure. Automatically resets the traversal pointers to the beginning of the trie.
UPDATE	Searches for a node with a specified key and checks if the nodes IN_USE field set is true in a specified trie and replaced the data field with a new value.
GET_DATA_FOR_KEY	Searches a specified trie for a node with a specified key pair and returns the associated data field.
EMPTY	Boolean-valued function that returns true if a specified trie has no nodes, or false otherwise.
FULL	Boolean-valued function that returns true if there is no more space to add any nodes to a tree, of false otherwise.
COUNT	Returns the number of key-data pairs in the trie. Note that the number of nodes is often different from the number of key-data pairs.
EQUAL	Boolean-valued function that returns true if both tries contain the same key-data pairs and both tries must have similar structures, or false otherwise.
KEY_IN_TRIE	Boolean-valued function that returns the IN_USE field of the node associated with the given key, or false otherwise.
NEXT_INORDER	Returns the key-data triple of the next node with a true valued IN_USE field. The traversal will be in ascending order of key components. When the traversal is finished it will return to the beginning. Any insertion or deletion of a key-data pair node will cause the sequence to be reset to the first node to be processed. WARNING. This operation returns a key of MAXIMUM_KEY_LENGTH even though only the first LENGTH_KEY_ components are valid.

Figure 8.6.2 Continues on page 280.

SET_INORDER   Sets the traversal sequence to start at the first node normally
                                     processed for an inorder traversal.

Exceptions

Five exceptions can occur: OVERFLOW, KEY_INDEX_ERROR, KEY_NOT_IN_TRIE,
KEY_IS_IN_TRIE, and TRIE_EMPTY. The exception OVERFLOW occurs when an attempt to
copy a trie, to insert a key-length-data triple is made, or to traverse the trie using NEXT_IN-
ORDER is made and a storage_error is raised. The exception KEY_INDEX_ERROR is raised
whenever the first index of a key is not equal to 1 or the last index is greater than MAX-
IMUM_KEY_INDEX. The exception KEY_NOT_IN_TRIE occurs when making a search in
DELETE, UPDATE, and GET_DATA_FOR_KEY for a given key and the key is not found. The
exception KEY_IS_IN_TRIE occurs when an attempt is made to insert the same key-length pair
that is already in the tree. The exception TRIE_EMPTY occurs when any operation requiring key-
length pair is attempted on an empty trie. The traversal also raises TRIE_EMPTY, when there is
no key-data pair to return.

Warnings

The key is implemented as an unconstrained array. However, the first index must always be 1 and
the last index must never be greater than MAXIMUM_KEY_LENGTH. Only the indices 1
through length are used. All other warnings are implementation dependent.

Figure 8.6.2   Concluded.

The reason that this trie is bounded is that the number of levels is limited to the maximum length of the key. If the key components are the 26 letters of the alphabet and the maximum length is 10, the trie could conceivably have 26**10 nodes. However, many letter
combinations don't appear. For example, all but three words that begin with the letter "q" must
be followed by the letter "u." This reduces the number of nodes by 25*26**8. According to
the flyleaf in *Webster's New Universal Unabridged Dictionary*, this unabridged version contains about 320,000 words or about 26*4 words. In this dictionary, all words that begin with
"z" must be followed by one of the following letters (a, e, i, n, o, r, u, w, y). This observation
eliminates 17*26**8 nodes. Certain letter combinations do not occur and this again reduces
the maximum trie.

```
generic
   MAXIMUM_KEY_LENGTH : in positive;
   type KEY_COMPONENTS is (<>);
   type DATA_TYPE is private;
package GENERIC_BOUNDED_SEARCH_TRIE is
   type KEY_TYPE is array ( positive range <>) of KEY_COMPONENTS;
   type TRIE is limited private;
   procedure COPY            (FROM_TRIE  : in      TRIE;
                              TO_TRIE    :     out TRIE);
   procedure CLEAR           (THIS_TRIE  : in out TRIE);
   procedure INSERT          (KEY        : in KEY_TYPE;
                              DATA       : in DATA_TYPE;
                              IN_TRIE    : in out TRIE );
```

Figure 8.6.3   GENERIC_BOUNDED_SEARCH_TRIE specification. Continues on page 281.

```
    procedure DELETE              (KEY       : in KEY_TYPE;
                                   FROM_TRIE : in out TRIE );
    procedure UPDATE              (KEY       : in KEY_TYPE;
                                   DATA      : in DATA_TYPE;
                                   IN_TRIE   : in out TRIE);
    procedure NEXT_INORDER        (KEY       : out KEY_TYPE;
                                   LENGTH    : out positive;
                                   DATA      : out DATA_TYPE;
                                   IN_TRIE   : in out TRIE);
    procedure SET_INORDER         (IN_TRIE   : in out TRIE);
    function EMPTY                (THIS_TRIE : TRIE ) return boolean;
    function FULL                 (THIS_TRIE : TRIE ) return booelan;
    function COUNT                (THIS_TRIE : TRIE ) return natural;
    function EQUAL                (LEFT, RIGHT : TRIE) return boolean;
    function KEY_IN_TRIE          (KEY : KEY_TYPE; IN_TRIE : TRIE ) return boolean;
    function GET_DATA_FOR_TRIE    (KEY : KEY_TYPE; IN_TRIE: TRIE) return DATA_TYPE;
    KEY_INDEX_ERROR    : exception;
    KEY_NOT_IN_TRIE    : exception;
    KEY_IS_IN_TRIE     : exception;
    TRIE_IS_EMPTY      : exception;
    OVERFLOW           : exception;
private
  type STACK_NODE;
  type TRIE_STACK is access STACK_NODE;
  type TRIE_NODE;
  type NEXT is access TRIE_NODE;
  type NEXT_ARRAY is array (KEY_COMPONENTS) of NEXT;
  type TRIE is
    record
      NEXT_COMPONENT : NEXT_ARRAY;
      COUNT          : natural := 0;
      NEXT_IN        : TRIE_STACK; -- USED in NEXT_INORDER
    end record;
end GENERIC_BOUNDED_SEARCH_TRIE;

package body GENERIC_BOUNDED_SEARCH_TRIE is

  type TRIE_NODE is
    record
      KEY_OBJECT     : KEY_COMPONENTS;
      IN_USE         : boolean := false;
      DATA           : DATA_TYPE;
      NEXT_COMPONENT : NEXT_ARRAY;
    end record;

  type STACK_NODE is
    record
      KEY     : KEY_TYPE (1..MAXIMUM_KEY_LENGTH);
      LENGTH  : positive;
```

Figure 8.6.3 Continues on page 282.

```
      NXT_NODE : NEXT;
      STACK    : TRIE_STACK;
    end record;


  ...................................
  end GENERIC_BOUNDED_SEARCH_TRIE;
```

Figure 8.6.3   GENERIC_BOUNDED_SEARCH_TRIE specification. Concluded.

The TRIE package is a little awkward as specified. If a trie implements as a spell checker, individual words must be converted into some object of type key before processing. After key conversion, the object can be inserted into the trie. The first KEY_COMPONENT determines which node on the first level is accessed. If there is no node that corresponds to the first component, one is created. This process continues for the length of the key. Once the node corresponding to the last KEY_COMPONENT is found or created, the boolean field IN_USE is checked. If IN_USE is already true, the exception KEY_IS_IN_TREE is raised. If IN_USE is false, it is set true and the data field is initialized. The implementation follows.

```
  procedure INSERT      ( KEY    : in KEY_TYPE;
                          DATA   : in DATA_TYPE;
                          IN_TRIE : in out TRIE) is
    -- Inserts a given key-data pair into the trie IN_TRIE. Nodes are created
    -- as required. Insertion causes the traversal to reset
    -- Exception KEY_IS_IN_TRIE raised if KEY already in trie.
    -- Exception OVERFLOW raised if no space to add KEY
    -- Exception KEY_INDEX_ERROR raised if KEY indices do not conform.
    TEMP : NEXT := IN_TRIE.NEXT_COMPONENT(KEY(1));
    LENGTH : positive := KEY'last;
  begin
    if KEY'first /= 1 or else LENGTH > MAXIMUM_KEY_LENGTH then
      raise KEY_INDEX_ERROR;
    elsif TEMP = null then
      -- No KEY with component KEY(1) in trie
      IN_TRIE.NEXT_COMPONENT(KEY(1)) := new TRIE_NODE;
      IN_TRIE.NEXT_COMPONENT(KEY(1)).KEY_OBJECT := KEY(1);
      TEMP := IN_TRIE.NEXT_COMPONENT(KEY(1));
    end if;
    for INDEX in positive range 2..LENGTH loop
      -- Go through the Trie KEY_ component by KEY component
      if TEMP.NEXT_COMPONENT(KEY(INDEX)) = null then
        -- New node needed
        TEMP.NEXT_COMPONENT(KEY(INDEX)) := new TRIE_NODE;
        TEMP.NEXT_COMPONENT(KEY(INDEX)).KEY_OBJECT := KEY(INDEX);
      end if;
      TEMP := TEMP.NEXT_COMPONENT(KEY(INDEX));
    end loop;
    -- TEMP references the TRIE_NODE where KEY should be.
    if TEMP.IN_USE then
      raise KEY_IS_IN_TRIE;
```

```
    else
      TEMP.IN_USE := true;
      TEMP.DATA := DATA;
      IN_TRIE.COUNT := IN_TRIE.COUNT + 1;
      IN_TRIE.NEXT_IN := null;
    end if;
exception
  when storage_error => raise OVERFLOW;
end INSERT;
```

The function KEY_IN_TRIE works its way down the trie to the proper node and then returns the IN_USE field. If the trek down the trie is interrupted at any point, a false is returned.

```
function KEY_IN_TRIE ( KEY : KEY_TYPE; IN_TRIE : TRIE) return boolean is
  -- Returns true if a key-data pair with specified key is in IN_TRIE.
  -- Exception KEY_INDEX_ERROR raised if KEY indices do not conform.
  TEMP : NEXT;
  LENGTH : positive := KEY'last;
begin
  if KEY'first /= 1 or else LENGTH > MAXIMUM_KEY_LENGTH then
    raise KEY_INDEX_ERROR;
  else
    -- traverse through Trie, set TEMP to proper subtrie
    TEMP := IN_TRIE.NEXT_COMPONENT(KEY(1));
    for INDEX in 2..LENGTH loop
      if TEMP = null then
        -- Subtrie empty, key is not there
        return false;
      end if;
      TEMP := TEMP.NEXT_COMPONENT(KEY(INDEX));
    end loop;
    -- Temp should reference the proper TREE_NODE
    if TEMP = null then
      return false;
    else
      return TEMP.IN_USE;
    end if;
  end if;
end KEY_IN_TRIE;
```

The operation DELETE differs from deleting a node in a binary tree. If the appropriate node at level length is in the tree, it cannot be deleted if it references any node (see Figure 8.6.4). The key is deleted by setting the IN_USE field to false and then checking to see if the node accesses any lower-level node. If it does not, only then can the node itself be deleted. The traversing of the trie is not difficult to implement. Again, suppose that the trie is a spell-checking dictionary. The object is to get a listing of all words in the dictionary and to output them in lexicographic order. That means that if a word is a prefix to a longer word, the shorter word is returned. The word *a* must be output before the word *at*, which is output before the word *attic*, and so on. This traversal is a modified preorder traversal. If the node is in use, its

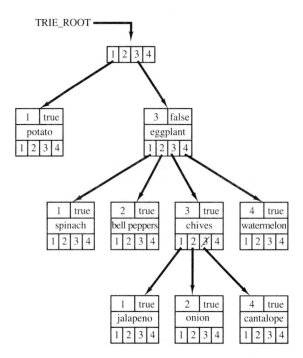

TRIE_ROOT

Figure 8.6.4 Consider the trie in Figure 8.6.1. The deletion of the node with key = "3" is done by setting the IN_USE field to false. The node itself cannot be physically deleted because other keys have prefix "3." The insertion of the key-data pair "33" - chives does not require the creation of a new node. The IN_USE field is merely set to true and the data field is initialized.

key-data pair is returned and then its subtrees are processed in proper order. The stack has the next node to process as its top element. This requires that the IN_USE field of the stack's top be true. If a node is a leaf, its IN_USE field must be true. The procedure FIX_TRIE_STACK takes a stack with an interior node that is not in use, and adds nodes to the stack until it finds a node with IN_USE is true. The procedure to reset the traversal becomes

```
procedure FIX_TRIE_STACK(T : in out TRIE) is
    -- Fixes traversal stack so next node to process has
    -- its IN_USE=true. This also leaves a valid key in the KEY component of
    -- the top stack node. This must terminate because every
    -- leaf of a trie is IN_USE; If this procedure is called, the
    -- stack is not empty.
    TEMP_NODE : NEXT;
    INDEX : positive;
    KEY_TEMP : KEY_TYPE (1..MAXIMUM_KEY_LENGTH);
begin
    -- Current key in top STACK_NODE is of specific length. There must
    -- be a key with longer length or this STACK_NODE would not be on the
    -- stack
    INDEX := T.NEXT_IN.LENGTH;
    -- Get the TRIE_NODE associated with top STACK_NODE
    TEMP_NODE := T.NEXT_IN.NXT_NODE;
    KEY_TEMP(1..INDEX) := T.NEXT_IN.KEY (1..INDEX);
    --Pop stack.  This stack node contains no more information of interest
    T.NEXT_IN := T.NEXT_IN.STACK;
```

```
      INDEX := INDEX + 1;
      if INDEX > MAXIMUM_KEY_LENGTH then
        raise OVERFLOW;
      end if;
      for I in reverse KEY_COMPONENTS loop
        -- Stack reverses order processed, so put on in reverse order
        if TEMP_NODE.NEXT_COMPONENT(I) /= null then
          -- Must be a valid key-data pair farther along, push it on the stack
          KEY_TEMP(INDEX) := I;
          T.NEXT_IN := new STACK_NODE' (KEY_TEMP, INDEX,
            TEMP_NODE.NEXT_COMPONENT(I), T.NEXT_IN);
        end if;
      end loop;
    -- Node referenced must contain valid key, if not, go to next level
    if not T.NEXT_IN.NXT_NODE.IN_USE then
      FIX_TRIE_STACK(T);
    end if;
  end FIX_TRIE_STACK;
  procedure SET_INORDER (IN_TRIE : in out TRIE) is
    -- Sets the traversal sequence to list the first valid key-data pair
    -- By convention, the top of the stack will reference a valid
    -- key-data pair
    -- Exception OVERFLOW raised if not enough space for the stack
    -- Exception TREE_IS_EMPTY raised if no key-data pairs to return
    KEY_TEMP : KEY_TYPE(1..MAXIMUM_KEY_LENGTH);
  begin
    if IN_TRIE.COUNT = 0 then
      raise TRIE_IS_EMPTY;
    else
      IN_TRIE.NEXT_IN := null;
      for INDEX in REVERSE KEY_COMPONENTS loop
        if IN_TRIE.NEXT_COMPONENT(INDEX) /= null then
          -- Subtrie found with valid data, put it on the trie
          KEY_TEMP(1) := INDEX;
          IN_TRIE.NEXT_IN := new STACK_NODE' (KEY_TEMP, 1,
                        IN_TRIE.NEXT_COMPONENT(INDEX), IN_TRIE.NEXT_IN);
        end if;
      end loop;
      if not IN_TRIE.NEXT_IN.NXT_NODE.IN_USE then
        -- By convention the top of the stack must reference a valid key-data
        FIX_TRIE_STACK(IN_TRIE);
      end if;
    end if;
  exception
    when storage_error => raise OVERFLOW;
  end SET_INORDER;
```

The procedure NEXT_INORDER returns the next key-data pair and leaves the stack with a node containing the next key-data pair to be processed or with the stack empty.

```
procedure NEXT_INORDER ( KEY         : out KEY_TYPE;
                         LENGTH_KEY : out positive;
                         DATA        : out DATA_TYPE;
                         IN_TRIE     : in out TRIE) is
   -- Returns the next key-data pair of the next node with IN_USE=true
   -- based on a traversal in ascending lexicographic order of KEY
   -- components. When the traversal is finished, it will repeat
   -- starting at the beginning. Any insertion or deletion resets the
   -- traversal. WARNING : KEY is returned as KEY_TYPE(1..MAXIMUM_KEY_LENGTH)
   -- even though only KEY(1..LENGTH_KEY) components are valid
   -- Exception OVERFLOW raised if not enough space for the stack
   -- Exception TREE_IS_EMPTY raised if no key-data pairs to return
   TEMP_STACK : TRIE_STACK;
   INDEX : positive;
   TEMP_NODE : NEXT;
   KEY_TEMP : KEY_TYPE(1..MAXIMUM_KEY_LENGTH);
begin --  NEXT_INORDER
   if IN_TRIE.COUNT = 0 then
      raise TRIE_IS_EMPTY;
   elsif IN_TRIE.NEXT_IN = null then
   -- Check to see if stack has been initialized.
      SET_INORDER(IN_TRIE);
   end if;
   -- By convention, the STACK_NODE on top contains a valid key and a
   -- reference to the TRIE_NODE where the associated data is located. Get
   -- key-data pair and pop the stack.
   KEY := IN_TRIE.NEXT_IN.KEY;
   LENGTH_KEY := IN_TRIE.NEXT_IN.LENGTH;
   DATA := IN_TRIE.NEXT_IN.NXT_NODE.DATA;
   -- Update stack so top points to next valid key-data pair.
   -- The node just processed can have subtries or it was a leaf.
   TEMP_STACK := IN_TRIE.NEXT_IN;
   IN_TRIE.NEXT_IN := IN_TRIE.NEXT_IN.STACK;
   if IN_TRIE.NEXT_IN = null then
      SET_INORDER (IN_TRIE);
   else
   if TEMP_STACK.LENGTH < MAXIMUM_KEY_LENGTH then
      TEMP_NODE := TEMP_STACK.NXT_NODE;
      -- The length of any keys in children will be one more their parent's
      INDEX := TEMP_STACK.LENGTH + 1;
      KEY_TEMP := TEMP_STACK.KEY;
      -- Check for all possible children
      for I in reverse KEY_COMPONENTS loop
         if TEMP_NODE.NEXT_COMPONENT(I) /= null then
            -- There is a child, put it on the stack
            KEY_TEMP(INDEX) := I;
            IN_TRIE.NEXT_IN := new STACK_NODE' (KEY_TEMP, INDEX,
                             TEMP_NODE.NEXT_COMPONENT(I), IN_TRIE.NEXT_IN);
         end if;
```

```
      end loop;
    end if;
    if not IN_TRIE.NEXT_IN.NXT_NODE.IN_USE then
      -- By convention the top of the stack must reference a valid key-data
      FIX_TRIE_STACK(IN_TRIE);
    end if;
    end if;
  exception
    when storage_error => raise overflow;
  end NEXT_INORDER;
```

The full implementation is left to the exercises.

Consider a standard spell checker, which is a trie instantiated as

```
type LETTERS is character range 'a'..'z';
SPELL_CHECK is new GENERIC_BOUNDED_SEARCH_TRIE (15, LETTERS, boolean);
use SPELL_CHECK;
```

The boolean variable is used as a data field. If words are implemented as strings, the function CONVERT_WORD takes a string of up to length to 15, puts all characters in lowercase, and then returns something of KEY_TYPE. After that the following procedure will list every word in the document whose first 15 letters is not in the dictionary.

```
procedure CHECK_FILE( FILE : in FILENAME;
                      T    : in TRIE ) is
begin
  SET_FILE_TO_START(FILE);
  while not END_OF_FILE(FILE) loop
    GET_NEXT_WORD(WORD);
    if not KEY_IN_TRIE(COVERT_WORD(WORD), WORD'length) then
      put(WORD);
      new_line;
    end if;
  end loop;
  put("Spell-Check finished");
end CHECK_FILE;
```

8.7 APPLICATIONS

Chapter 7 introduced the priority queue. Priority queues act like a queue when an item is dequeued because items come off the front of the queue. Normal queues insert an item at the rear of a queue. A priority queue places an item in a queue based on a priority. Every item in a priority queue has a priority greater than or equal to the item that follows it. When a priority queue is implemented as a queue, the operational overhead to add an item to a queue is $O(n)$. When a priority queue is implemented using a binary search tree, the operational overhead is reduced to $O(\log_2(n))$. The only problem is how to access the front of the queue. Assume the instantiation shown in Figure 8.7.1. Note that the private part has been replaced. As Figure 8.7.1 stands, it will not compile. Since the type TREE is limited private, the type

PRIORITY_QUEUE must also be limited private. When a component of a record type is limited private, the record itself is limited private. Records defined in this manner can never be a formal parameter of mode "out" [see ADA LRM 7.4.4(4)]. There are two ways to get this ADT to compile. One option is to recompile UNBOUNDED_BINARY_SEARCH_TREE with the type TREE defined as private. The second option is to change all formal parameters of type PRIORITY_QUEUE that are mode "out" to mode "in out." For no particular reason the second option is chosen.

```
with GENERIC_UNBOUNDED_BINARY_SEARCH_TREE;
generic
  type ITEM_TYPE is private;
  with function ">=" (LEFT, RIGHT : ITEM_TYPE) return boolean;
package GENERIC_UNBOUNDED_PRIORITY_QUEUE is
  type PRIORITY_QUEUE is limited private;
  procedure ADD_TO_Q  (ITEM       : in ITEM_TYPE;
                       TO_THE_Q    : in out PRIORITY_QUEUE);
  procedure DEQUEUE   (ITEM        : out ITEM_TYPE;
                       FROM_THE_Q : in out PRIORITY_QUEUE);
  procedure copy      (FROM_Q      : in     PRIORITY_QUEUE;
                       TO_Q        : in out PRIORITY_QUEUE);
  procedure MERGE     (FROM_Q1,
                       FROM_Q2     : in PRIORITY_QUEUE;
                       ONTO_Q      : in out PRIORITY_QUEUE);
  procedure CLEAR     (Q_TO_CLEAR : in out PRIORITY_QUEUE);
  procedure POP       (FROM_THE_Q : in out PRIORITY_QUEUE);
  function LENGTH     (Q_TO_COUNT : PRIORITY_QUEUE) return natural;
  function EMPTY      (Q_TO_CHECK : PRIORITY_QUEUE) return boolean;
  function FRONT_ITEM (FROM_THE_Q: PRIORITY_QUEUE) return ITEM_TYPE;
  function EQUAL      (LEFT, RIGHT : PRIORITY_QUEUE) return boolean;
  OVERFLOW : exception;
  Q_IS_EMPTY : exception;
private
  package P_Q is new
    GENERIC_UNBOUNDED_BINARY_SEARCH_TREE (ITEM_TYPE, boolean, ">=");
  use P_Q;
  type PRIORITY_QUEUE is
    record
      PQ : TREE;
    end record;
end GENERIC_UNBOUNDED_PRIORITY_QUEUE;
```

Figure 8.7.1 Package specification for GENERIC_UNBOUNDED_PRIORITY_QUEUE similar to Figure 7.5.1.

The procedure DEQUEUE must get an item from the front of the queue. Binary search trees work with key-data pairs. By making the data type boolean, the key-data pair becomes an item-boolean pair. The binary search tree that implements the priority queue inserts the item-boolean pair into the queue-tree in such a way as to preserve the inorder traversal of the tree. The inorder traversal is relative to the instantiated boolean operator supplied by the programmer at instantiation. If the programmer supplies a relational operator that orders keys in an ascending order, the inorder traversal will access the tree nodes so that the key-data pairs are accessed in ascending order. If the programmer supplies a relational operator that orders keys in a descending order, the inorder traversal will access that items by highest priority. The first item in the inorder traversal will be the highest-priority item in the tree. Two queue operations are implemented using operations from GENERIC_UNBOUNDED_BINARY_SEARCH_TREE. Figure 8.7.2 illustrates the situation.

```
procedure ADD_TO_Q       (ITEM     : in      ITEM_TYPE;
                          TO_THE_Q : in out PRIORITY_QUEUE) is
   --  Adds item to tree preserving the inorder traversal
begin
   INSERT_NODE (ITEM, true, TO_THE_Q.PQ);
end ADD_TO_Q;
procedure DEQUEUE (ITEM : out ITEM_TYPE;
                   FROM_THE_Q : in out PRIORITY_QUEUE) is
   --  Returns and deletes the first item in the inorder traversal.DUMMY : boolean;
   TEMP_X : ITEM_TYPE;
begin
   NEXT_INORDER(TEMP_X, DUMMY, FROM_THE_Q.PQ);
   ITEM := TEMP_X;
   DELETE_NODE(TEMP_X, FROM_THE_Q.PQ);
end DEQUEUE;
```

The exercises contain the remainder of the implementation.

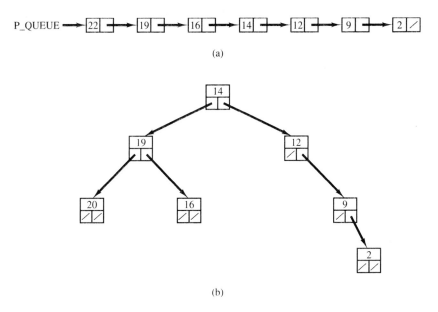

(a)

(b)

Figure 8.7.2 (a) Simple priority queue of integers implemented as a linear linked list. (b) Priority queue implemented as a binary search tree. Note that the inorder traversal of the tree is the same as the sequential traversal of the queue in (a).

Computers have a hierarchical file system. A directory may contain both files and sub-directories. At any directory files can be inserted or deleted, empty subdirectories can be created or deleted, or the home directory can be changed. Figure 8.7.3 shows how the basic ADT Unbounded_binary_tree can be used to implement a file directory system. Recall that a node is

```
type NODE is
  record
     ITEM : ITEM_TYPE;
     LEFT,
     RIGHT : TREE;
  end record;

type ITEM_TYPE is
  record
     DIR_NAME : String(1..8);
     DIR_Q    : BALKING_QUEUE;
  end record;
```

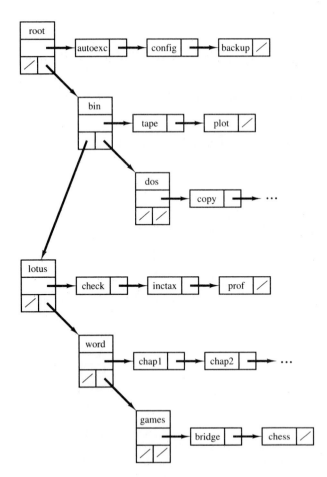

Figure 8.7.3 Simple file manager using a binary tree. The root directory has two sub-directories, bin and dos. The bin directory has three subdirectories: lotus, word, and games. Files in each directory are represented as balking queues.

Trees   Chap. 8

Suppose that a directory is a tree node. If ITEM_TYPE is a record composed of a directory name and a balking queue of files, then files and directories can be added, deleted, or listed. The right subtree can be defined as a queue of subdirectories. To change the directory the left tree access value is traversed like a queue until the required directory is found. The left access value is a queue of siblings.

Most applications using trees start with a basic binary search tree. These applications are characterized by large amounts of data that must be rapidly manipulated. If some sort of ordered listing is needed, the hash table option is not suitable. The chapter ends with a case study that builds a subject index.

8.8 TIME AND SPACE CONSTRAINTS

The tree structure is among the most efficient when the search, insert, and delete operations are considered. The ADT UNBOUNDED_BINARY_SEARCH_TREE, listed in Figure 8.2.3, and the ADT UNBOUNDED_BALANCED_BINARY_SEARCH_TREE, discussed in Section 3, differ only in the insert or delete procedures. The time and space constraints in Figure 8.8.1 assume that the tree is balanced. A balanced tree with n nodes has $\log_2(n)$ levels. Empirically, there is not much extra work involved in maintaining a balanced tree. As discussed previously, the insert and delete operations are $O(\log_2(n))$ in the balanced case. The insert and delete operations in the unmanaged case run from $O(\log_2(n))$, for random data that builds a nearly balanced tree, to $O(n)$ for data with an ascending or descending order. NEXT_INORDER can be $O(1)$ to $O(\log_2(n))$. The worst case is cited.

	Operation Overhead	Space Overhead
INSERT	$O(\log_2(n))$	$O(n)$
DELETE	$O(\log_2(n))$	$O(n)$
UPDATE	$O(\log_2(n))$	$O(n)$
COPY	$O(n)$	$O(n)$
NEXT_INORDER	$O(\log_2(n))$	$O(n)$
EQUAL	$O(n)$	$O(n)$
KEY_IN_TREE	$O(\log_2(n))$	$O(n)$
GET_DATA_FOR_TREE	$O(\log_2(n))$	$O(n)$

Figure 8.8.1   Constraints for the ADT GENERIC_UNBOUNDED_BALANCED_BINARY_SEARCH_TREE.

The operation EQUAL can be implemented in one of two ways. Recall that two binary search trees are equal if they contain the same set of key-data pairs. The hierarchical relationship between the nodes that contain the key-data pairs is not important. If two trees are equal, the inorder traversals of both trees will list the key-data pairs of both trees in the same order. If two trees are not equal, the key-data pairs will differ at some point in the traversal.

The constraints of the ADT GENERIC_BOUNDED_BALANCED_BINARY_SEARCH_TREE are similar, except that the space constraints are proportional to the maximum number of nodes, denoted size, but the operations are related to the number of active nodes, denoted by n. The time and space constraints for GENERIC_BOUNDED_BAL-ANCED_BINARY_SEARCH_TREE, listed in Figure 8.8.2, have the same or higher order.

	Operation Overhead	Space Overhead
INSERT	$O(n)$	$O(\text{Size})$
DELETE	$O(n)$	$O(\text{Size})$
UPDATE	$O(\log_2(n))$	$O(\text{Size})$
COPY	$O(n)$	$O(\text{Size})$
NEXT_INORDER	$O(1)$	$O(\text{Size})$
EQUAL	$O(n)$	$O(\text{Size})$
KEY_IN_TREE	$O(\log_2(n))$	$O(\text{Size})$
GET_DATA_FOR_TREE	$O(\log_2(n))$	$O(\text{Size})$

Figure 8.8.2 Constraints for the ADT GENERIC_BOUNDED_BALANCED_BINARY_SEARCH_TREE.

The time and space constraints for a TRIE depends on the maximum key length and the number of objects in the TRIE, denoted n. The maximum number of levels of a trie is the bound for insertion, deletion, and update. This observation yields Figure 8.8.3. The time and space constraints of the B-tree are left to the exercises.

	Operation Overhead	Space Overhead
INSERT	$O(\text{LENGTH})$	$O(n)$
DELETE	$O(\text{LENGTH})$	$O(n)$
UPDATE_KEY_DATA	$O(\text{LENGTH})$	$O(n)$
COPY	$O(n)$	$O(n)$
NEXT_INORDER	$O(1)$	$O(n)$
EQUAL	$O(n)$	$O(n)$
KEY_IN_TRIE	$O(\text{LENGTH})$	$O(n)$
GET_DATA_FOR_TRIE	$O(\text{LENGTH})$	$O(n)$

Figure 8.8.3 Constraints for the ADT BOUNDED_SEARCH_TRIE.

8.9 CASE STUDY: CREATING AN INDEX

At the end of this book is an index whose key is a word where the word's data is a list of page numbers where that word appears in this book. Not all words in this book appear in the index. The word *the* is an obvious example of a word that appears in the book but does not appear in the index. One way to build the index is to use a binary search tree. The tree would have the form shown in Figure 8.9.1. The inorder traversal of this index tree has the exact form of an index. Figure 8.9.2 lists one possible instantiation of a binary search tree that could build an index.

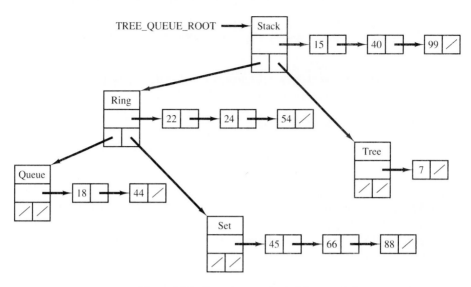

Figure 8.9.1 Tree of queues that builds a page index.

```
subtype WORD in string(1..10);
subtype PAGE_NUMBER is positive range 1..700;
type PAGE_ARRAY is array(positive range 1..20) of PAGE_NUMBER;
type PAGE_LIST is
  record
    LAST_USED : natural := 0;
    PAGE      : PAGE_ARRAY;
  end record;
package INDEX is new
    GENERIC_UNBOUNDED_BINARY_SEARCH_TREE(WORD, PAGE_LIST, "<");
use INDEX;
INDEX_TREE : TREE;
```

Figure 8.9.2 First instantiation of INDEX_TREE.

The package INDEX can build the index if no word in the index was referenced more than 20 times. Most words in the index are referenced fewer than five times. There is a considerable waste of memory with this structure. The type PAGE_ARRAY must be defined large enough to hold the page references of the most referenced word. An inorder traversal will return the key-data pairs in alphabetical order by the key word. Adding a reference is straightforward, as Figure 8.9.3 shows.

```
procedure ADD_ENTRY_TO_INDEX ( WORD_KEY : in   WORD;
                               PAGE_NUM : in   PAGE_NUMBER) is
  TEMP : PAGE_LIST;
begin
  if KEY_IN_TREE(WORD_KEY, INDEX_TREE) then
    TEMP := GET_DATA_FOR_TREE(WORD_KEY, INDEX_TREE);
    TEMP.LAST_USED := TEMP.LAST_USED + 1;
```

```
        TEMP.PAGE(TEMP.LAST_USED) := PAGE_NUM;
        UPDATE_NODE(WORD_KEY, TEMP, INDEX_TREE);
     else
        TEMP.LAST_USED := + 1;
        TEMP.PAGE(TEMP.LAST_USE) := PAGE_NUM;
        INSERT_NODE(WORD_KEY, TEMP, INDEX_TREE);
     end if;
  end ADD_ENTRY_TO_INDEX;
```

Figure 8.9.3   Procedure to add word to array-based index tree.

This structure wastes space. A method that does not waste space is to build a tree of queues. The node of a tree uses a word as a key and a queue of pages as the data. Unfortunately, the instantiation shown in Figure 8.9.4 fails. The reason the figure fails is that PAGE_NUMBER_QUEUE. QUEUE is a limited private type while the formal generic parameter KEY_TYPE in the TREE package is private. A limited private type cannot be instantiated into a private formal parameter. The formal generic parameter DATA_TYPE in the package GENERIC_UNBOUNDED_BINARY_SEARCH_TREE is private, not limited private. A private type allows reference, assignment, and comparison for equality.

```
subtype WORD is string(1..10);
subtype PAGE_NUMBER is positive range 1..700;
package PAGE_NUMBER_QUEUE is new GENERIC_UNBOUNDED_QUEUE(PAGE_NUMBER);
package INDEX is new GENERIC_UNBOUNDED_BINARY_SEARCH_TREE
                     ( WORD, PAGE_NUMBER_QUEUE.QUEUE, "<");
INDEX_TREE: INDEX_TREE.TREE;
```

Figure 8.9.4   Improper combination of two ADTs.

There is a simple solution. The ADT GENERIC_UNBOUNDED_BIN-ARY_SEARCH_TREE and the ADT GENERIC_UNBOUNDED_QUEUE can be combined as in Figure 8.9.4 if the queue type is private instead of limited private as defined in Figure 6.3.2. For this case study it will be assumed that both the package specification and the package body of GENERIC_UNBOUNDED_QUEUE have been recompiled with the queue defined as private, not limited private.

The next problem to consider is how to select words for entry into the index. The first method considered is to enter the words by hand. This is tedious. A second method would be to scan a file of text word by word. This would cause an index that references every occurrence of every word, including the words *the, it, is, a,* and *figure* if this text we used. The index could be edited when generated. A third method would be to maintain an index of words and page numbers that had been referenced previously and a table of words not to be referenced in the future. As the file of text is read, every word is checked against the index and the table. If the word is in the index, the page number is added to the queue of page numbers. If the word is in the table, it is ignored. If a word is not in either the index or the hash table, the system prompts the user and then the word is added to either the index or the table. This alternative is not entirely satisfactory. Consider the word *package* as used in this text. *Package* belongs in the index with references to pages where the concept is defined and enlarged. Unfortunately, the first word of any package specification or package body is the word *package*. These instances do not belong in the index. A fourth possibility is to generate a list of words to index. These words are initially read into the index, and then the text is scanned. Only words appearing previously in the index are updated. No new words are added. For simplicity's sake, the first alternative will be adopted for this case study.

The next consideration is how to save intermediate work and later to restart using previously saved work. The case study should prompt to see if there is any previously saved but partially completed index. If there is, it should read the words and page numbers and insert them into the index. At the end, a file of previous work should be saved. Since these would be text files, the format will be the word that is in the index, followed by the page numbers of that word, and the last page number is to be followed by an end-of-line marker. Note that unless one uses a balanced search tree, an inorder traversal of the index should not be used to save the intermediate work. If an intermediate file were generated using an inorder traversal, a totally right heavy index tree would result.

An inorder traversal of the tree will output the words in alphabetical order. When the index is generated, a text file generated by an inorder traversal in the same format as in the paragraph above will be saved for editing. Figure 8.9.5 lists the code for this case study.

```
with text_io;                              use text-io;
with GENERIC_UNBOUNDED_QUEUE;
with GENERIC-UNBOUNDED_BINARY_SEARCH_TREE;
procedure CASE_STUDY_8 is

   subtype WORD is string(1..15);
   subtype PAGE_NUMBER is positive range 1..700;

   NEXT_WORD : WORD;
   NEXT_PAGE : PAGE_NUMBER;
   DONE : boolean := false;

   package integer_text_io is new integer_io(integer);
                                          use integer_text_io;

   package PAGE_NUMBER_QUEUE is new
                   GENERIC_UNBOUNDED_QUEUE(PAGE_NUMBER)

   package INDEX is new GENERIC_UNBOUNDED_BINARY_SEARCH_TREE
                          ( WORD, PAGE_NUMBER_QUEUE.QUEUE, "<");
   use INDEX;

   INDEX_TREE : TREE;

   procedure GET_NEXT_WORD_AND_PAGE( DONE :    out boolean;
                                     NEXT_WORD :   out WORD;
                                     NEXT_PAGE :   out PAGE_NUMBER) is
      TEMP_WORD : WORD;
      LENGTH : natural;
   begin
      NEXT_WORD := TEMP_WORD;
```

Figure 8.9.5   Full listing of CASE_STUDY_8 to create an index. Continues on page 296.

```
    put ("Enter next word or Q to quit");
    get_Line (TEMP_WORD,LENGTH);
    skip_line;
    if LENGTH = 1 and then
              (TEMP_WORD(1) = 'Q' or TEMP_WORD(1) = 'q') then
      DONE := true;
      NEXT_PAGE := 1;
    else
      DONE := false;
      -- Pack the end of the word with blanks
      for COUNT in LENGTH+1..15 loop
        TEMP_WORD (COUNT) := ' ';
      end loop;
      NEXT_WORD := TEMP_WORD;
      put ("Enter the page number of next word");
      get (NEXT_PAGE); skip_line;
    end if;
end GET_NEXT_WORD_AND_PAGE;

procedure ADD_WORD_AND_PAGE (NEXT_WORD : in     WORD;
                             NEXT_PAGE : in     PAGE_NUMBER) is
  TEMP : PAGE_NUMBER_QUEUE.QUEUE;
begin
  if KEY_IN_TREE(NEXT_WORD, INDEX_TREE) then
    TEMP := GET_DATA_FOR_KEY(NEXT_WORD, INDEX_TREE);
    PAGE_NUMBER_QUEUE.ENQUEUE(NEXT_PAGE,TEMP);
    UPDATE( NEXT_WORD, TEMP, INDEX_TREE);
  else
    PAGE_NUMBER_QUEUE.ENQUEUE(NEXT_PAGE,TEMP);
    INSERT( NEXT_WORD, TEMP, INDEX_TREE);
  end if;
end ADD_WORD_AND_PAGE;

procedure RESTORE_SAVED_PARTIAL_INDEX is separate;
  -- get file name and open for reading
  -- get next word, pages, and add to tree
  -- close file

procedure SAVE_PARTIAL_INDEX is separate;
  -- Similar to Restore_saved_partial_index;
  -- saved for the exercises

procedure PRINT_AND_SAVE_FULL_INDEX is separate;
  -- get file name to open and open for writing
  -- do inorder traversal of the index.
  -- print a hard copy and write to file
  -- close the file
```

Figure 8.9.5 Continues on page 297.

```
begin -- CASE_STUDY_8
   RESTORE_SAVED_PARTIAL_INDEX;
   GET_NEXT_WORD_AND_PAGE(DONE, NEXT_WORD, NEXT_PAGE);
   while not DONE loop
      ADD_WORD_AND_PAGE(NEXT_WORD, NEXT_PAGE);
      GET_NEXT_WORD_AND_PAGE(DONE, NEXT_WORD, NEXT_PAGE);
   end loop;
   SAVE_PARTIAL_INDEX;
   PRINT_AND_SAVE_FULL_INDEX;
end CASE_STUDY_8;
```

Figure 8.9.5   Concluded.

The index for this book was generated using a program similar to Figure 8.9.5. Note that using a package for a balanced binary search tree would not alter the code since the operations have the same name and function.

EXERCISES

Section 8.1. Binary Trees and Their Operations

8.1.1 Implement the following operations for the ADT GENERIC_UNBOUNDED_BINARY_TREE as specified in Figure 8.1.7.
   a. Implement the operation CLEAR.
   b. Implement the operation SWAP_CHILDREN.
   c. Implement the operation EMPTY.
   d. Implement the operation RETURN_ITEM.
   e. Implement the operation RETURN_SUBTREE.
   f. Implement the operation UPDATE.
   g. Combine parts a through f with the operations implemented in the text to complete the package body for the package specification in Figure 8.1.7.
8.1.2 Use the ADT GENERIC_UNBOUNDED_BINARY_TREE to implement GENERIC_UN-BOUNDED_BINARY_SEARCH_TREE as specified in Figure 8.2.3.

Section 8.2 Binary Search Trees

8.2.1 Implement the following operations for the ADT GENERIC_UNBOUNDED_BIN-ARY_SEARCH_TREE as specified in Figure 8.2.3.
   a. Implement the operation COPY.
   b. Implement the operation CLEAR.
   c. Implement the operation UPDATE.
   d. Implement the operation NEXT_PREORDER.
   e. Implement the operation NEXT_POSTORDER.
   f. Implement the operation SET_INORDER.
   g. Implement the operation SET_PREORDER.
   h. Implement the operation SET_POSTORDER.
   i. Implement the operation EMPTY.
   j. Implement the operation EQUAL.
   k. Implement the operation KEY_IN_TREE.

l. Implement the operation GET_DATA_FOR_TREE.

m. Combine parts a through l with operations implemented in Section 2 to complete the body of the package specified in Figure 8.2.3.

Section 8.3 Balanced Trees

8.3.1 Implement the ADT GENERIC_UNBOUNDED_BALANCED_BINARY_SEARCH_TREE by modifying the specification of Figure 8.2.3 so as to require that insertion and deletion of nodes leaves the tree in balance.

Section 8.4. Bounded Trees

8.4.1 For the ADT GENERIC_BOUNDED_BINARY_SEARCH_TREE as specified in Figure 8.4.1, implement the following operations
   a. Implement the operation COPY.
   b. Implement the operation DELETE.
   c. Implement the operation UPDATE.
   d. Implement the operation NEXT_INORDER.
   e. Implement the operation SET_INORDER.
   f. Implement the operation EMPTY.
   g. Implement the operation FULL.
   h. Implement the operation EQUAL.
   i. Implement the operation KEY_IN_TREE.
   j. Implement the operation GET_DATA_FOR_TREE.
   k. Combine parts a through j with the operations implemented in the text to implement GENERIC_BOUNDED_BINARY_SEARCH_TREE as specified in Figure 8.4.1.

8.4.2 For the ADT GENERIC_BOUNDED_BINARY_SEARCH_TREE as specified in Figure 8.4.5, implement the following operations
   a. Implement the operation COPY.
   b. Implement the operation UPDATE.
   c. Implement the operation NEXT_INORDER.
   d. Implement the operation DELETE.
   e. Implement the operation SET_INORDER.
   f. Implement the operation EMPTY.
   g. Implement the operation FULL.
   h. Implement the operation EQUAL.
   i. Implement the operation KEY_IN_TREE.
   j. Implement the operation GET_DATA_FOR_TREE.
   k. Combine parts a through j with the operations implemented in the text to implement GENERIC_BOUNDED_BINARY_SEARCH_TREE as specified in Figure 8.4.5.

8.4.3 Fully implement the ADT specified in Figure 8.4.5 by making tree a variant record with discriminant equal to NUMBER_OF_NODES.

Section 8.5 B-Trees

8.5.1 Implement the following operations for the ADT M_WAY_B_TREE as specified in Figure 8.5.5.
   a. Implement the operation COPY.
   b. Implement the operation CREATE.
   c. Implement the operation CLEAR.

d. Implement the operation UPDATE.

e. Implement the operation SET_INORDER.

f. Implement the operation EMPTY.

g. Implement the operation EQUAL.

h. Implement the operation KEY_IN_B_TREE.

i. Combine parts a through i with the operations implemented in the text to implement M_WAY_B_TREE as specified in Figure 8.5.5.

8.5.2 Fully implement the ADT M_WAY_B_TREE based on the alternative definition given in Figure 8.5.11.

Section 8.6 Tries

8.6.1 Implement the following operations for the ADT GENERIC_BOUNDED_SEARCH_TRIE as specified in Figure 8.6.3.

a. Implement the operation COPY.

b. Implement the operation CLEAR.

c. Implement the operation DELETE.

d. Implement the operation UPDATE.

e. Implement the operation NEXT_INORDER.

f. Implement the operation SET_INORDER.

g. Implement the operation EMPTY.

h. Implement the operation FULL.

i. Implement the operation EQUAL.

j. Implement the operation GET_DATA_FOR_TRIE.

k. Combine parts a through j with the operations implemented in the text to implement GENERIC_BOUNDED_SEARCH_TRIE as specified in Figure 8.6.3.

Section 8.7 Applications

8.7.1 Implement GENERIC_UNBOUNDED_PRIORITY_QUEUE using GENERIC_UN-BOUNDED_BINARY_SEARCH_TREE.

8.7.2 Implement GENERIC_UNBOUNDED_PRIORITY_BALKING_QUEUE using GENERIC_UN-BOUNDED_BINARY_SEARCH_TREE.

Section 8.8 Time and Space Constraints

8.8.1 Complete A TABLE OF TIME AND SPACE CONSTRAINTS FOR

a. GENERIC_UNBOUNDED_PRIORITY_QUEUE as implemented in Exercise 8.7.1. Compare this results with the queue-based implementation developed in Chapter 7.

b. GENERIC_UNBOUNDED_PRIORITY_BALKING_QUEUE as implemented in Exercise 8.7.2. Compare this results with the queue-based implementation developed in Chapter 7.

Section 8.9 Case Study

8.9.1 Finish implementing CASE_STUDY_8.

8.9.2 Modify CASE_STUDY_8 so that a file is read. Whenever a new word is encountered, the user is prompted whether or not to put the word in the index. Your implementation must keep track of words to be indexed and words not to be indexed so that once a word is classified, it never reappears.

PROGRAMMING PROJECTS

P8.1 Modify the ADT GENERIC_UNBOUNDED_BALANCED_BINARY_SEARCH_TREE so that the number of rotations can be recorded at any time. Then build a tree whose keys are distinct random integers. Complete the following table.

NUMBER OF ROTATIONS DURING INSERTION

Number of Nodes	Number of Rotations
10	
20	
30	
40	
50	
100	
150	
200	
250	

Based on the table, conclude whether or not INSERT is $O(\log_2(n))$.

P8.2 Modify Project P8.1 and include a similar table for DELETE.

P8.3 Write a program using a tree to keep track of the number of times that a word appears in some text file. The output is to be an alphabetical listing of words and their frequencies.

P8.4 Repeat Project P8.3 using a trie.

NOTES AND REFERENCES

Balanced trees, sometimes called AVL trees, were first defined by Adelson-Velskii and Landis [2]. Knuth volumes 1 and 3 [27,29] contain a wealth of information about trees. Volume 1 contains material related to binary trees, and B-trees and tries are discussed in Volume 3. B-trees were first defined by Bayer and McCreight [6]. A good survey of B-trees is contained in Comer [13]. The diagrams in Section 8.3 dealing with balancing trees came from Wirth [52, pp. 218–224] and are adapted by permission of Prentice Hall, Englewood Cliffs, New Jersey.

9

Sets

Any upper division mathematics major will tell you that the language of mathematics is sets and relations on sets. A function or map is just a rule between two sets. In this chapter the focus will be on developing a bounded and an unbounded implementation of a set type. Sets have wide application in programming. In Chapter 10 the definition of a graph will be given in terms of a set of vertices and a set of edges. The breadth-first search of a graph requires the programmer to maintain a list of vertices already visited. Operating systems maintain a bit string for each file that indicates who has privileges to read or write or modify the file. This bit string is a set. Operating systems also have mechanisms for keeping track of nonsharable resources. While many users may share the data on a disk, only one user can control a tape drive. If another user requests the use of a tape drive, the operating system would deny the request. Collectors who want to have one of everything are maintaining a set. They either have it or they don't.

Sets are used to keep track of unique items. They are not used when an item may occur more than once. Card players keeping track of cards already played is an example of a possible set application. A program that does university class registration is another possibility. Students should not be able to double enroll in the same class. The class roll sheet represents the set of students enrolled in the class. The set of class roll sheets is the same as the set of all classes being offered. Clearly, a set can be composed of sets.

9.1 ADT SET

A *set* is a collection of elements from some universal set. Mathematically a *universal set* can be finite or infinite. A mathematical relation or a simple listing of the elements may define the universal set. Typical universal sets include the set of all integers, the letters in the alphabet, the valid words listed in a certain dictionary, or the names of students enrolled in a certain university. Examples of sets include the even integers, the vowels, all words in a certain dictionary that are five letters long, and the names of students majoring in computer science, respectively. For example, if the universal set U is the 26 letters in the alphabet, and S and T denote two sets, then

$$U = \{a,b,c,d,...,x,y,z\}$$

If $S = \{a,e,i,o,u\}$, then $S = \{i,a,o,u,e\}$, too. The listed order of elements in a set is not important. The important thing is whether an element is in the set or not in the set. The definition of set equality $S = T$ requires two things; every element in S must be in T and every element in T must be in S. There is no mention of the order. This definition also implies that

$$\{a,b,c\} = \{a,b,c,c,b,a,a,a,a\}$$

The number of times an element is listed in the set is not important. S is a subset of T, written

$$S <= T$$

if every element in S is also in T. S is a proper subset of T, written

$$S < T$$

if S is a subset of T and there is an element in T that is not in S. The basic set operation is a boolean function that answers the question "Is an element x in the set S?" The other basic set operations are defined in terms of membership. The union of two sets is a set composed of elements that are in one set or in the other set or in both sets. The intersection of two sets is a set made up of elements that are in both sets. The difference of two sets is a set whose elements are in the first set but not in the second set. The complement of a set is the set difference with the universal set.

$$S + T = \{x \mid x \text{ in } S \text{ or } x \text{ in } T \text{ or } x \text{ in both}\}$$
$$S * T = \{x \mid x \text{ in } S \text{ and } x \text{ in } T\}$$
$$S - T = \{x \mid x \text{ in } S \text{ but } x \text{ not in } T\}$$

For convenience, union will be denoted by "+" instead of "$\cup$" and intersection will be denoted "*" instead of "$\cap$". The complement of S will be denoted $-S$, not U–S. If $U = \{0,1,2,3,4,5,6,7,8,9\}$ and if $S = \{2,3,4,5\}$ and $T = \{4,5,6,7,8\}$, then

$$S + T = \{2,3,4,5,6,7\}$$
$$S * T = \{4,5\}$$
$$S - T = \{2,3\}$$
$$T - S = \{6,7,8\}$$
$$-S = \{0,1,6,7,8,9\}$$

With this discussion, the stage is set to list the documentation for the ADT set (see Figure 9.1.1).

GENERAL ADT SPECIFICATION FOR SET

Description

A SET is an unordered collection of elements. Elements are either in the set or not in the set. The number of times an element is listed or the order in which elements are listed is not important. For most applications the universal set or set of all possible elements is known. If the universal set is known, the bounded form is best. For other applications the general form of the elements is known but not the specific values. This requires the unbounded form.

Programmer-Supplied Data Structures or Specifications

Bounded form   The programmer must supply a discrete type that makes up the universal set. Only items listed in the discrete set can be referenced.

Figure 9.1.1   Documentation for ADT SET. Continues on page 303.

Unbounded form   The programmer must supply the general element type that makes up the set. Unlike the bounded form, this type need not be a discrete type. This type is implemented as a private type.

Operations

Name	Description
COPY	Makes a distinct copy of one set.
CLEAR	Removes all elements from a given set resulting in an empty set.
ADD_ELEMENT	Adds a new element to the set. Duplicate entries are not allowed.
REMOVE_ELEMENT	Removes a given element from the given set.
EQUAL	Boolean-valued function that returns true if two sets are equal, or false otherwise. Two sets are equal if all the elements in the first set are in the second set, and vice versa.
EMPTY	Boolean-valued function that returns true if the set contains no elements, and false otherwise.
ELEMENT_IN_SET	Boolean-valued function that returns true if a particular element is in the set, and false otherwise.
"+" or set union	Binary set operation that returns a set containing any element that is in the first set, the second set, or both sets.
"*" or set intersection	Binary set operation that returns a set containing any element that is in both sets.
"−" or set difference	Binary operation that returns a set containing any element that is in the first or left set but not in the second or right set.
"−" or set complement	(bounded version only) Unary set operation that returns a set made up of elements not in the given set.
"<=" or subset	Boolean-valued binary set operation that returns true when every element of the first or left set is in the second or right set, and false otherwise.
"<" or proper subset	Boolean-valued binary set operation that returns true if the first or left set is a subset of the second or right set but the first set is not equal to the second set, and false otherwise.
COUNT	Function that returns a natural number equal to the number of elements in a set.
NEXT_ELEMENT	Operation that returns the next element in the set. Repeated calls will eventually return every element in the set once before returning any element twice. Adding an element to the set or deleting an element from the set can cause some elements in

Figure 9.1.1 Continues on page 304.

the set to be listed twice before other elements are listed once.

Exceptions

Three exceptions can occur. The first exception is ELEMENT_IS_IN_SET, which can occur when an attempt is made to add an element to a set that already contains the element. The second exception, ELEMENT_NOT_IN_SET, occurs when an attempt is made to remove an element from a set, or list the next element in an empty set and the element is not there. An OVERFLOW can occur in the unbounded case when a storage error occurs. This condition results when an attempt to add an element data pair or copy a set is made with insufficient storage.

Warnings

All warnings are implementation dependent.

Figure 9.1.1 Concluded.

There are three differences between the discrete version and the unbounded version of the ADT SET. First, at instantiation the discrete version can only instantiate a discrete type, while the unbounded version can instantiate any valid Ada type. Second, the discrete type has one extra operation, the unary "–." Third, only the unbounded version can raise an overflow exception.

9.2 BOUNDED FORM

A better name for this implementation of the bounded form is the discrete form. Some enumeration type becomes the index of a boolean array. For example, if the universal set is defined by the enumerated type

```
type CLASS is (CS1, CS2, CS3, CS4, CS5, CALCULUS, ETHICS, ENGLISH);
```

then the set type is defined by

```
type SET is array ( CLASS ) of boolean;
```

All the operations can be specified in terms of the basic logical operations built into Ada. The abstract data type GENERIC_DISCRETE_SET is specified in Figure. 9.2.1.

```
generic
  type ELEMENT_TYPE IS (<>);
package GENERIC_DISCRETE_SET is
  type SET is private;
  procedure COPY         ( FROM_SET  : in      SET;
                           TO_SET    :     out SET );
  procedure CLEAR        ( TO_CLEAR  :     out SET );
  procedure ADD_ELEMENT  ( ELEMENT   : in      ELEMENT_TYPE;
                           ( TO_SET   : in out SET);
```

Figure 9.2.1 Package specification for GENERIC_DISCRETE_SET. Continues on page 305.

Sets   Chap. 9

```
          procedure REMOVE_ELEMENT ( ELEMENT    : in      ELEMENT_type;
                                     FROM_SET   : in out SET );
       function EQUAL            ( A, B : SET )                  return boolean;
       function EMPTY            ( A : SET )                     return boolean;
       function ELEMENT_IN_SET   ( ELEMENT    :        ELEMENT_TYPE;
                                   IN_SET     :        SET ) return boolean;
       function "+"              ( LEFT, RIGHT : SET )              return SET;
         -- computes the union of A and B
       function "*"              ( LEFT, RIGHT : SET )              return SET;
         -- computes the intersection of A and B
       function "-"              ( LEFT, RIGHT : SET )              return SET;
         -- computes the SET difference A - B
       function "-"              ( A : SET )                    return SET;
         -- computes the complement of A
       function "<="             ( A_subset, Of_B : SET ) return boolean;
         -- determines if A_subset is a subset of Of_B
       function "<"              ( A_proper, Of_B : SET ) return boolean;
         -- determines if A_proper is a proper subset of Of_B
       function COUNT            ( A : SET )                    return natural;
       procedure NEXT_ELEMENT (A : in out SET; ELEMENT: out ELEMENT_TYPE);
       ELEMENT_IS_IN_SET    : exception;
       ELEMENT_NOT_IN_SET   : exception;
   private
       type SET_ARRAY is array ( ELEMENT_TYPE ) of boolean;
       type SET is
         record
           S          : SET_ARRAY;
           COUNT      : natural := 0;
           LAST_LIST  : ELEMENT_TYPE
                          := ELEMENT_TYPE'last;--Last element listed
         end record;
   end GENERIC_DISCRETE_SET;
```

Figure 9.2.1 Concluded.

The exception ELEMENT_IN_SET is raised when the operation ADD_ELEMENT attempts to add an element that is already in the set. This exception could be ignored, as in the union or "+" function, but the primitive functions should raise exceptions. The intersection operation, for example, uses the "*" operator because this operator can be overloaded. The normal intersection operator, ∩, is not even in the Ada symbol set. This is the same reason that the other set operators are defined in terms of the Ada operators that can be overloaded. The same reasoning applies to the exception ELEMENT_NOT_IN_SET when REMOVE_ELEMENT tries to remove something not there, although intersection "*" and set difference "−" would not invoke the exception. Note that set is private.

The boolean operators and, or, xor, and not can be applied to one-dimensional boolean arrays. Recall that boolean-valued arrays with the same number of components can be used in boolean operations. The result is a boolean-valued array with the boolean operation applied on a component-by-component basis. If a discrete type is the boolean array's index, a simple implementation of many set operators results.

```
procedure COPY              ( FROM_SET : in      SET;
                              TO_SET   :    out SET ) is
   -- Makes a distinct copy of FROM_SET
   TEMP_SET : SET := FROM_SET;
begin
   TO_SET := TEMP_SET;
end COPY;


procedure CLEAR     ( TO_CLEAR :    out SET) is
   -- The set TO_CLEAR is cleared and contains no elements
begin
   TO_CLEAR := ((others => false), 0, ELEMENT_TYPE'last);
end CLEAR;

procedure ADD_ELEMENT        ( ELEMENT : in      ELEMENT_TYPE;
                               TO_SET   : in out SET ) is
   -- Adds ELEMENT to the set TO_SET.
   -- Exception ELEMENT_IS_IN_SET is raised when a duplicate entry
   --           is detected.
begin
   if TO_SET.S(ELEMENT) = true then
     raise ELEMENT_IS_IN_SET;
   else
      TO_SET.S(ELEMENT) := true;
      TO_SET.COUNT := TO_SET.COUNT + 1;
      TO_SET.LAST_LIST := ELEMENT_TYPE'last;
   end if;
end ADD_ELEMENT;


function ELEMENT_IN_SET ( ELEMENT   :  ELEMENT_TYPE;
                          IN_SET    :  SET ) return boolean is
   -- Returns true if ELEMENT is in IN_SET.
begin
   return IN_SET.S(ELEMENT);
end ELEMENT_IN_SET;


function "+" ( LEFT, RIGHT : SET)   return SET is
   -- Computes the union of two sets LEFT and RIGHT. The union
   -- of two sets is the set that contains elements that are in
   -- either set or both.
   ANS : SET;
begin
   ANS.S := LEFT.S or RIGHT.S;
   for i in ELEMENT_TYPE'first..ELEMENT_TYPE'last loop
     if ANS.S(i) then
       ANS.COUNT := ANS.COUNT + 1;
     end if;
   end loop;
   return ANS;
end "+";
```

```
function "-" ( LEFT, RIGHT : SET ) return SET is
  -- Computes the set difference LEFT - RIGHT. The result is a
  -- set that contains only those elements in LEFT that are not in
  -- Right.
  ANS : SET;
begin
  ANS.S := LEFT.S and (not RIGHT.S);
  for i in ELEMENT_TYPE'first..ELEMENT_TYPE'last loop
    if ANS.S(i) then
      ANS.COUNT := ANS.COUNT + 1;
    end if;
  end loop;
  return ANS;
end "-";

function "<" ( A_PROPER, OF_B : SET ) return boolean is
  -- Returns true if A_PROPER is a proper subset OF_B. A proper
  -- subset is a subset where equality is not allowed.
begin
  if A_PROPER.COUNT < OF_B.COUNT then
    return (A_PROPER.S = (A_PROPER.S and OF_B.S));
  else
    return false;
  end if;
end "<";
```

The remainder of the functions and procedures are left as an exercise.

9.3 UNBOUNDED FORM

There are several ways to implement the unbounded SET type. A large part of set operations involves determining if an element is or is not in a set. This is a search operation. Some sort of hashing scheme is an obvious candidate. Trees, the subject of Chapter 8, are also efficient at searching under certain circumstances. In this section a "brute force" implementation using a singly linked list will be used. Searching a linked list can be tedious, but the straightforward manner of implementing the other set operations overcomes this deficiency. Except for the three differences noted at the end of Section 9.2, the programmer would see no differences no matter what method of implementation is chosen. The set specification in Figure 9.3.1 has built these features into the set type.

```
generic
  type ELEMENT_TYPE is private;
package GENERIC_UNBOUNDED_SET is
  type SET is private;
  procedure COPY           ( FROM_SET : in      SET;
                             TO_SET   :      out SET );
  procedure CLEAR          ( TO_CLEAR :      out SET );
  procedure ADD_ELEMENT    ( ELEMENT  : in      ELEMENT_TYPE;
```

Figure 9.3.1 Package specification for GENERIC_UNBOUNDED_SET. Continues on page 308.

```
                                      TO_SET   : in out SET );
      procedure REMOVE_ELEMENT    ( ELEMENT  : in      ELEMENT_type;
                                    FROM_SET : in out SET );
      function EQUAL              ( A, B : SET )           return boolean;
      function EMPTY              (A : SET)                return boolean;
      function ELEMENT_IN_SET     ( ELEMENT  :      ELEMENT_TYPE;
                                    IN_SET   :      SET ) return boolean;
      function "+"                ( LEFT, RIGHT : SET)          return SET;
         -- computes the union of A and B
      function "*"                ( LEFT, RIGHT : SET )         return SET;
         -- computes the intersection of A and B
      function "-"                ( LEFT, RIGHT : SET )         return SET;
         -- computes the SET difference A - B
      function "<="               ( A_subset, Of_B : SET ) return boolean;
         -- determines if A_subset   is a subset of Of_B
      function "<"                ( A_proper, Of_B : SET ) return boolean;
         -- determines if A_proper is a proper subset of Of_B
      function COUNT              ( A : SET )              return natural;
      procedure NEXT_ELEMENT (A : in out SET; ELEMENT: out ELEMENT_TYPE);
      ELEMENT_IS_IN_SET     : exception;
      ELEMENT_NOT_IN_SET    : exception;
      OVERFLOW              : exception;
   private
      type SET_NODE;
      type NEXT_NODE is access SET_NODE;
      type SET is
        record
          FIRST      : NEXT_NODE;
          COUNT      : natural := 0;
          LAST_LIST  : NEXT_NODE; -- used by NEXT_ELEMENT to keep track of
                                  -- last set ELEMENT listed
        end record;
   end GENERIC_UNBOUNDED_SET;

   package body GENERIC_UNBOUNDED_SET IS
      type SET_NODE is
        record
          KEY  : ELEMENT_TYPE;
          NEXT : NEXT_NODE;
        end record;
      ...............
   end GENERIC_UNBOUNDED_SET;
```

Figure 9.3.1 Concluded.

From a theoretical point of view, all the functions in GENERIC_UNBOUNDED_SET can be implemented based on the boolean operation ELEMENT_IN_SET. This allows for a simple implementation of the operations in this ADT. Adding an element to the set is not simply an insertion onto its linked list. An element can be added to a set only if it is not already in the set. So the procedure ADD_ELEMENT must first make sure that the element is not already in the set.

```
procedure ADD_ELEMENT       ( ELEMENT : in       ELEMENT_TYPE;
                              TO_SET  : in out SET ) is
  -- Adds ELEMENT to the set TO_SET.
  -- Exception ELEMENT_IS_IN_SET is raised when a duplicate entry
  --           is detected.
  -- Exception OVERFLOW is raised if there is a storage_error.
begin
  if ELEMENT_IN_SET ( ELEMENT, TO_SET) then
    raise ELEMENT_IS_IN_SET;
  end if;
  TO_SET := (new SET_NODE'(ELEMENT, TO_SET.FIRST), TO_SET.COUNT+1, null);
end ADD_ELEMENT;
```

Many of the operations in this set require that a set be traversed element by element. The operation NEXT_ELEMENT will traverse a set if it is called repeatedly. The operation is listed below.

```
procedure NEXT_ELEMENT  ( A       : in out Set;
                            ELEMENT :    out ELEMENT_TYPE) is
  -- Returns the next element in an enumeration of the set A.
  -- Repeated calls will eventually list every element in A before
  -- before repeating the sequence provided that no elements have been
  -- added or deleted.
  -- Exception ELEMENT_NOT_IN_SET raised if A is empty.
begin
  if A.COUNT = 0 then
    raise ELEMENT_NOT_IN_SET;
  elsif A.LAST_LIST = null or else A.LAST_LIST.NEXT = null then
    A.LAST_LIST := A.FIRST;
  else
    A.LAST_LIST := A.LAST_LIST.NEXT;
  end if;
  ELEMENT := A.LAST_LIST.KEY;
end NEXT_ELEMENT;
```

NEXT_ELEMENT allows for simple implementations of many of the remaining set operations. The COPY operation is an example. An element is in the set no matter where it appears in the linked list. Order of appearance is not relevant.

```
procedure COPY              ( FROM_SET : in      SET;
                              TO_SET   :    out SET ) is
  -- Makes a distinct copy of FROM_SET
  -- Exception OVERFLOW can be raised by ADD_ELEMENT
  TEMP_FROM    : SET := FROM_SET;
  TEMP_TO      : SET;
  TEMP_ELEMENT : ELEMENT_TYPE;
begin
  -- Prevent operation NEXT_ELEMENT from raising an exception if
  -- FROM_SET is empty
  if FROM_SET.COUNT /= 0 then
    for COUNT in 1..TEMP_FROM.COUNT loop
```

```
          NEXT_ELEMENT (TEMP_FROM, TEMP_ELEMENT);
          ADD_ELEMENT (TEMP_ELEMENT, TEMP_TO);
       end loop;
    end if;
    TO_SET := TEMP_TO;
 exception
    when OVERFLOW      => raise OVERFLOW;
 end COPY;
```

The implementations of union, intersection, difference, subset, and proper subset follow the same idea. For union, it is not sufficient to append the two linked lists together. This could result in an element appearing in the set twice. The strategy is simple. Copy the first set onto a temporary set. For each element in the second set, check to see if it is in the second set, and add it to the temporary set only if it is not in the first set.

```
function "+" ( LEFT, RIGHT : SET ) return SET is
    -- Computes the union of two sets LEFT and RIGHT. The union
    -- of two sets is the set that contains elements that are in
    -- either set or both.
    -- Exception OVERFLOW can be raised by ADD_ELEMENT
    RIGHT_TEMP : NEXT_NODE := RIGHT.FIRST;
    RESULT : SET;
begin
    COPY (LEFT, RESULT);
    while RIGHT_TEMP /= null loop
       if not ELEMENT_IN_SET (RIGHT_TEMP.KEY, RESULT) then
          ADD_ELEMENT (RIGHT_TEMP.KEY, RESULT);
       end if;
       RIGHT_TEMP := RIGHT_TEMP.NEXT;
    end loop;
    return RESULT;
exception
    when OVERFLOW      => raise OVERFLOW;
end "+";
```

Intersection is implemented by searching both lists. If there is a match, there is an addition of the element. Difference is similar to union. The first set is traversed. If the element is in the second set, it is not added to the result. The implementation of the rest of the package is left as an exercise.

The union operation is $O(n**2)$, where n is the total number of elements. This follows from the fact that for each element in LEFT, RIGHT must be searched to see if that element should be added to the answer. Can this overhead be reduced? Recall that trees have search overhead of $O(\log_2(n))$ if the tree is treelike. The ADT SET uses a sequential search. This means that the union operation could be reduced to $O(\log_2(n)**2)$ from $O(n**2)$. Since unbounded trees have an unlimited capacity, trees are good candidates to implement an unbounded set. Consider the implementation of an unbounded set shown in Figure 9.3.2. The operations specified in Figure 9.3.1 and 9.3.2 are almost exactly the same. The only difference is that TO_SET in COPY and TO_CLEAR in CLEAR are now mode "in out" instead of mode "out." One new formal generic parameter has been introduced.

```
with GENERIC_UNBOUNDED_BINARY_SEARCH_TREE;
generic
  type ELEMENT_TYPE is private;
  with function "<" (LEFT, RIGHT : ELEMENT_TYPE) return boolean;
package GENERIC_UNBOUNDED_TREE_SET is
  type SET is private;
  procedure COPY            ( FROM_SET    : in     SET;
                              TO_SET      : in out SET );
  procedure CLEAR           ( TO_CLEAR    : in out SET );
  procedure ADD_ELEMENT     ( ELEMENT     : in     ELEMENT_TYPE;
                              TO_SET      : in out SET );
  procedure REMOVE_ELEMENT  ( ELEMENT     : in     ELEMENT_type;
                              FROM_SET    : in out SET );
  function EQUAL            ( A, B : SET )                return boolean;
  function EMPTY            (A : SET )                    return boolean;
  function ELEMENT_IN_SET   ( ELEMENT     :       ELEMENT_TYPE;
                              IN_SET      :       SET )return boolean;
  function "+"              ( LEFT, RIGHT : SET )               return SET;
    -- computes the union of A and B
  function "*"              ( LEFT, RIGHT : SET )               return SET;
    -- computes the intersection of A and B
  function "-"              ( LEFT, RIGHT : SET )               return SET;
    -- computes the SET difference A - B
  function "<="             ( A_subset, Of_B : SET )    return boolean;
    -- determines if A_subset is a subset of Of_B
  function "<"              ( A_proper, Of_B : SET )    return boolean;
    -- determines if A_proper is a proper subset of Of_B
  function COUNT            ( A : SET )                 return natural;
    -- determines the number of distinct elements in SET A
  procedure Next_ELEMENT (A : in out SET; ELEMENT: out ELEMENT_TYPE);
  ELEMENT_IS_IN_SET     : exception;
  ELEMENT_NOT_IN_SET    : exception;
  OVERFLOW              : exception;
private
  package NEW_SET is new
    GENERIC_UNBOUNDED_BINARY_SEARCH_TREE (ELEMENT_TYPE, boolean, "<");
  use NEW_SET;
  type SET is
    record
      TREE_SET : TREE;
    end record;
end GENERIC_UNBOUNDED_TREE_SET;
```

Figure 9.3.2   Implementation of an unbounded set using trees.

Unfortunately, the specification in Figure 9.3.2 will not compile until the ADT
GENERIC_UNBOUNDED_BINARY_SEARCH_TREE has been recompiled with type
TREE private instead of limited private. Ada requires that a type be limited private if any of
its components are limited private. The type SET is private, not limited private. If the type SET
is redefined to be limited private, statements of the form

$$A := B + C;$$

are not defined, where A, B, and C are sets. The loss of the binary set operations would change the character of this ADT. On the other hand, making TABLE private instead of limited private does not cause any problems. The encapsulation of ELEMENT_TYPE still holds, and the programmer cannot directly manipulate anything of type TREE. There are still some subtle details. Note that the mode of TO_SET has been changed from "in" to "in out."

```
procedure COPY              ( FROM_SET  : in      SET;
                              TO_SET    : in out SET ) is
   -- Makes a distinct copy of FROM_SET
   -- Exception OVERFLOW raised if insufficient storage
   TEMP : SET;
begin
   COPY (FROM_SET.TREE_SET, TEMP.TREE_SET);
   TO_SET := TEMP;
exception
   when OVERFLOW => raise OVERFLOW;
end COPY;
```

The two main operations in the set ADT are checking to see if an element is in a set and adding an element to a set. Both are listed below.

```
function ELEMENT_IN_SET  ( ELEMENT :       ELEMENT_TYPE;
                           IN_SET  :       SET ) return boolean is
   -- Returns true if ELEMENT is in IN_SET.
begin
   return KEY_IN_TREE (IN_SET.TREE_SET, ELEMENT);
end ELEMENT_IN_SET;


procedure ADD_ELEMENT    ( ELEMENT  : in     ELEMENT_TYPE;
                           TO_SET   : in out SET ) is
   -- Adds ELEMENT to the set TO_SET.
   -- Exception ELEMENT_IS_IN_SET is raised when a duplicate entry
   --           is detected.
   -- Exception OVERFLOW is raised if there is a storage_error.
begin
   if KEY_IN_TREE (ELEMENT, TO_SET.TREE_SET) then
      raise ELEMENT_IS_IN_SET;
   else
      INSERT (ELEMENT, true, TO_SET.TREE_SET);
   end if;
exception
   when OVERFLOW => raise OVERFLOW;
end ADD_ELEMENT;
```

The discussion of this implementation is closed by finding the union of two sets.

```
function "+" ( LEFT, RIGHT : SET ) return SET is
   -- Computes the union of two sets LEFT and RIGHT. The union
   -- of two sets is the set that contains elements that are in
   -- either set or both.
```

```
        -- Exception OVERFLOW can be raised by ADD_ELEMENT
    ELEMENT : ELEMENT_TYPE;
    DATA    : boolean;
    RESULT  : SET;
    TEMP    : SET;
begin
    -- By definition union contains all of LEFT.
    COPY (LEFT.TREE_SET, RESULT.TREE_SET);
    COPY (RIGHT.TREE_SET, TEMP.TREE_SET);
    -- For every element in RIGHT, add to result if it is not there
    for COUNT in 1..COUNT (TEMP.TREE_SET) loop
      NEXT_INORDER (ELEMENT, DATA TEMP.TREE_SET);
      if not KEY_IN_TREE (ELEMENT, LEFT.TREE_SET) then
        -- Element from RIGHT not in LEFT, so insert it.
        INSERT (ELEMENT, DATA, RESULT.TREE_SET);
      end if;
    end loop;
    return RESULT;
end "+";
```

The COPY operation is $O(n)$. The operation KEY_IN_TREE is $O(\log_2(n))$ assuming that the tree is balanced. If there are n elements in LEFT and RIGHT, the union operation above must loop through one set once while doing a search, so union is $O(n*\log_2(n))$ for sets implemented as trees. The rest of the operations, as well as the time and space constraints, are left to the exercises.

Some users feel that procedure and function should explicitly reflect their use. These users would have named the functions "+", "*", "<=", and "–" as UNION, INTERSECTION, SUBSET, and SET_DIFFERENCE, respectively. The decision as to whether to overload operators reflects a person's taste. The author favors overloading the operators because it leads to a more natural way of expressing certain set expressions.

9.4 APPLICATIONS

Many card games, such as bridge and 21, require both luck and skill. By keeping track of the cards already played plus the cards in his or her hand, an experienced card player can detect substantial shifts in the probabilities. By increasing the bet when odds are in your favor and decreasing the bet when the odds are against you, you minimize your potential losses while maximizing your potential winnings.

A deck of cards is divided into four suits (CLUBS, DIAMONDS, HEARTS, and SPADES) with each suit composed of 13 distinct cards (2, 3, 4, 5, 6, 7, 8, 9, 10, JACK, QUEEN KING, ACE) so one enumeration of a deck of cards is

```
type CARD_DECK is ( C_2, C_3, C_4, C_5, C_6, C_7, C_8, C_9, C_10,
                    C_JACK, C_QUEEN, C_KING, C_ACE, D_2, D_3, D_4,
                    D_5, D_6, D_7, D_8, D_9, D_10, D_JACK,
                    D_QUEEN, D_KING, D_ACE, H_2, H_3, H_4, H_5,
                    H_6, H_7, H_8, H_9, H_10, H_JACK, H_QUEEN,
```

```
                    H_KING, H_ACE, S_2, S_3, S_4, S_5, S_6, S_7,
                    S_8, S_9, S_10, S_JACK, S_QUEEN, S_KING,
                    S_ACE);
```

The set type can be used to keep track of cards in your hand. Consider the simple card game 21, which is sometimes called blackjack. The dealer and a player are dealt two cards. An ace can count 1 or 11. Kings, queens, and jacks all count 10. All other cards count their face value. A player tries to get as close as possible to 21 without exceeding 21. The player may request more cards until he or she either exceeds 21 and loses, or decides to hold with a value of 21 or under. If the player has 21 or less, the dealer must take cards until his or her hand exceeds 17. If the dealer's total exceeds 21, the player wins. If both the dealer and player both have valid hands, the one with the higher value wins. If the values are the same, the dealer wins. A procedure to simulate playing a game of 21 is given in Figure 9.4.1.

```
with GENERIC_DISCRETE_SET;
package CARDS is new GENERIC_DISCRETE_SET (CARD_DECK);
use CARDS:
procedure PLAY_21 is
  DECK, MY_HAND, DEALER_HAND : SET;
  MY_HAND_COUNT : natural;
begin
  --Make a complete Deck by applying set complement to any empty set
  CLEAR (DECK);
  DECK := -DECK;
  CLEAR (MY_HAND);
  CLEAR (DEALER_HAND);
  MY_HAND_COUNT := 0;
  loop
    exit when COUNT(DECK) <= 20 loop
    PLACE_BET;
    -- Pick a random card, return it, and delete it from deck
    -- Deal out player and dealer's first two cards
    DEAL_CARD (MY_HAND, DECK)
    DEAL_CARD (DEALER_HAND, DECK);
    DEAL_CARD (MY_HAND, DECK);
    MY_HAND_COUNT := EVALUATE( MY_HAND);
    DEAL_CARD (DEALER_HAND, DECK);
    -- Continue dealing cards to player until . . . . .
    while PROBABILITY_BUST (21 - MY_HAND_COUNT, DECK) <= 0.5 loop
      DEAL_CARD (MY_HAND, DECK);
      MY_HAND_COUNT := EVALUATE ( MY_HAND );
    end loop;
    if MY_HAND_COUNT <= 21 then
      -- Player has not gone bust, dealer takes cards until score >= 17
      while EVALUATE(DEALER_HAND) < 17 loop
        DEAL_CARD(MY_HAND, DECK);
      end loop;
      --See who won this hand
      if MY_HAND_COUNT > EVALUATE (DEALER_HAND) or
```

Figure 9.4.1 Procedure to simulate playing the card game 21. Continues on page 315.

```
            EVALUATE (DEALER_HAND) > 21 then
              PAY_BET;
          else
            CLEAR_BET;
          end if;
       else
          -- Player loses
          CLEAR_BET;
       end if
       PRINT_RESULT;
       --prepare for next hand
       CLEAR(MY_HAND);
       CLEAR(DEALER_HAND);
       MY_HAND_COUNT := 0;
     end loop;
   end PLAY_21;
```

Figure 9.4.1 Concluded.

The procedure PROBABILITY_BUST takes the first argument, the maximum card that can be drawn without exceeding 21, and computes the probability of a random card dealt from the deck exceeding that amount. If that probability is under 0.5, another card is drawn. This procedure scans the cards not yet dealt to compute this probability. Using Las Vegas rules, the dealer must continue dealing cards to himself or herself as long as his or her hand count is under 17. Although this example illustrates how a game of 21 might be simulated, various rules have been neglected. The knowledgeable student has already discerned that dealing a black-jack has been ignored.

The ADT SET is a natural choice when it is necessary to keep track of whether something has or has not been done.

9.5 TIME AND SPACE CONSTRAINTS

Constraints of the bounded form are similar to the constraints for any manipulation of an array. If n is the length of the array that implements the SET type, Figure 9.5.1 lists the time and space constraints for the ADT GENERIC_DISCRETE_SET as specified by Figure 9.2.1.

	Total Time Overhead	Space Overhead
ADD_ELEMENT	$O(1)$	$O(n)$
REMOVE_ELEMENT	$O(1)$	$O(n)$
EQUAL	$O(n)$	$O(n)$
ELEMENT_IN_SET	$O(1)$	$O(n)$
+ or union	$O(n)$	$O(n)$
* or intersection	$O(n)$	$O(n)$
<= or subset	$O(n)$	$O(n)$
< or proper subset	$O(n)$	$O(n)$

Figure 9.5.1 Time and space constraints for GENERIC_DISCRETE_SET.

An examination of the operations ADD_ELEMENT, ELEMENT_IN_SET, and RE-MOVE_ELEMENT in GENERIC_BOUNDED_SET shows that each operation looks at only one component of the boolean array holding the set. Clearly, these operations are $O(1)$. All the other operations must do boolean operations on every component, so they are $O(n)$.

The time and space constraints for the ADT GENERIC_UNBOUNDED_SET in Figure 9.3.1 are listed in Figure 9.5.2. GENERIC_UNBOUNDED_SET is implemented using linked lists. Some operations, such as intersection or union, require sequential searches of the set. The result is high CPU overhead. In Figure 9.5.1, n represents the number of elements in each set.

	Total Time Overhead	Space Overhead
ADD_ELEMENT	$O(n)$	$O(1)$
REMOVE_ELEMENT	$O(n)$	$O(1)$
EQUAL	$O(n**2)$	$O(1)$
ELEMENT_IN_SET	$O(n)$	$O(1)$
+ or union	$O(n**2)$	$O(1)$
* or intersection	$O(n**2)$	$O(1)$
<= or subset	$O(n**2)$	$O(1)$
< or proper subset	$O(n**2)$	$O(1)$

Figure 9.5.2   Time and space constraints for GENERIC_UNBOUNDED_SET.

Several of the operations in Figure 9.5.2 are "worst case" estimates. For example, if two sets have the same number of elements, they clearly cannot be proper subsets, and that operation is $O(1)$ in that case. ADD_ELEMENT, REMOVE_ELEMENT, and ELEMENT_IN_SET require a sequential search of the set in order to find or remove the element. Thus these operations are $O(n)$. The other listed operations require a search of one set for every element in the second set. If both sets have n elements, these operations are $O(n**2)$. In many applications, such as graph search algorithms, the techniques of using sets are often applied without implementing the full ADT.

In Chapter 10 the problem of finding paths through a graph is studied in detail. The case study in that chapter uses a combination of several ADTs, including GENERIC_BOUNDED_SET.

EXERCISES

Section 9.2 Bounded Form

9.2.1 Implement the following operations in the ADT GENERIC_DISCRETE_SET specified in Figure 9.2.1.
   a. The set operation REMOVE_ELEMENT
   b. The set operation EQUAL
   c. The set operation EMPTY
   d. The set operation "*", which computes the intersection of two sets A and B
   e. The set operation "–", which computes the complement of A
   f. The set operation "<=", which determines if the set A is a subset of the set B.
   g. The set operation NEXT_ELEMENT

h. Combine parts a through g with the set operations implemented in Section 9.2 into the package body of GENERIC_DISCRETE_SET to implement this ADT fully.

Section 9.3 Unbounded Form

9.3.1 Implement the following operations in the ADT GENERIC_UNBOUNDED_SET specified in Figure 9.3.1.
  a. The set operation CLEAR
  b. The set operation REMOVE_ELEMENT
  c. The set operation EQUAL
  d. The set operation EMPTY
  e. The set operation ELEMENT_IN_SET
  f. The set operation "∗", which computes the intersection of two sets A and B
  g. The set operation "−", which computes the set difference of two sets A − B
  h. The set operation "−", which computes the complement of A
  i. The set operation "<=", which determines if the set A is a subset of the set B
  j. The set operation "<", which determines if the set A is a proper subset of the set B
  k. The set operation COUNT
  l. The set operation NEXT_ELEMENT
  m. Combine parts a through l with the operations implemented in Section 9.3 into the package body GENERIC_UNBOUNDED_SET to implement this version of this ADT fully.

9.3.2 Implement the following operations in the ADT GENERIC_UNBOUNDED_TREE_SET specified in Figure 9.3.2.
  a. The set operation CLEAR
  b. The set operation REMOVE_ELEMENT
  c. The set operation EQUAL
  d. The set operation EMPTY
  e. The set operation "∗", which computes the intersection of two sets A and B
  f. The set operation "−", which computes the set difference of two sets A − B
  g. The set operation "−", which computes the complement of A
  h. The set operation "<=", which determines if the set A is a subset of the set B
  i. The set operation "<", which determines if the set A is a proper subset of the set B
  j. The set operation COUNT
  k. The set operation NEXT_ELEMENT
  l. Combine parts a through l with the operations implemented in Section 9.3 into the package body GENERIC_UNBOUNDED_SET to implement this version of this ADT fully.

Section 9.4 Applications

9.4.1 Implement one of the set packages and generate random sets to test whether or not the following set identifies from mathematics are true or false. Note that a single example of failure is enough to show that the identity is false but listing a number of cases where the identity holds does not prove that the identity is true.
  a. $A*(B + C) = A*B + A*C$
  b. $A + (B*C) = (A+ B)*(A + C)$
  c. $A <= A*B$
  d. $A*B < A$
  e. $A - (B + C) = (A - B)*(A - C)$

9.4.2 Finish implementing the program to play the game 21 as listed in Figure 9.4.1.

    a. Determine the number of games the player wins out of 1000.

    b. Modify the player's strategy by changing the loop

```
while PROBABILITY_BUST (21 - MY_HAND_COUNT, DECK) <= 0.5 loop
  DEAL_CARD(MY_HAND, DECK);
  MY_HAND_COUNT := EVALUATE( MY_HAND );
end loop;
```

to

```
while PROBABILITY_BUST (21 - MY_HAND_COUNT, DECK) <= 0.5
                    and then MY_HAND_COUNT < MAX_COUNT loop
  DEAL_CARD(MY_HAND, DECK);
  MY_HAND_COUNT := EVALUATE( MY_HAND );
end loop;
```

and determine how many hands out of 1000 the player wins for MAX_COUNT in the range 12 . . 20.

    c. Modify the players strategy to

```
while MY_HAND_COUNT < MAX_COUNT loop
  DEAL_CARD(MY_HAND, DECK);
  MY_HAND_COUNT := EVALUATE( MY_HAND );
end loop;
```

and determine how many hands out of 1000 the player wins for MAX_COUNT in the range 12 . . 20.

Section 9.5 Time and Space Constraints

9.5.1 Determine a table similar to the one in Figure 9.5.2 for the ADT in Exercise 9.3.2. Contrast these results with the ones contained in Figures 9.5.1 and 9.5.2.

NOTES AND REFERENCES

The notion of set introduced in this chapter is more mathematical than computational. Almost any introductory calculus textbook on discrete mathematics has more than enough background information.

10

Graphs and Digraphs

Formally, it takes two sets to make a graph. One set is a set of points, usually called *nodes* or *vertices*. The other set is a set of lines, sometimes called *edges*. Each edge joins two possibly distinct points together. Graphs can represent any relationship between objects. Stacks, queues, and trees are restricted graph forms. Because of their generality, graphs have many applications.

Consider a computer network. The vertices represent workstations or users, while the edges represent direct links between computers. Figure 10.0.1(a) shows a computer network in the token ring topology, and Figure 10.0.1(b) shows a computer network in the star topology. In the ring topology, the message is passed around the ring from one computer to the next computer until it reaches its destination. In the star topology all messages go through a central file server that relays messages to their final destination.

A road map is a type of graph. The vertices become street intersections and the edges represent the streets that join the intersections together. A road map illustrates one common graph property. Not every vertex is directly connected to every other vertex. In a road map an intersection typically connects to four other intersections.

An airline route map is another type of graph. When you phone up your travel agent and ask about flight information, the travel agent consults various airline route maps. The agent might respond that there is no direct flight from point *A* to point *C* but you can get there by laying over at point *B*. Here the vertices represent airports and the edges represent air service between the airports.

A graph can also represent a large construction job. Vertices represent the completion of certain tasks, such as digging the foundation or installing the heat ducts. The edges, which can be traversed in only one direction, represent task priorities. The task represented by a vertex cannot be started until the completion of all the tasks joined to it. Figure 10.0.2 shows a simple graph that represents the planting of a vegetable garden.

Even compilers use graphs. The syntax of many computer languages are defined using transition graphs. Figure 10.0.3 is a transition graph that determines if a particular character string is a valid Ada identifier. For each identifier, the transition graph starts at the start vertex. It must terminate at a final vertex or it is not a valid identifier. The vertices represent evaluation states and the edges are the transitions from one state to the next state.

Graph theory has a special vocabulary of its own. The points of a graph are interchangeably called nodes, points, or vertices. The lines joining the nodes of a graph are called

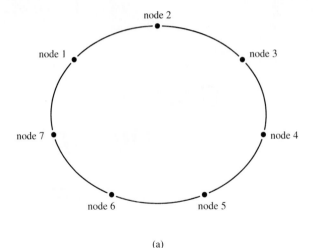

(a)

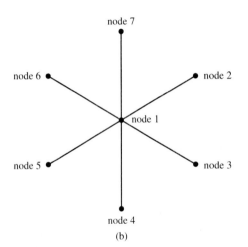

(b)

Figure 10.0.1 (a) Computer network implemented using a ring topology. Each node represents a computer. (b) Computer network using a star topology. Each message must be relayed through node 1.

edges, lines, or arcs. Any data structure used to represent a graph must represent both the vertices and the edges that join the vertices. If e_i is an edge that has v_k and v_l as endpoints (i.e., vertices), it is possible to move from v_k to v_l or from v_l to v_k. The edge of a graph is represented by the vertices at its endpoints. Formally,

$$e_i = (v_k, v_l) = (v_l, v_k)$$

Nothing prevents the case $v_k = v_l$.

A directed graph, which is usually called a digraph, is a graph where all the edges are "one way." An edge ei = <vk,vl> means that it is possible to move from vk to vl using the edge ei, but it not possible to move from vl to vk using ei. For this reason, edges in digraphs are visually represented as arrows. If ei = (vk,vl), then vk is the source vertex while vl is the destination vertex. The source vertex is always placed at the tail of the arrow and the destination vertex is placed at the head of the arrow. Clearly, in a digraph <vk,vl> /= <vl,vk>. Since

$$(vk,vl) = \{<vk,vl>, <vl,vk>\}$$

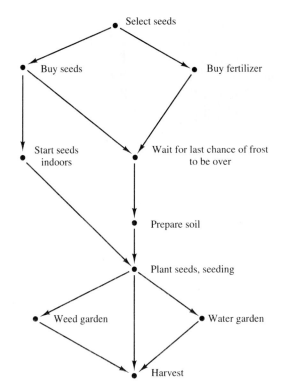

Figure 10.0.2 PERT graph that models a home vegetable garden.

the only graphs considered in this book will be digraphs. Figure 10.04(a) shows a simple graph, Figure 10.0.4(b) shows its formal representation as a set of vertices and a set of edges, and Figure 10.0.4(c) shows its formal digraph representation as a set of directed edges and a set of vertices.

If $e_i = <v_k, v_l>$, then v_l, the destination vertex, is said to be adjacent to v_k, the source vertex. The adjacency set of a vertex v_k is the set of all edges that are adjacent to v_k, that is,

$$\text{adjacency set}(v_k) = \{ v_j \mid \text{the edge } <v_k, v_j> \text{ exists} \}$$

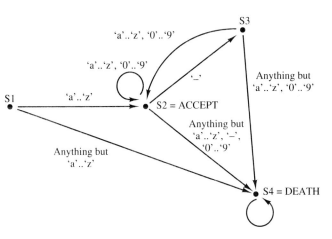

Figure 10.0.3 Finite-state machine represented as a transition graph. This finite-state machine recognizes any valid Ada identifier.

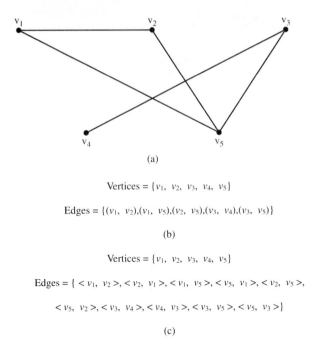

(a)

Vertices = {v_1, v_2, v_3, v_4, v_5}

Edges = {(v_1, v_2),(v_1, v_5),(v_2, v_5),(v_3, v_4),(v_3, v_5)}

(b)

Vertices = {v_1, v_2, v_3, v_4, v_5}

Edges = { < v_1, v_2 >, < v_2, v_1 >, < v_1, v_5 >, < v_5, v_1 >, < v_2, v_5 >,

< v_5, v_2 >, < v_3, v_4 >, < v_4, v_3 >, < v_3, v_5 >, < v_5, v_3 >}

(c)

Figure 10.0.4 (a) Simple graph of five vertices and five edges. (b) Representation of the graph in part (a) as a set of five vertices and a set of five edges. (c) Representation of the graph in part (a) with a set of five vertices and a set of 10 directed edges. Clearly, every graph can be represented as a digraph, but not every digraph can be represented as a graph.

The indegree of a vertex v_k is the number of edges that have v_k as a destination vertex. The outdegree of a vertex v_k is the number of edges that have v_k as a source vertex.

A *path* is a sequence of edges where the destination vertex of one edge is the source vertex of the next edge in the sequence. The digraph in Figure 10.0.5 has a path from v_2 to v_6 represented by the sequence of edges {v_2,v_3,v_7,v_6}, but there is no path from v_1 to v_4. A path is simple if the vertices in the path are distinct with the possible exception of the first and last vertices. The path

$$\{v_2, v_3, v_7, v_6, v_8\}$$

from v_2 to v_8 is simple but the path

$$\{v_2, v_4, v_7, v_2, v_4, v_7, v_6, v_8\}$$

is not simple. The length of a path is the number of edges in that path. If there is a path from v_i to v_j, then v_j is reachable from v_i. A cycle is a path where the source vertex of the first edge is the destination vertex of the last edge. A simple cycle is a simple path that is a cycle. A digraph is acyclic if has no cycles. Note that a tree can be defined as an acyclic digraph where every node has indegree 1 except the root, which has indegree 0. A graph is connected if and only if there is a path between any two vertices. Any graph that represents a computer network must be connected.

What are the typical operations on a graph? Obviously, there is a need to determine if there is an edge joining two vertices, and another need to be able to add and remove edges.

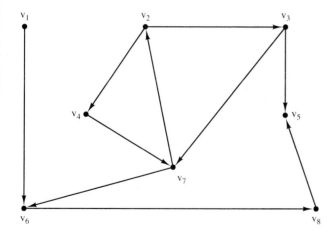

Figure 10.0.5 Simple nonconnected digraph.

Most applications involve finding a path from one vertex to another or determining if such a path exists. Other operations, such as determining the indegree of a vertex or copying the graph, can be built up from the first three. Operations such as listing all vertices with a common source vertex or a common destination vertex significantly reduce programming complexity. This is true when searching a graph to determine if there is a path from one vertex to another vertex.

The basic documentation for the ADT DIGRAPH is shown in Figure 10.0.6. Note that there are operations that can only be performed using the unbounded form. In the bounded or discrete version, the vertices are supplied at instantiation. The enumeration of the vertices is supplied by the programmer at instantiation. Only the type of vertices, not the vertices themselves, are supplied to the unbounded type at instantiation. This requires that the unbounded form have operations to add, delete, or list a graph's vertices.

GENERAL ADT SPECIFICATION FOR DISCRETE_DIGRAPH

Description

A digraph is a collection of two sets, vertices and edges. Every edge joins two, usually distinct, vertices. The edge joins one vertex, called the *source*, to the second vertex, called the *destination*. Digraph edges are one way in the sense that objects move from the source vertex to the destination vertex. In the discrete from every vertex is fixed. In the unbounded form vertices may be added or deleted. The type GRAPH is implemented as limited private.

Programmer-Supplied Data Structures
or Specifications

The programmer must supply a discrete type that makes up the vertex set. Only vertices listed in the discrete set can be referenced. The discrete type can be either an enumerated type or it may be a range subtype of integers.

Figure 10.0.6 Documentation for ADT DISCRETE_DIGRAPH. Continues on page 324.

Operations

Name	Description
COPY	Makes distinct exact copy of the graph. The boolean-valued function EQUAL returns true when the original and copy are compared.
CLEAR	Clears the graph. The result is a graph with an empty edge set. After the graph is cleared, VERTEX_IN_DE-GREE and VERTEX_OUT_DEGREE are all zero for any vertex.
ADD_EDGE	Adds an edge to a graph that joins a specified source vertex to a specified destination vertex.
REMOVE_EDGE	Removes an edge from a graph that joins a specified source vertex to a specified destination vertex.
EDGE_IN_GRAPH	Boolean-valued function that returns true if a specified graph has an edge joining a specified source vertex to a specified destination vertex, or false otherwise.
NEXT_SOURCE_VERTEX	For a given destination vertex, this operator returns a source vertex. Repeated calls will go through the complete sequence of vertices where each vertex is the source vertex to an edge with the given destination vertex before vertices before repeating the sequence.
NEXT_DESTINATION_VERTEX	For a given source vertex, this operator returns a destination vertex. Repeated calls will go through the complete sequence of vertices that are the destination vertex of an edge with a given source vertex before repeating the sequence.
VERTEX_IN_DEGREE	For a specified vertex in a given graph, returns a natural number equal to the number of edges that have the specified vertex as a destination vertex.
VERTEX_OUT_DEGREE	For a specified vertex in a given graph, returns a natural number equal to the number of edges that have the specified vertex as a source vertex.
EMPTY	Boolean-valued function that returns true if the specified graph is empty, or false otherwise. A discrete graph is empty if it has no edges.
EQUAL	Boolean-valued function that returns true if the two graphs are equal, or false otherwise. For a graph to be equal the nodes must have the same label and the edge set must be equal.

Exceptions

There are two exceptions. The exception NO_EDGE is raised by REMOVE_EDGE if there is no edge present to remove. The functions NEXT_SOURCE_VERTEX and NEXT_DESTI-NATION_VERTEX also raise NO_EDGE if a specified vertex has no edges, for which it is a

Figure 10.0.6 Continues on page 325.

source or destination vertex, respectively. The exception EDGE_EXISTS is raised by the operator ADD_EDGE if it attempts to add an edge that is already present.

Warnings

An exception to handle overflow has not been implemented. This exception could occur anytime an edge is added or the graph copied when the discrete digraph is implemented as a sparse matrix. The built-in exception storage_error will signal that an overflow has occurred.

Figure 10.0.6 Concluded.

10.1 ABSTRACT DATA TYPE DISCRETE_DIGRAPH

Recall that discrete forms come in two flavors. Any enumerated type is a discrete type. For example, an airline might fly between several cities and would want the vertices of the graph to be the names of the airports that they serve. The enumerated type cities does the job.

```
type CITY is (SAN_DIEGO, LA, BURBANK, SAN_FRANCISCO, ONTARIO);
```

The other discrete types are based on integer ranges, for example

```
subtype PINS is positive range 1..100;
```

All discrete graphs are bounded because the number of vertices and the names of the vertices are fixed.

For convenience the vertices of the graph will be labeled using positive values, but any enumerated type is feasible. The data structure is a boolean array where the element on the ith row and jth column is true if the edge $<v_i, v_j>$ exists. It is false otherwise. Such a representation is called an *adjacency matrix*. Figure 10.1.1 shows an adjacency matrix for the digraph in Figure 10.0.5.

Destination Vertices

Source Vertices	1	2	3	4	5	6	7	8
1	F	F	F	F	F	T	F	F
2	F	F	T	T	F	F	F	F
3	F	F	F	F	T	F	T	F
4	F	F	F	F	F	F	T	F
5	F	F	F	F	F	F	F	F
6	F	F	F	F	F	F	F	T
7	F	T	F	F	F	T	F	F
8	F	F	F	F	T	F	F	F

Figure 10.1.1 Adjacency matrix that represents the digraph in Figure 10.0.5.

Figure 10.1.2 specifies the abstract data type for a digraph implemented as an adjacency matrix.

```
generic
  type VERTEX is (<>);
  package GENERIC_DISCRETE_DIGRAPH is
  type GRAPH is limited private;
  procedure COPY            (FROM        : in    GRAPH;
                             TO          :   out GRAPH);
```

Figure 10.1.2 Specification for GENERIC_DISCRETE_DIGRAPH. Continues on page 326.

```
            procedure CLEAR              (GRAPH_TO_CLEAR   :     out GRAPH);
            procedure ADD_EDGE           (SOURCE,
                                          DESTINATION      : in      VERTEX;
                                          TO_GRAPH         : in out GRAPH);
            procedure REMOVE_EDGE        (SOURCE,
                                          DESTINATION      : in      VERTEX;
                                          FROM_GRAPH       : in out GRAPH);
            procedure NEXT_SOURCE_VERTEX (DESTINATION      : in      VERTEX;
                                          IN_GRAPH         : in out GRAPH;
                                          NEXT_SOURCE      :     out VERTEX);
            procedure NEXT_DESTINATION_VERTEX ( SOURCE     : in      VERTEX;
                                          IN_GRAPH         : in out GRAPH;
                                          NEXT_DESTINATION :     out VERTEX );
        function EDGE_IN_GRAPH       (SOURCE, DESTINATION : VERTEX;
                                          IN_GRAPH         : GRAPH) return boolean;
            function EMPTY               ( THIS_GRAPH      : GRAPH) return boolean;
            function EQUAL               ( LEFT, RIGHT     : GRAPH) return boolean;
            function VERTEX_IN_DEGREE    ( DESTINATION     : VERTEX;
                                          IN_GRAPH         : GRAPH ) return natural;
            function VERTEX_OUT_DEGREE ( SOURCE            : VERTEX;
                                          IN_GRAPH         : GRAPH ) return natural;
          NO_EDGE        : exception;
          EDGE_EXISTS    : exception;
      private
          type VERTEX_VECTOR is array (VERTEX) of VERTEX;
          type GRAPH_ARRAY is array (VERTEX, VERTEX ) of boolean;
          type GRAPH is
            record
              NEXT_SOURCE,
              NEXT_DEST : VERTEX_VECTOR :=(OTHERS => VERTEX'last);
              EDGE      : GRAPH_ARRAY   :=(others => (others => false));
            end record;
      end GENERIC_DISCRETE_DIGRAPH;
```

Figure 10.1.2 Concluded.

The implementation is straightforward except for the two procedures
NEXT_SOURCE_VERTEX and NEXT_DESTINATION_VERTEX. These procedures require two arrays to keep track of the last vertex returned. The two arrays NEXT_SOURCE and
NEXT_DEST of type VERTEX_VECTOR are used for this purpose. Initially, each element is
set to VERTEX' last. This value is arbitrary. This particular value will list the source or des-
tin-ation vertices by order of enumeration. The adjacency matrix is searched until either a true
value is found or it has been determined that the operation is undefined. This raises the
NO_EDGE exception.

Figure 10.1.3 contains a partial implementation of GENERIC_DISCRETE_DIGRAPH.
The remainder of GENERIC_DISCRETE_DIGRAPH is left as an exercise. As a simple application of GENERIC_DISCRETE_DIGRAPH, consider the problem of determining the
path graph P of the graph G. For a given graph G, the ijth element of the path graph P is true
if there is a path whose source vertex of the first edge is v_i and whose destination vertex of the

last edge is v_j. In other words, the path graph answers the question of which vertices are reachable from which vertices.

```
package body GENERIC_DISCRETE_DIGRAPH is
  NUMBER OF VERTICES : positive:= VERTEX VECTOR'length;


  ................


  procedure REMOVE_EDGE (SOURCE, DESTINATION :in  VERTEX;
                    FROM_GRAPH : in out GRAPH) is
    -- Removes the edge in a graph G with source vertex SOURCE and
    -- destination vertex DESTINATION.
    -- Exception NO_EDGE raised if the specified edge is
    --          not in the graph G.
  begin
    if FROM_GRAPH.EDGE (SOURCE, DESTINATION) then
      FROM_GRAPH.EDGE (SOURCE, DESTINATION) := false;
    else
      raise NO_EDGE;
    end if;
  end REMOVE_EDGE;

  function EDGE_IN_GRAPH (SOURCE, DESTINATION : VERTEX;
                        IN_GRAPH    : GRAPH ) return boolean is
    -- Returns true if an edge with source vertex SOURCE and destination
    -- vertex DESTINATION is in the graph
  begin
    return IN_GRAPH.EDGE (SOURCE, DESTINATION);
  end EDGE_IN_GRAPH;

  procedure NEXT_SOURCE_VERTEX( DESTINATION : in    VERTEX;
                              IN_GRAPH    : in out GRAPH;
                              NEXT_SOURCE :    out VERTEX) is
    -- Iterates through the edges of a specified destination vertex
    -- DESTINATION and returns the source vertex of the next edge.
    -- Exception NO_EDGE raised if the indegree of the specified
    --          vertex is 0.
  begin
    for COUNT in 1..NUMBER_OF_VERTICES loop
      if IN_GRAPH.NEXT_SOURCE (DESTINATION) = VERTEX'last then
        IN_GRAPH.NEXT_SOURCE(DESTINATION)    := VERTEX'first;
      else
        IN_GRAPH.NEXT_SOURCE(DESTINATION)    :=
          VERTEX'succ (IN_GRAPH.NEXT_SOURCE(DESTINATION));
      end if;
      if IN_GRAPH.EDGE(IN_GRAPH.NEXT_SOURCE(DESTINATION), DESTINATION) then
        NEXT_SOURCE := IN_GRAPH.NEXT_SOURCE(DESTINATION);
        return;
```

Figure 10.1.3 Partial implementation of GENERIC_DISCRETE_DIGRAPH. Continues on page 328.

```
      end if;
    end loop;
    raise NO_EDGE;
  end NEXT_SOURCE_VERTEX;

  . . . . . . . . . . . . . .


end GENERIC_DISCRETE_DIGRAPH;
```

Figure 10.1.3 Concluded.

For a given graph G, define $G**k$ to be a graph where $G**k$ (i,j) = true if there is a path of length k from v_i to v_j and false otherwise. If a graph G has n vertices, then

$$P = G \text{ or } G**2 \text{ or } G**3 \text{ or } \dots \text{ or } G**(n-1)$$

where the logical operation or is done element by element. Since the longest path without cycles through n vertices has length $n - 1$; there is a path from v_i to v_j of length less than n or there is no path. If G1 is a graph that lists vertices reachable by a path of length k, and if G2 is a graph that lists vertices that are reachable by length j, the procedure below will return a graph G3 that lists vertices that are reachable by paths of length $k + j$. Since the formal parameter G3 is of mode out, it is necessary to recompile DISCRETE_DIGRAPH in Figure 10.1.2 with the change that type GRAPH is private instead of limited private. It is assumed that the enumerated vertex type is called vertex, as the instantiation implies.

```
package THIS_GRAPH is new GENERIC_DISCRETE_DIGRAPH(VERTEX);
use THIS_GRAPH;

procedure COMPUTE_G1_AND_G2 ( G1, G2 : in     graph;
                              G3      :     out graph ) is
  G_TEMP : GRAPH;
begin
  for SOURCE in VERTEX loop
    for DESTINATION in VERTEX loop
      for TEMP_VERTEX in VERTEX loop
        if EDGE_IN_GRAPH (SOURCE, TEMP_VERTEX, G1) and then
             EDGE_IN_GRAPH (TEMP_VERTEX, DESTINATION, G2) and then
             not EDGE_IN_GRAPH(SCR,DST,G_TEMP) then
          ADD_EDGE(SOURCE, DESTINATION, G_TEMP);
        end if;
      end loop;
    end loop;
  end loop;
  COPY(G_TEMP, G3);
end COMPUTE_G1_AND_G2;
```

This procedure provides a straightforward way to compute the path graph. The procedure in Figure 10.1.4 provides a solution. Note that this solution is $O(n**5)$, where n is the number of vertices.

```
procedure COMPUTE_PATH_GRAPH ( OF_GRAPH : in     GRAPH;
                               PATH     :     out GRAPH ) is
  P1_TEMP, P2_TEMP : GRAPH;
```

Figure 10.1.4 Procedure to compute the path graph of a given graph G. Continues on page 329.

```
begin
  Copy(OF_GRAPH, P1_temp);
  -- Initialize with all paths of length 1
  COPY(OF_GRAPH, P2_TEMP);
  for INDEX IN 1..VERTEX'pos(VERTEX'last) loop
    -- Compute path of length i + 1
    COMPUTE_G1_AND_G2(OF_GRAPH, P1_TEMP, P1_TEMP);
    -- Add path of length i + 1 to all paths length <= i
    for SOURCE in VERTEX loop
      for DESTINATION in VERTEX loop
        -- If there is path from SRC to DST of length i+1
        if EDGE_IN_GRAPH(SOURCE,DESTINATION,P1_TEMP)and then
          -- and no path of length <= i
          not EDGE_IN_GRAPH(SOURCE,DESTINATION,P2_TEMP)then
          -- then add the new path
          ADD_EDGE(SOURCE,DESTINATION, P2_TEMP);
        end if;
      end loop;
    end loop;
  end loop;
  COPY (P2_TEMP, PATH);
end COMPUTE_PATH_GRAPH;
```

Figure 10.1.4 Concluded.

There is a similar but computationally simpler path algorithm due to Warshall. For a given graph G, define PATH$*0 = G$. Let PATH$**$ k (i,j) = true if and only if there is a simple path from v_i to v_j of any length that may or may not use any of the nodes $v_1, v_2, \ldots, v_k$ in any order. Clearly, the path graph PATH = PATH$**n$, where n is the number of nodes. Warshall's algorithm, given in Figure 10.1.5, is superior to procedure COMPUTE_PATH_GRAPH, given in Figure 10.1.4, because Warshall's algorithm is $O(n**3)$. It, too, requires that the type graph be private instead of limited private because the formal parameter PATH is mode out. Warshall's algorithm answers the question of the existence of a path, but it does not determine the path. This question is dealt with in Section 10.4.

```
procedure WARSHALL (THIS_GRAPH : in     GRAPH;
                    PATH        :     out GRAPH ) is
  P_TEMP : GRAPH;
begin
  -- Initialize with all paths length = 1
  COPY (THIS_GRAPH, P_TEMP);
  -- Compute PATH**K where K = VERTEX'pos (K)
  for INDEX in VERTEX loop
    for SOURCE in VERTEX loop
      for DESTINATION in VERTEX loop
        -- If there is a path from SOURCE to INDEX
        if EDGE_IN_GRAPH(SOURCE, INDEX, P_TEMP) and then
          -- and a path from INDEX to DESTINATION
          EDGE_IN_GRAPH(INDEX,DESTINATION,P_TEMP)and then
```

Figure 10.1.5 Warshall's path algorithm. Continues on page 330.

```
                    -- But no current path from SOURCE to
                    -- DESTINATION
               not EDGE_IN_GRAPH(SOURCE, DESTINATION, P_TEMP) then
                    -- Add the path from SRC to DST
                  ADD_EDGE(SOURCE, DESTINATION, P_TEMP);
             end if;
           end loop;
         end loop;
       end loop;
       COPY (P_TEMP, PATH);
     end WARSHALL;
```

Figure 10.1.5   Concluded.

The storage required to hold a graph using the data structure specified in Figure 10.1.2 is $O(n**2)$, where n is the number of vertices. Graphs are usually sparse. Sparse arrays are formally examined in Chapter 16. A sparse array keeps track of the edges in the graph, not the possible edges not in the graph. The data structure in Figure 10.1.6 implements a sparse array. Each row is a linked list of edges with the same source vertex and ordered by their destination vertex. Similarly, each column is a linked list of edges with the same destination vertex but ordered by their source vertex. If the private section of the graph specification in Figure 10.1.2 is replaced by Figure 10.1.6, the data structure is as shown in Figure 10.1.7.

```
type EDGE;
type NEXT_EDGE is access EDGE;
type EDGE is
  record
    SOURCE,
    DESTINATION       : VERTEX;
    NEXT_SOURCE,
    NEXT_DESTINATION  : NEXT_EDGE;
  end record;
type VERTICE is
  record
    FIRST_EDGE : NEXT_EDGE;
    DEGREE     : natural;
  end record;
type VERTEX_array is array (VERTEX) OF VERTICE;
type NEXT_ARRAY is array (VERTEX) of NEXT_EDGE;
type GRAPH is
  record
    NEXT_SOURCE,                      --used by NEXT_SOURCE_VERTEX
    NEXT_DESTINATION : NEXT_ARRAY;  --used by NEXT_DESTINATION_VERTEX
    SOURCE ARRAY,
    DESTINATION_ARRAY : VERTEX ARRAY := ( others => (null, 0));
  end record;
```

Figure 10.1.6   Second representation of GENERIC_DISCRETE_DIGRAPH.

The rows of the array GRAPH denote an ordered queue of edges that have the same source vertex. The columns in Figure 10.1.6 denote an ordered queue of edges that correspond

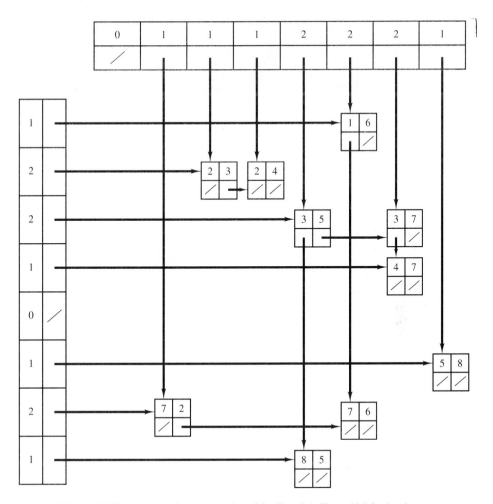

Figure 10.1.7   Sparse matrix representation of the digraph in Figure 10.0.5 using the
representation in Figure 10.1.6.

to edges with the same destination vertex. The graph operation ADD_EDGE is the same as the
sparse matrix operation ADD_MATRIX_ELEMENT. There is no value field to switch from
true to false in the edge record. If the edge record for a given edge is present in a variable
of type graph, the given edge is in the graph. Three operations, EDGE_IN_GRAPH,
ADD_EDGE, and NEXT_SOURCE_VERTEX, are listed below.

```
function EDGE_IN_GRAPH        (SOURCE,
                               DESTINATION : VERTEX;
                               IN_GRAPH    : GRAPH ) return boolean is
  --Adds an edge in a graph IN_GRAPH from vertex SOURCE to vertex DESTINATION.
  --Exception EDGE_EXISTS raised if the graph already
  --           contains the specified edge.
  TEMP_SOURCE : NEXT_EDGE := IN_GRAPH.SOURCE_ARRAY(SOURCE).FIRST_EDGE;
begin
```

```
      --Search the edge queue of all edges with a specified source
      loop
        exit when TEMP_SOURCE = null;
        if TEMP_SOURCE.DESTINATION = DESTINATION then
          return true;
        else
          TEMP_SOURCE := TEMP_SOURCE.NEXT_DESTINATION;
        end if;
      end loop;
      --Search fails, edge is not there.
      return false;
   end EDGE_IN_GRAPH;

   procedure ADD_EDGE ( SOURCE, DESTINATION : in      VERTEX;
                        TO_GRAPH                : in out GRAPH) is

     --Adds an edge in a graph TO_GRAPH from vertex SOURCE
     --to vertex DESTINATION.
     --Exception EDGE_EXISTS raised if the graph already
     -- contains the specified edge.
     TEMP_EDGE : NEXT_EDGE := new EDGE' (SOURCE, DESTINATION, null, null);

      procedure ADD_EDGE_TO_SOURCE_Q (EDGE : in      NEXT_EDGE;
                                      QUEUE : in out NEXT_EDGE) is
      -- Recursive insertion, similar to priority queue inorder insertion
      TEMP_EDGE : NEXT_EDGE := EDGE;
   begin
      if QUEUE = null or else EDGE.DESTINATION < QUEUE.DESTINATION then
        TEMP_EDGE.NEXT_DESTINATION := QUEUE;
        QUEUE := TEMP_EDGE;
      else
        ADD_EDGE_TO_SOURCE_Q (EDGE, QUEUE.NEXT_DESTINATION);
      end if;
   end ADD_EDGE_TO_SOURCE_Q;

   procedure ADD_EDGE_TO_DESTINATION_Q (EDGE : in      NEXT_EDGE;
                              QUEUE : in out NEXT_EDGE) is
      -- Recursive insertion, similar to priority queue inorder insertion
      TEMP_EDGE : NEXT_EDGE := EDGE;
   begin
      if QUEUE = null or else EDGE.SOURCE < QUEUE.SOURCE then
        TEMP_EDGE.NEXT_SOURCE := QUEUE;
        QUEUE := TEMP_EDGE;
      else
        ADD_EDGE_TO_DESTINATION_Q (EDGE, QUEUE.NEXT_SOURCE);
      end if;
   end ADD_EDGE_TO_DESTINATION_Q;
   begin
```

```
    if EDGE_IN_GRAPH (SOURCE, DESTINATION, TO_GRAPH) then
      raise EDGE_EXISTS;
    else
      ADD_EDGE_TO_SOURCE_Q (TEMP_EDGE,
          TO_GRAPH.SOURCE_ARRAY(SOURCE).FIRST_EDGE);
      TO_GRAPH.SOURCE_ARRAY(SOURCE).DEGREE :=
          TO_GRAPH.SOURCE_ARRAY(SOURCE).DEGREE + 1;
      ADD_EDGE_TO_DESTINATION_Q (TEMP_EDGE,
          TO_GRAPH.DESTINATION_ARRAY(DESTINATION).FIRST_EDGE);
      TO_GRAPH.DESTINATION_ARRAY(DESTINATION).DEGREE :=
          TO_GRAPH.DESTINATION_ARRAY(DESTINATION).DEGREE + 1;
    end if;
  end ADD_EDGE;

  procedure NEXT_SOURCE_VERTEX( DESTINATION : in      VERTEX;
                                IN_GRAPH     : in out GRAPH;
                                NEXT_SOURCE :     out VERTEX ) is
    -- Iterates through the edges of a specified destination vertex
    -- DESTINATION and returns the source vertex of the next edge.
    -- Exception NO_EDGE raised if the indegree of the specified
    --           vertex is 0.
  begin
    if IN_GRAPH.NEXT_SOURCE(DESTINATION) = null then
      IN_GRAPH.NEXT_SOURCE(DESTINATION) :=
          IN_GRAPH.DESTINATION_ARRAY(DESTINATION).FIRST_EDGE;
      if IN_GRAPH.NEXT_SOURCE(DESTINATION) = null then
        raise NO_EDGE;
      else
        NEXT_SOURCE := IN_GRAPH.NEXT_SOURCE(DESTINATION).SOURCE;
      end if;
    else
      IN_GRAPH.NEXT_SOURCE(DESTINATION) :=
          IN_GRAPH.NEXT_SOURCE(DESTINATION).NEXT_SOURCE;
      if IN_GRAPH.NEXT_SOURCE(DESTINATION) = null then
        IN_GRAPH.NEXT_SOURCE(DESTINATION) :=
            IN_GRAPH.DESTINATION_ARRAY(DESTINATION).FIRST_EDGE;
      end if;
      NEXT_SOURCE := IN_GRAPH.NEXT_SOURCE(DESTINATION).SOURCE;
    end if;
  end NEXT_SOURCE_VERTEX;
```

Any program that uses GENERIC_DISCRETE_DIGRAPH as specified in Figure 10.1.2 can use GENERIC_SPARSE_DISCRETE_DIGRAPH as specified in Figure 10.1.6. The rest of the operations are left to the exercises.

Many graph algorithms require that vertices be added and removed from the graph. It appears that neither GENERIC_DISCRETE_DIGRAPH nor GENERIC_SPARSE_DIS-CRETE_DIGRAPH would be suitable for these applications. The simplest way around this roadblock is to use GENERIC_DISCRETE_SET to keep track of the active vertices.

10.2 ABSTRACT DATA TYPE GENERIC_UNBOUNDED_DIGRAPH

The ADT GENERIC_DISCRETE_DIGRAPH specified in Figure 10.1.2 has three deficiencies. First, in many applications, the graph grows and the user does not know, in advance, the number of vertices or the names of the vertices. For the ADT GENERIC_DIS-CRETE_DIGRAPH, the number of vertices must be specified in advance. Second, many graph algorithms are easier to implement when it is possible to add or remove vertices. The ADT GENERIC_DISCRETE_DIGRAPH cannot remove vertices, although it is possible to use ADT SET to keep track of active vertices. The third and last deficiency, which was partially answered by using the graph representation in Figure 10.1.6, is the often excessive waste of space. Often, in practice, the adjacency matrix used to represent the graph in GENERIC_DISCRETE_DIGRAPH is a sparse matrix. This shortcoming was partially answered by GENERIC_SPARSE_DISCRETE_DIGRAPH. A given vertex will be the source vertex for a small, or sparse, number of edges joining other vertices. Eventually, most of the entries will be false.

The section "User-Supplied Data Structures or Specifications" must be modified. The vertices in the ADT GENERIC_UNBOUNDED_DIGRAPH are not known explicitly in advance. The set of vertices can increase or decrease.

The user must supply two parameters. The first is the vertex type and it is used as vertex names. The type VERTEX_TYPE is private within the package. The second parameter is a boolean-valued function "<" defined on VERTEX_TYPE that is used to order the priority queue of active vertices.

In addition to the operations already listed in GENERIC_DISCRETE_DIGRAPH, the ADT GENERIC_UNBOUNDED_DIGRAPH requires operations to add, delete, count, and list vertices. The names and descriptions of the additional operations follow.

ADD_VERTEX	Adds a vertex to both the source vertex queue and the destination vertex queue.
REMOVE_VERTEX	Removes a vertex from both the source vertex queue and the destination vertex queue. All edges must have been removed previously.
VERTEX_IN_GRAPH	Boolean-valued function that returns true if a specified graph contains a specified vertex.
VERTEX_COUNT	Returns a natural number equal to the number of vertices in the graph.
VERTEX_LIST	Returns the next vertex in the vertex queue. Repeated calls will eventually list all the vertices provided in a given graph provided that no vertex has been added or removed since the last call.

The two new exceptions NO_EDGE and EDGE_EXISTS are already contained in GENERIC_DISCRETE_DIGRAPH. The full description of the "Exception" section follows.

There are five exceptions for the unbounded case. The exception NO_EDGE is raised by REMOVE_EDGE if there is no edge present to remove. The functions NEXT_SOURCE_VER- TEX and NEXT_DEST_VERTEX also raise NO_EDGE if a specified vertex has no edges for which it is a source or destination vertex, respectively. The exception EDGE_EXISTS is raised by the operator ADD_EDGE if it attempts to add an edge that is already present. The operator REMOVE_VERTEX also will raise EDGE_EXISTS if the specified vertex is either the source or destination of any edge. The exception NO_VERTEX will be raised by ADD_EDGE and REMOVE_EDGE if the specified source or destination vertex is not in the vertex queue. NO_VER- TEX is also raised by VERTEX_LIST, VERTEX_IN_DEGREE, VERTEX_OUT_DEGREE, NEXT_SOURCE_EDGE, NEXT_DEST_EDGE, EDGE_IN_GRAPH, and REMOVE_VERTEX if the vertex is not present. ADD_VERTEX raises the exception VERTEX_EXISTS if the vertex is already present. The exception OVERFLOW is raised by ADD_VERTEX, and ADD_EDGE raises a storage_error due to lack of memory.

There are several reasons to use a sparse structure similar to the one proposed for GENERIC_UNBOUNDED_DIGRAPH. Consider the street map of a small town. The vertices represent intersections of streets and the edges represent a street that joins two intersections. As the town grows, the map grows. If n is the number of intersections, the adjacency matrix has $n**2$ entries. However, a typical vertex, which represents an intersection, has indegree 4 and outdegree 4. If there are 100 intersections in the small town, the adjacency matrix has 10,000 elements with less than 800, or 8 percent, used to represent various edges or streets.

One solution is to use linked lists of interlocking LIST_NODES. The two vertex queues will be a priority queue of source vertices and a priority queue of destination vertices. Each vertex node will be the header of a linked list of edges that has that vertex as either a source vertex or a destination vertex along with a field that denotes that vertex's degree. Figure 10.2.1(a) shows a small graph, Figure 10.2.1(b) shows the representation of this graph using the two priority queues of vertices that are themselves headers for priority queues of edges. The operations and exceptions include all DISCRETE_DIGRAPH operations and exceptions

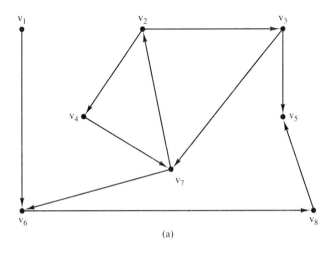

(a)

Figure 10.2.1 (a) Simple digraph.

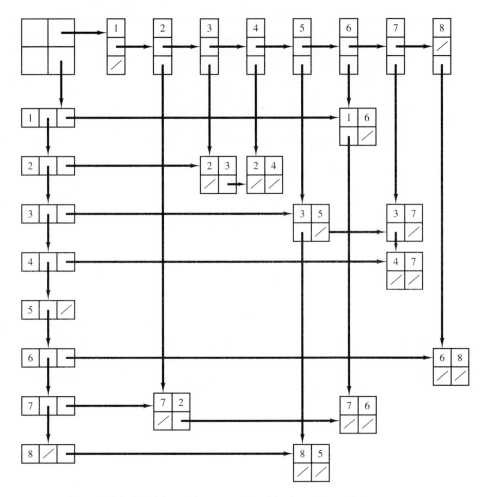

Figure 10.2.1 (b) Unbounded representation of the digraph in part (a).

plus four additional procedures and one additional boolean function described above. The generic specification for the package GENERIC_UNBOUNDED_DIGRAPH is listed in Figure 10.2.2.

```
generic
  type VERTEX_TYPE is private;
  WITH function "<" (LEFT, RIGHT : VERTEX_TYPE) return boolean is <>;
package GENERIC_UNBOUNDED_DIGRAPH is
  type GRAPH is limited private;
  procedure COPY            (FROM           : in      GRAPH;
                             TO             :     out GRAPH);
  procedure CLEAR           (GRAPH_TO_CLEAR :     out GRAPH);
  procedure ADD_EDGE        (SOURCE,
                             DESTINATION    : in      VERTEX_TYPE;
```

Figure 10.2.2 Specification for GENERIC_UNBOUNDED_DIGRAPH. Continues on page 337.

```
                                   TO_GRAPH           : in out GRAPH);
     procedure REMOVE_EDGE         (SOURCE,
                                   DESTINATION        : in      VERTEX_TYPE;
                                   FROM_GRAPH         : in out GRAPH);
     procedure ADD_VERTEX          (VERTEX            : in      VERTEX_TYPE;
                                   TO_GRAPH           : in out GRAPH);
     procedure REMOVE_VERTEX       (VERTEX            : in      VERTEX_TYPE;
                                   FROM_GRAPH         : in out GRAPH);
     function VERTEX_COUNT         (OF_GRAPH          : GRAPH ) return natural;
     procedure VERTEX_LIST         (OF_GRAPH          : in out GRAPH;
                                   VERTEX             :      out VERTEX_TYPE;
     function VERTEX_IN_GRAPH      (VERTEX            : VERTEX_TYPE;
                                   IN_GRAPH           : GRAPH ) return boolean;
     function EDGE_IN_GRAPH        (SOURCE, DESTINATION : VERTEX_TYPE;
                                   IN_GRAPH           : GRAPH ) return boolean;
     function NEXT_SOURCE_VERTEX   (DESTINATION       : VERTEX_TYPE;
                                   IN_GRAPH           : GRAPH ) return VERTEX_TYPE;
     function NEXT_DESTINATION_VERTEX (SOURCE         : VERTEX_TYPE;
                                   IN_GRAPH           : GRAPH ) return VERTEX_TYPE;
     function EMPTY                (THIS_GRAPH        : GRAPH) return boolean;
     function EQUAL                (LEFT, RIGHT       : GRAPH) return boolean;
     function VERTEX_IN_DEGREE     (DESTINATION       : VERTEX_TYPE;
                                   IN_GRAPH           : GRAPH ) return natural;
     function VERTEX_OUT_DEGREE    (SOURCE            : VERTEX_TYPE;
                                   IN_GRAPH           : GRAPH ) return natural;
   NO_EDGE         : exception;
   EDGE_EXISTS     : exception;
   NO_VERTEX       : exception;
   VERTEX_EXISTS   : exception;
   OVERFLOW        : exception;
private
   type EDGE;
   type NEXT_EDGE is access EDGE;
   type EDGE is
     record
       SOURCE,
       DESTINATION : VERTEX_TYPE;
       NEXT_SOURCE,
       NEXT_DESTINATION : NEXT_EDGE;
     end record;
   type VERTICE;
   type NEXT_VERTICE is access vertice;
   type VERTICE is
     record
       VERTEX : VERTEX_TYPE;
       DEGREE : natural;          -- USED BY VERTEX_IN_DEGREE, VERTEX_OUT_DEGREE
       LAST_LIST : NEXT_EDGE;     -- USED BY EITHER NEXT_SOURCE_EDGE or
                                  -- NEXT DESTINATION_EDGE
       FIRST_EDGE  : NEXT_EDGE;   -- first EDGE in SOURCE or DESTINATION list
```

Figure 10.2.2 Continues on page 338.

```
        NEXT_VERTEX : NEXT_VERTICE;
     end record;
   type GRAPH is
     record
        SOURCE_LIST         : NEXT_VERTICE; -- LIST OF SOURCE VERTICES
        DESTINATION_LIST    : NEXT_VERTICE; -- LIST OF DESTINATION VERTICES
        LAST_LIST           : NEXT_VERTICE;  -- USED BY VERTEX_TYPE_LIST
        COUNT : natural := 0;                       -- Number of vertices in graph
     end record;
end GENERIC_UNBOUNDED_DIGRAPH;
```

Figure 10.2.2   Concluded.

The implementation of the body is straightforward once the structure in Figure 10.2.1(b) is understood. Several utility operations are used repeatedly throughout the body. The function FIND_VERTEX searches either the source vertex queue or the destination vertex queue for a specific vertex node. This vertex node contains the pointer to the queue of edges and the degree of the vertex.

```
   function FIND_VERTEX (NEXT : NEXT_VERTICE; VERTEX : VERTEX_TYPE)
                                        return NEXT_VERTICE is
     -- RETURNS A PARTICULAR VERTEX.
     -- exception NO_VERTEX raised if the VERTEX is not found
     TEMP_VERTICE : NEXT_VERTICE := NEXT;
   begin
     -- Do a sequential search of a VERTEX queue
     loop
       exit when TEMP_VERTICE = null;
       if TEMP_VERTICE.VERTEX = VERTEX then
         return TEMP_VERTICE;
       elsif VERTEX < TEMP_VERTICE.VERTEX then
         raise NO_VERTEX;
       else
         TEMP_VERTICE := TEMP_VERTICE.NEXT_VERTEX;
       end if;
     end loop;
     -- Search unsuccessful
     raise NO_VERTEX;
   end FIND_VERTEX;
```

The function FIND_VERTEX makes the function VERTEX_IN_DEGREE a simple return statement.

```
   function VERTEX_IN_DEGREE   ( DESTINATION : VERTEX_TYPE;
                                 IN_GRAPH : GRAPH) return natural is
     -- Returns the number of edges in a graph with a specified
     -- destination vertex.
     -- Exception NO_VERTEX raised if the destination vertex
```

```
           --            is not in the vertex queue
      begin
        return FIND_VERTEX (IN_GRAPH.DESTINATION_LIST, DESTINATION).DEGREE;
      exception
        when NO_VERTEX = > raise NO_VERTEX;
      end VERTEX_IN_DEGREE;
```

The function FIND_VERTEX is also used in ADD_EDGE.

```
procedure ADD_EDGE ( SOURCE,
                     DESTINATION : in     VERTEX_TYPE;
                     TO_GRAPH    : in out GRAPH) is
    -- Adds an edge in a graph G from VERTEX SOURCE to VERTEX DESTINATION.
    -- Exception EDGE_EXISTS raised if the graph already
    --           contains the specified edge.
    -- Exception NO_VERTEX raised if either the source or destination
    --           VERTEX is not in the VERTEX queue


    SOURCE_VERTEX      : NEXT_VERTICE;
    DESTINATION_VERTEX : NEXT_VERTICE;
    NEW_EDGE_NODE : NEXT_EDGE := new EDGE'(SOURCE, DESTINATION, null, null);


    procedure INSERT_EDGE_INTO_SOURCE_Q (NEW_EDGE_NODE : in NEXT_EDGE;
                                         PLACE : in out NEXT_EDGE) is
    -- Inserts an edge in ascending order into the edge's source
    -- VERTEX Queue.
    TEMP: NEXT_EDGE := NEW_EDGE_NODE;
  begin
    if PLACE = null then
      PLACE := NEW_EDGE_NODE;
    elsif NEW_EDGE_NODE.DESTINATION < PLACE.DESTINATION then
      TEMP.NEXT_DESTINATION := PLACE;
      PLACE := TEMP;
    elsif PLACE.DESTINATION = NEW_EDGE_NODE.DESTINATION then
      raise EDGE_EXISTS;
    else
      INSERT_EDGE_INTO_SOURCE_Q (NEW_EDGE_NODE, PLACE.NEXT_DESTINATION);
    end if;
  end INSERT_EDGE_INTO_SOURCE_Q;


procedure INSERT_EDGE_INTO_DEST_Q (NEW_EDGE_NODE : in NEXT_EDGE;
                    PLACE : in out NEXT_EDGE) is
    -- Inserts an edge in ascending order into the edge's
    -- destination VERTEX queue.
    TEMP : NEXT_EDGE := NEW_EDGE_NODE;
  begin
    if PLACE = null then
      PLACE := NEW_EDGE_NODE;
    elsif NEW_EDGE_NODE.SOURCE_PLACE.SOURCE then
```

```
          TEMP.NEXT_SOURCE := PLACE;
          PLACE := TEMP;
        else
          INSERT_EDGE_INTO_DEST_Q (NEW_EDGE_NODE, PLACE.NEXT_SOURCE);
        end if;
    end INSERT_EDGE_INTO_DEST_Q;
begin
    -- Find beginning of queue of edges with SOURCE, DESTINATION
    SOURCE_VERTEX        := FIND_VERTEX (TO_GRAPH.SOURCE_LIST, SOURCE);
    DESTINATION_VERTEX := FIND_VERTEX (TO_GRAPH.DESTINATION_LIST, DESTINATION);
    -- Insert NEW_EDGE_NODE into ordered source queue of edges
    if SOURCE_VERTEX.FIRST_EDGE = null or else
          DESTINATION < SOURCE_VERTEX.FIRST_EDGE.DESTINATION then
        NEW_EDGE_NODE.NEXT_DESTINATION := SOURCE_VERTEX.FIRST_EDGE;
        SOURCE_VERTEX.FIRST_EDGE := NEW_EDGE_NODE;
    elsif DESTINATION = SOURCE_VERTEX.FIRST_EDGE.DESTINATION then
        raise EDGE_EXISTS;
    else
        INSERT_EDGE_INTO_SOURCE_Q
                        (NEW_EDGE_NODE, SOURCE_VERTEX.FIRST_EDGE);
    end if;
    -- Insert NEW_EDGE_NODE into ordered destination queue of edges
    if DESTINATION_VERTEX.FIRST_EDGE = null or else
          SOURCE < DESTINATION_VERTEX.FIRST_EDGE.SOURCE then
        NEW_EDGE_NODE.NEXT_SOURCE := DESTINATION_VERTEX.FIRST_EDGE;
        DESTINATION_VERTEX.FIRST_EDGE := NEW_EDGE_NODE;
    else
        INSERT_EDGE_INTO_DEST_Q (NEW_EDGE_NODE,
                DESTINATION_VERTEX.FIRST_EDGE);
    end if;
    -- Update degree of source VERTEX and destination VERTEX
    SOURCE_VERTEX.DEGREE        := SOURCE_VERTEX.DEGREE + 1;
    DESTINATION_VERTEX.DEGREE := DESTINATION_VERTEX.DEGREE + 1;
    SOURCE_VERTEX.LAST_LIST    := null;
    DESTINATION_VERTEX.LAST_LIST := null;
exception
    when storage_error => raise OVERFLOW;
    when NO_VERTEX => raise NO_VERTEX;
    when EDGE_EXISTS => raise EDGE_EXISTS;
end ADD_EDGE;
```

The two procedures INSERT_EDGE_INTO_DESTINATION_Q and IN-SERT_EDGE_INTO_SOURCE_Q are just recursive procedures to insert an object into a priority queue in priority order. The operation ADD_VERTEX is also a matter of inserting vertice nodes into the two priority queues of vertex nodes.

```
    procedure ADD_VERTEX (VERTEX   : in     VERTEX_TYPE;
                          TO_GRAPH : in out GRAPH ) is
      -- Adds a VERTEX to both the source queue and the destination queue.
      -- Exception VERTEX_EXISTS raised if VERTEX is already in either queue.
```

```
begin
  ADD_VERTEX_INORDER (TO_GRAPH.SOURCE_LIST, VERTEX);
  ADD_VERTEX_INORDER (TO_GRAPH.DESTINATION_LIST, VERTEX);
  TO_GRAPH.COUNT := TO_GRAPH.COUNT + 1;
exception
  when VERTEX_EXISTS => raise VERTEX_EXISTS;
  when storage_error => raise OVERFLOW;
end ADD_VERTEX;
```

The procedure ADD_VERTEX_INORDER inside the operation ADD_VERTEX is another example of an inorder priority queue insertion. It is similar to the procedure INSERT_EDGE_INTO_SOURCE_Q and INSERT_EDGE_INTO_DEST_Q in the operation INSERT_EDGE.

The function VERTEX_LIST uses a field in the graph structure to find the last vertex listed. This value just points to some vertex in the source vertex list. Similarly, the function to return the next edge in the list with a particular source or destination vertex uses a similar field in the vertex node.

```
procedure VERTEX_LIST       (OF_GRAPH          : in out GRAPH;
                             VERTEX            :     out VERTEX_TYPE ) is
  -- Returns the next vertex in the vertex queue.  Repeated calls
  -- will eventually list all vertices
  -- Exception NO_VERTEX raised if the VERTEX_TYPE set is empty.
begin
  if OF_GRAPH.LAST_LIST = null then
    OF_GRAPH.LAST_LIST := OF_GRAPH.SOURCE_LIST;
    if OF_GRAPH.LAST_LIST = null then
      raise NO_VERTEX;
    end if;
  else
    OF_GRAPH.LAST_LIST := OF_GRAPH.LAST_LIST.NEXT_VERTEX;
    if OF GRAPH.LAST_LIST = null then
      OF GRAPH.LAST_LIST := OF GRAPH.SOURCE_LIST;
    end if;
  end if;
  VERTEX := OF GRAPH.LAST_LIST.VERTEX;
end VERTEX_LIST;
function NEXT_SOURCE_VERTEX ( DESTINATION : VERTEX_TYPE;
                             IN_GRAPH : GRAPH) return VERTEX_TYPE is
  -- Iterates through the edges of a specified destination vertex
  -- DESTINATION and returns the source vertex of the next edge.
  -- Exception NO_EDGE raised if the indegree of the specified vertex is 0.
  -- Exception NO_VERTEX raised if either the destination vertex
  --           is not in the vertex queue.
  TEMP_V : NEXT_VERTICE;
begin
  TEMP_V := FIND_VERTEX (IN_GRAPH.DESTINATION_LIST, DESTINATION);
  if TEMP_V.LAST_LIST = null then
    TEMP_V.LAST_LIST := TEMP_V.FIRST_EDGE;
    if TEMP_V.LAST_LIST = null then
```

```
      raise NO_EDGE;
    end if;
  else
    TEMP_V.LAST_LIST := TEMP_V.LAST_LIST.NEXT_SOURCE;
    if TEMP_V.LAST_LIST = null then
      TEMP_V.LAST_LIST := TEMP_V.FIRST_EDGE;
    end if;
  end if;
  return TEMP_V.LAST_LIST.SOURCE;
exception
  when NO_VERTEX  => raise NO_VERTEX;
end NEXT_SOURCE_VERTEX;
```

The full implementa.tion of this ADT is left, as usual, to the exercises. Several operations in GENERIC_UNBOUNDED_GRAPH have some picky details. For example, when deleting an edge, care must be taken that the access type LAST_LIST in the VERTEX record does not point to a deleted edge. Since all the operations in GENERIC_DISCRETE_DI-GRAPH are also in GENERIC_UNBOUNDED_DIGRAPH, Warshall's algorithm, as implemented in Figure 10.1.5, works regardless of which ADT implements the graph.

Warshall's algorithm determines whether there is a path, but it does not find the path. In addition, if there are several paths, it does not find the shortest path. The algorithm in Figure 10.2.3, based on the breadth-first search, finds the shortest path. Since each edge is unweighted, the algorithm finds the path of shortest length. Recall that the length of a path is the number of edges in the path.

```
type VERTEX_TYPE is .....;
type VERTEX_DATA is
  record
    VISITED  : boolean := false;
    LENGTH   : natural := natural'last;
    PREVIOUS : VERTEX_TYPE;
  end record;
package VERTEX_TREE is new
    GENERIC_UNBOUNDED_SEARCH_TREE (VERTEX_TYPE, VERTEX_DATA, "<");
  use VERTEX_TREE;
package VERTEX_Q is new GENERIC_UNBOUNDED_QUEUE(VERTEX_TYPE);
  use VERTEX_Q;
package MY_GRAPH is new GENERIC_UNBOUNDED_DIGRAPH(VERTEX_TYPE);
  use MY_GRAPH;



.................


procedure SHORTEST_PATH ( THIS_GRAPH : in      GRAPH;
                          FIRST      : in      VERTEX_TYPE;
                          ANSWER     : in out TREE) is
  TEMP_TREE         : TREE;
```

Figure 10.2.3 SHORTEST_PATH algorithm for unweighted graph. Continues on page 343.

Graphs and Digraphs   Chap. 10

```
VERTEX_QUEUE        : QUEUE;
VERTEX1, VERTEX2 : VERTEX_TYPE;
V_DATA              : VERTEX_DATA;
TEMP_GRAPH          : GRAPH;
begin
COPY (THIS_GRAPH, TEMP_GRAPH);
-- add every vertex to tree with unvisited state
for index in 1..VERTEX_COUNT(TEMP_GRAPH) loop
  VERTEX_LIST (TEMP_GRAPH, VERTEX1);
  INSERT (VERTEX1, (false, natural'last, VERTEX1) TEMP_TREE);
end loop;
-- initialize VERTEX_QUEUE and TEMP_TREE
ENQUEUE(FIRST, VERTEX_QUEUE);
UPDATE (FIRST, (true, 0, FIRST), TEMP_TREE);
-- do breadth first search
loop
  exit when EMPTY (VERTEX_QUEUE);
  DEQUEUE(VERTEX1, VERTEX_QUEUE);
  for COUNT in 1..VERTEX_OUT_DEGREE(VERTEX1, THIS_GRAPH) loop
    VERTEX2 := NEXT_DESTINATION_VERTEX (VERTEX1, VERTEX_QUEUE);
    V_DATA := GET_DATA_FOR_KEY (VERTEX2, TEMP_TREE);
    if not V_DATA.VISITED then
      V_DATA.VISITED := true;
      V_DATA.LENGTH := GET_DATA_FOR_KEY (VERTEX1, TEMP_TREE).LENGTH + 1;
      V_DATA.PREVIOUS := VERTEX1;
      ENQUEUE (VERTEX2, VERTEX_QUEUE);
      UPDATE (VERTEX2, V_DATA, TEMP_TREE);
    end if;
  end loop;
end loop;
COPY(TEMP_TREE, ANSWER);
end SHORTEST_PATH;
```

Figure 10.2.3   Concluded.

The breadth-first search will visit, exactly once, every vertex that can be reached from a given vertex. The idea is simple. First the initial vertex is processed and marked as processed. Then all the adjacent vertices of the initial vertex are placed on a queue and marked as processed. A vertex is removed from the queue and each vertex adjacent to it is added to the queue provided that it has not been processed previously or placed on the queue. The process continues until the queue is empty. The breadth-first search answers the question "Which vertices can be reached from a specified vertex?" Without modification the breadth-first search does not answer the question by determining the path from the specified initial vertex to the final vertex of the path. A breadth-first search of a tree starting at the root will process the nodes level by level (see Figure 10.2.4).

This breadth-first search implementation assumes proper instantiation of GENERIC_UNBOUNDED_QUEUE and GENERIC_UNBOUNDED_SET to keep track of the vertices to be processed and the vertices visited. The elements in the sets defined in the package G_SET have their element field as vertex labels and the item field as boolean. If a

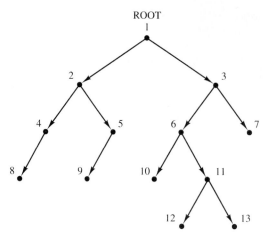

ROOT
1

Figure 10.2.4 Breadth-first search of a binary tree starting at the root. The number next to the vertex is the order of visit to that vertex by the search. Note that the tree is visited level by level.

particular vertex has its item field as true, it can be reached. The answer is obviously the set of elements and vertices with item field true. Repeated calls to the set operation NEXT_ELEMENT will list the set. The procedure first puts all the vertices into a set with item field marked false and then proceeds to do a breadth-first search.

```
type VERTEX_TYPE is .....;
Package VERTEX_SET is new GENERIC_UNBOUNDED_SET(VERTEX_TYPE,);
  use VERTEX_SET;
package VERTEX_Q is new GENERIC_UNBOUNDED_QUEUE(VERTEX_TYPE);
  use VERTEX_Q;
package MY_GRAPH is new GENERIC_UNBOUNDED_DIGRAPH(VERTEX_TYPE);
  use MY_GRAPH;


. . . . . . . . . . . . . .


procedure BREADTH_FIRST_SEARCH (THIS_GRAPH : in      GRAPH;
                                FIRST      : in      VERTEX_TYPE;
                                ANSWER     :     out SET ) is
  VERTEX_SET        : SET;
  VERTEX_QUEUE      : QUEUE;
  VERTEX1, VERTEX2  : VERTEX_TYPE;
begin
  -- initialize VERTEX_QUEUE and VERTEX_SET
  ENQUEUE(FIRST, VERTEX_QUEUE);
  ADD ELEMENT (FIRST, VERTEX_SET);
  -- do breadth first search
  loop
    exit when EMPTY (VERTEX_QUEUE);
    DEQUEUE(VERTEX1, VERTEX_QUEUE);
    for COUNT in 1..VERTEX_OUT_DEGREE(VERTEX1, THIS_GRAPH) loop
      VERTEX2 := NEXT_DESTINATION_VERTEX (VERTEX1, THIS_GRAPH);
      if not ELEMENT_IN_SET (VERTEX2, VERTEX_SET) then
        ENQUEUE (VERTEX2, VERTEX, QUEUE);
```

```
            ADD_ELEMENT (VERTEX2, VERTEX_SET);
        end if;
      end loop;
    end loop;
    COPY(VERTEX_SET, ANSWER);
  end BREADTH_FIRST_SEARCH;
```

For a given vertex FIRST, how can a path from FIRST to specific vertex LAST be determined? A modification to the breadth-first search algorithm will answer a much broader question, "What is the shortest path of any vertex reachable from the first vertex?" Consider the record for each vertex defined by

```
    type VERTEX_DATA is
      record
        VISITED    : boolean := false;
        LENGTH     : natural := natural'last;
        PREVIOUS   : VERTEX_TYPE;
      end record;
```

The field visited tells whether a vertex has been reached by some path. The first path that reaches a vertex during a breadth-first search will be the shortest path. The field length is the length of the path from the vertex first to the current vertex. The field previous is the vertex on the shortest path that precedes the current vertex. The problem of finding the shortest path from the vertex first to any vertex reachable by first is reduced to backtracking from the last vertex on the path until the vertex first is reached. Vertices not reachable from first will have a false value in the visited field (see Figure 10.2.5). Instead of a set to keep track of whether a vertex has been visited, as was used in the breadth first search, a tree will be used to keep track

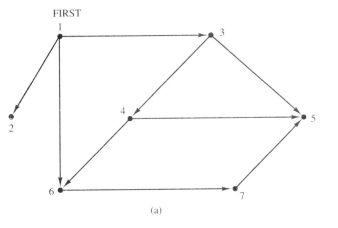

FIRST

(a)

vertice	1	2	3	4	5	6	7
visited	T	T	T	T	T	T	T
length	0	1	1	2	2	1	2
previous	1	1	1	3	3	1	6

(b)

Figure 10.2.5 (a) Digraph of seven vertices. (b) Values in set of VERTEX_DATA after the execution of the SHORTEST_PATH procedure in Figure 10.2.3.

of the VERTEX_TYPE-VERTEX_DATA pairs. It is assumed that "<" has been defined so that VERTEX_TYPE can be ordered. A traversal of the tree will retrieve all the information about every vertex in the graph.

In the next section a type of graph will be considered where the edges have weight. The procedure SHORTEST_PATH will not work unless every edge has the same weight.

10.3 ABSTRACT DATA TYPE WEIGHTED_DIGRAPH

Consider a road map for a vacation trip. The vertices represent cities and the edges represent highways. The ADT GENERIC_DISCRETE_DIGRAPH can tell whether there is a highway directly connecting two cites, but it cannot tell whether the cities are near or far. The adjacency matrix used in GENERIC_DISCRETE_DIGRAPH is now modified to be a weighted adjacency matrix. An element $G(i,j)$ in a weighted adjacency graph is defined to be

$$
\begin{aligned}
G(i,j) &= 0 && \text{if no edge from } v_i \text{ to } v_j \\
&= \text{weight} && \text{if there is an edge with a} \\
& && \text{given weight from } v_i \text{ to } v_j
\end{aligned}
$$

Figure 10.3.1(a) shows a simple road map, and Figure 10.3.1(b) shows the weighted adjacency matrix for that graph. A single modification in the ADT digraph incorporates this change. The function EDGE_WEIGHT is added that returns the edge's weight.

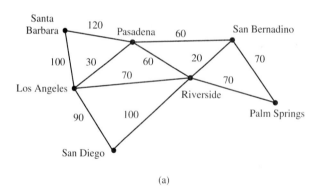

(a)

	S.D.	L.A.	S.Barb.	Pas.	River.	S.Bern.	P.S.
S.D.		90			100		
L.A.	90		100	30	70		
S.Barb.		100		120			
Pas.		30	120		60	60	
River.	100	70		60		20	70
S.Bern.				60	20		70
P.S.					70	70	

(b)

Figure 10.3.1   (a) Road map as a weighted graph. (b) Weighted adjacency matrix that represents the road map in part (a).

EDGE_WEIGHT　　　　　　Returns the weight of an edge that joins a specified source vertex to a specified destination vertex in a specified graph. If no edge joins the specified vertices, the exception NO_EDGE is raised.

The package in Figure 10.3.2 has the three needed modifications to allow for the weighted adjacency matrix data structure. The first is the addition of the operator EDGE_WEIGHT. The second modification is the formal generic parameters. The private type WEIGHT_TYPE has been added as well as a third formal generic constant ZERO_WEIGHT. In the private part of the graph is an array of weight instead of an array of boolean.

```
generic
  type VERTEX is (< >);
  type WEIGHT_TYPE is private;
  ZERO_WEIGHT : in WEIGHT_TYPE;
package GENERIC_DISCRETE_WEIGHTED_DIGRAPH is
  type GRAPH is limited private;
  procedure COPY              (FROM          : in     GRAPH;
                               TO            :    out GRAPH);
  procedure CLEAR             (GRAPH_TO_CLEAR :    out GRAPH);
  procedure ADD_EDGE          ( SOURCE,
                               DESTINATION   : in     VERTEX;
                               WEIGHT        : in     WEIGHT_TYPE;
                               TO_GRAPH      : in out GRAPH);
  procedure REMOVE_EDGE       ( SOURCE,
                               DESTINATION   : in     VERTEX;
                               FROM_GRAPH    : in out GRAPH);
  function EDGE_IN_GRAPH ( SOURCE, DESTINATION : VERTEX;
                          IN_GRAPH : GRAPH) return boolean;
  function EDGE_WEIGHT    ( SOURCE, DESTINATION : VERTEX;
                          IN_GRAPH : GRAPH) return WEIGHT_TYPE;
  procedure NEXT_SOURCE_VERTEX( DESTINATION   : in     VERTEX;
                               IN_GRAPH      : in out GRAPH;
                               VERTX         :    out VERTEX);
  procedure NEXT_DESTINATION_VERTEX (SOURCE   : in     VERTEX;
                               IN_GRAPH      : in out GRAPH;
                               VERTEX        :    out VERTEX);
  function EMPTY              (THIS_GRAPH    : GRAPH) return boolean;
  function EQUAL              (LEFT, RIGHT   : GRAPH) return boolean;
  function VERTEX_IN_DEGREE   ( DESTINATION:  VERTEX;
                               IN_GRAPH      : GRAPH) return natural;
  function VERTEX_OUT_DEGREE  ( SOURCE       :  VERTEX;
                               IN_GRAPH      : GRAPH) return natural;
  NO_EDGE        : exception;
  EDGE_EXISTS    : exception;
private
  type GRAPH_ARRAY is array (VERTEX, VERTEX) OF WEIGHT_TYPE;
  type VERTEX_VECTOR is array (VERTEX) OF VERTEX;
```

Figure 10.3.2　Specification for GENERIC_DISCRETE_WEIGHTED_DIGRAPH. Continues on page 348.

```
type GRAPH is
  record
    GRAPH : GRAPH_ARRAY := (others => (others => ZERO_WEIGHT));
    NEXT_SOURCE,
    NEXT_DEST : VERTEX_VECTOR := (others => VERTEX'LAST);
  end record;
end GENERIC_DISCRETE_WEIGHTED_DIGRAPH;
```

Figure 10.3.2   Concluded.

The implementation of GENERIC_DISCRETE_WEIGHTED_DIGRAPH is left to the exercises. The modifications discussed above plus one additional modification convert GENERIC_UNBOUNDED_GRAPH to GENERIC_UNBOUNDED_WEIGHTED_DI-GRAPH. The definition of edge in the private section must be changed to

```
type edge is
  record
    SOURCE,
    DESTINATION       : VERTEX;
    WEIGHT            : WEIGHT_TYPE;
    NEXT_SOURCE,
    NEXT_DESTINATION  : NEXT_EDGE;
  end record;
```

The specification and implementation for GENERIC_UNBOUNDED_WEIGHTED_DI-GRAPH is also left to the exercises.

In Section 10.2 an algorithm to determine shortest paths was developed for the case where every edge has weight 1. The algorithm, originally devised by Dijkstra, for weighted graphs is different. It uses the same data structure as that of the procedure SHORTEST_PATH in Figure 10.2.3. Consider Figure 10.3.3. The path $v_1 - v_2-v_3 - v_4$ is clearly shorter than v_1-v_4, but the shortest-path procedure would find v_1-v_4 first and never consider any alternatives.

Dijkstra's algorithm proceeds by stages. In the unweighted shortest-path algorithm case, once a vertex is visited, it is marked as visited and never reexamined. At each stage, Dijkstra's algorithm searches for a vertex that has not been marked as finished and has the minimum length. This vertex is marked as finished, and the distances adjusted from this vertex to any adjacent unfinished vertex as necessary. Suppose that v_i was just marked as finished and the

FIRST

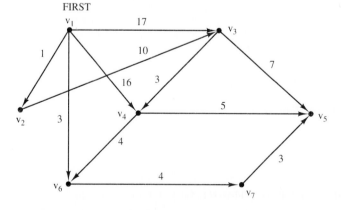

Figure 10.3.3   Weighted digraph where the path v_1-$v_4 = 16$ is longer than the path v_1-v_2-v_3-$v_4 = 13$.

vertice	1	2	3	4	5	6	7
finished	T	T	T	T	T	T	T
length	0	1	11	14	10	3	7
previous	1	1	2	3	7	1	6

Figure 10.3.4 Illustration of Dijkstra's algorithm to find the shortest path of the weighted matrix in Figure 10.3.3.

unfinished vertex v_j is the destination node of an edge with source vertex v_i; then two cases must be considered.

Let d_i denote the known shortest distance
  from the START vertex to v_i.

Let w_{ij} be the weight of the edge that joins v_i to v_j.

Let d_j denote the current estimate for the shortest distance from the start to v_j.

Case 1. $d_j <= d_i + w_{ij}$ then do nothing

Case 2. $d_i + w_{ij} < d_j$ then a. set $d_j := d_i + w_{ij}$;
                b. set v_j.previous $:= v_i$;

The algorithm continues until all remaining unfinished nodes have their distance field equal to WEIGHT'LARGE. Figure 10.3.4 illustrates the procedure under the assumption that edge weights are integers. The procedure is implemented in Figure 10.3.5.

```
type VERTEX_TYPE is .....;
type VERTEX_DATA is
  record
    VISITED  : boolean := false;
    LENGTH   : natural := natural'last;
    PREVIOUS : VERTEX_TYPE;
  end record;
package VERTEX_TREE is new
    GENERIC_UNBOUNDED_BINARY_SEARCH_TREE(VERTEX_TYPE, VERTEX_DATA, "<");
  use VERTEX_TREE;
package MY_GRAPH is new
    GENERIC_DISCRETE_WEIGHTED_DIGRAPH(VERTEX_TYPE, integer, 0);
use MY_GRAPH;


. . . . . . . . . . . .

procedure DIJKSTRA ( THIS_GRAPH : in      GRAPH;
              FIRST       : in      VERTEX_TYPE;
              ANSWER      :      out TREE) is
  TEMP_TREE          : TREE;
  VERTEX1, VERTEX2  : VERTEX_TYPE;
  V_DATA             : VERTEX_DATA;
  MAXIMUM_WEIGHT     : integer;
  LENGTH1, WEIGHT, LENGTH2 : integer;
  VERTEX_COUNT : integer := 1 + VERTEX_TYPE'pos(VERTEX_TYPE'last);
  TEMP_GRAPH : GRAPH;
```

Figure 10.3.5 Dijkstra's shortest-path algorithm for weighted graph. Continues on page 350.

```
begin
 COPY (THIS_GRAPH, TEMP_GRAPH);
  -- add every vertex to the tree with unvisited state
  for VERTEX1 in VERTEX_TYPE'first..VERTEX_TYPE'last loop
    if EDGE_IN_GRAPH (FIRST, VERTEX1, TEMP_GRAPH) then
      INSERT (VERTEX1, (false, EDGE_WEIGHT(FIRST, VERTEX1, TEMP_GRAPH),
FIRST), TEMP_TREE);
      else
        INSERT (VERTEX1, (false, integer'last, VERTEX1), TEMP_TREE);
      end if;

  end loop;
  -- initialize TEMP_TREE
  UPDATE (FIRST, (true, 0, FIRST), TEMP_TREE);
  -- process until all nodes that can be reached are processed
  loop
    -- Find unfinished vertex with minimum distance from First for
    MAXIMUM_WEIGHT := integer'last;
    for VERTEX1 in VERTEX_TYPE'first..VERTEX_TYPE'last loop;
      V_DATA := GET_DATA_FOR_KEY (VERTEX1, TEMP_TREE);
      if not V_DATA.FINISHED and then
          V_DATA.LENGTH < MAXIMUM_WEIGHT then
        VERTEX2 := VERTEX1;
        MAXIMUM_WEIGHT := V_DATA.LENGTH;
      end if;
      VER1 := VERTEX_TYPE'succ(VER1);
    end loop;
    -- if MAXIMUM_WEIGHT unchanged, then no more vertices to
    -- process
    exit when MAX_WEIGHT = integer'last;
    V_DATA := GET_DATA_FOR_KEY (VERTEX2, TEMP_TREE);
    V_DATA.FINISHED := true;
    LENGTH2 := V_DATA.LENGTH;
    UPDATE (VERTEX2, V_DATA, TEMP_TREE);
    -- process all vertices joined to vertex2 by an edge
    for COUNT in 1..VERTEX_OUT_DEGREE(VERTEX2, TEMP_GRAPH) loop
      VERTEX1 := NEXT_DEST_VERTEX(VERTEX2, TEMP_GRAPH);
      V_DATA := GET_DATA_FOR_KEY (VERTEX1, TEMP_TREE);
      LENGTH1 := LENGTH2 + EDGE_WEIGHT (VERTEX2, VERTEX1, TEMP_GRAPH);
      if not V_DATA.FINISHED and then LENGTH <V_DATA.LENTH then
        V_DATA.LENGTH := LENGTH1;
        V_DATA.PREVIOUS := VERTEX2;
        UPDATE (VERTEX1, V_DATA, TEMP_TREE);
      end if;
    end loop;
  end loop;
 COPY(TEMP_TREE, ANSWER);
end DIJKSTRA;
```

Figure 10.3.5 Concluded.

As was true in figure 10.2.5, the path of a reachable vertex is found by backtracking. Also note that the path algorithms illustrated in these last two sections can be implemented using discrete vertex types.

10.4 ABSTRACT DATA TYPE GENERIC_BOUNDED_TRANSITION_GRAPH

Figure 10.0.3 shows a transition graph to determine if a string is a valid Ada identifier. Transition graphs have many applications in theoretical computer science and compiler theory. The definition of a deterministic transition graph is:

1. A set of n states, exactly one of which is denoted as the initial state; none or more states are listed as accepting, or final, states; and exactly one is denoted as a death, or terminal, state.
2. An enumerated set of input characters.
3. A transition graph where the rows are indexed by states, the columns are indexed by the enumerated set of input characters, and the components of the graph are states.

Figure 10.4.1 shows the deterministic transition graph for Figure 10.0.3, where "letter" denotes an alphabetic character, whatever case; "digit" is any numeral, _denotes the underscore, and "other" denotes any other character, such as / or ;. The transition graph takes the state you are at and the next symbol on the input queue and returns the next state. By convention, the initial state is state 1 and the death state is the last state. Once the death state is entered it cannot be left. The death state can be a final state.

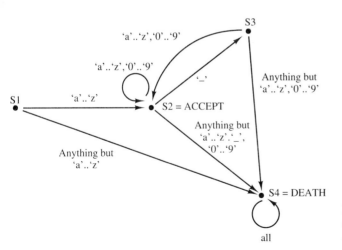

Figure 10.4.1 Deterministic transition graph used to recognize valid Ada identifiers.

Figure 10.4.2 illustrates how two strings are processed by the transition graph. Note that the first string, which is a valid Ada identifier, terminates in the single final state. The second string, whose third character is not a letter, numeral, or underscore, ends up in the death state where it is trapped. Since the death state is not a final, or accepting state, the string is rejected.

```
Example string = 'First_time'
Vertex sequence = $v_1-v_2-v_2-v_2-v_2-v_3-v_2-v_2-v_2-v_2$
Last vertex = $v_2$ = final state.
Accepted.
```

(a)

```
Example string = 'X_1_'
Vertex sequence = $v_1-v_2-v_3-v_4$
Last vertex = $v_4$ = nonaccepting.
Rejected.
```

(b)

Figure 10.4.2. Two examples of determining if strings form valid Ada identifiers using the transition graph, Figure 10.4.1. (a) Identifier 'First Time' accepted. (b) Identifier 'X_1_' rejected.

From automata theory it is known that these bounded transition graphs model finite-state machines. Finite-state machines can be thought of as very simple computers. Transition graphs can also be used to model various parlor games. Each state represents a position on the playing board, such as the space "Park Ave" in the game *Monopoly*. The input alphabet consists of the numbers that a pair of dice can take. The place your piece is at, plus the value of your dice roll, determines your next place on the board. The documentation for this ADT is shown in Figure 10.4.3.

General ADT Specification for BOUNDED_TRANSITION_GRAPH

Description

This ADT models a fully defined deterministic transition graph. A fully defined deterministic transition graph is defined as:

1. A set of n states numbered 1 to n. State 1 is labeled as the initial state. State n is always labeled as a dead state. Once a transition ends up in the dead state, it cannot leave. A possibly empty set F of states called final or accepting states.

2. An enumerated set of input characters.

3. A transition matrix where the rows are indexed by state labels, the columns are indexed by the enumerated set of input characters, and the components of the array are state labels.

The graph itself is of limited private type and can only be manipulated and accessed through the ADT operations supplied. The initial state label and the final state label are fixed once the ADT is instantiated.

Programmer-Supplied Data Structures or Specifications

The programmer must supply two actual generic parameters. The first is a positive constant equal to the number of states in the graph. This number must include the dead state. The second parameter is any discrete type. The second parameter serves as the input symbols of the transition graph.

Operations

Name	Description
COPY	Makes an exact copy of a given transition graph.

Figure 10.4.3 Documentation for ADT BOUNDED_TRANSITION_GRAPH. Continues on page 353.

CLEAR	If the transition graph has not been initialized, it initializes it first and then sets each component of the transition graph equal to NUMBER_STATES, the label of the dead state.
ADD_TRANSITION	Takes the specified state and specified symbol of a given transition graph and assigns a value of the input state to the state symbol component of the transition graph.
SET_FINAL_SET	For a specified state in a transition graph, the state is made a final state if the boolean value true is supplied. If the boolean value is false, the state is assigned to be a nonfinal state. The default is false for all states.
STATE_FINAL	Boolean-valued function that returns true if a specified state in a transition graph is a final state.
NEXT_STATE	Positive-valued function that returns the value of the component of the transition graph for a specified state and input symbol.
CLEAR	Boolean-valued function that returns true if the transition graph is either not initialized or if every state in the transition graph references the dead state.

Exceptions

The single exception NO_STATE is raised if the state parameter to any operation does not reference a valid state.

Warnings

This ADT will handle only deterministic transition graphs.

Figure 10.4.3 Concluded.

Figure 10.4.4 lists the specification for the ADT BOUNDED_TRANSITION_GRAPH.

```
generic
  NUMBER_STATES : in positive;
  type ALPHABET is (<>);
package GENERIC_BOUNDED_TRANSITION_GRAPH is
  type TRANSITION_GRAPH is limited private;
  procedure COPY              ( FROM           : in      TRANSITION_GRAPH;
                                TO             :     out TRANSITION_GRAPH);
  procedure CLEAR             ( GRAPH_TO_CLEAR :     out TRANSITION_GRAPH);
  procedure ADD_TRANSITION    ( STATE_AT       : in      positive;
                                SYMBOL         : in      ALPHABET;
                                STATE_TO       : in      positive;
                                TO_GRAPH       : in out TRANSITION_GRAPH);
  procedure SET_FINAL_SET     ( STATE          : in      positive;
                                IS_FINAL       : in      boolean;
                                IN_GRAPH       : in out TRANSITION_GRAPH);
  function STATE_FINAL        ( STATE          : positive;
                                IN_GRAPH       : TRANSITION_GRAPH) return boolean;
```

Figure 10.4.4 Specification for BOUNDED_TRANSITION_GRAPH. Continues on page 354.

```
function NEXT_STATE          ( STATE            : positive;
                               SYMBOL           : ALPHABET;
                               IN_GRAPH         : TRANSITION_GRAPH)return positive;
function CLEAR               ( GRAPH_TO_CHECK   : TRANSITION_GRAPH) return boolean;
NO_STATE         : exception;
private
  type FINAL_TYPE is array    ( positive range 1..NUMBER_STATES )  of boolean;
  type TRANSITION is array     ( positive range 1..NUMBER_STATES,
                                 ALPHABET                                ) of positive;
  type TRANSITION_GRAPH is
   record
       FINAL : FINAL_TYPE := (others => false);
       GRAPH : TRANSITION := (others =>( others :=> NUMBER_STATES));
    end record;
end GENERIC_BOUNDED_TRANSITION_GRAPH;
```

Figure 10.4.4 Concluded.

The implementation of this ADT is almost obvious. The function NEXT_STATE and the procedure CLEAR follow directly from the documentation in Figure 10.4.3.

```
procedure CLEAR (GRAPH_TO_CLEAR : out TRANSITION_GRAPH) is
  -- Returns a transition graph with all transitions to death state
  EMPTY_GRAPH : TRANSITION_GRAPH;
begin
  GRAPH_TO_CLEAR := EMPTY_GRAPH;
end CLEAR;


function NEXT_STATE ( STATE : positive;
                      SYMBOL: ALPHABET;
                      IN_GRAPH : TRANSITION_GRAPH) return positive is
  -- Returns the state that is transitioned to if currently at STATE
  -- with SYMBOL
  -- Exception NO_STATE raised if STATE does not
  -- reference a valid state
begin
  if STATE > NUMBER_STATES then
    raise NO_STATE;
  else
    return IN_GRAPH.GRAPH (STATE, SYMBOL);
  end if;
end NEXT_STATE;
```

The complete implementation is left to the exercises. As an application the function outlined in Figure 10.4.5 returns a boolean value for any transition graph that uses the ADT GENERIC_BOUNDED_TRANSITION_GRAPH. Assume that the transition graph has N states, including the death state, and that the following declarations have been made:

```
type INPUT-ALPHABET is . . . .; -- any discrete type
package T_GRAPH is new package
       GENERIC_BOUNDED_TRANSITION_GRAPH (N, INPUT_ALPHABET);
type INPUT_VECTOR is array (positive range <>) of INPUT_ALPHABET;
```

TG has been declared to be of type T_GRAPH.TRANSITION_GRAPH, and it has been properly defined. The function VALID_INPUT returns a true value if the string is accepted as valid by TG and false otherwise. A valid string is any string where the terminating state is a final state that is reached after processing the string.

```
function VALID_INPUT( TEST_STRING : INPUT_VECTOR;
                      GRAPH        : T_GRAPH.TRANSITION_GRAPH) return boolean is
  CURRENT_STATE : positive := 1;
begin
  for INDEX in TEST_STRING'range loop
    CURRENT_STATE := T_GRAPH.NEXT_STATE (CURRENT_STATE,TEST_STRING(INDEX));
  end loop;
  return STATE_FINAL(CURRENT_STATE, GRAPH);
end VALID_INPUT;
```

Figure 10.4.5 Function that traverses a transition graph.

10.5 APPLICATIONS

Many popular puzzle books have mazes to be traversed. A maze can be thought of as a series of rooms with doors leading from one room to adjacent rooms. The object is to find a path from a given initial room to a final room. The rooms can be thought of as vertices in a graph. The edges can be thought of as a path from one room to another through a given door. Clearly, the maze can be represented as a DISCRETE_DIGRAPH. Note that if there is a path from the *i*th room to the *j*th room, then there is a path back from the *j*th room to the *i*th room. Figure 10.5.1(a) shows a simple maze, and Figure 10.5.1(b) shows the DISCRETE_DIGRAPH representation of that maze.

There are two ways to find a path through a graph. One is the breadth-first search and the other is the depth-first search. Dijkstra's algorithm could be applied to the problem, but

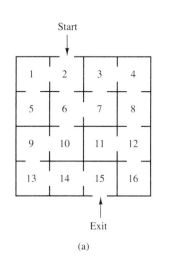

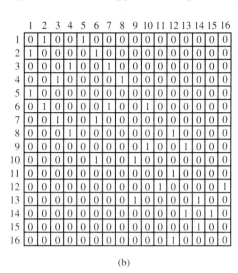

	1	2	3	4	5	6	7	8	9	10	11	12	13	14	15	16
1	0	1	0	0	1	0	0	0	0	0	0	0	0	0	0	0
2	1	0	0	0	0	1	0	0	0	0	0	0	0	0	0	0
3	0	0	0	1	0	0	1	0	0	0	0	0	0	0	0	0
4	0	0	1	0	0	0	0	1	0	0	0	0	0	0	0	0
5	1	0	0	0	0	0	0	0	0	0	0	0	0	0	0	0
6	0	1	0	0	0	0	1	0	0	1	0	0	0	0	0	0
7	0	0	1	0	0	1	0	0	0	0	0	0	0	0	0	0
8	0	0	0	1	0	0	0	0	0	0	0	0	1	0	0	0
9	0	0	0	0	0	0	0	0	0	1	0	0	1	0	0	0
10	0	0	0	0	0	1	0	0	1	0	0	0	0	0	0	0
11	0	0	0	0	0	0	0	0	0	0	0	1	0	0	0	0
12	0	0	0	0	0	0	0	0	0	0	1	0	0	0	0	1
13	0	0	0	0	0	0	0	0	1	0	0	0	0	1	0	0
14	0	0	0	0	0	0	0	0	0	0	0	0	1	0	1	0
15	0	0	0	0	0	0	0	0	0	0	0	0	0	1	0	0
16	0	0	0	0	0	0	0	0	0	0	0	1	0	0	0	0

(a)   (b)

Figure 10.5.1   (a) Simple 16-room maze. (b) Adjacency matrix for the maze in part (a).

there is no requirement to find the shortest path. Besides, Dijkstra's method is greedy. The depth-first search keeps on looking until it is successful or it encounters a node that it has visited previously. Here it backs up a bit and starts looking again. A related problem of determining all paths from an initial vertex to a terminal vertex is the subject of the case study at the end of the chapter.

The depth-first search uses a stack instead of a queue. It is similar to an inorder traversal of a tree. The starting vertex first placed on the stack, then marked as processed, and finally, processed. A random adjacent node not previously processed is placed on the stack, marked as processed, and then processed. This process continues until either all adjacent nodes are marked as processed or a dead end has been reached. If the process reaches a dead end, a vertex is popped from the stack and some unprocessed adjacent vertex is pushed onto the stack, marked as processed, processed, and the search continues. If no adjacent unprocessed node can be found, another node is popped from the stack and its adjacent nodes are examined. The process continues until the stack is empty. Both the breadth-first search and the depth-first search mark all the nodes that can be reached from an initial vertex. Neither finds a path. A depth-first search of a binary tree starting at its root results in an inorder traversal.

The depth-first search can be modified to stop after finding a particular node. Since unprocessed nodes are first pushed onto the stack, then marked as processed, and then processed, the stack has a path from the finish vertex back to the start vertex. This modification solves the maze traversal problem. Figure 10.5.2(a) outlines the breadth-first search of Figure 10.5.1(b), and figure 10.5.2(b) outlines the depth-first search.

Path Length	Paths on the Queue
1	{2}
2	{2,1} {2,6}
3	{2,1,5} {2,6,7} {2,6,10}
4	{2,6,7,3}{2,6,10,9}
5	{2,6,7,3,4} {2,6,10,9,13}
6	{2,6,7,3,4,8} {2,6,10,9,13,14}
7	{2,6,7,3,4,8,12} {2,6,10,9,13,14,15}

Process terminates: Path = {2,6,10,9,13,14,15} traverses the maze from start = 2 to exit = 15.

(a)

Step	Stack of Vertices in Path, Stack Top to the Left	
Initial	{2}	
1	{1,2}	
2	{5,1,2}	Dead end, start backtracking
3	{1,2}	
4	{2}	
5	{6,2}	Backtracked until found room not visited
6	{10,6,2}	
7	{9,10,6,2}	

Figure 10.5.2 (a) Breadth-first search of maze in Figure 10.5.1(a). (b) Depth-first search of maze in Figure 10.5.1(a). Continues on page 358.

Step	Stack of Vertices in Path, Stack Top to the Left
8	{13,9,10,6,2}
9	{14,13,9,10,6,2}
10	{15,14,13,9,10,6,2}

Process terminates: Stack holds path but in reverse order.

Path = $v_2-v_6-v_{10}-v_9-v_{13}-v_{14}-v_{15}$.

(b)

Figure 10.5.2 Concluded.

Assume that the following instantiations have been declared:

```
N_ROOMS : constant := . . . . ;
subtype MAZE_INDEX is positive range 1..N_ROOMS;
package MAZE_STACK is new GENERIC_UNBOUNDED_STACK (positive);
package MAZE_SET is new GENERIC_DISCRETE_SET (MAZE_INDEX);
package MAZE_GRAPH is new GENERIC_DISCRETE_DIGRAPH (MAZE_INDEX);
package POSITIVE_IO is new integer_io(positive); Use POSITIVE_IO;
```

and that a given maze with N_ROOMS has been converted to a graph in a manner similar to that illustrated in Figure 10.5.1. The procedure in Figure 10.5.3 does a depth-first search for a path joining two rooms labeled START and FINISH, and the path is printed out starting at finish.

```
procedure DEPTH_FIRST_MAZE_SEARCH ( START,
                                     FINISH : in positive;
                                     MAZE   : in MAZE_GRAPH.GRAPH) is
  ROOM_VISITED : MAZE_SET.SET;
  ROOM_NOW     : positive := START;
  ROOM_NEXT    : natural;
  ROOM_STACK   : MAZE_STACK.STACK;
  TEMP_MAZE    : MAZE_GRAPH.GRAPH;
begin
  MAZE_GRAPH.COPY(MAZE, TEMP_MAZE);
  MAZE_SET.ADD_ELEMENT (ROOM_NOW, ROOM_VISITED);
  MAZE_STACK.PUSH (ROOM_NOW, ROOM_STACK);
  loop
    if ROOM_NOW = FINISH then
      put_line ("One possible path from Finish to Start is ");
      while not MAZE_STACK.EMPTY(S) loop
        MAZE_STACK.POP(ROOM_NOW, S);
        put( ROOM_NOW );
        new_line;
      end loop;
      exit;
    else
      ROOM_NEXT := 0;
      for COUNT in 1..MAZE_GRAPH.VERTEX_OUT_DEGREE(ROOM_NOW, TEMP_MAZE)
      loop
```

Figure 10.5.3 Listing for depth-first maze search. Continues on page 358.

```
MAZE_GRAPH.NEXT_DESTINATION_VERTEX(ROOM_NOW,
                                TEMP_MAZE, ROOM_NEXT);
        if MAZE_SET.ELEMENT_IN_SET( ROOM_NEXT, ROOM_VISITED) then
          ROOM_NEXT := 0;
        else
          exit;
        end if;
      end loop;
      if ROOM_NEXT = 0 then
        -- reached dead end, backtrack
        -- First step, get dead end room from stack
        MAZE_STACK.POP(ROOM_NOW, ROOM_STACK);
        -- Check to see about the possibility of no path
        if MAZE_STACK.EMPTY(ROOM_STACK) then
          -- No path exists, so we are done and we failed
          put_line ("NO PATH FOUND!");
          exit;
        else
          -- Continue the quest, there still might be a path
          ROOM_NOW := MAZE_STACK.PEEK(ROOM_STACK);
        end if;
      else
        -- There was an unvisited room off of ROOM_NOW
        ROOM_NOW := ROOM_NEXT;
        MAZE_SET.ADD_ELEMENT( ROOM_NOW, ROOM_VISITED);
        MAZE_STACK.PUSH(ROOM_NOW, ROOM_STACK);
      end if;
    end if;
  end loop;
end DEPTH_FIRST_MAZE_SEARCH;
```

Figure 10.5.3   Concluded.

Figure 10.5.4(a) shows a directed graph that illustrates the classes that must be taken to earn a college degree. There is a single node of indegree 0, corresponding to being admitted to college, and a single node of outdegree 0, corresponding to completing the requirements of the degree. Note that the graph has no cycles. The problem is to list the classes in a sequential order so that every class is in the list exactly once, and no class appears on the list before any of its required prerequisites. Such a listing is not unique, as Figure 10.5.4(b) lists two different sequences with the desired property.

The graph G in Figure 10.5.4(a) has no cycles. If there were, it would be impossible to list the classes in prerequisite order. Such an ordering of the vertices in G is the result of a topological sort. The ordering of vertices $<$ is defined by $u < v$ if and only if there is no path starting at v and ending at u in G. The result of a topological sort is a partial ordering of vertices. A topological sort is possible only for a directed acyclic graph. Any directed acyclic graph (DAG) must have one or more nodes with indegree 0 and one or more nodes with outdegree 0. If no node had indegree 0 or outdegree 0 or both, the graph would not be acyclic; that is, it would contain at least one cycle.

The topological sort algorithm is easy to describe. All vertices of indegree 0 are randomly placed on a queue. The vertex at the front of the queue is dequeued and output. The sort

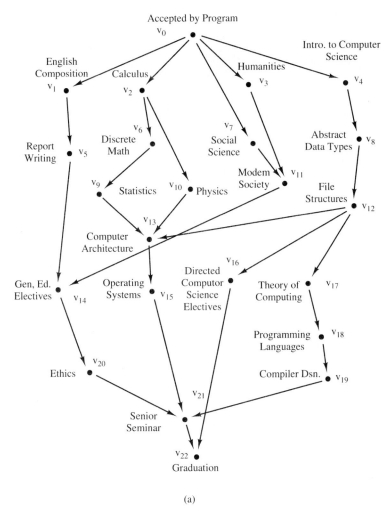

Accepted by Program
v_0

English Composition v_1

Calculus v_2

Humanities v_3

Intro. to Computer Science v_4

Report Writing v_5

v_6 Discrete Math

v_7 Social Science

Abstract Data Types v_8

Modem Society v_{11}

v_9 Statistics

v_{10} Physics

File Structures v_{12}

v_{13} Computer Architecture

v_{16} Directed Computor Science Electives

Gen, Ed. Electives v_{14}

Operating Systems v_{15}

Theory of Computing v_{17}

Programming Languages v_{18}

v_{20} Ethics

Compiler Dsn. v_{19}

v_{21} Senior Seminar

v_{22} Graduation

(a)

$v_0-v_1-v_5-v_2-v_6-v_9-v_{10}-v_{13}-v_7-v_3-v_{11}-v_4-v_8-v_{12}-v_{14}-v_{20}-v_{16}-v_{17}-v_{18}-v_{19}-v_{15}-v_{21}-v_{22}$

$v_0-v_4-v_8-v_{12}-v_3-v_7-v_{11}-v_2-v_6-v_{10}-v_9-v_{13}-v_1-v_5-v_{14}-v_{20}-v_{15}-v_{16}-v_{17}-v_{18}-v_{19}-v_{21}-v_{22}$

(b)

Figure 10.5.4 (a) Directed acyclic graph that illustrates requirements to graduate as a graph. (b) Two distinct but valid topological sorts of the directed acyclic digraph in part (a).

eliminates from the graph all edges that have this vertex as a source vertex, and any new nodes with indegree 0 are placed on the queue. The process continues until the graph and the queue are empty. If the vertices of the DAG are positive numbers and the following instantiations have been made

```
package TOPOLOGICAL_GRAPH is new GENERIC_UNBOUNDED_DIGRAPH (positive);
    use TOPOLOGICAL_GRAPH;
package TOPOLOGICAL_QUEUE is new GENERIC_UNBOUNDED_QUEUE (positive);
```

```
    use TOPOLOGICAL_QUEUE;
 package TOPOLOGICAL_TREE is new
    GENERIC_UNBOUNDED_BINARY_SEARCH_TREE(positive, boolean, "<");
  use TOPOLOGICAL_TREE;
```

then the procedure listed in Figure 10.5.5 performs a topological sort on a directed acyclic
graph. The answer is placed on global queue ANSWER by the procedure TOPOLOGICAL
SORT. If the queue package defines a queue as private instead of limited private, the queue AN-
SWER can be a formal parameter of mode out. The procedure destroys the graph, so a copy of
the graph must first be made before the sort begins. The result is returned as a queue of nodes.

```
  ANSWER : Queue; -- global to TOPOLOGICAL_SORT


procedure TOPOLOGICAL_SORT (OF_GRAPH : in GRAPH) is
   TEMP_GRAPH        : GRAPH;
   VERTEX_QUEUE      : QUEUE;
   VERTEX_TREE       : TREE;
   TEMP_VERTEX       : positive;
begin
   COPY (OF_GRAPH, TEMP_GRAPH);
   -- clear the queue where answer is stored
   CLEAR (ANSWER);
   -- find all vertices with indegree = 0, add all vertices to
   -- VERTEX_TABLE with false value, unless their indegree is 0
   for COUNT in positive range 1..VERTEX_COUNT(TEMP_GRAPH) loop
     TEMP_VERTEX := VERTEX_LIST (TEMP_GRAPH);
     INSERT (TEMP_VERTEX, false, VERTEX_TREE);
     if VERTEX_IN_DEGREE( TEMP_VERTEX, TEMP_GRAPH) = 0 then
        ENQUEUE (TEMP_VERTEX, VERTEX_QUEUE);
        UPDATE (TEMP_VERTEX, true, VERTEX_TREE);
     end if;
   end loop;
   loop
     exit when EMPTY(VERTEX_QUEUE);
     -- get next vertex with in_degree 0
     DEQUEUE(TEMP_VERTEX, VERTEX_QUEUE);
     -- vertex is now sorted, place on answer queue
     ENQUEUE(TEMP_VERTEX, ANSWER);
     -- delete all edges that have temp as a source vertice
     for INDEX in positive range
              1..VERTEX_OUT_DEGREE(TEMP_VERTEX,TEMP_GRAPH) loop
       REMOVE_EDGE(TEMP_VERTEX,
         NEXT_DESTINATION_VERTEX(TEMP_VERTEX, TEMP_GRAPH), TEMP_GRAPH);
     end loop;
     -- vertex temp now isolated, so remove it from the graph
     REMOVE_VERTEX (TEMP_VERTEX, TEMP_GRAPH);
     -- check to see if new vertices were created with indegree 0 exist
```

Figure 10.5.5 Listing for topological sort of a directed acyclic digraph. Continues on page 361.

```
    for COUNT in positive range 1..VERTEX_COUNT(TEMP_GRAPH) loop
        TEMP_VERTEX := VERTEX_LIST (TEMP_GRAPH);
        if VERTEX_IN_DEGREE (TEMP_VERTEX, TEMP_GRAPH) = 0 and then
              not GET_DATA_FOR_KEY (TEMP_VERTEX, VERTEX_TREE) then
          UPDATE (TEMP_VERTEX, true, VERTEX_TREE);
          ENQUEUE(TEMP_VERTEX, TEMP_GRAPH);
        end if;
      end loop;
    end loop;
  end TOPOLOGICAL_SORT;
```

Figure 10.5.5   Concluded.

Closely related to the idea of a topological sort is the determination of a critical path. Consider a graphical description of some type of project. Each vertex represents some event or subproject. No subproject can be started until the completion of all subprojects upon which it depends. This graph is a directed acyclic graph. It has exactly one start vertex of indegree 0, which denotes where the project starts, and one terminal vertex of outdegree 0, which denotes

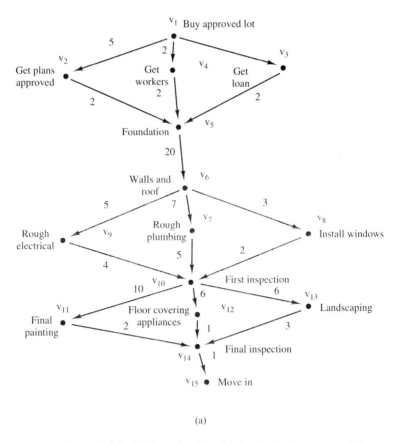

(a)

Figure 10.5.6   PERT graph and its critical path. Continues on page 362.

Vertex Number	Earliest Completion	Latest Completion
1	0	0
2	5	10
3	2	10
4	10	10
5	12	12
6	32	32
7	39	39
8	35	40
9	37	40
10	44	44
11	54	54
12	50	55
13	50	52
14	56	56
15	57	57

Critical path = v_1–v_4–v_5–v_6–v_7–v_{10}–v_{11}–v_{14}–v_{15}.

(b)

Figure 10.5.6 Concluded.

the job's completion. The edges for which a particular vertex is the destination all have the same weight, and these weights represent the time it takes to complete a project.

Figure 10.5.6(a) represents the building of a house. Note that the initial vertex, the only one with indegree 0, has edges leading to various tasks. The edge weight is the time it takes to complete a task. No job can start until the completion of every task depending on it. The terminal node, the one with outdegree zero, is the completion of the job. This graph is a directed acyclic graph (DAG). When a contractor bids the job, they naturally ask: What is the earliest time that the project can be completed? A related question is: When is the earliest time that any subproject can be finished? The job will be finished when the terminal vertex is reached. Another question is: When is the earliest time and when is the latest time that a particular subproject can be finished without affecting the completion time of the project? Vertices with the same earliest and latest completion times are the critical vertices. The path made by these critical vertices is the critical path. Any delay in completing any subproject in the critical path delays completion of the project. This problem is called the *critical path method* in PERT (performance evaluation and review technique) analysis. Figure 10.5.6(b) lists the earliest completion and latest completion times of each vertex.

Determining the critical path of a DAG G is done in three phases. First a topological sort of G is performed. The second part of the process determines the earliest completion time of each vertex. Since the completion time of the initial vertex is 0, it follows that earliest completion time of any other vertex *V* is given by

```
EARLIEST_TIME(V) :=
        max( EARLIEST_TIME(X) + EDGE_WEIGHT(X,V,G)):
```

where the maximum is taken over all vertices V_i that are less than *V* in the topological ordering and where there exists an edge from V_i to *V*. The third phase determines the latest completion time of each vertex. Since the latest completion time of the terminal vertex always equals the earliest completion time of the terminal vertex, it follows that the latest completion time of any other vertex V is given by

```
LATEST_TIME(V) := min (LATEST_TIME(Y) - EDGE_WEIGHT(V,Y));
```

where the minimum is taken over all vertices Y that appear after V in the topological sort and where there exists an edge from the vertex V to the vertex Y. Figure 10.5.7 contains a listing of CRITICAL_PATH that combines features of Dijkstra's algorithm and TOPOLOGI-CAL_SORT. The critical path algorithm searches using a topological sort method but does its bookkeeping in a manner similar to Dijkstra's shortest-path algorithm. Once completed the critical path is determined by backtracking from the terminal node. The path is in reverse order.

```
type VERTEX_DATA is
  record
    VISITED  : boolean := false;
    LENGTH   : integer;
    PREVIOUS : positive;
  end record;
package CRITICAL_PATH_TREE is new
    GENERIC_UNBOUNDED_BINARY_SEARCH_TREE (positive, VERTEX_DATA, "<");
  use CRITICAL_PATH_TREE;
package CRITICAL_PATH_GRAPH is new
    GENERIC_UNBOUNDED_WEIGHTED_DIGRAPH (positive, integer,0,"<");
  use CRITICAL_PATH_GRAPH;
package CRITICAL_PATH_QUEUE is new GENERIC_UNBOUNDED_QUEUE (positive);
  use CRITICAL_PATH_QUEUE;


CRITICAL_PATH : QUEUE; -- global variable where the critical path is stored


. . . . . . . . . . . . . . . . . .


procedure FIND_CRITICAL_PATH (START, TERMINAL : in    positive;
                              OF_GRAPH        : in    GRAPH) is
  TEMP_GRAPH : GRAPH;
  TEMP_Q     : QUEUE;
  WEIGHT     : integer;
  TEMP_VERTEX, DESTINATION_VERTEX : positive;
  TEMP_TREE  : TREE;
  VERTEX_VALUE, DESTINATION_VALUE : VERTEX_DATA;
begin
  -- Graph is destroyed, so make a copy
  COPY (OF_GRAPH, TEMP_GRAPH);
  -- Clear answer queue
  Clear (CRITICAL_PATH);
```

Figure 10.5.7   Finding a critical path. Continues on page 364.

```
-- add every vertex to table with unvisited state
for INDEX in 1..VERTEX_COUNT(OF_GRAPH) loop
  VERTEX_LIST (TEMP_GRAPH, TEMP_VERTEX);
  INSERT (TEMP_VERTEX, (false, 0, TEMP_VERTEX), TEMP_TREE);
end loop;
-- initialize TEMP_TREE with start, the only node with indegree 0
UPDATE (START, (true, 0, START), TEMP_TREE);
ENQUEUE(START, TEMP_Q);
loop
  exit when EMPTY (TEMP_Q);
  DEQUEUE(TEMP_VERTEX, TEMP_Q);
  VERTEX_VALUE := GET_DATA_FOR_KEY (TEMP_VERTEX, TEMP_TREE);
  -- for all edges with source TEMP_VERTEX
  for INDEX in
      positive range 1..VERTEX_OUT_DEGREE(TEMP_VERTEX, TEMP_GRAPH)loop
    DESTINATION_VERTEX :=
          NEXT_DESTINATION_VERTEX (TEMP_VERTEX, TEMP_GRAPH);
    DESTINATION_VALUE :=
              GET_DATA_FOR_KEY (DESTINATION_VERTEX, TEMP_TREE);
    WEIGHT := EDGE_WEIGHT(TEMP_VERTEX, DESTINATION_VERTEX, TEMP_GRAPH);
    if not DESTINATION_VALUE.VISITED then
      DESTINATION_VALUE :=
                (true, VERTEX_VALUE.LENGTH + WEIGHT, TEMP_VERTEX );
      UPDATE (DESTINATION_VERTEX, DESTINATION_VALUE, TEMP_TREE);
    elsif DESTINATION_VALUE.LENGTH < VERTEX_VALUE.LENGTH + WEIGHT then
      DESTINATION_VALUE :=
                (true, VERTEX_VALUE.LENGTH + WEIGHT, TEMP_VERTEX);
      UPDATE (DESTINATION_VERTEX, DESTINATION_VALUE, TEMP_TREE);
    end if;
    -- remove the edge
    REMOVE_EDGE (TEMP_VERTEX, DESTINATION_VERTEX, TEMP_GRAPH);
    -- if the in_degree of DESTINATION_VERTEX is 0, its ready to be sorted
    if VERTEX_IN_DEGREE(DESTINTATION_VERTEX, TEMP_GRAPH) = 0 then
      ENQUEUE (DESTINATION_VERTEX, TEMP_Q);
    end if;
  end loop;
end loop;
ENQUEUE(TERMINAL, CRITICAL_PATH);
-- backtrack to get the critical path
TEMP_VERTEX := GET_DATA_FOR_KEY (TERMINAL,TEMP_TREE).PREVIOUS;
while TEMP_VERTEX /= START loop
  ENQUEUE(TEMP_VERTEX, CRITICAL_PATH);
  TEMP_VERTEX := GET_DATA_FOR_KEY (TEMP_VERTEX, TEMP_TREE).PREVIOUS;
end loop;
ENQUEUE(START, CRITICAL_PATH);
end FIND_CRITICAL_PATH;
```

Figure 10.5.7 Concluded.

Next, consider a weighted graph that represents a highway map. Vertices represent cities. Edges joining two vertices represent the highways joining the cities. The edge weights represent the distance between two cities on that particular highway. Given two cities, what is the path of shortest length that joins the two cities? Warshall's algorithm can be modified to find the path of shortest length when implementing the graph using GENERIC_DIS-CRETE_WEIGHTED_GRAPH. If the inner loop of Warshall's algorithm is replaced by

```
EDGE(I,J) := min (EDGE(I,J), EDGE(I,K) + EDGE(K,J));
```

provided that the edges exist, this algorithm returns the length of the shortest path, but not the shortest path. Dijkstra's algorithm determines the shortest path. The extension of Warshall's algorithm is given in the exercises.

As a final example, consider the problem of network flow as set out in the weighted graph G in Figure 10.5.8. It might represent an electric power distribution system, data moving through a network, or the fluid flow through a system of pipes. Just as in the critical path problem, there is a vertex of indegree 0 called the *source* and a vertex of outdegree 0 called the *sink*. The network does not have to be a directed acyclic graph. The vertices represent distribution points of the flow, such as generating plants or distribution substations. The edge weights represent capacity, such as power transmission line capacity. The problem is to find the maximum flow between the source and sink. Except for the source and the sink, the flow into a vertex must equal the flow out of the vertex, and the flow through an edge cannot exceed the edge's capacity. In solving this problem two additional graphs, G_flow and G_residual, are defined with the

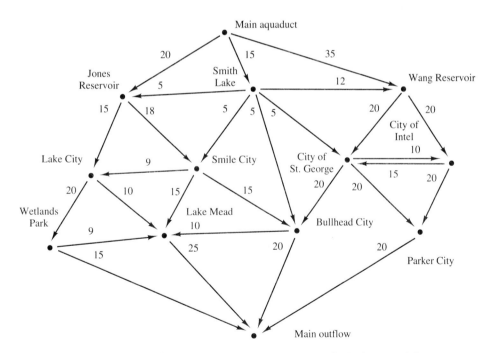

Figure 10.5.8   Weighted graph that models a water distribution network flow.

same vertices as G. The respective edge weights of G_flow and G_residual add up to the edge weight in G. Initially, G_residual equals G and all the edges of G_flow have weight 0.

The obvious way to try to solve the flow problem is first to determine a path from the source to the sink in G_residual, find the minimum edge weight of the path (the flow into a vertex must equal the flow out), and add edges or increase weights in the flow and subtract weights while eliminating at least one edge in G_residual. This continues until there is no path in from the source to the sink in G_residual. This simple algorithm doesn't always yield the best flow even in simple cases. The problem is that there might be several paths from the source to the sink to pick and the algorithm picks the wrong one. Consider the graph of four vertices in Figure 10.5.9(a) with the empty G_flow and exact copy G_residual. Clearly, the optimal flow [see Figure 10.5.9(b)] is 4. However, at the first stage there is a path of flow 2 from v_1–v_2–v_4, a second path of flow 2 from v_1–v_3–v_4, and one path of flow 1 from v_1–v_2–v_3–v_4. Choosing the third path results in the situation appearing in Figure 10.5.9(c). There are now two paths, v_1–v_2–v_4 and v_1–v_3–v_4, of flow 1. If either is picked, the algorithm cycles one more time and terminates with solution illustrated in Figure 10.5.9(d). Once this greedy algorithm makes a choice, the choice cannot be undone. The result can be a less than optimum solution.

There is a simple solution to this algorithm that allows for a bad choice to be undone. The change is to augment G_residual by using the following rule:

If an edge $<v_i, v_j>$ of weight w is added to G_flow or if an existing edge in G_flow from v_i to v_j has its weight increased by w, the edge in G_residual from v_i to v_j will have its weight reduced by w and an edge from v_j to v_i with weight w in G_residual will be added, or if already present, its weight will be increased by w.

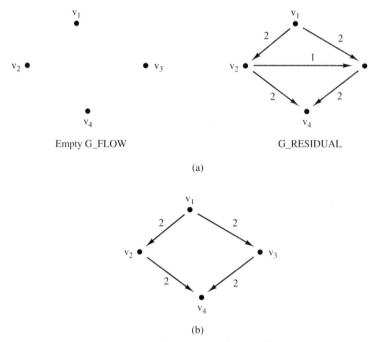

Empty G_FLOW

G_RESIDUAL

(a)

(b)

Figure 10.5.9 (a) Initial flow of a network. (b) Optimal flow of G_residual above. (c) Result after picking flow $v_1 - v_2$–$v_3 - v_4$ with flow = 1. (d) Suboptimal flow result caused by picking poor first choice and being unable to backtrack.

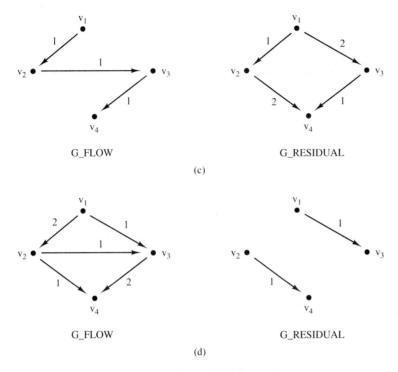

G_FLOW   G_RESIDUAL

(c)

G_FLOW   G_RESIDUAL

(d)

Figure 10.5.9 Concluded.

Figure 10.5.10(a) denotes the same initial situation as in 10.5.9(a). If the path v_1–v_2–v_3–v_4 is of flow 1, the result, with augmentations, is Figure 10.5.10(b). Figure 10.5.10(c) shows the situation after both paths $v_1 - v_2$–v_4 and v_1–$v_3 - v_4$ of flow 1 are chosen. This is the situation in Figure 10.5.9(d), where the first algorithm terminated, but there is still a path v_1–v_3–v_2–v_4 of flow 1 to be added, which results in the optimal solution in Figure 10.5.10(d). The program solution is left to the exercises.

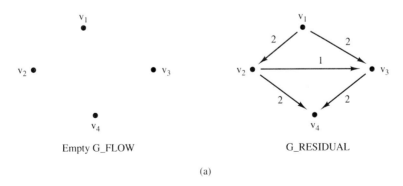

Empty G_FLOW   G_RESIDUAL

(a)

Figure 10.5.10 (a) Same initial flow as in Figure 10.5.9(a). (b) Result after picking flow v_1–v_2–v_3–v_4 with flow = 1. Note the shadow edges in reverse direction added to G_residual. (c) Result after adding two flows = 1. Note that G_residual still has a flow = 1 left, so the algorithm has not terminated. (d) Correct result in G_flow. After updating G_residual, not shown, has no path from v_1 to v_4.

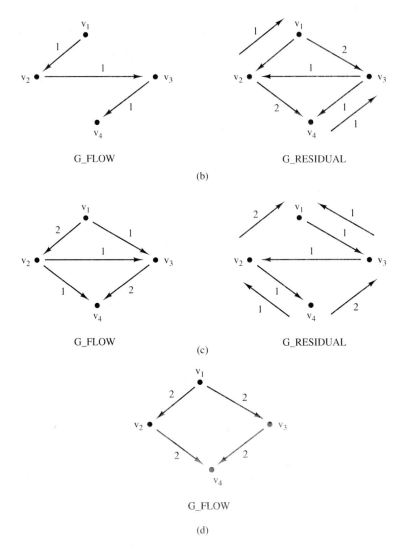

G_FLOW   G_RESIDUAL

(b)

G_FLOW   G_RESIDUAL

(c)

G_FLOW

(d)

Figure 10.5.10 Concluded.

10.6 TIME AND SPACE CONSTRAINTS

Let n_v be the number of vertices in a graph and let n_e be the number of edges in a graph. Figure 10.6.1 shows the constraints for the ADT DISCRETE_GRAPH listed in Figure 10.1.2. The constraint values are in line with array-implemented structures. Similar constraints hold for the ADT DISCRETE + WEIGHTED_DIGRAPH and for BOUNDED_TRANSITION_GRAPH. Figure 10.6.1 lists the worst-case values for the function NEXT_SOURCE_EDGE.

	Operation Overhead	Space Overhead
ADD_EDGE	$O(1)$	$O(n_v ** 2)$
REMOVE_EDGE	$O(1)$	$O(n_v ** 2)$
CLEAR	$O(n_v ** 2)$	$O(n_v ** 2)$
COPY	$O(n_v ** 2)$	$O(n_v ** 2)$
EDGE_IN_GRAPH	$O(1)$	$O(n_v ** 2)$
NEXT_SOURCE_EDGE	$O(n_v)$	$O(n_v ** 2)$
VERTEX_INDEGREE	$O(n_v)$	$O(n_v ** 2)$
EQUAL	$O(n_v ** 2)$	$O(n_v ** 2)$

Figure 10.6.1　Constraints for GENERIC_DISCRETE_DIGRAPH.

Figure 10.6.2 lists the constraints for the UNBOUNDED_DIGRAPH listed in Figure 10.2.2. While this structure is much more space efficient, operational overhead reflects the use of queue implementation of priority queues of vertices and edges. This overhead can be reduced by introducing tree implementations of priority queues of vertices and edges. A method to reduce this overhead is suggested in the exercises.

	Operation Overhead	Space Overhead
ADD_EDGE	$O(n_v)$	$O(n_e)$
REMOVE_EDGE	$O(n_v)$	$O(n_e)$
ADD_VERTEX	$O(n_v)$	$O(n_e)$
REMOVE_VERTEX	$O(n_v)$	$O(n_e)$
CLEAR	$O(n_v + n_e)$	$O(n_e)$
COPY	$O(n_v + n_e)$	$O(n_e)$
EDGE_IN_GRAPH	$O(n_v)$	$O(n_e)$
NEXT_SOURCE_EDGE	$O(n_v)$	$O(n_e)$
VERTEX_INDEGREE	$O(n_v)$	$O(n_e)$
VERTEX_COUNT	$O(1)$	$O(n_e)$
VERTEX_LIST	$O(n_v)$	$O(n_e)$
EQUAL	$O(n_v + n_e)$	$O(n_e)$

Figure 10.6.2　Constraints for GENERIC_UNBOUNDED_DIGRAPH.

The constraints for the unbounded case are not affected by adding information to the graph node, such as edge weight.

The discrete case is much more efficient operationally than the unbounded case. The opposite is true in the case of storage. Many algorithms require the addition and deletion of vertices which the unbounded case handles. Adding or deleting a node in the discrete case requires the programmer to set up a bookkeeping mechanism, like a boolean set, to keep track of active vertices.

10.7 CASE STUDY: FINDING ALL PATHS IN A MAZE

Previously, a maze has been searched for a path from the initial room to the finished room. The depth-first search (Figure 10.3.3) found some path, but not necessarily the shortest path. Figure 10.2.5 lists an algorithm that finds a shortest path in the underlying graph when the maze is unweighted. Dijkstra's algorithm (Figure 10.3.5) finds the shortest graph if the underlying graph is weighted. The problem considered here is to find all simple paths from a given initial vertex to a fixed final vertex. It is assumed that the start and final vertices are distinct. Recall that a path is simple if every vertex on the path is distinct. Simple paths have no loops.

The solution outlines here is a brute-force breadth-first search that uses three ADTs. The maze itself will be stored as a DISCRETE_DIGRAPH. Each path will be stored as a queue of vertices. Since all possible paths will be generated, a second queue of paths composed of records of the form

```
type PATH_TYPE is
   record
      THIS_PATH : VERTEX_QUEUE;
      VERTICES_USED : VERTEX_SET;
      PATH_LENGTH : natural := 0;
   end record;
```

will be needed. Note that in path_type the third ADT of set type is used to keep track of which vertices have already been visited. Clearly, the GENERIC_UNBOUNDED_QUEUE ADT and the GENERIC_DISCRETE_SET ADT must be recompiled, with queue and set being changed to private type instead of the default-limited private type. If VERTEX_QUEUE or VERTEX_SET were limited private, it would be impossible to assign objects of type path_type to each other. Ada forbids this (see Ada LRM 12.3.2/2). The discussion in previous chapters about passing limited private types as subprogram parameters applies.

The method is simple. A path record with the start vertex is enqueued onto the queues of paths. Although this queue is not empty, paths are removed from the queue of paths and another vertex is added to the end of the path provided that there is an adjacent unvisited vertex. Consider the simple maze in Figure 10.7.1. and suppose that room 3 is the initial room. Figure 10.7.2(a) shows the initial state of the queue of paths before entering the processing stage. The single path is removed from the queue. Note that rooms 2, 4, and 7 are adjacent to room

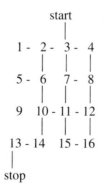

Figure 10.7.1   Example maze.

3 and that none of these rooms have previously been visited. Three paths of length 1 are enqueued on the path queue. One path goes from room 3 to room 2, one path goes from room 3 to room 4, and the final path goes from room 3 to room 7 [see Figure 10.7.2(b)].

```
                <3>
(a) queue_of_path -->      0
                {3}
                <32>      <34>      <37:
(b) queue_of_path -->      1    -->   1   -->   1
                {3,2}     {3,4}     {3,7}
                <321>     <326>     <348>      <378>      <37  11>
(c) queue_of_path -->      2    -->   2   -->   2   -->   2    -->      2
                {3,2,1}   {3,2,6}   {3,4,8}   {3,7,8}   {3,7,11}
                <3265>    <3487> <348  12>  <3784>
(d) queue_of_path -->      3    -->   3   -->   3 --> 3 -->
                {3,2,5,6} {3,4,7,8} {3,4,8,12}   {3,7,8,4}
                <378  12> <37   11   10>  <37   11   15>  <37   11   12>
                3    -->   3    -->   3 -->      3
                {3,7,8,12} {3,7,10,11}  {3,7,11,15}   {3,7,11,12}
```

Figure 10.7.2   (a) Initialized queue_of_path. (b) queue_of_path after processing part (a). (c) queue_of path after processing part (b). (d) queue_of_path after processing part (c).

Figure 10.7.2(c) shows the state of the path queue after every path of length 2 in Figure 10.7.2(b). The end node of the path <3–2–1> is adjacent to node 2, which has been visited previously. This path is dropped. The end node of path <3–2–6> is adjacent to a single node 5, so the path <3–2–6–5> of length 3 is added to the queue. The end node of the next path considered, <3–4–8>, is adjacent to nodes 4, 7, and 12. Node 4 has been used previously, which implies that the path <3–4–8–4> is not simple, and it is therefore dropped. Nodes 7 and 12 have not been used, so two paths, <3–4–8–7> and <3–4–8–12>, are added. At some point the end node of a path is adjacent to the terminating node, node 13. Node 13 is added to the path and that path is added to a queue of paths that go from the start to the terminating node. This process continues until the queue of partial paths is empty. Since there are only a finite number of nodes, it follows that there is only a finite number of simple paths, so the process terminates.

The nodes of the maze are represented as an integer range. With this last detail settled, the Ada code follows in Figure 10.7.3.

```
with text_io; use text_io;
with GENERIC_DISCRETE_DIGRAPH;
with GENERIC_UNBOUNDED_QUEUE;
with GENERIC_DISCRETE_SET;
Procedure CASE_STUDY_10 is
    NUMBER_OF_ROOMS : constant integer := 16;
    subtype VERTEX_RANGE is integer range 1..NUMBER_OF_ROOMS;

    package INTEGER_TEXT_IO is new integer_io(integer);
    use INTEGER_TEXT_IO;
```

Figure 10.7.3   Ada code for CASE_STUDY_10, a brute-force path search. Continues on page 372.

```
                       -- set up maze
                       package MAZE_GRAPH is new GENERIC_DISCRETE_DIGRAPH(VERTEX_RANGE);
                       use MAZE_GRAPH;

                       -- set up queue of vertices
                       package VERTEX_QUEUE is new
                                       GENERIC_UNBOUNDED_QUEUE(VERTEX_RANGE);

                       -- set up set type to keep track of referenced vertices
                       package VERTEX_SET is new GENERIC_DISCRETE_SET(VERTEX_RANGE);

                       -- set up queue of paths
                       type PATH_TYPE is
                         record
                           THIS_PATH : VERTEX_QUEUE.QUEUE;
                           VERTICES_USED : VERTEX_SET.SET;
                           PATH_LENGTH : natural := 0;
                         end record;
                   package PATH_QUEUE is new GENERIC_UNBOUNDED_QUEUE(PATH_TYPE);

                   MAZE : GRAPH;
                   QUEUE_OF_PATH,
                   QUEUE_OF_ANSWER : PATH_QUEUE.QUEUE;
                   START_ROOM   : VERTEX_RANGE  :=3;
                   FINISH_ROOM : VERTEX_RANGE :=3;
                   TEMP_PATH_NODE : PATH_TYPE;

                   procedure BUILD_MAZE is separate;
                     --builds up maze
                     --gets start, finish rooms
                     -- left to exercises

                   procedure PRINT_MAZE is separate;
                     --prints out maze in manner similar to Figure 10.7.1
                     --left to exercises

                   procedure PRINT_ALL_PATHS is
                     -- prints all paths in Queue_of_answer;
                     PATH_NUMBER : integer := 0;
                     TEMP_VERTEX : VERTEX_RANGE;
                   begin
                     if PATH_QUEUE.EMPTY (QUEUE_OF_ANSWER) then
                       put_line("Sorry, no paths exist!");
                     else
                       loop
                         exit when PATH_QUEUE.EMPTY(QUEUE_OF_ANSWER);
                         PATH_QUEUE.DEQUEUE(TEMP_PATH_NODE, QUEUE_OF_ANSWER);
```

Figure 10.7.3   Continues on page 373.

Graphs and Digraphs   Chap. 10

```
            PATH_NUMBER := PATH_NUMBER + 1;
            put("Path Number = ");
            put(Path_number,4);
            put(", Path Length = ");
            put(TEMP_PATH_NODE.PATH_LENGTH,4);
            put("Vertices of Path are ");
            loop
              exit when VERTEX_QUEUE.EMPTY(TEMP_PATH_NODE.THIS_PATH);
              VERTEX_QUEUE.DEQUEUE (TEMP_VERTEX, TEMP_PATH_NODE.THIS_PATH);
              put(TEMP_VERTEX,1);
              if not VERTEX_QUEUE.EMPTY(TEMP_PATH_NODE.THIS_PATH)then
                put(",");
              end if;
            end loop;
            new_line;
          end loop;
      end if;
  end PRINT_ALL_PATHS;

  procedure SET_UP_QUEUE_OF_PATH is
    -- sets up queue_of_path similar to Figure 10.7.2(a)
  begin
    VERTEX_SET.CLEAR(TEMP_PATH_NODE.VERTICES_USED);
    VERTEX_SET.ADD_ELEMENT
            (START_ROOM, TEMP_PATH_NODE.VERTICES_USED);
    VERTEX_QUEUE.CLEAR(TEMP_PATH_NODE.THIS_PATH);
    VERTEX_QUEUE.ENQUEUE(START_ROOM, TEMP_PATH_NODE.THIS_PATH);
    PATH_QUEUE.ENQUEUE(TEMP_PATH_NODE, QUEUE_OF_PATH);
  end SET_UP_QUEUE_OF_PATH;

  procedure PROCESS_TEMP_PATH_NODE( NODE : in        PATH_TYPE) is
    TEMP_NODE : PATH_TYPE;
    NEXT_VERTEX, END_VERTEX : VERTEX_RANGE;
    END_VERTEX_OUT_DEGREE : natural;
  begin
    END_VERTEX := VERTEX_QUEUE.REAR_ITEM(NODE.THIS_PATH);
    END_VERTEX_OUT_DEGREE := VERTEX_OUT_DEGREE(END_VERTEX,MAZE);
    for i in integer range 1..END_VERTEX_OUT_DEGREE loop
      NEXT_DESTINATION_VERTEX(END_VERTEX, MAZE, NEXT_VERTEX);
      if not VERTEX_SET.ELEMENT_IN_SET
              (NEXT_VERTEX, NODE.VERTICES_USED) then
        VERTEX_QUEUE.COPY(NODE.THIS_PATH, TEMP_NODE.THIS_PATH);
        VERTEX_QUEUE.ENQUEUE(NEXT_VERTEX, TEMP_NODE.THIS_PATH);
        TEMP_NODE.PATH_LENGTH := NODE.PATH_LENGTH + 1;
        VERTEX_SET.COPY
              (NODE.VERTICES_USED, TEMP_NODE.VERTICES_USED);
        VERTEX_SET.ADD_ELEMENT
              (NEXT_VERTEX, TEMP_NODE.VERTICES_USED);
```

Figure 10.7.3 Continues on page 374.

```
            if NEXT_VERTEX = FINISH_ROOM then
                PATH_QUEUE.ENQUEUE(TEMP_NODE, QUEUE_OF_ANSWER);
            else
                PATH_QUEUE.ENQUEUE(TEMP_NODE, QUEUE_OF_PATH);
            end if;
        end if;
      end loop;
   end PROCESS_TEMP_PATH_NODE;
 begin -- CASE_STUDY_10
    BUILD_MAZE;
    SET_UP-QUEUE_OF_PATH;
    loop
       exit when PATH_QUEUE.EMPTY(QUEUE_OF_PATH);
       PATH_QUEUE.DEQUEUE(TEMP_PATH_NODE, QUEUE_OF_PATH);
       PROCESS_TEMP_PATH_NODE(TEMP_PATH_NODE);
    end loop;
    PRINT_ALL_PATHS;
 end CASE_STUDY_10;
```

Figure 10.7.3 Concluded.

Figure 10.7.4 contains the output for this case study. Note that the paths are printed out in ascending order by length. This is a consequence of the breadth-first search on an un-weighted graph. The breadth-first search computes all paths of length 1, then all paths of length 2, and so on.

Path Number = 1, Path Length = 5, Vertices of Path are 3,2,6,5,9,13
Path Number = 2, Path Length = 5, Vertices of Path are 3,7,11,10,14,13
Path Number = 3, Path Length = 7, Vertices of Path are 3,4,8,7,11,10,14,13
Path Number = 4, Path Length = 7, Vertices of Path are 3,4,8,12,11,10,14,13
Path Number = 5, Path Length = 7, Vertices of Path are 3,7,8,12,11,10,14,13
Path Number = 6, Path Length = 9, Vertices of Path are 3,4,8,12,16,15,11,10,14,13
Path Number = 7, Path Length = 9, Vertices of Path are 3,7,8,12,16,15,11,10,14,13

Figure 10.7.4 Listing of all paths from START_ROOM = 3 and FINISH_ROOM = 13 for the maze in Figure 10.7.1.

The case study can easily be generalized to do breadth-first searches of weighted graphs. Instead of adding one to the length of the path for each edge added, the edge weight would be added. In that case the shortest path might not be the first path printed. The paths would be printed in ascending order, where the order is based on the number of edges. The order is not the total edge weight. By changing the variable QUEUE_OF_PATH to STACK_OF_PATH, and storing the intermediate paths on this stack instead of storing them on a queue, a depth-first search is obtained. These modifications are left to the exercises.

This algorithm is at least $o(n!)$, where n is the vertices. Consider a graph of n vertices where every vertex is connected to every other vertex. There is one path of length 1 joining the start vertex to the finish vertex. There are $n - 2$ paths of length 2. There are $(n - 2) * (n - 3)$ paths of length 3. Continuing, there are $(n - 2)!$ paths of length $(n - 1)$ joining the start vertex to the finish vertex. This is precisely the number of permutations of $(n - 2)$ objects. There are $(n - 2)!$ permutations of n vertices if the first and last vertex are fixed.

EXERCISES

Section 10.1 Abstract Data type DISCRETE_DIGRAPH

10.1.1 Implement the following operations for the ADT GENERIC_DISCRETE_DIGRAPH as specified in Figure 10.1.2.
- **a.** Implement the operation COPY.
- **b.** Implement the operation CLEAR.
- **c.** Implement the operation ADD_EDGE.
- **d.** Implement the operation NEXT_SOURCE_EDGE.
- **e.** Implement the operation EMPTY.
- **f.** Implement the operation EQUAL.
- **g.** Implement the operation VERTEX_IN_DEGREE.
- **h.** Implement the operation VERTEX_OUT_DEGREE.
- **i.** Combine the operations implemented in parts a through h with the operations implemented in the text to complete the package for the ADT GENERIC_DISCRETE_DIGRAPH.

10.1.2 Implement the following operations for the ADT GENERIC_SPARSE_DISCRETE_DIGRAPH with the same public section as in Figure 10.1.2 but with the private section listed in Figure 10.1.6.
- **a.** Implement the operation COPY.
- **b.** Implement the operation CLEAR.
- **c.** Implement the operation REMOVE_EDGE.
- **d.** Implement the operation ADD_EDGE.
- **e.** Implement the operation EDGE_IN_GRAPH.
- **f.** Implement the operation NEXT_DEST_EDGE.
- **g.** Implement the operation NEXT_SOURCE_EDGE.
- **h.** Implement the operation EMPTY.
- **i.** Implement the operation EQUAL.
- **j.** Implement the operation VERTEX_IN_DEGREE.
- **k.** Implement the operation VERTEX_OUT_DEGREE.
- **l.** Combine the operations implemented in parts a through k to complete the package for this version of the ADT GENERIC_SPARSE_DISCRETE_DIGRAPH.

Section 10.2 Abstract Data Type GENERIC_UNBOUNDED_DIGRAPH

10.2.1 Implement the following operations for the ADT GENERIC_UNBOUNDED_DIGRAPH as specified in Figure 10.2.2.
- **a.** Implement the operation COPY.
- **b.** Implement the operation CLEAR.
- **c.** Implement the operation REMOVE_EDGE.
- **d.** Implement the operation ADD_EDGE.
- **e.** Implement the operation REMOVE_VERTEX.
- **f.** Implement the operation VERTEX_COUNT.
- **g.** Implement the operation EDGE_IN_GRAPH.
- **h.** Implement the operation NEXT_DEST_EDGE.
- **i.** Implement the operation EMPTY.
- **j.** Implement the operation EQUAL.
- **k.** Implement the operation VERTEX_IN_DEGREE.
- **l.** Implement the operation VERTEX_IN_GRAPH.
- **m.** Implement the operation VERTEX_OUT_DEGREE.
- **n.** Combine the operations implemented in parts a through m with the operations implemented in Section 10.2 to complete the ADT GENERIC_UNBOUNDED_DIGRAPH.

Section 10.3 Abstract Data Type WEIGHTED_DIGRAPH

10.3.1 Implement the following operations for the ADT_GENERIC_SPARSE_DIS-CRETE_WEIGHTED_DIGRAPH as specified in Figure 10.3.2.

    a. Implement the operation ADD_VERTEX.
    b. Implement the operation COPY.
    c. Implement the operation CLEAR.
    d. Implement the operation REMOVE_EDGE.
    e. Implement the operation EDGE_IN_GRAPH.
    f. Implement the operation EDGE_WEIGHT.
    g. Implement the operation NEXT_SOURCE_EDGE.
    h. Implement the operation NEXT_DEST_EDGE.
    i. Implement the operation EMPTY.
    j. Implement the operation EQUAL.
    k. Implement the operation VERTEX_IN_DEGREE.
    l. Implement the operation VERTEX_OUT_DEGREE.
    m. Combine parts a through l into a package body that fully implements the ADT GENERIC_DISCRETE_WEIGHTED_DIGRAPH.

10.3.2 **a.** Design the documentation for the ADT GENERIC_UNBOUNDED_WEIGHTED_DIGRAPH.
    b. Design the specification for the ADT GENERIC_UNBOUNDED_WEIGHTED_DIGRAPH.
    c. Implement the operation ADD_VERTEX.
    d. Implement the operation REMOVE_VERTEX.
    e. Implement the operation VERTEX_COUNT.
    f. Implement the operation VERTEX_LIST.
    g. Implement the operation VERTEX_IN_GRAPH.
    h. Implement the operation COPY.
    i. Implement the operation CLEAR.
    j. Implement the operation ADD_EDGE.
    k. Implement the operation REMOVE_EDGE.
    l. Implement the operation EDGE_IN_GRAPH.
    m. Implement the operation EDGE_WEIGHT.
    n. Implement the operation NEXT_SOURCE_EDGE.
    o. Implement the operation NEXT_DEST_EDGE.
    p. Implement the operation EMPTY.
    q. Implement the operation EQUAL.
    r. Implement the operation VERTEX_IN_DEGREE.
    s. Implement the operation VERTEX_OUT_DEGREE.
    t. Combine parts c through s into a package body that fully implements the ADT GENERIC_UNBOUNDED_WEIGHTED_DIGRAPH.

Section 10.4 Abstract Data Type GENERIC_BOUNDED_TRANSITION_GRAPH

10.4.1 Implement the following operations for the ADT GENERIC_BOUNDED_TRANSITION_GRAPH as specified in Figure 10.4.4.

    a. Implement the operation COPY.
    b. Implement the operation ADD_TRANSITION.
    c. Implement the operation SET_FINAL_SET.

d. Implement the operation STATE_FINAL.

e. Implement the operation GRAPH_NOT_CLEAR.

f. Combine parts a through e and the operations already implemented in Section 10.4 into a package body that fully implements the ADT GENERIC_BOUNDED_TRANSITION_GRAPH.

10.4.2 Write a program that determines whether or not an Ada assignment statement is valid or not. Assume that the assignment statement contains no parenthesis.

10.4.3 Modify Exercise 10.4.2 to determine whether or not a given string composed only of *a*'s and *b*'s has an odd number of *a*'s and an even number of *b*'s.

10.4.4 Modify Exercise 10.4.2 to determine whether or not a string is composed of a sequence of *a*'s followed by a sequence of *b*'s followed by a single letter *a*.

Section 10.5 Applications

10.5.1 Let a vertex denote the entering of college and another vertex denote graduation from college. If additional vertices represent courses that must be taken and edges represent prerequisites, write a program that gives the order in which classes must be taken in order to get a degree. To test the program, use the degree requirements for a degree in computer science at your university.

10.5.2 Write a program to solve a "simple" network flow problem. Test your program using a network of about 10 vertices. What is your estimate of the running time in relation to the number of vertices?

Section 10.6 Time and Space Constraints

10.6.1 Construct a time and space constraint table for the ADT GENERIC_DISCRETE_DIGRAPH with the private part listed in Figure 10.1.6.

10.6.2 Construct a time and space constraint table for the ADT GENERIC_DIS-CRETE_WEIGHTED_DIGRAPH.

10.6.3 Construct a time and space constraint table for the ADT GENERIC_UN-BOUNDED_WEIGHTED_DIGRAPH.

10.6.4 Construct a time and space constraint table for the ADT GENERIC_BOUNDED_TRANSI-TION_GRAPH.

Section 10.7 Case Study: Finding All Paths in a Maze

10.7.1 **a.** Complete CASE_STUDY_10 as listed in Figure 10.7.3.
   b. Apply the program in part a to the graph in Figure 10.7.1.

10.7.2 Modify and complete the program listed in Figure 10.7.3 so that it handles weighted digraphs. The output should list the paths in ascending order by total weight.

10.7.3 **a.** Modify and complete the program listed in Figure 10.7.3 so that it performs a depth-first search for unweighted digraphs. The output should list the paths in ascending order by total length.
   b. Apply the program in part a to the graph in Figure 10.7.1.

10.7.4 Modify and complete the program listed in Figure 10.7.3 so that it handles unweighted digraphs using a depth-first search. The output should list the paths in ascending order by total weight.

PROGRAMMING PROJECTS

P10.1 Write a program that a travel agent might use to find the minimum ticket price. Here the vertices represent cities, the edges represent air service between two cities, and the edge weights represent air fares.

P10.2 Circuit boards can be thought of as graphs where the vertices represent places where various electronic devices can be attached and the edges represent wires. Write a program that lists which vertices are connected.

P10.3 The traveling salesman problem requires that a salesperson visit each city on his or her route exactly once at minimum cost. Assume that the salesperson has a map with the cities on the route clearly marked, and that he or she has computed a table of distances between every pair of cities on the route. Test your program on a suitable route. This problem is timewise $o(n!)$, where n is the number of cities on the route, so don't pick too large a route.

P10.4 Write a program that scans an Ada program and lists the valid Ada identifiers.

P10.5 Let $G = (V,E)$ be a graph. A spanning tree $T = (V,E')$ is a subgraph of a graph G that contains all the vertices of G and where E' is a subset of E. Write and test a procedure that finds a spanning tree if it exists and outputs a message if it does not.

P10.6 A graph is connected if there exists a path (not necessarily an edge) that joins every pair of vertices in the graph. Write a procedure that determines whether a given graph is connected. Your procedure should use GENERIC_UNBOUNDED_DIGRAPH.

NOTES AND REFERENCES

Knuth [27, Volume 1] is the basic reference for most graph algorithms. Weiss [49] contains a basic bibliography on the topic of network flow. The shortest-path algorithm is, as noted previously, due to Dijkstra [17]. Most texts on the design and analysis of algorithms, such as Baase [4], have at least a chapter devoted to applications of graphs. Any text on automata theory provides a reference for transition graphs and finite-state machines. See, in particular, Brookshear [10].

11

Sorting

Sorting a list, searching a list for a particular item of ITEM_TYPE, and searching a list for the occurrence of a particular pattern are three common problems arising in computer science. In this chapter we look at basic algorithms for sorting. Entire books have been written on each of these classes of algorithms. Sorts are classified as internal, where attention is restricted to one-dimensional arrays, and external, where data files are manipulated to yield a file of sorted elements.

Determining which sort method to use requires an awareness of the trade-offs. Some methods work well with random lists but perform poorly with nearly sorted lists. Some minimize interchanging elements while maximizing the comparison of elements. Some methods attempt to place elements in their final place early, while some methods attempt to move things closer to their final place at each step. Some perform well for short lists and poorly on long lists, or vice versa. Some obtain high performance in terms of time but at the cost of space.

11.1 INTERNAL SORTS

The sequential ordering of the elements in an array characterizes the goal of internal sorting. All the methods in this section have as a generic formal parameter list one of those shown in Figure 11.1.1. ITEM_TYPE is a programmer-supplied type. By suppling ITEM_TYPE as an array VECTOR, the sorting algorithms can be developed for general use. Any sort procedures developed in this section will work for any user-supplied array with integer indices. There are many other permutations and combinations of formal generic parameter lists. The implementation of all sorts using any of the formal generic parameter lists above is similar. The abstractness of the array attributes leads to equivalent implementations. For the rest of the section the implementations of the internal sorts will use the formal generic parameter list in Figure 11.1.1(a). The most general implementations, the discrete as seen in Figure 11.1.1 (b), are left to the exercises.

```
generic
  type ITEM_TYPE is private;
  type VECTOR is array (integer range < >) of ITEM_TYPE;
    with function "<" (LEFT, RIGHT : ITEM_TYPE) return boolean;
procedure NAME_SORT ( v : in out VECTOR );
```
(a)

Figure 11.1.1   (a) Formal parameter for integer range arrays.

```
generic
  type ITEM_TYPE is private;
  type INDEX is (< >);
  type VECTOR is array (INDEX range < >) of ITEM_TYPE;
  with function "<" (LEFT, RIGHT : ITEM_TYPE) return boolean;
procedure NAME_SORT (V: in out VECTOR);
```
(b)

Figure 11.1.1 (b) Formal parameter for discrete range arrays.

Bubble Sort

The brute-force approach to sorting uses the basic strategy of repeatedly comparing adjacent items and exchanging them when they are not in proper order. If V(I) and V(I+1) are out of order, they are swapped. This swapping continues until the VECTOR V is finally in order. The name of this algorithm is *exchange sort* or *bubble sort*. Bubble sort exchanges adjacent elements whenever the items are out of order. It is efficient in terms of space because all work is done in the initial array. Figure 11.1.2 lists the first version of this basic algorithm.

```
generic
  type ITEM_TYPE is private;
  type VECTOR is array (integer range < >) of ITEM_TYPE;
  with function "<"(LEFT, RIGHT : ITEM_TYPE) return boolean;
procedure BUBBLE_SORT (V : in out VECTOR);
procedure BUBBLE_SORT (V : in out VECTOR) is
  TEMP_ITEM : ITEM_TYPE;
begin
  for OUTER in V'first .. V'last-1 loop
    for INNER in V'first + 1 .. V'last loop
      if V(INNER) < V(INNER - 1) then
        TEMP_ITEM := V(INNER);
        V(INNER) := V(INNER - 1);
        V(INNER - 1) := TEMP_ITEM;
      end if;
    end loop;
  end loop;
end BUBBLE_SORT;
```

Figure 11.1.2 Bubble sort.

The number of comparisons is $O(n**2)$, where n is the length of the list. Recall from algebra that

$$n * (n - 1)/2 = (n - 1) + (n - 2) + (n - 3) + \cdots + 2 + 1$$

There are two loops in the BUBBLE_SORT algorithm. The outer loop executes $N - 1$ times, assuming that the indices of V have range 1..N. Thus there are $(N - 1)$ terms in the summation above. For each pass K through the inner loop, at most $K - 1$ compare and swaps are made. K goes from 1 through $N - 1$. Each term in the summation above represents the number of compares at that stage of the algorithm.

Consider the list of length 8 illustrated in Figure 11.1.3. The first row is the random list. The second row is the list after one completion of the inner loop. Each succeeding row shows the list after one additional completion of the inner loop. On the first pass through the inner loop, the largest element is moved to the last position, so there are at most $(n - 1)$ exchanges. On the second pass the next largest element is moved to the next-to-last position, so at most $(n - 2)$ exchanges can occur. After k passes of the inner loop, the k largest elements are in their final places in the sorted list. Continuing, and applying the formula above, it follows that the number of exchanges is $O(n * * 2)$.

$$
\begin{array}{cccccccc}
2 & 5 & 7 & 3 & 4 & 8 & 6 & 1 \\
2 & 5 & 3 & 4 & 7 & 6 & 1 & 8 \\
2 & 3 & 4 & 5 & 6 & 1 & 7 & 8 \\
2 & 3 & 4 & 5 & 1 & 6 & 7 & 8 \\
2 & 3 & 4 & 1 & 5 & 6 & 7 & 8 \\
2 & 3 & 1 & 4 & 5 & 6 & 7 & 8 \\
2 & 1 & 3 & 4 & 5 & 6 & 7 & 8 \\
1 & 2 & 3 & 4 & 5 & 6 & 7 & 8 \\
\end{array}
$$

Figure 11.1.3 Bubble sort on a random list.

The algorithm above sorts objects of ITEM_TYPE in the VECTOR V into ascending order. A simple modification of this, and any of the remaining sort methods discussed in this section, will sort the VECTOR V into descending order. At instantiation, insert the > function instead of the < function.

The number of exchanges varies from 0 for an already sorted list to $n * (n -1)/2$ to a list of n items in reverse order. BUBBLE_SORT can be modified easily to recognize when a VECTOR V is already sorted, and then stop. One method uses a boolean flag to signal if an exchange occurred in the previous pass. No exchange means that the vector was sorted. In addition, the observation was made in the preceding paragraph that the IN_PLACE largest elements were in their final place after IN_PLACE passes of the inner loop. Thus the inner loop can be shortened. This cuts the number of compares in half. Figure 11.1.4 lists the modified version.This version of bubble sort stops when the list is sorted. If a list is almost sorted, the algorithm will terminate before INNER = V'last. If the items in the vector are within IN_PLACE of their final position, bubble sort terminates after IN_PLACE + 1 passes. No sort algorithm has as poor a performance, as measured by the worse-case number of exchanges, as bubble sort. Unless the VECTOR V is nearly in sorted order, almost any other sorting method is preferable.

```
generic
   type ITEM_TYPE is private;
   type VECTOR is array (integer range < >) of ITEM_TYPE;
   with function "<" (LEFT, RIGHT : ITEM_TYPE) return boolean;
procedure BUBBLE_SORT (V : in out VECTOR);
procedure BUBBLE_SORT (V : in out VECTOR) is
   SORTED : boolean false;
   TEMP_ITEM : ITEM_TYPE;
   IN_PLACE : integer := 0;   -- keeps track of number of items known
```

Figure 11.1.4 Modified bubble sort. Continues on page 382.

```
                              -- to be in their final place at beginning
                              -- of each pass
        INDEX : integer := V'first;
    begin
      while not SORTED and then INDEX < V'last loop
        SORTED := true;
        INDEX := INDEX + 1;
        for INNER in V'first + 1 .. V'last - IN_PLACE loop
          if (V(INNER) < V(INNER - 1) then
            TEMP_ITEM := V(INNER);
            V(INNER) := V(INNER - 1);
            V(INNER - 1) := TEMP_ITEM;
            SORTED := false;
          end if;
        end loop;
        IN_PLACE := IN_PLACE + 1;
      end loop;
    end BUBBLE_SORT;
```

Figure 11.1.4 Concluded.

Shaker sort is another variation that replaces the single inner loop with two separate loops. The first loop runs from a low to a high index and the second loop runs from a high index to a low index. The first loop moves large items to the high side of the list quickly, but it does not move low items toward their final place by more than one place. The second loop behaves in just the opposite manner. At this point the slice to be sorted is reduced by one element at either end. This version of bubble sort is covered in the exercises.

Selection Sort

Selection sort is the next strategy examined. The idea is simple. In bubble sort, each pass placed the largest element out of place into its final position. Selection sort selects this largest element, makes one exchange per pass, and then sorts a diminished list. Its advantage over bubble sort is the reduced number of exchanges. An array is examined for the location of the largest element. This method exchanges the element at that location with the last element in the array. The whole process repeats for the array slice that ends at the next-to-last component. Using the same starting data as in Figure 11.1.3, the behavior shown in Figures 11.1.5 is encountered. Figure 11.1.6 lists the selection sort algorithm.

```
2  5  7  3  4  8  6  1
2  5  7  3  4  1  6  8
2  5  6  3  4  1  7  8
2  5  1  3  4  6  7  8
2  4  1  3  5  6  7  8
2  3  1  4  5  6  7  8
2  1  3  4  5  6  7  8
1  2  3  4  5  6  7  8
```

Figure 11.1.5   Selection sort on a random list.

```
generic
  type ITEM_TYPE is private;
  type VECTOR is array (integer range < >) of ITEM_TYPE;
  with function "<" (LEFT, RIGHT : ITEM_TYPE) return boolean;
procedure SELECTION_SORT (V : in out VECTOR);
procedure SELECTION_SORT (V : in out VECTOR) is
  MAX_LOC : integer;
  TEMP_ITEM : ITEM_TYPE;
begin
  for OUTER in reverse V'first + 1 .. V'last loop
    MAX_LOC := OUTER;
    for INNER in V'first..OUTER loop
      if V(MAX_LOC) < V(INNER) then
        MAX_LOC := INNER;
      end if;
    end loop;
    if MAX_LOC /= OUTER then
      TEMP_ITEM := V(OUTER);
      V(OUTER) := V(MAX_LOC);
      V(MAX_LOC) := TEMP_ITEM;
    end if;
  end loop;
end SELECTION_SORT;
```

Figure 11.1.6   Selection sort.

Suppose that the array contains n items. No more than one exchange takes place for each value of the loop index inner, so the number of exchanges is $O(n)$. For the first value of the index inner, $n - 1$ compares are made. The next pass through the inner loop requires $n - 2$ compares, and so on. The number of compares is $n * (n - 1)/2$ or $O(n ** 2)$. There isn't any way that selection sort can determine if a list is in order. Since it is usually quicker to compare items than to exchange them, selection sort is preferred over bubble sort.

Shell Sort

The next group of sorting algorithms offers both improved performance and some insight into determining the feasibility of trying a different approach. Before trying a different approach, one determines if some basic assumption has been made that was not necessary. This next sort algorithm does just that. It is natural, when sorting, to compare adjacent items. To determine if a list is in ascending order, the items are compared pairwise from one end of the list to the other end of the list. Why is it important to sort by checking adjacent items? The important thing is to terminate when everything is in order pairwise. The next sort (Figure 11.1.7) challenges the unnecessary assumption that sorts must always do adjacent pairwise exchanges and compares. It is a variation of class of sorting algorithms due to Shell

```
generic
  type ITEM_TYPE is private;
  type VECTOR is array (integer range < >) of ITEM_TYPE;
  with function "<" (LEFT, RIGHT : ITEM_TYPE) return boolean;
```

Figure 11.1.7   Speed sort, a version of shell sort. Continues on page 384.

```
procedure SPEED_SORT (V : in out VECTOR);
procedure SPEED_SORT (V : in out VECTOR) is
  TEMP_ITEM : ITEM_TYPE;
  COMPARE_DISTANCE : integer := (V'length + 1)/2;
begin
  loop
    for INDEX in V'first .. V'last- COMPARE_DISTANCE loop
      if V(INDEX + COMPARE_DISTANCE) < V(INDEX) then
        -- Two values COMPARE_DISTANCE apart in V are out
        -- of order with respect to each other.
        TEMP_ITEM := V(INDEX);
        V(INDEX) := V(INDEX + COMPARE_DISTANCE);
        V(INDEX + COMPARE_DISTANCE) := TEMP_ITEM;
      end if;
    end loop;
    if COMPARE_DISTANCE >1 then
      -- Must work COMPARE_DISTANCE down to 1
      COMPARE_DISTANCE := (COMPARE_DISTANCE + 1)/2;
    else
      -- All done
      return;
    end if;
  end loop;
end SPEED_SORT;
```

Figure 11.1.7 Concluded.

The value COMPARE_DISTANCE is the separation between elements in the VECTOR V that are being compared. Each pass tries to place an item within k places of its true spot. Each pass requires V'length - COMPARE_DISTANCE compares and performs no more than V'length - COMPARE_DISTANCE exchanges. The number of passes is $(1 + \log_2(n))$, so intuitively this algorithm is $O(n * \log_2(n))$ for compares and exchanges. The actual order of the algorithm depends on the strategy used to pick the compare distances. See Chapter 2 of Baase [4] for a fuller discussion. Figure 11.1.8 illustrates a list with 12 elements at the end of each pass.

$$
\begin{array}{ccccccccccccc}
 & 5 & 8 & 2 & 6 & 10 & 12 & 1 & 11 & 3 & 7 & 4 & 9 \\
k=6: & 1 & 8 & 2 & 6 & 4 & 9 & 5 & 11 & 3 & 7 & 10 & 12 \\
k=3: & 1 & 4 & 2 & 5 & 8 & 3 & 6 & 10 & 9 & 7 & 11 & 12 \\
k=2: & 1 & 4 & 2 & 3 & 6 & 5 & 8 & 7 & 9 & 10 & 11 & 12 \\
k=1: & 1 & 2 & 3 & 4 & 6 & 6 & 7 & 8 & 9 & 10 & 11 & 12 \\
\end{array}
$$

Figure 11.1.8 Operation of speed sort.

Quick Sort

Another method of devising a sort strategy asks whether a divide-and-conquer strategy can be developed. Suppose that a list of n elements is processed so that the four conditions listed in Figure 11.1.9 occur.

1. The original list is now divided into two lists.
2. The two new lists are unsorted.
3. Every element in the first list precedes every element in the second list.
4. The combined new lists are stored in the same area as the original list, with the first list appearing before the second.

Figure 11.1.9   Quick sort strategy.

Bubble sort is $O(n * * 2)$. It takes only half as much work to use bubble sort to sort two lists of length $(n/2)$. Taking this one step further, it only takes one-fourth the effort to sort four lists of length $(n/4)$ using BUBBLE_SORT as it does to sort a list of length n. This is the motivation of the QUICK_SORT algorithm (Figure 11.1.10).

```
generic
  type ITEM_TYPE is private;
  type VECTOR is array (integer range < >) of ITEM_TYPE;
  with function "<" (LEFT, RIGHT : ITEM_TYPE) return boolean;
procedure QUICK_SORT (V : in out VECTOR);
procedure QUICK_SORT (V : in out VECTOR) is
  TEMP_ITEM : ITEM_TYPE;
  SPLIT : integer ;

  procedure PARTITION (V : in out VECTOR, SPLIT : out integer) is separate;
  -- see discussion below

begin
  PARTITION (V, SPLIT);
  if SPLIT > V'first + 1 then
    QUICK_SORT (V(V'first..SPLIT-1));
  end if;
  if SPLIT < V'last-1 then
    QUICK_SORT (V(SPLIT + 1..V'Last));
  end if;
end QUICK_SORT;
```

Figure 11.1.10   Quick sort.

The procedure PARTITION rearranges the items in V so that all the items in the slice (V(V'first . . SPLIT-1) are less than or equal to V(SPLIT) and V(SPLIT) is less than or equal to all the items in the slice V(SPLIT + 1 . . V'last). The item V(SPLIT) is in its final place in V. There is no guarantee that the VECTOR V will be split in half by the partition procedure, but assume that, on average, it does. The QUICK_SORT procedure recursively calls itself as long as the slices of the partitioned VECTOR V have two or more components. How many times will QUICK_SORT be called? At the first level there are two vector slices of length $N/2$. At the second level, there are four slices of length $N/4$. This continues k times where k is the first integer such that $N < 2 * * k$. That is, k is the first integer where $\log_2(N) < = \log_2(2 * * k) = k$. Thus there are $\log_2(N)$ passes of QUICK_SORT. An examination of PARTITION will show that each pass requires $O(n)$ work so QUICK_SORT is $O(n * \log_2(n))$.

The procedure PARTITION (Figure 11.1.11) can be implemented in several ways. The strategy adopted here is to try to modify the VECTOR V so that V(V'first)) ends up somewhere in the "middle" of V with the four properties listed in Figure 11.1.10 being satisfied.

```
separate (QUICK_SORT)
procedure PARTITION (V : in out VECTOR; SPLIT : out integer) is
  LOWER : integer := V'first;
  UPPER : integer := V'last;
  MIDDLE_ITEM : ITEM_TYPE := V(V'first);
  TEMP_ITEM : ITEM_TYPE;
begin
  loop
    loop
      exit when V(LOWER) > MIDDLE_ITEM;
      LOWER := LOWER + 1;
      exit when LOWER = V'last;
    end loop;
    loop
      exit when V(UPPER) < MIDDLE_ITEM or else V(UPPER) = MIDDLE_ITEM;
      UPPER := UPPER + 1;
      exit when UPPER = V'first;
    end loop;
    if LOWER < UPPER then
      TEMP_ITEM := V(UPPER);
      V(UPPER) := V(LOWER);
      V(LOWER) := TEMP_ITEM;
    end if;
    exit when LOWER > = UPPER;
  end loop;
  SPLIT := UPPER;
  TEMP_ITEM := V(UPPER);
  V(UPPER := V(V'first);
  V(V'first) := TEMP_ITEM;
end PARTITION;
```

Figure 11.1.11 PARTITION procedure for QUICK_SORT.

Suppose that a random vector V that was to be sorted had length 9. Then Figure 11.1.12 shows how PARTITION works. QUICK_SORT is $O(n * \log_2(n))$ for random lists but it is $O(n ** 2)$ for a list already in order or in reverse order. QUICK_SORT sometimes suffers from system overhead because of its recursive nature. This can be cut down significantly. One way of reducing this overhead is to go to another sort routine when the length of v gets small. Clearly, for small n, there is not much difference, in effort, between a SELECTION_SORT routine and an $O(n * \log_2(n))$ routine. Another way to reduce this overhead is to implement QUICK_SORT without using recursion. Both methods are left as exercises. A final problem with QUICK_SORT occurs if the items in the list are not distinct. QUICK_SORT sometimes exchanges equal items.

```
Lower = 1,Upper = 9,Middle = 5  5  3  7  9  2  4  1  6  8  Initial Conditions
Lower = 2,Upper = 9,Middle = 5  5  3  7  9  2  4  1  6  8
Lower = 3,Upper = 9,Middle = 5  5  3  7  9  2  4  1  6  8
Lower = 3,Upper = 8,Middle = 5  5  3  7  9  2  4  1  6  8
Lower = 3,Upper = 7,Middle = 5  5  3  7  9  2  4  1  6  8
Lower = 3,Upper = 7,Middle = 5  5  3  1  9  2  4  7  6  8  Swap
                                                           V(Lower),V(Upper)
Lower = 4,Upper = 7,Middle = 5  5  3  1  9  2  4  7  6  8
Lower = 4,Upper = 6,Middle = 5  5  3  1  9  2  4  7  6  8
Lower = 4,Upper = 6,Middle = 5  5  3  1  4  2  9  7  6  8  Swap
                                                           V(Lower),V(Upper)
Lower = 5,Upper = 6,Middle = 5  5  3  1  4  2  9  7  6  8
Lower = 6,Upper = 6,Middle = 5  5  3  1  4  2  9  7  6  8  Exit loop,
Lower = 6,Upper = 6,Middle = 5  5  3  1  4  2  9  7  6  8  Set SPLIT := 5
Lower = 4,Upper = 6,Middle = 5  2  3  1  4  5  4  7  6  8  Swap

                                                           V(V'first),V (k)
                                                           End Partition
```

Figure 11.1.12 Concluded.

Internal Merge Sort

The next sort considered is a MERGE_SORT. MERGE_SORT requires a second array of equal length. It achieves its speed at the expense of memory. The algorithm merges two sorted array slices stored in one vector onto one slice stored on a second vector. Since lists of length 1 are sorted by definition, the first pass of MERGE_SORT creates half as many arrays of length 2, except that the last slice might be of length 1 if the original vector had odd length. The process continues. Vectors of length 2 are merged into vectors of length 4, 4 into 8, and so on. In each case the last vector might have shorter length.

The version of MERGE_SORT in Figure 11.1.13 has been tuned up as a divide-and-conquer recursive algorithm. Like QUICK_SORT, it first divides the vector into smaller vectors. This process repeats itself $\log_2(n)$ times, so the MERGE_SORT is $O(n * \log_2(n))$. The price paid for this performance is extra memory. If may not look like any extra memory has been created, but its creation is hidden in the declaration section of the function MERGE. The number of calls to MERGE_SORT is $2 * n - 1$, where n is the length of the vector. As usual with recursive algorithms, the system overhead associated with copying the formal parameters can be significant. A nonrecursive version is given in the exercises. The algorithm itself divides the vector in halves until a slice has length 1, then it starts merging slices together.

```
generic
  type ITEM_TYPE is private;
  type VECTOR is array (integer range < >) of ITEM_TYPE;
  with function "<" (LEFT, RIGHT : ITEM_TYPE) return boolean;
procedure MERGE_SORT (V : in out VECTOR);
procedure MERGE_SORT (V : in out VECTOR) is
```

Figure 11.1.13 Merge sort. Continues on page 388.

```
                MIDPOINT : integer;
                function MERGE (V1, V2 : VECTOR) return VECTOR is
                  V : VECTOR (V1'first..v2'last);
                  INDEX_V1 : integer := V1'first;
                  INDEX_V2 : integer := V2'first;
                begin
                  -- Merges two sorted vectors into one sorted vector
                  for INDEX in V'range loop
                    if INDEX_V1 in V1'range and INDEX_V2 in V2'range then
                      if V1(INDEX_V1) < V2(INDEX_V2) then
                        V(INDEX) := V1(INDEX_V1);
                        INDEX_V1 := INDEX_V1 + 1;
                      else
                        V(INDEX) := V2(INDEX_V2);
                        INDEX_V2 := INDEX_V2 + 1;
                      end if;
                    elsif INDEX_V1 in V1'range then
                      V(INDEX) := V1(INDEX_V1);
                      INDEX_V1 := INDEX_V1 + 1;
                    else
                      V(INDEX) := V2(INDEX_V2);
                      INDEX_V2 := INDEX_V2 + 1;
                    end if;
                  end loop;
                  return V;
                end MERGE;

            begin
              if V'first /= V'last then
                MIDPOINT := (V'first + V'LAST)/2;
                MERGE_SORT(V(V'FIRST..MIDPOINT));
                MERGE_SORT(V(MIDPOINT + 1..V'last));
                V := MERGE(V(V'first..MIDPOINT),V(MIDPOINT + 1..V'last));
              end if;
            end MERGE_SORT;
```

Figure 11.1.13 Concluded.

The generic procedure MERGE_SORT also illustrates a fine point about Ada programming. Consider the call to the function MERGE in Figure 11.1.13.

```
        V := MERGE(V(V'first..MIDPOINT),V(MIDPOINT + 1..V'last));
```

Suppose that this function were replaced by a procedure

```
        procedure MERGE (V1, V2 : in VECTOR; V : out VECTOR) is
```

and the call

```
        MERGE(V(V'first..MIDPOINT),V(MIDPOINT + 1..V'last),V);
```

replaced the function call above. If the entire parameter V were copied back at the end of the procedure MERGE, the result would be the same. However, if the formal parameter V was passed by reference, the generic procedure MERGE_SORT will usually yield incorrect results. If V is passed by reference, Ada will attempt to merge within V and not use a separate vector. The Ada LRM does not specify whether record or array parameters are to be passed by reference or by value. Most compilers pass by reference. The Ada Language Reference Manual does say that a program is erroneous if the program result depends on the mechanism in use (see Ada LRM 6.2).

Heap Sort

Given a VECTOR V with indices 1 through N, V is a HEAP if for each index I, $V(I) >= V(2 * I)$ and $V(I) >= V(2 * I + 1)$ for values of I where the relationship is defined. Clearly, the largest value in V is in $V(1)$ (see Figure 11.1.14). Figure 11.1.15 outlines the HEAP_SORT algorithm.

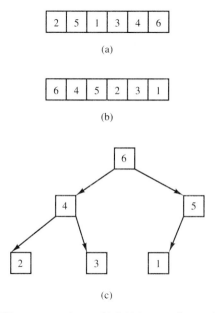

(a)

(b)

(c)

Figure 11.1.14 Binary tree as a heap. (a) Initial array to be sorted using heap sort. (b) Array from part (a) after being sorted to a heap. (c) Heap from part (b) represented as a tree.

1. Convert the VECTOR V into a HEAP.
2. While the HEAP is not empty:
   a. Swap the V(1) with the last component of V.
   b. Set LAST_NODE := LAST_NODE − 1.
   c. Rebuild Heap.

Figure 11.1.15 Outline of heap sort.

Converting a vector to a heap is straightforward. A vector of length 1 is trivially a heap. Elements are added to the heap at the bottom and filter up until the new vector is again a heap. The process continues until the vector becomes a heap. Consider the code in Figure 11.1.16. Then

```
for i in 2..V'last loop
   j := i;
   while j > 1 loop
      if V(j) > V(j/2) then
         TEMP_ITEM := V(j);
         V(j)      := V(j/2);
         V(j/2)    := TEMP_ITEM;
         j := j/2;
      else
         j := 0;
      end if;
   end loop;
end loop;
```

Figure 11.1.16   Ada code to put a vector into heap form.

Consider the vector in the first line of Figure 11.1.17. Figure 11.1.17 illustrates how the code above rearranges the vector V into a heap.

```
i = 2, j = 2:   2  5  1  3  4  6   Initial conditions
i = 2, j = 2:   5  2  1  3  4  6   Swap v(j), v(j/2)
i = 2, j = 1:   5  2  1  3  4  6   Leave while loop
i = 3, j = 3:   5  2  1  3  4  6   V(1..3) a heap, j set to 1,
                                              leave while loop
i = 4, j = 4:   5  3  1  2  4  6   Swap v(j/2), v(j/2), set j = 2
i = 4, j = 2:   5  3  1  2  4  6   V(1..4) a heap, j set to 1,
                                              leave while loop
i = 5, j = 5:   5  4  1  2  3  6   Swap v(j), v(j/2), set j = 2
i = 5, j = 2:   5  4  1  2  3  6   V(1..5) a heap, j set to 1,
                                              leave while loop
i = 6, j = 6:   5  4  6  2  3  1   Swap v(j), v(j/2), set j = 3
i = 6, j = 3:   6  4  5  2  3  1   Swap v(j), v(j/2), set j = 1,
                                              leave loop
                V(1..6) now a heap
```

Figure 11.1.17   Converting a vector to a heap.

The first element in a heap is always the largest. To do a HEAP_SORT, the first and last elements of the heap are swapped, the heap size is decreased by 1, and the heap is rebuilt. The new last element is the largest in the slice before decreasing the slice's size by 1. Figure 11.1.18 lists the HEAP_SORT algorithm. A word of warning is in order. HEAP_SORT assumes that the integer index range in VECTOR is of the form 1..VECTOR_LENGTH.

```
generic
   type ITEM_TYPE is private;
   type VECTOR is array (integer range < >) of ITEM_TYPE;
   with function "<" (LEFT, RIGHT : ITEM_TYPE) return boolean;
procedure HEAP_SORT (V : in out VECTOR);
procedure HEAP_SORT (V : in out VECTOR) is
   J : integer;
```

Figure 11.1.18   HEAP_SORT. Continues on page 391.

390   Sorting   Chap. 11

```
procedure SWAP_ITEM (A, B : in out ITEM_ITEM) is
  TEMP_ITEM : ITEM_TYPE := A;
begin
  A := B;
  B := TEMP_ITEM;
end SWAP_ITEM;

begin
  -- Turn V into a Heap
  for I in 2..V'last loop
    J := I;
    while J > 1 loop
      if V(J/2) < V(J) then
        SWAP_ITEM ( V(J), V(J/2) );
        J := J/2;
      else
        J := 0;
      end if;
    end loop;
  end loop;
  -- now that V is a heap, Sort by swapping the first and last,
  -- then rebuilding
  for I in reverse V'first + 1..V'last loop
    SWAP_ITEM ( V(1), V(I) );
    -- Rebuild V(1..I - 1) into a heap
    J := 1;
      -- while the current node has children
      while 2 * J < i loop
        -- node has 2 children
        if (2 * J + 1) < i then
          if (V(2 * J) < V(J) or V(2 * J) = V(J)) and
             (V(2 * J + 1) < V(J) or V(2 * J * 1) = V(J)) then
            --Heap restored, set J to get out
            J :=i;
          elsif V(2 * J + 1) < V(2 * J) then
            -- Not a Heap and V(2 * J) largest child
            SWAP_ITEM ( V(J), V(2 * J) );
            J := 2 * J;
          else
            --Not a Heap and V(2 * J + 1) largest child
            SWAP_ITEM (V(J), V(2 * J + 1) );
            J := 2 * J + 1;
          end if;
        else -- only one child
          if V(J) < V(2 * J) then
            --not a heap, swap and reset J
            SWAP_ITEM ( V(J), V(2 * J) );
            J := 2 * J;
```

Figure 11.1.18 Continues on page 392.

```
        else
            J := I; -- it's a heap, get out
        end if;
      end if;
    end loop;
  end loop;
end HEAP_SORT;
```

Figure 11.1.18 Concluded.

Like QUICK_SORT and MERGE_SORT, HEAP_SORT is $O(n * \log_2(n))$. Unlike QUICK_SORT, HEAP_SORT is $O(n * \log_2(n))$ for all cases. In practice, QUICK_SORT usually gives better performance because its proportionality constant in $O(N * \log_2(N))$ is lower. However, HEAP_SORT does not use recursion like QUICK_SORT, nor does it need an extra array such as MERGE_SORT.

Radix Sort

Are there any sort algorithms that can operate in $O(n)$, where n is the number of items to be sorted? Under some very restricted conditions, the answer is yes but the cost is extra memory, and the main requirement is a fixed-length key. The key is examined bit by bit from the least significant bit to the most significant bit. The result of the first pass is two lists, one where each key ends in 0 and one where each key ends in 1. The lists are adjoined and the process is repeated for the next least significant bit. Again the result is two lists to be adjoined. An examination shows that the least two significant digits of the key are in order. After k passes, the keys of the least significant k digits are in order. If the key has m bits, the list is sorted after m passes (see Figure 11.1.19).

Assuming that the number of items to be sorted is n, then each pass is $O(n)$. After m passes, the result is a sort algorithm that is $O(n)$. The name of this sort is radix sort. It has its origins back in the days of the mechanical card sorter. The only time the author has seen the algorithm used was in the mid-1960s when decks of punched cards were being sorted using a mechanical card sorter.

The package GENERIC_UNBOUNDED_BINARY_SEARCH_TREE can be used to implement a sort. The elements of V are inserted into a binary search tree. Once the elements of V have been inserted into the tree, an inorder traversal returns the elements back in sorted order. The same method can be used to sort a linked list. This application was described in Chapter 8. The main drawback is the extra storage needed to build the tree.

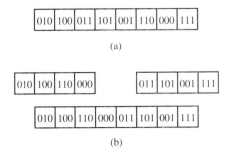

Figure 11.1.19 Simple radix sort on a binary key of length 3. (a) Array of eight objects with a 3-bit binary key. (b) Radix sort after first pass of ISB. Note that left array has ISB 0, right array ISB 1. Bottom adjoined.

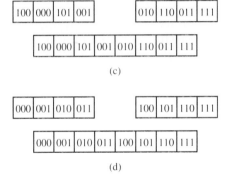

(c)

Figure 11.1.19 (c) Radix sort after second pass on middle bit. Top arrays adjoined to make bottom array. (d) Radix sort after third pass on the MSB. After top arrays adjoined, bottom array sorted.

(d)

11.2 EXTERNAL SORTS

The material in this section is typically part of a course in file and memory management. External sorts correspond to sorting of a sequential file of unknown length composed of records when a function exists to determine which one of two records precedes the other. Two methods will be sketched. Surprisingly, one is $O(n)$ and the other is $O(n*\log_2(n))$. The reader should keep in mind that internal sorts are done in memory. The record swaps, record accesses, and compares are all relatively quick. External sorts are done on external files. Record accesses and swaps correspond to reading and writing of files. Although the order of operations compares favorably between internal and external swaps, the time for each operation does not. Accesses for internal sorts occur in microseconds, while accesses for external sorts occur in milliseconds. The interested reader is referred to the Bibliography.

Consider the problem the telephone company has when preparing bills of customer long-distance toll charges. After completing a call, a data record is written to a file. This data would include the time the call was placed, the length of the call, the mode (operator assisted, collect, 800, etc.), the number called, the number making the call, and the billing number. At the end of the month every telephone subscriber gets their bill. Clearly, this file of calls has been sorted by billing number. Even the file for all toll calls made in a 1-hour period through a major switchboard is probably too long to be sorted in the memory of a computer. Eventually, all the month's calls must be sorted by billing number before the customers' bills can be prepared.

One method of sorting the phone company's billing files would be to perform an *external radix sort* on the file using the 10-digit phone number as a key. (Remember that the three-digit area code plus the seven-digit number equals a 10-digit key.) This radix sort takes 10 passes because the key is 10 digits long. Starting with the original unsorted file, the kth pass takes the $(11 - k)$th digit of the phone number and reads a record "call by call" until the end-of-file marker is reached. Each call is placed on one of 10 files. The first file contains all calls whose $(11 - k)$th digit ends in "0." The second file contains all calls whose $(11 - k)$th digit ends in "1," and so on. Once the end-of-file marker of the original file has been reached, a new file is created that equals the first file concatenated with the second file, which is concatenated with the third file, and so on. This file is the input to the next pass if more passes are to be made and the sorted file after all passes have been made.

The second method sketched is related to MERGE_SORT. Consider the simple problem of merging two external files that are already in order into a third file while preserving the order. An analogous problem was discussed in Chapter 7 when writing a nonrecursive merge procedure for two priority queues in the package GENERIC_UNBOUNDED_PRI-ORITY_QUEUE. The algorithm for merging files looks something like the pseudocode in Figure 11.2.1.

```
procedure MERGE_2_ORDERED_FILES ( FILE1 : in out FILE;
                                  FILE2 : in out FILE;
                                  FILE3 : in out FILE ) is

begin
  OPEN FIRST FILE FOR READING ITEMS;
  OPEN SECOND FILE FOR READING ITEMS;
  OPEN THIRD FILE FOR WRITING ITEMS;
  READ(FILE1, ITEM1);
  READ(FILE2, ITEM2)
  while not end_of_file(FILE1) and not end_of_file(FILE2) loop
    if ITEM1 < ITEM2 then
      WRITE(FILE3, ITEM1);
      READ(FILE1, ITEM1);
    else
      WRITE(FILE3, ITEM2);
      READ(FILE2, ITEM2);
    end if;
  end loop;
  if not end_of_file(FILE1) then
    -- copies remainder of file 1 to file 3
    COPY(FILE1, FILE3);
  else
    COPY(FILE2, FILE3);
  end if;
  CLOSE FILE1;
  CLOSE FILE2;
  CLOSE FILE3;
end MERGE_2_ORDERED_FILES;
```

Figure 11.2.1 Outline for external merge sort of two sorted files.

The algorithm is really quite simple. Yet it requires a data type item, a limited private type to pass files, procedures to open files of items for reading and writing, a procedure to get an item from the input file and put it on the output file, a way to compare two items for order, a way to check for the end of file, and a procedure to close files.

How can external files that are not already in order be sorted? The unsorted file is "distributed" into two temporary files, and these two files are merged into a third file. The process is repeated until the file is in order. A run is an ordered subsequence of items. When a file is distributed, a complete run is copied to the first file, the next run is copied to the second file, and so on. The process continues until the end-of-file marker for the file to be distributed is encountered. At this point the two files are merged run by run. Figure 11.2.2 illustrates the process. The beginning of the runs are marked accordingly.

File to Sort		File1		File2		Merged Files	
R1	21	R1	21	R2	55	R1,R2	21
	25		25		65		25
	44		44		90		44
	87		87	R4	13		55
R2	55	R3	12	R6	42		65
	65		16		91		87
	90		23		98		90
R3	12		35			R3,R4	12
	16		45				13
	23		61				16
	35		81				23
	45	R5	10				35
	61		39				45
	81		49				61
R4	13						81
R5	10					R5,R6	10
	39						39
	49						42
R6	42						49
	91						91
	98						98

Figure 11.2.2 Sort by distribution.

Note that the list in column 4 of Figure 11.2.2 has half as many runs in it as the list in column 1. If the process is repeated starting with the list in column 4, the result will have fewer runs. The number of runs is cut in half at each iteration while the average length of each run is doubled. Thus $\log_2(n)$ is the upper bound for the number of times that this process must be repeated for the case of a file in perfect reverse order. In this pathological case, each initial run will have length 1. Thus this sort is $O(n * \log_2(n))$. The pseudocode for this process is listed in Figure 11.2.3.

```
SORTED := false;
while not SORTED loop
  SORTED := true;
  OPEN FILE_TO_SORT TO READ;
  OPEN TEMP_FILE1 TO WRITE;
  OPEN TEMP_FILE2 TO WRITE;
  DISTRIBUTE FILE_TO_SORT OVER TEMP_FILE1 AND TEMP_FILE2;
  REWIND TEMP_FILE1 AND CHANGE STATUS TO READ;
  REWIND TEMP_FILE2 AND CHANGE STATUS TO READ;
  REWIND FILE_TO_SORT AND CHANGE STATUS TO WRITE;
  MERGE TEMP_FILE1 AND TEMP_FILE2 ONTO FILE_TO_SORT;
    -- Merge sets the the global flag sorted to false if it
    -- writes a record to Temp_file2
```

Figure 11.2.3 Pseudocode for external merge sort. Continues on page 396.

```
            CLOSE FILE_TO_SORT;
            CLOSE TEMP_FILE1;
            CLOSE TEMP_FILE2;
        end loop;
```

Figure 11.2.3   Concluded.

The actual Ada code is left as an exercise for the motivated student to develop. The implementation is more tedious than challenging. A generalization, called a polyphase sort, is needed for truly massive files. Polyphase distributes the unsorted file over *k* temporary files. When the distributing file is empty, it becomes one of the files distributed into, and one of the previous files is selected, rewound, and starts distributing over the new set of *k* files.

11.3 SORTING LINKED LISTS

Let ITEM_TYPE be some programmer-defined type that has a well-defined boolean operator < defined on it. Given the basic list data structure

```
type LIST_NODE;
type LIST is access LIST_NODE;
type LIST_NODE is
record
    ITEM : ITEM_TYPE;
    NEXT : LIST;
end record;
```

the question arises about how to sort a given linked list that uses the foregoing structure in ascending order. In a single linked list, nodes cannot be directly accessed, as was done in the arrays of Section 11.1.

One solution would be to note the similarity between a singly linked list and an external file. Both the file and the list can only be traversed in a forward manner. Once a node has been skipped past, it cannot be referenced without again starting at the beginning. This implies that the polyphase sort outlined in Section 11.2 can be mimicked. This is left to the exercises.

Another idea is to try to mimic various sorting methods from Section 11.1. Recall that the bubble sort compares adjacent items and swaps them if they are out of order. The main difference between the linked list bubble sort and the array-based bubble sort is that the length of the list is unknown. The following procedure transforms a bubble sort to sort lists.

```
procedure BUBBLE_SORT_LIST (L : in out LIST) is
    TEMP,                   -- References the current node
    TEMP_FIRST,             -- References the next node past TEMP in the list
    TEMP_SECOND,            -- References the second node past TEMP in the list
    TEMP_THIRD : LIST;  -- References the third node past TEMP in the lists
    SORTED : boolean    -- Signals when the list is finally sorted
begin
    -- Nothing to do if L is empty or has exactly one node
    if L /= null and then L.NEXT /= null then
        loop
            -- Assume the list is sorted
            SORTED := true;
            -- Check and see if the first two nodes are out of order
```

```
    if L.NEXT.ITEM < L.ITEM then
        -- Interchange the order of nodes 1 and 2 and reset L
        TEMP_FIRST := L;
        TEMP_SECOND := L.NEXT;
        TEMP_THIRD := TEMP_SECOND.NEXT;
        -- Make L reference old second node
        L := TEMP_SECOND;
        -- Make the second node the old first
        L.NEXT := TEMP_FIRST;
        -- Add the rest of the list on after the new second
        TEMP_FIRST.NEXT := TEMP_THIRD;
        -- Signal the list was not sorted after all
        SORTED := false;
    end if;
    -- Sort the rest of the list by comparing adjacent nodes.
    TEMP := L;
    while TEMP.NEXT.NEXT /= null loop
        -- Does the node two past TEMP belong one past TEMP
        if TEMP.NEXT.NEXT.ITEM < TEMP_L.NEXT.ITEM loop
            -- Swap similar to above
            TEMP_FIRST := TEMP.NEXT;
            TEMP_SECOND := TEMP_FIRST.NEXT;
            TEMP_THIRD := TEMP_SECOND.NEXT;
            TEMP := TEMP_SECOND;
            TEMP_SECOND.NEXT := TEMP_FIRST;
            TEMP_FIRST.NEXT := TEMP_THIRD;
            SORTED := false;
        end if
        -- GO TO NEXT NODE ON THE LIST
            TEMP := TEMP.NEXT;
        end loop;
        -- If the list was sorted, no swaps were made.
        exit when SORTED;
    end loop;
  end if;
end BUBBLE_SORT_LIST;
```

Note that BUBBLE_SORT_LIST swapped access types; it did not swap objects of ITEM_TYPE. Nothing is known about the structure of ITEM_TYPE. It could be something as simple as an integer or it could be a gigantic record. For a list of length n, BUBBLE_SORT_LIST is $O(n)$ for an already sorted list, and $O(n**2)$ for a random list.

It is easy to program a method that removes a node from one list and inserts it, in ascending order, onto a second list. This second list behaves like a priority queue. If the first list were in reverse order, any node taken off the front of this list would precede every node already inserted onto the second list. If the first list were already sorted, any element removed from the front of the first list would be placed at the end of the second list. Sorting a list in reverse order is $O(n)$, while sorting an already sorted list is $O(n**2)$. If the key being used to sort is a fixed-length array of items, the radix sorting algorithm outlined at the end of Section 1 can be a very efficient method for sorting a list. Other methods are outlined in the literature.

Sec. 11.3   Sorting Linked Lists

One of the goals of this book is to express all operations and algorithms in a reusable generic form. This particular problem does not allow for this. Consider the following generic subprogram formal parameter list:

```
generic
  type ITEM_TYPE is private;
  type NODE is private;
  type LIST is access NODE;
  with function "<" (LEFT, RIGHT : ITEM_TYPE) return boolean;
procedure LIST_SORT . . . . . . . .
```

The problem is that even though LIST is access NODE, there is no way to send the structure of NODE to the generic procedure. There is no concept of a formal record type for NODE. The internal structure of records is somewhat arbitrary, and the resulting probability of a match would be rare. Hopefully, this problem will be solved by Ada 9X when full inheritance and object-oriented capabilities are added to the language.

EXERCISES

Section 11.1 Internal Sorts

11.1.1 For the sort procedures indicated, replace the formal generic parameter list in the original generic procedure and implement the same procedures using the format generic parameter list below.

```
generic
  type ITEM_TYPE is private;
  type INDEX is (< >);
  type VECTOR is array (INDEX range < >) of ITEM_TYPE;
  with function "<" (LEFT, RIGHT : ITEM_TYPE) return boolean;
procedure NAME_SORT (V : in out VECTOR);
```

  a. BUBBLE_SORT as specified in Figure 11.1.2
  b. BUBBLE_SORT as specified in Figure 11.1.4
  c. SELECTION_SORT as specified in Figure 11.1.6
  d. SPEED_SORT as specified in Figure 11.1.7
  e. QUICK_SORT as specified in Figure 11.1.10
  f. MERGE_SORT as specified in Figure 11.1.13

11.1.2 For each of the generic sort procedures below, modify the formal procedure parameter list to include two additional mode out parameters of the form

```
procedure NAME_SORT ( V : in out VECTOR;
                  NUMBER_SWAPS :    out natural;
                  NUMBER_COMPS :    out natural);
```

where NUMBER_SWAPS is the number of swaps that the procedure did in sorting the vector V, and NUMBER_COMPS is the number of compares done in sorting the vector V.
  a. BUBBLE_SORT as specified in Figure 11.1.2
  b. BUBBLE_SORT as specified in Figure 11.1.4
  c. SELECTION_SORT as specified in Figure 11.1.6

d. SPEED_SORT as specified in Figure 11.1.7

e. QUICK_SORT as specified in Figure 11.1.10

f. MERGE_SORT as specified in Figure 11.1.13

g. HEAP_SORT as specified in Figure 11.1.17

h. If V_INORDER is a vector of *n* elements where the elements are in ascending order, if V_RE-VERSE is a vector of *n* elements in descending order, and if V_RANDOM is a vector of *n* elements placed in random order, then for a fixed value of *n*, finish the following two tables.

```
                       NUMBER COMPARES FOR N = _.


                              V_INORDER V_REVERSE V_RANDOM
BUBBLE_SORT,Figure 11.1.2
BUBBLE_SORT,Figure 11.1.4
SELECTION_SORT
SPEED_SORT
QUICK_SORT
MERGE_SORT
HEAP_SORT


                    NUMBER SWAPS FOR N =  _.


                              V_INORDER V_REVERSE V_RANDOM
BUBBLE_SORT,Figure 11.1.2
BUBBLE_SORT,Figure 11.1.4
SELECTION_SORT
SPEED_SORT
QUICK_SORT
MERGE_SORT
HEAP_SORT
```

11.1.3 Consider QUICK_SORT as specified in Figures 11.1.10 and 11.1.11.

    a. Modify the partition procedure so that the first, middle and last element in a vector are sorted and then the vector is partitioned. This strategy prevents intervals of length one from occurring.

    b. Compare the number of compares and swaps for your procedure in part a with the procedure in Figure 11.1.10. Use the test vectors listed in Exercise 11.1.2.

    c. Modify QUICK_SORT as specified in Figure 11.1.10 so that QUICK_SORT calls a bubble sort procedure if V'length < = 8.

    d. Compare the number of compares and swaps for your procedure in part c with the procedure in Figure 11.1.10. Use the test vectors listed in Exercise 11.1.2.

    e. Implement QUICK_SORT in Figure 11.1.10 without using recursion.

11.1.4 Implement MERGE_SORT as specified in Figure 11.1.13 without using recursion.

Section 11.2 External Sorts

11.2.1 Implement the external sort routine specified in Figure 11.2.3. Test your procedure for a file of random integers of unknown length.

Section 11.3 Sorting Linked Lists

Assume the following for all problems in this section:

```
type LIST_NODE;
type LIST is access LIST_NODE;
type LIST_NODE is
  record
     ITEM : INTEGER;
     NEXT : LIST;
  end record;
```

11.3.1 Devise an "insertion sort" algorithm to sort a LIST by deleting nodes from a first list and adding them in order to a second list.

11.3.2 Consider

```
package MY_QUEUE is new GENERIC_UNBOUNDED_QUEUE (ITEM_TYPE);
SPECIAL_QUEUE : MY_QUEUE.QUEUE;
```

where ITEM_TYPE is an arbirary programmer-defined structure that has a well-defined boolean function < defined on it. Instantiate GENERIC_UNBOUNDED_PRIORITY_QUEUE and write a procedure that sorts SPECIAL_QUEUE.

11.3.3 Suppose that

```
subtype DIGIT is integer range 0..9;
type ITEM_TYPE is array (integer range 1..5) of DIGIT;
type LIST_NODE;
type LIST is access LIST_NODE;
type LIST_NODE is
  record
     ITEM : ITEM_TYPE;
     NEXT : LIST;
  end record;
```

Write a procedure RADIX_LIST_SORT that sorts a list of this type using a radix sort outlined at the end of Section 11.3.

NOTES AND REFERENCES

There is an extensive literature available about sorting. Volume 2 of Knuth [28] is a good place to start. Miller and Petersen [38] have an excellent introduction to external sorts that focus on Ada implementations. The original sources for TREESORT are Floyd [19, 20] and Williams [50], while Hoare [23] was the first to investigate QUICKSORT. Shell [45] was the basis for SPEEDSORT. Baase [4], Aho, Hopcroft, and Ullman [3], and Sedgewick [44] all contain material related to sorting linked lists as well as time estimates for the methods listed in section 11.1. Another version of the package GENERIC_UNBOUNDED_PRIORITY_QUEUE was built up in Chapter 8, where a simple sort procedure based on binary trees is outlined.

12

Search Tables

Searching and sorting are two of the most common tasks in programming. Chapter 11 covered sorting. A restricted form of this problem is considered in Section 8.2, where binary search trees are examined in detail. In this chapter we concentrate on looking through some universal table to return data related to some key. The table, which is just an array of key-data pairs, will be composed of components of the form

```
type ELEMENT is
   record
      KEY  : KEY_TYPE;
      DATA : DATA_TYPE;
   end record;
```

Keys are a unique designator of an item and data is information associated with the key. Consider a phone book from an imaginary town where everyone has a unique name. The key used in the phone book is the person's last name followed by an optional first name or initial. The data associated with the key is the telephone number and an optional address.

When a compiler converts program text into computer instructions, the compiler must keep track of all the identifiers in the program. The compiler generates a symbol table, which is another example of a search table. The keys are the valid identifiers or reserved words for the language. The data includes information about the identifier's type, the possible attributes, the storage location of the value, and so on.

Simple databases with one key can also be implemented as a search table. Whether it is a system to record checks drawn on savings account organized by check number, the price and description of a file of items stocked by the friendly grocer organized by universal bar code identifiers, or information about doctors on call at a major hospital, the organizing of information for later retrieval and the timely accessing of that information are major tasks of search tables. For this chapter a search table is an ADT implemented as an array of key-data pairs. Figure 12.0.1(a) illustrates a search table set up for a sequential search, and Figure 12.0.1(b) illustrates a search table similar to one a hash function might access. In both cases the key is the student's last name and the data is the student's advisor.

What types of operations are performed on a search table? There are five major operations. First, there must be a mechanism for inserting a new key-data pair into the table.

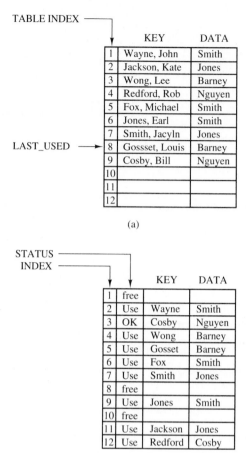

TABLE INDEX

	KEY	DATA
1	Wayne, John	Smith
2	Jackson, Kate	Jones
3	Wong, Lee	Barney
4	Redford, Rob	Nguyen
5	Fox, Michael	Smith
6	Jones, Earl	Smith
7	Smith, Jacyln	Jones
8	Gossset, Louis	Barney	← LAST_USED
9	Cosby, Bill	Nguyen
10		
11		
12		

(a)

STATUS INDEX

	STATUS	KEY	DATA
1	free		
2	Use	Wayne	Smith
3	OK	Cosby	Nguyen
4	Use	Wong	Barney
5	Use	Gosset	Barney
6	Use	Fox	Smith
7	Use	Smith	Jones
8	free		
9	Use	Jones	Smith
10	free		
11	Use	Jackson	Jones
12	Use	Redford	Cosby

(b)

Figure 12.0.1 (a) Sequential search table of size = 12 and with eight current entries stored randomly in locations 1 through 8. (b) Search table set up as a hash table. Each array element has one of three states: free and available for use, OK once used and no longer in use, and in use. Access and retrieval based on a function whose argument is a key. This table has the same entries as those in part (a).

Second, for a given key, there must be a procedure that allows the data for that particular key to be retrieved. Third, there must be a way to update the data associated with a key. Fourth, there must be a way delete a key-data pair from the table. Fifth and last, there must be a way of listing the elements in the table.

Consider the phone company's information service. All the operators must have access to a list of current subscribers. As new subscribers get their phones, their names, addresses, and numbers must be added to the table. Once a subscriber is in the directory, the operator must be able to get a person's number. There must be a way to change the information about a subscriber in case the subscriber moves or changes their number. If the subscriber moves out of the area, their name would be removed. Every so often the phone company prints a directory for customer use, so it is necessary to get the latest list to make up the new directory.

Some comments are in order about the last function, the listing of everything in the table. There are a variety of ways of organizing the data within the table. The first requirement for the list function is that eventually, each key-data pair in the search table is listed. The second requirement for the list function is that no key-data pair be listed twice until every key-data pair has been listed once. There is no requirement to list this sequence in any particular order.

The basic documentation associated with a search table is shown in Figure 12.0.2. Four operations help to maintain the table. Four distinct variations of search tables are developed in this chapter. The operations in all four varieties are exactly the same. The only difference that the programmer sees in the four abstract data types are variations in the formal generic parameters. Except for minor variations at instantiation, any program that uses one type of search table will work with any of the other three.

GENERAL ADT SPECIFICATION FOR SEARCH_TABLE

Description

A search table is a structure for storing and retrieval of data based on a programmer-supplied key. The five basic operations that allow a new key-data pair to be inserted, updated, retrieved, deleted, or listed are provided. All entries are pairs composed of a key and the data associated with that key. Certain other utility functions are provided. These allow the programmer to see if an entry with a given key is in the table, to copy one table into a table that may be of different size, or to reset a pointer that marks the last entry listed to the beginning of the list. Tables of any specified size can be created. Entries with duplicate keys are not allowed.

Programmer-Supplied Data Structures or Specifications

The programmer must supply a KEY_TYPE and a DATA_TYPE at instantiation. The table is composed of records that are made up of both types.

Operations

Name	Description
CREATE	Takes a positive number size and a variable T of table type and returns a table with size entries.
INSERT	Takes a pair (KEY, DATA) and inserts this entry into the table. All keys in the table must be distinct.
GET_DATA_FOR_KEY	For a given key-data pair already in the table, this operation returns the data associated with an exact match of key.
UPDATE	For a given key-data pair already in the table, this operation replaces the field associated with the data with a newly supplied data value provided that there is an exact match of the supplied key.
DELETE	Deletes a given key-data pair already in the table if there is an exact match with the supplied key.
CLEAR	Deletes all key-data pairs from the table.
COPY	Copies the key-data pairs from one table to a second table. The tables do not need to be the same size.
LIST_NEXT_KEY_DATA	Returns the next key-data pair in the table. Eventually returns all key-data pairs before starting to repeat itself.

Figure 12.0.2 Documentation for SEARCH_TABLE. Continues on page 404.

KEY_IN_TABLE	Returns true if the supplied key corresponds to any key of a key-data pair already in the table.
SET_TO_START	Used in conjunction with LIST_NEXT_KEY_DATA in order to start at the beginning of the table.
LOAD_FACTOR	Function that returns the ratio of the number of key-data pairs in the table to the size of the table.
TABLE_SIZE	Function that returns the size of the table.
COUNT	Function that returns the number of key-data pairs in the table.

Exceptions

Five exceptions can occur. The exception TABLE_NOT_DEFINED can be raised by any operation except CREATE. This exception occurs when an operation is attempted on a table with unknown size. If a table has no room in it for an additional entry during an attempt to insert or to copy, a TABLE_FULL entry is raised. TABLE_FULL also occurs if CREATE raises a storage error when creating a table. An attempt to get data associated with a given key or to update the data portion of a pair with a given key or to delete a pair with a given key will raise KEY_IS_NOT_FOUND if no entry with the given key is included in the table. The exception KEY_IS_IN_TABLE is raised when an attempt is made to insert another pair with the same key. TABLE_EMPTY is raised only when an attempt to list an empty table occurs.

Warnings

The first operation on any table must be a call to CREATE in order to set the SIZE of the TABLE. When using the closed hash table, SIZE must be chosen so that SIZE rem 13 /= 0 or the collision strategy will fail. All other warnings are implemented dependent.

Figure 12.0.2 Concluded.

One major operation, UPDATE, is redundant, but the need for this operation occurs so often that it is included. A call to DELETE followed by a call to INSERT accomplishes the same thing, usually at considerable extra overhead.

12.1 SEQUENTIAL IMPLEMENTATIONS

Sequential search tables are carried out in one of two ways. They are either arrays of components of key-data pairs or they are arrays of priority lists of nodes of key-data pairs. The list implementations are left to the exercises. The basic common data structure of the three sequential implementations of the search table ADT array is shown in Figure 12.1.1. For all three implementations, the first component of type TABLE, here the variable LAST_USED, refers to the number of key-data pairs in the table. The defined pairs are stored in LIST(1 .. LAST_USED), and the components in LIST(LAST+1 .. SIZE) are not in use. The variable LIST_LAST is the index of the last pair returned by the procedure LIST_NEXT_KEY_DATA. Figure 12.1.2 contains the basic specification for the ADT GENERIC_UNORDERED_ARRAY_SEARCH table. The formal parameter "TO" of the operation COPY must in "in out." This is necessary to order to reference the size parameter of the variant record TO.

```
type ELEMENT is
  record
    KEY  : KEY_TYPE;
    DATA : DATA_TYPE;
  end record;
type SEARCH_ARRAY is array (positive range <>) of ELEMENT;
type SEARCH_TABLE (SIZE : positive) is
  record
    LAST_USED : natural := 0;
    LIST_LAST : natural := 0;
    LIST      : SEARCH_ARRAY (1..SIZE);
  end record;
type TABLE is access SEARCH_TABLE;
```

Figure 12.1.1 Sequential array implemented data structure.

```
generic
  type KEY_TYPE is private;
  type DATA_TYPE is private;
package GENERIC_UNORDERED_ARRAY_SEARCH_TABLE is
  type TABLE is limited private;
  procedure CREATE             ( THIS_TABLE :    out TABLE;
                                 SIZE       : in     positive);
  procedure INSERT             ( INTO_TABLE : in out TABLE;
                                 KEY        : in     KEY_TYPE;
                                 DATA       : in     DATA_TYPE);
  procedure UPDATE             ( THIS_TABLE : in out TABLE;
                                 KEY        : in     KEY_TYPE;
                                 DATA       : in     DATA_TYPE);
  procedure DELETE             ( FROM_TABLE : in out TABLE;
                                 KEY        : in     KEY_TYPE);
  procedure LIST_NEXT_KEY_DATA ( IN_TABLE   : in out TABLE;
                                 KEY        :    out KEY_TYPE;
                                 DATA       :    out DATA_TYPE);
  procedure CLEAR              ( THIS_TABLE : in out TABLE);
  procedure COPY               ( FROM       : in     TABLE;
                                 TO         : in out TABLE);
  procedure SET_TO_START       ( THIS_TABLE : in out TABLE);
  function LOAD_FACTOR         ( OF_TABLE   : TABLE ) return float;
  function TABLE_SIZE          ( OF_TABLE   : TABLE ) return natural;
  function COUNT               ( OF_TABLE   : TABLE ) return natural;
  function GET_DATA_FOR_KEY    ( FROM_TABLE : TABLE;
                                 KEY        : KEY_TYPE) return DATA_TYPE;
  function KEY_IN_TABLE        ( IN_TABLE   : TABLE;
                                 KEY        : KEY_TYPE) return boolean;


  TABLE_NOT_DEFINED : exception;
  TABLE_FULL        : exception;
  TABLE_EMPTY       : exception;
```

Figure 12.1.2 ADT GENERIC_UNORDERED_ARRAY_SEARCH_TABLE. Continues on page 406.

Sec. 12.1   Sequential Implementations

```
KEY_IS_NOT_FOUND   : exception;
KEY_IS_IN_TABLE    : exception;

private
  type ELEMENT is
    record
      KEY  : KEY_TYPE;
      DATA : DATA_TYPE;
    end record;
  type SEARCH_LIST is array (positive range <>) of ELEMENT;
  type SEARCH_TABLE (SIZE : positive) is
    record
      LAST_USED  : natural := 0;
      LIST_LAST  : natural := 0;
      LIST       : SEARCH_LIST (1..SIZE);
    end record;
  type TABLE is access SEARCH_TABLE;
end GENERIC_UNORDERED_ARRAY_SEARCH_TABLE;
```

Figure 12.1.2   Concluded.

Figure 12.1.3 lays out an array-based search table used by the ADT GENERIC_UN-ORDERED_ARRAY_SEARCH_TABLE. Implementation of this package is straightforward. Every table must first have its size set. This is done by a call to the procedure CREATE that follows.

```
procedure CREATE        ( THIS_TABLE :    out TABLE;
                          SIZE        : in positive) is
  --Returns a table that will hold SIZE KEY-data pairs.
  --Exception TABLE_FULL raised if a storage_error occurs
begin
  THIS_TABLE := new SEARCH_TABLE (SIZE);
exception
  when storage_error =>
    raise TABLE_FULL;
end CREATE;
```

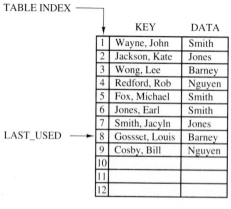

TABLE INDEX

LAST_USED

	KEY	DATA
1	Wayne, John	Smith
2	Jackson, Kate	Jones
3	Wong, Lee	Barney
4	Redford, Rob	Nguyen
5	Fox, Michael	Smith
6	Jones, Earl	Smith
7	Smith, Jacyln	Jones
8	Gossset, Louis	Barney
9	Cosby, Bill	Nguyen
10		
11		
12		

Figure 12.1.3   Unordered array-based search table set up using the private part in Figure 12.1.2 with T. SIZE = 2 and T.LAST_USED = 8. Insertion or deletion of a key-data pair first requires a sequential search and often a shift of a slice of T.LIST to make room or cover a deleted item.

An element is added onto the list at index LAST_USED+1. Since keys must be unique, the table must first be searched to ensure that the key is not already present. To return the data associated with a given key, the list is sequentially searched until the key is found. These two equations are listed below.

```
procedure INSERT     ( INTO_TABLE : in out TABLE;
                       KEY         : in    KEY_TYPE;
                       DATA        : in    DATA_TYPE) is
  -- Inserts a KEY-data pair (KEY,Data) into a table.
  -- Entries with duplicate keys are not allowed.
  -- Exception TABLE_NOT_DEFINED raised if SIZE of INTO_TABLE undefined,
  --           which occurs when INTO_TABLE = null.
  -- Exception TABLE_FULL raised if no space is available
  -- Exception KEY_IS_IN_TABLE raised if a key-data pair with a
  --           given specific KEY is already in the table
begin
  if INTO_TABLE = null then
    raise TABLE_NOT_DEFINED;
  elsif INTO_TABLE.LAST_USED = INTO_TABLE.SIZE then
    raise TABLE_FULL;
  else
    -- Make sure that key is not already in the table
    for INDEX in 1..INTO_TABLE.LAST_USED loop
      if KEY = INTO_TABLE.LIST (INDEX).KEY then
        raise KEY_IS_IN_TABLE;
      end if;
    end loop;
    -- Key not in table, insert at the first available slot
    INTO_TABLE.LAST_USED := INTO_TABLE.LAST_USED + 1;
    INTO_TABLE.LIST(INTO_TABLE.LAST_USED) := (KEY, DATA);
    INTO_TABLE.LIST_LAST := 0;
  end if;
end INSERT;


function GET_DATA_FOR_KEY (FROM_TABLE : TABLE;
                           KEY        : KEY_TYPE) return DATA_TYPE is
  -- Returns the data field for a given KEY-data pair already in
  -- the table.
  -- Exception TABLE_NOT_DEFINED raised if SIZE of FROM_TABLE undefined,
  --           which occurs when FROM_TABLE = null.
  -- Exception KEY_IS_NOT_FOUND raised if no key-data pair with
  --           the specific KEY is in the table FROM_TABLE.
begin
  if FROM_TABLE = null then
    raise TABLE_NOT_DEFINED;
  else
    for INDEX in positive range 1..FROM_TABLE.LAST_USED loop
      if KEY = FROM_TABLE.LIST(INDEX).KEY then
        return FROM_TABLE.LIST(INDEX).DATA;
      end if;
```

```
      end loop;
        raise KEY_IS_NOT_FOUND;
    end if;
  end GET_DATA_FOR_KEY;
```

Those two operations reveal the shortcomings of this implementation. The elements appear in the table roughly in the order inserted. There is no way to determine if a key is in the table except by searching the entire table. If the table is stable, the operation GET_DATA_FOR_KEY is the most used operation, and the implementation should optimize this operation. The instance of GET_DATA_FOR_KEY above is $O(n)$, and it is clearly not optimized.

One way to optimize GET_DATA_FOR_KEY is to arrange the table so that all the key-data pairs are in ascending order by key (see Figure 12.1.4). To insert key-data pairs into the table in ascending order, a boolean procedure < must be added to the formal generic parameter listed in Figure 12.1.2. No other changes need to be made to Figure 12.1.2; the private section of the figure remains unchanged. The formal generic parameter list becomes as shown in Figure 12.1.5.

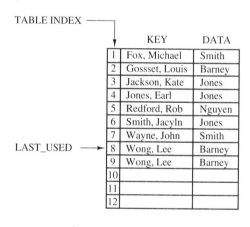

TABLE INDEX

	KEY	DATA
1	Fox, Michael	Smith
2	Gossset, Louis	Barney
3	Jackson, Kate	Jones
4	Jones, Earl	Jones
5	Redford, Rob	Nguyen
6	Smith, Jacyln	Jones
7	Wayne, John	Smith
8	Wong, Lee	Barney
9	Wong, Lee	Barney
10		
11		
12		

LAST_USED → 8

Figure 12.1.4 Search table T ordered by key. A binary search strategy can be used during insertion, deletion, update, and retrieval. Insertion or deletion may still result in a shift of a slice of T.List. This is what happened when "Cosby, Bill" was deleted and "Wong, Lee" moved from index = 9 to index = 8 T.List(2..9) was assigned to T.List(1..8).

```
generic
  type KEY_TYPE is private;
  type DATA_TYPE is private;
  with function "<" (LEFT, RIGHT) return boolean is <>;
  package GENERIC_ORDERED_ARRAY_SEARCH_TABLE is
GENERIC_ORDERED_ARRAY_SEARCH_TABLE.
```

Figure 12.1.5 Formal generic parameters list for GENERIC_ORDERED_ARRAY_SEARCH_TABLE.

If the key is some built-in Ada type with a defined built-in function "<" the function does not need to be referenced at instantiation. Now that the list is in order, a divide-and-conquer strategy called *binary search* can be implemented. Binary search attempts to divide the part of the table being searched in half at each pass. At the kth pass, $N/2**k$ key-data pairs in the table remain to be searched. Searching goes on until $N <= 2**k$, or at most $\log_2(n)$ times. Binary search compares the key being searched for with the key-data pair in the middle of the region of the table being searched. There are three possibilities. If they are equal, the search is successful. If the key being searched for is less than the middle key, repeat the process on the first half or the region in the table. If not, search the last half of the region of the table. The function GET_DATA_FOR_KEY can be coded using a binary search strategy as follows:

```
function GET_DATA_FOR_KEY  ( FROM TABLE : TABLE;
                             KEY        : KEY_TYPE) return DATA_TYPE is
  -- Returns the data field for a given KEY-DATA pair already in the table
  -- Exception TABLE_NOT_DEFINED raised if SIZE of FROM_TABLE undefined,
  --           which occurs when FROM_TABLE = null.
  -- Exception KEY_IS_NOT_FOUND raised if no key-data pair with
  --           the specific KEY is in the table FROM_TABLE.
  LEFT    : natural := 1;
  RIGHT   : natural := FROM_TABLE.LAST_USED;
  MIDDLE  : natural;
begin
  if FROM_TABLE = null then
    raise TABLE_NOT_DEFINED;
  elsif FROM_TABLE.LAST_USED = 0 then
    --If table is empty
    raise KEY_IS_NOT_FOUND;
  else
    --Do a binary search for the correct position
    loop
      MIDDLE := (LEFT + RIGHT)/2;
      if LEFT > RIGHT then
        raise KEY_IS_NOT_FOUND;
      elsif KEY = FROM_TABLE.LIST(MIDDLE).KEY then
        return FROM_TABLE.LIST(MIDDLE).DATA;
      elsif KEY < FROM_TABLE.LIST(MIDDLE).KEY then
        RIGHT := MIDDLE - 1;
      else
        LEFT := MIDDLE + 1;
      end if;
    end loop;
  end if;
end GET_DATA_FOR_KEY;
```

If n is the number of key-data pairs in the table, the previous linear table's search strategy operation count is $O(n)$. The binary search strategy operation count is $O(\log_2 n)$ for both returning the data field associated with a given key or for determining that a given key is not in the table. Five of the seven major operations in this ADT can be optimized. Both the ordered array and the unordered array versions of this search ADT are fully implemented in the exercises.

12.2 HASHING METHODS

In Section 12.1 the search tables used arrays where the key-data pairs were stored sequentially in an array. All the operations that insert, update, delete, or retrieve data from a table based on a given key value execute between $O(\log_2 n)$ and $O(n)$, where n is the number of entries in the table. Suppose that instead of doing a sequential or binary search on the table, a function that uses the key type as an argument returns the place in the table to insert or to locate the key-data pair. Such a function would operate in $O(1)$ or constant time.

Let KEY be one the possible values of a variable of KEY_TYPE. The programmer-supplied function, called a *hash function*, must compute a positive number based on this value. Let SIZE denote the number of elements that the hash table can hold, and suppose that the index of the table ranges from 1 to SIZE. Once the function computes this positive hash value, the place in the table where the key-data pair is is found by

```
INDEX := 1 + (HASH(KEY) rem SIZE);
```

If A is the set of all addresses, the hash function has the mathematical notation

```
HASH : KEY_TYPE ⟶ A
```

The number of possible key values is usually much, much larger than the size of the table, so the problem of what to do when

```
(HASH(KEY_1) rem SIZE) = (HASH(KEY_2) rem SIZE)
```

must be addressed. *Synonyms* are keys that are mapped into the same place. Handling the synonym problem is called *collision resolution*. Collision resolution strategies find other locations in the array in which to store the key-data pair. The resolution must be done so that the key-data pair can always be updated, deleted, or retrieved later.

What are the characteristics of a good hashing function? First, a good hashing function should be easy to compute. The second requirement is that the hash function should map any key-data pair into any table location with equal probability. In other words, the hash function must uniformly distribute the key-data pairs over the index space. Suppose that the keys are three-digit integers. The keys 123, 223, 113, and 122 all have, pairwise, two digits in common. The third digit, pairwise, differs by one. A good hashing function would not map these keys into the same index neighborhood. A bad hashing function for valid Ada identifiers would be the simple function that returns a value based only on the first character's place in the alphabet. If so, then

```
H('Ada') = H('Al_Steak') = ('algebra') = 1
H('zoo') = H('Zebra') = H('Z2') = 26
```

A quick look at any dictionary shows that the distribution of words by first letter is not even. The same is true of Ada identifiers.

The first requirement is computing the table location is a hashing function that converts the key to a positive integer. If the key is a string type, then

```
function HASH (KEY : string ) return positive is
   ANSWER : positive := 1;
   MULTIPLIER : constant positive := 29;
   DIVISOR    : constant positive := integer'last/31;
begin
   for INDEX in KEY'length loop
      ANSWER := ANSWER rem DIVISOR;
      ANSWER := MULTIPLIER*ANSWER + character'pos(KEY(INDEX));
   end loop;
   return ANSWER;
end HASH;
```

is one possible choice. Picking the table size, the value of MULTIPLIER, and the value of DIVISOR is more art than science. Clearly, the choice of MULTIPLIER and DIVISOR should not ever raise a numeric_error. What is known is that the three numbers should be relatively prime. Two numbers are relative prime if the only number that divides each exactly is 1. The easiest way to ensure this is to choose numbers TABLE_SIZE, MULTIPLIER, and DIVISOR all to be prime.

The second requirement, often omitted by naive programmers, is systematically to scatter the positive computed hash value. The name *hash* comes from chopping the number into parts, performing an intermediate operation on each part, combining the results, and then scaling the value to the table size. The midsquare method first squares the number and then extracts digits from both ends before scaling. For example, if HASH(KEY) is four digits long, HASH(KEY)$**2$ is eight digits long. The function shown in Figure 12.2.1 takes a four-digit positive number, squares the number, and takes two digits off each end. It returns the middle four digits. The two assumptions in Figure 12.2.1 are that SIZE is less than 10000, and L$*$L is less than positive'last.

```
function MID_SQ(KEY : positive) return natural is
begin
  -- extract two leftmost digits
  --throw out right two digits, keep the middle four
  return (KEY*KEY/100) rem 10000;
end MID_SQ;
```

Figure 12.2.1 Midsquare hashing method of a four-digit number.

The last method examined is folding (Figure 12.2.2). After converting a key to a natural number P, the number P is "chopped" into *m*-digit pieces. These pieces are somehow combined. The first function repeatedly peels off the two right-hand digits of P and adds them together while ignoring the carry into the hundreds digit. The second repeatedly adds and divides by SIZE. The method FOLD_1. assumes that TABLE_SIZE is less than 100.

```
function FOLD_1(KEY : positive) return natural is
  TEMP   : positive := KEY / 100;
  ANSWER : positive := KEY rem 100;
begin
  while TEMP > 0 loop
    ANSWER := (ANSWER + TEMP rem 100) rem 100;
    TEMP := TEMP/100;
  end loop
  return ANSWER;
end FOLD_1;

function FOLD_2(KEY, TABLE_SIZE : positive) return natural is
  TEMP   : positive := KEY / TABLE_SIZE;
  ANSWER : positive := KEY rem TABLE_SIZE;
begin
  while TEMP > 0 loop
    ANSWER := (ANSWER + TEMP rem TABLE_SIZE) rem TABLE_SIZE;
```

Figure 12.2.2 Two examples of hashing by folding. Continues on page 412.

```
      TEMP := TEMP/TABLE_SIZE;
   end loop
   return ANSWER;
end FOLD_2;
```

Figure 12.2.2   Concluded.

Once the positive hashed key value has been converted to a positive number it must be mapped into the interval [1,SIZE]. The easiest way is to add one to the remainder after dividing by SIZE, that is, use

```
1 + (HASH(KEY) REM SIZE)
```

This is the last step unless the hash value is processed further.

The problem of collision resolution is examined next. Recall that a collision occurs when making an attempt to insert two distinct keys into the same location. This does not mean that

```
HASH(KEY_1) = HASH(KEY_2)
```

but it does mean that

```
1 + HASH(KEY_1) rem TABLE_SIZE) = INDEX = 1 + (HASH(KEY_2) rem TABLE_SIZE)
```

No matter how it occurs, there must be a consistent method for finding a place to insert the second key. This process is called *collision resolution.*

The possibility of collisions must be recognized and allowed for in all the basic search operations that use a hashing strategy. If the operation GET_DATA_FOR_KEY is used and finds the table location filled with another key-data pair that contains a different key than the one being searched for, it must continue its search. The same is true for the UPDATE operation.

One simple but largely ineffective method of resolving collisions is called *linear probing.* Linear probing starts looking for an empty table element by examining the next table location. If that location is full, it goes on to the next index. A simple loop that implements this strategy is

```
INDEX := 1 + (HASH(KEY) rem TABLE_SIZE);
if TABLE(INDEX) /= EMPTY then
  for COUNT in 1..TABLE_SIZE loop
    INDEX := 1 + (INDEX rem TABLE_SIZE);
    exit when TABLE(INDEX) = EMPTY;
  end loop;
end if;
```

This method has the unfortunate side effect of clustering. Clustering occurs when a large contiguous sequence of table entries are all in use. This is bad, for two reasons. A good hashing function attempts to place key-data pairs randomly into the hash table. When a table has several large clusters, the probability of a collision increases. The collision resolution process may cause either one cluster to grow larger or two large clusters to join. This leads to a larger cluster. The result is that the hashing function behaves less randomly while spending more time resolving collisions. As collisions become more common, the hashing behaves more like $O(n)$ instead of $O(1)$. Once a key is hashed into a cluster, the cluster must be searched, sequentially, for the key. If a new key-data pair is to be inserted in the cluster, it ends up being inserted at the boundary of the cluster. Sequentially searching a cluster becomes an $O(\text{size})$ operation, where "size" refers to the number of key-data pairs in the cluster.

Prime probing is a simple modification of linear probing. A prime number, such as 13, is selected as a package constant. Every thirteenth entry is examined until a place to insert the key-data pair is found. It is important that the prime number selected not divide the TABLE_SIZE. To understand why, suppose that the prime selected is 5 and the TABLE_SIZE is 15. If index = 3 is full, the only other entries probed are 8 and 13. If the prime 7 had been selected, eventually every table entry is probed. Note that 7 does not divide 15, but 5 does divide 15.

Quadratic probing is a third collision resolution method. If TABLE_SIZE is a prime number and

```
INDEX := 1 + (HASH(KEY) rem TABLE_SIZE)
```

is occupied, the search proceeds using the square of the number of probes attempted; that is, the locations

```
INDEX+1, INDEX+4, INDEX+9, INDEX+16 , ...
```

are probed to see if they are free. The one problem with quadratic probing is that only half the number of entries in the table are examined.

A fourth simple collision resolution strategy is *double hashing*. If a collision occurs with the first function, a second function computes a number between 1 and TABLE_SIZE. Let H' denotes a number between 1 and TABLE_SIZE-1, double hashing probes the following locations:

```
INDEX + H', INDEX + 2*H', INDEX + 3*H', ...
```

If TABLE_SIZE and H' are relatively prime, the double hashing sequence will eventually probe every location in the hash table.

The strategies described above are called *open addressing*. Any successful collision resolution strategy must be both computationally simple to implement and simultaneously scattering the key-data pairs throughout the table. Scattering preserves the randomness of the hash function.

12.3 IMPLEMENTING A CLOSED HASH TABLE

A hash table is a closed table if the number of key-data pairs that the table can hold is fixed. Because of the insert and delete operations, every element in a closed hash table has three states. The element has either never been used, is now in use, or is now free but was once used. The "now free but once used" state is important in retrieval operations. Consider the case where KEY_1 is inserted at INDEX_1. Later, the hash function attempts to put KEY_2 into the same index, but the collision resolution strategy places it at INDEX_2. Later still, KEY_1 is deleted, freeing INDEX_1, and an attempt to access the key-data pair with key KEY_2 is made. The first place looked is the empty location at INDEX_1. If the retrieval operation does not know that INDEX_1 was once used, it would raise an exception because it could not find the key-data pair.

The data structure for the implementation of the closed hash table must look like

```
type ELEMENT_STATUS is (FREE, IN_USE, NOW_FREE);
type ELEMENT is
   record
      STATUS : ELEMENT_STATUS := FREE;
      KEY    : KEY_TYPE;
      DATA   : DATA_TYPE;
   end record;
type HASH_TABLE is array (positive range <>) of ELEMENT;
type SEARCH_TABLE (SIZE : positive) is
   record
      COUNT     : NATURAL := 0;
      LIST_LAST : NATURAL := SIZE;
      LIST      : HASH_TABLE (1..SIZE);
   end record;
type TABLE is access SEARCH_TABLE;
```

This data structure is similar to the data structure of previous tables. Figure 12.3.1 exhibits a simple example structure. COUNT is merely the number of entries in the table. LIST_LAST is the index of the last key-data pair listed. The full specification for the ADT GENERIC_CLOSED_HASH_TABLE is given in Figure 12.3.2.

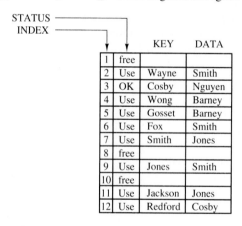

Figure 12.3.1 Closed hash search table T set up using the data structure in Figure 12.3.2. The table T can hold 12 key-data pairs, but it currently has only eight pairs in it. Note the status component of each element. This is necessary during hashing so that the correct cell can be found.

```
generic
   type KEY_TYPE is private;
   type DATA_TYPE is private;
   with function HASH (KEY : KEY_TYPE) return natural;
package GENERIC_CLOSED_HASH_SEARCH_TABLE is
   type TABLE is limited private;
   procedure CREATE        ( THIS_TABLE :    out TABLE;
                             SIZE       : in     positive);
   procedure INSERT        ( INTO_TABLE : in out TABLE;
                             KEY        : in     KEY_TYPE);
                             DATA       : in     DATA_TYPE);
   procedure UPDATE        ( THIS_TABLE : in out TABLE;
```

Figure 12.3.2 ADT GENERIC_CLOSED_HASH_TABLE. Continues on page 415.

```
                                           KEY          : in      KEY_TYPE;
                                           DATA         : in      DATA_TYPE);
      procedure DELETE               ( FROM_TABLE : in out TABLE;
                                           KEY          : in      KEY_TYPE);
      procedure LIST_NEXT_KEY_DATA   ( IN_TABLE   : in out TABLE;
                                           KEY          :    out KEY_TYPE);
                                           DATA         :    out DATA_TYPE);
      procedure CLEAR                ( THIS_TABLE : in out TABLE);
      procedure COPY                 ( FROM       : in      TABLE;
                                           TO           : in out TABLE);
      procedure SET_TO_START         ( THIS_TABLE : in out TABLE);
      function LOAD_FACTOR           ( OF_TABLE   : TABLE ) return float;
      function TABLE_SIZE            ( OF_TABLE   : TABLE ) return natural;
      function COUNT                 ( OF_TABLE   : TABLE ) return natural;
      function GET_DATA_FOR_KEY      ( FROM_TABLE : TABLE;
                                           KEY          : KEY_TYPE) return DATA_TYPE;
      function KEY_IN_TABLE          ( IN_TABLE   : TABLE;
                                           KEY          : KEY_TYPE) return boolean;

   TABLE_NOT_DEFINED : exception;
   TABLE_FULL        : exception;
   TABLE_EMPTY       : exception;
   KEY_IS_NOT_FOUND  : exception;
   KEY_IS_IN_TABLE   : exception;


private
   type ELEMENT_STATUS is (FREE, IN_USE, NOW_FREE);
   type ELEMENT is
     record
       STATUS : ELEMENT_STATUS := FREE;
       KEY    : KEY_TYPE;
       DATA   : DATA_TYPE;
     end record;
   type HASH_TABLE is array(natural range <>) of ELEMENT;
   type SEARCH_TABLE (SIZE : positive) is
     record
       COUNT     : natural := 0;
       LIST_LAST : natural := SIZE;
       LIST      : HASH_TABLE (1..SIZE);
     end record;
   type TABLE is access SEARCH_TABLE;
end GENERIC_CLOSED_HASH_SEARCH_TABLE;
```

Figure 12.3.2   Concluded.

The operation LOAD FACTOR is particularly important for the ADT GEN-
ERIC_CLOSED_HASH_SEARCH_TABLE. The operation count for this ADT is a function
of the load factor. Once the load factor gets above 0.7, the operation count goes from $O(1)$ to
$O(n)$ as the load factor tends to 1. The function LOAD_FACTOR is trivial.

```
function LOAD_FACTOR ( OF_TABLE : TABLE) return float is
    -- Returns the ratio of the number KEY-data pairs in the table
    -- to the size of the table.
    -- Exception TABLE_NOT_DEFINED raised if SIZE of OF_TABLE undefined,
    --          which occurs when OF_TABLE = null.
  begin
    if OF_TABLE = null then
      raise TABLE_NOT_DEFINED;
    else
      return float(OF_TABLE.COUNT)/float(OF_TABLE.SIZE);
    end if;
  end LOAD_FACTOR;
```

Intuitively, as a closed hash table fills, it is more likely that collisions will occur. As more collisions occur, the more likely it is that the basic ADT operations will begin to mimic their counterparts in the unordered search array case. This reason for this change in complexity is that as the hash table fills up, it acts more like an unordered sequential search with a random starting point. The solution is to copy the hash table into a larger table which results in reduced overhead.

The implementation depends on the collision resolution strategy chosen. For example, the implementation that follows uses a prime probing strategy with prime factor 13. (All closed hash operations illustrated here and in the exercises use prime probing with factor 13 unless otherwise noted.) Assuming that TABLE_SIZE is not divisible by 13 and that the hash table is not full, this strategy will always result in an insertion.

```
procedure DELETE ( FROM_TABLE : in out TABLE;
                   KEY         : in     KEY_TYPE) is
  -- Deletes a given KEY-DATA pair already in the table FROM_TABLE. The
  -- KEY field must match the supplied KEY.
  -- Exception TABLE_NOT_DEFINED raised if SIZE of FROM_TABLE undefined,
  --          which occurs when FROM_TABLE = null.
  -- Exception KEY_IS_NOT_FOUND raised if no key-data pair with
  --          the specific KEY is in the table FROM_TABLE.
  INDEX : natural;
begin
  if FROM_TABLE = null then
    raise TABLE_NOT_DEFINED;
  else
    INDEX := 1 + (HASH (KEY) rem FROM_TABLE.SIZE);
    for COUNT in 1..FROM_TABLE.SIZE loop
      if FROM_TABLE.LIST(INDEX).STATUS = FREE then
        raise KEY_IS_NOT_FOUND;
      elsif FROM_TABLE.LIST(INDEX).STATUS = IN_USE and then
            FROM_TABLE.LIST(INDEX).KEY = KEY then
        FROM_TABLE.LIST(INDEX).STATUS := NOW_FREE;
        FROM_TABLE.COUNT := FROM_TABLE.COUNT - 1;
        FROM_TABLE.LIST_LAST := FROM_TABLE.SIZE;
        return;
      else
        --collision resolution uses prime probing
```

```
        INDEX := 1 + ((INDEX + 12) rem FROM_TABLE.SIZE);
      end if;
    end loop;
    raise KEY_IS_NOT_FOUND;
  end if;
end DELETE;
```

The for loop is necessary in DELETE because the key-data pair to be deleted might have been inserted at a place other than where it was first hashed because of collisions. It appears that this operation could be made more efficient by replacing the end range of the for loop FROM_TABLE.SIZE with FROM_TABLE.COUNT, the number of key-data pairs in the table. This is not so. Suppose that the table size is 10 and suppose further that 10 distinct key-data pairs were hashed into the table. The table is full. If all 10 keys hashed to index 1, every key-data pair except the first was placed after one or more collisions occurred. If the first five key-data pairs that were inserted are now deleted, there are five key-data pairs left in the table. The five empty locations have status NOW_FREE. A search for any of the remaining keys will examine each of these five places. The last key-data pair inserted will examine every place in the table before it is found.

The function LIST_NEXT_KEY_DATA starts searching the hash table at the last value listed and continues searching until encountering the next element with status IN_USE.

```
procedure LIST_NEXT_KEY_DATA ( IN_TABLE : in out TABLE;
                               KEY       :    out KEY_TYPE;
                               DATA      :    out DATA_TYPE) is
  -- Returns the next key-data pair in the table. Repeated calls
  -- will eventually returns all key-data pairs before any pair is
  -- listed again.
  -- Exception TABLE_NOT_DEFINED raised if SIZE of IN_TABLE undefined,
  --           which occurs when IN_TABLE = null.
  -- Exception TABLE_EMPTY raised if no key-data pairs are in the
  --           to be listed.
begin
  if IN_TABLE = null then
    raise TABLE_NOT_DEFINED;
  elsif IN_TABLE.COUNT = 0 then
    raise TABLE_EMPTY;
  else
    --IN_TABLE.LIST_LAST contains the last key-data pair returned.
    --Sequentially search the table until next location IN_USE
    --found, and then return the key-data pair
    loop
      IN_TABLE.LIST_LAST := 1 + (IN_TABLE.LIST_LAST rem IN_TABLE.SIZE);
      if IN_TABLE.LIST(IN_TABLE.LIST_LAST).STATUS = IN_USE then
        KEY := IN_TABLE.LIST(IN_TABLE.LIST_LAST).KEY;
        DATA := IN_TABLE.LIST(IN_TABLE.LIST_LAST).DATA;
        exit;
      end if;
    end loop;
  end if;
end LIST_NEXT_KEY_DATA;
```

The operation COPY has several uses. As noted previously, it can be used to copy the given table to a larger table when the load factor gets near 1. A second use is to reduce search overhead. If every component of the table has status NOW_FREE or IN_USE, an unsuccessful search would look at every component. If a table has a large number of components with status NOW_FREE, copying the table into a separate identically sized table will result in a table without any components with status NOW_FREE.

```
procedure COPY          (FROM : in      TABLE;
                         TO   : in out TABLE) is
     -- Copies the key-data pairs from the table FROM to the table
     -- TO.  The tables do not need to be the same size.
     -- Exception TABLE_NOT_DEFINED raised if SIZE of FROM or TO
     --           are undefined, which occurs when they = null.
     -- Exception TABLE_FULL raised if TO.SIZE is too small to hold
     --           the data in FROM
   begin
      if FROM = null or TO = null then
         raise TABLE_NOT_DEFINED;
      elsif FROM.COUNT > TO.SIZE then
         raise TABLE_FULL;
      else
         CLEAR(TO);
         for INDEX in 1..FROM.SIZE loop
            if FROM.LIST(INDEX).STATUS = IN_USE then
               INSERT (TO, FROM.LIST(INDEX).KEY, FROM.LIST(INDEX).DATA);
            end if;
         end loop;
      end if;
   end COPY;
```

The process of retrieving data from a hash table is similar to inserting a key-data pair except that the search must continue if the cell has status NOW_FREE or IN_USE.

```
function GET_DATA_FOR_KEY ( FROM_TABLE : TABLE;
                            KEY        : KEY_TYPE) return DATA_TYPE is
   -- Returns the data field for a given key-data pair already in
   -- the table.
   -- Exception TABLE_NOT_DEFINED raised if SIZE of FROM_TABLE undefined,
   --           which occurs when FROM_TABLE = null.
   -- Exception KEY_IS_NOT_FOUND raised if no key-data pair with
   --           the specific KEY is in the table FROM_TABLE.
   INDEX : natural;
begin
   if FROM_TABLE = null then
      raise TABLE_NOT_DEFINED;
   else
      INDEX := 1 + (HASH(KEY) rem FROM_TABLE.SIZE);
      for COUNT in 1..FROM_TABLE.SIZE loop
         if FROM_TABLE.LIST(INDEX).STATUS = IN_USE and then
              FROM_TABLE.LIST(INDEX).KEY = KEY then
            return FROM_TABLE.LIST(INDEX).DATA;
```

```
      elsif FROM_TABLE.LIST(INDEX).STATUS = FREE then
         --A FREE list location has been found. KEY is hashed to
         --an empty location so the KEY is not in the table.
         raise KEY_IS_NOT_FOUND;
      else
         --Collision resolution uses prime probing
         INDEX := 1 + ((INDEX + 12) rem FROM_TABLE.SIZE);
      end if;
   end loop;
   raise KEY_IS_NOT_FOUND;
  end if;
 end GET_DATA_FOR_KEY;
```

All of the examples of closed hashing used a prime probing collision strategy. Remember, the documentation of all the operations is the same as in the ADT GENERIC_CLOSED_HASH_SEARCH_TABLE as in the other search ADTs in this chapter.

12.4 IMPLEMENTING AN OPEN HASH TABLE

An open hash table is one where there is no upper limit on capacity. Like the closed hashing method implemented in Section 12.3, the hash strategy maps a key to an index. The open hash table is an array of linked lists (see Figure 12.4.1). Each component in the array is called a *bucket*. Each node of every linked list is a key-data pair along with an access variable that points to the next node.

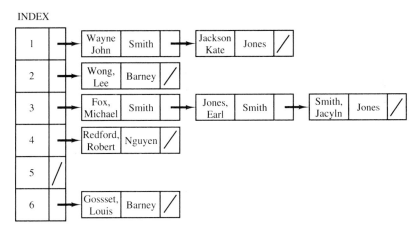

Figure 12.4.1 Open hash table T similar to the table specified in Figure 12.4.2. Even though T.SIZE = 6, the capacity of T is unbounded or "open." This open nature means that there is no need for a collision strategy as in the "closed" case.

Every key-data pair hashed to the same bucket is inserted onto the linked list accessed by that bucket. There is no further attempt to scatter the key-data pairs about the table; no collision strategy is necessary. However, this does not mean that the number of buckets is not important. The goal of a hash-based search is still to be able to locate a given key-data pair in $O(1)$ time. If b equals the number of buckets and if n equals the number of items on the list, there will be

b lists with an average length of n/b. Locating the proper bucket is an $O(1)$ operation and searching the bucket sequentially is an $O(n/b)$ operation for a combined process of $O(1 + n/b)$. Consider the case where $b = 100$, $n = 1000$; then the search operation is $O(11)$. Since $\log_2(1000)$ is approximately 10, the GET_DATA_FOR_KEY operation using an open hash table is no better than the basic binary search strategy.

The specification for the ADT GENERIC_OPEN_HASH_SEARCH_TABLE is shown in Figure 12.4.2. The only difference between this specification and the one for the closed table lies in the private section. As a result, the programmer would see no difference in their program except that the exception TABLE_FULL now means that a storage error has occurred.

```
generic
  type KEY_TYPE is private;
  type DATA_TYPE is private;
  with function HASH (KEY : KEY_TYPE) return natural;
package GENERIC_OPEN_HASH_SEARCH_TABLE is
  type TABLE is limited private;
  procedure CREATE              ( THIS_TABLE :    out TABLE;
                                  SIZE       : in      positive);
  procedure INSERT              ( INTO_TABLE : in out TABLE;
                                  KEY        : in      KEY_TYPE);
                                  DATA       : in      DATA_TYPE);
  procedure UPDATE              ( THIS_TABLE : in out TABLE;
                                  KEY        : in      KEY_TYPE;
                                  DATA       : in      DATA_TYPE);
  procedure DELETE              ( FROM_TABLE : in out TABLE;
                                  KEY        : in      KEY_TYPE);
  procedure LIST_NEXT_KEY_DATA  ( IN_TABLE   : in out TABLE;
                                  KEY        : in      KEY_TYPE);
                                  DATA       :    out DATA_TYPE);
  procedure CLEAR               ( THIS_TABLE : in out TABLE);
  procedure COPY                ( FROM       : in      TABLE;
                                  TO         : in out TABLE);
  procedure SET_TO_START        ( THIS_TABLE : in out TABLE);
  function LOAD_FACTOR          ( OF_TABLE   : TABLE )return float;
  function TABLE_SIZE           ( OF_TABLE   : TABLE )return natural;
  function COUNT                ( OF_TABLE   : TABLE) return natural;
  function GET_DATA_FOR_KEY     ( FROM_TABLE : TABLE;
                                  KEY        : KEY_TYPE) return DATA_TYPE;
  function KEY_IN_TABLE         ( IN_TABLE   : TABLE;
                                  KEY        : KEY_TYPE) return boolean;
  TABLE_NOT_DEFINED : exception;
  TABLE_FULL        : exception;
  TABLE_EMPTY       : exception;
  KEY_IS_NOT_FOUND  : exception;
  KEY_IS_IN_TABLE   : exception;

private
  type ELEMENT;
```

Figure 12.4.2 ADT GENERIC_OPEN_HASH_SEARCH_TABLE. Continues on page 421.

```
      type NEXT_ELEMENT is access ELEMENT;
      type ELEMENT is
        record
          KEY  : KEY_TYPE;
          DATA : DATA_TYPE;
          NEXT : NEXT_ELEMENT;
        end record;
      type HASH_TABLE is array(natural range <>) of NEXT_ELEMENT;
      type SEARCH_TABLE (SIZE : positive) is
        record
          COUNT             : natural := 0;
          LIST_LAST_BUCKET  : natural := 0;
          LIST_LAST_ELEMENT : NEXT_ELEMENT;
          LIST              : HASH_TABLE (1..SIZE);
        end record;
      type TABLE is access SEARCH_TABLE;
    end GENERIC_OPEN_HASH_SEARCH_TABLE;
```

Figure 12.4.2 Concluded.

The operation LOAD_FACTOR is defined exactly as in the closed case, but the interpretation of the load factor is now the expected length of each bucket's queue. To list the elements in an open hash table, both the bucket index and the access value of the last element listed in that bucket must be saved. The implementation combines features from the closed hash table case with principles from the implementation of unbounded lists. For example, the retrieval function follows:

```
function GET_DATA_FOR_KEY   (FROM_TABLE : TABLE;
                             KEY        : KEY_TYPE) return DATA_TYPE is
    -- Returns the data field for a given key-data pair already
    -- in the table.
    -- Exception TABLE_NOT_DEFINED raised if SIZE of FROM_TABLE
    --           is undefined which occurs when FROM_TABLE = null.
    -- Exception KEY_IS_NOT_FOUND raised if no key-data pair
    --           with the specific KEY is in FROM_TABLE.
  TEMP_ELEMENT : NEXT_ELEMENT;
begin
  if FROM_TABLE = null then
    raise TABLE_NOT_DEFINED;
  else
    --Get the bucket the key-data pair should be in
    TEMP_ELEMENT := FROM_TABLE.LIST (1 + (HASH(KEY) rem FROM_TABLE.SIZE));
    --Search the bucket sequentially for key
    loop
      if TEMP_ELEMENT = null then
        raise KEY_IS_NOT_FOUND;
      elsif TEMP_ELEMENT.KEY = KEY then
        return TEMP_ELEMENT.DATA;
      else
        TEMP_ELEMENT := TEMP_ELEMENT.NEXT;
```

```
        end if;
      end loop;
    end if;
  end GET_DATA_FOR_KEY;
```

The operation DELETE illustrates several possibilities that must be allowed for. If the bucket is empty, the key is not there. If the bucket is not empty, the entire list must be searched. The key-data pair can be anywhere in the list, or it may not be in the list at all.

```
procedure DELETE     ( FROM_TABLE : in out TABLE;
                       KEY        : in KEY_TYPE) is
  -- Deletes a given KEY-data pair already in the table FROM_TABLE.
  -- The KEY field must match the supplied KEY.
  -- Exception TABLE_NOT_DEFINED raised if SIZE of FROM_TABLE
  --           undefined, which occurs when FROM_TABLE = null.
  -- Exception KEY_IS_NOT_FOUND raised if no key-data pair
  --           with the specific KEY is in FROM_TABLE.
  INDEX        : natural;
  TEMP_ELEMENT : NEXT_ELEMENT;
begin
  if FROM_TABLE = null then
    raise TABLE_NOT_DEFINED;
  else
    INDEX := 1 + (HASH(KEY) rem FROM_TABLE.SIZE);
    TEMP_ELEMENT := FROM_TABLE.LIST(INDEX);
    if TEMP_ELEMENT = null then
      -- Bucket is empty, noting found
      raise KEY_IS_NOT_FOUND;
    elsif TEMP_ELEMENT.KEY = KEY then
      -- Key is first key-data pair in bucket, delete and return
      FROM_TABLE.LIST(INDEX) := TEMP_ELEMENT.NEXT;
      FROM_TABLE.LIST_LAST_BUCKET := 0;
      FROM_TABLE.LIST_LAST_ELEMENT := null;
      FROM_TABLE.COUNT := FROM_TABLE.COUNT - 1;
      return;
    else
      -- key data pair is not first in bucket, search and update
      loop
        if TEMP_ELEMENT.NEXT.KEY = null then
          raise KEY_IS_NOT_FOUND;
        elsif TEMP_ELEMENT.NEXT.KEY = KEY then
          TEMP_ELEMENT := TEMP_ELEMENT.NEXT;
          FROM_TABLE.LIST_LAST_BUCKET := 0;
          FROM_TABLE.LIST_LAST_ELEMENT := null;
          FROM_TABLE.COUNT := T.COUNT - 1;
          return;
        else
          TEMP_ELEMENT := TEMP_ELEMENT.NEXT;
        end if;
      end loop;
```

```
        end if;
      end if;
    end DELETE;
```

The complete implementation of the rest of the package is covered in the exercises.

Various strategies have been proposed to shorten the bucket search time. If the list in the bucket is organized as a priority queue with the most frequently accessed key-data pairs given the highest priority, decreases in search time could be expected in cases where n/b is large. Unfortunately, the probability of access of any pair is seldom known at insertion. Any successful strategy must move the more frequently referenced items toward the front of the list. One method puts the last referenced item at the front of the list. A second possible strategy would move an item up one position toward the front of the queue every time it was referenced. This assumes that the item is not already the front item.

12.5 APPLICATIONS

Hash tables have wide application. The characteristic of all applications is the need for quick search, update, delete, and insert. Compilers must keep track of all variables declared in the program by using a data structure known as a symbol table. The key in the symbol table is the identifier itself, while the data is the type, the attributes of the identifier, and the memory address associated with the identifier. There are no deletions in the building of a compiler symbol table, and since identifiers are typically short, the computation of the hash value is typically fast.

Many grocery stores are converting to a system where an optical scanner reads the bar code of a product and a computer converts this to an itemized register receipt. An example of an itemized receipt from a grocery store might look as follows:

Milk, half-gallon		1.90
Pepsi, six-pack	2@01.49	2.98
Produce, lettuce		0.49
Aspirin, generic		0.75T
1 oz Hershey Almond	4@00.60	2.40T
Subtotal		8.52
Sales tax		
0.0825*3.15		0.26
Total		8.78
Amount tendered		10.00
Change		1.22
Thank You for Shopping at		
ADA's Market		

Such a system would be easy to implement. One method considered in Chapter 17 was the use of a sparse vector data structure. Hash tables can also be used. The inventory is entered into a hash table with the bar code as key and the data_type as

```
type ITEM is
  record
    DESCRIPTION  : String(1..17);
    UNIT_PRICE   : PRICE_TYPE;
    TAXABLE      : boolean := false;
    INVENTORY    : natural;
  end record;
```

As an item is scanned, the bar code is hashed to find the matching item in the table. The description and price are first printed, then the inventory count is adjusted, and the price is added to the subtotal for the total purchase and to the subtotal for taxable items if necessary. The process continues until the checker indicates that the last item has been scanned. The totals are then printed and the purchase is paid for. This scenario works in any inventory situation, whether it is the local video store or the parts department of a major factory.

Another application of a hash table is a spelling checker. Suppose that WEBSTER is the name of a dictionary of words placed in memory using a hash table. The key is the word. The data field is a simple boolean in order to take up minimum space. The data is not important in this crude application, only whether the word is in the dictionary. The spell checker checks all words in the working word processing file. A crude spelling checker that only highlights words not in its dictionary might look as follows:

```
procedure SPELLER (WEBSTER : DICTIONARY) is
  TEMP: WORD_TYPE;
begin
  LOAD_DICTIONARY(DICT);
  while POSITION /= LAST_WORD loop
    GET_NEXT_WORD(TEMP);
    if not KEY_IN_TABHE(DICT, TEMP) then
      SET_ATTRIBUTE(TEMP, HIGHLIGHT);
    end if;
  end loop;
end SPELLER;
```

Spell checkers are much more sophisticated than the one in this crude example. A good spell checker would not only highlight the word, it would list alternative words in the dictionary that might be substituted for the word wanted or it could allow the word to be added to the dictionary or its warnings might be ignored.

As a final application, consider the multiplication of two polynomials $P_1(x)$ and $P_2(x)$ of degree m and n, respectively. The product

$$P_3(x) = P_1(x)*P_2(x)$$

will be of degree $m + n$. To form the product of two polynomials, every term of the first polynomial is multiplied by every term in the second, resulting in up to $(n + 1)*(m + 1)$ terms. Suppose that the polynomials were stored as a queue of terms (see Chapter 6).

```
type TERM;
type POLYNOMIAL is access TERM;
type TERM is
  record
    EXPONENT     : natural;
```

```
                    COEFFICIENT : float;
                    NEXT        : POLYNOMIAL;
                 end record;
```

The product would have $O(m*n)$ terms in its queue. Since the degree of the product is $m + n + 1$, there are at most $m + n + 1$ terms with distinct exponents in the queue. The product queue must be sorted so that terms with like exponents can be combined, an operation that is at best $O((m + n)*\log_2 (m + n))$. The following procedure uses hashing to eliminate the need to sort the queue where the product is stored. It is assumed that polynomials are stored in a priority order with larger exponents located nearer the front of the queue.

```
function POLY_HASH( K : natural) return natural is
  --map terms degree i into table location i
begin
  return K;
end Poly_hash;
package PRODUCT_HASH is new
     GENERIC_CLOSED_HASH_TABLE (natural, float, POLY_HASH);
Use PRODUCT_HASH;


function "*" (LEFT, RIGHT : POLYNOMIAL;
               DEG_LEFT, DEG_RIGHT : natural) return POLYNOMIAL is
  TEMP       : TABLE;
  TEMP_POLY : POLYNOMIAL;
  TEMP_LEFT : POLYNOMIAL := LEFT;
  TEMP_RIGHT: POLYNOMIAL := RIGHT;
  EXP, T_EXP: natural := 2*(DEG_LEFT+DEG_RIGHT);
  T_COEF     : float;
begin
  -- Create a table of exactly the right size
  CREATE (TEMP, DEG_LEFT+DEG_RIGHT+1);
  while TEMP_LEFT /= null loop
    -- For each term in the polynomial LEFT
    TEMP_LEFT := LEFT;
    -- Multiply each term of LEFT by each term in RIGHT.
    while TEMP_LEFT /= null loop
      -- Compute the next term
      EXP :- TEMP_LEFT.EXPONENT + TEMP_LEFT.EXPONENT;
      if KEY_IN_TABLE(TEMP, EXP) then
      -- Get the old coefficient for that exponent, add coefficient, update
      UPDATE (TEMP, EXP, GET_DATA_FOR_KEY (TEMP, EXP) +
             TEMP_LEFT.COEFFICIENT*TEMP_RIGHT.COEFFICIENT);
    else
      INSERT (TEMP, EXP, TEMP_LEFT.COEFFICIENT*TEMP_RIGHT.COEFFICIENT);
    end if;
    -- Get next term of RIGHT
    TEMP_RIGHT := TEMP_RIGHT.NEXT;
  end loop;
  -- Get next term of LEFT
  TEMP_LEFT := TEMP_LEFT.NEXT;
```

```
      end loop;
      -- Polynomial product is in the table, put it into a linked list
      LIST_NEXT_KEY_DATA(TEMP, EXP, T_COEF);
      TEMP_POLY := NEW TERM'(EXP, T_COEF, NULL);
      LIST_NEXT_KEY_DATA(TEMP, T_EXP, T_COEF);
      while T_EXP /= EXP loop
         TEMP_POLY := new TERM'(T_EXP, T_COEF, TEMP_POLY);
         LIST_NEXT_KEY_DATA(TEMP, T_EXP, T_COEF);
      end loop;
      return TEMP_POLY;
   end "*";
```

Note that the hash function put terms of degree i into table location i. The hash function never had a collision, although the load factor was 1.0. The chosen hash function fits the application. The answer is placed in priority ordered by highest exponent. In the exercises this example will be generalized by an instantiation of one of the queue packages.

12.6 TIME AND SPACE CONSTRAINTS

Hash table performance is heavily dependent on the load factor. For open hashing the load factor should be close to 1, but larger load factors do not significantly degrade performance. The load factor of a closed hash table should never exceed 0.5 because the performance starts to degrade rapidly. Figures 12.6.1 and 12.6.2 bear this out. Unless the load factor is large, the hash implementations are computationally better than the array methods, even with binary search implemented. Figure 12.6.3 summarizes these details.

The question of when to rehash, that is, copy the hash table into a larger table, must be well thought out. Rehashing is an $O(n)$ process where n is the number of elements. Hopefully, the need to rehash will seldom occur. The decision is often based on the collision strategy. Proposed strategies might be to rehash whenever the table is half full, or to rehash anytime an insertion fails, or to rehash based on the load factor. The central goal of any hashing scheme is to be able to insert or search in $O(1)$. When the hashing scheme loses this behavior, it also loses its advantage. The ease of rehashing by just a simple COPY makes it an attractive option whenever the need arises, but the programmer must watch table growth in large systems where memory is at a premium.

The ADTs developed in this chapter were all implemented using tables that are in memory. The concepts extend to developing search schemes that reside in external storage devices such as disks. Instead of components of an array, the key-data pair is hashed to a disk address. The time savings between a sequential search and direct access often make the effort mandatory.

Let Lf denote the load factor of a closed hash table with linear probing. Let $S(Lf)$ denote the expected number of probes for a successful search of a key, and let $U(Lf)$ be the expected number of probes for an unsuccessful search for a given key. The formulas for $S(Lf)$ and $U(Lf)$ along with a computed table are given in Figure 12.6.1. Clearly, higher load factors result in higher overhead.

Lf	S(Lf)	U(Lf)
0.1	1.06	2.23
0.3	1.21	3.04
0.5	1.5	5.0
0.6	1.75	7.25
0.8	3.0	26.0
0.9	5.5	101.0
0.95	11.0	401.0
0.99	50.5	10001.0

Figure 12.6.1 Efficiency of linear probing

Lf	S(Lf)	U(Lf)
0.5	1.25	1.1
0.75	1.38	1.22
1.0	1.5	1.37
1.5	1.75	1.72
2.0	2.0	2.14
3.0	2.5	3.05
5.0	3.5	5.0

Figure 12.6.2 Efficiency of open hash tables.

$$S(Lf) = \{1/(1 - Lf)\}/2 \qquad U(Lf) = \{1 + 1/(1 - Lf)**2\}$$

The formulas for $S(Lf)$ and $U(Lf)$ for open hash tables are given above in Figure 12.6.2. Note that very acceptable results can be achieved in the case where the load factors are larger than 1.0.

$$S(Lf) = 1 + Lf/2 \qquad U(Lf) = Lf + exp(-Lf)$$

The complexity of the different operations is shown in Figure 12.6.3. Note that n is the number of key-data pairs in the table, not the table size.

ADT	INSERT	UPDATE	DELETE	KEY_IN_TABLE
Unordered array	$O(n)$	$O(n)$	$O(n)$	$O(n)$
Ordered array sequential	$O(n)$	$O(n)$	$O(n)$	$O(n)$
Ordered array binary	$O(n)$	$O(\log_2 n)$	$O(n)$	$O(\log_2 n)$
Binary search tree	$O(\log_2 n)$	$O(\log_2 n)$	$O(\log_2 n)$	$O(\log_2 n)$
Closed hash Lf = 0.5	$O(1)$	$O(1)$	$O(1)$	$O(1)$
Open hash Lf = 1	$O(1)$	$O(1)$	$O(1)$	$O(1)$

Figure 12.6.3 Relative operatinal complexity.

12.7 CASE STUDY: A SIMPLE LIBRARY

Libraries are places where items are checked out and returned by individuals authorized to borrow these items. This case study specifically considers a simple program to manage a videotape rental store. A customer comes into the store to check out some videotapes. The customer selects the tapes that he or she wants to rent and presents his or her customer identification card at the checkout stand. The clerk enters the customer's id number into the computer to get the customer's current status. Then the tape number for each tape being checked out is entered, the customer file and the inventory table are updated, and a bill is prepared. When the customer is finished viewing the tapes, they are returned, and both files are updated.

Normally, programs like this would be handled using a database, but this case study will use two open hash tables. One hash table will hold the inventory of videotapes, while the other hash table will contain the current customers. Some of the low-level details involving input and output will be left to the student. Other enhancements will be suggested in the exercises.

The first step is to specify the key-data pairs for the customer table and for the video table. Each customer and each videotape will have a unique identification number as a key.

```
subtype CUSTOMER_ID is integer range 1..9999;
subtype VIDEO_ID   is integer range 1..32000;
```

When a customer is added to the base, a unique number is assigned to them. It is probably already printed on the video store's customer id card. The same holds true for each videotape for rent in the store.

Every customer is more than a number. The data field for the customer must have the customer's name, address, and phone number. In addition, the data field must include the amount of any previously owed bills, how many tapes the customer has checked out, the video_id number of each tape checked out, and the date each tape was checked out. A management decision has been made that limits to five the number of tapes that a customer can check out. The details of keeping track of dates are made easier by the standard Ada package Calendar. The necessary data structures to implement CUSTOMER_DATA are

```
type VIDEO_OUT is
  record
    TAPE     : VIDEO_ID;
    DAY_OUT  : DAY_NUMBER; --defined in Calendar
    MON_OUT  : MONTH_NUMBER;
    YEAR_OUT : YEAR_NUMBER;
  end record;
type VIDEO_ARRAY is array( integer range 1..5 ) of VIDEO;
type CUSTOMER_DATA is
  record
    CUS_ID      : CUSTOMER_ID;
    LAST_NAME   : string(1..15);
    FULL_NAME   : string(1..30);
```

```
        STREET_LINE_1 : string(1..30);
        STREET_LINE_2 : string(1..30);
        CITY          : string(1..20);
        ZIP           : positive;
        HOME_PHONE    : string(1..12);
        OFFICE_PHONE  : string(1..12);
        PREVIOUS_BILL : float := 0.0;
        TAPES_OUT     : positive := 0;
        CHECKED_OUT   : video_array;
    end record;
```

The information about each videotape must also be combined into a VIDEO_DATA type. Obviously, the tape's id number, its status, the CUSTOMER_ID number of who currently has the tape, the id number of who last had the tape, type subject of the tape, its title, its rental fee per day, when it was purchased, how many times it has been checked out, and its selling price must be available. Combining this into a record yields

```
type STATUS is (CHECKED_OUT, IN_STORE, MISSING, ON_ORDER)
type TAPE_TYPE is (COMEDY, DRAMA, MYSTERY, SCI_FI, CHILDREN,
                   INFORMATION);
type TAPE_DATA is
  record
    ID_OF_TAPE      : VIDEO_ID;
    TAPE_TITLE      : string(1..30);
    CURRENT_STATUS  : STATUS;
    CATEGORY        : TAPE_TYPE;
    CHECKED_OUT_TO  : CUSTOMER_ID;
      DAY_OUT       : DAY_NUMBER;
      MON_OUT       : MONTH_NUMBER;
      YR_OUT        : YEAR_NUMBER;
    LAST_CHKED_TO   : CUSTOMER_ID;
    RENTAL_BY_DAY   : float;
    PURCHASE_PRICE  : float;
      DAY_PUR       : DAY_NUMBER;
      MON_PUR       : MONTH_NUMBER;
      YR_PUR        : YEAR_NUMBER;
    TIMES_RENTED    : natural := 0;
  end record;
```

The case study is outlined in Figure 12.7.1. The hash tables are instantiated first. Note that the hash functions are simply functions that return either the VIDEO_ID or the CUSTOMER_ID. The hash tables are implemented as open hash tables, so there is no danger of overflow because the table is full. Assuming that both CUSTOMER_ID and VIDEO_ID numbers are assigned sequentially, the key-data pairs are spread out uniformly through the hash tables. Next in the outline are procedures and functions without their bodies. Some procedures are implemented in the discussion that follows, while others are part of the exercises.

The case study in Figure 12.7.1 starts out with a simple package that contains the hash functions needed for CUSTOMER_ID and VIDEO_ID.

```
package CASE_12_HASH is
   function CUSTOMER_HASH (KEY : integer) return natural;
   function VIDEO_HASH (KEY : integer) return natural;
end CASE_12_HASH;

package body CASE_12_HASH is

   function CUSTOMER_HASH (KEY : integer) return natural is
   begin
     return KEY;
   end CUSTOMER_HASH;

   function VIDEO_HASH (KEY : integer) return natural is
   begin
     return KEY;
   end VIDEO_HASH;
end CASE_12_HASH;

   with text_io;                    use text_io;
   with CASE_12_HASH;               use CASE_12_HASH;
   with calendar;                   use calendar;
   with GENERIC_OPEN_HASH_SEARCH_TABLE;
   with QUICK_SORT;    --generic sort procedure from Chapter 11

   procedure CASE_STUDY_12 is

   package MY_IO is new integer_io(integer); use my_io;

     -- program constants
        CUSTOMER_TABLE_SIZE : constant positive := 250;
        VIDEO_TABLE_SIZE    : constant positive := 1000;

     -- program defined types
        subtype CUSTOMER_ID is integer range 1..9999;
        subtype VIDEO_ID    is integer range 1..32000;
        type ACTION_TYPE is (ADD_NEW_CUSTOMER, ADD_NEW_VIDEO,
                             CHECK_OUT, RETURN_VIDEO,
                             UPDATE_CUSTOMER, UPDATE_VIDEO,
                             PRINT_CUSTOMER_LIST,
                             PRINT_OVERDUE_VIDEO_LIST,
                             PRINT_VIDEO_INVENTORY, QUIT);

     -- Create Customer open hashing table
        type VIDEO_OUT is
          record
```

Figure 12.7.1 CASE_STUDY_12, a video library program. Continues on page 431.

```
          TAPE     : VIDEO_ID;
          DAY_OUT  : DAY_NUMBER;
          MON_OUT  : MONTH_NUMBER;
          YEAR_OUT : YEAR_NUMBER;
       end record;
    type VIDEO_ARRAY is array(integer range 1..5) of VIDEO_OUT;
    type CUSTOMER_DATA is
       record
          CUS_ID  : CUSTOMER_ID;
          LAST_NAME  : STRING(1..15);
          FULL_NAME  : string(1..30);
          STREET_LINE_1 : string(1..30);
          STREET_LINE_2 : string(1..30);
          CITY          : string(1..20);
          ZIP           : positive;
          HOME_PHONE    : string(1..12);
          OFFICE_PHONE  : string(1..12);
          PREVIOUS_BILL : float := 0.0;
          TAPES_OUT     : natural := 0;
          CHECKED_OUT   : VIDEO_ARRAY;
       end record;


    package CUSTOMER is new GENERIC_OPEN_HASH_SEARCH_TABLE
                            ( KEY_TYPE  => CUSTOMER_ID,
                              DATA_TYPE => CUSTOMER_DATA,
                              HASH      => CUSTOMER_HASH);


-- Create Video open hashing table

    type STATUS is (CHECKED_OUT, IN_STORE, MISSING, ON_ORDER);
    type TAPE_TYPE is (COMEDY, DRAMA, MYSTERY, SCI_FI,CHILDREN,
                       INFORMATION);
    type TAPE_DATA is
       record
          ID_OF_TAPE      : VIDEO_ID;
          TAPE_TITLE      : string(1..30);
          CURRENT_STATUS : STATUS;
          CATEGORY        : TAPE_TYPE;
          CHECKED_OUT_TO : CUSTOMER_ID;
            DAY_OUT       : DAY_NUMBER;
            MON_OUT       : MONTH_NUMBER;
            YR_OUT        : YEAR_NUMBER;
          LAST_CHKED_TO  : CUSTOMER_ID;
          RENTAL_BY_DAY  : float;
          PURCHASE_PRICE : float;
            DAY_PUR       : DAY_NUMBER;
            MON_PUR       : MONTH_NUMBER;
            YR_PUR        : YEAR_NUMBER;
```

Figure 12.7.1   Continues on page 432.

Sec. 12.7   Case Study: A Simple Library

```
        TIMES_RENTED   : natural := 0;
      end record;
    package VIDEO is new GENERIC_OPEN_HASH_SEARCH_TABLE
                            (KEY_TYPE  => VIDEO_ID,
                             DATA_TYPE => TAPE_DATA,
                             HASH      => VIDEO_HASH);


-- program defined variables
    THIS_DAY          : day_number; --from package calendar
    THIS_MON          : month_number;
    THIS_YR           : year_number;
    ACTION            : ACTION_TYPE;
    OPEN_FOR_BUSINESS : boolean := true;


    CUSTOMER_TABLE : CUSTOMER.TABLE;


    VIDEO_TABLE : VIDEO.TABLE;

-- program-defined procedures and functions


procedure LOAD_CUSTOMER_DATA is separate;
    --prompts clerk for the secondary file where the customer
    --data is stored, opens that file,
    --loads that file of customer_data into
    --the hash table CUSTOMER_TABLE. Note that the key
    --CUSTOMER_ID is part of the customer_data record
    --See Figure 12.7.2


procedure LOAD_VIDEO_DATA is separate;
    --prompts clerk for the secondary file where the video
    --data is stored, opens that file,
    --loads that file of video key-data pairs into
    --the hash table VIDEO_TABLE
    --Similar to LOAD_CUSTOMER_DATA, deferred to the exercises


procedure SAVE_CUSTOMER_DATA is separate;
    --prompts clerk for the secondary file where the customer
    --data is to be stored, opens that file,
    --Saves to a secondary file the customer key-data pairs
    --from the hash table CUSTOMER_TABLE
    --Similar to LOAD_CUSTOMER_DATA, deferred to the exercises


procedure SAVE_VIDEO_DATA is separate;
    --prompts clerk for the secondary file where the video
    --data is to be stored, opens that file,
    --Saves to a secondary file the video key-data pairs from
```

Figure 12.7.1   Continues on page 433.

```
--the hash table VIDEO_TABLE
--Similar to LOAD_CUSTOMER_FILE, deferred to the exercises


procedure OPEN_ARCHIVE_TRANSACTION_FILE is separate;
  --opens three files to save daily business so tables can
  --be reconstructed if need be.
  -- file 1. all video rentals and returns
  -- file 2. all customer file updates
  -- file 3. all tapes added or removed from inventory
  --Simple IO procedure, not implemented


procedure CLOSE_AND_SAVE_TRANSACTION_FILE is separate;
  --closes and saves the three files open in the procedure
  --OPEN_ARCHIVE_TRANSACTION_FILE
  --Simple IO procedure, not implemented


procedure DISPLAY_MENU_AND_GET_RESPONSE
                  (ACTION :    out ACTION_TYPE) is separate;
  --Displays menu of options to clerk, gets clerk
  --response, and returns response to main program
  --for action.
  --Simple IO procedure, not implemented


procedure ADD_CUSTOMER is separate;
  -- Adds a new customer to Customer_table
  -- Adds customer to customer file updates
  -- See figure 12.7.3


procedure ADD_VIDEO is separate;
  -- Adds a new videotape to Video_table
  -- Adds video to video file update
  --Similar to Add_customer, deferred to the exercises


procedure GET_CUSTOMER_ID ( CUS_ID:  out CUSTOMER_ID) is separate;
begin
  -- prompts clerk for the customer's id number
end Get_Customer_id;


procedure GET_NUMBER_OF_TAPES_TO_CHECK (NUM :    out positive) is
  --prompts clerk for the number of tapes that are being
  --checked out or returned


procedure GET_TAPE_ID( CUS_ID:   out VIDEO_ID) is separate;
  --prompts clerk for the id of the tape being checked out
  -- or returned. Similar to GET_CUSTOMER_ID
procedure START_CUSTOMER_BILL (CUS_DATA : out CUSTOMER_DATA) is separate;
```

Figure 12.7.1 Continues on page 434.

```
         --prepares bill to be printed
      procedure UPDATE_BILL (TAPE_TITLE     : in string;
                             RENTAL_BY_DAY  : in float;
                             ID_OF_TAPE     : in Video_id) is separate;
         -- adds items to bill

      procedure PRINT_BILL is separate;
         --prints customer bill, updates various transaction files

      procedure CHECK_OUT_TAPES is separate;
         --gets CUSTOMER id, determines if customer in good
         --standing. if ok, tape checked out added to CUSTOMER_DATA
         --in CUSTOMER_TABLE and TAPE_DATA updated in VIDEO_TABLE.
         --All appropriate actions archived and bill prepared.
         -- See Figure 12.7.4

      procedure RETURN_TAPES is separate;
         --opposite of CHECK_OUT_TAPES. For each TAPE_ID entered,
         --sets STATUS of tape to IN_STORE, updates who last
         --checked tape out, checks if tape was overdue and updates
         --CUSTOMER_ID by removing tape from list of those checked
         --out to that CUSTOMER_ID.
         --Similar to CHECK_OUT_TAPES, deferred to the exercises

      procedure UPDATE_CUSTOMER_DATA is separate;
         --Gets CUSTOMER_ID from clerk and CUSTOMER_DATA from
         --CUSTOMER_VIDEO. All fields can be modified for any
         --reason such as change of address, payment of overdue
         --bill, or modification of tapes checked out. All changes
         --are saved.
         --Similar to CHECK_OUT_TAPES, deferred to the exercises

      procedure UPDATE_VIDEO_DATA is separate;
         --Gets VIDEO_ID from clerk and VIDEO_DATA from VIDEO_TABLE.
         --All fields can be modified for any reason. Changes are
         --saved.
         --Similar to CHECK_OUT_TAPES, deferred to the exercises

      procedure PRINT_CUSTOMER is separate;
         -- Prints customer list in one of two forms.
         -- form 1.  Mailing labels sorted by zip code
         -- form 2.  General list sorted by last name
         --Similar to PRINT_OVERDUE, deferred to the exercises

      procedure PRINT_OVERDUE is separate;
         --prints a list of all video titles along with customer
         --names and phone numbers of all overdue videos. List is
         --sorted by CUSTOMER_ID.
```

Figure 12.7.1 Continues on page 435.

```
    --See Figure 12.7.5

procedure PRINT_INVENTORY is separate;
    -- prints an inventory sorted by VIDEO_ID in one of two forms
    -- Form 1   entire inventory.
    -- Form 2   Inventory based on tape_type.
    --Similar to PRINT_OVERDUE, deferred to the exercises


begin --Case study 12;
    CUSTOMER.CREATE (CUSTOMER_TABLE, 250 );
    VIDEO.CREATE ( VIDEO_TABLE, 1000);
    LOAD_CUSTOMER_DATA;
    LOAD_VIDEO_DATA;
    --Get today's date by using package Calendar
    THIS_DAY := DAY(CLOCK);
    THIS_MON := MONTH(CLOCK);
    THIS_YR   := YEAR(CLOCK);
    OPEN_ARCHIVE_TRANSACTION_FILE;
    while OPEN_FOR_BUSINESS loop
      DISPLAY_MENU_AND_GET_RESPONSE(ACTION);
      case ACTION is
        when ADD_NEW_CUSTOMER         => ADD_CUSTOMER;
        when ADD_NEW_VIDEO            => ADD_VIDEO;
        when CHECK_OUT                => CHECK_OUT_TAPES;
        when RETURN_VIDEO             => RETURN_TAPES;
        when UPDATE_CUSTOMER          => UPDATE_CUSTOMER_DATA;
        when UPDATE_VIDEO             => UPDATE_VIDEO_DATA;
        when PRINT_CUSTOMER_LIST       => PRINT_CUSTOMER;
        when PRINT_OVERDUE_VIDEO_LIST => PRINT_OVERDUE;
        when PRINT_VIDEO_INVENTORY    => PRINT_INVENTORY;
        when QUIT                     =>
                                     OPEN_FOR_BUSINESS := false;
      end case;
    end loop;
    SAVE_VIDEO_DATA;
    SAVE_CUSTOMER_DATA;
    CLOSE_AND_SAVE_TRANSACTION_FILE;
  end CASE_STUDY_12;
```

Figure 12.7.1   Concluded.

Only four of the procedures in Figure 12.7.1 will be implemented in any detail. Most of the rest of the procedures are similar to other procedures in the case study or they do not use the operations of an open hash table. In the four examples that follow, certain utility procedures are not implemented. Their function is as obvious as their name.

Note that the procedure CASE_STUDY_12 is a simple case statement embedded in a while loop. All the procedure body does is open the inventory and customer files, then it creates the two hash tables, and performs operations on these tables until the store closes. Finally, it saves the current state of the two hash tables as well as all of the day's transactions.

The procedure LOAD_CUSTOMER_DATA (Figure 12.7.2) first opens a file of CUSTOMER_DATA for reading. A record is read from the file until the file is empty. For each record read, the CUSTOMER_ID is extracted from the record, and the key-data pair is inserted into the customer table.

```
separate (CASE_STUDY_12)
procedure LOAD_CUSTOMER_FILE is
  --prompts clerk for the secondary file where the customer
  --data is stored, opens that file,
  --loads that file of CUSTOMER_DATA into
  --the hash table CUSTOMER_TABLE. Note that the key
  --CUSTOMER_ID is part of the CUSTOMER_DATA record
  TEMP : CUSTOMER_DATA;
begin
  OPEN_CUSTOMER_FILE_FOR_READING(FILE_NAME1);
  while not end_of_file(FILE_NAME1) loop
    GET_ONE_RECORD(FILE_NAME1, TEMP);
    CUSTOMER.INSERT (CUSTOMER_TABLE, TEMP.CUS_ID, TEMP);
  end loop;
  CLOSE_CUSTOMER_FILE
end LOAD_CUSTOMER_FILE;
```

Figure 12.7.2 Procedure LOAD_CUSTOMER_FILE.

The procedure ADD_CUSTOMER (Figure 12.7.3) is similar to the procedure LOAD_CUSTOMER_FILE. Instead of getting a record from the file of CUSTOMER_DATA, the next CUSTOMER_ID value is read, the address and phone data are determined, and then the key-data pair is inserted into CUSTOMER_TABLE.

```
separate (CASE_STUDY_12)
procedure ADD_CUSTOMER is
-- Adds a new customer to CUSTOMER_TABLE
-- Adds customer to customer file updates
  TEMP : CUSTOMER_DATA;
begin
  GET_NEXT_CUSTOMER_ID( TEMP.CUS_ID );
  GET_ADDRESS_PHONE_DATA ( TEMP );
  CUSTOMER.INSERT (CUSTOMER_TABLE; TEMP.CUS_ID, TEMP);
end ADD_CUSTOMER;
```

Figure 12.7.3 Procedure ADD_CUSTOMER.

The procedure CHECKOUT_TAPES in Figure 12.7.4 makes sure that the CUSTOMER_ID is valid. The operation KEY_IN_ TABLE is done in GET_CUSTOMER_ID to ensure a valid id. The procedure GET_CUSTOMER_ID raises the exception KEY_NOT_FOUND, which is handled in CHECK_OUT_TAPES by printing a warning message and returning to the main procedure without taking any action. Note that records in both tables are extracted by key, updated, and then put back in their respective tables.

```
separate (CASE_STUDY_12)
procedure CHECKOUT_TABLES is
  --gets CUSTOMER_ID, determines if customer in good
  --standing. if ok, tape checked out added to CUSTOMER_DATA
  --in CUSTOMER_TABLE and TAPE_DATA updated in VIDEO_TABLE.
  --All appropriate actions archived and bill prepared.
  NUMBER_OF_TAPES : positive;
  TEMP_CUS_ID      : CUSTOMER_ID;
  TEMP_TAPE_ID     : VIDEO_ID;
  TEMP_CUS_DATA    : CUSTOMER_DATA;
  TEMP_TAPE_DATA   : TAPE_DATA;
begin
  -- GET_CUSTOMER_ID gets a CUSTOMER_ID and determines
  -- that the id is valid
  GET_CUSTOMER_ID( TEMP_CUS_ID );
  GET_NUMBER_OF_TAPES_TO_CHECK( NUMBER_OF_TAPES );
  TEMP_CUS_DATA := CUSTOMER.GET_DATA_FOR_KEY(CUSTOMER_TABLE,
                              TEMP_CUS_ID);
  if NUMBER_OF_TAPES + TEMP_CUS_DATA.TAPES_OUT > 5 then
    put(" Customer already has ");
    put( integer(Temp_cus_data.Tapes_out) );
    put(". Tape quota would be exceeded. No Action Taken");
    new line;
  else --complete checkout
    -- prepare final customer bill
    START_CUSTOMER_BILL(TEMP_CUS_DATA);
    for i in integer range 1..NUMBER_OF_TAPES loop
      --update video tape record
      GET_TAPE_ID(TEMP_TAPE_ID);
      TEMP_TAPE_DATA := VIDEO.GET_DATA_FOR_KEY(VIDEO_TABLE,
                                TEMP_TAPE_ID);
      TEMP_TAPE_DATA.CURRENT_STATUS := CHECKED_OUT;
      TEMP_TAPE_DATA.LAST_CHKED_TO
                        := TEMP_TAPE_DATA.CHECKED_OUT_TO;
      TEMP_TAPE_DATA.CHECKED_OUT_TO := TEMP_CUS_ID;
      TEMP_TAPE_DATA.DAY_OUT := THIS_DAY;
      TEMP_TAPE_DATA.MON_OUT := THIS_MON;
      TEMP_TAPE_DATA.YR_OUT   := THIS_YR;
      TEMP_TAPE_DATA.TIMES_RENTED :=
                  TEMP_TAPE_DATA.TIMES_RENTED + 1;
      VIDEO.UPDATE (VIDEO_TABLE,
              TEMP_TAPE_DATA.ID_OF_TAPE, TEMP_TAPE_DATA);
      --update customer record
      TEMP_CUS_DATA.TAPES_OUT := TEMP_CUS_DATA.TAPES_OUT+1;
      TEMP_CUS_DATA.CHECKED_OUT(TEMP_CUS_DATA.TAPES_OUT) :=
                  (TEMP_TAPE_ID, THIS_DAY, THIS_MON, THIS_YR);
      -- update amount owed on bill
      UPDATE_BILL(TEMP_TAPE_DATA.TAPE_TITLE,
```

Figure 12.7.4   Procedure CHECKOUT_TAPES. Continues on page 438.

```
      TEMP_TAPE_DATA.RENTAL_BY_DAY,
      TEMP_TAPE_DATA.ID_OF_TAPE);
   end loop;
   CUSTOMER.UPDATE (CUSTOMER_TABLE, TEMP_CUS_ID, TEMP_CUS_DATA);
   PRINT_BILL;
   put_line(" Tape Checkout complete");
  end if;
 exception
  when VIDEO.KEY_IS_NOT_FOUND =>
   put("Tape Key not found, No action taken, ");
   put_line("Try again!");
  when CUSTOMER.KEY_IS_NOT_FOUND =>
   put("Customer id not found,No action taken,");
   put_line(" Try_again!");
end CHECKOUT_TAPES;
```

Figure 12.7.4   Concluded.

The final procedure implemented is PRINT_OVERDUE. There are two basic ways to implement this procedure. One uses an internal sort and one uses an external sort. The implementation listed in Figure 12.7.5 uses an internal implementation. The procedure body first determines the number of entries in VIDEO_TABLE. The table is traversed and those entries that are overdue are processed further. An array of overdue records is created, sorted by a generic sort procedure, and then printed. Note the instantiation of the generic sort procedure QUICK_SORT.

```
separate (CASE_STUDY_12)
procedure PRINT_OVERDUE is
   --prints a list of all video titles along with customer
   --names and phone numbers of all overdue videos. List is
   --sorted by CUSTOMER_ID.

   SIZE : integer;

   procedure PRINT_SORTED_LIST (N : in    integer) is

     type OVERDUE is
       record
         CUS_ID     : CUSTOMER_ID;
         FULL_NAME : string(1..30);
         OFFICE     : string(1..12);
         HOME       : string(1..12);
         VID_TITLE : string(1..30);
         VID_ID     : VIDEO_ID;
         DAY_OUT    : DAY_NUMBER;
         MON_OUT    : MONTH_NUMBER;
         YR_OUT     : YEAR_NUMBER;
       end record;
```

Figure 12.7.5   Procedure PRINT_OVERDUE. Continues on page 439.

```
type VECTOR is array (integer range <>) of OVERDUE;
V        : VECTOR(1..N);
CUS_DATA : CUSTOMER_DATA;
VID_DATA : TAPE_DATA;
VID_ID   : VIDEO_ID;
COUNT    : integer := 0;
SIZE     : integer;

function "<" (LEFT, RIGHT : OVER_DUE) return boolean is
begin
  return L.FULL_NAME < R.FULL_NAME;
end "<";

procedure SORT_OVERDUE is new
                   QUICK_SORT (OVERDUE, VECTOR, "<");

Procedure PRINT_ELEMENT ( ELEMENT : in OVERDUE) is
begin
  null; --not implemented
end PRINT_ELEMENT;

Procedure PRINT_OVERDUE_ELEMENT(ELEMENT: in OVERDUE) is
begin
  null; --not implemented
end PRINT_OVERDUE_ELEMENT;

function TAPE_IS_OVERDUE(DAYOUT:DAY_NUMBER;
                MONOUT:MONTH_NUMBER;
                YROUT:YEAR_NUMBER) return boolean is
begin
    null; --not implemented
end TAPE_IS_OVERDUE;

begin
  VIDEO.SET_TO_START(VIDEO_TABLE);
  for INDEX in integer range 1..N loop
    VIDEO.LIST_NEXT_KEY_DATA(VIDEO_TABLE, VID_ID, VID_DATA);
    if VID_DATA.CURRENT_STATUS = CHECKED_OUT and then
      TAPE_IS_OVERDUE(VID_DATA.DAY_OUT, VID_DATA.MON_OUT,
            VID_DATA.YR_OUT) THEN
      COUNT := COUNT + 1;
      V(COUNT).CUS_ID    := VID_DATA.CHECKED_OUT_TO;
      V(COUNT).VID_TITLE    := VID_DATA.TAPE_TITLE;
      V(COUNT).VID_ID    := VID_DATA.ID_OF_TAPE;
      V(COUNT).DAY_OUT := VID_DATA.DAY_OUT;
      V(COUNT).MON_OUT := VID_DATA.MON_OUT;
      V(COUNT).YR_OUT  := VID_DATA.YR_OUT;
      CUS_DATA := CUSTOMER.GET_DATA_FOR_KEY (CUSTOMER_TABLE,
```

Figure 12.7.5 Continues on page 440.

```
                         VID_DATA.CHECKED_OUT_TO);
          V(COUNT).FULL_NAME := CUS_DATA.FULL_NAME;
          V(COUNT).OFFICE    := CUS_DATA.OFFICE_PHONE;
          V(COUNT).HOME      := CUS_DATA.HOME_PHONE;
       end if;
     end loop;
     SORT_OVERDUE( V(1..COUNT) );
     for INEDEX in integer range 1..COUNT loop
       PRINT_OVERDUE_ELEMENT( V(INDEX) );
     end loop;
   end PRINT_SORTED_LIST;

begin --PRINT_OVERDUE
  --Determine length of Video_Table and sort
  SIZE := VIDEO.TABLE_COUNT (VIDEO_TABLE);
  PRINT_SORTED_LIST(SIZE);
end PRINT_OVERDUE;
```

Figure 12.7.5   Concluded.

The full implementation of this case study uses all the operations of the abstract data type OPEN_HASH_SEARCH_TABLE except CLEAR and COPY. Two different hash tables were defined and manipulated. Data from tables was exchanged, deleted, and combined. A generic procedure to sort was properly instantiated, and its use saved much effort. If there was not enough room in memory to perform the sort, an easy modification of the program would have allowed an external sort. A different search type, the binary search tree, was implemented in Chapter 8. This case study can easily be modified to replace the open hash type with a binary search tree type. The full implementation of this case study is left to the exercises.

EXERCISES

Section 12.1 Sequential Implementations

12.1.1 Implement the following operations from the ADT GENERIC_UNORDERED_AR-RAY_SEARCH_TABLE as specified in Figure 12.1.2.
  a. UPDATE
  b. DELETE
  c. LIST_NEXT_KEY_DATA
  d. CLEAR
  e. COPY
  f. SET_TO_START
  g. KEY_IN_TABLE
  h. Combine parts a through g with the operations INSERT and GET_DATA_FOR_KEY already done in the text into a package body that implements GENERIC_UNORDERED_AR-RAY_SEARCH_TABLE.
  i. For the operations in GENERIC_UNORDERED_ARRAY_SEARCH_TABLE, determine the time and space constraints.

12.1.2 Implement the following operations from the ADT GENERIC_ORDERED_AR-RAY_SEARCH_TABLE which has the formal parameter list as in Figure 12.1.5 but the same package specification and private part as in Figure 12.1.2. Note that all the operations must use a binary search strategy whenever possible.

   a. UPDATE
   b. DELETE
   c. LIST_NEXT_KEY_DATA
   d. CLEAR
   e. COPY
   f. SET_TO_START
   g. KEY_IN_TABLE
   h. INSERT
   i. Combine parts a through h with the operation GET_DATA_FOR_KEY already done in the text into a package body that implements GENERIC_UNORDERED_ARRAY_SEARCH__TABLE.
   j. Determine the time and space constraints for the operations in GENERIC_ORDERED_ARRAY_SEARCH_TABLE.

Section 12.2 Hashing Methods

12.2.1 For each key type listed below, write a hashing procedure that transforms the key into a natural number. Include in your answer why the hashing method is acceptable and how it prevents almost similar keys from being hashed next into table locations that are next to each other.

   a. Individuals' last names
   b. Valid Ada identifiers of arbitrary length
   c. Social security numbers of the form *xxx-xx-xxxx*, where *x* is any digit in the range 0..9
   d. Zipcodes
   e. First and last names

12.2.2 A spell checker must be designed to determine if a word is in a dictionary or not. No attempt is made to correct misspelled words. Instead of storing character strings, the hash table stores a unique LONG_INTEGER for each word. Devise a function that determines a word's unique LONG_INTEGER. (If LONG_INTEGER is implemented as a 32-bit number, there are over $2**31$ values. There are fewer than 500,000 or $2**19$ words in the English language.)

Section 12.3 Implementing a Closed Hash Table

12.3.1 Implement the operations from the ADT GENERIC_CLOSED_HASH_SEARCH_TABLE below as specified in Figure 12.3.2.

   a. UPDATE
   b. CREATE
   c. CLEAR
   d. SET_TO_START
   e. KEY_IN_TABLE
   f. INSERT
   g. Combine parts a through f with the operations listed in this chapter into a package body that implements GENERIC_CLOSED_HASH_SEARCH_TABLE.
   h. Write the full documentation of Section 12.3.2.
   i. For the operations in GENERIC_CLOSED_HASH_SEARCH_TABLE determine the time and space constraints.

12.3.2 As the load factor increases the number of probes before successful insertion or search goes up exponentially. Add an operation to GENERIC_CLOSED_HASH_SEARCH_TABLE called REBUILD. REBUILD copies a given hash table into a larger table and returns the new table with the old name.

12.3.3 Define two search tables as equal if they contain the same key-data pairs. Note that this definition of equal does not depend on the size of the tables. Implement the boolean-valued operation EQUAL and add it to GENERIC_CLOSED_HASH_SEARCH_TABLE.

Section 12.4 Implementing an Open Hash Table

12.4.1 Implement the operations from the ADT GENERIC_OPEN_HASH_SEARCH_TABLE shown below as specified in Figure 12.4.2.
  a. UPDATE
  b. CREATE
  c. CLEAR
  d. SET_TO_START
  e. KEY_IN_TABLE
  f. INSERT
  g. UPDATE
  h. DELETE
  i. LIST_NEXT_KEY_DATA
  j. COPY
  k. LOAD_FACTOR
  l. Combine parts a through k with the operations listed in this chapter into a package body that implements GENERIC_OPEN_HASH_SEARCH_TABLE.
  m. Write the full documentation of Figure 12.4.2.
  n. For the operations in GENERIC_OPEN_HASH_SEARCH_TABLE determine the time and space constraints.

Section 12.5 Applications

12.5.1 Implement a simple spell checker that uses the ADT from Exercise 12.1.1.

12.5.2 Implement a simple spell checker that uses the ADT from Exercise 12.1.3

12.5.3 Implement a simple spell checker that uses the ADT from Exercise 12.4.1.

12.5.4 What is the difference that would be expected in the procedures that implemented Exercises 12.5.1, 12.5.2, and 12.5.3?

12.5.5 Implement a package using a hash-based ADT that does polynomial arithmetic.

12.5.6 The ADT GENERIC_UNBOUNDED_SET can be implemented using hashing. Do so.

Section 12.7 Case Study: A Simple Library

12.7.1 Implement the following procedures and functions from CASE_STUDY_12.
  a. LOAD_VIDEO_DATA
  b. SAVE_CUSTOMER_DATA
  c. ADD_VIDEO
  d. RETURN_TAPES
  e. UPDATE_CUSTOMER_DATA
  f. PRINT_CUSTOMER
  g. PRINT_INVENTORY

PROGRAMMING PROJECTS

P12.1 In Shakesperian scholarship, one of the problems that is often encountered is trying to determine if a newly discovered poem was written by the Bard. The object is to determine the frequency of words used in the newly discovered works and compare this to the frequency of words used in known works.

    a. Write a procedure that sets up a hash table for words in a file. A word is scanned, then is checked to see if it is in the table. If it is there, the data field is incremented by 1. If it is not there, a key-data pair of word-positive is inserted into the table.

    b. Write a procedure that sorts all the entries generated by part a and prints a table with three columns. Column 1 is the words, in sorted order. Column 2 is the number of times the word is in the poem. Column 3 is the percentage of times the word appears in the poem.

P12.2 Modify GENERIC_CLOSED_HASH_SEARCH_TABLE to keep track of the number of collisions during hashing. Write a program to insert randomly generated keys and insert them into the hash table. What does this information tell you about hashing? (*Note:* Most random number generators, including the one in Appendix C, can be set to repeat the same random sequence. This allows the same keys to be tested for each hash function.)

P12.3 A compiler must keep track of the valid identifiers. Write a program that scans an Ada file and enters all valid Ada identifiers into the table. Nonvalid identifiers are rejected and output. (*Hint:* Check out the transition graph ADT in Section 10.4 and review Exercise 12.2.2.)

P12.4 The specification for search tables forbids duplicate keys. This same restriction is true for the ADT TREE. At the end of Chapter 8 a tree of indices was used to build an index. Modify CASE_STUDY_8 so that it uses an open hash table instead of a tree.

NOTES AND REFERENCES

Volume 3 of Knuth [29] is a good place to start when considering any searching or sorting problem. Mauer and Lewis [36] is an excellent survey. Exercise 12.2.2 is motivated by the Rabin–Karp [26] pattern-matching scheme, which is considered in Section 13.4. Even though the concept of hashing is basic, the performance analysis is quite complicated and many questions remain unresolved. Knuth does a considerable amount of analysis on various hashing schemes, including the formulas that were cited in Section 12.6.

13

Strings

Strings typically invoke the idea of sequences of characters used in applications related to word processing. Ada has a predefined character string type

```
type string is array (positive range <>) of character;
```

in the Ada Standard package which reinforces this stereotype. The abstract data structure for strings is much more general than this. First, a string is not just a linear list of characters; strings are lists of items. These items can be any discrete set, such as characters, numerals, bits, or any group of symbols. Second, the Ada predefined string type is static: defining an object as type string fixes its length.

A string is an unbounded list of items. Using this definition, a string could be defined by the instantiation

```
package STRING is new GENERIC_UNBOUNDED_LIST (ITEM_TYPE);
```

but this definition has serious shortcomings. One string operation requires a list of items to be inserted into a second list starting at a specified position. The built-in operations of the ADT GENERIC_UNBOUNDED_LIST, defined in Chapter 5, do not allow for the simple insertion of one list into another except at the beginning or the end of the list. There is no simple way of using list operations to insert another list in its middle. The brute-force method resorts to multiple calls to the "tail" operation to get the proper spot, catenating the list to be inserted in the middle, then catenating the tail back (see Figure 13.0.1).

The package definition of string does remove one shortcoming of the Ada predefined string definition. Strings now have dynamic length instead of fixed length. Following the traditional approach, a distinction will be made between a string and a substring throughout this chapter. Substrings are defined as

```
type SUBSTRING is array (positive range <>) of ITEM_TYPE;
```

This implies that all substrings have fixed lengths. This is the main difference between a string and a substring. Strings do not have a fixed length; substrings have fixed length. All string operations must be able to work on any combination of strings and substrings.

What are the typical operations on strings? The string operations must have several forms. The operations relate strings to strings, strings to substrings, and substrings to strings.

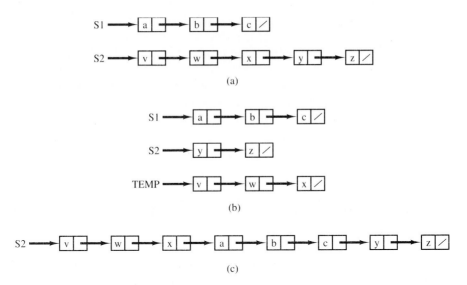

Figure 13.0.1 (a) Problem is to insert the string S1 into S2 after the third node and before the fourth node if S1 and S2 are implemented as lists of characters. (b) The result after three iterations of the string operations X := GET_HEAD(S2), S2 := TAIL_OF_LIST(S2), ADD_ITEM_TO_HEAD(TEMP2.X), CONCATENATE(TEMP. TEMP2. TEMP), and CLEAR(TEMP2) of the lists in part (a). (c) Final result after concatenating the three lists in part (b) together and copying the result to S2.

Operations with several forms perform the same function. Consider the typical operations of an editor or word processor. Strings and substrings must be copied. Operations that build larger strings by catenating stings and substrings are another class of string operations. Operations to insert a string or substring into a second string at a specified point, or replacing the occurrence of any pattern substring by a target substring are another set of operations. Operations that compare two strings are needed. When are two strings equal? Is one string "less" than another string? Other operations that find the current length of a string or return the substring between two given places in the string are also required.

Applications of strings are widespread. Strings of characters and operations on these strings of characters form the basis of all editors and word processing programs. A computer program in machine language is a string of bits. Different programs have different lengths. Similarly, in genetics, genes and chromosomes can be represented by strings of bits that can have lengths in excess of 1 million bits. Biologists are interested in the location where some particular substring starts or in the existence and placement of substrings where the first half of the string equals the reverse of the second half of the string. Integers are strings of numeric digits of arbitrary length. This representation is useful when it is necessary to determine if a certain long sequence of digits represents a prime number.

13.1 ADT STRING

The string and substring were both defined above. Again, the main difference is that a string is a sequence of zero or more items maintained as a linearly ordered list of items, while a substring is a sequence of items with fixed length. Substrings are typically represented as arrays of items. A string is null if it has length zero. The front of a string is the first item in a string. The position of an item is its location with respect to the front of the string. The length of a string can be defined as either the position of the last item in the string or the number of items in the string.

One way to motivate the operations on strings and substrings is to think of the built-in features of a typical text editor or word processor. Text must be copied. Once copied, text must be moved from one part of the string and then inserted into another portion of the text or document. The usual order of moving or copying text is first to fix a substring and then to copy it beginning at another position. If the desired result is just to move the text, the original substring is then deleted. Sometimes two documents are joined together to make a larger document. This involves appending one document onto the end of the second document.

Another group of typical word processing operations is the searching for a pattern string and then replacing it with a target string. This involves a systematic search. Each possible substring in the string is tested for equality with the pattern string. When a match is found, the substring that matched the pattern is replaced by the target string. Writing over text causes a particular item at a particular position to be replaced. A text editor displays a portion of a file of text on a CRT. In the absence of a CRT there must be a way of extracting items or strings or substrings that start at a certain position.

Finally, there is a need for utility type operations. Sometimes there is a need to clear the string and start all over. How can it be determined if a string is empty? How much space needs to be allocated on a storage device in order to store a particular string? Finally, consider the possibility of having an array of strings. Each array component might represent an entry in the index of this text, for example. If the array is to be sorted, there must be a way of comparing strings and substrings.

Many operations mentioned above must have several versions. Consider the testing for equality. There are three cases: When does one string equal a second string, when does a string equal a substring, and when does a substring equal a string? Substrings are not be declared as a private type, so determining when one substring equals a second substring can be done outside the ADT. This also allows the programmer to manipulate substrings directly without using any package operations. Each operator version will be listed in the documentation for completeness. Another consideration is the name of the operations. If every operator is overloaded, either a "use" clause or a renaming convention must be used. Which is more convenient, 'S1 = S2', 'ITEM_STRING."="(S1,S2)', or 'ITEM_STRING.EQUAL(S1, S2)'? The first option requires a use clause, which some Ada programmers feel should be avoided when possible. Without the use clause, the second or third options involving renaming are left. Figure 13.1.1 lists the documentation for the ADT STRING. With the documentation completed the specification and implementation of a bounded and unbounded form can proceed.

GENERAL ADT SPECIFICATION FOR STRING

Description

A STRING is an unbounded list of objects of ITEM_TYPE maintained in linear order by position. Items can be inserted or deleted from any position within the string based on position within the

Figure 13.1.1   Documentation for GENERIC_UNBOUNDED_STRING. Continues on page 447.

string. There are three structures in the ADT string. The first is the programmer-supplied ITEM_TYPE. Items of type ITEM_TYPE are typically symbols. Examples are characters, digits, bits, or objects from some programmer-defined enumerated type. The second structure is the SUB-STRING. A SUBSTRING is a STRING of fixed length. Substrings are represented as an unconstrained array of ITEM_TYPE. SUBSTRINGS are not private and can be manipulated by the programmer without using ADT operations. The third structure is the STRING. The maximum length of a STRING is not fixed. Operations on strings include insertion, deletion, modification, and comparison of strings and substrings as well as operations for extracting strings, substrings, and items from strings, and operations to clear strings and to find the length of strings are supplied.

Programmer-Supplied Data Structures or Specifications

The programmer must supply two generic parameters. The first is the type of items, denoted ITEM_TYPE, that make up the types STRING and SUBSTRING that the package manipulates. ITEM_TYPE is private within the package. The second programmer-supplied component is a boolean-valued function that returns true when the first object of type ITEM_TYPE is less than the second object of type ITEM_TYPE.

Operations

Name	Description
COPY	(Two versions) Makes an exact copy of one STRING to another STRING or from a SUBSTRING to a string. A SUBSTRING can be copied to another SUBSTRING outside the package by a simple assignment statement.
APPEND	(Four versions) (1) Takes the first STRING argument and adjoins a copy of it to the end of the second STRING argument and returns the modified second STRING; (2) takes first SUBSTRING argument and copies it onto the end of the second STRING argument and returns the modified second STRING; (3) makes a STRING copy of the second SUBSTRING argument and adjoins onto it the first STRING argument, which is then returned; and (4) takes an object of ITEM_TYPE and adjoins it onto the end of a STRING that is returned. The programmer can append one SUBSTRING onto another SUBSTRING by using the array catenation operator.
INSERT	(Three versions) Inserts a copy of either a STRING, a SUBSTRING, or an object of ITEM_TYPE into a STRING at a given position.
DELETE	Deletes all objects of ITEM_TYPE in a given STRING starting at the first position and ending at a second position.
CLEAR	Returns a STRING of length 0.
REPLACE	(Three versions) Delete all objects of ITEM_TYPE starting at a specified position through the end of a given STRING and then appends a given STRING, SUBSTRING, or object of ITEM_TYPE on the end of the remaining STRING.
EQUAL	(Three versions) Returns true if (1) two STRINGs of equal length have the same item in every position, or if (2) a SUBSTRING and STRING of equal length have the same items in the same position, or if (3) a STRING and a SUBSTRING of equal length have the same items in the same position;

Figure 13.1.1 Continues on page 448.

	otherwise returns false. The programmer can check for equality of two SUBSTRINGs using the "=" operator.
LESS	(Three versions) Compares the left STRING with the right STRING or the left SUBSTRING with the right STRING of the left STRING with the right SUBSTRING on an item-by-item basis. If the left item is less than the right item, returns true, or if the right item is less than the left item, returns false, or if both items are equal, goes on to the next position. A null string is always less than a nonnull string. The user can check two SUBSTRINGs directly using a function built with the < operator.
GREATER	(Three versions) Similar in operation to LESS. Compares the left STRING with the right STRING or the left SUBSTRING with the right STRING of the left STRING with the right SUBSTRING on an item-by-item basis. If the left item is greater than the right item, returns true, or if the right item is greater than the left item, returns false, or if both items are equal, goes on to the next position. A nonnull string is always greater than a null string. The user can check directly for two SUBSTRINGs by using the > operator.
LENGTH	Returns a natural number equal to the number of items in the STRING. The programmer can find the length of a SUBSTRING directly by using the array attribute length.
EMPTY	Boolean-valued function that returns true if the STRING has length 0, otherwise returns false.
GET_ITEM	Function that returns an object of ITEM_TYPE at given position in a STRING.
GET_STRING	Function that returns a STRING that equals the tail of a given STRING starting from a specified position of the given STRING.
GET_SUBSTRING	(Two versions) One function returns a SUBSTRING that equals the tail of a given STRING starting from a specified position, or it returns a SUBSTRING that starts at a specified position and ends at a second specified position.

Exceptions

Two exceptions can occur. The exception "OVERFLOW" occurs when no storage space is left to perform a valid STRING operation. The operators COPY, APPEND, INSERT, REPLACE, GET__STRING, and GET_SUBSTRING can raise an OVERFLOW exception. A "POSITION_ERROR" indicates that a position has been specified that is not in the current string. Any operator that specifies a position can raise this exception.

Warnings

This ADT defines two objects, STRING and SUBSTRING. All operations involving a STRING must use ADT operators defined in the package. All operations done on only SUBSTRINGS must be performed by the programmer. All other warnings are implementation dependent.

Figure 13.1.1 Concluded.

13.2 STRINGS WITH MAXIMUM FIXED LENGTH: BOUNDED FORM

The definition of the string type implies that the string can have any length. Strings come in two flavors. The unbounded flavor is dynamic. The maximum length of the string is limited only by memory and other system resources. The bounded flavor fixes the maximum length of the string. The length of a bounded string is not fixed. It varies between null, that is length 0, and the set maximum length (see Figure 13.2.1).

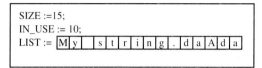

Figure 13.2.1 BOUNDED_STRING implementation holding the string 'My string'. Note that List(11..15) is not in use.

The documentation does not require the programmer to set the maximum length of the string at instantiation, so the maximum length must be set at declaration. This requires the use of a discriminant record with variant SIZE. Making the last field in the definition of the STRING to be a SUBSTRING with length SIZE eases implementation of the ADT GENERIC_BOUNDED_STRING. Slices of STRINGS can be directly assigned to SUBSTRINGS or SUBSTRINGS can be assigned to slices of STRINGS.

The ADT GENERIC_BOUNDED_STRING is specified in Figure 13.2.2. The implementation is more tedious than challenging. Consider the two COPY operations. Both use the array slice assignment statement. The only difference is the use of the array attribute length in the second version that copies a SUBSTRING to a STRING.

```
generic
  type ITEM_TYPE is private;
  with function "<" (LEFT, RIGHT : ITEM_TYPE) return boolean is <>;
package GENERIC_BOUNDED_STRING is
  type STRING (SIZE : positive) is limited private;
  type SUBSTRING is array (positive range <> ) of ITEM_TYPE;
  procedure COPY        (FROM      : in      STRING;
                         TO        : in out STRING);
  procedure COPY        (FROM      : in      SUBSTRING;
                         TO        : in out STRING);
  procedure APPEND      (FROM      : in      ITEM_TYPE;
                         TO        : in out STRING);
  procedure APPEND      (FROM      : in      STRING;
                         TO        : in out STRING);
  procedure APPEND      (FROM      : in      SUBSTRING;
                         TO        : in out STRING);
  procedure APPEND      (FROM      : in      STRING;
                         TO        : in out SUBSTRING;
                         TARGET    : in out STRING);
  procedure INSERT      (FROM      : in      STRING;
                         INTO      : in out STRING;
                         POSITION  : in      positive);
```

Figure 13.2.2 Specification of ADT GENERIC_BOUNDED_STRING. Continues on page 451.

```
procedure INSERT        (FROM     : in    SUBSTRING;
                         INTO      : in out STRING;
                         POSITION  : in    positive);
procedure INSERT        (FROM     : in    ITEM_TYPE;
                         INTO      : in out STRING;
                         POSITION  : in    positive);
procedure DELETE        (FROM     : in out STRING;
                         START_AT  : in    positive;
                         END_AT    : in    positive);
procedure CLEAR         (S        : in out STRING);
procedure REPLACE       (IN_STRING: in out STRING;
                         USING     : in    STRING;
                         START_AT  : in    positive);
procedure REPLACE       (IN_STRING: in out STRING;
                         USING     : in    SUBSTRING;
                         START_AT  : in    positive);
procedure REPLACE       (IN_STRING: in out STRING;
                         USING     : in    ITEM_TYPE;
                         START_AT  : in    positive);
function EMPTY          (S        : STRING ) return boolean;
function EQUAL          (LEFT     : STRING;
                         RIGHT     : STRING ) return boolean;
function EQUAL          (LEFT     : SUBSTRING;
                         RIGHT     : STRING ) return boolean;
function EQUAL          (LEFT     : STRING;
                         RIGHT     : SUBSTRING ) return boolean;
function LESS           (LEFT     : STRING;
                         RIGHT     : STRING ) return boolean;
function LESS           (LEFT     : SUBSTRING;
                         RIGHT     : STRING ) return boolean;
function LESS           (LEFT     : STRING;
                         RIGHT     : SUBSTRING ) return boolean;
function GREATER        (LEFT     : STRING;
                         RIGHT     : STRING ) return boolean;
function GREATER        (LEFT     : SUBSTRING;
                         RIGHT     : STRING ) return boolean;
function GREATER        (LEFT     : STRING;
                         RIGHT     : SUBSTRING ) return boolean;
function LENGTH         (IN_STRING: STRING ) return natural;
function GET_ITEM       (FROM     : STRING;
                         POSITION  : positive ) return ITEM_TYPE;
function GET_STRING     (FROM     : STRING;
                         POSITION  : positive ) return STRING;
function GET_SUBSTRING (FROM      : STRING;
                         START_AT  : positive ) return SUBSTRING;
function GET_SUBSTRING (FROM      : STRING;
                         START_AT  : positive;
                         END_AT    : positive ) return SUBSTRING;
OVERFLOW      : exception;
```

Figure 13.2.2   Continues on page 451.

```
      POSITION_ERROR : exception;
   private
     type STRING (SIZE : positive) is
       RECORD
         LENGTH : natural := 0;
         LIST   : SUBSTRING (1..SIZE);
       end RECORD;
     end GENERIC_BOUNDED_STRING;
```

Figure 13.2.2   Concluded.

All the operations with multiple versions behave this way. There are only minor variations in the implementation of each, so once one version of an operation is understood, the others will follow easily. The one slight exception is the procedure APPEND. It is not possible to
APPEND a STRING onto the end of the SUBSTRING because a SUBSTRING's length is
fixed, so both are copied onto a STRING.

```
      procedure COPY ( FROM : in      STRING;
                       TO   : in out STRING) is
        -- Makes exact copy of the string FROM
        -- Exception OVERFLOW raised if there is FROM.LENGTH > TO.SIZE
      begin
        if FROM.LENGTH > TO.SIZE then
          raise OVERFLOW;
        else
          TO.LIST (1..FROM.LENGTH) := FROM.LIST (1..FROM.LENGTH);
          TO.LENGTH := FROM.LENGTH;
        end if;
      end COPY;

      procedure COPY ( FROM : in      SUBSTRING;
                       TO   : in out STRING) is
        -- Converts the substring FROM to a string TO.
        -- Exception OVERFLOW raised if FROM'length > TO.SIZE
      begin
        if FROM'length > TO.SIZE then
          raise OVERFLOW;
        else
          TO.LIST (1..FROM'length) := FROM (1..FROM'length);
          TO.LENGTH := FROM'length;
        end if;
      end COPY;

      procedure APPEND (FROM   : in      STRING;
                        TO     : in      SUBSTRING;
                        TARGET : in out STRING) is
        -- Converts the substring ONTO to a string and then adjoins
        -- a copy of the string FROM onto its end and returns the
        -- combined string as TARGET.
        -- Exception OVERFLOW raised if there is insufficient space
      begin
        if FROM.LENGTH + TO'length > TARGET.SIZE then
```

```
      raise OVERFLOW;
    else
      -- Copy TO to TARGET
      TARGET.LIST (1..TO'length) := TO (1..TO'length);
      -- Append FROM onto the end of TARGET
      TARGET.LIST(TO'length+1..TO'length+FROM.LENGTH);
                  FROM.LIST(1..FROM.LENGTH);
      TARGET.LENGTH := FROM.LENGTH + TO'length;
    end if;
  end APPEND;
```

INSERT and REPLACE are similarly implemented. Both require that conditions that raise exceptions be tested for initially. INSERT makes room for the STRING or SUBSTRING at the given point, while REPLACE essentially truncates the STRING starting at the specified position and then appends the second STRING.

```
procedure INSERT (FROM     : in     STRING;
                  INTO     : in out STRING;
                  POSITION : in     positive) is
  -- Inserts a copy of the a string FROM at a given position
  -- in the string INTO.
  -- Exception OVERFLOW raised if there is insufficient room.
  -- Exception POSITION_ERROR raised if POSITION > LENGTH
begin
  if FROM.LENGTH + INTO.LENGTH > INTO.SIZE then
    raise OVERFLOW
  elsif POSITION > INTO.LENGTH then
    raise POSITION ERROR;
  else
    -- Make room for FROM.LENGTH items in INTO starting at POSITION
    INTO.LIST (POSITION+FROM.LENGTH..INTO.LENGTH+FROM.LENGTH) :=
               INTO.LIST (POSITION..INTO.LENGTH);
    -- Put FROM into the hkle in INTO
    INTO.LIST(POSITION..POSITION+FROM.LENGTH-1) :=
               FROM.LIST(1..FROM.LENGTH);
    INTO.LENGTH := INTO.LENGTH + FROM.LENGTH;
  end if;
end INSERT;

procedure REPLACE (IN_STRING: in out STRING;
                   USING    : in     STRING;
                   START_AT : in     positive) is
  -- Deletes all items starting at the position START_AT through the
  -- end of the string IN_S. Then appends the string USING onto the
  -- end of the result.
  -- Exception OVERFLOW raised if there is insufficient room.
  -- Exception POSITION_ERROR raised if START_AT > LENGTH
begin
  if START_AT + USING.LENGTH - 1 > IN_STRING.SIZE then
    raise OVERFLOW;
```

```
      elsif START_AT > IN_STRING.LENGTH then
         raise POSITION_ERROR;
      else
         IN_STRING.LIST(START_AT..START_AT + USING.LENGTH-1) :=
                        USING.LIST(1..USING.LENGTH);
         IN_STRING.LENGTH := START_AT + USING.LENGTH - 1;
      end if;
   end REPLACE;
```

The boolean-valued functions are easy to implement. Since both strings and substrings are arrays, the Ada equality operator = for arrays can be used for equal. The two functions LESS and GREATER are mirrors of each other. If A is LESS than B, it follows that B is GREATER than A. To implement GREATER, simply reverse the arguments in LESS. As has occurred previously, the two available compare operations are "=" because the formal generic parameter ITEM_TYPE is private, and ">" which uses the programmer-supplied function at instantiation.

```
   function EQUAL (LEFT    : STRING;
                   RIGHT   : SUBSTRING ) return boolean is
      -- Returns true if two strings of equal length have the same items
      -- in the same position.
   begin
      return LEFT.LENGTH = RIGHT'length and then
                 LEFT.LIST(1..LEFT.LENGTH) = RIGHT;
   end EQUAL;

   function LESS (LEFT   : STRING;
                  RIGHT : STRING ) return boolean is
      -- Returns true if the string LEFT is less than the string
      -- RIGHT when using the standard lexicographic orderings
      MIN : natural := LEFT.LENGTH;
   begin
      -- Adjust minimum length if necessary
      if MIN < RIGHT.LENGTH then
        MIN := RIGHT.LENGTH;
      end if;
      -- Check item by item using lexicographic ordering with respect to
      -- ITEM_TYPE
      for I in natural range 1..MIN loop
        if LEFT.LIST(I) < RIGHT.LIST(I) then
           return true;
        elsif RIGHT.LIST(I) < LEFT.LIST(I) then
           return false;
        end if;
      end loop;
      -- ITEMS are equal in range 1..MIN, so check to if RIGHT is longer
      return MIN = LEFT.LENGTH AND MIN /= RIGHT.LENGTH;
   end LESS;

   function GREATER (LEFT   : SUBSTRING;
                     RIGHT  : STRING ) return boolean is
      -- Returns true if the substring LEFT is greater than the string
```

```
                 -- RIGHT when using the standard lexicographic orderings
                 MIN : natural :=LEFT'length;
            begin
                 -- Adjust value of minimum length if necessary
                 if MIN < RIGHT.LENGTH then
                    MIN := RIGHT.LENGTH;
                 end if;
                 -- Compare item by item using lexicographic ordering
                 for I in natural range 1..MIN loop
                    if LEFT(I) < RIGHT.LIST(I) then
                       return false;
                    elsif RIGHT.LIST(I) < LEFT(I) then
                       return true;
                    end if;
                 end loop;
                 -- First items in slices in 1..MIN are equal
                 return MIN = RIGHT.LENGTH AND MIN /= LEFT'length;
            end GREATER;
```

of course, GREATER could be implemented directly by

```
            function GREATER (LEFT     : STRING;
                              RIGHT    : STRING ) return boolean is
               -- Returns true ib the string LEFT is greater than the string
               -- RIGHT when using the standard lexicographic orderings
            begin
               -- Note LEFT > RIGHT iff RIGHT < LEFT
               return LESS (RIGHT, LEFT);
            end GREATER;
```

The last example is the operator GET_SUBSTRING. This function is almost like an adjustable tail function in the list operators. It returns a SUBSTRING that is everything from a specified position onward.

```
            function GET_SUBSTRING (FROM    : STRING;
                                    START_AT : positive ) return SUBSTRING is
               -- Returns a substring that starts at a given point in
               -- the string and goes to the end of the string.
               -- Exception POSITION_ERROR raised if START_AT > LENGTH
               ANSWER : SUBSTRING (1..FROM.LENGTH – START_AT + 1);
            begin
               if START_AT > FROM.LENGTH then
                  raise POSITION_ERROR;
               else
                  ANS := FROM.LIST(START_AT..FROM.LENGTH);
                  return ANSWER;
               end if;
            end CET_SUBSTRING;
```

The implementation of the rest of the operations in GENERIC_BOUNDED_STRING is left to the exercises.

13.3 UNBOUNDED FORM

The data structure for the unbounded form will be a linked list structure with a separate field for storing the length of the list (see Figure 13.3.1). When declaring an unbounded STRING, there is no need to declare its maximum length. These two changes are the only differences between the specification for the bounded form in Figure 13.2.2 and the specification for the unbounded form in Figure 13.3.2.

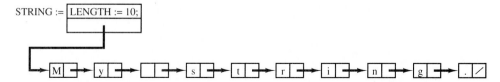

Figure 13.3.1 Unbounded_string Implementation holding the string 'My string'.

```
generic
   type ITEM_TYPE is private;
   with function "<" (LEFT, RIGHT : ITEM_TYPE) return boolean is  <> ;
package GENERIC_UNBOUNDED_STRING is
   type STRING is limited private;
   type SUBSTRING is array (positive range  <> ) OF ITEM_TYPE;
   procedure COPY          (FROM      : in     STRING;
                            TO        :     out STRING);
   procedure COPY          (FROM      : in     SUBSTRING;
                            TO        :     out STRING);
   procedure APPEND        (FROM      : in     ITEM_TYPE;
                            ONTO      : in out STRING);
   procedure APPEND        (FROM      : in     STRING;
                            ONTO      : in out STRING);
   procedure APPEND        (FROM      : in     SUBSTRING;
                            ONTO      : in out STRING);
   procedure APPEND        (FROM      : in     STRING;
                            ONTO      : in     SUBSTRING;
                            TARGET    : in out STRING);
   procedure INSERT        (FROM      : in     STRING;
                            INTO      : in out STRING;
                            POSITION : in     positive);
   procedure INSERT        (FROM      : in     SUBSTRING;
                            INTO      : in out STRING;
                            POSITION : in     positive);
   procedure INSERT        (FROM      : in     ITEM_TYPE;
                            INTO      : in out STRING;
                            POSITION : in     positive);
   procedure DELETE        (FROM      : in out STRING;
                            START_AT : in     positive;
                            END_AT   : in     positive);
   procedure CLEAR         (S         :     out STRING);
   procedure REPLACE       (IN_STRING: in out STRING;
```

Figure 13.3.2 Specification of ADT GENERIC_UNBOUNDED_STRING. Continues on page 456.

```
                              USING     : in     STRING;
                              START_AT : in     positive);
     procedure REPLACE        (IN_STRING: in out STRING;
                              USING     : in     SUBSTRING;
                              START_AT : in     positive);
     procedure REPLACE        (IN_STRING: in out STRING;
                              USING     : in     ITEM_TYPE;
                              START_AT : in     positive);
     function EMPTY           (S         : STRING ) return boolean;
     function EQUAL           (LEFT      : STRING;
                              RIGHT     : STRING ) return boolean;
     function EQUAL           (LEFT      : SUBSTRING;
                              RIGHT     : STRING ) return boolean;
     function EQUAL           (LEFT      : STRING;
                              RIGHT     : SUBSTRING ) return boolean;
     function LESS            (LEFT      : STRING;
                              RIGHT     : STRING ) return boolean;
     function LESS            (LEFT      : SUBSTRING;
                              RIGHT     : STRING ) return boolean;
     function LESS            (LEFT      : STRING;
                              RIGHT     : SUBSTRING ) return boolean;
     function GREATER         (LEFT      : STRING;
                              RIGHT     : STRING ) return boolean;
     function GREATER         (LEFT      : SUBSTRING;
                              RIGHT     : STRING ) return boolean;
     function GREATER         (LEFT      : STRING;
                              RIGHT     : SUBSTRING ) return boolean;
     function LENGTH          (S         : STRING ) return natural;
     function GET_ITEM        (FROM      : STRING;
                              POSITION : positive ) return ITEM_TYPE;
     function GET_STRING      (FROM      : STRING;
                              POSITION : positive ) return STRING;
     function GET_SUBSTRING (FROM       : STRING;
                              START_AT : positive ) return SUBSTRING;
     function GET_SUBSTRING (FROM       : STRING;
                              START_AT : positive;
                              END_AT   : positive ) return SUBSTRING;
   OVERFLOW        : exception;
   POSITION_ERROR : exception;
 private
   type STRING_NODE;
   type NEXT_NODE is access STRING_NODE;
   type STRING_NODE is
     RECORD
       ITEM : ITEM_TYPE;
       NEXT : NEXT_NODE;
     end RECORD;
```

Figure 13.3.2 Continues on page 457.

```
    type STRING is
      RECORD
        LENGTH : natural := 0;
        FIRST  : NEXT_NODE;
      end RECORD;
  end GENERIC_UNBOUNDED_STRING;
```

Figure 13.3.2 Concluded

It is not enough to adjust access values when implementing GENERIC_UN-BOUNDED_STRING. Consider two possible versions of the operation INSERT. Each inserts one STRING into a second STRING at a specified position. Figure 13.3.3(a) shows one possible implementation that just adjusts pointers of the STRING_NODEs. Figure 13.3.3(b) shows a second implementation where the items in the first STRING are first copied and then inserted. The second implementation must be used for unbounded strings, or the value of the first string can be modified anytime the second string is modified. Recall that it should make no difference to the programmer whether GENERIC_BOUNDED_STRING or GENERIC_UN-BOUNDED_STRING is instantiated and then applied to the problem under consideration.

To simplify the implementation of the operations in GENERIC_UN-BOUNDED_STRING, two procedures and one function will be added to the package body. By definition and design, these utilities will be available only inside the body of the package. These utilities make the implementation of the unbounded case similar to the implementation of the bounded case. The two procedures, both called COPY_TO_TEMPORARY, copy the list of items in a STRING or SUBSTRING to a temporary list. The length of the list is not computed. Their code is listed below.

```
    procedure COPY_TO_TEMPORARY (FROM : in    NEXT_NODE;
                                 TO   :    out NEXT_NODE ) is
      -- Make an exact copy of the string list FROM and returns it as TO
      -- Exception OVERFLOW raised if there is insufficient memory to
      --           store the result.
      TEMP_FROM : NEXT_NODE := FROM;
      TEMP_TO   : NEXT_NODE;
    begin
      if FROM = null then
        TO := null;
      else
        TEMP_TO := new STRING_NODE'(FROM.ITEM, null);
        TO := TEMP_TO;
        loop
          exit when TEMP_FROM.NEXT = null;
          TEMP_FROM := TEMP_FROM.NEXT;
          TEMP_TO.NEXT := new STRING_NODE'(TEMP_FROM.ITEM, null);
          TEMP_TO := TEMP_TO.NEXT;
        end loop;
      end if;
    exception
      when storage_error => raise OVERFLOW;
    end COPY_TO_TEMPORARY;
```

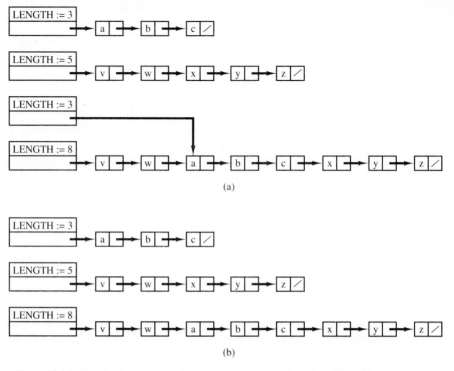

Figure 13.3.3 Two implementations of the procedure insert. (a) Insertion of first string into second at position = 3 without copying, resulting in second string looking like the third. (b) First string copied into second at position = 3, resulting in the third string.

```
procedure COPY_TO_TEMPORARY (FROM : in      SUBSTRING;
                                TO   :    out NEXT_NODE ) is
  -- Converts the substring FROM to a string and returns that string
  -- as TO
  -- Exception OVERFLOW raised if there is insufficient memory to
  --           store the result.
  TEMP_TO   : NEXT_NODE;
begin
  if FROM'length = 0 then
    TO := null;
  else
    TEMP_TO := new STRING_NODE'(FROM(1), null);
    TO := TEMP_TO;
    for INDEX in positive range 2..FROM'last loop
      TEMP_TO.NEXT := new STRING_NODE'( FROM(INDEX), null);
      TEMP_TO := TEMP_TO.NEXT;
    end loop;
  end if;
exception
  when storage_error => raise OVERFLOW;
end COPY_TO_TEMPORARY;
```

The additional function LOCATE_NODE returns the pointer to the STRING_NODE at a given position of a STRING. The typical use is to get the STRING_NODE at the position preceding the one you are modifying and then access the desired node by using the "next" field. For example,

```
TEMP_NEXT := LOCATE_NODE (S, 9);
```

returns the pointer to the ninth node, but TEMP_NEXT.NEXT points to the tenth node. This function locates the specified STRING_NODE when other STRING_NODES are to be deleted, inserted, or replaced.

```
function LOCATE_NODE (S_IN  : STRING;
                      PLACE : positive) return NEXT_NODE is
  -- Returns a reference to the STRING_NODE is S_IN at position PLACE
  TEMP : NEXT_NODE := S_IN.FIRST;
begin
  if PLACE > S_IN.LENGTH then
    raise POSITION_ERROR;
  elsE
    for INDEX in natural range 2..PLACE loop
      TEMP := TEMP.NEXT;
    end loop;
  end if;
  return TEMP;
end LOCATE_NODE;
```

These three utility operations essentially replace most needs for loops in the implementation. The same operations, that is, procedures and functions, implemented in the bounded case are shown for the unbounded case. This will allow the reader to compare implementations. To help understand the code, some comments using array notation have been added. The special cases occur at position equal to 1. The rest are left as an exercise.

The two versions of copy are essentially the same as COPY_TO_TEMPORARY except that the lengths need adjusting.

```
procedure COPY (FROM : in     STRING;
                TO   :     out STRING) is
  -- Makes exact copy of the string FROM
  -- Exception OVERFLOW raised if there is insufficient memory to
  --          store the result
  TEMP : NEXT_NODE;
begin
  COPY_TO_TEMPORARY (FROM.FIRST, TEMP);
  TO := (FROM.LENGTH, TEMP);
exception
  when OVERFLOW => raise OVERFLOW;
end COPY;
procedure COPY (FROM : in     SUBSTRING;
                TO   :     out STRING) is
  -- Makes exact copy of the substring FROM and converts it to a
```

```
  -- string
  -- Exception OVERFLOW raised if there is insufficient memory to
  --            store the result.
  TEMP : NEXT_NODE;
begin
  COPY_TO_TEMPORARY (FROM, TEMP);
  TO := (FROM'length, TEMP);
exception
  when OVERFLOW => raise OVERFLOW;
end COPY;
```

The APPEND procedure just finds the pointer to the next-to-last node and then copies the second STRING or SUBSTRING as appropriate.

```
procedure APPEND (FROM   : in      STRING;
                  ONTO   : in      SUBSTRING;
                  TARGET : in out STRING) is
  -- Converts the substring ONTO a string and then adjoins
  -- a copy of the string FROM onto its end and returns the
  -- combined string as TARGET.
  -- Exception OVERFLOW raised if there is insufficient
  --            memory to store the result
  TEMP : NEXT_NODE;
begin
  -- Convert substring to string
  COPY_TO_TEMPORARY (ONTO, TEMP);
  TARGET := (ONTO'length, TEMP);
  -- Find the last STRING_NODE in the list TARGET.FIRST
  TEMP := LOCATE_NODE (TARGET, ONTO'length);
  -- Copy string from to last element of string TEMP
  COPY_TO_TEMPORARY (FROM.FIRST, TEMP.NEXT);
  TARGET.LENGTH := FROM.LENGTH + ONTO'length;
exception
  when OVERFLOW => raise OVERFLOW;
end APPEND;
```

INSERT and REPLACE are easily implemented. Both require that the position exception be tested and then the appropriate copies are inserted into the result at the appropriate place.

```
procedure INSERT (FROM     : in      STRING;
                  INTO     : in out STRING;
                  POSITION : in      positive) is
  -- Inserts a copy of the a string FROM at a given position
  -- in the string INTO.
  -- Exception OVERFLOW raised if there is insufficient
  --           memory to store the result
  -- Exception POSITION_ERROR raised if POSITION > LENGTH
  TEMP1, TEMP2 : NEXT_NODE;
begin
  if POSITION > INTO.LENGTH then
    raise POSITION_ERROR;
```

```
    else
      -- Copy from position to end of string into temp2
      TEMP1 := LOCATE_NODE(INTO, POSITION-1);
      TEMP2 := TEMP1.NEXT;
      -- Copy entire string FROM to INTO starting at POSITION
      COPY_TO_TEMPORARY (FROM.FIRST, TEMP1.NEXT);
      -- Put rest of into stored in temp2 back onto into
      TEMP1 := LOCATE_NODE (INTO, FROM.LENGTH+POSITION-1);
      TEMP1.NEXT := TEMP2;
      INTO.LENGTH := INTO.LENGTH + FROM.LENGTH;
    end if;
  exception
    when OVERFLOW => raise OVERFLOW;
  end INSERT;

  procedure REPLACE (IN_STRING: in out STRING;
                     USING    : in     STRING;
                     START_AT : in     positive) is
    -- Deletes all items starting at the position START_AT through the
    -- end of the string IN_S.  Then appends the string USING onto the
    -- end of the result.
    -- Exception OVERFLOW raised if there is insufficient
    --            memory to store the result
    -- Exception POSITION_ERROR raised if START_AT > LENGTH
    TEMP : NEXT_NODE;
  begin
    if START_AT > IN_STRING.LENGTH then
      raise POSITION_ERROR;
    elsif START_AT = 1 then
      -- If START_AT = 1, effect is to clear IN_S and copy USING
      COPY_TO_TEMPORARY (USING.FIRST, IN_STRING.FIRST);
      IN_STRING.LENGTH := USING.LENGTH;
    else
      -- Find node before START_AT in IN_STRING
      TEMP := LOCATE_NODE (IN_STRING, START_AT-1);
      -- Copy string using at START_AT node, adjust length
      COPY_TO_TEMPORARY (USING.FIRST, TEMP.NEXT);
      IN_SSTRING.LENGTH := START_AT + USING.LENGTH - 1;
    end if;
  exception
    when OVERFLOW => raise OVERFLOW;
  end REPLACE;
```

The boolean-valued functions must traverse the given STRINGs or SUBSTRINGs item by item. After implementing LESS, GREATER follows by reversing the arguments.

```
  function EQUAL (LEFT  : STRING;
                  RIGHT : SUBSTRING ) return boolean is
    -- Returns true if two strings of equal length have the same items
    -- in the same position.
    TEMP : NEXT_NODE := LEFT.FIRST;
```

```
begin
  if LEFT.LENGTH = RIGHT'length then
    -- LEFT and RIGHT have same length, check item by item
    for I in RIGHT'range loop
      if TEMP.ITEM /= RIGHT(I) then
        return false;
      else
        TEMP := TEMP.NEXT;
      end if;
    end loop;
    -- All items are equal
    return true;
  else
    -- Lengths are different, can't be equal
    return false;
  end if;
end EQUAL;


function LESS (LEFT  : STRING;
              RIGHT : STRING ) return boolean is
  -- Returns true if the string LEFT is less than the string
  -- RIGHT when using the standard lexicographic orderings
  MIN : natural := LEFT.LENGTH;
  TEMP_L : NEXT_NODE := LEFT.FIRST;
  TEMP_R : NEXT_NODE := RIGHT.FIRST;
begin
  if TEMP_L = null and then TEMP_R = null then
    return false;
  elsif TEMP_L = null then
    return true;
  else
    -- Make sure that the minimum length is correctly defined
    if MIN < RIGHT.LENGTH then
      MIN := RIGHT.LENGTH;
    end if;
    --Compare ITEM by ITEM based on lexicographic order
    for I in natural range 1..MIN loop
      if TEMP_L.ITEM < TEMP.R.ITEM then
        return true;
      elsif TEMP_R.ITEM < TEMP_L.ITEM then
        return false;
      else
        TEMP_L := TEMP_L.NEXT;
        TEMP_R := TEMP_R.NEXT;
      end if;
    end loop;
    -- The first MIN characteristics of LEFT and RIGHT are equal
    return MIN = LEFT.LENGTH and MIN /= RIGHT.LENGTH;
  end if;
end LESS;
```

```
function GREATER (LEFT  : STRING;
                  RIGHT : STRING ) return boolean is
  -- Returns true if the string LEFT is greater than the string
  -- RIGHT when using the standard lexicographic orderings
begin
  -- Note LEFT > RIGHT iff RIGHT < LEFT
  return LESS (RIGHT, LEFT);
end GREATER;
```

The last example is the function GET_SUBSTRING.

```
function GET_SUBSTRING (FROM     : STRING;
                        START_AT : positive ) return SUBSTRING is
  -- Returns a substring that starts at a given point in
  -- the string and goes to the end of the string.
  -- Exception POSITION_ERROR raised if START_AT > LENGTH
  -- or if START_AT > END_AT.
  ANS : SUBSTRING (1..FROM.LENGTH – START_AT + 1);
  TEMP : NEXT_NODE;
begin
  if START_AT > FROM.LENGTH then
    raise POSITION_ERROR;
  else
    TEMP := LOCATE_NODE (FROM, START_AT);
      -- TEMP references the START_AT the STRING_NODE, copy item by
      -- item
    for I in positive range 1..FROM.LENGTH – START_AT + 1 loop
      ANS(I) := TEMP.ITEM;
      TEMP := TEMP.NEXT;
    end loop;
    return ANS;
  end if;
exception
  when OVERFLOW => raise OVERFLOW;
end GET_SUBSTRING;
```

Just as in the bounded string case, the rest of the implementation is left to the exercises.

13.4 PATTERN MATCHING

One major editor operation that is not in either string package might be called "find." This operation starts searching a target string at a given position for a match of a pattern string. After finding a match, the position where the first item matches is returned. If there is no match, zero is returned. Using the ADT STRING operations, the function FIND can be implemented as

```
function FIND (S        : STRING;
               PATTERN  : STRING;
               START_AT : positive ) return natural is
begin
```

```
     if LENGTH(PATTERN) > LENGTH(S) - START_AT + 1 then
        return 0;
     else
        for INDEX in positive range START_AT..LENGTH(S)-LENGTH(PATTERN)+1 loop
          if EQUAL(GET_STRING(S, INDEX, INDEX+LENGTH(PATTERN)-1),PATTERN))then
             return INDEX;
          end if;
        end loop;
        return 0;
     end if
  end FIND;
```

This is an example of a brute-force type of pattern-matching algorithm. In this section several pattern-matching strategies are examined. In the exercises, two operations, FIND and FIND_AND_REPLACE, will be added to the STRING ADT. For the rest of this section only, all strings are defined by

```
          type STRING is array (positive range <>) of ITEM_TYPE;
```

For simplicity S' first is always 1 for any string S. The implementation of these algorithms using the basic definitions of string in either GENERIC_BOUNDED_STRING or GENERIC_UNBOUNDED_STRING is straightforward once the basic ideas are understood.

The basic brute-force string pattern-matching function becomes

```
     function FIND ( SOURCE   : STRING;
                     PATTERN  : STRING;
                     START_AT : positive ) return natural is
        INDEX : positive;
        FAIL : boolean := false;
        LENGTH_PATTERN : positive := LENGTH (PATTERN);
        LENGTH_SOURCE  : positive := LENGTH (SOURCE);
     begin
        for POSITION in START_AT..LENGTH_SOURCE - LENGTH_PATTERN + 1 loop
          INDEX := 1;
          while not FAIL and then INDEX <= LENGTH_PATTERN loop
             if PATTERN (INDEX) = SOURCE (POSITION + INDEX - 1), then
                INDEX := INDEX + 1;
             else
                fail := true;
             end if;
          end loop;
          if not FAIL then
             return POSITION;
          end if;
          FAIL := false;
        end loop;
        return 0;
     end FIND;
```

In the algorithm above (LENGTH_S – LENGTH_PATTERN + 1), attempts are made to find a match. Determining if there is a match at a given position is an O(LENGTH_PAT-TERN) process. Depending on the value of START_AT, this process can range from O(LENGTH_PATTERN + LENGTH_S) to O(LENGTH_PATTERN * LENGTH_S). The reason for this wide range of complexity is that in most calls, complete execution of the inner loop is rare. The reason is that the first mismatch causes it to jump out. If PATTERN = 'zoo' and S = 'No news is not necessarily good news', the inner loop fails on the first character every time. If the PATTERN is 'aaaaaaaaaab' and the string SOURCE is

SOURCE = 'aaaaaaaaaaaaaaaaaaaaaaaaaaaaaaaaaaaaaaaaab'

the inner loop executes 10*30 times before finding a match.

There are several approaches to improve the efficiency of this search problem. Three of the more famous are the Knuth–Morris–Pratt algorithm, the Boyer–Moore algorithm, and the Rabin–Karp algorithm. The first two require some preprocessing, while the last uses hashing techniques. Most word processors' search operations have been speeded up significantly using one of these methods because they often run in O(LENGTH_PATTERN + LENGTH_S) time.

The *Knuth–Morris–Pratt* (KMP) *algorithm* is formulated so that the pointer in the target string is never backed up. The insight that allows this is to use some preprocessed information about the pattern string. Suppose that

SOURCE = cdbababacdabab
PATTERN = baba'cda

The first character of SOURCE and pattern do not line up until the third character of SOURCE. Then the third through sixth characters of SOURCE match the first through fourth characters of PATTERN, with a mismatch occurring at the seventh character of SOURCE and the fifth character of PATTERN. The brute-force search would start all over at the third character of SOURCE. The KMP search uses its knowledge of the partial match and the knowledge gained from preprocessing of the PATTERN to start a search at the seventh character of SOURCE and the third character of

SOURCE = cdbababacdabab
PATTERN =   ba'bacda

Note that the pointer of SOURCE has not been decremented. The preprocessed information about PATTERN and facts about the previous match make it unnecessary to check out the known two-symbol matches starting at the fifth position of SOURCE.

An array NEXT with range 1 . . LENGTH_PATTERN determines how far to back up after detecting a mismatch. For POSITION > 1, the distance to back up at a mismatch of the character at place POSITION, NEXT(POSITION), is one plus the number of overlapping characters. The value of NEXT(1) is set to 0. In Figure 13.4.1, the first column is place, the POSITION, in the pattern string above where the mismatch occurred, the second column is the first POSITION-1 characters of PATTERN that matched, the third column is the number of overlapping characters in the second column, and the fourth column is the value of NEXT(POSITION). Note that the value of NEXT(POSITION) depends only on the PATTERN and not on the string that is being matched.

POSITION	PATTERN(1..POSITION-1)	Overlapping Characters	NEXT(POSITION)
1		0	0
2	b	0	1
3	ba	0	1
4	bab	1	2
5	baba	2	3
6	babac	0	1
7	babacd	0	1

Figure 13.4.1   Example of NEXT function in KMP algorithm.

It is relatively simple to visualize how to find the values in NEXT(POSITION). If a mismatch has occurred at the POSITION place of PATTERN, imagine sliding a copy of the first POSITION-1 characters of PATTERN over itself, moving from left to right, until either a match occurs or the string has slid beyond itself. Figure 13.4.2 shows the cases for POSITION=5 and POSITION=6. The value of NEXT(POSITION), for POSITION > 1, is the value INDEX < POSITION for which the first INDEX-1 characters of the PATTERN match the last INDEX-1 characters of first POSITION-1 characters of the PATTERN.

```
POSITION=5                        POSITION=6
baba      initial                 babac     initial position
baba                              babac


baba      overlap=0               babac     overlap=0
 baba                              babac
baba      overlap=2               babac     overlap=0
  baba                             babac


                                  babac     overlap=0
                                   babac


                                  babac     overlap=0
                                   babac
```

Figure 13.4.2   Example of computing overlap in NEXT.

Suppose that the NEXT table has been computed for some PATTERN. If a mismatch occurs at the symbol in position PLACE of SOURCE and the symbol in position INDEX of PATTERN, the brute-force search resets the value of PLACE to PLACE-INDEX+1, and resets INDEX to 1. The KMP search algorithm uses the information in the NEXT table. This table knows that the first NEXT(INDEX)-1 characters at position PLACE-INDEX+1 match the first NEXT(INDEX)-1 of PATTERN, so there is no need to decrement PLACE. The value of INDEX is reset to NEXT(INDEX). The KMP search algorithm is

```
function KMP_SEARCH ( SOURCE, PATTERN : STRING) return natural is

    type NEXT_TYPE is array (PATTERN'range) of natural;

    SOURCE_INDEX : natural := SOURCE'first;
```

```
      PATTERN_INDEX : natural := 1;
      LENGTH_PATTERN : natural := LENGTH (PATTERN);
      LENGTH_SOURCE  : natural := LENGTH (SOURCE);
      NEXT : NEXT_TYPE;

      procedure FIND_NEXT (PATTERN : in      STRING;
                           NEXT     : in out NEXT_TYPE ) is
        INDEX : natural := 1;
        MATCH : natural := 0;
  begin
      NEXT(1) := 0;
      while INDEX < PATTERN'last loop
        if MATCH = 0 or else PATTERN (INDEX) = PATTERN (MATCH) then
          INDEX := INDEX + 1;
          MATCH := MATCH + 1;
          NEXT(INDEX) := MATCH;
        else
          MATCH := NEXT (MATCH);
        end if;
      end loop;
    end FIND_NEXT;

begin
  FIND_NEXT (PATTERN, NEXT);
  while PATTERN_INDEX <= LENGTH_PATTERN and SOURCE_INDEX <= LENGTH_SOURCE
    loop
      if PATTERN_INDEX = 0 or else
           SOURCE(SOURCE_INDEX := PATTERN(PATTERN_INDEX) then
      SOURCE_INDEX := SOURCE_INDEX +1;
      PATTERN_INDEX := PATTERN_INDEX + 1;
    else
      PATTERN_INDEX := NEXT(PATTERN_INDEX);
    end if;
  end loop;
  if PATTERN_INDEX > LENGTH_PATTERN then
    return SOURCE_INDEX - LENGTH_PATTERN;
  else
    return 0;
  end if;
end KMP_SEARCH;
```

When PATTERN_INDEX = 1 and there is no match with S(SOURCE_INDEX), there is no overlap, so SOURCE_INDEX must be incremented and PATTERN_INDEX set to point to the first symbol in pattern. By defining NEXT(1) equal to 0, the next pass through the loop increments SOURCE_INDEX and sets PATTERN_INDEX equal to 1. This is why NEXT(1) is 0. This program is functionally the same as the brute-force search, but it will run much faster if PATTERN has repetitive subsequences. PATTERN strings with repetitive sequences occur often, particularly when trying to match strings of bits.

Since the pointer to the string SOURCE is never backed up, the KMP search algorithm is attractive for the unbounded implementation, which uses a single linked list. Implementing this algorithm is left to the exercises. Using the operation GET_SUBSTRING to convert PATTERN to a SUBSTRING makes for a straightforward implementation.

If backing the pointer up is not a problem, the *Boyer–Moore algorithm* can speed up searching significantly. Instead of comparing and scanning left to right, Boyer–Moore scans right to left. Instead of working from left to right and resetting the pattern based on partial matches, Boyer–Moore looks for mismatches from right to left and uses this information to skip ahead to the first place a match might occur. Boyer–Moore uses both the character in the text SOURCE that caused the mismatch and knowledge about what characters appear where in PATTERN to decide how far to skip ahead. Consider the initial situation at SOURCE_INDEX=PATTERN_INDEX=7.

```
SOURCE  =  cdbababacdabab
PATTERN = babacda (note)
```

The character at location SOURCE_INDEX of SOURCE is a "b" while the character at location PATTERN_INDEX of PATTERN is an "a," a mismatch. The knowledge that the character at SOURCE_INDEX of SOURCE is a "b" is used to shift PATTERN four places to the right. Here a match occurs and the process of comparing starting at the end of PATTERN resumes, that is,

```
SOURCE  =  cdbababacdabab
PATTERN = babacda (note)
```

If the character in SOURCE that caused the mismatch did not appear in PATTERN, the shift would have been LENGTH_PATTERN. Recall that for every enumerated type (most strings are lists of some enumerated type) the attribute Pos takes a value of the enumeration and returns a natural corresponding to the position number of the value in the enumeration. (T'Pos(T'first) is 0 for any enumerated type T. In other words, the position number of the first listed enumerated value is 0, the second is 1, and so on. See Appendix A or the LRM Sections 3.5.1 and 3.5.5). Assuming that the compacts of STRING are of some enumerated type (characters and symbols are always enumerated types), the B_M_SKIP_SEARCH algorithm can be implemented as follows:

```
function B_M_SKIP_SEARCH (SOURCE, PATTERN : STRING ) return natural is

   subtype ITEM_INDEX is character range
          character'first..character'last;
   type SKIP_ARRAY is array (ITEM_INDEX) of natural;
   SKIP : SKIP_ARRAY;
   LENGTH_PATTERN,
   SOURCE_INDEX,
   PATTERN_INDEX : natural := LENGTH (PATTERN);
   SOURCE_LENGTH : natural := LENGTH (SOURCE);

   procedure GET_SKIP ( PATTERN : in     STRING;
                        SKIP    :    out SKIP_ARRAY ) is
      PATTERN_LENGTH : natural := LENGTH (PATTERN);
   begin
      SKIP (SKIP'range) := (others => PATTERN_LENGTH);
```

```
        for INDEX in PATTERN'range loop
          SKIP (PATTERN (INDEX)) := LENGTH_PATTERN - natural(INDEX);
        end loop;
      end GET_SKIP;

    begin
      GET_SKIP (PATTERN, SKIP);
      loop
        if PATTERN_INDEX = 0 then
          --success
          return SOURCE_INDEX + 1;
        elsif SOURCE_INDEX > SOURCE_LENGTH then
          -- Pattern not found
          return 0;
        elsif SOURCE (SOURCE_INDEX) = PATTERN (PATTERN_INDEX) then
          SOURCE_INDEX := SOURCE_INDEX - 1;
          PATTERN_INDEX := PATTERN_INDEX - 1;
        else
          PATTERN_INDEX := LENGTH_PATTERN;
          SOURCE_INDEX := SOURCE_INDEX + SKIP (SOURCE (SOURCE_INDEX));
        end if;
      end loop;
    end B_M_SKIP_SEARCH;
```

The procedure GET_SKIP makes up an array equal in length to the number of values in the enumerated type and indexed by the values in the enumeration. Every element in SKIP is either the length of PATTERN, which means that the index value is not in PATTERN, so skip forward the full length of PATTERN, or it is the number of places to skip so that the rightmost occurrence is the PATTERN of the value that matches the value in SOURCE (SOURCE_INDEX).

The Boyer–Moore algorithm increases in efficiency as both the number of symbols in the enumeration gets larger and as the PATTERN length increases. A match takes, on average, about *M/N* steps. Because of the need to back up string indices, Boyer–Moore is not a good candidate for unbounded strings unless the data structure is a doubly linked list. Boyer–Moore is an ideal candidate for bounded strings.

The last method examined, the *Rabin–Karp algorithm,* converts the pattern string and each substring with the same length in the string to be searched to a number and compares this number. The method is similar to hashing, which was covered in Chapter 12. The trick is arriving at the number that corresponds to the substring in an efficient manner. Suppose that A denotes an array of N positive numbers, where N is a fixed integer. Let WL be a fixed positive number. For each integer I between 1 and N-4, define

$$p(I) = A(I)*WL**4 + A(I+1)*WL**3 + A(I+2)*WL**2 + A(I+3)*WL + A(I+4)$$

The Rabin–Karp algorithm notes that if p(I) is known, p(I+1) can easily be computed. Note that

$$p(I+1) = (p(I) - A(I)*WL**4)*WL + A(I+5)$$

If WL**4 is computed beforehand and stored, then p(I+1) follows from p(I) by two multiplications, one addition and one subtraction. In this example the length of PATTERN was of N=5, hence the fourth-degree polynomial, which has five coefficients. Obviously, patterns of PATTERN_LENGTH would generate a polynomial of degree PATTERN_LENGTH-1.

In the Rabin–Karp algorithm, A(I) is the ASCII value of the Ith character in the string and WL corresponds to the integer word length. There is an apparent problem that must be addressed. In computing p(I) it is possible that one of the operations might cause the rising of the exception NUMERIC_ERROR when the value for a partially computed p(I) exceeds the largest value that can be stored. This difficulty is overcome by using modular arithmetic. A large prime Q is selected.

The value of p(I) should always be positive. At any step in the process, it is not p(I) that is not stored or compared, it is p(I) mod Q. When p(I+1) is computed, it is possible that

$$p(I) - A(I)*WL**4$$

is negative. To guarantee that p(I+1) is always positive, a large positive value that drops out in the mod process will be added before the mod operation is performed. Clearly, for any number X,

$$(X*Q) \bmod Q = 0$$

In fact, the reader should verify that for all X and P such that $0 < P < Q$,

$$(P + X*Q) \bmod Q = P$$

This implies that the final step in computing p(I+1) from p(I) should be

$$p(I+1) = (((p(I) + X*Q - A(I)*WL**4) * WL) \bmod Q) + A(I+5)) \bmod Q$$

for a suitable value of X that depends on the word length used to store an integer in a particular computer, and the length of the pattern string that is being matched. It appears that the string PATTERN and some other distinct string of the same length as PATTERN might have values that are equal. Although this is possible, it is not very likely. The possibility is ignored.

How does the Rabin–Karp pattern matching algorithm work? First, a value is found for the string PATTERN using the ideas outlined above. If SOURCE is the string to be searched, a value for every substring of SOURCE that has the same length as PATTERN is computed. If two values are equal, a match has been found. If the values are not equal, the value for the next substring in SOURCE is computed in much the same manner as p(I + 1) is computed from p(I). This continues until the end of SOURCE is reached or a match has been found. The full implementation follows.

```
function RK_SEARCH (SOURCE, PATTERN : STRING ) return natural is
   LARGE_PRIME        : constant long_integer := 33554393;
   WL                 : constant long_integer := 32;
   PATTERN_VALUE,
   SUBSTRING_VALUE    : long_integer := 0;
   DM                 : long_integer := 1;
   SOURCE_INDEX       : integer := 1;
   LENGTH_SOURCE      : integer := LENGTH (SOURCE);
   LENGTH_PATTERN     : integer := LENGTH (PATTERN);
begin
   -- DM needed when subtracting off first character. Compute it once
   -- and save it.
   for INDEX in 1..LENGTH_PATTERN - 1 loop
     DM := (DM*WL) mod LARGE_PRIME;
   end loop;
   -- Compute values for PATTERN and first substring in SOURCE.
   for INDEX in positive range 1..LENGTH_PATTERN loop
```

```
-- Compute hash value for pattern
PATTERN_VALUE := (PATTERN_VALUE*WL + character'pos ( PATTERN(INDEX)))
                                        mod LARGE_PRIME;
-- Compute hash value for first possible match in S
SUBSTRING_VALUE := (SUBSTRING_VALUE*WL +
                 character'pos ( SOURCE(INDEX))) mod LARGE_PRIME;
end loop;
while PATTERN_VALUE /= SUBSTRING_VALUE and
        SOURCE_INDEX <= LENGTH_SOURCE - LENGTH_PATTERN loop
-- extra WL*LARGE_PRIME term keeps SUBSTRING_VALUE term positive but
-- drops out in mod operation as (WL*LARGE_PRIME) mod LARGE_PRIME = 0
-- First, subtract off the value of the first character in old
-- SUBSTRING_VALUE
SUBSTRING_VALUE := (SUBSTRING_VALUE + WL*LARGE_PRIME
                     - character'pos (SOURCE(SOURCE_INDEX)) *DM)
                                        mod LARGE_PRIME;
-- And then multiply by WL and add the next term
SUBSTRING_VALUE := (SUBSTRING_VALUE + WL +
                character'pos (SOURCE(SOURCE_INDEX+ LENGTH_PATTERN)))
                                        mod LARGE_PRIME;
    -- Update SOURCE_INDEX to first character of substring to be
    -- examined.
  SOURCE_INDEX := SOURCE_INDEX + 1;
end loop;
if SUBSTRING_VALUE = PATTERN_VALUE then
  return SOURCE_INDEX;
else
  return 0;
end if;
end RK_SEARCH;
```

This algorithm is typically $O(\text{LENGTH}(S) + \text{LENGTH}(\text{PATTERN}))$.

There are other pattern-matching schemes that can be used successfully, including methods based on binary search trees. The four covered here each have strengths and weaknesses.

13.5 APPLICATIONS

The obvious applications of the ADT STRING would be in developing editors and word processing packages. The basis of all editors and word processors is string processing. If the instantiation

```
package WP_STRING is new GENERIC_UNBOUNDED_STRING (character);
```

then the following function would return the next word in a string, starting at a given position.

```
function NEXT_WORD(SOURCE : WP_STRING.STRING; AT : positive)
            return WP_STRING.STRING is
  -- At is assumed to be the location of the first character of
  -- the word. Blank should cause function to terminate.
  WORD  : WP_STRING.STRING;
```

```
            NEXT_CH : character;
        begin
          for PLACE in AT..WP_STRING.LENGTH (SOURCE) loop
            NEXT_CH := GET_ITEM(S, PLACE);
            case NEXT_CH is
              when 'a'..'z' | 'A'..'Z' | '.' | '?' | ',' | '!' =>
                APPEND(NEXT_CH, WORD);
              when others =>
                return WORD;
            end case;
          end loop;
        end NEXT_WORD;
```

A function GET_NEXT_LINE can be built up by repeated calls to GET_WORD while inserting blanks between words until finding an end-of-line character or the next word overflowed the line length. After implementing GET_LINE, procedures to get a screen or get a page follow. Eventually, a word processor or editor is the result.

    Strings also can be used to implement packages that do arithmetic operations to any precision. To pass strings as procedure parameters with mode "out" or "in out," the package GENERIC_UNBOUNDED_STRING must be recompiled with type STRING declared as private instead of limited private. Recall that a syntax error results if a limited private type is passed back [see LRM 7.4.4(4)]. If a package of digits were defined as

```
        subtype DIGIT is integer range 0..9;
        package HIGH_PRECISION_INTEGER is new GENERIC_UNBOUNDED_STRING (DIGIT);
```

an integer of arbitrary precision can be represented as a string. Figure 13.5.1 illustrates the representation of two integers of arbitrary magnitude. Note that the least significant digit is at the far end of the string. Addition is easy to implement. Addition is performed digit by digit, from right to left. Since it is unknown if the integers are of the same magnitude, the programmer must exercise caution not to reference undefined digit positions.

X := 923457;
Y := 246801357;

(a)

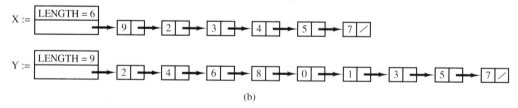

(b)

Figure 13.5.1 String representation of high-precision integers (a) Two arbitrary integers. (b) String representation of integers in part (a).

```
        Procedure ADD_X_TO_Y (X   : in      HIGH_PRECISION_INTEGER.STRING;
                              Y   : in      HIGH_PRECISION_INTEGER.STRING;
                              ANS :      out HIGH_PRECISION_INTEGER.STRING) is
```

```
    CARRY     : integer := 0;
    LENGTH_X : natural := HIGH_PRECISION_INTEGER.LENGTH(X);
    LENGTH_Y : natural := HIGH_PRECISION_INTEGER.LENGTH(Y);
    TEMP      : HIGH_PRECISION_INTEGER.STRING;
begin
  -- Get least significant digit, initialize the carry
  CARRY := HIGH_PRECISION_INTEGER.GET_ITEM (X, LENGTH_X) +
             HIGH_PRECISION_INTEGER.GET_ITEM (Y, LENGTH_Y);
  HIGH_PRECISION_INTEGER.APPEND (CARRY rem 10, TEMP);
  CARRY := (CARRY - (CARRY rem 10))/10;
  LENGTH_X := LENGTH_X - 1;
  LENGTH_Y := LENGTH_Y - 1;
  loop
    if LENGTH_Y = 0 then
      loop
        -- Add the rest of X if length of X exceeds length of Y
        exit when LENGTH_X = 0;
        CARRY := CARRY+ HIGH_PRECISION_INTEGER.GET_ITEM (X, LENGTH_X);
        HIGH_PRECISION_INTEGER.INSERT( CARRY rem 10, TEMP, 1);
        CARRY := (CARRY - (CARRY rem 10))/10;
        LENGTH_X := LENGTH_X - ;
      end loop;
      exit;
    elsif LENGTH_X = 0 then
      loop
        -- Add the rest of Y ...
        exit when LENGTH_Y = 0;
        CARRY := CARRY+ HIGH_PRECISION_INTEGER.GET_ITEM (Y, LENGTH_Y);
        HIGH_PRECISION_INTEGER.INSERT( CARRY rem 10, TEMP, 1);
        CARRY := (CARRY - (CARRY rem 10))/10;
        LENGTH_Y := LENGTH_Y - 1;
      end loop;
      exit;
    else
      -- Get next digit in X and Y, Add, Compute Carry
      CARRY := CARRY + HIGH_PRECISION_INTEGER.GET_ITEM (X, LENGTH_X)
                 + HIGH_PRECISION_INTEGER.GET_ITEM (Y, LENGTH_Y);
      -- Put result in the answer TEMP
      HIGH_PRECISION_INTEGER.INSERT (CARRY rem 10, TEMP, 1);
      CARRY := (CARRY - (CARRY rem 10))/10;
      LENGTH_X := LENGTH_X - 1;
      LENGTH_Y := LENGTH_Y - 1;
    end if;
  end loop;
  -- May still be carrying a carry digit
  if CARRY /= 0 then
    HIGH_PRECISION_INTEGER.INSERT(CARRY, TEMP, 1);
  end if;
    HIGH_PRECISION_INTEGER.COPY (TEMP, ANS);
end ADD_X_TO_Y;
```

Multiplication follows immediately once a procedure is used that multiplies an integer by a digit. The multiplication algorithm is the same as the one taught in grade school. For each digit, one term is multiplied by the digit, and the shifted result is added to the running total (see Figure 13.5.2).

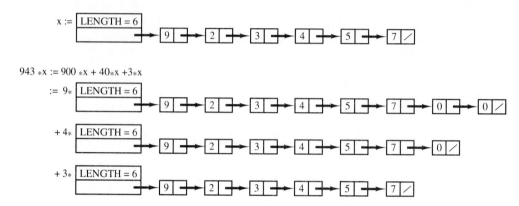

Figure 13.5.2 Multiplication of two high-precision integers where the integers are stored as strings.

```
procedure MUL_X_BY_DIGIT ( X    :    in HIGH_PRECISION_INTEGER.STRING;
                           D    :    in DIGIT;
                           ANS  :    out HIGH_PRECISION_INTEGER.STRING )
                           is
   CARRY : integer := 0;
   LENGTH_X : natural := HIGH_PRECISION_INTEGER.LENGTH(X);
   TEMP : HIGH_PRECISION_INTEGER.STRING;
begin
   -- Get least significant digit, multiply by D, and compute Carry digit
   CARRY := HIGH_PRECISION_INTEGER.GET_ITEM (X, LENGTH_X)*D;
   HIGH_PRECISION_INTEGER.APPEND (CARRY rem 10, TEMP);
   CARRY := (CARRY - (CARRY rem 10))/10;
   LENGTH_X := LENGTH_X - 1;
   -- For each digit from right to left
   while Length_X /= 0 loop
      -- Get next digit, multiply by D
      CARRY := CARRY + HIGH_PRECISION_INTEGER.GET_ITEM (X, LENGTH_X)*D;
      -- Insert the answer minus the carry intk TEMP
      HIGH_PRECISION_INTEGER.INSERT (CARRY rem 10, TEMP, 1);
      -- Update Carry digit and number of digits remaing
      CARRY := (CARRY - (CARRY rem 10))/10;
      LENGTH_X := LENGTH_X - 1;
   end loop;
   -- If there is still a carry digit
   if CARRY /= 0 then
      HIGH_PRECISION_INTEGER.INSERT(CARRY,TEMP,1);
   end if;
   HIGH_PRECISION_INTEGER.COPY(TEMP, ANS);
end MUL_X_BY_DIGIT;
```

```
procedure MUL_X_BY_Y (X    : in     HIGH_PRECISION_INTEGER.STRING;
                      Y    : in     HIGH_PRECISION_INTEGER.STRING;
                      ANS :    out HIGH_PRECISION_INTEGER.STRING) is
     D : DIGIT;
     TEMP1, TEMP2, TEMP3 : HIGH_PRECISION_INTEGER.STRING;
     LENGTH_Y : natural := HIGH_PRECISION_INTEGER.LENGTH(Y);
begin
     -- Copy X to a temporary string
     HIGH_PRECISION_INTEGER.COPY (X, TEMP1);
     -- Multiply X by least significant digit, store in TEMP3, which
     -- accumulates the answer.
     MUL_X_BY_DIGIT(TEMP1,
             HIGH_PRECISION_INTEGER.GET_ITEM (Y,LENGTH_Y), TEMP3);
     LENGTH_Y := LENGTH_Y - 1;
     -- For each digit place in Y from right to left
     for PLACE in reverse 1..Length_Y loop
       -- Multiply X by 10, same as shift
       HIGH_PRECISION_INTEGER.APPEND (0,TEMP1);
       -- Multiply next digit in Y by properly shifted X
       -- with result placed in a temporary string TEMP2.
       MUL_X_BY_DIGIT(TEMP1,
           HIGH_PRECISION_INTEGER.GET_ITEM (Y, PLACE), TEMP2);
       -- Add the result to the accumulator TEMP3
       ADD_X_TO_Y(TEMP2, TEMP3, TEMP3);
     end loop;
     HIGH_PRECISION_INTEGER.COPY(TEMP3, ANS);
end MUL_X_BY_Y;
```

The procedures to subtract and divide are left to the exercises. While addition and multiplication can be defined using the procedures ADD_X_TO_Y and MUL_X_BY_Y, they are not very efficient. GET_ITEM is $O(n)$, where n is the length of the string. If both X and Y are n digits long, then ADD_X_TO_Y is $O(n**2)$. Since MUL_X_BY_Y calls ADD_X_TO_Y once for each digit in Y, MUL_X_BY_Y is $O(n**3)$. Even switching to GENERIC_BOUNDED_STRING does not help. In GENERIC_BOUNDED_STRING, GET ITEM is $O(1)$, but INSERT goes from being $O(1)$ in GENERIC_UNBOUNDED_STRING to $O(n)$ in GENERIC_BOUNDED_STRING. The problem of high-precision integer arithmetic is related to polynomial manipulation. A more efficient implementation is suggested in Chapter 14.

13.6 TIME AND SPACE CONSTRAINTS

The package GENERIC_BOUNDED_STRING is implemented using arrays, so the time and space constraints reflect this fact. Operations that just access are fast, whereas those that insert or append require the shifting of array slices. Figure 13.6.1 uses the implementation of GENERIC_BOUNDED_STRING that was specified in Figure 13.2.3.

Figure 13.6.2 shows the constraints for GENERIC_UNBOUNDED_STRING specified in Figure 13.3.2. The constraints represent the listlike nature of the representation. Compare these constraints with those for GENERIC_UNBOUNDED_LIST in Chapter 5.

	Operation Overhead	Space Overhead
COPY	$O(n)$	$O(\text{SIZE})$
APPEND	$O(n)$	$O(\text{SIZE})$
INSERT	$O(n)$	$O(\text{SIZE})$
LENGTH	$O(1)$	$O(\text{SIZE})$
REPLACE	$O(n)$	$O(\text{SIZE})$
EQUAL	$O(n)$	$O(\text{SIZE})$
LESS	$O(n)$	$O(\text{SIZE})$
GET_ITEM	$O(1)$	$O(\text{SIZE})$

Figure 13.6.1 Constraints for GENERIC_BOUNDED_STRING.

In both Figures 13.6.1 and 13.6.2, worst-case constraints are given. For example, if two strings are not equal in length, the operation EQUAL is $O(1)$. If the first items on two strings being compared are distinct, LESS is also $O(1)$.

	Operation Overhead	Space Overhead
COPY	$O(n)$	$O(n)$
APPEND	$O(n)$	$O(n)$
INSERT	$O(n)$	$O(n)$
LENGTH	$O(1)$	$O(n)$
REPLACE	$O(n)$	$O(n)$
EQUAL	$O(n)$	$O(n)$
LESS	$O(n)$	$O(n)$
GET_ITEM	$O(n)$	$O(n)$

Figure 13.6.2 Constraints for GENERIC_UNBOUNDED_STRING.

13.7. CASE STUDY: SIMPLE CRYPTOGRAPHY

Cryptography literally means "hidden writing." The process is simple to explain but hard to implement. A message, called the *plain text*, is altered, a process called *encrypting,* using a secret key or cipher. The goal is to hide the meaning of the plain text. The altered message, called *cipher text,* is transmitted and received. The cipher text is restored to plain text by a decrypting process using the key. Ciphers usually include a key and a method. Distinct keys applied with the same method yield distinct codes. Often the method is public, but the key is not. A good cipher is easy to use but hard to break. The measure of the security of a cipher is the effort it takes to break the cipher. There are simple unbreakable ciphers that use a *one-time pad.*

Codes and code breaking have wide applications. Military and intelligence applications are obvious. Every government or military commander wants to know what the other side is doing or thinking. Cryptography has other wide commercial applications as well as basic applications to computer science. Consider a multiuser operating system. Every operating system has certain security features built into the logon process. The password file is often stored in an encrypted format. As the user logs in, the password is encrypted first and then compared against the encrypted form in the password file. Gaining access to the password file does not get access to the passwords. Most multiuser operating systems also offer ways of encrypting sensitive data so that it can be stored on secondary storage devices or shared with only those authorized to have access.

There are also commercial applications. Large sums of money are routinely transferred through international computer networks. Not only is the authorization to transfer money encrypted, but a digital signature can be added and acknowledged. This assures the sender that the transfer was received by the proper bank, while the receiver knows that only the sender could have transmitted the message.

As a final example, consider the basic data types themselves. An integer in base 10 is converted, or enciphered, to a binary form, before the computer can operate on it directly. After operating on it, the computer decrypts it back to base 10. Floating-point numbers are altered before they are stored. Similarly, characters have the ASCII representation. These last examples are not very good ciphers because both the key and the method is known. There is nothing secret about the method.

One of the first known ciphers was attributed to Julius Caesar. It is a simple shift cipher. A number between 1 and 26 is selected. This number is the key. Every letter is shifted by this number. Letters are wrapped around. If the key is five, the letter D becomes the letter I and the letter X becomes the letter C. In cryptography, letters are usually capitalized. Figure 13.7.1a is a simple message and Figure 13.7.1b is the same message enciphered by the Caesar cipher with key=7.

```
BRUTUS
ATTACK THE ENEMIES RIGHT FLANK AT DAWN
YOUR
BUDDY
JULIUS
                        (a)


IZBABZ
HAAHJR AOL LULTPLZ YPNOA MSHUR HA KHDU
FVBY IBKKF
QBSPBZ
                        (b)
```

Figure 13.7.1(a) Plain text message from Julius Caesar to Brutus. (b) Message in part (a) ciphered with key=7.

Figure 13.7.2 contains functions that encrypt and decrypt messages using a Caesar cipher. The Caesar cipher is simple and is simple to break. There are 25 distinct keys. It is a simple matter to try them all.

```
package MY_TEXT is new GENERIC_UNBOUNDED_STRING(CHARACTER);
subtype KEY_TYPE is integer range 1..25;
    ...........
function CODE_TEXT_USING_CAESAR (KEY    : KEY_TYPE;
                                 PLAIN  : MY_TEXT.STRING)
                                 RETURN MY_TEXT.STRING is
```

Figure 13.7.2 Functions to cipher a String of Characters using the Caesar cipher. It is assumed that all letters are capitalized. Continues on page 478.

```
ANSWER    : MY_TEXT.STRING;
CHAR      : character;
TEMP      : integer;
begin
  if not MY_TEXT.EMPTY (PLAIN) then
    -- For each character in the plain text
    for PLACE in positive range 1..MY_TEXT.LENGTH (PLAIN) loop
      CHAR := MY_TEXT.GET_ITEM (PLAIN, PLACE);
      -- If it is a character only
      if CHAR in 'A'..'Z' then
        -- Shift and wrap around if necessary
        TEMP := character'pos (CHAR) + KEY;
        if TEMP > character'pos ('Z') then
          TEMP := TEMP - 26;
        end if;
      end if;
      CHAR := character'val (TEMP);
      -- Add coded character to cipher text
      MY_TEXT.APPEND (char, ANSWER);
    end loop;
  end if;
  return ANSWER;
end CODE_TEXT_USING_CAESAR;;


function DECODE_TEXT_USING_CAESAR (KEY     : KEY_TYPE;
                                   CODED   : MY_TEXT.STRING)
                                   return MY_TEXT.STRING is
begin
  return CODE_TEXT_USING_CAESAR( 26 - KEY, CODED);
end DECODE_TEXT_USING CAESAR;
```

Figure 13.7.2 Concluded.

The Caesar cipher is a special case of the *substitution cipher*. For each letter in the alphabet, another letter is selected in such a way that no letter is repeated. There are 26 choices for the letter A. Once a choice has been made, there are 25 choices for a letter B, then 24 choices for the letter C, and so on. It would appear that there are 26! keys for the substitution cipher. Even if a computer could check 1 billion keys a second, this system seems relatively secure. It isn't. Figure 13.7.3(a) lists a short piece of text from the Introduction of the *Ada Language Reference Manual*. Note that the punctuation and numbers have been spelled out. How many words made up of one character are there, and which of these words appear in this book? What about words of made up of two or three characters? Words made up of one character (i.e., the words "a" and "I") give a lot of information to the codebreaker. This can be obscured by grouping letters in groups of five as was done in Figure 13.7.3(b). Unfortunately, letters are not used with the same frequency in words in the English language. Figure 13.7.3(c) contains the letter count of the original passage, and Figure 13.7.3(d) contains the frequency of letters used in this chapter.

ADA IS A PROGRAMMING LANGUAGE DESIGNED IN ACCORDANCE WITH
REQUIREMENTS DEFINED BY THE UNITED STATES DEPARTMENT OF
DEFENSE COLON THE SO CALLED STEELMAN REQUIREMENTS PERIOD
OVERALL COMA THESE REQUIREMENTS CALL FOR A LANGUAGE WITH
CONSIDERABLE EXPRESSIVE POWER COVERING A WIDE APPLICATION
DOMAIN PERIOD AS A RESULT COMA THE LANGUAGE INCLUDES
FACILITIES OFFERED BY CLASSICAL LANGUAGES SUCH AS PASCAL AS
WELL AS FACILITIES OFTEN FOUND ONLY IN SPECIALIZED
LANGUAGES PERIOD THUS THE LANGUAGE IS A MODERN ALGORITHMIC
LANGUAGE WITH THE USUAL CONTROL STRUCTURES COMA AND WITH
THE ABILITY TO DEFINE TYPES AND SUBPROGRAMS PERIOD IT ALSO
SERVES THE NEED FOR MODULARITY COMA WHEREBY DATA COMA TYPES
COMA AND SUBPROGRAMS CAN BE PACKAGED PERIOD IT TREATS
MODULARITY IN THE PHYSICAL SENSE AS WELL COMA WITH A FACILITY
TO SUPPORT SEPARATE COMPILATION PERIOD

(a)

ADAIS APROG RAMMI NGLAN GUAGE DESIG NEDIN ACCOR DANCE WITHR
EQUIR EMENT SDEFI NEDBY THEUN ITEDS TATES DEPAR TMENT OFDEF
ENSEC OLONT HESOC ALLED STEEL MANRE QUIRE MENTS PERIO DOVER
ALLCO MATHE SEREQ UIREM ENTSC ALLFO RALAN GUAGE WITHC ONSID
ERABL EEXPR ESSIV EPOWE RCOVE RINGA WIDEA PPLIC ATION DOMAI
NPERI ODASA RESUL TCOMA THELA NGUAG EINCL UDESF ACILI TIESO
FFERE DBYCL ASSIC ALLAN GUAGE SSUCH ASPAS CALAS WELLA SFACI
LITIE SOFTE NFOUN DONLY INSPE CIALI ZEDLA NGUAG ESPER IODTH
USTHE LANGU AGEIS AMODE RNALG ORITH MICLA NGUAG EWITH THEUS
UALCO NTROL STRUC TURES COMAA NDWIT HTHEA BILIT YTODE FINET
YPESA NDSUB PROGR AMSPE RIODI TALSO SERVE STHEN EEDFO RMODU
LARIT YCOMA WHERE BYDAT ACOMA TYPES COMAA NDSUB PROGR AMSCA
NBEPA CKAGE DPERI ODITT REATS MODUL ARITY INTHE PHYSI CALSE
NSEAS WELLC OMAWI THAFA CILIT YTOSU PPORT SEPAR ATECO MPILA
TIONP ERIOD

(b)

A = 74	F = 13	K = 0	Q = 3	V = 4
B = 8	G = 22	L = 38	R = 39	W = 10
C = 30	H = 19	M = 22	S = 46	X = 1
D = 32	I = 54	N = 39	T = 47	Y = 10
E = 85	J = 0	O = 44	U = 24	Z = 1
		P = 20		

(c)

A = 0.062	F = 0.024	K = 0.005	Q = 0.002	V = 0.007
B = 0.015	G = 0.031	L = 0.033	R = 0.072	W = 0.007
C = 0.036	H = 0.041	M = 0.024	S = 0.066	X = 0.007

Figure 13.7.3 Text from ADA LRM.(a)Text from ADA LRM.(b) Text blocked into groups of 5. (c) Character frequency distribution of text. (d) Frequency of letters in Chapter 13. Continues on page 480.

D = 0.031	I = 0.083	N = 0.080	T = 0.110	Y = 0.012
E = 0.128	J = 0.002	O = 0.064	U = 0.027	Z = 0.001
		P = 0.033		

(d)

Figure 13.7.3 Concluded.

Substitution ciphers can be broken by a systematic attack based on frequency analysis. Given enough text, certain substitutions become obvious. Any substitution cipher applied to Figure 13.7.3(a) will have the same character distribution as Figure 13.7.3(c). Certain characters are used more often than others. In a coded message, some letters such as vowels and the letters r, s, and t, will be used more often than others. This allows the text to be deciphered, and the text of the message become clear. Once certain letters are known others follow. If the letter t is known, t is often followed by h, as in "the" or "that," or by "ion," as in "substitution" or "separation." Figure 13.7.4 contains two procedures to cipher and decipher text for a given key. Note that the key is an array of characters indexed by a character range. CODE_TEXT_BY_SUBSTITUTION assumes that all characters are capitals.

```
package MY_TEXT is new GENERIC_UNBOUNDED_STRING (character);
type LETTERS is character range 'A'..'Z';
type KEY_TYPE is array (LETTERS) of LETTERS;
   ..........
function CODE_TEXT_BY_SUBSTITUTION (KEY   : KEY_TYPE;
                                    PLAIN : MY_TEXT.STRING)
                                    return MY_TEXT.STRING is
  ANSWER : MY_TEXT.STRING;
  CHAR   : character;
begin
  if not MY_TEXT.EMPTY (PLAIN) then
    -- For each character in the plain text
    for PLACE in positive range 1..MY_TEXT.LENGTH (PLAIN) loop
      CHAR := MY_TEXT.GET_ITEM (PLAIN, PLACE);
      if CHAR in 'A'..'Z' then
        -- Get the substitution for CHAR from the key K
        CHAR := KEY (CHAR);
      end if;
        -- Insert the coded character into the cipher text
        MY_TEXT.APPEND(CHAR, ANSWER);
      end loop;
  end if;
  return ANSWER;
end CODE_TEXT_BY_SUBSTITUTION;

function DECODE_TEXT_BY_SUBSTITUTION (KEY   : KEY_TYPE;
                                      CODED : MY_TEXT.STRING)
                                      return MY_TEXT.STRING is
  NEW_KEY : KEY_TYPE;
begin
  -- Make reverse key to decode the message
  for INDEX in 'A'..'Z' loop
```

Figure 13.7.4 Functions to cipher and decipher text using substitution ciphers. Continues on page 481.

```
        NEW_KEY (KEY(INDEX)) := INDEX;
    end loop;
    -- Change cipher text back to plain text using reverse key
    return CODE_TEXT_BY_SUBSTITUTION (NEW_KEY, CODED);
 end DECODE_TEXT_BY_SUBSTITUTION;
```

Figure 13.7.4   Concluded.

To prevent the breaking of the substitution code, something must be done to prevent an attack using frequency analysis. The *Vignere cipher* combines the simplicity of the Caesar cipher while significantly reducing the probability of a successful attack by a code breaker. The Vignere cipher uses a keyword, key phrase, or string as its key. Suppose that the key phrase is "computer science." This phrase is 15 characters long. The first and every fifteenth character thereafter is shifted by three, because C is the third letter in the alphabet. The second and every fifteenth character thereafter is shifted by 15 because the second letter in the key is an o, the fifteenth letter in the alphabet. In general, the kth letter and every fifteenth letter are shifted by the place in the alphabet of the kth letter in the key. Consider the message in Figure 13.7.1(a). Figure 13.7.5(a) illustrates the message with the key written under it, Figure 13.7.5(b) illustrates the cipher text, and Figure 13.7.5(c) shows the cipher text grouped in blocks of 5.

```
BRUTUS ATTACK THE ENEMIES RIGHT FLANK AT DAWN YOUR BUDDY JULIUS
COMPUT ERSCIE NCE COMPUTE RSCIE NCECO MP UTER SCIE NCECO MPUTER
EGHJPM FLMDLP HKJ HCRCDYX JBJQY TOFQZ NJ YUBF RRDW PXIGN WKGCZK
```

(b)

```
EGHJP MFLMD LPHKJ
HCRCD YXJBJ QYTOF
QZNJY UBFRR DWPXI
GNWKG CZK
```

(c)

Figure 13.7.5   (a) Plain text message with key written underneath. (b) Cipher Text of part (a). (c) Cipher text grouped in blocks of 5.

The procedure CASE_STUDY_13 in Figure 13.7.6 illustrates a procedure that either codes or decodes a plain text message using the Vignere cipher. The case study first asks for a key composed of capital letters or blanks. All characters in the key must be uppercase and all blanks are removed. Then a message, either in cipher or in plain text, is read in and converted to the same format as the key. The message is either coded or decoded, and the result is printed in groups of 5 characters. The program will repeat until the user indicates that all ciphering is completed.

```
with text_io;      use text_io;
with GENERIC_UNBOUNDED_STRING;
procedure CASE_STUDY_13 is
  package CIPHER is new GENERIC_UNBOUNDED_STRING (character);

    KEY, --string used to hold key of Vignere cipher
    PLAIN_TEXT,  --string to hold text to be ciphered, or text
                 --that was deciphered
```

Figure 13.7.6   CASE_STUDY_13, the Vignere cipher. Continues on page 482.

```
              CIPHER_TEXT,              --string for ciphered text
              TEMP_TEXT : CIPHER.STRING;
              CODE_FLAG : boolean;
              MORE      : boolean := TRUE; -- More messages to decode

              procedure PRINT_TEMP_TEXT is
                --Prints to screen the string Temp_text on screen
                --using the format of 12 blocks of 5 characters
                --separated by a single space until the end of the string
                TEMP_LENGTH : natural := CIPHER.LENGTH (TEMP_TEXT);
                J, PLACE : natural := 1;
                CHAR : character;
              begin
                loop
                  exit when PLACE > TEMP_LENGTH;
                  J := 1;
                  while J <= 60 and PLACE <= TEMP_LENGTH loop
                    put (CIPHER.GET_ITEM (TEMP_TEXT, PLACE));
                    if J rem 5 = 0 then
                      -- Put blank between each group of 5
                      put (' ');
                    end if;
                    J := J + 1;
                    PLACE := PLACE + 1;
                  end loop;
                  new_line;
                end loop;
              end PRINT_TEMP_TEXT;

              procedure REMOVE_BLANKS is
                -- Removes all blanks from Temp_Text
                TEMP_LENGTH : natural := CIPHER.LENGTH(TEMP_TEXT);
                INDEX       : natural := 1;
              begin
                while INDEX <= TEMP_LENGTH loop
                  if CIPHER.GET_ITEM(TEMP_TEXT, INDEX) = ' ' THEN
                    -- Blank found, delete it from message and adjust string length
                    CIPHER.DELETE (TEMP_TEXT, INDEX, INDEX);
                    TEMP_LENGTH := TEMP_LENGTH - 1;
                  else
                    INDEX := INDEX + 1;
                  end if;
                end loop;
              end REMOVE_BLANKS;

              function CHECK_TEXT return boolean is
                -- Returns true if all items in Temp_text are in 'A'..'Z'
              begin
```

Figure 13.7.6 Continues on page 483.

```
    for PLACE in natural range 1..CIPHER.LENGTH(TEMP_TEXT) loop
      if CIPHER.GET_ITEM (TEMP_TEXT, PLACE) not in 'A'..'Z' then
        return false;
      end if;
    end loop;
    return true;
  end CHECK_TEXT;

  procedure CODE_OR_DECODE( FLAG : out boolean) is
    --Returns true if string PLAIN_TEXT is to be coded or false
    --if string CIPHER_TEXT is to be decoded
    ANSWER : character;
  begin
    loop
      new_line;
      skip_line;
      put ("Enter 'C' if you want to code,");
      put (" 'D' if you want to decode.");
      get (ANSWER);
      skip_line;          if ANSWER = 'C' or ANS = 'c' then
        FLAG := true;
        return;
      elsif ANSWER = 'D' or ANS = 'd' then
        FLAG := false;
        return;
      else
        put_line ("Improper response, try again.");
      end if;
    end loop;
  end CODE_OR_DECODE;

  procedure GET_TEXT is
    -- Gets a string TEMP_TEXT of arbitrary length where
    -- input is any object of character type.
    -- A slash / ends input
    STRNG : string (1..81) := (others => ' ');
    LENGTH : natural := 0;
    CHAR : character := ' ';
  begin
    CIPHER.CLEAR (TEMP_TEXT);
    put_line ( "Input text one line at a time.");
    put_line ( "Only capital letters and blanks are allowed.");
    put_line ( "Input ends with a slash /.");
    while CHAR /= '/' loop
      get (CHAR);
      LENGTH := LENGTH + 1;
      STRNG (LENGTH) := CHAR;
    end loop;
```

Figure 13.7.6 Continues on page 484.

```
    for INDEX in 1..LENGTH loop
      if STRNG(INDEX) /= '/' then
        CIPHER.APPEND (STRNG(INDEX), TEMP_TEXT);
      end if;
    end loop;
end GET_TEXT;

procedure GET_KEY is
  -- Gets the string KEY for Vignere cipher.
  -- String can be any length, must have only capitals or blanks
begin
  put_line ( "Now input text to act as a key.");
  loop
    GET_TEXT;
    REMOVE_BLANKS;
    if CHECK_TEXT then
      exit;
    else
      put_line("Improper characters in key, try again.");
    end if;
  end loop;
  CIPHER.COPY (TEMP_TEXT, KEY);
end GET_KEY;

procedure GET_CIPHER_TEXT is
  -- Gets string CIPHER_TEXT that contains a message
  -- of any length to decode
  -- Only capital letters or blanks allowed
begin
  put_line ( "Now input cipher text to decode.");
  loop
    GET_TEXT;
    REMOVE_BLANKS;
    if CHECK_TEXT then
      exit;
    else
      put ("Improper characters in cipher string,");
      put_line ( "try again.");
    end if;
  end loop;
  CIPHER.COPY (TEMP_TEXT, CIPHER_TEXT);
end GET_CIPHER_TEXT;

procedure GET_PLAIN_TEXT is
  -- Gets string PLAIN_TEXT that contains message to code
  -- Only capital letters or blanks allowed
begin
  put_line ( "Now input plain text to code.");
  loop
```

Figure 13.7.6 Continues on page 485.

```
      GET_TEXT;
      REMOVE_BLANKS;
      if CHECK_TEXT then
        exit;
      else
        put ("Improper characters in plain text,");
        put_line ( "try again.");
      end if; end loop;
    CIPHER.COPY (TEMP_TEXT, PLAIN_TEXT);
  end GET_PLAIN_TEXT;


  procedure IS_THERE_MORE (FLAG : out boolean ) is
    ANS : character;    .
  begin
    loop
      put("Enter 'Y' if there is more to code or decode,");
      put(" 'N' if you are finished.");
      get (ANS);
      if ANS = 'Y' or ANS = 'y' then
        FLAG := true;
        return;
      elsif ANS = 'N' or ANS = 'n' then
        Flag := false;
        return;
      else
        put_line("Improper response, try again.");
      end if;
    end loop;
  end IS_THERE_MORE;


  function USE_NEW_KEY return boolean is
    ANS : character;
  begin
    loop
      put("Enter 'Y' if there is more to code or decode,");
      put(" 'N' if you are finished.");
      get (ANS);
      if ANS = 'Y' or ANS = 'y' then
        return true;
      elsif ANS = 'N' or ANS = 'n' then
        return false;
      else
        put_line("Improper response, try again.");
      end if;
    end loop;
  end USE_NEW_KEY;


  procedure CODE_PLAIN_TEXT is
```

Figure 13.7.6   Continues on page 486.

```
                --Codes the string PLAIN_TEXT and puts result in CIPHER_TEXT
                KEY_LENGTH : natural := CIPHER.LENGTH (KEY);
                PLAIN_TEXT_LENGTH : natural := CIPHER.LENGTH (PLAIN_TEXT);
                CHAR : character ;
                SHIFT : natural;
                TEMP : natural;
            begin
                CIPHER.CLEAR (CIPHER_TEXT);
                for PLACE in positive range 1..PLAIN_TEXT_LENGTH loop
                    -- Get next character to code from plain text
                    CHAR := CIPHER.GET_ITEM (PLAIN_TEXT, PLACE);
                    -- Get shift from proper place in KEY
                    SHIFT := 1 + character'pos
                            (CIPHER.GET_ITEM(KEY, ((PLACE-1) rem KEY_LENGTH) + 1))
                                - character'pos('A');
                    -- Code the character using the shift above
                    TEMP := character'pos (CHAR) + SHIFT;
                    if TEMP > character'pos('Z') then
                        TEMP := TEMP - 26;
                    end if;
                    -- Add the coded character to the end of the cipher text
                    CIPHER.APPEND (character'val(TEMP), CIPHER_TEXT);
                end loop;
                CIPHER.COPY(CIPHER_TEXT, TEMP_TEXT);
            end CODE_PLAIN_TEXT;


            procedure DECODE_CIPHER_TEXT is
                -- Decodes the string CIPHER_TEXT and puts result in
                -- the string PLAIN_TEXT. Idea is the same as CODE_PLAIN_TEXT
                -- except that the complement of the key is used.
                KEY_LENGTH : natural := CIPHER.LENGTH(KEY);
                CIPHER_TEXT_LENGTH : natural := CIPHER.LENGTH (CIPHER_TEXT);
                CHAR : character ;
                SHIFT : natural;
                TEMP : natural;
            begin
                CIPHER.CLEAR (PLAIN_TEXT);
                for PLACE in positive range 1..CIPHER_TEXT_LENGTH loop
                    CHAR := CIPHER.GET_ITEM (CIPHER_TEXT, PLACE);
                    SHIFT := 25 - character'pos
                            (CIPHER.GET_ITEM(KEY, ((PLACE-1) rem KEY_LENGTH) + 1))
                                + character'pos(char);
                    TEMP := character'pos(char) + SHIFT;
                    if TEMP > character'Pos('Z') then
                        TEMP := TEMP - 26;
                    end if;
                    CIPHER.APPEND (character'val(TEMP), PLAIN_TEXT);
                end loop;
```

Figure 13.7.6 Continues on page 487.

```
      CIPHER.COPY (PLAIN_TEXT, TEMP_TEXT);
   end DECODE_CIPHER_TEXT;


begin --CASE_STUDY_13
   GET_KEY;
   while MORE loop
      CODE_OR_DECODE (CODE_FLAG);
      if CODE_FLAG then
         GET_PLAIN_TEXT;
         CODE_PLAIN_TEXT;
         PRINT_TEMP_TEXT;
      else
         GET_CIPHER_TEXT;
         DECODE_CIPHER_TEXT;
         PRINT_TEMP_TEXT;
      end if;
      IS_THERE_MORE (MORE);
      if MORE and then USE_NEW_KEY then
         GET_KEY;
      end if;
   end loop;
end CASE_STUDY_13;
```

Figure 13.7.6 Concluded.

The Vignere cipher can be broken under some conditions. If the amount of text ciphered is large compared to the length of the key, classical methods to determine the length of the key can be applied. If n denotes the length of the key, the cipher text is grouped into n groups of characters. The kth group starts from the kth character in the cipher text and includes every nth character that follows. A frequency analysis is done on each group to determine the shift. Remember that there are only 26 possibilities for each group. Once the shift is known, the key can be reconstructed.

Assuming that keys can be kept secret, the Vignere cipher forms the basis for a totally secure cipher, the one-time pad. In the one-time pad, the length of the key equals the length of the message. Once a key is used, it is never used again. To break the code, the key must be compromised. Hollywood has made spy thrillers where two spies would send messages back and forth. Both spies have a copy of the same edition and same printing of a particular novel. Based on the date/time stamp of the message, a special character on a certain line on a particular page would be the first character of the key. Starting from that point, text from the novel that is the same length as the message is used as the key of the one-time pad. As long as the title, printing, and edition of the novel are unknown to the code breaker, the code is secure.

Modern ciphers are designed to be secure and easy to implement. A cipher's security is an estimate of the time it would take to break the cipher. There are ciphers based on a large number that equals the product of two large prime numbers. The number is public but the factors are not. A simple program that uses modular arithmetic based on the public number is used to cipher the plain text. To decipher the message, the prime factors must be known. Currently numbers of about 70 digits can be factored in an acceptable time. Since factoring is $O(\exp(n))$, where n is the number of digits, numbers of 100 digits or more are considered temporarily secure. Another well-known cipher is DES (data encryption standard). DES takes blocks of bits and performs logical binary operations on the string of bits. It is thought to be secure but is not known to be secure.

There are ciphers with two keys, one listed as a public key and one kept secret as a private key. A message ciphered using one key can be deciphered only by using the other key. Two banks want to exchange confidential information. Bank *A* looks up the public key of bank *B* in the directory. Bank *A* codes a message to bank *B* by first ciphering it using *A*'s private key and then ciphers the message a second time using bank *B*'s published key. Upon receipt, bank *B* uses its private key to decode the message and sees that it contains a coded message from bank *A*. Bank *B* then decodes the message using bank *A*'s public key. Both banks are happy. Bank *A* knows that only bank *B* can decode the message, and bank *B* knows that only bank *A* could have sent the message.

This case study may seem more recreational than professional, but the rumored leading user of supercomputers in the United States is the National Security Agency. This agency is in charge of the security of U.S. codes while trying to break other government's codes.

EXERCISES

Section 13.2 Bounded Form

13.2.1 Consider the generic package listed in Figure 13.2.2.
    a. Implement both versions of the procedure COPY.
    b. Implement the four versions of the procedure APPEND.
    c. Implement the three versions of the procedure INSERT.
    d. Implement the procedure DELETE.
    e. Implement the procedure CLEAR.
    f. Implement the three versions of the procedure REPLACE.
    g. Implement the function EMPTY.
    h. Implement the three versions of the function EQUAL.
    i. Implement the three versions of the function LESS.
    j. Implement the three versions of the function GREATER.
    k. Implement the function LENGTH.
    l. Implement the function GET_ITEM.
    m. Implement the function GET_STRING.
    n. Implement the versions of the function GET_SUBSTRING.
    o. Combine parts a through n into a generic package body for the generic package specification listed in Figure 8.2.2.

Section 13.3 Unbounded Form

13.3.1 Implement GENERIC_UNBOUNDED_STRING as specified in Figure 13.3.2.
    a. Implement both versions of the procedure COPY.
    b. Implement the four versions of the procedure APPEND.
    c. Implement the three versions of the procedure INSERT.
    d. Implement the procedure DELETE.
    e. Implement the procedure CLEAR.
    f. Implement the three versions of the procedure REPLACE.
    g. Implement the function EMPTY.
    h. Implement the three versions of the function EQUAL.

i. Implement the three versions of the function LESS.

j. Implement the three versions of the function GREATER.

k. Implement the function LENGTH.

l. Implement the function GET_ITEM.

m. Implement the function GET_STRING.

n. Implement the versions of the function GET_SUBSTRING.

o. Combine parts a through n into a generic package body for the generic package specification listed in Figure 13.3.2.

13.3.2 Replace the data structure in the private section of Figure 13.3.2 by

```
type NODE;
type NEXT_NODE is access NODE;
type NODE is
   record
      X : ITEM_TYPE;
      PREVIOUS,
      NEXT : NEXT_NODE;
   end record;
type STRING is
   record
      LENGTH : natural :=0;
      FIRST,
      LAST : NEXT_NODE;
   end record;
```

The data structure above forms a doubly linked list.

a. Implement both versions of the procedure COPY.

b. Implement the four versions of the procedure APPEND.

c. Implement the three versions of the procedure INSERT.

d. Implement the procedure DELETE.

e. Implement the procedure CLEAR.

f. Implement the three versions of the procedure REPLACE.

g. Implement the function EMPTY.

h. Implement the three versions of the function EQUAL.

i. Implement the three versions of the function LESS.

j. Implement the three versions of the function GREATER.

k. Implement the function LENGTH.

l. Implement the function GET_ITEM.

m. Implement the function GET_STRING.

n. Implement the versions of the function GET_SUBSTRING.

o. Combine parts a through n into a generic package body for a similar generic package specification to the one listed in Figure 13.3.2.

13.3.3 An alternative form of an unbounded string can be implemented by using a variant record structure similar to

```
type ITEM_ARRAY is array (positive range <>) of ITEM_TYPE;
type STRING (SIZE : positive ) is
   record
      S : ITEM_ARRAY(1..SIZE);
   end record;
```

Exercises

Each string is full. When two strings are operated on, a new string is created. For example, the procedure Append might look like

```
procedure Append ( From : in     String;
                      To  : in out String) is
  TEMP : STRING (FROM.SIZE+TO.SIZE);
begin
  TEMP.S(1..TO.SIZE) := TO.S;
  TEMP.S(TO.SIZE+1..TEMP.SIZE) := FROM.S;
  TO :=TEMP;
exception
  when storage_error =>
    raise overflow;
end Append;
```

Implement GENERIC_UNBOUNDED_STRING using this data structure.

Section 13.4 Pattern Matching

13.4.1 a. Write a version of the brute-force procedure called FIND and add it to the ADT developed in Exercise 13.2.1.
  b. Write a version of the brute-force procedure called FIND and add it to the ADT developed in Exercise 13.3.1.
  c. Write a version of the brute-force procedure called FIND and add it to the ADT developed in Exercise 13.3.2.
  d. Write a version of the brute-force procedure called FIND and add it to the ADT developed in Exercise 13.3.3.

13.4.2 Repeat Exercise 13.4.1 for the Knuth–Morris–Pratt algorithm.

13.4.3 a. Write a version of the Boyer–Moore procedure called FIND and add it to the ADT developed in Exercise 13.2.1.
  b. Write a version of the Boyer–Moore procedure called FIND and add it to the ADT developed in Exercise 13.3.2.
  c. Write a version of the Boyer–Moore procedure called FIND and add it to the ADT developed in Exercise 13.3.3.

13.4.4 Repeat Exercise 13.4.1 for the Rabin–Karp algorithm.

Section 13.5 Applications

13.5.1 Complete a package to do high-precision arithmetic.

PROGRAMMING PROJECTS

P13.1 Complete a project that codes, decodes, and breaks a basic substitution cipher.

NOTES AND REFERENCES

The original source for the Knuth–Morris–Pratt algorithm is [30], for Boyer–Moore is [7], and for Rabin–Karp is [26]. All three pattern-matching methods as well as a short introduction to cryptography are contained in Sedgewick [44]. Cryptography has a wide and varied history.

Kahn's history of codebreaking [25] reads like a novel. Dewdney [15] is a readable account of DES. Gardner [21] has two chapters devoted to the trapdoor cipher and other public key algorithms. A reference for actual public key algorithms is Diffie [16].

14

Rings

Suppose that a program monitors a series of entry points in a home or business. Such a program, in reality a burglar alarm system, would endlessly loop through a sequence of sensors at each window, door, skylight, and so on, in a predefined order. As each sensor is encountered, its status is checked. Unauthorized entry would be detected and reported. One method of implementing this program would be to use a queue of SENSOR_TYPE. A queue item, composed of an object of SENSOR_TYPE and an access value referencing the next queue item, is dequeued, then the sensor object is extracted, processed, and enqueued at the end of the queue.

A standard queue is a linear structure, in the sense that items follow one another. Every item in the queue except the first has an item preceding it. Every item in the queue except the last has an item following it. A *ring* is a sequence of items arranged in a circular fashion. Every item in a ring has both a predecessor and a successor. Rings have no first or last item. The burglar alarm application checks the sensors in a circular fashion. It is a natural application for a ring. Other possible applications include a multitasking operating system where each task executes for a given time slice before control transfers to the next task, an industrial process control system where the building of the same part involves a series of repetitive steps, or a video game that has some sort of wheel of chance, such as roulette.

14.1 ADT RING

A ring is a sequence of zero or more items arranged as a circular linear list (see Figure 14.1.1). Operations on the ring are easier to visualize than to describe. The addition and deletion of items is from one point on the ring called the TOP. The added item becomes the new top item and the previous top item becomes the successor of the top item (see Figure 14.1.2).

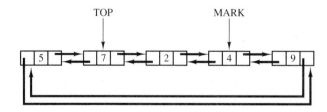

Figure 14.1.1 Typical ring implemented as a doubly linked list.

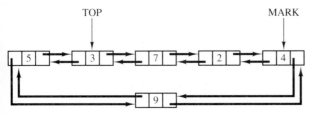

Figure 14.1.2   Insertion of the integer 3 into the ring in Figure 14.1.1. Note that the inserted item becomes the new top item.

The TOP can be rotated in either direction, which is why the RING must be a doubly linked list. An item is deleted by an operation called POP. POP deletes the item from the top position and the top's successor becomes the new top item. Popping does not return the item that was previously at the top (see Figure 14.1.3). Popping removes an item, but the operation PEEK returns the item's data field without modifying the ring. Adding and deleting items proceeds just as on a stack, where the inserted item becomes the new top item and deletion of an item from the ring removes the top item. The length of the ring, sometimes called the *extent*, is the number of items in the ring. The documentation for the ADT ring in given in Figure 14.1.4.

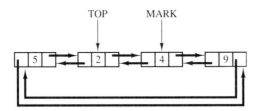

Figure 14.1.3   Popping an item from the ring in Figure 14.1.1. Note that the item at the top is deleted and TOP's successor becomes the new TOP.

General ADT Specification for Ring

Description

A ring is a linear sequence of items arranged as a circle. Every item in the ring has a unique predecessor and a unique successor. A ring with only one item in it has only the item itself as its own predecessor and successor. A ring has one point of access called the TOP. An item is added to the top while the old top item becomes the successor of the added item. When the top item is removed or popped, its successor becomes the new top item. A second item can be marked, but there is no access to the marked item unless the marked item is the top item. The top item can be rotated either clockwise toward its successor or counterclockwise towards its predecessor.

Programmer-Supplied Data Structures
or Specifications

The programmer must supply a single type name ITEM_TYPE at instantiation. This programmer-supplied data structure defines the objects that are on the ring, added to the ring, or deleted from the ring. The supplied type is a private formal generic parameter. No ring operation modifies the programmer-supplied object in any way.

Figure 14.1.4   Documentation for a ring. Continues on page 494.

Operations

Name	Description
ADD_ITEM	Adds an item to the ring at the top position. The new item becomes the new top item, its successor is the old top item, and its predecessor is the predecessor of the old top item. The marked item is not affected unless the ring was previously empty. In that case the single item on the ring is both the top item and the marked item.
POP	Deletes the item referenced by TOP. The new top item is the successor item of the previous TOP. The marked item is not affected by the deletion unless it is the marked item that was deleted. Then the new marked item is the new top item. If the new ring is empty, both TOP and MARK are undefined.
CLEAR	Clears the ring of all items by setting both top and mark references to null and then dereferencing all items in the ring.
COPY	Makes a distinct copy of a ring with items referenced by TOP and MARK preserved. The operation RINGS_EQUAL returns true when the original and its copy are compared.
ROTATE_RING	Sets the new top to be the current top's successor if clockwise direction is specified or to the current top's predecessor if the counterclockwise direction is specified. The item referenced by MARK is not affected.
MARK_TOP_ITEM	Sets the marked item equal to the current top item.
PEEK	Returns the item at the top of the ring. The ring is unaltered.
LENGTH	Returns a natural number equal to the number of items in the ring.
MARK_AT_TOP	Boolean-valued function that returns true if both TOP and MARK reference the same item.
EQUAL	Boolean-valued function that returns true when two rings have the same length, and the items on both rings are equal item by item when the comparison starts at the top of both rings and when the same item is marked with reference to the top of both rings, otherwise returns false.
EMPTY	Boolean-valued function that returns true if there are no items on the ring, and false otherwise.
FULL	Boolean-valued function that returns true if there is no space available to add an item, and false if more items can be added to the ring.

Exceptions

There are two conditions that raise exceptions. An OVERFLOW occurs when there is insufficient space to add an item to the ring. Overflows can occur only while adding items to a ring or while copying rings. The exception EMPTY_RING occurs when the ring is empty and an attempt is made to MARK_TOP_ITEM, to MARK_AT_TOP, to POP, to PEEK, or to ROTATE_RING.

Figure 14.1.4 Continues on page 495.

Warnings

The operation ROTATE_RING uses an enumerated type direction with two values, CLOCKWISE and COUNTER_CLOCKWISE. These values must be specified exactly.

Figure 14.1.4 Concluded.

Although it is possible to build a bounded form of a ring using an array, it is not often done. Specification and implementation of the bounded implementation are the subject of Section 3.

14.2 UNBOUNDED IMPLEMENTATION

An unbounded ring must be implemented using access types. Clearly, it takes two access types to keep track of the nodes in a ring. The data structure for a ring looks as shown in Figure 14.2.1.

```
type RING_NODE;
type NEXT_NODE is access RING_NODE;
type RING_NODE is
  record
    ITEM     : ITEM_TYPE;
    NEXT_CW,                   -- Next clockwise or successor
    NEXT_CCW : NEXT_NODE;  -- Next counterclockwise or predecessor
  end record;
type RING is
  record
    TOP     : NEXT_NODE;
    MARK    : NEXT_NODE;
    LENGTH  : natural := 0;
  end record;
```

Figure 14.2.1 Data Structure for ADT GENERIC_UNBOUNDED_RING.

As usual, ring will be declared as a limited private type. The generic package in Figure 14.2.2 implements the ADT GENERIC_UNBOUNDED_RING.

```
generic
  type ITEM_TYPE is private;
package GENERIC_UNBOUNDED_RING is
  type RING is limited private;
  type DIRECTION is (CLOCKWISE, COUNTERCLOCKWISE);
  procedure ADD_ITEM     (TO          : in out RING;
                          ITEM        : in     ITEM_TYPE);
  procedure POP          (FROM        : in out RING );
  procedure CLEAR        (THIS_RING   : in out RING );
  procedure COPY         (FROM        : in     RING;
```

Figure 14.2.2 ADT GENERIC_UNBOUNDED_RING. Continues on page 496.

```
                                       TO          :    out RING );
      procedure ROTATE_RING     (THIS_RING   : in out RING;
                                 WAY         : in      DIRECTION );
      procedure MARK_TOP_ITEM (THIS_RING     : in out RING );
      function PEEK            (AT_THIS_RING : RING ) return ITEM_TYPE;
      function LENGTH          (OF_THIS_RING : RING ) return natural;
      function MARK_AT_TOP     (OF_THIS_RING : RING ) return boolean;
      function EQUAL           (LEFT, RIGHT  : RING ) return boolean;
      function EMPTY           (THIS_RING    : RING ) return boolean;
      function FULL            (THIS_RING    : RING ) return boolean;
      OVERFLOW    : exception;
      EMPTY_RING : exception;
   private
      type RING_NODE;
      type NEXT_NODE is ACCESS RING_NODE;
        record
          ITEM      : ITEM_TYPE;
          NEXT_CW,                 -- Next item clockwise on the ring
          NEXT_CCW : NEXT_NODE; -- Next item counterclockwise on the ring
        end record;
      type RING is
        record
          TOP  : NEXT_NODE;
          MARK : NEXT_NODE;
          LENGTH : natural := 0;
        end record;
   end GENERIC_UNBOUNDED_RING;
```

Figure 14.2.2 Concluded.

The operations in Figure 14.2.2 are sufficient to write a function to process every item
in the list exactly once. If the procedure PROCESS_ITEM is defined, the procedure in Figure
14.2.3 processes every item in the ring in a specified direction.

```
      procedure PROCESS_RING_ONCE (R   : in   RING;
                                   WAY : in   DIRECTION) is
         TEMP : RING;
      begin
        if EMPTY(R) then
          raise EMPTY_RING;
        else
          COPY(R, TEMP);
          for COUNT in 1..LENGTH (TEMP) loop
            PROCESS_ITEM (PEEK (TEMP));
            ROTATE_RING (TEMP, WAY);
          end loop;
        end if;
      end PROCESS_RING_ONCE;
```

Figure 14.2.3 Procedure that processes every item in a ring.

Most of the procedures and functions are easy to implement. Some are trivial. Note that clearing a ring requires clearing the individual nodes. Ada will not automatically deallocate any node that is referenced. Since the ring is a doubly linked list, every node is always referenced. After breaking up the nodes of the ring, Ada can recover the nodes after the procedure is left. This is why the formal parameter THIS_RING in the operation CLEAR must be in mode in out.

```
procedure CLEAR (THIS_RING : in out RING ) is
  -- Clears the ring of all items
  TEMP : NEXT_NODE := THIS_RING.TOP;
begin
  THIS_RING := (null, null, 0);
  -- De-reference all the nodes
  loop
     exit when TEMP = null;
     TEMP.NEXT_CCW.NEXT_CW := null;
     TEMP.NEXT_CCW          := null;
     TEMP := TEMP.NEXT_CW;
  end loop;
end CLEAR;


procedure MARK_TOP_ITEM (THIS_RING : in out RING ) is
  -- Sets MARK equal to TOP
  -- Exception EMPTY_RING raised if the ring is empty.
begin
  if THIS_RING.TOP = null then
     raise EMPTY_RING;
  else
     THIS_RING.MARK := THIS_RING.TOP;
  end if;
end MARK_TOP_ITEM;


function MARK_AT_TOP (OF_THIS_RING : RING ) return boolean is
  -- Returns true if both TOP and MARK reference the same item
  -- Exception EMPTY_RING raised if the ring is empty.
begin
  if OF_THIS_RING.TOP = null then
     raise EMPTY_RING;
  else
     return OF_THIS_RING.MARK = OF_THIS_RING.TOP;
  end if;
end MARK_AT_TOP;


function PEEK (AT_THIS_RING : RING ) return ITEM_TYPE is
  -- Returns the ITEM at the top of the ring.
  -- The ring remains unchanged after a peek.
  -- Exception EMPTY_RING raised if the ring is empty.
begin
  if AT_THIS_RING.LENGTH = 0 then
```

```
                raise EMPTY_RING;
           else
              return AT_THIS_RING.TOP.ITEM;
           end if;
        end PEEK;

        procedure ROTATE_RING (THIS_RING : in out RING;
                               WAY        : in      DIRECTION ) is
           -- Sets TOP to be the current TOP's successor if CLOCKWISE is
           -- specified or to the current TOP's predecessor if
           -- COUNTERCLOCKWISE direction is specified. MARK is not
           -- affected
           -- Exception EMPTY_RING raised if the ring is empty.
        begin
           if THIS_RING.TOP = null then
              raise EMPTY_RING;
           elsif WAY = CLOCKWISE then
              THIS_RING.TOP := THIS_RING.TOP.NEXT_CW;
           else
              THIS_RING.TOP := THIS_RING.TOP.NEXT_CCW;
           end if;
        end ROTATE_RING;
```

The procedure PEEK could have determined if the list was empty by a call to the function EMPTY, but checking the length directly saves some system overhead. The procedure ADD_ITEM must consider the possibility of an empty ring. ADD_ITEM also must set all access types in the doubly linked list. Figure 14.2.4 illustrates the situation.

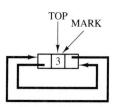

Figure 14.2.4 Result after adding 3 to a previously empty ring.

The procedure POP must do the same access-type bookkeeping that ADD_ITEM did but in reverse. The one detail in POP that is easiest to overlook is the case where the deleted RING_NODE is also the marked RING_NODE. Setting the new marked node as the top node is the convention used to solve this problem.

```
        procedure ADD_ITEM (TO   : in out RING;
                            ITEM : in      ITEM_TYPE) is
           -- Adds an item to the ring at the top position. The added
           -- item becomes the new top item, the added item's successor is
           -- the old top item and the added item's predecessor is the
           -- predecessor of the old top item. If the ring was empty
           -- before the item was added, MARK is set to TOP, otherwise the
           --.value of mark is not affected.
           -- Exception OVERFLOW raised if there is no space to add an item
        begin
```

```
    if TO.TOP = null then
       --Ring empty
       TO.TOP := new RING_NODE' (ITEM, null, null);
       TO.TOP.NEXT_CW; := TO.TOP;
       TO.TOP.NEXT_CCW := TO.TOP;
       TO.MARK := TO.TOP;
       TO.LENGTH := 1;
    else
       -- Ring not empty
       TO.TOP := new RING_NODE' (ITEM, TO.TOP, TO.TOP.NEXT_CCW);
       TO.TOP.NEXT_CW.NEXT_CCW := TO.TOP;
       TO.TOP.NEXT_CCW.NEXT_CW := TO.TOP;
       TO.LENGTH := TO.LENGTH + 1;
    end if;
exception
  when storage_error =>
     raise OVERFLOW;
end ADD_ITEM;

procedure POP (FROM : in out RING ) is
   -- Deletes the item referenced by TOP. The new TOP item
   -- is the successor item of the previous TOP. The marked
   -- item is unaffected by the deletion unless the marked
   -- item is also deleted. In this case new marked item is the
   -- new TOP item. TOP and MARK are null if the ring is empty.
   -- Exception EMPTY_RING raised if the ring is empty.
begin
   if R.LENGTH = 0 then
     raise EMPTY_RING;
   elsif FROM.LENGTH = 1 then
     -- Ring has length 1, result after deletion is empty ring
     FROM := (null, null, 0);
   else
     FROM.TOP.NEXT_CCW.NEXT_CW := FROM.TOP.NEXT_CW;
     FROM.TOP.NEXT_CW.NEXT_CCW := FROM.TOP.NEXT_CCW;
     if FROM.MARK = FROM.TOP then
        FROM.MARK := FROM.TOP.NEXT_CW;
     end if;
     FROM.TOP := FROM.TOP.NEXT_CW;
     FROM.LENGTH := FROM.LENGTH - 1;
   end if;
end POP;
```

The procedure COPY is the final procedure illustrated. The result is two identical rings. Two identical rings must satisfy four conditions. First, they must have the same number of RING_NODES. Second, the top RING_NODES must have the same item in them. Third, the marked RING_NODES must have the same item in them and be at the same point in the ring with respect to top. Fourth, both rings must contain identical sequences of items when the top item is considered to be the first item. Since a ring is a circular structure, some method of keeping track of where copying started must be done or there is a risk of an endless loop. The motivation for COPY is to start at the top and COPY just as you would copy a doubly linked list. After reaching the end, the end item is wrapped around and linked to the front item.

```
procedure COPY (FROM : in      RING;
                TO   :    out RING ) is
  -- Makes a distinct copy of a FROM that preserves both TOP and
  -- MARK.
  -- Exception OVERFLOW raised if there is not enough space in TO
  --           hold the ring FROM.
  TEMP_FROM : NEXT_NODE := FROM.TOP;
  FIRST_NODE,
  TEMP_TO    : NEXT_NODE;
begin
  if FROM.TOP = null then
    -- RING EMPTY
    TO := (null, null, 0);
  else
    -- Copy first ring_node
    TEMP_TO := new RING_NODE' (TEMP_FROM.ITEM, null, null);
    TO := (TEMP_TO, null, FROM.LENGTH);
    FIRST_NODE := TEMP_TO;
    if FROM.MARK = TEMP_FROM then
      TO.MARK := TEMP_TO;
    end if;
    TEMP_FROM := TEMP_FROM.NEXT_CW;
    -- Copy remaining ring_nodes into doubly linked list
    for COUNT in 1..FROM.LENGTH - 1 loop
      -- Make a new successor node with next FROM.ITEM.
      TEMP_TO.NEXT_CW :=
          new RING_NODE' (TEMP_FROM.ITEM, null, TEMP_TO);
      -- Set up NEXT_CCW of new node to its precedecessor
      TEMP_TO.NEXT_CW.NEXT_CCW := TEMP_TO;
      -- Move to next node on TO ring.
      TEMP_TO := TEMP_TO.NEXT_CW;
      -- If at FROM.MARK, Mark TEMP_TO
      if FROM.MARK := TEMP_FROM then
        TO.MARK := TEMP_TO;
      end if;
      -- Get next ITEM from FROM to copy
      TEMP_FROM := TEMP_FROM.NEXT_CW;
    end loop;
    -- Tie end of doubly linked list to front to make into ring
    FIRST_NODE.NEXT_CCW := TEMP_TO;
    TEMP_TO.NEXT_CW := FIRST_NODE;
  end if;
exception
  when storage_error =>
    raise OVERFLOW;
end COPY;
```

The function RINGS_EQUAL checks that the four required conditions identified when copying two rings occur. Full implementation of the package is covered in the exercises.

14.3 BOUNDED FORM

There are many ways to implement the bounded ring. All use the array type. One way to represent the ring data structure is to modify the structure used in GENERIC_BOUNDED_STACK, and a second method is to build a structure that would allow the algorithms used in GENERIC_UNBOUNDED_RING to be the pattern for the implementation. The basic structural difference is the way the ring data structure keeps track of the unused array components.

Consider the record with variant part that was first proposed in Exercise 5.2.4 to implement one form of GENERIC_BOUNDED_STACK and later used in Figure 13.2.3 to implement the bounded form of a string.

```
type STACK_ARRAY is array (positive range <> ) of ITEM_TYPE;
type STACK (SIZE   : positive ) is
  record
    TOP : natural := 0;
    STK : STACK_ARRAY (1..SIZE);
  end record;
```

Unused components in STK were located in the slice TOP + 1..SIZE. Adding to this structure a mark field and a field to tell where unused items start would allow the ring to be divided into two slices. The lower slice contains the RING_NODES of the ring, and the upper slice contains the unused components of ITEM_TYPE. The data structure would look as follows:

```
type RING_ARRAY is array (positive range  <> ) of ITEM_TYPE;
type RING (SIZE : positive ) is
  record
    TOP        : natural := 0;
    MARK       : natural := 0;
    TOP_USED   : natural := 0;
    ITEM_ARRAY : RING_ARRAY(1..SIZE);
  end record;
```

TOP and MARK have the same function as they did before. The array ITEM_ARRAY is divided into two disjoint slices ITEM_ARRAY(1..TOP_USED), which is the actual ring itself, and ITEM_ARRAY(TOP_USED + 1..SIZE), composed of unused components. A ring is empty when TOP_USED = 0, and it is full when TOP_USED = SIZE. TOP_USED is the length of the ring. Again the mode of the formal parameter "TO" in the operation COPY has been changed to "in out." This is necessary because the SIZE parameter of the record must be accessible. This implementation leads to the specification in Figure 14.3.1.

```
generic
  type ITEM_TYPE is private;
package GENERIC_BOUNDED_RING is
```

Figure 14.3.1   ADT GENERIC_BOUNDED_RING. Continues on page 502.

```
type RING (SIZE : positive) is limited private;
type DIRECTION is (CLOCKWISE, COUNTERCLOCKWISE);
procedure ADD_ITEM          (TO              : in out RING;
                             ITEM            : in     ITEM_TYPE);
procedure POP               (FROM            : in out RING;
procedure CLEAR             (THIS_RING       : in out RING );
procedure COPY              (FROM            : in     RING;
                             TO              :    out RING );
procedure ROTATE_RING       (THIS_RING       : in out RING;
                             WAY             : in     DIRECTION );
procedure MARK_TOP_ITEM     (THIS_RING       : in out RING );
function PEEK               (AT_THIS_RING : RING ) return ITEM_TYPE;
function LENGTH             (OF_THIS_RING : RING ) return natural;
function MARK_AT_TOP        (OF_THIS_RING : RING ) return boolean;
function EQUAL              (LEFT, RIGHT   : RING ) return boolean;
function EMPTY              (THIS_RING    : RING ) return boolean;
function FULL               (THIS_RING    : RING ) return boolean;
OVERFLOW     : exception;
EMPTY_RING : exception;
private
   type RING_ARRAY is array (positive range  <> ) of ITEM_TYPE;
   type RING (SIZE: positive ) is
      record
         TOP           : natural := 0;
         MARK          : natural := 0;
         TOP_USED      : natural := 0;
         ITEM_ARRAY : RING_ARRAY(1..SIZE);
      end record;
end GENERIC_BOUNDED_RING;
```

Figure 14.3.1   Concluded.

The use of array operations and attributes make the implementation straightforward. The biggest wrinkle is the observation that two rings can be equal without having equal-size ring structures. Consider the following case, where R1 is a ring of size 20 and R2 is a ring size of 30. The two rings R1 and R2 would be equal if

```
R1.TOP = R2.TOP
R1.MARK = R2.MARK
R1.TOP_USED = R2.TOP_USED
R1.ITEM_ARRAY (1..R1.TOP_USED) = R2.ITEM_ARRAY (1..R2.TOP_USED)
```

Unfortunately, this case does not cover all the possibilities. It is true if both R1.TOP = R2.TOP. Rings can be equal when R1.TOP does not equal R2.TOP. It does provide a correct strategy for copying one ring onto a second ring. The operation COPY provides a second illustration of how a ring can be copied into a smaller or a larger structure.

```
procedure COPY (FROM : in     RING;
                TO   : in out RING ) is
   -- Makes a distinct copy of a FROM that preserves both TOP and
   -- MARK.
```

```
--  Exception OVERFLOW raised if there is not enough space in
--            TO to hold the ring FROM.
begin
  if FROM.TOP_USED > TO.SIZE then
    --Not enough room in TO to hold FROM
    raise OVERFLOW;
  elsif FROM.TOP_USED = 0 then
    --FROM is empty
    TO.TOP := 0;
    TO.TOP_USED := 0;
    TO.MARK := 0;
  else
    TO.ITEM_ARRAY (1..FROM.TOP_USED) :=
              FROM.ITEM_ARRAY (1..FROM.TOP_USED);
    TO.TOP := FROM.TOP;
    TO.TOP_USED := FROM.TOP_USED;
    TO.MARK := FROM.MARK;
  end if;
end COPY;
```

For two rings to be equal, the ITEM R1.ITEM_ARRAY (R1.TOP) must equal the ITEM R2.ITEM_ARRAY (R2.TOP), but this does not require that R1.TOP equal R2.TOP. Two identical rings have the same number of components in use; that is, R1.TOP_USED equals R2.TOP_USED. The component in R1.ITEM_ARRAY (R1.MARK) must equal the component in R2.ITEM_ARRAY (R2.MARK), but that does not require R1.MARK to equal R2.MARK. In equal rings, each ring has identical items in identical sequences where the first item of each sequence is at the TOP position in the array. This does not require that the items be stored in the same position in their respective arrays. The function EQUAL is as follows:

```
function EQUAL (LEFT, RIGHT : RING) return boolean is
  -- Returns true for two rings of the same length when the
  -- rings are equal item are item when the comparison starts
  -- at the TOP of both rings, and the same item is marked with
  -- with reference to the TOP of both rings.
  TEMP_LEFT_INDEX : natural := LEFT.TOP;
  TEMP_RIGHT_INDEX : natural := RIGHT.TOP;
begin
  if LEFT.TOP_USED = 0 then
    -- Empty rings are equal
    return RIGHT.TOP_USED = 0;
  elsif LEFT.TOP_USED /= RIGHT.TOP_USED then
    -- Rings of different length are not equal
    return false;
  else
    -- Check to see in rings are equal item by item starting at
    -- their respective top
    for COUNT in 1..LEFT.TOP_USED loop
      if LEFT.ITEM_ARRAY (TEMP_LEFT_INDEX)  /=
              RIGHT.ITEM_ARRAY (TEMP_RIGHT_INDEX) then
        -- ITEM at this place not equal
```

```
          return false;
        end if;
        -- Check to see if both have same MARK'ed ITEM
        if (LEFT.MARK = TEMP_LEFT_INDEX) xor
              (RIGHT.MARK = TEMP_RIGHT_INDEX) then
          --Oops, one ITEM marked but other is not relative to TOP
          return false;
        end if;
        -- Update indices for LEFT and RIGHT subject to TOP_USED
        TEMP_LEFT_INDEX := TEMP_LEFT_INDEX + 1;
        if TEMP_LEFT_INDEX > LEFT.TOP_USED then
          TEMP_LEFT_INDEX := 1;
        end if;
        TEMP_RIGHT_INDEX := TEMP_RIGHT_INDEX + 1;
        if TEMP_RIGHT_INDEX > RIGHT.TOP_USED then
          TEMP_RIGHT_INDEX := 1;
        end if;
      end loop;
      return true;
    end if;
  end EQUAL;
```

To implement the procedure ROTATE, a convention must be adopted that defines what CLOCKWISE and COUNTERCLOCKWISE means. CLOCKWISE will be defined to mean increasing the value of TOP.

```
    procedure ROTATE_RING (THIS_RING : in out RING;
                          WAY       : in      DIRECTION) is
    -- Sets TOP to be the current TOP's successor if CLOCKWISE is
    -- specified or to the current TOP's predecessor if
    -- COUNTERCLOCKWISE direction is specified. MARK is not
    -- affected
    -- Exception EMPTY_RING raised if the ring is empty.
    begin
      if THIS_RING.TOP_USED = 0 then
        raise EMPTY_RING;
      elsif WAY = CLOCKWISE then
        -- Clockwise rotation sets TOP equal to old TOP's successor
        THIS_RING.TOP := THIS_RING.TOP + 1;
        if THIS_RING.TOP > THIS_RING.TOP_USED then
          THIS_RING.TOP := 1;
        end if;
      else
        -- COUNTERCLOCKWISE rotation specified
        THIS_RING.TOP := THIS_RING.TOP - 1;
        if THIS_RING.TOP = 0 then
          THIS_RING.TOP := THIS_RING.TOP_USED;
        end if;
      end if;
    end ROTATE_RING;
```

With the convention on direction now defined, the procedure to ADD_ITEM can be listed. Recall that an object is inserted at location TOP. All items with indices greater than TOP must be moved and the value of MARK readjusted if necessary.

```
procedure ADD_ITEM (TO    : in out RING;
                     ITEM  : in       ITEM_TYPE) is
   -- Adds an item to the ring at the top position. The added
   -- item becomes the new top item, the added items' successor is
   -- the old TOP item, and the added item's predecessor is the
   -- predecessor of the old TOP item. If the ring was empty
   -- before the item was added, MARK is set to TOP, otherwise the
   -- value of MARK is not affected.
   -- Exception OVERFLOW raised if there is no space to add an item
begin
   if TO.TOP_USED = TO.SIZE then
      -- ITEM_ARRAY is full
      raise OVERFLOW;
   elsif TO.TOP_USED = 0 then
      -- RING EMPTY
      TO.TOP := 1;
      TO.MARK := 1;
      TO.TOP_USED := 1;
      TO.ITEM_ARRAY (1) := ITEM;
   else
      -- Shift ITEM_ARRAY slice to make room for ITEM
      TO.ITEM_ARRAY (TO.TOP + 1..TO.TOP_USED + 1) :=
              TO.ITEM_ARRAY (TO.TOP..TO.TOP_USED);
      TO.ITEM_ARRAY (TO.TOP) := ITEM;
      -- If marked item shifted, adjust MARK
      if TO.MARK >= TO.TOP then
         TO.MARK := TO.MARK + 1;
      end if;
      TO.TOP_USED := TO.TOP_USED + 1;
   end if;
end ADD_ITEM;
```

The remainder of the procedures and functions are covered in the exercises.

14.4 APPLICATIONS

In Chapter 13 the ADT STRING implemented an arbitrary precision package to manipulate integers of any length. The addition and multiplication operations were developed. The ADT GENERIC_UNBOUNDED_RING will be used to implement the same procedures. For convenience GENERIC_UNBOUNDED_RING will be recompiled with type RING now private instead of limited private. This allows the type RING to be passed in all modes, including the mode out.

Suppose that a new package LARGE_NUMBERS is instantiated as

```
subtype DIGIT is integer range 0..9;
package LARGE_NUMBERS is new GENERIC_UNBOUNDED_RING (DIGIT);
use LARGE_NUMBERS;
```

Figure 14.4.1 shows how an integer or arbitrary length can be represented by a ring of DIGIT. Note that the ring's mark keeps track of the unit's digit. The ten's digit is the unit's digit predecessor; that is, it is the next counterclockwise entry on the ring. The hundred's digit is the ten's digit predecessor, and so on. (It must be the predecessor item because ADD_ITEM inserts an item at the top and the old top becomes the new top item's successor.) An integer with n digits can be represented by a ring with n RING_NODE. The integer with value zero can be represented by either an empty ring or a ring where every element contains the zero digit. To add together two integers represented by rings, both rings are first rotated so that their top and mark line up. Then the two digits in each ring's first node, which represents the unit digit of each integer, are added together and that result is added to the ring containing the result. Next both rings are rotated counterclockwise to the unit's digit predecessor, the ten's digit. The programmer must allow for the case where the two integers have different lengths.

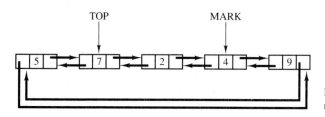

Figure 14.4.1 High-precision integer representation of 95724.

```
procedure ADD_X_TO_Y (X    : in      RING;
                      Y    : in      RING;
                      ANS :     out RING) is
  CARRY       : integer := 0;
  TEMP_X, TEMP_Y, TEMP : RING;
  LENGTH_X    : natural := LENGTH (X);
  LENGTH_Y    : natural := LENGTH (Y);
  MIN_LENGTH  : natural := LENGTH_X;
begin
  COPY(X, TEMP_X);
  COPY(Y, TEMP_Y);
  -- If the ring Y is shorter than ring X, adjust MIN_LENGTH
  if LENGTH_Y < MIN_LENGTH then
    MIN_LENGTH := LENGTH_Y;
  end if;
  -- Put the units digit of both rings at TOP
  while not MARK_AT_TOP (TEMP_X) loop
    ROTATE_RING (TEMP_X, COUNTERCLOCKWISE);
  end loop;
  while not MARK_AT_TOP (TEMP_Y) loop
    ROTATE_RING (TEMP_Y, COUNTERCLOCKWISE);
  end loop;
  -- Add first MIN_LENGTH digits of both numbers together
  for COUNT in 1..MIN_LENGTH loop
    CARRY := CARRY + PEEK (TEMP_X) + PEEK (TEMP_Y);
    -- Note that 0 <= CARRY <= 18, strip off units, and update
    ADD_ITEM (TEMP, (CARRY rem 10));
    CARRY := (CARRY - (CARRY rem 10)) / 10;
```

```
          ROTATE_RING (TEMP_X, COUNTERCLOCKWISE);
          ROTATE_RING (TEMP_Y, COUNTERCLOCKWISE);
        end loop;
        -- Allow for case where integers have different length
        if MIN_LENGTH < LENGTH_X then
          -- Add the remaining digits of X to the answer
          for i in MIN_LENGTH + 1..LENGTH_X loop
            CARRY := CARRY + PEEK (TEMP_X);
            ADD_ITEM(TEMP, (CARRY rem 10));
            CARRY := (CARRY - (CARRY rem 10)) / 10;
            ROTATE_RING (TEMP_X, COUNTERCLOCKWISE);
          end loop;
        elsif MIN_LENGTH < LENGTH_Y then
          -- Y is the longer
          for i in MIN_LENGTH + 1..LENGTH_Y loop
            CARRY := CARRY + PEEK (TEMP_Y);
            ADD_ITEM(TEMP, (CARRY rem 10));
            CARRY := (CARRY - (CARRY rem 10)) / 10;
            ROTATE_RING (TEMP_Y, COUNTERCLOCKWISE);
          end loop;
        end if;
        -- There may still be a digit in the carry
        if CARRY /= 0 then
          ADD_ITEM (TEMP, CARRY);
        end if;
        -- Copy results to the ANSWER
        Copy (Temp, Ans);
      end ADD_X_TO_Y;
```

Just as in the previous case, multiplication follows immediately once a procedure that multiplies an integer by a digit is defined. The multiplication algorithm is the same as the one in Chapter 13.

```
        procedure MUL_X_BY_DIGIT (X   : in      RING;
                                  D   : in      DIGIT;
                                  ANS :     out RING ) is
          CARRY        : integer := 0;
          LENGTH_X     : natural := LENGTH (X);
          TEMP_X, TEMP : RING;
        begin
          Copy(X, Temp_X);
          -- Put TOP at the unit's digit;
          while not MARK_AT_TOP (TEMP_X) loop
            ROTATE_RING (TEMP_X, COUNTERCLOCKWISE);
          end loop;
          -- Multiply each digit and add result to the answer
          for i in 1..LENGTH_X loop
            CARRY := CARRY + PEEK (TEMP_X) * D;
            ADD_ITEM (TEMP. (CARRY rem 10));
            CARRY := (CARRY - (CARRY rem 10)) / 10;
```

```
        ROTATE_RING (TEMP_X, COUNTERCLOCKWISE);
      end loop;
      -- Allow for the possibility of a nonzero carry
      if CARRY /= 0 then
        ADD_ITEM (TEMP, CARRY);
      end if;
      COPY (TEMP, ANS);
    end MUL_X_BY_DIGIT;

    procedure MUL_X_BY_Y (X   : in     RING;
                          Y   : in     RING;
                          ANS :     out RING ) is
      D : DIGIT;
      TEMP_X, TEMP_Y, TEMP, TEMP_ANS : RING;
      LENGTH_Y : natural := LENGTH (Y);
    begin
      -- TEMP_ANS is used as an accumulator, it can't be empty
      ADD_ITEM (TEMP_ANS, 0);
      -- Get X and Y and locate unit's digit at the top
      COPY (X, TEMP_X);
      while not MARK_AT_TOP (TEMP_X) loop
        ROTATE_RING (TEMP_X, COUNTERCLOCKWISE);
      end loop;
      COPY (Y, TEMP_Y);
      while not MARK_AT_TOP (TEMP_Y) loop
        ROTATE_RING (TEMP_Y, COUNTERCLOCKWISE);
      end loop;
      -- Now multiply
      for COUNT in 1..LENGTH_Y loop
        MUL_X_BY_DIGIT (TEMP_X, PEEK (TEMP_Y), TEMP);
        --Get next digit
        ROTATE_RING (TEMP_Y, COUNTERCLOCKWISE);
        ROTATE_RING(TEMP_X,CLOCKWISE)
        -- Adding an 0 has the effect of multiplying X by 10
        ADD_ITEM (TEMP_X, 0);
        -- Digit added above is new unit's digit
        MARK_TOP_ITEM (TEMP_X);
        -- Add the temporary product to the accumulator
        ADD_X_TO_Y (TEMP, TEMP_ANS, TEMP_ANS);
      end loop;
      COPY (TEMP_ANS, ANS);
    end MUL_X_BY_Y;
```

If the length of the integers X and Y is n, then ADD_X_TO_Y is $O(n)$ and MUL_X_BY_Y is $O(n**2)$. This is a reduction of one order from $O(n**2)$, when strings were used to represent integers in Chapter 13, to $O(n)$ for addition and from $O(n**3)$ to $O(n**2)$ for multiplication. A reduction of one order of magnitude is significant. The reason for this reduction is that the ring does not have to be searched for the next digit on a digit-by-digit basis.

There are significant applications of rings to the implementation of parallel processing and concurrency. There are possible applications in a multitasking environment. Let the ring NEXT_TASK contain all the active tasks. The operation

PEEK (NEXT_TASK)

is the current active task. After the procedure

ROTATE_RING (NEXT_TASK, CLOCKWISE);

executes, the next task is at the top of the ring. A new task is added to the ring by the operation

ADD_ITEM (NEXT_TASK, TASK);

Figure 14.4.2 illustrates this situation.

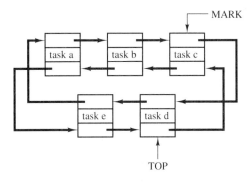

Figure 14.4.2 Tasks in a multitasking environment stored on a ring. The pointer top points to the current task being executed.

Many operating systems and editors have the facility to keep track of the last few commands. This record is kept on a bounded ring. As a command executes, the last command on the ring is popped and the most recent command is added to the top of the ring. Typically, the "up arrow" key gets the preceding command, and the "down arrow" key gets the succeeding command (see Figure 14.4.3).

Figure 14.4.3 Bounded ring used to keep track of the six most recent commands. Mark is the place of the last command executed. The next command executed goes into the successor of MARK. TOP points to the command that will be executed if the "Enter" key is pressed without typing in a new command.

In Chapter 7 the package GENERIC_UNBOUNDED_DEQUE was described (see Figure 7.4.2). Recall that a deque is a queue type ADT where an item can be inserted at either the front or the rear of the queue. Figure 14.4.4 shows the specifications of the GENERIC_UN-BOUNDED _DEQUE when it is implemented using GENERIC_UNBOUNDED_RING.

```
with GENERIC_UNBOUNDED_RING;
generic
  type ITEM_TYPE is private;
package GENERIC_UNBOUNDED_DEQUE is
  type DEQUE is limited private;
  type PLACE_TO_ADD is (IN_FRONT, IN_REAR);
```

Figure 14.4.4 GENERIC_UNBOUNDED_DEQUE implemented using GENERIC_UNBOUNDED_RING. Continues on page 510.

Sec. 14.4   Applications   **509**

```
procedure ENQUEUE          (ITEM                    : in      ITEM_TYPE;
                            WHERE                    : in      PLACE_TO_ADD;
                            TO                       : in out DEQUE);
procedure DEQUEUE          (ITEM                    :     out ITEM_TYPE;
                            FROM                     : in out DEQUE);
procedure COPY             (FROM                     : in      DEQUE;
                            TO                       : in out QUEUE);
procedure APPEND           (FROM                     : in      DEQUE;
                            ONTO                     : in out DEQUE);
procedure CLEAR            (Q_TO_CLEAR               : in out DEQUE);
procedure POP              (FROM_THE_Q               : in out DEQUE);
function LENGTH            (Q_TO_COUNT  : DEQUE) return natural;
function EMPTY             (Q_TO_CHECK  : DEQUE) return boolean;
function FRONT_ITEM        (FROM_THE_Q  : DEQUE) return ITEM_TYPE;
function REAR_ITEM         (FROM_THE_Q  : DEQUE) return ITEM_TYPE;
function EQUAL             (LEFT, RIGHT : DEQUE) return boolean;
OVERFLOW     : exception;
Q_IS_EMPTY : exception;
private
   Package NEW_DEQUE is new GENERIC_UNBOUNDED_RING (ITEM_TYPE);
   type DEQUE is new NEW_DEQUE.RING;
end GENERIC_UNBOUNDED_DEQUE;
```

Figure 14.4.4   Concluded.

Figure 14.4.5 illustrates how a ring can be identified as a deque.

Adding an item to the front of the deque is the same as adding an item to the ring using ADD_ITEM. To add an item to the end of the deque, the ring rotates once, the item is then inserted using ADD_ITEM, and finally, the ring is rotated back to its original position. Figure 14.4.6 lists the partial implementation of GENERIC_UNBOUNDED_DEQUE.

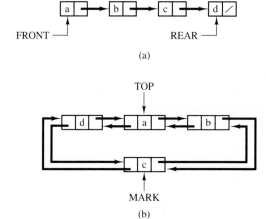

(a)

(b)

Figure 14.4.5   Using a ring to implement the ADT deque. (a) Typical deque from Chapter 7. Recall that an item can be added to either the front or the rear of a deque. (b) The deque in part (a) represented as a ring. TOP points to the front of the deque. To add an item to the front requires a call to ADD_ITEM. To add an item to the rear requires a call to ADD_ITEM followed by a rotation of the ring one place clockwise.

```
package body GENERIC_UNBOUNDED_DEQUE is

  . . . . . . . . . . .

  procedure DEQUEUE (ITEM :    out ITEM_TYPE);
                     FROM : in out DEQUE) is
  -- Returns the item at the front of the queue, or TOP of the ring
  -- Exception Q_IS_EMPTY returned when EMPTY_RING raised
  begin
    ITEM := NEW_DEQUE.PEEK (NEW_DEQUE.RING (FROM));
    NEW_DEQUE.POP (NEW_DEQUE.RING (FROM));
  exception
    when NEW_DEQUE.EMPTY_RING => raise Q_IS_EMPTY;
  end DEQUEUE;


  procedure COPY (FROM : in    DEQUE;
                  TO   : in out DEQUE) is
    -- Makes an exact copy of FROM_Q and returns it as TO_Q
    -- Exception OVERFLOW returned when NEW_DEQUE>OVERFLOW raised
  begin
    NEW_DEQUE.COPY (NEW_DEQUE.RING (FROM), NEW_DEQUE.RING (TO));
  exception
    when NEW_DEQUE.OVERFLOW => raise OVERFLOW;
  end COPY;


  . . . . . . . . . . .

end GENERIC_UNBOUNDED_DEQUE;
```

Figure 14.4.6   Implementation of GENERIC_UNBOUNDED_DEQUE using GENERIC_UNBOUNDED_RING.

The rest of the implementation is covered in the exercises.

14.5 TIME AND SPACE CONSTRAINTS

Let n be the number of items on the ring. Since any item on a ring can access both its predecessor and its successor, the ring can be a very efficient ADT. Figure 14.5.1 shows the constraints of GENERIC_BOUNDED_RING specified in Figure 14.3.1. The operational overhead of POP and ROTATE_RING can be reduced to $O(1)$ by using the specification in Figure 14.3.3. The constraints for GENERIC_UNBOUNDED_RING specified in Figure 14.2.2 are listed in Figure 14.5.2. For most applications, GENERIC_UNBOUNDED_RING is preferred. The operational overhead for the major operations is smaller than the same operations for the bounded cause.

	Operation Overhead	Space Overhead
ADD_ITEM	$O(1)$	$O(\text{SIZE})$
POP	$O(n)$	$O(\text{SIZE})$
COPY	$O(n)$	$O(\text{SIZE})$
LENGTH	$O(1)$	$O(\text{SIZE})$
ROTATE_RING	$O(n)$	$O(\text{SIZE})$
Peek	$O(1)$	$O(\text{SIZE})$
EQUAL	$O(n)$	$O(\text{SIZE})$

Figure 14.5.1   Constraints for GENERIC_BOUNDED_RING.

	Operation Overhead	Space Overhead
ADD_ITEM	$O(1)$	$O(n)$
POP	$O(1)$	$O(n)$
COPY	$O(n)$	$O(n)$
LENGTH	$O(1)$	$O(n)$
ROTATE_RING	$O(1)$	$O(n)$
PEEK	$O(1)$	$O(n)$
EQUAL	$O(n)$	$O(n)$

Figure 14.5.2   Constraints for GENERIC_UNBOUNDED_RING.

EXERCISES

Section 14.2 Unbounded Implementation

14.2.1 Implement the following operations for the ADT GENERIC_UNBOUNDED_RING as specified in Figure 14.2.2.
  a. The ring operation LENGTH
  b. The ring operation EQUAL
  c. The ring operation EMPTY
  d. Combine parts a through c with the ring operations implemented in Section 14.2 into a package body that completes the implementation of GENERIC_UNBOUNDED_RING.

14.2.2 Change the private part in Figure 14.2.2 to

```
type RING_NODE;
type NEXT is access RING_NODE;
type RING is
  record
    TOP  : NEXT;
    MARK : NEXT;
    LENGTH : natural := 0;
  end record;
type RING_NODE is
  record
    ITEM    : ITEM_TYPE;
    NEXT_CW : NEXT;      -- Next clockwise item
  end record;
```

Implement the following operations for the ADT GENERIC_UNBOUNDED_RING with the new private part.
  a. The ring operation ADD_ITEM
  b. The ring operation POP
  c. The ring operation CLEAR
  d. The ring operation COPY
  e. The ring operation ROTATE_RING
  f. The ring operation MARK_TOP_ITEM
  g. The ring operation PEEK
  h. The ring operation LENGTH
  i. The ring operation MARK_AT_TOP
  j. The ring operation EQUAL
  k. The ring operation EMPTY
  l. Combine parts a to k into a package body that completes this implementation of GENERIC__UNBOUNDED_RING.
  m. Complete a time and space constraint table for the ADT above. Use Figure 14.5.2.

Section 14.3 Bounded Form

14.3.1 Implement the following operations for the ADT GENERIC_UNBOUNDED_RING as specified in Figure 14.3.1.
  a. The ring operation POP
  b. The ring operation CLEAR
  c. The ring operation MARK_TOP_ITEM
  d. The ring operation PEEK
  e. The ring operation LENGTH
  f. The ring operation MARK_AT_TOP
  g. The ring operation EMPTY
  h. The ring operation FULL
  i. Combine parts a through j along with the operations implemented in Section 14.3 into a package body that completes this implementation of GENERIC_UNBOUNDED_RING.

Section 14.4 Applications

14.4.1 Suppose that integers of arbitrary length are implemented using lists defined by the instantiation

```
subtype DIGIT is integer range 0..9;
package LARGE_NUMBERS is new GENERIC_UNBOUNDED_RING (DIGIT);
use LARGE_NUMBERS;
```

In Section 4 two procedures, ADD_X_TO_Y and MUL_X_BY_Y, were implemented.
  a. Implement a boolean function X_LESS_THAN_Y that returns true if the first argument is less than the second argument and false otherwise.
  b. Implement a boolean function X_EQUAL_Y that returns true if X = Y and false otherwise.
  c. Implement a procedure SUB_X_FROM_Y that subtracts X from Y under the assumption that X <= Y.
  d. Implement a procedure DIV_X_BY_Y that divides X by Y and returns the answer and the remainder.
  e. Implement a procedure SHIFT_X_BY_P that returns a long integer equal to $X*10**p$.
  f. Devise a time and space constraint table for the seven LONG_NUMBER operations. Use $n =$ length of LONG_NUMBER.

g. A prime number is a number that is divisible by itself and by 1. Using parts a through f and the operations implemented in Section 14.4, write a procedure that returns two values. If the number is prime, the boolean value flag is true, and the LONG_INTEGER divisor returns the number 1. If the number is not prime, the boolean value flag is set to false, and the LONG_INTEGER divisor returns a divisor of the number.

14.4.2 Implemented the package GENERIC_UNBOUNDED_DEQUE by using a rename GENERIC_UNBOUNDED_RING as illustrated in Figure 14.4.4.

PROGRAMMING PROJECTS

P14.1 Many games, such as roulette, wheel of fortune, and spin the bottle, use some sort of spinner to determine the next outcome. Write a program that simulates such a game.

NOTES AND REFERENCES

Knuth [27] is a good reference for rings. Booch [8] discusses some applications to operating systems and concurrency.

15

Arrays and Matrices with Numeric Components

In Chapter 1 we reviewed the array type. In this chapter we concentrate on one- and two-dimensional arrays of numeric type. The Ada built-in numeric types are floats and integers. There are programmer-defined numeric types such as the rational and complex types. The goal is to develop several simple packages that will allow expressions involving arrays to be expressed in a natural mathematical fashion. This makes arrays and matrices into an ADT by adding the missing operations. Some familiarity with linear algebra is helpful but is not necessary.

Manipulating matrix expressions is very important in many fields of science, engineering, and computational science. Every physics student is familiar with the three-dimensional vector space. Three-dimensional vectors of float type represent points in space. The transforms, which move these vectors around from one point in space to another point in space, are three-dimensional square matrices of float type. Graphics programming uses similar representations.

A variety of significant problems in science and engineering use matrix representation. A computer model uses the equations of three-dimensional fluid flow to determine the flight characteristics of an experimental airplane wing design. The wing might never be built, but aerospace engineers will gain enough insight to progress to the next design phase. Geologists trying to find the next major oil field examine seismic data in an attempt to discern the earth's structure to locate probable oil deposits. The model uses equations of sound traveling through a solid to unravel the seismic data recorded by the geologists. The goal is to determine the earth's structure. An environmentalist concerned with air pollution, global warming, and the ozone layer uses a meteorological model of the earth's atmosphere to try to predict future long-range trends. An economist uses a model of the economy based on the relationships between such things as federal budgets and deficits, home mortgage rates, steel production, and the price of a barrel of oil to predict the future growth rate of the economy. These problems all involve the use of matrix algebra.

Problems using matrix algebra are natural problems for parallel computation and multitasking. Evaluating a matrix expression involves repeating some basic task. Adding up two n-dimensional square matrices involves solving the problem of adding two vectors together n times. If the ith processor adds the ith rows together, the process can be speeded up at a rate proportional to the number of processors assigned to the problem. Packages such as these are available commercially. Although the specifications are similar, the implementation of the package minimizes the time needed to solve the problem. The architecture of supercomputers and vector processors requires that the programmer pay special attention to the details of the program. Simple changes to programming code that do not affect the validity of solution can cause program execution speed-ups of several magnitudes. These specialized details are best left to the experts, but the programmer can achieve these same benefits by using a properly implemented package.

In Section 15.1 we review basic matrix algebra operations and develop a basic package of overloaded matrix operations. In Section 15.2 we develop elementary matrix operations. All the vectors and matrices defined in this chapter are assumed to index ranges whose first index is always 1.

15.1 MATRIX ALGEBRA

Let N be some positive constant. The types vector and matrix are defined as

```
type VECTOR is array (positive range <> ) of float;
type MATRIX is array (positive range <>,
                      positive range <> ) of float;
V1, V2, V3 : VECTOR (1..N);
M1, M2, M3 : MATRIX (1..N, 1..N);
K1, K2, K3 : FLOAT;
```

Throughout this chapter, it is assumed that V'first = 1 for any VECTOR V, and that M'first(1) = 1 and M'first(2) = 1 for any MATRIX M. With this assumption, all index ranges of any VECTOR or MATRIX are of the form 1..N. The dimension of a VECTOR is the number of components, sometimes called elements, in the VECTOR. From the mathematical point of view, a VECTOR with index range 1..3 is the same as the case for arbitrary index range 1..N. The one additional thing that the case N = 3 supplies is the vector product, sometimes called the cross product. Abstractly, the VECTOR V1 is the location of a point in n-dimensional space. The MATRIX M1, commonly called a linear transformation, shifts a point from one location to another location. The VECTOR expression

```
V1 := K1*V2*V3*K2*M1*M2*V3 - V2;
```

is a valid mathematical expression, but it is not defined in Ada. The goal of this section is to define the basic matrix vector operations and then to build an ADT composed of overloaded operators. The implementation of this package would allow the expression above to be defined. Figure 15.1.1 provides a basic ADT documentation for matrix-vector type.

GENERAL ADT SPECIFICATION FOR MATRIX AND VECTOR OPERATIONS

Description

This ADT builds a package that overloads the binary operators "+", "*", and "−" to create a package of standard matrix and vector operations. Two types, VECTOR and MATRIX, are created.

Figure 15.1.1   Documentation for MATRIX and VECTOR operations. Continues on page 517.

Neither is private to the package. A VECTOR is a one-dimensional array with positive range index of the form 1..N. A MATRIX is a two-dimensional array with indices that have the same range pattern as a vector's range. It is not necessary that a MATRIX be square. Operations are implemented for the MATRIX-MATRIX, MATRIX-VECTOR, SCALAR-MATRIX, and SCALAR-VECTOR cases. Standard mathematical conventions define all operations.

Programmer-Supplied Data Structures or Specifications

The programmer must supply the ranges of all VECTORS and MATRICES at declaration. All ranges must be in the form 1..N for N a positive number. All operations will raise an INDEX_ERROR if the index range is not in this form.

Operations

Name	Description
VECTOR operations	
"*"	(Three versions) Two versions, constant*VECTOR and VECTOR*constant, return a VECTOR whose components are defined by multiplying each component in the VECTOR times the constant. The third version, VECTOR*VECTOR, is the scalar or dot product that returns a float defined as the sum of the product of the respective VECTOR elements.
"+"	returns a VECTOR whose components are the sum of the respective components.
"−"	returns a VECTOR whose components are the difference of the respective components.
MATRIX operations	
"*"	(Three versions) Two versions, constant*MATRIX and MATRIX*constant, return a MATRIX whose components are defined by multiplying each component in the MATRIX times the constant. The third version, MATRIX*MATRIX, is the standard product that returns a MATRIX.
"+"	returns a MATRIX whose components are the sum of the respective components.
"−"	returns a MATRIX whose components are the difference of the respective components.
MATRIX-VECTOR operations	
"*"	returns a VECTOR that is the result of multiplying a MATRIX*VECTOR.

Exceptions

The exception INDEX_ERROR is raised whenever the index of any VECTOR or MATRIX is not of the form 1..N, or if the indices of any VECTOR-VECTOR operation, MATRIX-VECTOR operation, or MATRIX-MATRIX operation do not result in a well-defined object.

Figure 15.1.1 Continues on page 518.

Warnings

The type VECTOR and the type MATRIX are not private. They may be modified, operated on, or assigned without using operations defined within the package.

Figure 15.1.1 Concluded.

It appears that the cross product of two vectors is missing from the specification in Figure 15.1.1. The cross product is defined only for N = 3.

Multiplying a VECTOR by a constant SCALAR is the same as multiplying each component of that VECTOR by that constant. Note that the relation "SCALAR*V" = "V*SCALAR" defines the second function.

```
    function "*" (SCALAR : float; V : VECTOR ) return VECTOR is
      -- Returns a vector whose components are a constant multiple of the
      -- corresponding components of V
      -- Exception INDEX_ERROR raised if V'range not of the form 1..N
      ANSWER : VECTOR (V'range);
    begin
      if V'first /= 1 then
        -- Since V'last is positive, it need not be checked.
        raise INDEX_ERROR;
      else
        for INDEX in V'range loop
          ANSWER (INDEX) := SCALAR * V(INDEX);
        end LOOP
        return ANSWER
      end if
    end "*";

function "*" (V: VECTOR; SCALAR : float) return VECTOR is
      -- Returns a vector whose components are a constant multiple of the
      -- corresponding components of V
      -- Exception INDEX_ERROR raised if V'range not of the form 1..N
      begin
        if V'first /= 1 then
          -- Since V'last is positive, it need not be checked.
          raise INDEX_ERROR;
        else
          return SCALAR*V;
        end if;
      end "*";
```

The expression V2*V3 is called the 'dot product' or 'scalar product' of two vectors. The physical interpretation is the length of the vector LEFT multiplied by the length of the vector RIGHT multiplied by the cosine of the angle between the vectors. The computation itself is easy. The result is a float that is the sum of the product of the two vectors, component by components.

```
    function "*" (LEFT, RIGHT : VECTOR) return float is
      -- Returns the dot product of two vectors LEFT and RIGHT.
      -- Exception INDEX_ERROR raised if LEFT'range or RIGHT'range are both
```

```
            --            not of the form 1..N
      ANSWER : float := 0.0;
   begin
      if LEFT'first /= one or else RIGHT'first /= 1
                        or else LEFT'last /= RIGHT'last then
        raise INDEX_ERROR;
      else
        for INDEX in LEFT'range loop
          ANSWER := ANSWER + LEFT(INDEX) * RIGHT(INDEX);
        end loop;
        return ANSWER;
      end if;
   end "*";
```

The expression "K1∗V2∗V3∗K2" is a float value, thus "K1∗V2∗V3∗K2∗M1" is the same as "K3∗M1" where K3 = K1∗V2∗V3∗K2. The multiplication of any array, whatever the dimension, by a constant is the product of every element in the array by that constant. Operations are needed for the cases "K∗M" and "M∗K." The expression "M1∗M2" is the multiplying of two matrices. The result is also a MATRIX. The product of two matrices is not defined if the number of columns of M1 does not equal the number of rows of M2. The *ij*th element in the answer is defined to be the dot product of the *i*th row of the left operand where the *j*th column of the right operand.

```
function "*" (LEFT, RIGHT : MATRIX) return MATRIX is
   -- Returns a matrix defined by the matrix product LEFT * RIGHT
   -- Exception INDEX_ERROR raised if LEFT'range(1) or LEFT'range(2) or
   --           RIGHT'range(1) or RIGHT'range(2) is not of the form 1..N
   --           or LEFT'last(2) does not equal RIGHT'last(1).
   ANSWER : MATRIX (LEFT'range(1), RIGHT'range(2));
begin
   if LEFT'first(1) /= 1 or else LEFT'first(2) /= 1 or else
      RIGHT'first(1) /= 1 or else RIGHT'first(2) /= 1 or else
      LEFT'last(2) /= RIGHT'last(1) then
    raise INDEX_ERROR;
   else
     for ROW_INDEX in LEFT'range(1) loop
       for COL_INDEX in RIGHT'range(2) loop
         ANSWER(ROW_INDEX, COL_INDEX) := 0.0;
         for INDEX in LEFT'range(2) loop
           ANSWER (ROW_INDEX, COL_INDEX) := ANSWER (ROW_INDEX, COL_INDEX) +
                       LEFT (ROW_INDEX, INDEX) * RIGHT (INDEX, COL_INDEX);
         end loop;
       end loop;
     end loop;
     return ANSWER;
   end if;
end "*";
```

Finally, the expression "M2 ∗ V3" is the multiplying of a VECTOR by a MATRIX. The product of a MATRIX times a VECTOR is not defined if the number of columns of the MATRIX does not equal the number of elements of the VECTOR. The result is a VECTOR whose *i*th element equals the dot product of the *i*th row of the MATRIX times the VECTOR.

```
function "*" (M : MATRIX; V : VECTOR ) return VECTOR is
  -- Returns a vector whose components are defined by M * V.
  -- Exception INDEX_ERROR raised if M'range(1) or M'range(2) or
  --        V'range is not of the form 1..N or if V'last does not
  --        equal M'last(2).
  ANSWER : VECTOR (V'range);
begin
  if M'first(1) /= 1 or else V'first(1) /= 1 or else
     M'first(2) /= 1 or else M'last(2) /= V'last then
    raise INDEX_ERROR;
  else
    for INDEX in M'range(1) loop
      ANSWER(INDEX) := 0.0;
      for COL_INDEX in M'range(2) loop
        ANSWER(INDEX) := ANSWER(INDEX) + M (INDEX, COL_INDEX)*V(COL_INDEX);
      end loop;
    end loop;
    return ANSWER;
  end if;
end "*";
```

The subtraction of two VECTORS or the subtraction of two matrices is also done element by element. One way of defining subtraction is to note that if V1 and V2 are vectors, then

$$V1 - V2 = V1 + (-1.0) * V2$$

A similar observation applies to matrices.

Several words of warning are in order, particularly for people who are not familiar with the rules of matrix-vector algebra. Division of VECTORS with two or more components is not defined. The division of one MATRIX by another MATRIX is not defined unless the identification

$$M1/M2 = M1 * inv(M2)$$

is made where inv(M2) is defined as the inverse of M2. Only a square MATRIX can have an inverse, but not all square matrices have inverses. Every element of a square MATRIX can be nonzero without the inverse of the MATRIX being defined. MATRIX multiplication is not commutative. Sometimes

$$M1*M2 = M2*M1$$

but not always. The only time that V1*M1 is defined is if $n = 1$.

The package in Figure 15.1.2 is the specification of the ADT MATRIX_VECTOR_OPERATIONS listed in Figure 15.1.1. One difference between this ADT implemented as a package and others in this book is that there are two data types defined in the package. A second difference is that the two defined data types VECTOR and MATRIX are not private or limited private. Often, the individual elements in the arrays have meanings. Declaring vectors and matrices as private types would not allow their components to be accessed or modified without using additionally defined operations in the package. The purpose of this package is to provide the operations for the natural expression of matrix vector operations. This last problem could be remedied by the addition of two procedures to assign a value to the component of a matrix or vector and two functions to return the value of a component of a vector or matrix, but nothing significant is gained.

```
package MATRIX_VECTOR_OPERATIONS is
   type VECTOR is array (positive range <> ) of float;
   type MATRIX is array (positive range <>,
                         positive range <>) of float;
   -- VECTOR operations
   function "*" (SCALAR : float; V      : VECTOR ) return VECTOR;
   function "*" (V      : VECTOR; SCALAR : float ) return VECTOR;
   function "*" (LEFT, RIGHT : VECTOR ) return float;
   function "+" (LEFT, RIGHT : VECTOR ) return VECTOR;
   function "-" (LEFT, RIGHT : VECTOR ) return VECTOR;
   -- MATRIX operations
   function "*" (SCALAR : float; M      : MATRIX ) return MATRIX;
   function "*" (M      : MATRIX; SCALAR : float ) return MATRIX;
   function "*" (LEFT, RIGHT : MATRIX ) return MATRIX;
   function "+" (LEFT, RIGHT : MATRIX ) return MATRIX;
   function "-" (LEFT, RIGHT : MATRIX ) return MATRIX;

   -- MATRIX VECTOR operations
   function "*" (M : MATRIX; V : VECTOR) return VECTOR;

   INDEX_ERROR : exception;

end MATRIX_VECTOR_OPERATIONS;
```

Figure 15.1.2   Concluded.

With the completion of this package the expression

```
V1 := K1*V2*V3*K2*M1*M2*V3 - V2;
```

can be evaluated directly. There are other operations that could be added to this package. Functions to find the maximum or minimum value of the elements in a VECTOR or the index of the VECTOR element where the maximum or minimum value occurs are four such operations.

The package in Figure 15.1.2 is defined only for vectors and matrices whose component type is float. Figure 15.1.3 lists a generic package that works for any component of ITEM_TYPE provided that ITEM_TYPE has a zero value and the addition, subtraction, and multiplication of two objects of ITEM_TYPE can be defined. This generalization of Figure 15.1.2 is trivial, so it is deferred to the exercises.

```
generic
   type ITEM_TYPE is private;
   ZERO_VALUE : ITEM_TYPE;
   with function "+" (LEFT, RIGHT : ITEM_TYPE) return ITEM_TYPE is <>;
   with function "-" (LEFT, RIGHT : ITEM_TYPE) return ITEM_TYPE is <>;
   with function "*" (LEFT, RIGHT : ITEM_TYPE) return ITEM_TYPE is <>;
package GENERIC_MATRIX_VECTOR_OPERATIONS is
   type VECTOR is array (positive range <>) of ITEM_TYPE;
   type MATRIX is array (positive range <>,
                         positive range <>) of ITEM_TYPE;
```

Figure 15.1.3   Specification for GENERIC_MATRIX_VECTOR_OPERATIONS. Continues on page 522.

```
-- VECTOR operations
function "*" (SCALAR : ITEM_TYPE ; V      : VECTOR ) return VECTOR;
function "*" (V       : VECTOR;    SCALAR : ITEM_TYPE ) return VECTOR;
function "*" (LEFT, RIGHT : VECTOR ) return ITEM_TYPE;
function "+" (LEFT, RIGHT : VECTOR ) return VECTOR;
function "-" (LEFT, RIGHT : VECTOR ) return VECTOR;

-- MATRIX operations
function "*" (SCALAR : ITEM_TYPE ; M  : MATRIX ) return MATRIX;
function "*" (M      : MATRIX; SCALAR : ITEM_TYPE ) return MATRIX;
function "*" (LEFT, RIGHT : MATRIX ) return MATRIX;
function "+" (LEFT, RIGHT : MATRIX ) return MATRIX;
function "-" (LEFT, RIGHT : MATRIX ) return MATRIX;

-- MATRIX VECTOR operations
function "*" (M : MATRIX; V : VECTOR ) return VECTOR;

INDEX_ERROR : exception;

end GENERIC_MATRIX_VECTOR_OPERATIONS;
```

Figure 15.1.3   Concluded.

In the next section we expand these basic matrix arithmetic operations by adding some additional elementary matrix operations.

15.2 MATRIX OPERATIONS

Recall that the type matrix was defined as

```
type MATRIX is array (positive range <>,
                      positive range <>) of float;
```

The theory of matrix algebra defines the "elementary operations" on a MATRIX as the multiplying of a row or column by a constant, the interchanging of two rows or columns, and the addition of a scalar multiple of one row or column to another row or column. The procedures to perform these operations are also elementary. Figure 15.1.1 expands the ADT documentation to include the basic elementary operations whose documentation is listed in Figure 15.2.1.

Operations	Description
MUL_ROW_BY_SCALAR	Multiplies every component in a specified row of a specified MATRIX by a specified constant.
EXCHANGE_ROWS	Swaps two specified rows, component by component in the same column, in a specified MATRIX.
ADD_SCALAR_MUL_ROW1_TO_ROW2	For a specified MATRIX multiplies every component in row 1 and adds the result to the corresponding component in row 2. Row 1 is not modified.
MUL_COL_BY_SCALAR	Multiplies every component in a specified column of a

Figure 15.2.1   ADT documentation for elementary matrix operations. Continues on page 523.

	specified MATRIX by a specified constant.
EXCHANGE_COLS	Swaps two specified columns, component by component in the same row, in a specified matrix.
ADD_SCALAR_MUL_COL1_TO_COL2	For a specified MATRIX, multiplies every component in column 1 and adds the result to the corresponding component in column 2. Column 1 is not modified.
MAX_VECTOR_VAL_AND_LOC	Searches a given VECTOR for its maximum value. The maximum value and its location are returned.
MIN_VECTOR_VAL_AND_LOC	Searches a given VECTOR for its minimum value. The minimum value and its location are returned.
MAX_MATRIX_VAL_AND_LOC	Searches a given MATRIX for its maximum value. The maximum value and its location are returned.
MIN_MATRIX_VAL_AND_LOC	Searches a given MATRIX for its minimum value. The minimum value and its location are returned.
MAX_MATRIX_COL_VAL_AND_LOC	Searches a specific column of a given MATRIX for the column's maximum value. The maximum value and its row index are returned.
MIN_MATRIX_COL_VAL_AND_LOC	Searches a specific column of a given matrix for the column's minimum value. The minimum value and its column index are returned.
MAX_MATRIX_ROL_VAL_AND_LOC	Searches a specific row of a given MATRIX for the row's maximum value. The maximum value and its column index are returned.
MIN_MATRIX_ROW_VAL_AND_LOC	Searches a specific row of a given MATRIX for the row's minimum value. The minimum value and its row index are returned.
ADJOIN_M2_TO_M1	If two matrices M1 and M2 have the same number of rows, a third MATRIX M is created where columns 1 through M1'last(2) are M1 and columns M1'last(2) + 1 through M1'last(2) + M2'last(2) are M2.
ADJOIN_V_TO_M1	If the number of rows in MATRIX M1 equals the number of components in the vector V, a MATRIX M is created where columns 1 through M1'last(2) contain M1 and column M1'last(2) + 1 contains V.

Figure 15.2.1 Concluded.

The implementation of the elementary row operations is listed below.

```
procedure MUL_ROW_BY_SCALAR (M        : in out MATRIX;
                             ROW      : in      positive;
                             SCALAR   : in      float  ) is
  -- Multiplies every component in a specified row of M by the constant K
  -- Exception INDEX_ERROR raised if M'range(1) is not of the form 1..N,
  --          or if ROW not in M'range(1).
begin
  if M'first(1) /= 1 or else M'first(2) /= 1 or else
    ROW > M'last(1) then
      raise INDEX_ERROR;
  else
    for COLUMN in M'range(2) loop
      M(ROW, COLUMN) := SCALAR * M(ROW,COLUMN);
```

```
      end loop;
    end if;
end MUL_ROW_BY_SCALAR;


procedure EXCHANGE_ROWS ( M         : in out MATRIX;
                          ROW1, ROW2 : in      positive) is
  -- Swaps two specified rows, component by component in M.
  -- Exception INDEX_ERROR raised if M'range(1) is not of the form 1..N.
  --           or if ROW1 and Row2 not in M'range(1).
  TEMP : float;
begin
  if M'first(1) /= 1 or else M'first(2) /= 1 or else
    ROW1 > M'last(1) or else ROW2 > M'last(1) then
      raise INDEX_ERROR;
else
    for COLUMN in M'range(2) loop
      TEMP := M(ROW2,COLUMN);
      M(ROW1,COLUMN) := M(ROW2,COLUMN);
      M(ROW1,COLUMN) := TEMP;
    end loop;
  end if;
end EXCHANGE_ROWS;


procedure ADD_SCALAR_MUL_ROW1_TO_ROW2
                          ( M      : in out MATRIX;
                            SCALAR : in      float;
                            ROW1, ROW2 : in positive) is
  -- For a specified matrix M adds a constant multiple of every component
  -- in row1 and adds the result to the corresponding component in row2.
  -- No component in Row1 is modified.
  -- Exception INDEX_ERROR raised if M'range(1) is not of the form 1..N.
  --           or if ROW1 and Row2 not in M'range(1).
begin
  if M'first(1) /= 1 or else M'first(2) /= 1 or else
    ROW1 > M'last(1) or else ROW2 > M'last(1) then
      raise INDEX_ERROR;
  else
    for COLUMN in M'range(2) loop
      M(ROW2,COLUMN) := M(ROW2,COLUMN) + SCALAR * M(ROW1,COLUMN);
    end loop;
  end if;
end ADD_SCALAR_MUL_ROW1_TO_ROW2;
```

These elementary operations appear trivial, but all MATRIX manipulations can be defined in terms of them. Consider the linear system of n equations in n unknowns.

$$5*x_1 + 7*x_2 - 2*x_3 + x_4 = 11$$
$$2*x_1 + 3*x_2 + 4*x_3 + 7*x_4 = 16$$
$$-6*x_1 - 5*x_2 + 5*x_3 + 9*x_4 = 3$$
$$x_1 + x_2 + 2*x_3 - 2*x_4 = 2$$

This system can be expressed as a matrix equation $A * x = b$, where the solution vector is to be determined. The system is defined by

$$\begin{bmatrix} 5 & 7 & -2 & 1 \\ 2 & 3 & 4 & 7 \\ -6 & -5 & 5 & 9 \\ 1 & 1 & 2 & -2 \end{bmatrix} \begin{bmatrix} x_1 \\ x_2 \\ x_3 \\ x_4 \end{bmatrix} = \begin{bmatrix} 11 \\ 6 \\ 3 \\ 2 \end{bmatrix}$$

The solution of this system can be found by using two elementary operations. The solution below assumes that the diagonal element is never zero at any stage. One way to guarantee this is to start with a square matrix A that is strongly diagonally dominate, or for each diagonal element $A(i,i)$,

$$\operatorname{abs}(A(i,i)) > \operatorname{abs}(A(i,1)) \quad + \cdots + \operatorname{abs}(A(i,i-1))$$
$$+ \operatorname{abs}(A(i,i+1)) + \cdots + \operatorname{abs}(A(i,n))$$
$$\operatorname{abs}(A(i,i)) > \operatorname{abs}(A(1,i)) \quad + \cdots + \operatorname{abs}(A(i-1,i))$$
$$+ \operatorname{abs}(A(i+1,i)) + \cdots + \operatorname{abs}(A(n,i))$$

This condition guarantees that both the inverse of the matrix A exists and that there is a solution to the system. Diagonal dominance is a very strong condition. Less restrictive conditions and more general algorithms for this problem are part of any standard numerical analysis course. The algorithm below is simple. It adds suitable multiples of one row to another until a solution is found. This solution mimics the naive method used by high school students. One equation reduces the system of n equations in n unknowns to a system of $n-1$ equations in $n-1$ unknowns. This process continues until the system is reduced to a single equation in a single unknown.

```
procedure NAIVE_SOLUTION (A : in      MATRIX;
                          X :     out VECTOR;
                          B : in      VECTOR) is
  M : MATRIX (A'range(1), A'first(2)..A'last(2) + 1);
begin
  -- Adjoin A and B into M
  for ROW_INDEX in A'range(1) loop
    for COL_INDEX in A'range(2) loop
      M(ROW_INDEX, COL_INDEX) := A(ROW_INDEX, COL_INDEX);
    end loop;
    M(ROW_INDEX,A'last(2)+ 1) := B(ROW_INDEX);
  end loop;
  -- Zero out every value in every column except the diagonal
  -- element and the last column in M by adding constant multiples
  -- of one row to another.
  for ROW_INDEX in M'range(1) loop
    for COL_INDEX in M'range(1) loop
      if ROW_INDEX /= COL_INDEX then
        ADD_SCALAR_MUL_ROW1_TO_ROW2
          (M, -M(COL_INDEX, ROW_INDEX) / M(ROW_INDEX, ROW_INDEX),
                      ROW_INDEX, COLUMN_INDEX);
      end if;
    end loop;
```

```
    end loop;
      for INDEX in M'range(1) loop
         X(INDEX) := B(INDEX) / M(INDEX, INDEX);
      end loop;
   end NAIVE_SOLUTION;
```

Again, the requirement of diagonal dominance guarantees that the diagonal elements are never zero, so division by a diagonal element is always defined.

The procedure to solve a system of equations suggests the need for procedures to adjoin a VECTOR to a MATRIX and a MATRIX to a MATRIX. To adjoin a VECTOR or MATRIX to a MATRIX is to add addition columns to the target matrix and then place the VECTOR or MATRIX in these additional columns. If the identity MATRIX, a MATRIX of zeros except for ones on the diagonal, were adjoined to *A* in the procedure NAIVE_SOLUTION, the area occupied by the adjoined MATRIX becomes the inverse MATRIX of *A* (see the exercises). The adjoin function for two matrices looks as follows:

```
function ADJOIN_M2_TO_M1 (M1, M2 : MATRIX) return MATRIX is
  -- For two matrices M1 and M2 that have the same number of rows, this
  -- function returns a matrix M where columns 1 through M1'last(2) are M1
  -- and columns M1'last(2)+1 through M1'last(2)+M2'last(2) are M2
  -- Exception INDEX_ERROR raised if all indices of M1 and M2 are not of
  --           form 1..N, or the number of rows of M1 does not equal the
  --           number of rows of M2.
  ANSWER : MATRIX( M1'range(1), 1..M1'last(2)+M2'length(2));
begin
  if M1'first(1) /= 1 or else M1'first(2) /= 1 or else
     M2'first(1) /= 1 or else M2'first(2) /= 1 or else
     M1'last(1) /= M2'last(1) then
       raise INDEX_ERROR;
  else
     for ROW_INDEX in M1'range(1) loop
       for COL_INDEX in M1'range(2) loop
         ANSWER(ROW_INDEX, COL_INDEX) := M1(ROW_INDEX, COL_INDEX);
       end loop;
       for COL_INDEX in M1'last(2)+1..M1'last(2)+M2'last(2) loop
         ANSWER(ROW_INDEX, COL_INDEX) := M2(ROW_INDEX, COL_INDEX);
       end loop;
     end loop;
     return ANSWER;
  end if;
end ADJOIN_M2_TO_M1;
```

The elementary matrix operations are now added to the package MATRIX_VECTOR_OPERATIONS (Figure 15.2.2). Also added are functions to find the maximum and minimum value in a VECTOR, and the index value of that maximum or minimum value. Similar added functions find the maximum and minimum value of a MATRIX, and procedures to find the indices of the maximum or minimum value are also added. Note that this is not a generic package. Any ranges may be substituted for the vectors and the matrices, but the exception INDEX_ERROR is raised if any range is not of the form 1..N. It is not necessary that the matrices have the same number of rows and columns. When implementing this package it is important to check that index ranges match up. The implementation of the package and completion of the ADT documentation are left to the exercises. Also left to the exercises are some applications of the package.

```
package MATRIX_VECTOR_OPERATIONS is

    type VECTOR is array (positive range <>) of float;
    type MATRIX is array (positive range <>,
                          positive range <>) of float;


    -- VECTOR OPERATIONS
    function "*" (SCALAR : float; V      : VECTOR) return VECTOR;
    function "*" (V      : VECTOR; SCALAR : float) return VECTOR;
    function "*" (LEFT, RIGHT : VECTOR) return float;
    function "+" (LEFT,RIGHT  : VECTOR) return VECTOR;
    function "-" (LEFT,RIGHT  : VECTOR) return VECTOR;


    -- MATRIX OPERATIONS
    function "*" (SCALAR : float; M      : MATRIX) return MATRIX;
    function "*" (M      : MATRIX; SCALAR : float) return MATRIX;
    function "*" (LEFT, RIGHT : MATRIX) return MATRIX;
    function "+" (LEFT, RIGHT : MATRIX) return MATRIX;
    function "-" (LEFT, RIGHT : MATRIX) return MATRIX;


    -- MATRIX VECTOR OPERATIONS
    function "*" (M : MATRIX; V : VECTOR) return VECTOR;


    -- ELEMENTARY MATRIX OPERATIONS
    procedure MUL_ROW_BY_SCALAR (M           : in out MATRIX;
                                 ROW         : in     positive;
                                 SCALAR      : in     float );
    procedure EXCHANGE_ROWS     (M           : in out MATRIX;
                                 ROW1, ROW2  : in     positive);
    procedure ADD_SCALAR_MUL_ROW1_TO_ROW2
                                (M           : in out MATRIX;
                                 SCALAR      : in     float;
                                 ROW1, ROW2  : in     positive);
    procedure MUL_COL_BY_SCALAR (M           : in out MATRIX;
                                 COL         : in     positive;
                                 SCALAR      : in     float );
    procedure EXCHANGE_COLS     (M           : in out MATRIX;
                                 COL1, COL2  : in     positive);
    procedure ADD_SCALAR_MUL_COL1_TO_COL2
                                (M           : in out MATRIX;
                                 SCALAR      : in     float;
                                 COL1, COL2  : in     positive)
    -- PROCEDURES TO return MAXIMUM AND MINIMUM VALUES AND LOCATIONS
```

Figure 15.2.2 Specification for ADT matrix and vector operations augmented with elementary matrix operations. Continues on page 528.

```
        procedure MAX_VECTOR_VALUE_AND_LOCATION (V          : in      VECTOR;
                                                 MAXIMUM   :    out float;
                                                 LOCATION  :    out positive);
        procedure MIN_VECTOR_VALUE_AND_LOCATION (V          : in      VECTOR;
                                                 MINIMUM   :    out float;
                                                 LOCATION  :    out positive);
        procedure MAX_MATRIX_VALUE_AND_LOCATION (M          : in      MATRIX;
                                                 MAXIMUM   :    out float;
                                                 ROW, COL  :    out positive);
        procedure MIN_MATRIX_VALUE_AND_LOCATION (M          : in      MATRIX;
                                                 MINIMUM   :    out float;
                                                 ROW, COL  :    out positive);
        procedure MAX_MATRIX_COLUMN_VALUE_AND_LOCATION
                                                (M          : in      MATRIX;
                                                 MAXIMUM   :    out float;
                                                 COL        : in      positive;
                                                 ROW        :    out positive);
        procedure MIN_MATRIX_COLUMN_VALUE_AND_LOCATION
                                                (M          : in      MATRIX;
                                                 MINIMUM   :    out float;
                                                 COL        : in      positive;
                                                 ROW        :    out positive);
        procedure MAX_MATRIX_ROW_VALUE_AND_LOCATION
                                                (M          : in      MATRIX;
                                                 MAXIMUM   :    out float;
                                                 ROW        : in      positive;
                                                 COL        :    out positive);
        procedure MIN_MATRIX_ROW_VALUE_AND_LOCATION
                                                (M          : in      MATRIX;
                                                 MINIMUM   :    out float;
                                                 ROW        : in      positive;
                                                 COL        :    out positive);
    -- OPERATIONS TO ADJOIN MATRIX or VECTOR TO MATRIX
    function ADJOIN_M2_TO_M1 (M1, M2 : MATRIX) return MATRIX;
    function ADJOIN_V_TO_M (M : MATRIX; V : VECTOR) return MATRIX;

    INDEX_ERROR : EXCEPTION;

end MATRIX_VECTOR_OPERATIONS;
```

Figure 15.2.2 Concluded.

This type of package is a small example of the libraries of operations that vector and array processors use to achieve high CPU performance. The package bodies, previously called subroutine libraries, were implemented in either assembly language or microcode on these special-purpose machines. Even today these packages are part of the system software of many supercomputers. However, in this age of efficient optimizing compilers, high-level-language programmers seldom bother using these packages unless performance issues are critical. When that situation occurs, other options exist. These options include using mathematics packages such as LINPACK, ICEPACK, or IMSL. The routines in these packages uses operations and algorithms fully optimized to minimize numerical error and while obtaining maximum CPU performance.

15.3 TIME AND SPACE CONSTRAINTS

The time and space trade-offs for MATRIX and VECTOR operations are easy to determine by examining the functions and procedures that implement the operations. For example, when multiplying two square matrices together, the result is a square matrix with $n**2$ elements. To compute each element requires n multiplications and n additions, so the number of operations is $O(n**3)$. The result required $n**2$ words to store, so it is $O(n**2)$. In Figure 15.3.1, M denotes a square MATRIX with n rows, V denotes a VECTOR of n elements, and k is a float constant. Figure 15.3.1 conveys the time and space constraints for various operations using the MATRIX and VECTOR data structure specified in Figure 15.1.2.

Operation	Time	Space
$k*V$	$O(n)$	$O(n)$
$V*V$	$O(n)$	$O(n)$
$M*V$	$O(n**2)$	$O(n**2)$
$M*M$	$O(n**3)$	$O(n**2)$
$M+M$	$O(n**2)$	$O(n**2)$
$k*M$	$O(n**2)$	$O(n**2)$

Figure 15.3.1   Time and space constraints for vectors and matrices defined as array types.

These packages can be optimized further. For a parallel machine, tasking and parallelism will speed up execution. In Chapter 16 representation strategies for sparse matrices, those whose elements are mostly zero, are examined as a way of reducing space overhead.

15.4 ITERATIVE SOLUTIONS OF SYSTEMS OF EQUATIONS

Mathematical modeling is becoming an increasingly important part of applied computer science. The area has grown so large that it has its own name, *computational science*. The common misconception in finding solutions to mathematical models is that an exact solution is found by direct methods. Most interesting models are not simple. The basic high school student's conception that all algebraic equations are simple equations in one variable with exact solutions is wrong. The equation

$$3x = 9$$

with solution $x = 3$ is so trivial as not to be interesting.

In Section 2 a very naive method of solving systems of equations was listed. Most students can solve systems of three or four equations in three or four linear equations but would be hard pressed to solve a simple system of two nonlinear equations in two unknowns. Figure 15.4.1(a) shows the graph of the two nonlinear equations listed in Figure 15.4.1(b). Most computer solutions try to approximate the solution to some required degree of accuracy. This approximation takes the form of iteration. An iterative scheme inserts a good guess into an algorithm that returns, hopefully, a better guess. This process continues until the "better guess"

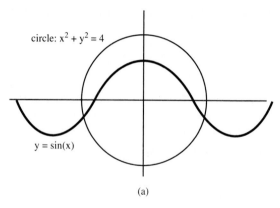

circle: $x^2 + y^2 = 4$

$y = \sin(x)$

(a)

$$x ** 2 + y ** 2 = 4$$
$$\sin(x) - y = 0$$
(b)

Figure 15.4.1 (a) System of two nonlinear equations in two unknowns. The two solutions are the two points of intersection. (b) System of two nonlinear equations shown in part (a).

is good enough. Consider the general problem of finding the positive square root of any positive number A. The solution of

$$f(x) = x**2 - A = 0$$

provides the correct answer.

Perhaps the most famous iterative method is Newton's method. Newton's method can find the solution of $f(x) = 0$ provided that the derivative of f can be easily computed and $f'(x)$ is continuous and it does not equal zero near the solution. Figure 15.4.2 lists Newton's method. Figure 15.4.3 applies Newton's method to finding the square root of 2. Figure 15.4.4 illustrates several characteristics of iterative methods. First, an exact solution is not found. The goal is a good approximation to the true solution. Second, each iteration should provide a better answer. There are functions where the method either does not converge, or the convergence is very slow. Iterative solutions often converge under very restrictive conditions.

$$x_{n+1} = x_n - f(x_n)/f'(x_n) \qquad n = 1, 2, 3, \ldots$$
$$x_0 \text{ arbitrary}$$

Figure 15.4.2 Definition of Newton's method.

$$
\begin{aligned}
x_0 \quad &= 1\\
x_{n+1} &= x_n - f(x_n)/f'(x_n)\\
&= x_n - (x_n**2 - 2)/(2*x_n)\\
&= (x_n**2 + 2)/(2*x_n)\\
x_1 \quad &= (1**2 + 2)/(2*1) = 1.5\\
x_2 \quad &= (2.25 + 2)/3 \qquad = 1.4167\\
x_3 \quad &= (2.0069 + 2)/2.8334 = 1.4142
\end{aligned}
$$

Figure 15.4.4 Iterative computation of the square root of 2 using Newton's method.

The first step in developing most iterative methods is to put them in fixed-point form. The value x is a fixed point of the function $y = f(x)$ if and only if $x = f(x)$. In a fixed-point form the solution put in yields the same answer out. For the function $f(x) = x**2 - 2$, the fixed-point form is

$$x = g(x) = x + 2 - x**2$$

This form will not yield an iterative solution, but the auxiliary form

$$x_{n+1} = ((L-1)/L)*x_n + g(x_n)/L$$

does converge. The constant L is any value larger than the maximum of the first derivative in a neighborhood of the solution. Figure 15.4.5 illustrates the case where $L=5$.

$$
\begin{aligned}
x_{n+1} &= (4/5*x_n + (x_n + 2 - x_n**2)/5 \\
&= 0.8*x_n + 0.2*(x_n + 2 - x_n**2) \\
&= x_n + 0.4 - 0.2*x_n**2 \\
x_1 &= 1 \\
x_2 &= 1 + 0.4 - 0.2*1.2**2 = 1.2 \\
x_3 &= 1.2 + 0.4 - 0.2*1**2 = 1.3120 \\
x_4 &= 1.3120 + 0.4 - 0.2*1.3120**2 = 1.367731 \\
x_5 &= 1.393593 \\
x_6 &= 1.405173 \\
x_7 &= 1.410271 \\
x_8 &= 1.412498 \\
x_9 &= 1.413468 \\
x_{10} &= 1.413890 \\
x_{15} &= 1.414209
\end{aligned}
$$

Figure 15.4.5 Alternative solution to find the square root of 2.

In the alternative method, note that the convergence was much slower. What is not obvious is that an alternative fixed-point form of $f(x) = x**2 - 2$,

$$x = g(x) = x + 2 - x**2$$

does not converge using this method.

Consider the MATRIX-VECTOR equation $A*x = b$, where A is a square coefficient MATRIX, b is a known VECTOR, and x is the solution VECTOR. This situation was considered earlier when the procedure NAIVE_SOLUTION was developed. Let D denote the diagonal MATRIX whose elements are zero except on the diagonal, and for $i=1,2,\ldots,n, d_{ii} = a_{ii}$. Then

$$Ax = (A - D + D)x = b$$

from which it follows that

$$Dx = b - (A - D)x$$

Since D is a diagonal matrix, its inverse is easily computed. The definition of the inverse of a square matrix D requires that

$$D*\text{inverse}(D) = \text{inverse}(D)*D = I$$

where I is the identity matrix. For a diagonal matrix, the matrix inverse (D) is another diagonal matrix where the element on the ith diagonal of the inverse is equal to $1/d_{ii}$. Multiplying both sides of the equation by inverse (D) puts the equation into fixed-point form,

$$x = Ix = \text{inverse}(D)*Dx = \text{inverse}(D)*(b - (A - D)*x)$$

This matrix equation is the basis of the Jacobi algorithm for finding the solution to $Ax = b$ by iteration. The Jacobi algorithm is given in Figure 15.4.6.

$$x_0 = b$$
$$x_{n+1} = \text{inverse}(D)*(b - (A - D)*x_n) \quad n = 1, 2, 3, \ldots$$

Figure 15.4.6 Jacobi method for finding the solution of $Ax = b$.

Some method for determining if the sequence of iterates is converging must be specified. One method is to measure the maximum difference between components of x_{n+1} and x_n. Unfortunately, the difference between two successive iterates might be small, although any one iterate makes a poor approximation to the solution. Another option is to compute the residual vector

$$r_n = b - A*x_n$$

and determine how close r_n is to the zero vector. This is the approach taken in Figure 15.4.7. Instead of developing a full program for this case study, a procedure to do the iteration will be developed. Besides passing the coefficient matrix A and the vector b, the maximum error of the residual and the maximum number of iterations are passed. The solution vector x and a boolean flag are returned. Figure 15.4.7 lists the procedure.

```
with MATRIX_VECTOR_OPERATIONS;
use MATRIX_VECTOR_OPERATIONS;
    . . . . . . . . . . . . .
procedure JACOBI ( A                : in      MATRIX;
                   B                : in      VECTOR;
                   ERROR            : in      float;
                   MAX_ITERATIONS : in        natural;
                   SOLUTION_FOUND :          out boolean;
                   X                :          out VECTOR) is
  TEMP_A : MATRIX (A'range(1), A'range(2)) := A;
    --A must be square, so A'range(1) = A'range(2)
  D_INVERSE : MATRIX (A'range(1), A'range(1)) :=
                              (others => (others => 0.0));
  SOLUTION,
  RESIDUAL : VECTOR (B'range);
begin
  --Set up TEMP_A, D_INVERSE
  for ROW_INDEX in A'range(1) loop
    D_INVERSE(ROW_INDEX, ROW_INDEX) := 1.0 / TEMP_A(ROW_INDEX, ROW_INDEX);
    TEMP_A(ROW_INDEX, ROW_INDEX) := 0.0;
  end loop;
  -- Initialize the solution vector and the residual vector
  SOLUTION := B;
  SOLUTION_FOUND := true;
  -- iterate until eith MAX_ITERATIONS exceeded, or dot product of
  -- the residual vector is arbitrarily small
```

Figure 15.4.7 Jacobi method for finding a solution to $A * x = b$. Continues on page 533.

```
    for COUNT in 1..MAX_ITERATIONS loop
      SOLUTION := D_INVERSE*(B - TEMP_A*SOLUTION);
      RESIDUAL := B - A * SOLUTION;
      if RESIDUAL * RESIDUAL < ERROR then
        X := SOLUTION;
        return;
      end if;
    end loop;
    SOLUTION_FOUND := false;
  end JACOBI;
```

Figure 15.4.7 Concluded.

The conditions on the matrix *A* that guarantee convergence are technical and best left to a course in numerical methods. If the coefficient matrix *A* is diagonally dominant, the method will converge. There are less restrictive conditions than diagonal dominance that guarantee convergence.

Why use an iterative method instead of a direct method? There are two basic reasons. First, the direct method has an $O(n ** 4)$ operation count. Each iteration of the Jacobi method has an $O(n ** 3)$ operation count, so there are situations where it is faster to do iteration. The second reason has to do with the fundamental hope of iteration. Each iterate is a more accurate approximation than the last. Often, the direct solution is fed into the iterative method as the initial guess. The direct solution is often just an approximation to the true solution. The resulting iterates "polish" the direct solution. One unwanted problem in the solution of linear systems of equations is the random appearance of roundoff error, which makes the direct solution meaningless. This is usually not as large a problem with iterative methods.

Except for the nonlinear system in Figure 15.4.1, all the systems considered so far have been linear. Linear systems can usually be solved. If a solution exists, it is unique. Most modeled phenomena are in the form of nonlinear systems. Nonlinear systems may or may not have a solutions. If a solution exists, it may not be unique. Most solutions to nonlinear systems are found by developing a linear approximation to the nonlinear system. The solution of the approximated linear system is considered an approximation to the solution of the nonlinear system.

The use of ADT packages developed in this chapter allow for more natural mathematical expression of problems. An examination of most advanced science and engineering texts shows that, particularly in engineering and physics, they use matrix algebra expressions. Computer graphics is a related area of computer science that makes heavy use of linear algebra.

Many large matrices are sparse, the subject of Chapter 16. A *sparse matrix* is one where most array components are zero. In the example above, the diagonal matrix was sparse. A diagonal matrix with *n* rows and *n* columns has $n ** 2$ elements, $n ** 2 - n$ of which are zero. Some of the space inefficiencies of the Jacobi method in Figure 15.4.7 may be eliminated by using the proper equivalent sparse matrix representation.

Almost any significant numerical application implemented on the computer involves matrix algebra. Computational science, previously called scientific programming, is a legitimate area of computer science research in its own right. A cornerstone of computational science is the study of numerical linear algebra.

EXERCISES

Section 15.1 Matrix Algebra

15.1.1 Implement the following operations specified in the generic package MATRIX_VECTOR_OP-ERATIONS listed in Figure 15.1.2.

    a. The operation function "+" (LEFT, RIGHT : vector) return vector;

    b. The operation function "–" (LEFT, RIGHT : vector) return vector;

    c. The operation function "*" (SCALAR : float; M : matrix) return matrix;

    d. The operation function "*" (M : matrix; SCALAR : float) return matrix;

    e. The operation function "+" (LEFT, RIGHT : matrix) return matrix;

    f. The operation function "–" (LEFT, RIGHT : matrix) return matrix;

    g. Combine the operations implemented in a through f with those implemented in the text and put them into a package body to complete this version of the ADT MATRIX_VECTOR_OP-ERATIONS.

15.1.2 **a.** Implement the package specified in Figure 15.1.3.

    b. Explain how the ADT generated in part a can be used to solve problems where ITEM_TYPE is float, integer, COMPLEX, RATIONAL, or boolean.

Section 15.2 Matrix Operations

15.2.1 Implement the following operations specified in the generic package MATRIX_VECTOR_OP-ERATIONS listed in Figure 15.2.2.

    a. The operation function "*" (SCALAR : float; V : VECTOR) return VECTOR

    b. The operation function "*" (V : VECTOR; SCALAR : float) return VECTOR

    c. The operation function "*" (LEFT, RIGHT : VECTOR) return float

    d. The operation function "+" (LEFT, RIGHT : VECTOR) return VECTOR

    e. The operation function "–" (LEFT, RIGHT : VECTOR) return VECTOR

    f. The operation function "abs" (V : VECTOR) return float

    g. The operation function "*" (SCALAR : float; M : MATRIX) return MATRIX

    h. The operation function "*" (M : MATRIX; SCALAR : float) return MATRIX

    i. The operation function "*" (LEFT, RIGHT : MATRIX) return MATRIX

    j. The operation function "+" (LEFT, RIGHT : MATRIX) return MATRIX

    k. The operation function "–" (LEFT, RIGHT : MATRIX) return MATRIX

    l. The operation function "*" (M : MATRIX; V : VECTOR) return VECTOR

    m. The operation MUL_COL_BY_SCALAR

    n. The operation EXCHANGE_COLS

    o. The operation ADD_SCALAR_MUL_COL

    p. The operation MAX_VECTOR_VAL_AND_LOC

    q. The operation MIN_VECTOR_VAL_AND_LOC

    r. The operation MAX_MATRIX_VAL_AND_LOC

    s. The operation MIN_MATRIX_VAL_AND_LOC

    t. The operation MAX_MATRIX_COL_VAL_AND_LOC

    u. The operation MIN_MATRIX_COL_VAL_AND_LOC

    v. The operation MAX_MATRIX_ROW_VAL_AND_LOC

    w. The operation MIN_MATRIX_ROW_VAL_AND_LOC

    x. The operation ADJOIN_V2_TO_M1

    y. Combine the operations implemented in a through z with those implemented in the text and put them into a package body to complete this version of the ADT MATRIX_VECTOR_OP-ERATIONS.

Section 15.4 Iterative Solutions of Systems of Equations

15.4.1 Solve the system of four equations in four unknowns in Section 15.2 by using the procedure NAIVE_SOLUTION.

15.4.2 Solve the system in Exercise 15.5.1 by use of the Jacobi method.

PROGRAMMING PROJECTS

P15.1 The procedure NAIVE_SOLUTION can suffer from roundoff error. The solution is to use "pivoting." Consult a basic numerical methods text and implement pivoting using one of the packages in this chapter.

P15.2 Given $n + 1$ points (x_i, y_i) for $i = 0, 1, \ldots, n$, where the x_i are distinct, an interpolating polynomial is any polynomial of degree $<= n$ where $p(x) = y$ for all i. Use the procedure in Project P15.1 to determine the coefficients of an interpolating polynomial.

NOTES AND REFERENCES

There are many texts that contain additional material on numerical methods. Cheney and Kincaid [12] is a good basic introduction. Press et al. [42] is more advanced, covers more topics, and contains a good bibliography. Stewart [47] is devoted solely to numerical linear algebra. The algorithm in Figure 15.4.5 is due to Hillam [22].

16

Sparse Vectors and Matrices

A matrix or vector is *sparse* if most of its elements are zero. Sparse matrices and vectors appear in many applications. Since so many matrix or vector elements are zero, there are two possible optimizations. The first is memory space. If a data structure can be devised that contains only the nonzero elements, memory space is conserved. A second efficiency is processing time. Zero multiplied by any number is still zero, and zero added or subtracted from any number does not change the value of the number. If these unnecessary operations can be avoided, processing time can be saved.

As a simple application, consider finding the total and printing the items purchased at the checkout counter of a large grocery store. Many grocery stores stock more than 10,000 items, making allowances for all brands and sizes. Any one customer seldom buys more than 50 items. Most large grocery stores use a computer interfaced to an array of holographic scanners at the checkout lines to read bar codes and prepare bills. As the purchase's bar codes are scanned, the computer records the item's inventory bar code, and the clerk enters quantity of that item purchased, which the computer also records. The computer stores this information as a linked priority list of items purchased, with the key being the inventory number. This linked list represents a sparse vector. Only items purchased appear on the list. Items not purchased, these that would have zero in the vector entry, do not appear in the list. To compute the bill and print the customer order requires two nonsparse vectors, both of which are indexed by inventory numbers. The first vector is a vector of strings. The ith entry is a short description of the item. The second vector is the unit cost of each item (see Figure 16.0.1). The bill is computed by taking the scalar vector product. The bill is printed using the nonzero items as a key.

As a second application, consider the problem of trying to model a road map of the streets and intersections in a city. If the intersections are numbered from 1 to N, then setting the ith row, jth column entry to 1 indicates that there is a road from the ith intersection to the jth intersection. A typical intersection is joined to four other intersections. If a city has N intersections, the matrix will have $N**2$ entries, but only about $4*N$ of them will not be zero. For example, if $N = 1000$, then 4000 entries will not be zero, or about 0.4% of the matrix. We consider this problem in depth in this chapter.

Our goal is to design and implement a package similar to the ADT GENERIC_MATRIX_VECTOR_OPERATIONS in Chapter 15. This goal requires that the eventual sparse representation chosen support the basic matrix and vector operations. Figure 16.0.2 lists the

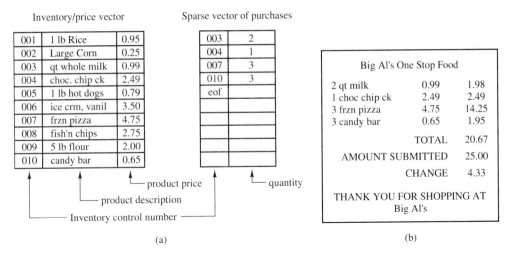

Figure 16.0.1 Preparing a grocery bill using a sparse vector. (a) Data structure to store inventory and purchase. Note that both data structures key on the inventory number. (b) Final grocery bill.

documentation for this package. Note that it is almost identical with the documentation for GENERIC_MATRIX_VECTOR_OPERATIONS in Figure 15.1.1, except for two points. The first point is the inclusion of two additional functions to return the value of a particular component in a matrix or vector, and the inclusion of two procedures that either change the value in the matrix or vector, or to insert a nonzero value in a sparse vector or matrix. The second point is that all vectors and matrices will have indices with ranges of the form 1..MAXIMUM_INDEX. This forces all matrices to be square.

GENERAL ADT SPECIFICATION FOR SPARSE MATRIX AND VECTOR OPERATIONS

Description

This ADT builds a package that overloads the binary operators "+," "*," and "–" to create a package of standard matrix vector operations. Two types, VECTOR and MATRIX, are created. Both are limited private to the package. By default, a VECTOR is a one-dimensional array with integer range 1 . . N. Similarly, a MATRIX is a two-dimensional array with indices with the same range as a vector's range. Binary operations must be implemented for up to four cases: the MATRIX-MATRIX, MATRIX-VECTOR, SCALAR-MATRIX, and SCALAR-VECTOR. Since MATRIX-VECTOR representations are limited private, two built-in assignment operations must be used for normal assignment. All operations use conventional mathematical definitions.

Programmer-Supplied Data Structures or Specifications

The programmer must supply six formal generic parameters. The first is a positive integer, MAXIMUM_INDEX, equal to the dimension of the vectors and matrices to be operated upon. The

Figure 16.0.2 Documentation for matrix and vector operations. Continues on page 538.

component type, called ITEM_TYPE (such as float, integer, boolean, complex, etc.), is the second formal parameter. A default zero element, called ZERO_ITEM, of the second parameter is also needed. Sparse matrices and vectors do not store the zero values. Three binary operations for objects of ITEM_TYPE, equivalent to "*," "+," and "–," are the last three formal generic parameters.

Operations

Name	Description
Vector operations	
"*"	(Three versions) Two versions, constant*VECTOR and VECTOR*constant, return a VECTOR whose components are defined by multiplying each component in the VECTOR times the constant. The third version, VECTOR*VECTOR, is the standard or dot product that returns an object of ITEM_TYPE defined as the sum of the product of the respective vector components.
"+"	returns a VECTOR whose components are the sum of the respective components.
"–"	returns a VECTOR whose components are the difference of the respective components.
MATRIX operations	
"*"	(Three versions) Two versions, constant*Matrix and MATRIX*constant, return a MATRIX whose components are defined by multiplying each component in the given matrix times the constant. The third version, MATRIX*MATRIX is the standard product that returns a MATRIX.
"+"	returns a MATRIX whose components are the sum of the respective components.
"–"	returns a MATRIX whose components are the difference of the respective components.
MATRIX-VECTOR operations	
"*"	returns a VECTOR that is the result of multiplying a MATRIX*VECTOR.
MATRIX-VECTOR access operations	
CLEAR_VECTOR	Deletes all components from a VECTOR. Effectively assigns zero to every component in the VECTOR.
CLEAR_MATRIX	Deletes all components from a MATRIX. Effectively assigns zero to every component in the MATRIX.
ADD_VECTOR_VALUE	Takes a value of ITEM_TYPE and VECTOR index and performs one of three tasks. If no component with that index is in the vector, a node with that index and value is added if the value is not zero. If a node with that index is already there, the value in the node is updated if the value is not zero, or the node is deleted if the value is zero. No action is taken if the value is zero and the node does not exist.
ADD_MATRIX_VALUE	Takes a value of ITEM_TYPE and MATRIX row and column

Figure 16.0.2   Continues on page 539.

Sparse Vectors and Matrices   Chap. 16

index and performs one of three tasks. If no component with those indices is in the MATRIX, a node with those indices and value is added if the value is not zero. If a node with those indices is already there, the value in the value is updated if the value is not zero, or the node is deleted if the value is zero. No action is taken if the value is zero and the node does not exist.

GET_VECTOR_ELEMENT	Returns the component with a given index in the given VECTOR. Returns ZERO_ITEM if no component with that index is present.
GET_MATRIX_ELEMENT	Returns the component at a specified row-column index in a given MATRIX. Returns ZERO_ITEM if no component is in the MATRIX.
ASSIGN_TO_VECTOR	This operation assigns the result of a package operation that results in a VECTOR to a given VECTOR. Needed because type VECTOR is limited private.
ASSIGN_TO_MATRIX	This operation assigns the result of a package operation that results in a MATRIX to a given MATRIX. Needed because type MATRIX is limited private.

Exception

Two exceptions can occur. The exception OVERFLOW occurs if there is insufficient memory to add an element or to complete an operation. The exception INDEX_ERROR occurs when a supplied vector or matrix index is not in the range 1 .. MAXIMUM_INDEX.

Warnings

None.

Figure 16.0.2   Concluded.

An extensive literature is available on sparse matrices and sparse vectors as well as algorithms that operate on sparse structures. These variations on the representations and operations typically consider the maximization or minimization of some problem constraint.

16.1 SPARSE VECTORS: TWO REPRESENTATIONS

There are two requirements for any representation for a sparse vector or matrix. The first is that it must save memory, and the second is that it must be easy to use. Recall that if

```
type VECTOR is array (positive range 1..SIZE) of float;
```

then the addition of two vectors returns a vector where the addition is defined component by component, that is,

```
function "+" (LEFT, RIGHT : VECTOR) return VECTOR is
  SUM : VECTOR
begin
  for INDEX in V1'range loop
    SUM(INDEX) := V1(INDEX) + V2(INDEX);
```

```
                end loop;
                return ANS;
            end "+";
```

The addition function above is straightforward. The second goal of the sparse vector representation is to have a representation that allows for straightforward implementations of all the scalar-VECTOR (such as k∗v for scalar k, VECTOR V), VECTOR-VECTOR (such as V1+V2 for two vectors V1 and V2), and MATRIX-VECTOR (M∗V for M a MATRIX and V a VECTOR) operations.

Specifically what comes to mind is a linked list or array of vector components. Each component contains the nonzero value and the index of a vector element. Elements with zero value are not in the list or the array. If a particular component is not in the list, it must be zero. The representations from Chapter 7 for GENERIC_BOUNDED_QUEUE and GENERIC_UNBOUNDED_QUEUE immediately come to mind. Consider the representation shown in Figure 16.1.1.

```
            type ELEMENT;
            type SPARSE_VECTOR is access ELEMENT;
            type ELEMENT is
              record
                 INDEX : integer;
                 VALUE : float;
                 NEXT  : SPARSE_VECTOR;
              end record;
```

Figure 16.1.1   Linked Representation for SPARSE_VECTOR.

Now consider two vectors V1 and V2 as shown in Figure 16.1.2(a). Note that the indices of V1 and V2 appear in random order. This representation is not optimal. Since only nonzero entries are in the queue, it does minimize space but it does not make the binary operations minimal. To add V1 and V2 requires the full search of the vector V2 for each nonzero element in the vector V1. If there is an element in V2 with the same index, the respective values are added and a new element with the common index is inserted on the queue that represents the answer. If the search is unsuccessful, a copy of the current index and value of the present element in V1 is inserted into the answer. The function is still not finished because elements in V2 with

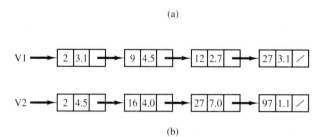

Figure 16.1.2   Two representations of a sparse vector. (a) Two four-element sparse vectors with elements stored in random order. (b) The sparse vectors from part (a) stored in ascending order by index. Note how much simpler the binary vector operations are.

nonzero values and indices that do not correspond to any index in V1 must be copied to the result. Addition is no longer $O(n)$, where n is the length of the vector, but is $O(m*n)$, where $m = V1$ ' length and $n = V2$ ' length.

One way of reducing the time spent adding two sparse vectors would be to store the elements in a priority queue where an element's index determines its place in the queue. Figure 16.1.2(b) shows V1 and V2 represented as priority queues with priority based on the index. Addition can be implemented easily by using two variables NEXT_V1 and NEXT_V2 to keep track of the next nodes in V1 and V2. Three cases can occur:

$$NEXT\_V1.INDEX < NEXT\_V2.INDEX$$
$$NEXT\_V1.INDEX = NEXT\_V2.INDEX$$
$$NEXT\_V1.INDEX > NEXT\_V2.INDEX$$

This addition operation strategy is $O(n)$, where n is the sum of the total number of nonzero elements in the two sparse vectors. An algorithm to add two sparse vectors stored in priority index order is given as follows:

```
function "+" (V1, V2 : SPARSE_VECTOR) return SPARSE_VECTOR is
  TEMP, SUM : SPARSE_VECTOR;
  NEXT_V1   : SPARSE_VECTOR := V1;
  NEXT_V2   : SPARSE_VECTOR := V2;
begin
  -- Check to see if either V1 or V2 is null
  if V1 = null then
    -- V1 has no entries, must be zero vector.
    COPY (NEXT_V2, SUM);
    return SUM;
  else
    -- V2 has no entries, must be zero vector.
    COPY (NEXT_V1, SUM);
    return SUM;
  -- Neither V1 or V2 null vector.
  -- Initialize SUM by finding component with least index
  elsif NEXT_V1.INDEX = NEXT_V2.INDEX then
    -- Index in both vectors the same; add, insert, and update
    SUM := new ELEMENT' (V1.INDEX, V1.VALUE + V2.VALUE,null);
    NEXT_V1 := NEXT_V1.NEXT;
    NEXT_V2 := NEXT_V2.NEXT;
  elsif NEXT_V1.INDEX < NEXT_V2.INDEX then
    -- Index in vector V1 smallest
    SUM := new ELEMENT' (V2.INDEX,V2.VALUE, null);
    NEXT_V1 := NEXT_V1.NEXT;
  else
    -- Index in vector V2 smallest
    SUM := new ELEMENT' (V2.INDEX, V2.VALUE, null);
    NEXT_V2 := NEXT_V2.NEXT;
  end if;
  TEMP := SUM;
  -- Traverse both vectors until one or both null
  while (NEXT_V1 /= null) and (NEXT_V2 /= null) loop
    if NEXT_V1.INDEX = NEXT_V2.INDEX then
```

```
         TEMP.next := new ELEMENT '
                    (NEXT_V1.INDEX, NEXT_V1.VALUE + NEXT_V2.VALUE, null);
         NEXT_V1 := NEXT_V1.NEXT;
         NEXT_V2 := NEXT_V2.NEXT;
       elsif NEXT_V1.INDEX < NEXT_V2.INDEX then
         TEMP.NEXT := new ELEMENT' (NEXT_V1.INDEX, NEXT_V1.VALUE, null);
         NEXT_V1 := NEXT_V1.NEXT;
       else
         TEMP.NEXT := new ELEMENT' (NEXT_V2.INDEX, NEXT_V2.VALUE, null);
         NEXT_V2 := NEXT_V2.NEXT;
       end if;
       TEMP := TEMP.NEXT;
     end loop;
     -- Finish adding V1 if V2 fully traversed
     while NEXT_V1 /= null loop
       TEMP.NEXT := new ELEMENT' (NEXT_V1.INDEX, NEXT_V1.VALUE, null);
       NEXT_V1 := NEXT_V1.NEXT;
       TEMP := TEMP.NEXT;
     end loop;
     -- Finish adding V2 if V1 fully traversed
     while NEXT_V2 /= null loop
       TEMP.NEXT := new ELEMENT' (NEXT_V2.INDEX, NEXT_V2.VALUE, null);
       NEXT_V2 := NEXT_V2.NEXT;
       TEMP := TEMP.NEXT;
     end loop;
   end "+";
```

The idea behind this algorithm is to "merge" the sum together. This representation based on the priority queue allows all SCALAR-VECTOR or VECTOR-VECTOR operations to be defined in $O(n)$, where n is either the number of nonzero elements in the VECTOR in the SCALAR-VECTOR operation case or the total number of nonzero elements in both VECTORs in the VECTOR-VECTOR operation case. There is a subtle error in the algorithm above. It is possible to add two nonzero values, get zero, and still insert a zero component. This will be corrected in the ADT implementation.

A second representation would use a smaller array to store the nonzero elements. This basis of this method is the bounded priority queue. If V1 is a sparse VECTOR using the definition in Figure 16.1.3, some elements might not be used. The following two conventions will be adopted. First, the nonzero elements are stored in V1 in priority order, using the index field as the key while starting at the first element of V1. Second, if the value in the index field is zero, that particular element in that sparse vector V1 is not in use. Note that these conventions divide the vector V1 into two contiguous groups of elements. The first group, which appears in the lower index range of V1, represents the nonzero elements of V1. The second group, which appears after the first group, represents the unused elements. Figure 16.1.4 illustrates a VECTOR V1 with both a linked and an array representation.

```
   type ELEMENT is
     record
       INDEX : natural := 0;
```

Figure 16.1.3 Array representation for SPARSE_VECTOR. Continues on page 543.

Sparse Vectors and Matrices   Chap. 16

```
        VALUE : float;
   end record;
 type SPARSE_VECTOR is array (positive range 1..SIZE) of ELEMENT;
```

Figure 16.1.3 Concluded.

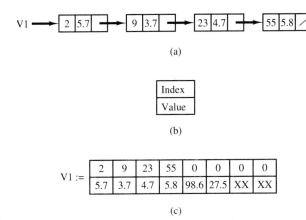

(a)

(b)

(c)

Figure 16.1.4 Sparse vector V1 stored as either a linked list, illustrated in part (a), or as a bounded array-based structure, illustrated in part (b). (a) Sparse vector V1 that uses a priority queue structure. (b) Individual subcomponent of an array-based structure. (c) Sparse vector V1 from part a stored in a bounded or array-based structure.

Which representation is best? There are two problems with the array representation. When adding two arrays, the total number of nonzero elements must be less than the fixed formal parameter SIZE. The number of nonzero elements can vary between zero and 2*SIZE. The linked representation can expand or contract to fit the problem's needs precisely. The fixed-size array representation must set the value of SIZE high enough so that there is always room to insert that extra nonzero element. The ADT built in Section 16.3 uses the representation that implements a sparse VECTOR as an unbounded priority queue.

16.2 SPARSE MATRICES AS MULTILISTS

The same criteria that applied to finding an optimum data representation for a sparse VECTOR apply to the data representation for a sparse MATRIX. The data structure chosen must minimize both the storage required to hold the MATRIX and the order of the operations on a sparse MATRIX. The three types of operations that must be minimized with respect to complexity are SCALAR-MATRIX operations (such as k*M, where k is a scalar and M is a MATRIX), MATRIX-MATRIX operations (such as M1 + M2 or M1*M2, where M1 and M2 are matrices) and MATRIX-VECTOR operations (such as M*V, where M is a MATRIX and V is a sparse VECTOR). All SCALAR-MATRIX operations are done on an element-by-element basis, so any representation where the elements can be examined systematically will minimize the SCALAR-MATRIX case. A VECTOR can be thought of as a MATRIX with one column, so any data structure that minimizes the complexity of the MATRIX-MATRIX case will minimize the MATRIX-VECTOR case. The problem of finding the proper data structure for a sparse matrix reduces to finding a structure that minimizes the storage required to hold the matrix while simultaneously minimizing the complexity of the two MATRIX-MATRIX operations M1 + M2 and M1*M2.

A MATRIX can be thought of as a one-dimensional array of one-dimensional row vectors. If the row vectors are implemented as indexed-based priority queues of elements, a data structure that uses the representation for a sparse vector defined in Figure 16.1.1 with an array of row sparse vectors is a possibility. Figure 16.2.1 lists an example of such a structure.

```
type ELEMENT;
type SPARSE_VECTOR is access ELEMENT;
type ELEMENT is
  record
    INDEX : integer;
    VALUE : float;
    NEXT  : SPARSE_VECTOR;
  end record;
type SPARSE_MATRIX is array(positive range 1..MAXIMUM_INDEX) of
                                          SPARSE_VECTOR;
```

Figure 16.2.1   First representation of SPARSE_MATRIX.

Figure 16.2.2 shows a sparse representation of a small matrix using this representation. This first representation is initially quite appealing. It is simple, easy to understand, and in the case of matrix addition quite effective. The matrix addition algorithm is quite easy to visualize. The algorithm would add the two matrices together row by row. Since each row is just a sparse VECTOR, the function to add two sparse vectors defined in Section 16.1 could be used to add two rows. The use of a previously defined function to add two rows just adds to the appeal of this data structure. The implementation of addition of two sparse matrices is trivial.

```
function "+" (LEFT, RIGHT : SPARSE_MATRIX) return SPARSE_MATRIX is
    SUM : SPARSE_MATRIX;
begin
    for ROW_INDEX in positive range 1..MAXIMUM_INDEX loop
      -- Addition operator below is for SPARSE_VECTORS
      SUM(ROW_INDEX) := LEFT(ROW_INDEX) + RIGHT(ROW_INDEX);
    end loop;
    return SUM;
end "+";
```

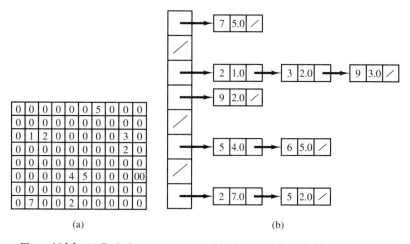

(a)   (b)

Figure 16.2.2   (a) Typical sparse matrix stored in the conventional fashion. (b) Sparse matrix representation of the matrix in part (a) using the data structure in Figure 16.2.1.

The normal complexity order for adding two square matrices is O(MAXIMUM_INDEX∗∗2). This function adds MAXIMUM_INDEX rows together, and each row is at most O(n), so this representation allows two matrices to be summed with a maximum of O(n∗MAXIMUM_IN-DEX) operations.

The other operation that must be minimized is the product of two matrices. Recall that two matrices can only be multiplied if the number of columns of the first equals the number of rows of the second. Each element in the answer equals the vector or dot product of a row in the first matrix with a column in the second matrix.

Thus if PRODUCT := LEFT ∗ RIGHT; the element in the ith row, jth column would be defined as

```
M3(ROW_INDEX, COL_INDEX) := 0.0;
for INDEX in M1(2) ' range loop
  M3 (ROW_INDEX, COLUMN_INDEX) := M3 (ROW_INDEX, COL_INDEX) +
                    M1 (ROW_INDEX, INDEX) * M2 (INDEX, COL_INDEX);
end loop;
```

In computing M3(ROW_INDEX, COL_INDEX), the sequential access of the elements of M1 is along the row ROW_INDEX, which the data structure in Figure 16.2.1 allows. Simultaneously, however, the elements of M2 must be accessed sequentially down the column COL_INDEX, which the data structure does not support. The only way that this access can be done is to go to the kth row of M2 and search that row to see if there is a nonzero entry of the column COL_INDEX. Every row must be searched whether or not there is a nonzero entry in the corresponding column. Matrix multiplication of normal arrays is on the order $O(n∗∗3)$. The need to search each row sequentially would make this operation $O(n∗∗4)$.

One way to eliminate the need to search every row during the multiplication operation is if every element could be referenced by two priority queues, one using the row index as a key and the other using the column index as a key. Figure 16.2.3 lists one possible data structure with this property. Note that every element is in two queues. Every nonzero element can be accessed through a row queue and a column queue. All queues are in priority order. Elements that are in the same row are ordered by their column index. Elements that are in the same column are ordered by their row index. Such a structure is commonly called a *multilist*. A multilist is any structure where it is possible for an element to appear in more than one list. Multilists have wide application in databases. Figure 16.2.4 illustrates a simple matrix that uses this representation. This structure is clearly minimal in the sense that only nonzero elements are stored. It is also minimal with respect to the addition of two matrices because the rows of elements can be accessed. It is not necessary to access the columns. It also allows for the accessing of matrix components along both the row and the column, so the matrix multiplication operation will be minimized.

```
type ELEMENT;
type NEXT_ELEMENT is access ELEMENT;
type ELEMENT is
  record
    ROW,
    COL      : positive;
    VALUE    : float;
    NEXT_ROW,
    NEXT_COL : NEXT_ELEMENT;
```

Figure 16.2.3 Second representation of SPARSE_MATRIX. Continues on page 546.

```
  end record;
type SPARSE_ARRAY is array (positive range 1..MAXIMUM_INDEX) of NEXT_ELEMENT;
type SPARSE_MATRIX is
  record
    ROW_ARRAY,
    COL_ARRAY : SPARSE_ARRAY;
  end record;
```

Figure 16.2.3 Concluded.

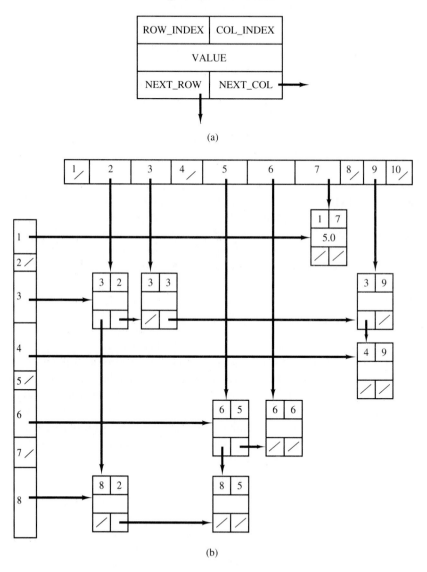

(a)

(b)

Figure 16.2.4 Second sparse matrix representation that is now optimized for matrix multiplication because elements are now accessible by either row or columns. (a) Sparse matrix element structure from Figure 16.2.3. (b) Sparse matrix from Figure 16.2.2(a) represented by the data structure in Figure 16.2.3. Note the array of queues of elements for both rows and columns.

16.3 ADT SPARSE_MATRIX_VECTOR_OPERATIONS

The ADT to be developed here is essentially an augmented form of the ADT GENERIC_MATRIX_VECTOR_OPERATIONS that was completed in Chapter 15. The ADT uses the linked list access representation for vectors and the sparse matrix representation listed in Figure 16.2.4. Several functions and procedures have been added in order to add, modify, update, delete, or access VECTOR or MATRIX elements. Unlike the nonsparse form, both VECTOR and MATRIX are limited private types because of their data structures. It would be tempting to make the types VECTOR and MATRIX private, but this would allow assignment and comparison for equality. The assignment and comparison would be misleading. What are being assigned and compared are access values, not VECTOR or MATRIX component values. Two distinct equal sparse vectors would fail the test for equality using = because only the access values to the first component are being compared. This requires the additional operator for assignment (Figure 16.3.1).

```
generic
  MAXIMUM_INDEX : positive;
  type ITEM_TYPE is private;
  ZERO_ITEM : in ITEM_TYPE;
  with function "*" (LEFT, RIGHT : ITEM_TYPE) return ITEM_TYPE IS <>;
  with function "+" (LEFT, RIGHT : ITEM_TYPE) return ITEM_TYPE IS <>;
  with function "-" (LEFT, RIGHT : ITEM_TYPE) return ITEM_TYPE IS <>;
package GENERIC_SPARSE_MATRIX_VECTOR_OPERATIONS is
  type VECTOR is limited private;
  type MATRIX is limited private;

--VECTOR OPERATIONS
function "*" (K : ITEM_TYPE ; V :VECTOR) return VECTOR;
function "*" (V :VECTOR; K : ITEM_TYPE) return VECTOR;
function "*" (LEFT, RIGHT : VECTOR) return ITEM_TYPE;
function "+" (LEFT, RIGHT : VECTOR) return VECTOR;
function "-" (LEFT, RIGHT : VECTOR) return VECTOR;

--MATRIX OPERATIONS
function "*" (K : ITEM_TYPE ; M : MATRIX) return MATRIX;
function "*" (M : MATRIX; K : ITEM_TYPE) return MATRIX;
function "*" (LEFT, RIGHT : MATRIX) return MATRIX;
function "+" (LEFT, RIGHT : MATRIX) return MATRIX;
function "-" (LEFT, RIGHT : MATRIX) return MATRIX;

--MATRIX VECTOR OPERATIONS
function "*" (M : MATRIX; V : VECTOR) return VECTOR;

--MATRIX VECTOR ACCESS OPERATIONS
procedure CLEAR_VECTOR (V : in out VECTOR);
procedure CLEAR_MATRIX (M : in out MATRIX);
function GET_VECTOR_ELEMENT (V : VECTOR; INDEX : positive )
                                          return ITEM_TYPE;
function GET_MATRIX_ELEMENT (M : MATRIX; ROW, COL :positive)
                                          return ITEM_TYPE;
```

Figure 16.3.1 ADT specification for GENERIC_SPARSE_MATRIX_VECTOR_OPERATIONS. Continues on page 548.

Sec. 16.3   ADT Sparse_Matrix_Vector_Operations   **547**

```
procedure ADD_VECTOR_ELEMENT (V      : in out VECTOR;
                              ITEM   : in     ITEM_TYPE;
                              INDEX  : in     positive);
procedure ADD_MATRIX_ELEMENT (M      : in out MATRIX;
                              ITEM   : in     ITEM_TYPE;
                              ROW,
                              COL    : in positive);

  --ASSIGNMENT OPERATIONS
  procedure ASSIGN_TO_VECTOR (RIGHT_SIDE_EXP : in      VECTOR);
                              LEFT_SIDE      :     out VECTOR);
  procedure ASSIGN_TO_MATRIX (RIGHT_SIDE_EXP : in      MATRIX);
                              LEFT_SIDE      :     out MATRIX);

  OVERFLOW       : exception;
  INDEX_ERROR    : exception;
private
  type VECTOR_NODE;
  type VECTOR is access VECTOR_NODE;
  type MATRIX_NODE;
  type NEXT_NODE is access MATRIX_NODE;
  type SPARSE_LIST is array (positive range 1..MAXIMUM_INDEX) of
                                    NEXT_NODE;
  type MATRIX is
    record
      ROW_LIST
      COL_LIST : SPARSE_LIST;
    end record;
end GENERIC_SPARSE_MATRIX_VECTOR_OPERATIONS;

package body GENERIC_SPARSE_MATRIX_VECTOR_OPERATIONS is
  type VECTOR_NODE is
    record
      INDEX : positive;
      VALUE : ITEM_TYPE;
      NEXT  : VECTOR;
    end record;
  type MATRIX_NODE is
    record
      ROW,
      COL      : positive;
      VALUE    : ITEM_TYPE;
      NEXT_ROW;
      NEXT_COL : NEXT_NODE;
    end record;

. . . . . . . . . . . . . . . . .

end GENERIC_SPARSE_MATRIX_VECTOR_OPERATIONS;
```

Figure 16.3.1 Concluded.

A basic understanding of access types and typical vector-matrix scalar operations is all that is needed now to implement this ADT. In Chapter 15 we reviewed the necessary operations. The vector operation defining vector addition illustrated in Section 16.1 can be simplified by use of the vector operation ADD_VECTOR_ELEMENT to insert and element with value ITEM and given INDEX into the vector ANSWER. The addition operator below can be used as a model for addition, subtraction, and scalar product for objects of type VECTOR.

```
function "+" (LEFT, RIGHT : VECTOR) return VECTOR is
  -- Returns a vector equal to the sum of two vectors
   -- Exception OVERFLOW raised if there is not enough memory to complete
  -- this operation
  SUM : VECTOR;
  TEMP_LEFT  : VECTOR := LEFT;
  TEMP_RIGHT : VECTOR := RIGHT;
  TEMP_VALUE : ITEM_TYPE;
begin
  -- Traverse both vectors until one is null.
  while TEMP_LEFT /= null and TEMP_RIGHT /= null loop
    -- Both indices the same
    if TEMP_LEFT.INDEX = TEMP_RIGHT.INDEX then
      --Both indices the same..
      TEMP_VALUE := TEMP_LEFT.VALUE + TEMP_RIGHT.VALUE;
      -- if TEMP_VALUE not equal to ZERO_ITEM it belongs in ANSWER
      if TEMP_VALUE /= ZERO_ITEM then
        ADD_VECTOR_ELEMENT (SUM, TEMP_VALUE, TEMP_LEFT.INDEX);
      end if;
      TEMP_LEFT := TEMP_LEFT.NEXT;
      TEMP_RIGHT := TEMP_RIGHT.NEXT;
    elsif TEMP_LEFT.INDEX < TEMP_RIGHT.INDEX then
      -- Indices do not line up, copy and add next LEFT
      ADD_VECTOR_ELEMENT (SUM, TEMP_LEFT.VALUE, TEMP_LEFT.INDEX);
      TEMP_LEFT := TEMP_LEFT.NEXT;
    else
      -- Indices do not line up, copy and add next RIGHT
      ADD_VECTOR_ELEMENT (SUM, TEMP_RIGHT.VALUE, TEMP_RIGHT.INDEX);
      TEMP_RIGHT := TEMP_RIGHT.NEXT;
    end if;
  end loop;
  -- Left vector not fully traversed, add the rest of LEFT to ANSWER
  while TEMP_LEFT /= null loop
    ADD_VECTOR_ELEMENT (SUM, TEMP_LEFT.VALUE, TEMP_LEFT.INDEX);
    TEMP_LEFT := TEMP_LEFT.NEXT;
  end loop;
  -- Right vector not fully traversed, add the rest of RIGHT to ANSWER
  while TEMP_RIGHT /= null loop
    ADD_VECTOR_ELEMENT (SUM, TEMP_RIGHT.VALUE, TEMP_RIGHT.INDEX);
    TEMP_RIGHT := TEMP_RIGHT.NEXT;
  end loop;
  return SUM;
```

```
exception
   when OVERFLOW => raise OVERFLOW;
end "+";
```

Illustrated below is the vector-scalar product, the sum of the product of nonzero components with the same index. To compute the scalar product, both vectors must be traversed until one or both is null. Clearly, no components in both vectors can be found with the same index if one vector is null.

```
function "*" (LEFT, RIGHT : VECTOR) return ITEM_TYPE is
   -- Returns the dot or scalar product of two vectors. The dot product
   -- is the sum of products of components with the same index.
   ANSWER      : ITEM_TYPE := ZERO_ITEM;
   NEXT_LEFT   : VECTOR    := LEFT;
   NEXT_RIGHT  : VECTOR    := RIGHT;
begin
   -- Traverse both vectors until one or both is null
   while (NEXT_LEFT /= null) AND (NEXT_RIGHT /= null) loop
      if NEXT_LEFT.INDEX = NEXT_RIGHT.INDEX then
         -- Indices are the same, form product, and add to ANSWER
         ANSWER := ANSWER + LEFT.VALUE * RIGHT.VALUE;
         -- Get the next component with nonzero value
         NEXT_LEFT := NEXT_LEFT.NEXT;
         NEXT_RIGHT := NEXT_RIGHT.NEXT;
      elsif NEXT_LEFT.INDEX < NEXT_RIGHT.INDEX then
         -- Indices do not line up, update NEXT_LEFT
         NEXT_LEFT := NEXT_LEFT.NEXT;
      else
         -- Indices do not line up, update NEXT_RIGHT
         NEXT_RIGHT := NEXT_RIGHT.NEXT;
      end if;
   end loop;
   return ANSWER;
end "*";
```

The implementation of the matrix operations for sparse matrices parallels the implementation of their standard analogs. Scalar multiplication of a matrix requires that every element in the matrix be multiplied by the scalar. Two matrices are added together by adding their corresponding elements together. There are three cases to consider for sparse matrix addition. The first is that both matrices have a nonzero element at the same location, the second is that the first matrix does not have a nonzero entry for a particular location while the second matrix does, and finally, the first matrix has a nonzero element at a location but the second matrix does not. Scalar matrix multiplication is the simplest case. Since only nonzero elements are in nodes, this operation is $O(n)$, where n is the number of nonzero elements.

```
function "*" (K : ITEM_TYPE; M : MATRIX) return MATRIX is
   -- Returns a matrix where every has been multiplied by K
   -- Exception OVERFLOW raised if there is not enough memory to complete
   --          this operation
   ANSWER : MATRIX;
   TEMP_ROW : NEXT_NODE;
```

```
begin
  for ROW_INDEX in 1..MAXIMUM_INDEX loop
    TEMP_ROW := M.ROW_LIST (ROW_INDEX);
    while TEMP_ROW /= null loop
      ADD_MATRIX_ELEMENT
             (ANSWER, K*TEMP_ROW.VALUE, TEMP_ROW.ROW, TEMP_ROW.COL);
      TEMP_ROW := TEMP_ROW.NEXT_COL;
    end loop;
  end loop;
  return ANSWER;
exception
  when OVERFLOW => raise OVERFLOW;
end "*";
```

Note that the procedure goes through each row of the matrix. For each node, where the nonzero values are stored, it multiplies the value by the scalar and calls ADD_MATRIX_EL-EMENT. The operation ADD_MATRIX_ELEMENT does several things. It can update a previously defined value with a new value, delete the node if the value is zero, or insert a node if it is not present.

```
procedure ADD_MATRIX_ELEMENT (M : in out MATRIX;
                              ITEM : in      ITEM_TYPE;
                              ROW,
                              COL  : in       positive) is
  -- Inserts a MATRIX_NODE at a specified ROW and COL with value ITEM.
  -- If a node with same ROW_COL is there, it is updated unless
  -- ITEM = ZERO_ITEM in which case the node is deleted.
   -- Exception OVERFLOW raised if there is not enough memory to complete
  -- this operation
  -- Exception INDEX_ERROR raised in ROW or COL > MAXIMUM_INDEX
  TEMP_NEXT : NEXT_NODE;
  TEMP_NODE : NEXT_NODE;
  FOUND : boolean := false;
begin
  if ROW > MAXIMUM_INDEX or COL > MAXIMUM_INDEX then
    raise INDEX_ERROR;
  else
    -- Create the MATRIX_NODE to be inserted in M
    TEMP_NODE := new MATRIX_NODE' (ROW, COL, ITEM, null, null);
    -- First place the node in the proper row, or update, or delete
    TEMP_NEXT := M.ROW_LIST (ROW);
    if TEMP_NEXT = null then
      -- Row is empty, add node and go to place in proper column
      if ITEM /= ZERO_ITEM then
        M.ROW_LIST (ROW) := TEMP_NODE;
      end if;
    elsif COL = TEMP_NEXT.COL then
      -- Node with same ROW-COL already exists
      if ITEM /= ZERO_ITEM then
        -- All done after updating node with new nonzero ITEM
        TEMP_NEXT.VALUE := ITEM;
```

```
            return;
        else
          -- ITEM is zero, by definition of SPARSE matrix, must delete node.
          -- Note node must be deleted from column list, too.
          M.ROW_LIST (ROW) := TEMP_NEXT.NEXT_COL;
        end if;
    elsif COL < TEMP_NEXT.COL then
      -- Node belongs before first node in current row, provided that ITEM /=
      -- ZERO_ITEM.
      if ITEM /= ZERO_ITEM then
        TEMP_NODE.NEXT_COL := M.ROW_LIST (ROW);
        M.ROW_LIST (ROW) := TEMP_NODE;
      end if;
    else
      -- Node not placed, search and insert, update, or delete as required.
      while TEMP_NEXT.NEXT_COL /= null loop
        if COL < TEMP_NEXT.NEXT_COL.COL then
          -- Node not in matrix, but place found . . . .
          if ITEM /= ZERO_ITEM then
            TEMP_NODE.NEXT_COL := TEMP_NEXT.NEXT_COL;
            TEMP_NEXT.NEXT_COL := TEMP_NODE;
          end if;
          FOUND := true;
          exit;
        elsif COL = TEMP_NEXT.NEXT_COL.COL then
          -- Node in row, so update and return if ITEM /= ZERO_ITEM
          if ITEM /= ZERO_ITEM then
            TEMP_NEXT.NEXT_COL.VALUE := ITEM;
            return;
          else
            -- Delete the node in row because ITEM = ZERO_ITEM
            TEMP_NEXT.NEXT_COL := TEMP_NEXT.NEXT_COL.NEXT_COL;
          end if;
        else
          TEMP_NEXT := TEMP_NEXT.NEXT_COL;
        end if;
      end loop;
      if not FOUND and ITEM /= ZERO_ITEM then
        -- Consider case if node to be the end node in the row.
        TEMP_NEXT.NEXT_COL := TEMP_NODE;
      end if;
    end if;
  end if;
-- If the node was already there and ITEM /= ZERO_ITEM, the value has
-- been updated and procedure terminated. If the node is there, and
-- ITEM = ZERO_ITEM it still must be deleted from column list but updating
-- the value in an already existing node has been completed.
FOUND := false;
-- Get correct column
TEMP_NEXT := M.COL_LIST (COL);
```

```
        if TEMP_NEXT = null then
          -- Column empty, insert and leave
          if ITEM /= ZERO_ITEM then
            M.COL_LIST (COL) := TEMP_NODE;
          end if;
        elsif ROW = TEMP_NEXT.ROW then
          -- If node already there, it was updated previously, so this one
          -- must need to be deleted.
          M.COL_LIST(COL) := TEMP_NEXT.NEXT_ROW;
        elsif ROW < TEMP_NEXT.ROW then
          if ITEM /= ZERO_ITEM then
            TEMP_NODE.NEXT_ROW := M.COL_LIST (COL);
            M.COL_LIST (COL) := TEMP_NODE;
          end if;
        else
          -- Search the column . . .
          while TEMP_NEXT.NEXT_ROW /= null loop
            if ROW < TEMP_NEXT.NEXT_ROW.ROW then
              if ITEM /= ZERO_ITEM then
                TEMP_NODE.NEXT_ROW := TEMP_NEXT.NEXT_ROW;
                TEMP_NEXT.NEXT_ROW := TEMP_NODE;
              end if;
              FOUND := true;
              exit;
            elsif ROW = TEMP_NEXT.NEXT_ROW.ROW then
              -- Node was updated previously, so it must need to be deleted
              TEMP_NEXT.NEXT_ROW := TEMP_NEXT.NEXT_ROW.NEXT_ROW;
              return;
            else
              TEMP_NEXT := TEMP_NEXT.NEXT_ROW;
            end if;
          end loop;
          if not FOUND and ITEM /= ZERO_ITEM then
            TEMP_NEXT.NEXT_ROW := TEMP_NODE;
          end if;
        end if;
    exception
      when storage_error => raise OVERFLOW;
    end ADD_MATRIX_ELEMENT;
```

The operational complexity of ADD_MATRIX_ELEMENT is proportional to the length of the longest row or column queue in M.

The multiplication of two matrices is a straightforward adaptation of the case for non-sparse matrices. A value is computed that might be nonzero. If it is not zero, it is inserted into the answer.

```
    function "*" ( LEFT, RIGHT : MATRIX) return MATRIX is
      -- Returns a matrix equal to the conventional product of two matrices.
      -- Exception OVERFLOW raised if there is not enough memory to complete
      -- this operation
```

```
ANSWER    : MATRIX;
TEMP_VALUE : ITEM_TYPE;


function LEFT_ROW_WITH_RIGHT_COL_PRODUCT (LEFT, RIGHT : NEXT_NODE)
                            return ITEM_TYPE is
  -- Auxillary function used to compute the value of the element in the
  -- LEFT row and RIGHT column. Method is dot product of LEFT row with
  -- RIGHT column.
  TEMP_LEFT : NEXT_NODE := LEFT;
  TEMP_RIGHT : NEXT_NODE := RIGHT;
  ANSWER : ITEM_TYPE := ZERO_ITEM;
begin
  while TEMP_LEFT /= null and TEMP_RIGHT /= null loop
    if TEMP_LEFT.COL = TEMP_RIGHT.ROW then
      ANSWER := ANSWER + TEMP_LEFT.VALUE * TEMP_RIGHT.VALUE;
      TEMP_LEFT := TEMP_LEFT.NEXT_COL;
      TEMP_RIGHT := TEMP_RIGHT.NEXT_ROW;
    elsif TEMP_LEFT.COL < TEMP_RIGHT.ROW then
      TEMP_LEFT := TEMP_LEFT.NEXT_COL;
    else
      TEMP_RIGHT := TEMP_RIGHT.NEXT_ROW;
    end if;
  end loop;
  return ANSWER;
end LEFT_ROW_WITH_RIGHT_COL_PRODUCT;


begin
  for ROW_INDEX in positive range 1..MAXIMUM_INDEX loop
    for COL_INDEX in positive range 1..MAXIMUM_INDEX loop
      TEMP_VALUE := LEFT_ROW_WITH_RIGHT_COL_PRODUCT
                      (LEFT.ROW_LIST(ROW_INDEX), RIGHT.COL_LIST(COL_INDEX));
      if TEMP_VALUE /= ZERO_ITEM then
        ADD_MATRIX_ELEMENT (ANSWER, TEMP_VALUE, ROW_INDEX, COL_INDEX);
      end if;
    end loop;
  end loop;
  return ANSWER;
exception
  when OVERFLOW => raise OVERFLOW;
end "*";
```

Normally, matrix multiplication is $O(n**3)$. If k is the maximum number of nonzero nodes in any row or column, the sparse version is $O(k* n**2) = O(n**2)$, which is an order of magnitude less. In most applications, the MAXIMUM_INDEX n is very large and k is relatively small, so the savings can be significant.

When adding two sparse matrices together or when subtracting two sparse matrices, there is a possibility that the sum of two values will be zero. Note how this is checked for in the addition operation.

```
function "+" (LEFT, RIGHT : MATRIX) return MATRIX is
  -- Returns a matrix equal to the sum of LEFT and RIGHT
  -- Exception OVERFLOW raised if there is not enough memory to complete
  --           this operation
  ANSWER     : MATRIX;
  TEMP_LEFT : NEXT_NODE;
  TEMP_RIGHT : NEXT_NODE;
  TEMP_VALUE : ITEM_TYPE;
begin
  -- For each row in LEFT and RIGHT . . .
  for INDEX in positive range 1..MAXIMUM_INDEX loop
    TEMP_LEFT := LEFT.ROW_LIST (INDEX);
    TEMP_RIGHT := RIGHT.ROW_LIST (INDEX);
    -- Traverse both rows as long as both are not empty
    while TEMP_LEFT /= null and TEMP_RIGHT /= null loop
      if TEMP_LEFT.COL = TEMP_RIGHT.COL then
        -- If the column indices are equal, add and insert if the sum is
        -- not the ZERO_ITEM, then go to next node in both rows
        TEMP_VALUE := TEMP_LEFT.VALUE + TEMP_RIGHT.VALUE;
        if TEMP_VALUE /= ZERO_ITEM then
          ADD_MATRIX_ELEMENT (ANSWER, TEMP_VALUE, INDEX, TEMP_LEFT.COL);
        end if;
        TEMP_LEFT := TEMP_LEFT.NEXT_COL;
        TEMP_RIGHT := TEMP_RIGHT.NEXT_COL;
      elsif TEMP_LEFT.COL < TEMP_RIGHT.COL then
          -- Node indices do not match. Insert the nonzero value from
          -- LEFT and update.
                     ADD_MATRIX_ELEMENT (ANSWER, TEMP_LEFT.VALUE, INDEX,
        TEMP_LEFT.COL);
        TEMP_LEFT := TEMP_LEFT.NEXT_C0L;
      else
          -- Node indices do not match. Insert the nonzero value from
          -- RIGHT and update.
        ADD_MATRIX_ELEMENT
                     (ANSWER,TEMP_RIGHT.VALUE,INDEX,TEMP_RIGHT.COL);
        TEMP_RIGHT := TEMP_RIGHT.NEXT_COL;
      end if;
    end loop;
    -- One or both rows are now empty, add the remaining values
    while TEMP_LEFT /= null loop
      ADD_MATRIX_ELEMENT (ANSWER, TEMP_LEFT.VALUE, INDEX, TEMP_LEFT.COL);
      TEMP_LEFT := TEMP_LEFT.NEXT_COL;
    end loop;
    while TEMP_RIGHT /= null loop
      ADD_MATRIX_ELEMENT (ANSWER,TEMP_RIGHT.VALUE,INDEX,TEMP_RIGHT.COL);
      TEMP_RIGHT := TEMP_RIGHT.NEXT_COL;
    end loop;
  end loop;
  return ANSWER;
```

```
exception
  when OVERFLOW => raise OVERFLOW;
end "+";
```

A common mistake is to access every node in every row, as was done above, and then every node in every column. After all, each node is in a row list and in a column list. This results in every node being "double counted."

Since types VECTOR and MATRIX are limited private, all access to any variable of type VECTOR or of type MATRIX must be through a function or procedure listed in the specification. Procedures CLEAR_VECTOR and CLEAR_MATRIX set the respective access types to null. Since a sparse VECTOR or sparse MATRIX lists only the nonzero elements, the VECTORs and MATRIXs are effectively zeroed out.

The function GET_MATRIX_ELEMENT returns the value of the specified element if it is in the array or ZERO_ITEM if it is not there.

```
function GET_MATRIX_ELEMENT (M        : MATRIX;
                            ROW, COL : positive ) return ITEM_TYPE is
  -- Returns the value of M(ROW,COL) if it is in M or ZERO_ITEM otherwise
  -- Exception INDEX_ERROR raised if ROW or COL > MAXIMUM_INDEX
  TEMP_ROW : NEXT_NODE;
begin
  if ROW > MAXIMUM_INDEX or COL > MAXIMUM_INDEX then
    raise INDEX_ERROR;
  else
    TEMP_ROW := M.ROW_LIST (ROW);
    while TEMP_ROW /= null loop
      if TEMP_ROW.COL = COL then
        return TEMP_ROW.VALUE;
      elsif COL < TEMP_ROW.COL then
        return ZERO_ITEM;
      else
        TEMP_ROW := TEMP_ROW.NEXT_COL;
      end if;
    end loop;
    return ZERO_ITEM;
  end if;
end GET_MATRIX_ELEMENT;
```

Note again that only the particular row is searched. It is not necessary to search both the row and the column.

The implementation is more tedious than challenging. The full implementation details are left to the exercises. Several operations appear to be left out. For example, there are no procedures to copy sparse vectors or sparse matrices. This can be done in one of two ways. If an exact copy is needed, an application of the scalar multiplication function will work. The trick is to multiply the vector or matrix by the constant 1. If a second reference is needed, the appropriate assign operations will work.

All vectors and matrices in this package have index ranges of 1 to MAXIMUM_INDEX. The vector and matrix elements can be any type as long as addition, multiplication, and subtraction can be defined. Being able to define addition or subtraction requires a ZERO_ITEM, since the result may yield zero. Another problem can occur during subtraction. If A and B are objects of ITEM_TYPE, A – B is defined but (–B) is not. Note how this problem is handled when two VECTORS are subtracted.

```
function "-" (LEFT, RIGHT : VECTOR) return VECTOR is
  -- Returns a vector equal to the difference of two vectors
   -- Exception OVERFLOW raised if there is not enough memory to complete
  -- this operation
  ANSWER : VECTOR;
  TEMP_LEFT  : VECTOR := LEFT;
  TEMP_RIGHT : VECTOR := RIGHT;
  TEMP_VALUE : ITEM_TYPE;
begin
  --Traverse both vectors until one is empty . . .
  while TEMP_LEFT /= null and TEMP_RIGHT /= null loop
    if TEMP_LEFT.INDEX = TEMP_RIGHT.INDEX then
      TEMP_VALUE := TEMP_LEFT.VALUE - TEMP_RIGHT.VALUE;
      if TEMP_VALUE /= ZERO_ITEM then
        ADD_VECTOR_ELEMENT (ANSWER, TEMP_VALUE, TEMP_LEFT.INDEX);
      end if;
      TEMP_LEFT := TEMP_LEFT.NEXT;
      TEMP_RIGHT := TEMP_RIGHT.NEXT;
    elsif TEMP_LEFT.INDEX < TEMP_RIGHT.INDEX then
      ADD_VECTOR_ELEMENT (ANSWER, TEMP_LEFT.VALUE, TEMP_LEFT.INDEX);
      TEMP_LEFT := TEMP_LEFT.NEXT;
    else
      -- Note that -TEMP_RIGHT.VALUE not defined, but ZERO_ITEM-TEMP_RIGHT.VALUE
      -- is defined
      ADD_VECTOR_ELEMENT
            (ANSWER, ZERO_ITEM - TEMP_RIGHT.VALUE, TEMP_RIGHT.INDEX);
      TEMP_RIGHT := TEMP_RIGHT.NEXT;
    end if;
  end loop;
  -- If LEFT has not been fully traversed, add the remaining nodes to the
  -- answer
  while TEMP_LEFT /= null loop
    ADD_VECTOR_ELEMENT (ANSWER, TEMP_LEFT.VALUE, TEMP_LEFT.INDEX);
    TEMP_LEFT := TEMP_LEFT.NEXT;
  end loop;
  -- If RIGHT has not been fully traversed, negate and add the remaining
  -- nodes to the answer
  while TEMP_RIGHT /= null loop
    ADD_VECTOR_ELEMENT
          (ANSWER, ZERO_ITEM - TEMP_RIGHT.VALUE, TEMP_RIGHT.INDEX);
    TEMP_RIGHT := TEMP_RIGHT.NEXT;
  end loop;
```

```
    return ANSWER;
  exception
    when OVERFLOW => raise OVERFLOW;
  end "-";
```

The problem above is that only the binary subtraction operator was instantiated, not the unary operator.

16.4 ADVANTAGES OF THE SPARSE REPRESENTATION

The matrix applications highlighted in Chapter 15 can be performed using sparse matrices. This representation allows for the typical MATRIX-VECTOR equations to be formed and computed using a natural, mathematical type notation. The basis for this discussion is the MATRIX-VECTOR statement that forms the statement inside the loop in the solution of a linear system by the Jacobi method listed in Figure 15.7.5.

```
SOLUTION := D_INVERSE*(B - TEMP_A*SOLUTION);
```

Recall that both TEMP_A and D_INVERSE are two square matrices with n rows while SOLUTION and B are VECTORS with MAXIMUM_INDEX = n. The MATRIX-VECTOR product TEMP_A*SOLUTION is $O(n**2)$. The expression inside the parentheses is the difference of two VECTORS, which results in a VECTOR. It is $O(n)$. Finally, D_INVERSE*(B-TEMP_A*SOLUTION) is another MATRIX-VECTOR product that is $O(n**2)$. Computing one iteration is an $O(n**2)$ process. Using the methods of Chapter 15, this process is $O(n**2)$ in both time and method for all problems.

Consider the problem shown in Figure 16.4.1. The particular problem appears often in the solution of differential equations.

$$
\begin{aligned}
a_{1,1}{}^*x_1 + a_{1,2*}x_2 \qquad\qquad\qquad &= b_1 \\
a_{2,1}{}^*x_1 + a_{2,2}{}^*x_2 + a_{2,3}{}^*x_3 \qquad &= b_2 \\
a_{3,2}{}^*x_3 + a_{3,3}{}^*x_3 + a_{3,4}{}^*x_4 &= b_3 \\
\cdots\cdots\cdots\cdots\cdots\cdots \qquad\qquad & \\
a_{k,k-1}{}^*x_{k-1} + a_{k,k}{}^*x_k + a_{k,k+1}{}^*x_{k+1} &= b_k \\
\cdots\cdots\cdots\cdots\cdots\cdots \qquad\qquad & \\
a_{n-1,n}{}^*x_{n-1} + a_{n,n}{}^*x_n \qquad\quad &= b_n
\end{aligned}
$$

Figure 16.4.1   Tridiagonal system of linear equations.

For large n, this system is sparse. The coefficient matrix has $3 * n - 2$ nonzero elements. Recall that TEMP_A = A − D is a matrix with a diagonal of all zeros. Thus TEMP_A has $2*n - 2$ nonzero elements. The matrix D_INVERSE is also a diagonal matrix that has n elements. The first conclusion is that the sparse representation requires memory of the order of $O(n)$ instead of memory on the order $O(n**2)$. This order-of-magnitude reduction in memory is significant.

The computational reduction is also significant. Note that the MATRIX-VECTOR, MATRIX-MATRIX, and SCALAR-MATRIX products do not attempt an arithmetic operation unless both operands are nonzero. The MATRIX and VECTOR addition and subtraction operations are performed only when at least one term is not zero. For this particular tridiagonal system, the two MATRIX-VECTOR products are $O(n)$ instead of $O(n**2)$. This order-of-magnitude reduction in computational effort is also significant.

Banded or diagonal systems are not normally solved using SPARSE methods. There are methods based on the structure or these special matrix systems that give exact $O(n)$ solutions in both time and memory. The naive direct solution is $O(n**3)$. These specialized methods, which are studied in any numerical linear algebra course, are the preferred method. The tridiagonal system does provide an excellent example of the power of sparse methods when applied appropriately.

16.5 TIME AND SPACE CONSTRAINTS

The time and storage overhead of sparse matrix operations depend on how "sparse" the matrices and vectors under consideration are. For the two tables below, let N = number of rows and columns in a matrix and the number of elements in a vector be fixed. Let M1 and M2 be two sparse matrices with $m1$ and $m2$ nonzero elements, respectively. Let V1 and V2 be two sparse vectors with $v1$ and $v2$ elements, respectively.

Adding two vectors or two matrices is clearly $O(m1 + m2)$ or $O(v1 + v2)$, respectively. The reason for this is that there is no guarantee that the same elements in the matrices or vectors are not zero. Under the assumption that the elements in a sparse matrix are "uniformly distributed" so that ml/N nonzero elements appear in each row and in each column of M1, an estimate for the product M1*M2 can be made. Each of the $N**2$ possible elements in M1*M2 must be computed, but only the nonzero are kept. Since each row of M1 has about ml/N nonzero elements and each column of M2 has about $m2/N$, the calculation of each of the possible $N**2$ nonzero elements involves $O((ml + m2)/N)$ additions and multiplications, or the computation of the sparse matrix product is proportional to $O(N*(m1 + m2))$. The traditional matrix product is $O(N**3)$ if M1 and M2 are 99% sparse and $N = 1000$, then $N**3 = 10**9$ but $N(ml + m2) = 2.0*10**7$, a difference of two orders of magnitude in computational complexity that is well worth the effort.

If the sparse matrix data representation is the one listed in Figure 16.2.3, then Figure 16.5.1 summarizes the time space and parameter overhead of selected sparse matrix operations.

Operation	Time	Space
V1*V2	$O(v1 + v2)$	$O(v1 + v2)$
k*v2	$O(v2)$	$O(v2)$
V1 + V2	$O(v1 + v2)$	$O(v1 + v2)$
M1 + M2	$O(ml + m2)$	$O(ml + m2)$
M1*V1	$O(ml + v2)$	$O(ml + v1)$
k*M2	$O(m2)$	$O(m2)$
M1*M2	$O(N (ml + m2))$	$O(ml + m2)$
ADD_MATRIX_ELEMENT	$O(N)$	$O(1)$
GET_MATRIX_ELEMENT	$O(N)$	$O(1)$

Figure 16.5.1 Time and space overhead for sparse matrices using as defined in Figure 16.2.3.

EXERCISES

SECTION 16.1 SPARSE VECTORS: TWO REPRESENTATIONS

16.1.1 Consider the representation of a sparse vector listed in Figure 16.1.1. Implement the following operations without using a priority queue.
  a. Scalar multiplication
  b. Vector addition
  c. Vector product

16.1.2 Consider the bounded or array-based representation of a sparse vector listed in Figure 16.1.3. Implement the following operations.
  a. Scalar multiplication
  b. Vector addition
  c. Vector product

Section 16.2 Sparse Matrices as Multilists

16.2.1 Consider the representation of a sparse matrix listed in Figure 16.2.1. Implement the following matrix operations.
  a. Scalar multiplication
  b. Matrix addition
  c. Matrix product

16.2.2 Consider the representation of a sparse matrix listed in Figure 16.2.3. Implement the following matrix operations.
  a. Scalar multiplication
  b. Matrix addition
  c. Matrix product

16.2.3 Consider the representation of a sparse matrix listed in Figure 16.2.5. Implement the following matrix operations.
  a. Scalar multiplication
  b. Matrix addition
  c. Matrix product

Section 16.3 ADT SPARSE_MATRIX_VECTOR_OPERATIONS

16.3.1 Implement the following operations in the package GENERIC_SPARSE_MATRIX_VEC-TOR_OPERATIONS as listed in Figure 16.3.1.
  a. Function "*" (K : ITEM_TYPE ; V :VECTOR) return VECTOR;
  b. Function "*" (V : VECTOR; K : ITEM_TYPE) return VECTOR;
  c. Function "+" (LEFT, RIGHT : VECTOR) return VECTOR;
  d. Function "*" (M : MATRIX; K : ITEM_TYPE) return MATRIX;
  e. Function "−" (LEFT, RIGHT : MATRIX) return MATRIX;
  f. Function "*" (M : MATRIX; V : VECTOR) return VECTOR;
  g. Procedure CLEAR_VECTOR (V : in out VECTOR);
  h. Procedure CLEAR_MATRIX (M : in out MATRIX);
  i. Function GET_VECTOR_ELEMENT (V : VECTOR; INDEX : positive)
                                                                                return ITEM_TYPE;
  j. Procedure ADD_VECTOR_ELEMENT (V   : in out VECTOR;
                                       ITEM   : in   ITEM_TYPE;
                                       INDEX : in   positive);

k. Procedure ASSIGN_TO_VECTOR (RIGHT_SIDE_EXP : in   VECTOR;
                                 LEFT_SIDE   :   out VECTOR);

l. Procedure ASSIGN_TO_MATRIX (RIGHT_SIDE_EXP : in   MATRIX;
                                 LEFT_SIDE   :   out MATRIX);

m. Combine parts a through l and the operations implemented in this section into a package body that completes implementation of the ADT GENERIC_SPARSE_MATRIX_VECTOR_OPERATIONS.

NOTES AND REFERENCES

Most numerical methods texts discuss banded matrices and their representation as vectors. See, in particular, Cheney and Kincaid [12] or Press et al. [42]. The literature for sparse matrices is very specific and often optimized to a particular application. The representations here are meant only as an introduction.

17

Putting It
All Together

17.1 WHAT HAS BEEN ACCOMPLISHED

Every reader of this book has, hopefully, acquired an understanding of the basic abstract data types and their Ada implementation. According to McCracken [35], students who complete a first computer science course generically titled "Introduction to Programming and Computer Science" and a second course in data types should have acquired several skills and insights. These acquired skills include the mastery of a needed tool to study other areas of computer science, such as algorithms and compiler construction, the mastery of a tool for describing things and actions, and a basic insight into an algorithmic way of thinking. Admittedly, there is a lot more to computer science.

After a bit of reflection, the reader may have already deduced that there are basically two abstract data structures. They are the linear list implemented as either a linked list or an array, and the nonlinear structures such as trees and graphs. Operations on these structures make them into distinct data types. The goals of this book have been to introduce the reader to basic abstract data types and to help the reader to create, to understand, and to learn to use a basic library of abstract data types. During this course of study, the reader should have learned to appreciate that programming or software engineering is a discipline. The discipline used in this book can be stated as (1) understanding the problem, (2) recognizing the structure within the problem and knowing how to take advantage of the structure, (3) planning the attack on the problem, (4) coding, and (5) testing and validation of the program. The actual software life cycle includes other steps, such as formal specification and documentation.

17.2 GENERALIZING ABSTRACT DATA TYPES

By its nature, programming is a bootstrap process. The use of primitives results in nonprimitives. Nonprimitives combine with other actions to become types. Types combine with algorithms to become modules. Interfaced modules become programs. The programming process is a process of layers.

Like most programming languages, Ada supplies some basic types. Integers, floats, characters, and the user-defined enumerated types are the primitives. The record type allows the primitives to be combined into nonprimitives data structures. The operations on these user-defined record structures make these structures and operations into types. Algorithms use type operations to manipulate the type structures. These manipulations become the modules.

Any moderately complex program will use several types. Several case studies at the end of the chapters used three or more abstract data types. As a person becomes more experienced, programming becomes less of an art and more of a discipline. The experienced programmer knows that stacks, queues, lists, trees, graphs, and other types are all necessary program components. The disciplined programmer does not reinvent these basic types. When the disciplined Ada programmer recognizes a need for a concrete data type, the instantiation of an abstract data type results in a suitable user-defined type. This increases productivity while making validation and testing easier.

Insight follows experience. As experience grows, insight into program structure follows. This insight enables a programmer to specify, implement, and test specialized abstract data types. Just as the primitive types of integers, floats, characters, and user-defined enumerated types can be combined to form nonprimitive record data structures, data types can be combined to meet unique requirements.

17.3 DESIGNING YOUR OWN ABSTRACT DATA TYPE

Correct Ada programming style requires the implementation of abstract data types as generic packages. New data types arise out of need. The open hashing scheme is an example of two combined data types. The result was the ADT GENERIC_OPEN_HASH_SEARCH_TABLE. Closed hash tables are arrays of key-data pairs. As the table fills, collisions result. By combining an array-based hashing scheme with a queue of key-data pairs, an open hashing scheme results. Collisions do not occur in open hashing data types and there is no worry about the table becoming full. There may be some sacrifice in search efficiency. The open hashing data type is an example of a generalized data type. Its repeated use had made it a basic primitive data type.

The sparse matrix is another example of the power of combining data types to meet a special need. If a large matrix has mostly zero elements in it, why is storage wasted storing these null values? As shown in Chapter 16, this problem can be solved by either two arrays whose elements are priority queues with interlocking elements, or by two priority queues whose elements are themselves priority queues of interlocking elements. After defining the structure, matrix addition, multiplication, and other matrix operations were developed. The combined structure and operations implement the data type.

How can one learn to recognize the need for new abstract data types? Experience is a good teacher. Consider the case study at the end of Chapter 8. The tree type requires that all keys must be unique. What if the keys are not unique? To develop an index, the search operations and structure organization for the keys of a binary search tree was combined with the queue structure for storing data. An alternative strategy would be to define, specify, and develop a new ADT called GENERIC_UNBOUNDED_BINARY_SEARCH_TREE_QUEUE. Each tree node would look as shown in Figure 17.3.1.

```
type QUEUE_NODE;
type QUEUE is access QUEUE_NODE;
type QUEUE_NODE is
   record
```

Figure 17.3.1 Data structure for a TREE_QUEUE. Continues on page 564.

```
            DATA : DATA_TYPE;
            NEXT : QUEUE;
          end record;
      type TREE_NODE;
      type TREE is access TREE_NODE;
      type TREE_NODE is
        record
          KEY : KEY_TYPE;
          DATA_QUEUE : QUEUE;
          LEFT,
          RIGHT : TREE;
        end record;
```

Figure 17.3.1 Concluded.

There would be no insert operation. The operation ADD_KEY_DATA would do a search for a node with a given key. If there were no such node, one would be created, the key inserted, and the data would be the first item on the queue. If a node with the given key were present, those data would be added to the end of the queue. Other operations would be added as needed. An inorder iterative traversal to get the next key would be needed as well as an operation to list the data sequentially. The full definition and specification is easy to visualize (see Figure 17.3.2). This book is meant only as an introduction to data types. We described the basic types and some of their variations, but the coverage is hardly exhaustive. Most abstract data types fall into three categories: generalizations, specializations, and advanced applications.

A map is a specialization of a set. An element is either in or not in a set. Sets do not cover the case of an item being in the set several times. Consider a shopping list. If the list is a set, the

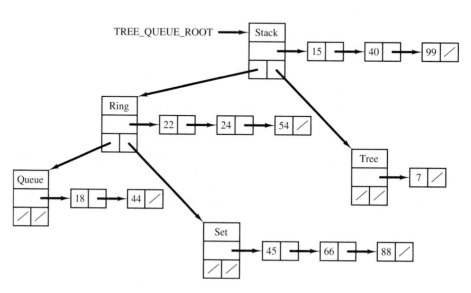

Figure 17.3.2 Tree queue that uses the structure in Figure 17.3.1.

"apples" could be one apple or a dozen. Removing an apple and eating it leaves other apples in the bag. A set cannot handle this scenario, but a map can. An example of an advanced application is the virtual memory manager in many modern operating systems. This application must keep track of all memory allocated to any user or system utility active on a computer. Finally, the binary search tree is a specialization of the general *m*-way tree.

17.4 THE NEXT STEP

The purpose of this book is to introduce the concept of the abstract data type within the framework of Ada to the reader. Hopefully, the book will stand alone as a basic reference. The case studies provided examples of advanced programming, but this is not a textbook in advanced programming. A course in advanced programming cannot be taught without using abstract data types. All the abstract data types covered in this book were encapsulated within a package. This encapsulation is a major principle of software engineering, but it is only a small part.

Abstract data structures serve as a good introduction to the power of abstraction. One lesson that mathematics teaches is that the abstract general solution is often easier to find than a particular solution. The method is simple. First, restate the problem in its abstract setting, then solve the restated problem in that setting, and finally, extrapolate the particular solution from the general solution. The manipulation of data types is often stated in the abstract setting. A queue is a queue is a queue. Whenever there is a need for a queue, it is easier to instantiate the proper ITEM_TYPE into the proper abstract data type than it is to develop a separate new, but functionally equivalent, queue.

An exhaustive study of this book would have created a library of abstract data types, but this library is not complete or exhaustive. Consider the case of the queue as outlined in Figure 17.4.1. Queues can be bounded or unbounded. Queues can store an item or they can store a key-data pair with operations for updating the data. The standard definition of a queue grants access only to the front element. In some applications, memory management, for example, it is necessary to examine every node. Thus operations to iterate through a queue are often necessary. Counting all possible combinations yields a minimum of 48 possible variations of the ADT queue.

1. Two choices of storage: bounded versus unbounded.
2. Three choices for inserting items into a queue: queues versus dequeues versus priority queues.
3. Two choices for removing an item from a queue: queue versus balking queue
4. Two choices on storage: item versus key-data
5. Two choices on iteration: iterated versus noniterated

Figure 17.4.1 Sample catalog of 48 queues. Total variations = 48 = 2 * 3 * 2 * 2 * 2.

There are commercial libraries of Ada abstract data types developed as generic packages available. Figure 17.4.2 lists the partial contents of the Grady Booch library. In addition, the Booch library has many generic algorithms for sorting, searching, and other applications. The Meridian Ada complier even comes with a small subset of the Booch library.

Stacks	26 types
Lists	8 types
Strings	26 types
Queues	92 types
Rings	26 types
Maps	58 types
Sets	34 types
Bags	34 types
Trees	16 types
Graphs	8 types

Total types sampled, 328

Figure 17.4.2   Concluded.

The Introduction opened with the assertion that

Programming = Abstract Data Types + Algorithms

The case studies presented at the ends of the chapters stressed fundamental algorithms operating on the abstract data types developed in this book. The goal was clear, simple, powerful applications. The next step in this process is the development of an understanding of the fundamental algorithms of computer science followed by a rigorous introduction to the methods and discipline of software engineering. Finally, practice and experience will yield the insights and discipline of a professional programmer, as discussed in Chapter 5.

What issues have been avoided? The main issue that was avoided was how Ada handles memory deallocation. When a stack is popped, a STACK_NODE is dereferenced. What happens to this STACK_NODE? There are several explicit ways of handling this situation. One way is to maintain a list of available nodes within a package. Whenever a new STACK_NODE is needed, the list is first checked to see if it is empty. If it is empty, the "new" operator allocates a new STACK_NODE. If it is not empty, a once-used STACK_NODE is recycled. The other method is to deallocate the STACK_NODE explicitly by using the Ada generic procedure UNCHECKED_DEALLOCATION (see Ada LRM 13.10.1). A second issue that was avoided was systematic validation of the abstract data types. This issue is beyond the scope of this introduction.

The first revision of Ada, called Ada 9X, will make Ada a fully object-oriented language. The usefulness of the ADT packages will be enhanced further when full inheritance comes to Ada.

NOTES AND REFERENCES

The Booch library is described in Booch [8]. Many books provide an introduction to more data types, including Kruse [31], Naps [39], and Weiss [49]. None of the latter texts are Ada based, but each has additional topics, types, and structures not covered in this book.

A

Summary of Ada Attributes for Scalar Types

To write general routines, Ada has required that most types have attributes. The reason for attributes is that many features of Ada, such as the range of an integer or the number of significant digits in the float type, are implementation dependent. To help the programmer overcome these limitations, Ada has attributes. Annex A of the Ada LRM contains a complete summary of attributes.

Scalar types include the integer types, the enumeration types, and the real types. All scalar types or subtypes have the following two attributes, where T is the name of any scalar type or subtype:

T'first   Lower bound of T. The value of this attribute is the same type or subtype as T.

T'last   Upper bound of T.

Examples:integer'first, boolean'last

Discrete types include the integer and the enumerated types. They do not include the real types. Besides the integer type, most Ada implementations include a short_integer and a long_integer type. Integer type and subtype definitions are of the form

```
type NEW_TYPE is range L..R;
subtype NEW_TYPE is integer_type range L..R;
```

where new_type and integer_type are valid Ada identifiers and L and R are discrete values.

For discrete types the following attributes are really functions. Constraint_error exceptions are raised if the argument is not defined.

T'pos(X)   The parameter X is of type T. The result is an integer. The result is the position number of the value of X when the values of T are enumerated.

T'val(X)   The parameter X can be of any integer type. The result is of type T and corresponds to the value whose position number is X.

T'succ(X)   The parameter X and the result are of type T. The result is the next value in the enumeration after X. X cannot be T'last.

T'pred(X)   The parameter X and the result are of type T. The result is the previous or preceding value in the enumeration before X. X cannot be T'first.

T'image(X) The parameter X is of type T. The result is of string type. The result is the character image that would be printed by a printer or displayed on a screen after a string "put" call.

T'value(X) The parameter X is a string that is in values assumed by variables of type T. All leading and trailing blanks are ignored. The result is of type T. This attribute converts the string to the literal.

Real types include numeric types with decimal points. Besides float, most Ada implementations have the built-in extensions Short_float and Long_float. A floating-point type and subtype are defined by

```
type T is digits D;
type TT is digits dd range L..R;
subtype TTT is some_floating_type digits D;
subtype TTT is some_floating_type digits D range L..R;
```

The following are attributes of real types.

T'digits Yields an integer equal to the number of decimal digits of T.

T'mantissa Yields an integer equal to the number of binary bits used to hold the decimal part of the type T.

T'epsilon Yields a float number equal to the absolute value between 1.0 and the next model number of type T larger than 1.0.

T'emax Yields an integer equal to the largest exponent.

T'small Yields a float equal to the smallest positive value of type T.

T'large Yields the largest positive number of subtype T.

Not defined are the attributes SIZE and ADDRESS, which are implementation dependent.

B

ADTs in this Book

The following is a list of ADTs by name, documentation, and package specification.

ADT NAME	ADT DOCUMENTATION	ADT PACKAGE SPECIFICATION
RATIONAL		Exercise 3.1.8
COMPLEX		Figure 3.1.6
GENERIC_COMPLEX		Figure 3.3.4
GENERIC_UNBOUNDED_LIST	Figure 5.5.3	Figure 5.5.4
GENERIC_BOUNDED_LIST		Figure 5.5.8
GENERIC_BOUNDED_STACK	Figure 6.1.1	Figure 6.2.2
		Figure 6.2.4
GENERIC_UNBOUNDED_STACK		Figure 6.3.1
GENERIC_UNBOUNDED_QUEUE	Figure 7.1.1	Figure 7.3.2
GENERIC_BOUNDED_QUEUE	Figure 7.1.1	Figure 7.2.3
		Exercise 7.2.2
		Exercise 7.2.3
		Exercise 7.2.4
GENERIC_UNBOUNDED_BALKING_QUEUE		Figure 7.4.3
GENERIC_UNBOUNDED_DEQUE		Figure 7.4.2
GENERIC_UNBOUNDED_ PRIORITY_QUEUE	Figure 7.5.4	Figure 7.5.5
GENERIC_UNBOUNDED_PRIORITY_BALKING_QUEUE		Figure 8.7.1
		Figure 7.5.7
GENERIC_UNBOUNDED_TREE	Figure 8.1.6	Figure 8.1.7
GENERIC_UNBOUNDED_BINARY_SEARCH_TREE	Figure 8.2.2	Figure 8.2.3
GENERIC_UNBOUNDED_BALANCED_BINARY_SEARCH_TREE		Figure 8.2.3
GENERIC_BOUNDED_BALANCED_BINARY_SEARCH_TREE		Figure 8.4.5
GENERIC_UNBOUNDED_M_WAY_ SEARCH_TREE	Figure 8.5.4	Figure 8.5.5
GENERIC_BOUNDED_SEARCH_TREE	Figure 8.6.2	Figure 8.6.3
GENERIC_DISCRETE_SET	Figure 9.1.1	Figure 9.2.1
GENERIC_UNBOUNDED_SET		Figure 9.3.1
		Figure 9.3.2

C

Special Functions and Procedures

C.1. UNIFORMLY DISTRIBUTED RANDOM NUMBER

A number is uniformly distributed over an interval $[a,b]$ if any number in the interval is equally likely to be returned. Computer-generated numbers are really pseudorandom or cyclic. Hopefully, the cycle is long enough that the numbers do not start to repeat. The procedure SET_SEED allows for getting the same sequence again. Different seeds start the sequence at different points. This procedure is sometimes important in simulation when it is desirable to get the same sequence of events for different simulations. The function SELECT_INTEGER returns a random integer in the range low..high. The picking of the seed is often critical. The seed in this routine has been chosen so as not to raise a numeric_error when using the Meridian Ada compiler, where long_integer'last = 2147483647. For more details, see Pike and Hill [41]

```
generic
  SEED  : long_integer := 13421773;
  LOWER : float := 0.0;
  UPPER : float := 1.0;
package UNIFORM_RANDOM is
  procedure SET_SEED ( S : in     long_integer );
  function RANDOM return float;
  function SELECT_INTEGER (LOW, HIGH : integer) return integer;
end UNIFORM_RANDOM;

package body UNIFORM_RANDOM is

  X, Y, FACTOR : long_integer;

  procedure SET_SEED (S : in long_integer ) is
  begin
    Y := S;
  end SET_SEED;

  function RANDOM return float is
  begin
```

```
      Y := Y * FACTOR;
      Y := Y rem X;
      return float(Y)/float(X) * (UPPER - LOWER) + LOWER;
   end RANDOM;

   function SELECT_INTEGER (LOW, HIGH : integer) return integer is
   begin
      return integer (Random * float (HIGH - LOW)) + LOW;
   end SELECT_INTEGER;

begin
   Y := SEED;
   X := 67108864;
   FACTOR := 25;
end UNIFORM_RANDOM;
```

The value X is really $2**26$. For this value, Y will be some odd long_integer in the range 1 .. X–1. The seed must be odd and less than X. Factor can be any odd number not divisible by 2 as long as FACTOR∗X <long_integer'last. If this condition is not met, a numeric_error will eventually arise.

These are not the only values of Y, X, and FACTOR allowed, but these are suitable. The designing of random number generators with long periods is as much an art as a science (see Press et al. [42]).

C.2. NORMALLY DISTRIBUTED RANDOM NUMBER

The function NORMAL_RANDOM returns a normally distributed random number with specified mean and standard deviation. The normal distribution is the basis of the bell-shaped grading curve that many students fear. Note that the package UNIFORM_RANDOM must be instantiated with its range set to [0,1].

```
package MY_RANDOM is new UNIFORM_RANDOM; use MY_RANDOM;


function NORM_RANDOM ( MEAN, SIGMA : float) return float is

  SUM :float := 0.0;

begin
  for i in integer range 1..12 loop
    SUM := SUM + RANDOM;
  end loop;
  return MEAN + SIGMA * (SUM - 6.0);
end NORM_Random;
```

This function works because the means of a sample of a uniform distribution are normally distributed. See any intermediate-level statistics text.

C.3. PERMUATION OF *n* DISCRETE OBJECTS

A permutation of a set is a listing of the set where the order of appearance within the set must be taken into account. A set of *n* objects can be expressed in *n*! ways if order is taken into account. The following procedure, which is due to Peck and Schrack [40], systematically returns the next permutation while keeping track of the permutations already returned.

```
generic
  SIZE : positive;
  type ITEM_TYPE is (<>);
  type NEXT is array (positive range <>) of ITEM_TYPE;
package PERMUTATION is
  procedure PERMUTE ( X : in out NEXT );
end PERMUTATION;
package body PERMUTATION is
  type P_ARRAY is array ( positive range 2..Size ) of natural;
  FLAG : boolean := true;
  P    : P_ARRAY;

  procedure INITIALIZE is
  begin
    for INDEX in P'range loop
      P(INDEX) := INDEX;
    end loop;
  end INITIALIZE;

  Procedure PERMUTE ( X : in out NEXT ) is
    TEMP : ITEM_TYPE;
  begin
    if FLAG then
      INITIALIZE;
      FLAG := false;
    end if;
    for INDEX in 2..SIZE loop
      TEMP := X(1);
      X(1..(INDEX-1) := X(2..INDEX);
      X(INDEX) := TEMP;
      P(INDEX) := P(INDEX) -1;
      if P(INDEX) /= 0 then
        FLAG := false;
        exit;
      else
        FLAG := true;
        P(INDEX) := INDEX;
      end if;
    end loop;
  end PERMUTE;
end PERMUTATION;
```

Figure C.3.1   Procedure to generate permutations systematically.

The procedure PERMUTE initializes itself every SIZE n! calls. At every call the items in the vector X are permuted and returned. The vector P keeps track of what permutations have been returned. Note that this package allows the systematic generation of an exhaustive search of all possible orderings of SIZE objects. The vector X can hold any discrete type.

Another situation that often arises is the need to generate random permutations of a set. Suppose that test cases for a new sorting procedure need to be developed. One strategy would be to take an already sorted vector and generate a random permutation. Obviously, the random permutation should not depend on the input. The same input (e.g., a sorted vector) should produce distinct permutations. The procedure PERMUTE in Figure C.3.1 cannot be used because it generates a systematic permutation. If the test vector for the sort routines is 1000 long, there are 1000! permutations.

If SELECT_INTEGER (I,J) from the package UNIFORM_RANDOM is used to return a random integer between I and J with uniform probability, the simple loop in Figure C.3.2 generates a random permutation of a vector V.

```
for INDEX in 2..N loop
   SWAP ( V(1), V (SELECT_RANDOM(1,INDEX)) );
end loop;
```

Figure C.3.2   Method to permute an arbitrary vector.

C.4 COMBINATION OF *k* FROM A GROUP OF *n* OBJECTS

A combination is a group where the order of enumeration is not important. The sequences *abc* and *bac* are different permutations but they are the same combination. Given a positive number *n* and a second positive number *m* <= *n*, the number of distinct groupings of *m* objects out of *n* is given by the binomial coefficient.

$$\binom{n}{m} = \frac{n!}{m!* \ (n-m)!}$$

The need to generate combinations of possibilities arises in a wide variety of applications. Many states have institutionalized lotteries where *m* numbers are selected out of *n* possibilities. All lucky players who selected all *m* drawn numbers share equally in the total prize, which has exceeded $100 million. It is a rather simple procedure to select a random group of *m* out of *n* objects. Every element in a boolean array of *n* elements is initialized to false. A random number generator is used to set *m* distinct indexes to true. If V is a vector of boolean indexed from 1 to N, the procedure might be implemented as follows:

```
procedure RANDOM_M_OUT_OF_N( V : in out VECTOR;
                             N : in     positive;
                             M : in     positive ) is
   COUNT : integer := 0;
   J     : integer;
begin
   V := ( others => false );
   while COUNT < M loop
      J := SELECT_INTEGER(1,N);
      if not V(J) then
         V(J) := true;
```

```
      COUNT := COUNT + 1;
    end if;
  end loop;
end RANDOM_M_OUT_OF_N;
```

SELECT_INTEGER(I,J) is an integer-valued function that returns a random integer between I and J. This algorithm will not systematically generate all combinations of m out of n objects. It would be suitable in sampling problems. For example, a company makes a specialized part. The tests that determine if this part meets its specifications destroy the part. Total testing is clearly out of the question. A random method to select a sample is needed. If the sample meets the acceptance criteria, the lot is accepted. If the sample fails the test, the lot is rejected. The random procedure above could be used to select the items to be tested.

Some applications require that all possible groups be generated systematically. Suppose that a tournament is being organized. N players have entered the tournament but the table holds only M players. Tournament rules require that every player must compete against every combination of opponents. A program that systematically generates all playing combinations is needed. One method would be to try to convert the permutation procedure to generate combinations. As an example of one strategy, consider the case of trying to generate groups of $m = 3$ integers out of a group of $n = 7$ integers. Since permutations generate groupings where the enumerated order is important, it seems that the only thing you would have to do is devise a strategy that uniquely picks out a new grouping. Figure C.4.1(a) shows a situation where the first three integers are different permutations but the same combination. One method is to pick out the new group whenever its permutation is in ascending order. Only one $n = 7$ integer grouping has the first $m = 3$ integers in order. But Figure C.4.1(b) implies that each m = 3 grouping has $4! = 24$ integer groupings following it with the same $m = 3$ first grouping. The heuristic can be extended to repeat looking until both the first $m = 3$ and the last $n - m = 4$ length slices are in order. If VECTOR_IN_ORDER is a boolean-valued function, the loop in Figure C.4.1c will detect a new group from repeated calls to the procedure PERMUTE in Section C.3.

| (3,4,5,1,6,2,7) | (3,5,4,1,6,2,7) | (4,3,5,1,6,2,7) |
| (4,5,3,1,6,2,7) | (5,4,3,1,6,2,7) | (5,3,4,1,6,2,7) |

(a)

(3,4,5,1,2,6,7)	(3,4,5,1,2,7,6)	(3,4,5,1,7,2,6)
(3,4,5,1,7,6,2)	(3,4,5,1,6,2,7)	(3,4,5,1,6,7,2)
(3,4,5,2,1,6,7)	(3,4,5,2,1,7,6)	(3,4,5,2,7,1,6)
(3,4,5,2,7,1,6)	(3,4,5,2,6,7,1)	(3,4,5,2,6,1,7)
(3,4,5,6,1,2,7)	(3,4,5,6,1,7,2)	(3,4,5,6,2,1,7)
(3,4,5,6,2,7,1)	(3,4,5,6,7,1,2)	(3,4,5,6,7,2,1)
(3,4,5,7,1,2,6)	(3,4,5,7,1,6,2)	(3,4,5,7,2,1,6)
(3,4,5,7,2,6,1)	(3,4,5,7,6,1,2)	(3,4,5,7,6,2,1)

(b)

Figure C.4.1 (a) Six different permutations with same first three combinations.
(b) Twenty-four different permutations with same first three integers. **(c)** Procedure to generate all combinations of M out of N. Continues on page 577.

```
                procedure M_OUT_OF_N ( m : in      integer;
                                       n : in      integer;
                                       X : in out Vector ) is
            begin
              PERMUTE(X);
              while (not VECTOR_IN_ORDER(X(1..m)) or
                    (not VECTOR_IN_ORDER(X(m+1..n)) loop
                PERMUTE(X);
              end loop;
            end M_OUT_OF_N;
```

(c)

Figure C.4.1 Concluded.

Although the procedure M_OUT_OF_N in Figure C.4.1(c) works, it has enormous computational overhead. For the case of $m = 3$ and $n = 7$, it makes on average $m!*(n - m)! = 3!*4! = 144$ calls to PERMUTE for each combination generated. For $m = 3$ and $n = 10$, $m!* (n - m)! = 3!*7! = 6*5040 = 30,240$ subroutine calls are made to permute.

Several algorithms have been developed to generate combinations directly. Figure C.4.2 lists one such method (see Kurtzberg [32]). After all combinations have been returned, the process starts again. This procedure generates the next combination of n integers taken m at a time. The arguments are m, n, and a vector type with an integer index from 1 to n that contains the preceding combination. The m integers in the vector slice J(1) through J(m) range in value from 0 through $n - 1$. They are enumerated as a monotonically increasing sequence, both at input and output. If the vector J is set to 0, the first combination produced is $n - m, n - m + 1, \ldots, n - 1$. This same initial value is produced after $0, 1, 2, \ldots, n - 1$, which is the last value in the cycle. If m is not a proper value, no action is taken.

As an application, support that $n = 52$, the number of cards in a deck of cards. A brute-force method of determining a card game strategy is to generate all hands and compare them to a fixed hand. The probability of generating a winning hand compared to the given hand can be determined.

```
            type VECTOR is array (positive range <>) of integer;

            procedure M_OUT_OF_N(M, N : in      integer;
                                 C      : in out VECTOR) is
              --This procedure assumes C'first=1 and C'last=n
              A, B, L : integer := 1;
              DONE : boolean := false;
            begin
              if M <= N and M > 1 then
                while not DONE and B<=N loop
                  if C(B) >= B then
                    A := C(B) - B - 1;
                    for L in 1..B loop
                      C(L) := L+A;
```

Figure C.4.2 Procedure to generate systematically m out of n combinations of integers in the range $0 \ldots n - 1$. Continues on page 578.

Special Functions and Procedures   Appendix C

```
        end loop;
          DONE:=true;
      elsif B=M then
        for bb in 1..M loop
          C(bb) := n-M-1+bb;
        end loop;
      else
        B := B + 1;
      end if;
    end loop;
  end if;
end M_OUT_OF_N;
```

Figure C.4.2   Concluded.

D

Example of an Ada Procedure to Check an ADT against Its Specification

The Ada procedure that follows tests all the requirements listed in Figure 5.5.3 against a package UNBOUNDED_LIST_ADT. This procedure is by no means exhaustive. The first test of an ADT package is answered by the question, "Does it compile without errors or warnings?" All that is guaranteed by a yes answer is that the Ada code does not have any syntax errors, so more testing is needed. After the generic package has compiled error free, the next step is to read the code and compare it against the ADT requirements. Are all required operations in the package? Are all exceptions properly handled? Does each operation conform to the requirements? The next step would be to set aside the generic package and write a simple test program that uses the generic package. The only guide to writing this test program, other than experience, is the list of ADT requirements.

Experience has taught the author that testing of linear structures requires that an empty list, a list with exactly one item in it, and a list with more than one item in it are the basic testing structures. Experience has also taught that those operations that have the potential to combine or meld two structures, creating a third, must be examined carefully. For this reason, CATENATE and SWAP_TAIL are examined to see if circular references can result.

Building any test procedure is a bootstrap process. There is often an operation that must be assumed correct. It is often an operation that builds the objects being created. The procedure that is shown below is a case in point. The operation ADD_ITEM_TO_HEAD is assumed correct. The operation ADD_ITEM_TO_HEAD cannot be validated first by using any other operation that has previously been validated, for the simple reason that any list that is created must use ADD_ITEM_TO_HEAD. For the ADT list, ADD_ITEM_TO_HEAD is used as a primitive.

Each operation's function is tested in a separate procedure. Any operation that might generate an exception is tested twice, once for function and once to see if the exception is properly raised. Comments have been added where appropriate.

```
with text_io; use text_io;
with GENERIC_UNBOUNDED_LIST;

procedure LIST_TST is

package CHAR_LIST is new with GENERIC_UNBOUNDED_LIST; (character); use CHAR_LIST;
```

```
EMPTY_LIST, ONE_ELEMENT_LIST, FIVE_ELEMENT_LIST : LIST;

procedure BUILD_LISTS is
begin
  --ONE_ELEMENT_LIST ->'A'
  ADD_ITEM_TO_HEAD(ONE_ELEMENT_LIST, 'A');
  --FIVE_ELEMENT_LIST ->'A'->'B'->'C'->'D'->'E'
  ADD_ITEM_TO_HEAD(FIVE_ELEMENT_LIST, 'E');
  ADD_ITEM_TO_HEAD(FIVE_ELEMENT_LIST, 'D');
  ADD_ITEM_TO_HEAD(FIVE_ELEMENT_LIST, 'C');
  ADD_ITEM_TO_HEAD(FIVE_ELEMENT_LIST, 'B');
  ADD_ITEM_TO_HEAD(FIVE_ELEMENT_LIST, 'A');
end BUILD_LISTS;

procedure TEST_LIST_EMPTY is
begin
  if not EMPTY(EMPTY_LIST) then
    put_line("EMPTY fails for an empty list!");
  elsif EMPTY(ONE_ELEMENT_LIST) then
    put_line("Either EMPTY fails on nonempty list");
    put_line("or ADD_ITEM_TO_HEAD has failed.");
  else
    put_line("List_empty passes!");
  end if;
end TEST_LIST_EMPTY;

procedure TEST_LIST_LENGTH is
begin
  if not (LENGTH(EMPTY_LIST) = 0) then
    put_line("LENGTH fails for an empty list.");
  elsif not (LENGTH(ONE_ELEMENT_LIST) = 1) then
    put_line("LENGTH fails for a one element list,");
  elsif not (LENGTH(FIVE_ELEMENT_LIST) = 5) then
    put_line("LENGTH fails for a five element list,");
    put_line("or ADD_ITEM_TO_HEAD has failed.");
  else
    put_line("LENGTH passes!");
  end if;
end TEST_LIST_LENGTH;

procedure TEST_LISTS_EQUAL is
begin
  if not EQUAL(EMPTY_LIST, EMPTY_LIST) then
    put_line ("EQUAL fails for two empty lists!");
  elsif not EQUAL(ONE_ELEMENT_LIST, ONE_ELEMENT_LIST) then
    put_line("Either EQUAL fails for two one element lists");
    put_line("or ADD_ITEM_TO_HEAD has failed.");
  elsif not EQUAL(FIVE_ELEMENT_LIST, FIVE_ELEMENT_LIST) then
    put_line("EQUAL fails for two five element lists list!");
  elsif EQUAL(ONE_ELEMENT_LIST, EMPTY_LIST) then
    put_line("EQUAL fails for one empty, one nonempty list");
```

```
    elseif EQUAL(ONE_ELEMENT_LIST, FIVE_ELEMENT_LIST) then
      put_line("EQUAL fails for two distinct nonempty list");
    else
      put_line("EQUAL passes!");
    end if; end TEST_LISTS_EQUAL;

procedure TEST_CLEAR is
  T1 : List := ONE_ELEMENT_LIST:
  T5 : LIST := FIVE_ELEMENT_LIST;
begin
  CLEAR(T1);
  CLEAR(T5);
  if EMPTY(T1) and EMPTY(T5) then
    put_line("CLEAR passes!");
  else
    put_line("CLEAR fails!");
  end if;
end TEST_CLEAR;

procedure TEST_HEAD_AND_TAIL_OF_LIST is
begin
  if HEAD_OF_LIST(FIVE_ELEMENT_LIST) /= 'A' then
    put_line("HEAD_OF_LIST fails");
  else
    put_line("HEAD_OF_LIST passes");
  end if;
  if HEAD_OF_LIST(TAIL_OF_LIST(FIVE_ELEMENT_LIST)) /= 'B' then
    put_line("TAIL_OF_LIST fails");
  else
    put_line("TAIL_OF_LIST passes");
  end if;
end TEST_HEAD_AND_TAIL_OF_LIST;

procedure TEST_COPY is
  T0, T1, T5 : LIST;
begin
  COPY(EMPTY_LIST, T0);
  COPY(ONE_ELEMENT_LIST, T1);
  COPY(FIVE_ELEMENT_LIST, T5);
  if ONE_ELEMENT_LIST = T1 or FIVE_ELEMENT_LIST = T5 then
    put_line("COPY fails! Lists must be distinct");
  elsif EQUAL(EMPTY_LIST, T0) and
    EQUAL(ONE_ELEMENT_LIST, T1) and
    EQUAL(FIVE_ELEMENT_LIST, T5) then
    put_line("COPY passes!");
  else
    put_line("COPY fails!");
  end if;
end TEST_COPY;

procedure TEST_CATENATE is
  T0, T1, T5 : LIST;
```

```
      FLAG : boolean := true;
  begin
    COPY(ONE_ELEMENT_LIST, T1);
    COPY(FIVE_ELEMENT_LIST, T5);
    --Test for circular list when concatenated onto itself
    CATENATE(T1, T1);
    if not EQUAL(TAIL_OF_LIST(TAIL_OF_LIST(T1)),EMPTY_LIST) then
      put("CATENATE fails! Circular list without end");
      put_line(" has been created ");
      put_line(" by catenating a list onto itself.");
      FLAG := false;
    end if;
    if flag then
      CLEAR(T1);
      COPY(ONE_ELEMENT_LIST, T1);
      CATENATE(T1, T0);
      CATENATE(T0, T1);
      CATENATE(T5, T1);
      if EQUAL(T0, T1) and then LENGTH(T5) = 6 then
        put_line("CATENATE passes!");
      else
        put_line("CATENATE fails!");
      end if;
    end if;
  end TEST_CATENATE;

  procedure TEST_SWAP_TAIL is
    T0, T1, T4, T5, TEMP : LIST;
  begin
    COPY(ONE_ELEMENT_LIST, T1);
    COPY(FIVE_ELEMENT_LIST, T5);
    SWAP_TAIL(T1, T5);
    if TAIL_OF_LIST(T5) = EMPTY_LIST and
       EQUAL(T1, FIVE_ELEMENT_LIST) then
      put_line ("SWAP_TAIL passes first test");
    else
      put_line("SWAP_TAIL fails first test");
    end if;
    --circular reference possible if SWAP_TAIL follows concatenation
    ADD_ITEM_TO_HEAD(TEMP, 'A');
    ADD_ITEM_TO_HEAD(TEMP, 'A');
    COPY(TEMP, T1);
    CATENATE(TEMP, T1);
    ADD_ITEM_TO_HEAD(T4, 'A');
    ADD_ITEM_TO_HEAD(T4, 'A');
    ADD_ITEM_TO_HEAD(T4, 'A');
    ADD_ITEM_TO_HEAD(T4, 'A');
    --T4, Temp both length 4, all 'A'
    --T1 length 2 all 'A'
    SWAP_TAIL(TEMP, T1);
```

```
    --if correct, T1 has length 4, Temp length 2, T1 = T4
    if EQUAL(T1, T4) and then LENGTH(TEMP) = 2 then
      put_line("SWAP_TAIL passes second test.");
    else
      put_line("SWAP_TAIL fails second test. Circular reference ");
      put_line("is generated when SWAP_TAIL follows concatenation.");
    end if;
end TEST_SWAP_TAIL;

procedure TEST_EXCEPTION_LIST_NULL is
  TEMP : LIST;
  CHAR : character;

  function SWAP_TEST(L1, L2: List) return boolean is
    T1 : LIST := L1;
    T2 : LIST := L2;
  begin
    SWAP_TAIL(T1,T2);
    return false;
    exception
      when LIST_NULL => return true;
  end SWAP_TEST;
begin
  --define individual blocks to localize exceptions
  begin
    TEMP := TAIL_OF_LIST(TEMP);
    put_line("LIST_NULL exception not raised by TAIL_OF_LIST.");
    exception
      when LIST_NULL =>;
      put("List_null exception correctly raised by ");
      put_line("TAIL_OF_LIST.");
  end;
  begin
    CHAR := HEAD_OF_LIST(TEMP);
    put_line("LIST_NULL exception not raised by HEAD_OF_LIST.");
    exception
      when LIST_NULL =>
          put("LIST_NULL exception corrected raised by ");
          put_line("HEAD_OF_LIST.");
  end;
  if SWAP_TEST(TEMP, ONE_ELEMENT_LIST) and
     SWAP_TEST(ONE_ELEMENT_LIST, TEMP) and
     SWAP_TEST(TEMP, EMPTY_LIST) then
    put("LIST_NULL exception correctly raised by ");
    put_line("SWAP_TAIL.");
  else
    put_line("LIST_NULL exception not raised by Swap_Tail.");
  end if;
end TEST_EXCEPTION_LIST_NULL;
```

```
begin
   put("This procedure does basic testing of the generic package ");
   put_line("GENERIC_UNBOUNDED_LIST.");
   put_line("WARNING! The procedure ADD_ITEM_TO_HEAD is used as a ");
   put_line("primitive and it is not directly tested.");
   BUILD_LISTS; --also tests Add_item_to_head
   TEST_LIST_EMPTY;
   TEST_LIST_LENGTH;
   TEST_CLEAR;
   TEST_LISTS_EQUAL;
   TEST_HEAD_AND_TAIL_OF_LIST;
   TEST_COPY;
   TEST_CATENATE;
   TEST_SWAP_TAIL;
   TEST_EXCEPTION_LIST_NULL;
end LIST_TST;
```

The procedure LIST_TST has a subtle flaw if it is used to test a bounded list. The "if" statement in the procedure TEST_COPY

```
         if ONE_ELEMENT_LIST = T1 or FIVE_ELEMENT_LIST = T5 then
```

is designed to test and make sure that in the case of an unbounded list implemented as a linked list, COPY is not a simple assignment statement. In the bounded case that uses an array to store a list, a simple assignment statement defines a distinct list, yet the test above fails. The type list is private, so testing for equality is allowed. If the procedure TEST_COPY is replaced by

```
         procedure TEST_COPY is
            T0, T1, T5 : List;
         begin
            COPY(EMPTY_LIST, T0);
            COPY(ONE_ELEMENT_LIST, T1);
            COPY(FIVE_ELEMENT_LIST, T5);
            --add and remove front element to see if the same list results
            ADD_ITEM_TO_HEAD(T1, 'Z');
            ADD_ITEM_TO_HEAD(T5, 'Z');
            T1 := TAIL_OF_LIST(T1);
            T5 := TAIL_OF_LIST(T5);
            if ONE_ELEMENT_LIST = T1 or FIVE_ELEMENT_LIST = T5 then
               put_line("COPY fails! Lists must be distinct");
            elsif EQUAL(EMPTY_LIST, T0) and
                  EQUAL(ONE_ELEMENT_LIST, T1) and
                  EQUAL(FIVE_ELEMENT_LIST, T5) then
               put_line(:"COPY passes!");
            else
                put_line("COPY fails!");
            end if;
         end TEST_COPY;
```

then TEST_COPY will work in both cases.

Bibliography

1. *Reference Manual for the Ada Programming Language,* ANSI/MIL-STD-1815A-1983. Washington, D.C.: U.S. Department of Defense, 1983.

2. Adelson-Velskii, G. M., and E. M. Landis, *Doklady Akademia Nauk SSSR,* Vol. 146 (1962), pp. 263–266. [English translation in *Soviet Math,* Vol. 3 (1963), pp. 1259–1263.]

3. Aho, A., J. Hopcroft, and J. Ullman, *The Design and Analysis of Computer Algorithms.* Reading, Mass.: Addison-Wesley, 1974.

4. Baase, S. *Computer Algorithms,* 2nd ed. Englewood Cliffs, N.J.: Prentice Hall, 1988.

5. Barnes, J. *Programming in Ada Plus Language Reference Manual,* 3rd ed. Reading, Mass.: Addison-Wesley, 1991.

6. Bayer, R., and E. McCreight, "Organization and Maintenance of Large Ordered Indexes," *Acta Informatica,* Vol. 1 (1972), pp. 173–189.

7. Booch, G., *Software Engineering with Ada,* 2nd ed. Redwood City, Calif.: Benjamin-Cummings, 1986.

8. Booch, G., *Software Components with Ada.* Redwood City, Calif.: Benjamin-Cummings, 1987.

9. Boyer, R. S., and J. S. Moore, "A Fast String Searching Algorithm," *Communications of the ACM,* Vol. 20, No. 10 (1977), pp. 762–772.

10. Brookshear, J. G., *Theory of Computation: Formal Languages, Automata, and Complexity.* Redwood City, Calif.: Benjamin-Cummings, 1989.

11. Bryan, D., and G. Mendal, *Exploring Ada,* Vols. 1 and 2. Englewood Cliffs, N.J.: Prentice Hall, 1992.

12. Cheney, W., and D. Kincaid, *Numerical Mathematics and Computing,* 2nd ed. Pacific Grove, Calif.: Brooks/Cole, 1985.

13. Comer, D., "The Ubiquitous B-Tree," *Computing Surveys,* Vol. 11, No. 2 (1979), pp. 121–137.

14. Degrace, P., and L. H. Stahl, *Wicked Problems, Righteous Solutions.* Englewood Cliffs, N.J.: Yourdon Press, 1990.

15. Dewdney, A. K., "Computer Recreations. On Making and Breaking Codes: Part II," *Scientific American,* November 1988, pp. 142–145.

16. Diffie, W., "The First Ten Years of Public-Key Cryptography," *Proceedings of the IEEE,* Vol. 75, No. 5 (1988), pp. 560–577.

17. Dijkstra, E. W., "A Note on Two Problems in Connexion with Graphs," *Numerishe Mathematik,* Vol. 1 (1959), pp. 269–271.

18. Dijkstra, E. W., *A Discipline of Programming.* Englewood Cliffs, N.J.: Prentice Hall, 1976.

19. Floyd, R. W., "Treesort: Algorithm 113," *Communications of the ACM,* Vol. 5, No. 8 (1962), p. 432.

20. Floyd, R. W., "Treesort: Algorithm 243," *Communications of the ACM,* Vol. 7, No. 12 (1964), p. 701.
21. Gardner, M., *Penrose Tiles to Trapdoor Ciphers.* New York: W.H. Freeman, 1989.
22. Hillam, B., "A Generalization of Krasnoselski's Theorem on the Real Line," *Mathematics Magazine,* Vol. 48, No. 3 (1978), p. 167.
23. Hoare, C. A. R., "Quicksort," *Computer Journal,* Vol. 5, No. 1 (1962), pp. 10–15.
24. Johnson, K., E. Simmons, and F. Stluka, *Ada Quality and Style: Guidelines for Professional Programmers.* Herndon, Va.: Software Productivity Consortium, 1991.
25. Kahn, D., *The Codebreakers: The Story of Secret Writing.* New York: Macmillan, 1967.
26. Karp, R. M., and M. O. Rabin, *Efficient Randomized Pattern Mathing Algorithms,* Aiken Computer Laboratory Report TR-31-81. Cambridge, Mass.: Harvard University, 1981.
27. Knuth, D. E., *The Art of Computer Programming,* Vol. 1, *Fundamental Algorithms.* Reading, Mass.: Addison-Wesley, 1973.
28. Knuth, D. E., *The Art of Computer Programming,* Vol. 2, *Semi-numerical Algorithms.* Reading, Mass.: Addison-Wesley, 1973.
29. Knuth, D. E., *The Art of Computer Programming,* Vol. 3, *Sorting and Searching.* Reading, Mass.: Addison-Wesley, 1973.
30. Knuth, D. E., J. H. Morris, and V. R. Pratt, "Fast Pattern Matching in Strings," *SIAM Journal of Computing,* Vol. 6, No. 2 (June 1977), pp. 323–349.
31. Kruse, R. L., *Data Structures and Program Design,* 2nd ed. Englewood Cliffs, N.J.: Prentice Hall, 1987.
32. Kurtzberg, J., "Algorithm 94; Combination," in *Collected Algorithms from ACM,* Vol. 1. New York: ACM.
33. Ledgard, H., *Professional Software: Software Engineering Concepts.* Reading, Mass.: Addison-Wesley, 1987.
34. Ledgard, H., *Programming Proverbs.* Rochelle Park, N.J.: Hayden, 1975.
35. McCracken, D., "Programming Languages in the Computer Science Curriculum," *SIGCSE Bulletin,* Vol. 24, No. 1 (March 1992), pp. 1–8.
36. Mauer, W. D., and T. G. Lewis, "Hash Table Methods," *Computing Surveys,* Vol. 7 (1975), pp. 5–20.
37. Meyer, B., *Object Oriented Software Construction.* Englewood Cliffs, N.J.: Prentice Hall, 1988.
38. Miller, N. E., and C. G. Petersen, *File Structures with Ada.* Redwood City, Calif.: Benjamin-Cummings, 1990.
39. Naps, T., *Introduction to Data Structures and Algorithm Analysis,* 2nd ed. St. Paul, Minn.: West Publishing, 1992.
40. Peck, J. E. L., and G. F. Schrack, "Algorithm 86: Permute," in *Collected Algorithms from the ACM,* Vol. 1. New York: ACM.
41. Pike, M. C., and I. D. Hill, "Algorithm 266 : Pseudo-random Numbers," in *Collected Algorithms from ACM,* Vol. 2. New York, N.Y.: ACM.
42. Press, W. H., B. P. Flannery, S. A. Teukolsky, and W. T. Vetterling, *Numerical Recipes: The Art of Scientific Programming.* New York: Cambridge University Press, 1989.
43. Savitch, W. J., and C. G. Petersen, *Ada: An Introduction to the Art and Science of Programming.* Redwood City, Calif.: Benjamin-Cummings, 1992.
44. Sedgewick, R, *Algorithms.* Reading, Mass.: Addison-Wesley, 1983.
45. Shell, D. L., "A Highspeed Sorting Procedure," *Communications of the ACM,* Vol. 2, No. 7 (1959), pp. 30–32.
46. Sommerville, J., *Software Engineering,* 4th ed. Reading, Mass.: Addison-Wesley, 1992.
47. Stewart, G. W., *Introduction to Matrix Computations.* New York: Academic Press, 1973.
48. Volper, D., and M. Katz, *Introduction to Programming Using Ada.* Englewood Cliffs, N.J.: Prentice Hall, 1990.

49. Weiss, M. A. *Data Structures and Algorithm Analysis.* Redwood City, Calif.: Benjamin-Cummings, 1992.
50. Williams, J., "Heapsort: Algorithm 232," *Communications of the ACM,* Vol. 7, No. 6 (1964), pp. 347–348.
51. Wirth, N., *Algorithms + Data Structures = Programs.* Englewood Cliffs, N.J.: Prentice Hall, 1976.
52. Wirth, N., *Algorithms and Data Structures.* Englewood Cliffs, N.J.: Prentice Hall, 1976.

Glossary

Abstract data type Generic data structure and the operations on the generic data structure that encapsulates a user-defined data structure.

Acyclic graph Digraph without any cycles.

Adjacency graph Matrix representation of a graph where the existence of an edge, or an edge weight, is stored as an element in an array.

Algorithm Well-defined sequence of operations that manipulates objects in order to solve a given problem in a finite amount of time.

Attribute Characteristic of the objects in a data type. The attribute is often a value taken on by the object.

AVL tree *See* Balanced tree.

Balanced tree Binary tree where each node of the tree has a left subtree and a right subtree whose height differ by at most one.

Balking Ability to remove a specific object or an object at a specific location from a structure. Most often used with queues.

"Big O" A process is $O(f(n))$, read "Big O of $f(n)$" if there is a constant C and N such that for $n > N$, the process is less than $C*f(n)$. Used when discussing size and performance of a data type and its operations.

Binary Search Divide-and-conquer strategy that examines the midpoint of an array to see which half contains the answer.

Binary search tree Binary tree where every node in the tree has the property that all keys in the left subtree are less than the node's key and all keys in the right subtree are greater than the node's key.

Bounded Structure that can hold a maximum number of components. Most often implemented using an array or other static structure.

Breadth-first search Graph or tree-searching process that examines all nodes adjacent to a given node before visiting any other node.

B-tree Efficient balanced key search structure where each node has a minimum number of key-data pairs.

Bubble sort Sorting algorithm that compares adjacent items and swaps the items if they are out of order.

Bucket Array index of a linked list of key-data pairs in an open hash table.

Circular linked list Sequential linked list where the last item in the list references the first item.

Cluster Result of a collision resolution method in a closed hashing scheme that places key-data pairs with the same initial hash address into a contiguous part of the table.

Component Well-defined object of some data type. Most often used as an "array of components," or a subroutine, package, or part of a program.

COPY Data type operation that reproduces the object.

Correctness Measure of certainty of an algorithm executing as specified.

Cycle Path with nonzero length that starts and ends with the same vertex in a digraph.

Data structure Form of the objects that a data type, algorithm, or program manipulates.

Data type Group of objects or values and the operations on those objects.

Degree of a node In trees, the number of nodes referenced by a given node. In graphs, the number of edges that start or terminate at a given vertex.

DELETE Tree or search table operation that removes an item or key-data pair from a structure.

Depth-first search Strategy to visit all nodes in a graph by searching for a path as long as possible from the starting node.

Deque Linear sequence of objects where new objects can be added at either end of the sequence, but can only be removed from one end.

DEQUEUE Operation that removes an item from the front of the queue and returns it to the program.

Digraph Graph where the initial vertex of an edge is distinguished from the terminal node of an edge.

Dijkstra's algorithm Algorithm to find the shortest path between two nodes.

Directed Denotes an edge of the graph where the order of the endpoints of the edge is important. Typically, action can flow in only one direction on an edge in a digraph.

Discrete Any enumerated or integer type.

Divide and conquer Programming strategy where each problem is divided into two or more simpler subproblems.

Doubly linked list Linear sequential list structure where each node references its predecessor and its successor.

Dynamic Structure whose capacity changes depending on need.

Encapsulate Ability to either hide or control access to a user-supplied type inside a generic type. Private and limited private types are often used to build encapsulated types.

ENQUEUE Queue operation that adds an item to the rear of the queue.

FIFO (first in, first out) Characterization of how items are added and deleted from a queue.

Generic Package or subroutine with formal parameters that serves as a template to meet a program need.

Graph Collection of points or vertices, and the edges or arcs that join the vertices.

Hashing Search strategy that uses a function defined from the key space to the table address space with the goal of placing a key-data pair into its final place as soon as possible.

Heap Portion of computer memory used for allocating dynamic memory requests, or a binary tree implemented as an array where each node's left subtree index has twice its index, and the index of the right subtree is one plus twice the node's index.

Hierarchy Relationship between nodes where one node is viewed as above or with higher priority than the other node.

Indegree of a vertex Number of edges in a digraph that terminate at a given vertex.

Information hiding Package that manipulates information without the program knowing the implementation details of the package.

Inorder traversal Binary tree traversal where every node in the left subtree is recursively processed before the node is processed, and then every node in the right subtree is recursive processed. The inorder traversal lists all keys of a tree in either ascending or descending order.

INSERT Tree or search table operation that adds a key-data pair to a table.

Insertion sort Sort strategy that starts with an empty array and inserts elements into their final place.

Internal sort Any sort algorithm where the array or list being sorted stays in internal memory.

Intersection Set, denoted A*B, whose elements are common to both A and B.

ITEM Any object of ITEM_TYPE.

ITEM_TYPE Name given to a user-supplied data structure that is encapsulated inside an abstract data type.

Iterator Operation that returns an item or key-data pair. Repeated calls will list every item or key-data pair once before listing any item or key-data pair twice.

LIFO (last in, first out) Item access strategy of a stack.

List Abstract data type composed of a linear sequence of zero or more objects of some ITEM_TYPE.

Matrix Collection of data of the same component type arranged as a rectangular grid whose rows and columns have a separate contiguous index of some enumerated range type.

Merge Process of combining lists where the priority is preserved.

Node Structure used to encapsulate an item in a linked list, tree, or graph.

Object Name given to a specific value of some data type.

Operation Action that modifies the value of a data type, or returns an attribute of an object in a data type.

Outdegree of a vertex Number of edges in a digraph that have a particular vertex as their initial vertex.

Pattern matching Operation that examines a contiguous region of a structure for matches.

Pointer Another name for an access value. A pointer references the memory location of another data item.

POP Stack operation that removes and returns an item from the TOP of a stack, or a ring or queue operation that removes an item without returning its value.

Postorder traversal Binary tree traversal where every node's left subtree is recursively processed, then the node's right subtree is recursively processed, and then finally, the node itself is processed.

Preorder traversal Binary tree traversal where the node itself is first processed, then the node's left subtree is recursively processed, and finally, the node's right subtree is recursively processed.

Priority Place that an item or object will occupy after it is inserted into a queue or deque.

Priority queue Linear sequential structure where an item is added to the queue after all items of equal or higher priority but in front of items of lower priority. Items are removed from the front of the queue.

PROPER_SUBSET Denoted $A < B$, A is a proper subset of B if A is a subset of B but A is not equal to B.

PUSH Stack operation that adds a new item on the TOP of the stack.

Queue Linear sequence of items where items can be added at one end, the rear, and removed from the other end, the front.

Random number generator Function that returns a number between 0 and 1 in such a way as repeated calls will be eventually uniformly distributed in [0,1].

Recursion Process that calls itself until it reaches a state not defined in terms of itself.

Relatively prime Two integers are relatively prime if the only positive number that divides both is 1.

Reusable Data type that has been designed to be usable in a variety of applications. Reusable data types are often implemented as generic abstract data types.

Ring Circular sequence of zero or more objects, with one object denoted as the TOP, where every object precedes exactly one object and follows exactly one object.

Sequential Denotes a structure where every object can follow at most one object and precedes at most one object.

Sequential search Sequential examination of all elements in a list, which starts at the first item in the list until a match is found.

Set Collection of objects from some universe where duplication is not allowed.

Software engineering Disciplined approach to software design, implementation, validation, and maintenance with the goal of developing reliable, cost-effective software.

Sort Operation or algorithm that puts items into a specific order.

Sparse Matrix or graph where most of the components have the same value, typically zero.

Specification Visible part of a package, or the requirement that a program component must satisfy.

Stack Linear sequence of items where items are added or deleted from one end of the sequence called the TOP.

Static Structure that is fixed, or an object whose location is fixed.

String Sequence of zero or more discrete items. The items on a string can be ordered, which distinguishes a string from a list.

SUBSET Denoted $A <= B$, A is a subset of B if every element of A is in B.

Synonyms Two distinct keys that hash to the same location.

TOP In a stack, the TOP is the place where the next item is added or the current item is removed.

Topological ordering Usually nonunique linear ordering of vertices in a directed acyclic graph where no vertex v appears before another vertex w if there is an edge joining with initial vertex w and final vertex v.

Traversal Listing of all items or key-data pairs in a structure in such a way that no item or pair is listed twice until every item or pair has been listed once.

Tree Collection of nodes that preserve a hierarchical order. Nodes may be referenced by only one node, but nodes may reference zero or more nodes. Every node but one, called the ROOT, must be referenced by another node.

Unbounded Structure whose size changes depending on need. The opposite of static.

UNION Set operation, denoted $A + B$, where a set containing all the elements that are in A or B or both.

UPDATE Tree or search table operation that replaces the data part of a key-data pair already in the tree or search table.

Validation Process of determining whether an operation, subroutine, or program executes as specified.

Warshall's algorithm Algorithm that finds the transitive closure of a graph or digraph: that is, a graph that contains all the edges and vertices of the original graph plus initial edges joining any two vertices that can be joined by a path in the original graph.

Worst case Arrangement of a data set that causes an algorithm to take the longest time to complete.

Answers to Selected Exercises

Chapter 1

1.1.2
```
function CHANGE_CASE (CHAR : character) return character is
begin
  if CHAR in 'a'..'z' then
    return character'val (character'pos(CHAR) - character'pos('a') +
                          character'pos('A'));
  else
    return CHAR;
  end if;
end CHANGE CASE;
```

1.1.4 All the operations involve overloading the arithmetic operators.

```
function "+" (LEFT : integer; RIGHT : float) return float is
  -- returns LEFT + RIGHT
begin
  return float(LEFT) + RIGHT;
end "+";


function "+" (LEFT : float; RIGHT : integer) return float is
  -- returns LEFT + RIGHT
begin
  return X + float(I);
end "+";
```

Similar functions are needed for subtraction, multiplication, division, unary minus, and exponentiation.

1.3.5
```
procedure MAXIMUM_GRID_INDICES ( G       : in      GRID;
                                 ROW     :      out natural;
                                 COLUMN :      out character) is
  TEMP_ROW : natural   := G'first(1);
  TEMP_COL : character := G'first(2);
begin
  for ROW_INDEX in G'range(1) loop
```

```
            for COL_INDEX in G'range(2) loop
              if G(TEMP_ROW, TEMP_COL) < G(ROW_INDEX, COL_INDEX) then
                TEMP_ROW := ROW_INDEX;
                TEMP_COL := COL_INDEX;
              end if;
            end loop;
          end loop;
          ROW    := TEMP_ROW;
          COLUMN := TEMP_COL;
        end MAXIMUM_GRID_INDICES;
```

1.4.3 a.
```
        type DIRECTORY_ARRAY is array (positive range <>) of PERSON;
        type DIRECTORY (SIZE : POSITIVE) is
          record
            LIST : DIRECTORY_ARRAY (1..SIZE);
          end record;
```
b.
```
        function PHONE EXTENSION (PHONE : DIRECTORY;
                                 FIRST, LAST : string (1..15))
                                    return string is
        begin
          for INDEX in positive range 1..T.SIZE loop
            if PHONE.LIST(INDEX).LAST = LAST and then
                    PHONE.LIST(INDEX).FIRST = FIRST then
              return PHONE.LIST (INDEX).PHONE;
            end if;
          end loop;
          -- Name is not in list, must return something
          return "9999999";
        end PHONE_EXTENSION;
```

Chapter 2

2.4.1
```
        procedure PUSH (VALUE_TO_ADD : in integer;
                        FRONT        : in out NEXT_ELEMENT) is
        begin
          FRONT := new ELEMENT'(VALUE_TO_ADD, FRONT);
        end PUSH;
```

2.4.3
```
        function LIST_EQUAL (LEFT, RIGHT : NEXT_ELEMENT) return boolean is
          TEMP_LEFT  := NEXT_ELEMENT := LEFT;
          TEMP_RIGHT := NEXT_ELEMENT := RIGHT;
        begin
          loop
            if TEMP_LEFT = null and the TEMP_RIGHT = null then
              -- List have same length and content
              return true;
            elsif TEMP_LEFT = null xor TEMP_RIGHT = null then
              -- Lists have different length as one empty, other isn't
              return false;
            elsif TEMP_LEFT.DATA /= TEMP_RIGHT.DATA then
              return false;
            else
```

```
                -- Everything equal so far, get next ELEMENT in both lists
                TEMP_LEFT  := TEMP_LEFT.NEXT;
                TEMP_RIGHT := TEMP_RIGHT.NEXT;
            end if;
        end loop;
    end LIST_EQUAL;
2.4.7 procedure SORT_LIST (LIST : in out NEXT_ELEMENT) is

        TEMP_LIST    : NEXT_ELEMENT := LIST;
        TEMP_ELEMENT : NEXT_ELEMENT;

        procedure INSERT_INTO_LIST(ELEMENT_TO_INSERT : in NEXT_ELEMENT) is
            -- Inserts ELEMENT in ascending order into nonempty LIST
            -- Note list is global
            TEMP_PLACE : NEXT_ELEMENT := ELEMENT_TO_INSERT;
            TEMP       : NEXT_ELEMENT := LIST;
        begin
            if TEMP_PLACE.DATA <= LIST.DATA then
                -- Belongs up front
                TEMP_PLACE.NEXT := LIST;
                LIST := TEMP_PLACE;
            else
                -- Must find place between second and last
                while TEMP.NEXT /= null loop
                    if TEMP_PLACE.DATA <= TEMP.DATA then
                        -- ELEMENT belongs between TEMP and TEMP.NEXT
                        TEMP_PLACE.NEXT := TEMP.NEXT;
                        TEMP.NEXT := TEMP_PLACE;
                        -- all done so return
                        return;
                    else
                        TEMP := TEMP.NEXT;
                    end if;
                end loop; -- ELEMENT belongs at the end of list
                TEMP.NEXT := TEMP_PLACE;
            end if;
        end INSERT_INTO_LIST;

    begin --SORT_LIST
        if TEMP /= null then
            --List to sort is not empty, put first ELEMENT on LIST
            LIST.NEXT := null;
            TEMP := TEMP_NEXT;
            loop
                exit when TEMP = null;
                -- Get next element in the list
                TEMP_ELEMENT := TEMP_LIST;
                -- Remove first element from list
                TEMP_LIST := TEMP_LIST.NEXT;
                -- Remove TEMP_ELEMENT from referencing the LIST
                TEMP_ELEMENT.NEXT := null;
```

```
          INSERT_INTO_LIST (TEMP_ELEMENT);
      end loop;
    end SORT_LIST;
```

2.5.1
```
procedure REMOVE_ELEMENT (LIST  :  in out NEXT_ELEMENT;
                          PLACE : in positive ) is
    TEMP : NEXT_ELEMENT := LIST;
  begin
    If PLACE = 1 then
      -- Must remove the first ELEMENT
      LIST := LIST.NEXT;
      LIST.PREVIOUS := null;
    else
      for COUNT in integer range 1..PLACE - 1 loop
        TEMP := TEMP.NEXT;
      end loop;
      -- TEMP now references the ELEMENT in front of the one to be
      -- removed
      TEMP.NEXT := TEMP.NEXT.NEXT;
      TEMP.NEXT.PREVIOUS := TEMP;
    end if;
  end REMOVE_ELEMENT;
```

2.5.3
```
procedure REMOVE_VALUE (LIST            : in out NEXT_ELEMENT;
                        VALUE_TO_REMOVE : in      float        ) is
    TEMP : NEXT_ELEMENT;
  begin
    -- One or more consecutive values at the front of the list may
    -- need to be removed
    loop
      exit when LIST = null or else LIST.DATA /= VALUE_TO_REMOVE;
      LIST.NEXT.PREVIOUS := null;
      LIST := LIST.NEXT;
    end loop;
    -- Value in first ELEMENT is not to be removed, but others maybe
    TEMP := LIST;
    loop
      exit when TEMP = null;
      if TEMP.NEXT.DATA = VALUE_TO_REMOVE then
        -- Allow that ELEMENT to be deleted is the last in the list
        if TEMP.NEXT.NEXT /= null then
          -- ELEMENT to be removed is not the last
          TEMP.NEXT.NEXT.PREVIOUS := TEMP;
        end if;
        TEMP.NEXT := TEMP.NEXT.NEXT;
      else
        TEMP := TEMP.NEXT;
      end if;
    end loop;
  end REMOVE_VALUE;
```

2.6.2
```
function SMALLEST_VALUE_IN_TREE (T : in out TREE) return integer is
    TEMP_TREE : TREE := T;
begin
  -- The smallest value is always to the left
  loop
    if TEMP_TREE.LEFT = null then
      return TEMP_TREE.DATA;
    else
      TEMP_TREE := TEMP_TREE.LEFT;
    end if;
  end loop;
end SMALLEST_VALUE_IN_TREE;
```

Chapter 3

3.1.2 a.
```
function "-" (LEFT, RIGHT : COMPLEX_NUMBER ) return COMPLEX_NUMBER is
  begin
    return (LEFT.REAL - RIGHT.REAL, LEFT.IMAGINARY - RIGHT.IMAGINARY);
  end "-";
```
d.
```
function REAL_PART ( Z : COMPLEX_NUMBER ) return float is
  begin
    return Z.REAL;
  end REAL_PART;
```
g.
```
function COMPLEX (X : float ) return COMPLEX_NUMBER is
  -- returns complex number with real part X
  begin
    return (X, 0.0);
  end COMPLEX;
```
3.1.6
```
package TWO_D is
    type POINT is
      record
        X_COORDINATE,
        Y_COORDINATE : float := 0.0;
      end record;
    function "+" (LEFT, RIGHT : POINT) return POINT;
    function "*" (SCALAR : float; PLACE : POINT) return POINT;
    function "*" (PLACE : POINT: SCALAR : float) return POINT;
    function TRANSLATE (X_SHIFT, Y_SHIFT : float;
                        PLACE : POINT ) return POINT;
    function ROTATE (COS_ANGLE, SIN_ANGLE : float;
                     PLACE              : POINT) return POINT;
    function SKEW_X function SKEW_X_CORDINATE (SCALAR : float;
                                PLACE : POINT) return POINT;
    function SKEW_Y function SKEW_X_CORDINATE (SCALAR : float;
                                PLACE : POINT) return POINT;
  end TWO_D;

  package body TWO_D is
    function "+" (LEFT, RIGHT : POINT) return POINT is
```

```
         -- Returns the vector sum of two points
      begin
         return (LEFT.X_COORDINATE + RIGHT.X_COORDINATE,
                 LEFT.Y_COORDINATE + RIGHT.Y_COORDINATE);
      end "+";


      function "*" (SCALAR : float; PLACE : POINT) return POINT is
         --Returns the vector scalar product
      begin
         return (SCALAR*PLACE.X_CORDINATE, SCALAR*PLACE.Y_COORDINATE);
      end "*";


      function "*" (PLACE : POINT: SCALAR : float) return POINT is
      begin
         return SCALAR*POINT;
      end "*";


      function TRANSLATE (X_SHIFT, Y_SHIFT : float;
                          PLACE : POINT ) return POINT is
         --Returns point shifted by (X_SHIFT,Y_SHIFT)
      begin
         return (PLACE.X_COORDINATE + X_SHIFT,
                 PLACE.Y_COORDINATE + Y_SHIFT);
      end TRANSLATE;


      function ROTATE   (COS_ANGLE, SIN_ANGLE  : float;
                         PLACE             : POINT) return POINT is
         -- Returns given point rotated by ANGLE
         -- Note COS_ANGLE**2 + SIN_ANGLE**2 must equal 1
      begin
         return(COS_ANGLE*PLACE.X_COORDINATE+SIN_ANGLE*PLACE.Y_COORDINATE,
              -SIN_ANGLE*PLACE.X_COORDINATE+COS_ANGLE*PLACE.Y_COORDINATE);
      end ROTATE;


      function SKEW_X_COORDINATE (SCALAR : float;
                                  PLACE : POINT) return POINT is
         -- Returns point with x coordinate multiplied by SCALAR
      begin
         return (SCALAR*PLACE.X_COORDINATE, PLACE.Y_COORDINATE);
      end SKEW_X_COORDINATE;


      function SKEW_Y_COORDINATE (SCALAR : float;
                                  PLACE : POINT) return POINT is
         -- Returns point with y coordinate multiplied by SCALAR
      begin
         return (PLACE.X_COORDINATE, SCALAR*PLACE.Y_COORDINATE);
      end SKEW_Y_COORDINATE;


   end TWO_D;
```

3.2.1 generic

```
      type ARRAY_INDEX is (<>);
      type ITEM_TYPE is private;
      type VECTOR_ARRAY is array (ARRAY_INDEX <>) of ITEM_TYPE;
   function FIND_LOCATION (VECTOR : VECTOR_ARRAY; ITEM : ITEM_TYPE)
                   return ARRAY_INDEX;
   function FIND_LOCATION (VECTOR : VECTOR_ARRAY; ITEM : ITEM_TYPE)
                   return ARRAY_INDEX is
     -- Returns the array index of a given item
     -- Function fails if ITEM not in array
   begin
     for INDEX in VECTOR'range loop
       if VECTOR (INDEX) = ITEM then
         return INDEX;
       end if;
     end loop;
   end FIND_LOCATION;
```

3.2.3 generic

```
      with function F (X : float) return float;
   function SIMPSON_RULE (LEFT,
                          RIGHT            : float;
                          NUMBER_INTERVALS : positive) return float;
   function SIMPSON_RULE (LEFT,
                          RIGHT            : float;
                          NUMBER_INTERVALS : positive) return float is
     --Uses Simpson's rule to estimate the area under a given
     --curve F and between the LEFT and RIGHT interval endpoints
     -- NUMBER_INTERVALS must be even so multiplied by 2 when
     -- computing H
     H : float := (RIGHT - LEFT)/float(2*NUMBER_INTERVALS);
     SUM : float := (F(LEFT) + F(RIGHT));
     X   : float := LEFT;
   begin
     for COUNT in positive range 1 .. NUMBER_INTERVALS - 1 loop
       X := X + H;
       SUM := SUM + 4.0*F(X);
       X := X + H;
       SUM := SUM + 2.0*F(X);
     end loop;
       X := X + H;
       SUM := SUM + 4.0*F(X);
       return SUM * H;
   end SIMPSON_RULE;
```

3.2.5 generic

```
      type ITEM_TYPE is private;
      ZERO_ITEM : in ITEM_TYPE;
      type INDEX is (<>);
      type ITEM_MATRIX is array (INDEX, INDEX) of  ITEM_TYPE;
      with function "+" (LEFT, RIGHT : ITEM_TYPE) return ITEM_TYPE;
```

```
      with function "*" (LEFT, RIGHT : ITEM_TYPE) return ITEM_TYPE;
  function "*" (LEFT, RIGHT : ITEM_MATRIX ) return ITEM_MATRIX;
  function "*" (LEFT, RIGHT : ITEM_MATRIX ) return ITEM_MATRIX is
    ANSWER : ITEM_MATRIX;
begin
  for ROW in INDEX loop
    for COLUMN in INDEX loop
      ANSWER(ROW, COLUMN) := ZERO_ITEM;
      for COUNT in INDEX loop
        ANSWER(ROW, COLUMN) := ANSWER(ROW, COLUMN)
                          + LEFT(ROW, COUNT)*RIGHT(COUNT, COLUMN)
      end loop;
    end loop;
  end loop;
  return ANSWER;
end "*";
```

3.3.2
```
generic
    type ITEM_TYPE is private;
pacakage GENERIC_QUEUE is
  type QUEUE is limited private;
  procedure ENQUEUE ( THIS_QUEUE : in out QUEUE;
                      ITEM       : in     ITEM_TYPE);
  procedure DEQUEUE ( THIS_QUEUE : in out QUEUE;
                      ITEM       :    out ITEM_TYPE);
  function QUEUE_EMPTY (THIS_QUEUE : QUEUE ) return boolean;
private
  type NODE;
  type NEXT_NODE is access NODE;
  type NODE is
    record
      DATA : ITEM_TYPE;
      NEXT : NEXT_NODE;
    end record;
  type QUEUE is
    record
      FRONT,
      REAR : NEXT_NODE;
    end record;
end GENERIC_QUEUE;


package body GENERIC_QUEUE is

  procedure ENQUEUE ( THIS_QUEUE : in out QUEUE;
                      ITEM       : in     ITEM_TYPE) is
  begin
    if THIS_QUEUE.FRONT = null then
      -- QUEUE is empty
      THIS_QUEUE.FRONT := new NODE'(ITEM, null);
      THIS_QUEUE.REAR  := THIS_QUEUE.FRONT;
    else
```

```
            THIS_QUEUE.REAR.NEXT: new NODE'(ITEM,null);
            THIS_QUEUE.REAR     : THIS_QUEUE.REAR.NEXT;
        end if;
    end ENQUEUE;

    procedure DEQUEUE ( THIS_QUEUE : in out QUEUE;
                        ITEM       :    out ITEM_TYPE) is
    begin
      ITEM := THIS_QUEUE.FRONT.DATA;
      if THIS_QUEUE.FRONT = THIS_QUEUE.REAR then
        -- Queue only has one node it
        THIS_QUEUE REAR := null;
      end if;
      THIS_QUEUE.FRONT := THIS_QUEUE.FRONT.NEXT;
    end DEQUEUE;

    function QUEUE_EMPTY (THIS_QUEUE : QUEUE ) return boolean is
    begin
      return THIS_QUEUE.FRONT = null;
    end if;

end GENERIC QUEUE;
```

Chapter 4

4.2.1 a. The function "+" has a loop within a loop. The order is proportional to the product of the ranges of the loops, or O(LEFT'range(1)* RIGHT'range(2)).

c. The function MINIMUM_VECTOR_VALUE in Figure 2.2.1 has an if statement inside a loop. The "big O" is a "worst case" measure, so it is assumed the if statement executes everytime, the answer is O(V'length).

e. The function ADD_INORDER_TO_LIST in Section 2.4 must put an item in order someplace in the list. It is assumed, that on average, the item will be placed in the middle of the list. If the list is n long, then this procedure is $O(n/2)$, but $O(n/2) = O(n)$, so the better answer is $O(n)$.

Chapter 5

5.5.1 a.
```
procedure CLEAR (THIS_LIST : out LIST) is
      -- Returns a list with no items in it
      TEMP : LIST;
begin
  LIST := TEMP;
end CLEAR;
```
c.
```
function TAIL_OF_LIST (THIS_LIST : LIST) return LIST is
      -- Returns a list starting at the second ITEM and going through the
      -- last ITEM.
      -- Exception LIST_IS_EMPTY raised if the list is empty.
      TEMP : LIST := THIS_LIST;
begin
  if THIS_LIST.LENGTH = 0 then
    raise LIST_IS_EMPTY;
  else
    TEMP.LENGTH := TEMP.LENGTH - 1;
```

```
                TEMP.FRONT := TEMP.FRONT.NEXT;
                  return TEMP;
              end if;
          end TAIL_OF_LIST;
```

h.
```
    function LENGTH (OF_LIST : LIST) return natural is
        -- Returns the number of LIST_NODES in the list.
    begin
        return OF_LIST.LENGTH;
    end LENGTH;
```

j.
```
    procedure ADD_ITEM_TO_HEAD (OF_LIST : in out LIST;
                                ITEM    : in     ITEM_TYPE) is
        -- Adds an ITEM to the front of the list
        -- Exception OVERFLOW raised if there is no storage left to
        --         add an item to the head of the list.
    begin
        OF_LIST.FRONT := new LIST_NODE'(ITEM, OF_LIST.FRONT);
        if OF_LIST.LENGTH = 0 then
          OF_LIST.REAR := OF_LIST.FRONT;
        end if;
        OF_LIST.LENGTH := OF_LIST.LENGTH + 1;
    exception
        when storage_eror =>
          raise OVERFLOW;
    end ADD_ITEM_TO_HEAD;
```

k.
```
    procedure ADD_ITEM_TO_REAR (OF_LIST : in out LIST;
                                ITEM    : in     ITEM_TYPE) is
        -- Adds an Item to the end of the list.
        -- Exception OVERFLOW raised if there is no storage left to
        --         add an item to the tail of the list.
    begin
        if OF_LIST.LENGTH = 0 then
          OF_LIST.FRONT  := new LIST_NODE'(ITEM, null);
          OF_LIST.REAR   := OF_LIST.REAR;
          OF_LIST.LENGTH := 1;
        else
          OF_LIST.REAR.NEXT := new LIST_NODE'(ITEM, null);
          OF_LIST.REAR      := OF_LIST.REAR.NEXT;
          OF_LIST.LENGTH    := OF_LIST.LENGTH + 1;
        end if;
    exception
        when storage error =>
        raise OVERFLOW;
    end ADD_ITEM_TO_REAR;
```

5.5.2 a.
```
    procedure CLEAR (THIS_LIST : out LIST) is
        -- Returns a list with no items in it
        TEMP : LIST;
    begin
        LIST := TEMP;
    end CLEAR;
```

d.
```
    procedure COPY        (FROM  : in     LIST;
```

```
                              TO      :    out LIST) is
        --Returns an exact copy of FROM with same items in the same order
        --Exception OVERFLOW raised if there is no storage left to
        --          copy the list.
        TEMP_TO : LIST;
        TEMP_FROM : LIST := FROM;
    begin
        if FROM = null then
          TO := null;
        else
          TEMP_TO := new LIST_NODE'(TEMP_FROM.ITEM, null, null);
          TO := TEMP_TO;
          TEMP_FROM := TEMP_FROM.NEXT;
          while TEMP_FROM /= null loop
            TEMP_TO.NEXT := new LIST_NODE'(TEMP_FROM.ITEM, null, null);
            TEMP_TO.NEXT.PREVIOUS := TEMP_TO;
            TEMP_FROM := TEMP_FROM.NEXT;
            TEMP_TO := TEMP_TO.NEXT;
          end loop;
        end if;
    exception
        when storage_error =>
          raise OVERFLOW;
    end COPY;
```

Chapter 6

6.2.1 a.
```
procedure COPY          (FROM_STACK : in     STACK;
                          TO_STACK   :    out STACK) is
    -- Makes an exacy copy of the FROM_STACK and returns it as TO_STACK.
    -- The result is two stacks with same items in the same order.
    TEMP : STACK := FROM_STACK;
begin
    TO_STACK := TEMP;
end COPY;
```

e.
```
function EQUAL (STACK1, STACK2 : STACK) return boolean is
    -- Returns true if two stacks have the same depth and the two
    -- sequences of items are equal when compared item by item starting
    -- at from their respective tops.
begin
    if STACK1.TOP = 0 THEN
      return STACK2.TOP = 0;
    else
      return STACK1.TOP = STACK2.TOP AND THEN
           STACK1.STACK(1..STACK1.TOP) = STACK2.STACK (1..STACK2.TOP);
    end if;
end EQUAL;
```

6.2.3 a.
```
procedure CREATE (SIZE        : in     positive;
                   NEW_STACK   :    out STACK) is
    -- Creates a new stack of specified size
```

```
begin
  NEW_STACK := new STACK_NODE'(SIZE);
end CREATE;
```
b. procedure COPY (FROM_STACK : in   STACK;
                      TO_STACK   : in out STACK) is
```
-- Copies the data in FROM_STACK
-- exception STACK_NOT_DEFINED raised if FROM_STACK or
--           TO_STACK = null
-- exception overflow raised if TO_STACK is not large
--           enough
begin
  if FROM_STACK = null or TO_STACK = null then
    raise STACK_NOT_DEFINED;
  elsif FROM_STACK.TOP > TO_STACK.SIZE then
    --There isn't room in TO_STACK
    raise overflow;
  else
    TO_STACK.TOP := FROM_STACK.TOP;
    TO_STACK.STACK(1..TO_STACK.TOP) :=
             FROM_STACK.STACK(1..FROM_STACK.TOP);
  end if;
end COPY;
```
f. procedure PUSH (ITEM   : in   ITEM_TYPE;
                      ONTO_THE_STK : in out STACK) is
```
-- Adds ITEM to TOP of ONTO_THE_STACK
-- exception STACK_NOT_DEFINED raised if ONTO_THE_STACK = null
-- exception overflow raised if TO_STACK is not large
--           enough
begin
  if ONTO_THE_STACK = null then
    raise STACK_NOT_DEFINED;
  elsif ONTO_THE_STACK.TOP = ONTO_THE _STACK.SIZE then
    --There isn't room in TO_STACK raise overflow;
    raise overflow;
  else
    ONTO_THE_STACK.TOP := ONTO_THE_STACK.TOP + 1;
    ONTO_THE_STACK.STACK(ONTO_THE_STACK.TOP) := ITEM;
  end if;
end PUSH;
```
6.3.1 c. function EMPTY (STACK_TO_CHECK : STACK) return boolean is
```
-- Returns true if the stack is empty.
begin
  return STACK_TO_CHECK.DEPTH = 0;
end EMPTY;
```
e. procedure COPY (FROM STACK : in   STACK;
                      TO_STACK   :   out STACK) is
```
-- Makes an exact copy of the FROM_STACK and returns it as TO_STACK.
-- The result is two stacks with same items in the same order.
-- Exception OVERFLOW is raised if there is not enough memory to
--           copy the stack
```

```
      TEMP_FROM : STACK_NEXT := FROM_STACK.TOP;
      TEMP_TO : STACK_NEXT;
   begin
      if FROM_STACK.DEPTH = 0 then
         TO_STACK : (0, null);
      else
         TEMP_TO := new STACK_NODE'(TEMP_FROM.ITEM, null);
         TO_STACK := (FROM_STACK.DEPTH, TEMP_TO);
         loop
            exit when TEMP_FROM.NEXT = null;
            TEMP_FROM := TEMP_FROM.NEXT;
            TEMP_TO.NEXT := new STACK_NODE'(TEMP_FROM.ITEM, null);
            TEMP_TO := TEMP_TO.NEXT;
         end loop;
      end if;
   exception
      when storage_error =>
         raise OVERFLOW;
   end COPY;
```

6.5.3 This procedure can be implemented by pushing an "a" on the stack if the stack is empty or if the top of the stack is an "a." If the top of the stack is a "b," then one element is popped and discarded from the stack. The same rules apply for the letter "b." The program outputs "equal" if the stack is empty, and "not equal" otherwise.

Chapter 7

7.2.1 a.
```
procedure ENQUEUE ( ITEM     : in    ITEM_TYPE;
                    TO_THE_Q : in out QUEUE) is
   -- Add ITEM after the last object at the rear of TO_THE_Q
   -- preserving the FIFO behavior. The previous rear object
   -- the queue is now the next-to-last object.
   -- Exception OVERFLOW raised if there is no space left to add an
   --            ITEM to the queue.
   REAR : natural := 1 +
            (TO_THE_Q.FRONT + TO_THE_Q.IN_USE - 2) mod MAXIMUM_Q_SIZE;
begin
   if TO_THE_Q.IN_USE = MAXIMUM_Q_SIZE then
      raise OVERFLOW;
   else
      if TO_THE_FRONT = 0 then
         TO_THE_Q.FRONT := 1;
      end if;
      TO_THE_Q.IN_USE := TO_THE_Q.IN USE + 1;
      TO_THE_Q.QUE(REAR) := ITEM;
   end if;
end ENQUEUE;
```
c.
```
procedure COPY  (FROM_Q : in    QUEUE;
                 TO_Q   :    out QUEUE) is
   -- Makes an exact copy of the queue FROM_Q
   -- Exception OVERFLOW raised if there is no space
   --            left to add an ITEM to the queue.
```

```
        TEMP : QUEUE := FROM_Q;
begin
    TO_Q := TEMP;
    end COPY;
```

k. `function REAR_OBJECT (FROM_THE_Q : QUEUE) return ITEM_TYPE is`
```
        -- Returns the last ITEM added to the queue without modifying
        -- the queue.
        -- Exception Q_IS_EMPTY raised if there is no item to return
        REAR : natural := 1 +
                (TO_THE_Q.FRONT + TO_THE_Q.IN_USE - 2) mod MAXIMUM_Q_SIZE;
begin
    if FROM_THE_Q.IN_USE = 0 then
        raise Q_IS_EMPTY;
    else
        return FROM_THE_Q.QUE(REAR);
    end if;
    end REAR_OBJECT;
```

7.2.3 a. `procedure ENQUEUE ( ITEM        : in      ITEM_TYPE;`
```
                    TO_THE_Q : in out QUEUE) is
    -- Add ITEM after the last object at the rear of TO_THE_Q
    -- preserving the 'fifo' behavior. The previous rear object
    -- the queue is now the next-to-last object.
    -- Exception OVERFLOW raised if there is no space left to add an
    --           ITEM to the queue.
    REAR : natural := 1 +
            (TO_THE_Q.FRONT + TO_THE_Q.IN_USE - 2) mod MAXIMUM_Q_SIZE;
begin
    if TO_THE_Q = null then
        -- TO_THE_Q must be initialized
        TO_THE_Q : new QUEUE_NODE;
    end if;
    if TO_THE_Q.IN_USE = MAXIMUM_Q_SIZE then
        raise OVERFLOW;
    else
        if TO_THE_Q.FRONT = 0 then
            TO_THE_Q.FRONT := 1;
            TO_THE_Q.REAR := 1;
            TO_THE_Q.QUE(1) := ITEM;
        else
            TO_THE_Q.REAR := 1 + (TO_THE_Q.REAR mod MAXIMUM_Q_SIZE);
            TO_THE_Q.QUE (TO_THE_Q.REAR) := ITEM;
        end if;
    end if;
    end ENQUEUE;
```

c. `procedure COPY  (FROM_Q    : in     QUEUE;`
```
                    TO_Q       :      out QUEUE) is
    -- Makes an exact copy of the queue FROM_Q
    -- Exception OVERFLOW raised if there is no space
    --           left to add an ITEM to the queue.
```

```
begin
  if FROM_Q = null then
    -- FROM_Q must be initialized
    FROM_Q := new QUEUE_NODE;
  end if;
  if TO_Q = null then
    -- TO__Q must be initialized
    TO_Q := new QUEUE_NODE
  end if;
  TO_Q.all := FROM_Q.all;
end COPY;
```

k.
```
function REAR_OBJECT (FROM_THE_Q : QUEUE) return ITEM_TYPE is
  -- Returns the last ITEM added to the queue without modifying
  -- the queue.
  -- Exception Q_IS_EMPTY raised if there is no item to return
begin
  if FROM_THE_Q = null or else FROM_THE_Q.IN_USE = 0 then
    raise Q_IS_EMPTY;
  else
    return FROM_THE_Q.QUE(FROM_THE_Q.REAR);
  end if;
end REAR_OBJECT;
```

7.2.4 a.
```
procedure ENQUEUE ( ITEM       : in ITEM_TYPE;
                    TO_THE_Q : in out QUEUE) is
  -- Add ITEM after the last object at the rear of TO_THE_Q
  -- preserving the FIFO behavior. The previous rear object
  -- the queue is now the next-to-last object.
  -- Exception OVERFLOW raised if there is no space left to add an
  --           ITEM to the queue.
  REAR : natural := 1 +
         (TO_THE_Q.FRONT + TO_THE_Q.IN_USE - 2) mod MAXIMUM_Q _SIZE;
begin
  if TO_THE_Q = null then
    raise QUEUE_NOT_DEFINED;
  elsif TO_THE_Q.FRONT < TO_THE_Q.REAR and then
        TO_THE_Q.REAR - TO_THE_Q.FRONT + 1 = TO_THE_Q.SIZE then
    raise OVERFLOW;
  elsif TO_THE_Q.REAR < TO_THE_Q.FRONT and then
        TO_THE_Q.REAR = TO_THE_Q.FRONT - 1 then
    -- Front has wrapped around, see if Q full
    raise OVERFLOW;
  else
    if TO_THE_Q.FRONT = 0 then
      TO_THE_Q.FRONT := 1;
      TO_THE_Q.REAR := 1;
      TO_THE_Q.QUE(1) := ITEM;
    else
      TO_THE_Q.REAR := 1 + (TO_THE_Q.REAR mod TO_THE_Q.SIZE);
      TO_THE_Q.QUE (TO_THE_Q.REAR) := ITEM;
```

```
          end if;
        end if;
      end ENQUEUE;
  c. procedure COPY (FROM_Q   : in      QUEUE;
                     TO_Q      : in out QUEUE) is
     -- Makes an exact copy of the queue FROM_Q
     -- Exception OVERFLOW raised if there is no space
     --           left to add an ITEM to the queue.
     begin
       if FROM_Q = null or TO_Q = null then
         raise QUEUE_NOT_DEFINED;
       elsif FROM_Q.FRONT < FROM_Q.REAR and then
           FROM_Q.REAR - FROM_Q.FRONT + 1 > TO_Q.SIZE then
         raise OVERFLOW;
       elsif FROM_Q.REAR < FROM_Q.FRONT and then
           FROM_Q.REAR + FROM_Q.SIZE - FROM_Q.FRONT + 1 > TO Q.SIZE then
           -- Front has wrapped around
         raise OVERFLOW;
       else
         if FROM_Q.FRONT <= FROM_Q.REAR and then
           TO_Q.FRONT := 1;
           TO_Q.REAR := FROM_Q.REAR - FROM_Q.FRONT + 1;
           TO_Q.QUE(1..TO_Q.REAR) :=
                   FROM_Q.QUE(FROM_Q.FRONT..FROM_Q.REAR);
         else
           TO_Q.FRONT := 1;
           TO_Q.REAR := FROM_Q.REAR + FROM_Q.SIZE - FROM_Q.FRONT + 1;
           TO_Q.QUE(1..FROM_Q.SIZE -FROM_Q.FRONT+1) :=
                   FROM_Q.QUE(FROM_Q.FRONT..FROM_Q.SIZE);
           TO_Q.QUE(FROM_Q.SIZE - FROM_Q.FRONT + 2..TO_Q.REAR) :=
                   FROM_Q.QUE(1..FROM_Q.REAR);
         end if;
       end if;
     end COPY;
  k. function REAR_OBJECT (FROM_THE_Q : QUEUE) return ITEM_TYPE is
     -- Returns the last ITEM added to the queue without modifying
     -- the queue.
     -- Exception Q_IS_EMPTY raised if there is no item to return
     begin
       if FROM_THE_Q = null or else FROM_THE_Q.IN_USE = 0 then
         raise Q_IS_EMPTY;
       else
         return FROM_THE_Q.QUE(FROM_THE_Q.REAR);
       end if;
     end REAR_OBJECT;
7.3.1 a. procedure ENQUEUE ( ITEM      : in      ITEM_TYPE;
                             TO_THE_Q : in out QUEUE) is
     -- Add ITEM after the last object at the rear of TO_THE_Q
     -- preserving the 'fifo' behavior. The previous rear object
     -- the queue is now the next-to-last object.
```

```
    -- Exception OVERFLOW raised if there is no space left to add an
    --            ITEM to the queue.
    TEMP : QUEUE := TO_THE_QUEUE;
begin
    if TO_THE_Q = null then
      -- TO_THE_Q is empty
      TO_THE_Q := new QUEUE_NODE'(ITEM null);
    else
      --Find last node in queue
      while TEMP.NEXT /= null loop
        TEMP := TEMP.NEXT;
      end loop;
      TEMP.NEXT := new QUEUE_NODE'(ITEM, null);
    end if;
exception
    when storage_error =>
      raise OVERFLOW;
end ENQUEUE;
c. procedure COPY (FROM_Q      : in    QUEUE;
                   TO_Q        :    out QUEUE) is
    -- Makes an exact copy of the queue FROM_Q
    -- Exception OVERFLOW raised if there is no space
    --            left to add an ITEM to the queue.
    TEMP_FROM : QUEUE := FROM_Q;
    TEMP_TO   : QUEUE;
begin
    if FROM_Q = null then
      TO_Q := null;
    else
      TEMP_TO := new QUEUE_NODE' (TEMP_FROM.ITEM, null);
      TO_Q := TEMP_TO;
      TEMP_FROM := TEMP_FROM.NEXT;
      loop
        exit when TEMP_FROM = null;
        TEMP_TO.NEXT := new QUEUE_NODE' (TEMP_FROM.ITEM, null);
        TEMP_TO := TEMP_TO.NEXT;
        TEMP_FROM := TEMP_FROM.NEXT:
      end loop;
    exception
      when storage_error =>
        raise OVERFLOW;
    end COPY;
k. function REAR_OBJECT (FROM_THE_Q : QUEUE) return ITEM_TYPE is
    -- Returns the last ITEM added to the queue without modifying
    -- the queue.
    -- Exception Q_IS_EMPTY raised if there is no item to return
    TEMP : QUEUE := FROM_THE_Q;
begin
    if FROM_THE_Q = null then
      raise Q_IS_EMPTY;
```

```
          else
            --Find last node in queue
            while TEMP.NEXT /= null loop
              TEMP := TEMP.NEXT;
            end loop;
            return TEMP.ITEM;
          end if;
        exception
          when storage_error =>
            raise OVERFLOW;
      end REAR_OBJECT;
```

7.5.1 a.
```
      procedure Add_TO_QUEUE( KEY    : in     KEY_TYPE;
                              DATA   : in     DATA_TYPE;
                              TO_THE_Q : in out QUEUE) is
      begin
        if TO_THE_Q = null then
          TO_THE_Q := new Q_ITEM'(KEY, DATA, null);
        elsif (TO_THE_Q.KEY <= KEY) and then not (KEY<=TO_THE_Q.KEY) then
          TO_THE_Q := new Q_ITEM'(KEY, DATA, TO_THE_Q);
        else
          ADD_TO_QUEUE (KEY, DATA, TO_THE_Q.NEXT);
        end if;
      exception
        when storage_error =>
          raise OVERFLOW;
      end Add_to_QUEUE;
```

c.
```
      procedure Copy ( From_Q    : in     QUEUE;
                       TO_Q      :    out QUEUE) is
        FROM_TEMP   : QUEUE := FROM_Q;
        TO_TEMP : QUEUE;
      begin
        if FROM_TEMP = null then
          TO_Q := null;
        else
          TO_TEMP :=new Q_ITEM'(FROM_TEMP.KEY, FROM_TEMP.DATA, null);
          TO_Q := TO_TEMP;
          FROM_TEMP := FROM_TEMP.NEXT;
          while FROM_TEMP /= null loop
            TO_TEMP.NEXT
              := new Q_ITEM'(FROM_TEMP.KEY, FROM_TEMP.DATA, null);
            FROM_TEMP := FROM_TEMP.NEXT;
            TO_TEMP := TO_TEMP.NEXT;
          end loop;
        end if;
      exception
        when storage_error =>
          raise OVERFLOW;
      end COPY;
```

j.
```
      procedure REAR_PAIR    ( FROM_THE_Q : in     QUEUE;
                               KEY        :    out KEY_TYPE;
```

```
                        DATA       : out DATA_TYPE) is
   begin
     if FROM_THE_Q = null then
       raise Q_IS_EMPTY;
     elsif FROM_THE_Q.NEXT = null then
       KEY := FROM_THE_Q.KEY;
       DATA := FROM_THE_Q.DATA;
     else
       REAR_PAIR (FROM_THE_Q_NEXT, KEY, DATA);
     end if;
   end REAR_PAIR;
```

Chapter 8

8.2.1 a.
```
   procedure COPY (FROM_TREE: in     TREE;
                   TO_TREE   :    out TREE) is
   -- Makes an exact copy of a specified tree that preserves structure
   -- and shares no nodes. The traversals of the tree TO_TREE start
   -- at the first node of the particular traversal
   -- Exception OVERFLOW raised if insufficient memory left to add a
   --          node
   TEMP_ROOT : NEXT;

     procedure COPY (FROM : in NEXT; TO : out NEXT) is
       -- Recursive procedure that first copies the current node,
       -- then the node's left subtree, then the node's right subtree
       TEMP_NODE : NEXT;
     begin
       if FROM = null then
         TO := null;
       else
         TEMP_NODE := new NODE'(FROM.KEY, FROM.DATA, null, null);
         COPY (FROM.LEFT, TEMP_NODE.LEFT);
         COPY (FROM.RIGHT, TEMP_NODE.RIGHT);
         TO := TEMP_NODE;
       end if;
     end COPY;


   begin
     if FROM_TREE.ROOT /= null then
       COPY (FROM_TREE.ROOT, TEMP_ROOT);
     end if;
     TO_TREE := (TEMP_ROOT, FROM_TREE.COUNT, null, null, null);
   exception
     when storage_error => raise OVERFLOW;
   end COPY;
```
c.
```
   procedure UPDATE (KEY : in     KEY_TYPE;
                     DATA : in     DATA_TYPE;
                     T : in     TREE) is
     -- Searches for a node with a specified key in T and replaces the
```

```
-- data field with the new value.
-- Exception KEY_NOT_IN_TREE raised if no node contains specified
--          key.

procedure UPDATE ( KEY  : in     KEY_TYPE;
                   DATA : in     DATA_TYPE;
                   R    : in     NEXT) is
    -- Recursive procedure to search tree for a node with a given key
    -- and to then replace its data field
    TEMP_NODE : NEXT := R;
begin
  if R = null then
    raise KEY_NOT_IN_TREE;
  elsif R.KEY = KEY then
    TEMP_NODE.DATA := DATA;
  elsif R.KEY < KEY then
    UPDATE (KEY, DATA, R.LEFT);
  else
    UPDATE (KEY, DATA, R.RIGHT);
  end if;
end UPDATE;

begin
  UPDATE (KEY, DATA, T.ROOT);
exception
  when KEY_NOT_IN_TREE => raise KEY_NOT_IN_TREE;
end UPDATE;
```

e.
```
procedure NEXT_POSTORDER (KEY :    out KEY_TYPE;
                          DATA :   out DATA_TYPE;
                          T    : in out TREE) is
  -- Returns the key-data pair of the next node to be processed with a
  -- postorder traversal of T. When the traversal is finished, it
  -- will start at the beginning. Any insertion or deletion of a
  -- node will cause the traversal to be reset. A postorder traversal
  -- processes the left subtree, the right subtree, and then the root
  -- recursively.
  -- Exception TREE_IS_EMPTY raised if there is no key-data pair to
  --           return
  TEMP : NEXT;
  AUX_STACK : NEXT_TRAVERSAL := null;
begin
  if T.COUNT = 0 then
    -- No key-data pairs to return
    raise TREE_IS_EMPTY;
  end if;
  -- T.NEXT_POST points to the top of a stack of nodes that performs a
  -- postorder traversal of T. The top always references the next node
  -- to process.
  if T.NEXT_POST = null then
    -- The stack is null, so it must be initialized. The entire
```

```
      -- postorder traversal must be put onto the stack. The last node
      -- to be processed is put on first (i.e., the root)
      T.NEXT_POST := new TRAVERSAL'(T.ROOT, null);
      TEMP := T.ROOT;
      -- The left subtree and then the right subtree are processed in
      -- that order. An auxiliary stack is formed to keep track of the
      -- next subtree not the next node to process. Remember that stacks
      -- reverse, so must come off the auxiliary stack first to be
      -- processed and placed on the regular stack
      if TEMP.LEFT /= null then
        -- Put root's left subtree on the stack
        AUX_STACK := new TRAVERSAL'(TEMP.LEFT, AUX_STACK);
      end if;
      if TEMP.RIGHT /= null then
        -- Put root's right subtree on the stack
        AUX_STACK := new TRAVERSAL'(TEMP.RIGHT, AUX_STACK);
      end if;
      while AUX_STACK /= null loop
        -- There are more subtrees to process, so pop the next subtree
        TEMP := AUX_STACK.PROCESS;
        AUX_STACK := AUX_STACK.NEXT_PROC;
        -- The root node of that subtree goes on the regular stack
        -- (because of reverse order) and the left and right subtrees, if
        -- they exist, go onto the auxiliary stack of subtrees
        T.NEXT_POST :- new TRAVERSAL'(TEMP, T.NEXT_POST);
        if TEMP.LEFT /= null then
          AUX_STACK := new TRAVERSAL'(TEMP.LEFT, AUX_STACK);
        end if;
        if TEMP.RIGHT /= null then
          AUX_STACK := new TRAVERSAL'(TEMP.RIGHT, AUX_STACK);
        end if;
        end loop;
      end if;
      --The NODE on top of the stack is next to process;
      TEMP := T.NEXT_POST.PROCESS;
      KEY    := TEMP.KEY;
      DATA      := TEMP.DATA;
      -- Pop the node stack because it must contain the next node to
      -- process
      T.NEXT_POST := T.NEXT_POST.NEXT_PROC;
    end NEXT_POSTORDER;
 1. function KEY_IN_TREE ( KEY : KEY_TYPE; T : TREE) return boolean is
    -- Returns true if a specified key is in T.
    function KEY_TREE(KEY : KEY_TYPE; R : NEXT) return boolean is
      -- Recursive search of a tree for some key
    begin
      if R = null then
        return false;
      elsif R.KEY = KEY then
        return true;
```

```
                elsif KEY < R.KEY then
                    return KEY_TREE (KEY, R.LEFT);
                else
                    return KEY_TREE (KEY, R.RIGHT);
                end if;
            end KEY_TREE;
        begin
            return KEY_TREE(KEY, T.ROOT);
        end KEY_IN_TREE;
```

8.4.2 b.
```
    procedure UPDATE (KEY  : in      KEY_TYPE;
                      DATA : in      DATA_TYPE;
                      T    : in out TREE) is
        -- Procedure that searches for a node with a key and updates it.
        -- Exception KEY_NOT_IN_TREE raised if key cannot be deleted.
        INDEX : positive := 1;
    begin
        loop
            if INDEX > T.NODES_IN_USE then
                raise KEY_NOT_IN_TREE;
            elsif T.T(INDEX).KEY = KEY then
                T.T.(INDEX).DATA := DATA;
                return;
            elsif KEY < T.T.(INDEX).KEY then
                INDEX := 2 * INDEX;
            else
                INDEX := 2 * INDEX + 1;
            end if;
        end loop;
    end UPDATE;
```

i.
```
    function KEY_IN_TREE(KEY : KEY_TYPE; T : TREE) return boolean is
        -- Returns true if a specified key is in T.
        INDEX : positive := 1;
    begin
        loop
            if INDEX > T.NODES_IN_USE then
                return false;
            elsif T.T.(INDEX).KEY = KEY then
                return true;
            elsif KEY < T.T(INDEX).KEY then
                INDEX := 2 * INDEX;
            else
                INDEX := 2 * INDEX + 1;
            end if;
        end loop;
    end KEY_IN_TREE;
```

8.7.1
```
    with UNBOUNDED_BINARY_SEARCH_TREE;
    generic
        type ITEM_TYPE is private;
        with function "<=" (LEFT, RIGHT : ITEM_TYPE) return boolean;
    package GENERIC_UNBOUNDED_PRIORITY_QUEUE is
```

```
type PRIORITY_QUEUE is limited private;
procedure ADD_TO_Q (ITEM        : in     ITEM_TYPE;
                    TO_THE_Q     : in out PRIORITY_QUEUE);
procedure DEQUEUE   (ITEM        :     out ITEM_TYPE;
                    FROM_THE_Q   : in out PRIORITY_QUEUE);
procedure COPY      (FROM_Q      : in     PRIORITY_QUEUE;
                    TO_Q         : in out PRIORITY_QUEUE);
procedure MERGE     (FROM_Q1,
                    FROM_Q2      : in     PRIORITY_QUEUE;
                    ONTO_Q       : in out PRIORITY_QUEUE);
procedure CLEAR     (Q_TO_CLEAR  : in out PRIORITY_QUEUE);
procedure POP       (FROM_THE_Q  : in out PRIORITY_QUEUE);
function LENGTH     (Q_TO_COUNT  : PRIORITY_QUEUE) return natural;
function EMPTY      (Q_TO_CHECK  : PRIORITY_QUEUE) return boolean;
function FRONT_ITEM (From_the_Q: PRIORITY_QUEUE) return ITEM_TYPE;
function EQUAL      (Q1, Q2      : PRIORITY_QUEUE) return boolean;
OVERFLOW   : exception;
Q_IS_EMPTY : exception;
private
  package P_Q is new
    UNBOUNDED_BINARY_SEARCH_TREE (ITEM_TYPE, boolean, "<=");
  use P_Q;
  type PRIORITY_QUEUE is
    record
      PQ : TREE;
    end record;
end GENERIC_UNBOUNDED_PRIORITY_QUEUE;


package body Generic_unbounded_PRIORITY_QUEUE is

  procedure ADD_TO_Q (ITEM    : in     ITEM_TYPE;
                      TO_THE_Q : in out PRIORITY_QUEUE) is
  begin
    INSERT (ITEM, true, TO_THE_Q.PQ);
  end ADD_TO_Q;
  procedure DEQUEUE (ITEM       : in     ITEM_TYPE;
                     FROM_THE_Q : in out PRIORITY_QUEUE) is
    DUMMY : boolean;
    TEMP_X : ITEM_TYPE;
  begin
    NEXT_INORDER(TEMP_X, DUMMY, FROM_THE_Q.PQ);
    ITEM := TEMP_X;
    DELETE(TEMP_X, FROM_THE_Q.PQ);
  end DEQUEUE;

  procedure COPY ( FROM_Q : in     PRIORITY_QUEUE;
                   TO_Q   : in out PRIORITY_QUEUE) is
  begin
    COPY (FROM_Q.PQ, TO_Q.PQ);
  end COPY;
```

```
procedure MERGE ( FROM_Q1,
                  FROM_Q2 : in      PRIORITY_QUEUE;
                  ONTO_Q  : in out PRIORITY_QUEUE) is
  KEY : ITEM_TYPE;
  DATA : boolean;
  TEMP_Q : PRIORITY_QUEUE;
begin
  COPY_TREE (FROM_Q1.PQ, ONTO_Q.PQ);
  COPY_TREE (FROM_Q2.PQ, TEMP_Q.PQ);
  SET_INORDER (TEMP_Q.PQ);
  for COUNT in 1..COUNT (TEMP_Q.PQ) loop
    NEXT_INORDER (KEY, DATA, TEMP_Q.PQ);
    INSERT (KEY, DATA, ONTO_Q.PQ);
  end loop;
end MERGE;

procedure CLEAR ( Q_TO_CLEAR : in out PRIORITY_QUEUE) is
begin
  CLEAR (Q_TO_CLEAR.PQ);
end CLEAR;

procedure POP (FROM_THE_Q : in out PRIORITY_QUEUE) is
  dummy : boolean;
  TEMP_X : ITEM_TYPE;
begin
  SET_INORDER (FROM_THE_Q.PQ);
  NEXT_INORDER(TEMP_X, DUMMY, FROM_THE_Q.PQ);
  DELETE (TEMP_X, FROM_THE_Q.PQ);
end POP;

function LENGTH (Q_TO_COUNT : PRIORITY_QUEUE) return natural is
begin
  return COUNT (Q_TO_COUNT.PQ);
end LENGTH;

function EMPTY (Q_TO_CHECK : PRIORITY_QUEUE) return boolean is
begin
  return COUNT (Q_TO_CHECK.PQ) = 0;
end EMPTY;

function FRONT_ITEM (FROM_THE_Q; PRIORITY_QUEUE) return ITEM_TYPE is
  ANS : ITEM_TYPE;
  DATA : boolean;
  TEMP_Q : PRIORITY_QUEUE;
begin
  COPY (FROM_THE_Q.PQ, TEMP_Q.PQ);
  SET_INORDER (TEMP_Q.PQ);
  NEXT_INORDER (ANS, DATA, TEMP_Q.PQ);
  return ANS;
end FRONT_ITEM;
```

```
      function EQUAL (Q1, Q2 : PRIORITY_QUEUE) return boolean is
      begin
        return EQUAL (Q1.PQ, Q2.PQ);
      end EQUAL;


  end GENERIC_UNBOUNDED_PRIORITY_QUEUE;
```

Chapter 9

9.2.1 b.
```
      function EQUAL (A, B : SET ) return boolean is
          -- Returns true if two sets are equal. Two sets are equal if all
          -- the elements in set A are in set B, and vice versa.
      begin
        if A.COUNT = B.COUNT then
          return A.S. = B.S.;
        else
          return false;
        end if;
      end EQUAL;
```

d.
```
      function "*" ( LEFT, RIGHT: SET ) return SET is
          -- Computes the intersection of the sets LEFT and RIGHT. The
          -- intersection of two sets is a set that contains elements
          -- common to both sets.
        ANS : SET;
      begin
        ANS.S := LEFT.S and RIGHT.S;
        for i in ELEMENT_TYPE'first..ELEMENT_TYPE'last loop
          if ANS.S(i) then
            ANS.COUNT := ANS.COUNT + 1;
          end if;
        end loop;
        return ANS;
      end "*";
```

g.
```
      procedure NEXT_ELEMENT ( A       : in out SET;
                                ELEMENT :    out ELEMENT_TYPE ) is
          -- Returns the next element in an enumeration of the set A.
          -- Repeated calls will eventually list every element in A before
          -- before repeating the sequence provided that no elements have been
          -- added or deleted.
          -- Exception ELEMENT_NOT_IN_SET raised if A is empty.
      begin
        if A.COUNT = 0 then
          raise ELEMENT_NOT_IN_SET;
        else
          for COUNT in 1..A.S'length loop
            if A.LAST_LIST = A.S.'last then
              A.LAST_LIST := A.S.'first;
            else
              A.LAST_LIST :=ELEMENT_TYPE'succ(A.LAST_LIST);
            end if;
```

```
            if A.S.(A.LAST_LIST) then
               ELEMENT := A.LAST_LIST;
               return;
            end if;
         end loop;
      end if;
   end NEXT_ELEMENT;
```

9.2.2 d.
```
procedure REMOVE_ELEMENT ( ELEMENT  : in      ELEMENT_TYPE;
                           FROM SET : in out SET ) is
   PLACE : NEXT_NODE := FROM_SET.FIRST;
begin
   From_SET.LAST_LIST := null;
   if PLACE = null then
      -- FROM_SET is empty, so element is not there
      raise ELEMENT_NOT_IN_SET;
   elsif PLACE.KEY = ELEMENT then
      --ELEMENT is the first item in the list
      FROM_SET.FIRST := PLACE.NEXT;
      FROM_SET.COUNT := FROM_SET.COUNT - 1;
      return;
   else
      --Element is assumed in list but not at the head of the list
      while PLACE.NEXT /= null loop
         if PLACE.NEXT.KEY = ELEMENT then
            PLACE.NEXT := PLACE.NEXT.NEXT;
            FROM_SET.COUNT := FROM_SET.COUNT - 1;
            return;
         end if;
         PLACE := PLACE.NEXT;
      end loop;
      -- Arrived at end of set list without finding the element.
      raise ELEMENT_NOT_IN_SET;
   end if;
end REMOVE_ELEMENT;
```

g.
```
function ELEMENT_IN_SET (ELEMENT :    ELEMENT_TYPE;
                         IN_SET  :    SET ) return boolean is
   PLACE : NEXT_NODE := IN_SET.FIRST;
begin
   while PLACE /= null loop
      if PLACE.KEY = ELEMENT then
         return true;
      else
         PLACE := PLACE.NEXT;
      end if;
   end loop;
   return false;
end ELEMENT_IN_SET;
```

9.3.1 e.
```
function ELEMENT_IN_SET (ELEMENT    : ELEMENT_TYPE;
                         IN_SET     : SET ) return boolean is
```

```
     -- Returns true if ELEMENT is in IN_SET.
    PLACE : NEXT_NODE := IN_SET.FIRST;
  begin
    while PLACE /= null loop
       if PLACE.KEY = ELEMENT then
          return true;
       else
          PLACE := PLACE.NEXT;
       end if;
    end loop;
    return false;
  end ELEMENT_IN_SET;
f. function "*" ( LEFT, RIGHT : SET ) return SET is
     -- Computes the intersection of the sets LEFT and RIGHT. The
     -- intersection of two sets is a set that contains elements
     -- common to both sets.
     -- Exception OVERFLOW can be raised by ADD_ELEMENT
    PLACE : NEXT_NODE := LEFT.FIRST;
    RESULT : SET;
  begin
    while PLACE /= null loop
       if ELEMENT_IN_SET (PLACE.KEY, RIGHT) then
          ADD_ELEMENT(PLACE.KEY, RESULT);
       end if;
       PLACE := PLACE.NEXT;
    end loop;
    return RESULT;
  exception
    when OVERFLOW => raise OVERFLOW;
  end "*";
```

9.3.2 b.
```
procedure REMOVE_ELEMENT ( ELEMENT  : in     ELEMENT_TYPE;
                           FROM_SET : in out SET ) is
     -- Removes ELEMENT from the set FROM_SET.
     -- Exception ELEMENT_NOT_IN_SET raised if ELEMENT not in FROM_SET
  begin
    if KEY_IN_TREE (ELEMENT, TO_SET.TREE_SET) then
       DELETE (ELEMENT, FROM_SET.TREE_SET);
    else
       raise ELEMENT_NOT_IN_SET;
    end if;
  end REMOVE_ELEMENT;
```

h.
```
function "<=" ( A_subset, of_B : SET ) return boolean is
     -- Returns true if the set A_SUBSET is a subset of the set OF_B.
     -- Every element in A_Subset must be in OF_B.
    ELEMENT : ELEMENT_TYPE;
    DATA    : boolean;
    TEMP_A  : SET;
  begin
     -- By definition of subset, everything in A_SUBSET must be in OF_B
```

```
          COPY (A_SUBSET.TREE_SET, TEMP_A.TREE_SET);
          -- Check everything in A_SUBSET
          for COUNT in 1..COUNT (TEMP_A.TREE_SET) loop
            NEXT_INORDER (ELEMENT, DATA TEMP_A.TREE_SET);
            if not KEY_IN_TREE (ELEMENT, OF_B.TREE_SET) then
              -- Element from TEMP_A not in OF_B
              return false;
            end if;
          end loop;
          return false;
       end "<=";
```

Chapter 10

10.1.1
```
       procedure ADD_EDGE (SOURCE, DESTINATION : in    VERTEX;
                           TO_GRAPH            : in out GRAPH) is
          -- Adds an edge in a graph G from vertex SOURCE to vertex
          -- DESTINATION.
          -- Exception EDGE_EXISTS raised if the graph already
          --           contains the specified edge.
       begin
          if TO_GRAPH.EDGE (SOURCE, DESTINATION) then
            raise EDGE_EXISTS;
          else
            TO_GRAPH.EDGE (SOURCE, DESTINATION) := true;
          end if;
       end ADD_EDGE;
```

d.
```
       procedure NEXT_SOURCE_VERTEX( DESTINATION : in    VERTEX;
                                     IN_GRAPH    : in out GRAPH;
                                     NEXT_SOURCE :    out VERTEX ) is
          -- Iterates through the edges of a specified destination vertex
          -- DESTINATION and returns the source vertex of the next edge.
          -- Exception NO_EDGE raised if the indegree of the specified
          --           vertex is 0.
       begin
          for COUNT in 1..NUMBER_OF_VERTICES loop
            if IN_GRAPH.NEXT_SOURCE(DESTINATION) = VERTEX'last then
            IN_GRAPH.NEXT_SOURCE(DESTINATION) := VERTEX'first;
            else
              IN_GRAPH.NEXT_SOURCE(DESTINATION) :=
                  VERTEX'succ (IN_GRAPH.NEXT_SOURCE(DESTINATION));
            end if;
            if IN_GRAPH.EDGE(IN_GRAPH.NEXT_SOURCE(DESTINATION), DESTINATION)
                then
              NEXT_SOURCE := IN_GRAPH.NEXT_SOURCE(DESTINATION);
              return;
            end if;
          end loop;
          raise NO_EDGE;
       end NEXT_SOURCE_VERTEX;
```

```
    g. function VERTEX_IN_DEGREE(DESTINATION : VERTEX;
                                 IN_GRAPH    : GRAPH) return natural is
       -- Returns the number of edges in a graph with a specified
       -- destination vertex.
       COUNT : natural := 0;
    begin
       for SOURCE in VERTEX loop
         if IN_GRAPH.EDGE(SOURCE, DESTINATION) then
           COUNT := COUNT + 1;
         end if;
       end loop;
       return COUNT;
    end VERTEX_IN_DEGREE;
```

10.1.2 a.
```
    procedure COPY (FROM : in GRAPH; TO: out GRAPH) is
            -- Makes an exact copy TO of the graph FROM.
            TEMP : GRAPH;
            TEMP_FROM : GRAPH := FROM;
            DESTINATION : VERTEX;
        begin
          --For each source vertex in the graph
          for SOURCE in VERTEX loop
            --Get all edges with that source vertex and add to TO.
            for COUNT in 1..VERTEX_OUT_DEGREE(SOURCE, TEMP_FROM) loop
              NEXT_DESTINATION_VERTEX (SOURCE, TEMP_FROM, DESTINATION);
              ADD_EDGE(SOURCE, DESTINATION, TEMP);
            end loop;
          end loop;
            TO := TEMP;
        end COPY;
```

d.
```
    procedure ADD_EDGE ( SOURCE, DESTINATION : in     VERTEX;
                         TO_GRAPH             : in out GRAPH) is
       -- Adds an edge in a graph TO_GRAPH from vertex SOURCE to vertex
       -- DESTINATION.
       -- Exception EDGE_EXISTS raised if the graph already
       --           contains the specified edge.
       TEMP_EDGE : NEXT_EDGE := new EDGE'(SOURCE,DESTINATION,null,null);

        procedure ADD_EDGE_TO_SOURCE_Q (EDGE  : in     NEXT_EDGE;
                                        QUEUE : in out NEXT_EDGE) is
       TEMP_EDGE : NEXT_EDGE := EDGE;
    begin
       if QUEUE = null or else EDGE.DESTINATION < QUEUE.DESTINATION then
         TEMP_EDGE.NEXT_DESTINATION := QUEUE;
         QUEUE := TEMP_EDGE;
       else
         ADD_EDGE_TO_SOURCE_Q (EDGE, QUEUE.NEXT_DESTINATION);
       end if;
    end ADD_EDGE_TO_SOURCE_Q;

    procedure ADD_EDGE_TO_DESTINATION_Q (EDGE  : in     NEXT_EDGE;
                                         QUEUE : in out NEXT_EDGE) is
```

```
    TEMP_EDGE : NEXT_EDGE := EDGE;
  begin
    if QUEUE = null or else EDGE.SOURCE < QUEUE.SOURCE then
        TEMP_EDGE.NEXT_SOURCE := QUEUE;
        QUEUE := TEMP_EDGE;
      else
        ADD_EDGE_TO_DESTINATION_Q (EDGE, QUEUE.NEXT_SOURCE);
      end if;
    end ADD_EDGE_TO_DESTINATION_Q;
  begin
    if EDGE_IN_GRAPH (SOURCE, DESTINATION, TO_GRAPH) then
      raise EDGE_EXISTS;
    else
      ADD_EDGE_TO_SOURCE_Q (TEMP_EDGE,
      TO_GRAPH.SOURCE_ARRAY(SOURCE).FIRST_EDGE);
      TO_GRAPH.SOURCE_ARRAY(SOURCE).DEGREE :=
          TO_GRAPH.SOURCE_ARRAY (SOURCE).DEGREE + 1;
      ADD_EDGE_TO_DESTINATION_Q (TEMP_EDGE,
          TO_GRAPH.DESTINATION_ARRAY(DESTINATION).FIRST_EDGE);
      TO_GRAPH. DESTINATION_ARRAY(DESTINATION).DEGREE :=
          TO_GRAPH.DESTINATION_ARRAY(DESTINATION).DEGREE + 1;
    end if;
  end ADD_EDGE;
```

f.
```
  procedure NEXT_DESTINATION_VERTEX (SOURCE    : in     VERTEX;
                                     IN_GRAPH : in out GRAPH;
                              NEXT_DESTINATION :    out VERTEX ) is
    -- Iterates through the edges with a specified source vertex SOURCE
    -- and returns the destination vertex DESTINATION of the next edge.
    -- Exception NO_EDGE raised if the outdegree of the specified
    --          vertex is 0.
  begin
    if IN_GRAPH.NEXT_DESTINATION(SOURCE) = null then
      IN_GRAPH.NEXT_DESTINATION(SOURCE) :=
            IN_GRAPH.SOURCE_ARRAY(SOURCE).FIRST_EDGE;
      if IN_GRAPH.NEXT_DESTINATION(SOURCE) = null then
        RAISE NO_EDGE;
      else
        NEXT_DESTINATION :=
            IN_GRAPH.NEXT_DESTINATION(SOURCE).DESTINATION;
      end if;
    else
      IN_GRAPH.NEXT_DESTINATION(SOURCE) :=
          IN_GRAPH.NEXT_DESTINATION(SOURCE).NEXT_DESTINATION;
      if IN_GRAPH.NEXT_DESTINATION(SOURCE) : null then
        IN_GRAPH.NEXT_DESTINATION(SOURCE) :=
            IN_GRAPH.SOURCE_ARRAY(SOURCE).FIRST_EDGE;
      end if;
      NEXT_DESTINATION :=
          IN_GRAPH.NEXT_DESTINATION(SOURCE).DESTINATION;
    end if;
```

```
        end NEXT_DESTINATION_VERTEX;
    k. function VERTEX_OUT_DEGREE (SOURCE   : VERTEX;
                                   IN_GRAPH : GRAPH) return natural is
       -- Returns the number of edges in a graph with a specified
       -- source vertex.
       begin
         return IN_GRAPH.SOURCE_ARRAY(SOURCE).DEGREE;
       end VERTEX_OUT_DEGREE;
10.2.1 c. procedure REMOVE_EDGE  (SOURCE,
                                  DESTINATION : in    VERTEX_TYPE;
                                  FROM_GRAPH  : in out GRAPH) is
       -- Removes the edge in a graph G with source VERTEX SOURCE and
       -- destination VERTEX DESTINATION.
       -- Exception NO_EDGE raised if the specified edge is
       --          not in the graph FROM_GRAPH.
       -- Exception NO_VERTEX raised if either the source or destination
       --          VERTEX is not in the VERTEX queue
       SOURCE_VERTEX      : NEXT_VERTICE;
       DESTINATION_VERTEX : NEXT_VERTICE;

       procedure REMOVE_EDGE_FROM_SOURCE_Q
                      (DESTINATION : in    VERTEX_TYPE;
                       PLACE       : in out NEXT_EDGE) IS
       begin
         if PLACE = null or else DESTINATION < PLACE.DESTINATION then
           raise NO_EDGE;
         elsif DESTINATION = PLACE.DESTINATION then
           PLACE := PLACE.NEXT_DESTINATION;
         else
           REMOVE_EDGE_FROM_SOURCE_Q(DESTINATION,
                      PLACE.NEXT_DESTINATION);
         end if;
       end REMOVE_EDGE_FROM_SOURCE_Q;

       procedure REMOVE_EDGE_FROM_DEST_Q (SOURCE : in    VERTEX_TYPE;
                                          PLACE  : in out NEXT_EDGE ) IS
         -- Exception NO_VERTEX raised if the source VERTEX SOURCE
         --          is not in the VERTEX queue
       begin
         if SOURCE = PLACE.SOURCE then
           PLACE := PLACE.NEXT_SOURCE;
         else
           REMOVE_EDGE_FROM_DEST_Q (SOURCE, PLACE.NEXT_SOURCE);
         end if;
       end REMOVE_EDGE_FROM_DEST_Q;

       begin
         --Find beginning of queue of edges with src, dst
         SOURCE_VERTEX := FIND_VERTEX (FROM GRAPH.SOURCE LIST, SOURCE);
         DESTINATION_VERTEX := FIND_VERTEX(FROM_GRAPH.DESTINATION_LIST,
                                           DESTINATION);
```

```
       -- Remove edge_node from ordered source queue of edges
       if SOURCE_VERTEX := FIRST_EDGE = null or else
           DESTINATION < SOURCE_VERTEX.FIRST_EDGE.DESTINATION then
         raise NO_EDGE;
       elsif DESTINATION = SOURCE_VERTEX.FIRST_EDGE.DESTINATION then
         SOURCE_VERTEX.FIRST_EDGE :=
               SOURCE_VERTEX.FIRST_EDGE.NEXT_DESTINATION;
       else
         REMOVE_EDGE_FROM_SOURCE_Q
               (DESTINATION, SOURCE_VERTEX.FIRST_EDGE);
       end if;
       -- Remove edge_node from ordered destination queue of edges
       if DESTINATION_VERTEX.FIRST_EDGE.SOURCE = SOURCE then
         DESTINATION_VERTEX.FIRST_EDGE :=
               DESTINATION_VERTEX.FIRST_EDGE.NEXT_SOURCE;
       else
         REMOVE_EDGE_FROM_DEST_Q (SOURCE, SOURCE_VERTEX.FIRST_EDGE);
       end if;
       SOURCE_VERTEX.DEGREE      := SOURCE_VERTEX.DEGREE - 1;
       DESTINATION_VERTEX.DEGREE := DESTINATION_VERTEX.DEGREE - 1;
       SOURCE_VERTEX.LAST_LIST   := null;
       DESTINATION_VERTEX.LAST_LIST := null;
     exception
       when NO_VERTEX => raise NO_VERTEX;
       when NO_EDGE   => raise NO_EDGE;
     end REMOVE_EDGE;
  g. function EDGE_IN_GRAPH (SOURCE, DESTINATION : VERTEX_TYPE;
                             IN_GRAPH : GRAPH ) return boolean is
       -- Returns true if an edge with SOURCE and DESTINATION is in
       -- IN_GRAPH
       -- Exception NO_VERTEX raised if either the source or destination
       --           vertices are not in the vertex queue
       TEMP_SOURCE_VERTICE : NEXT_VERTICE;
       TEMP_EDGE : NEXT_EDGE;
     begin
       -- Determine if both vertices in graph
       TEMP_SOURCE_VERTICE := FIND_VERTEX(IN_GRAPH.DESTINATION_LIST, DESTINATION)
       TEMP_SOURCE_VERTICE := FIND_VERTEX (IN_GRAPH.SOURCE_LIST, SOURCE);
       TEMP_EDGE := TEMP_SOURCE_VERTICE.FIRST_EDGE;
       loop
         if TEMP_EDGE = null then
           return false;
         elsif TEMP_EDGE.DESTINATION = DESTINATION then
           return true;
         else
           TEMP_EDGE := TEMP_EDGE.NEXT_DESTINATION;
         end if;
       end loop;
     exception
       when NO_VERTEX => raise NO_VERTEX;
     end EDGE_IN_GRAPH;
```

```
   h. function NEXT_DESTINATION_VERTEX ( SOURCE : VERTEX_TYPE;
                              IN_GRAPH : GRAPH ) return VERTEX_TYPE is
      -- Iterates through the edges with a specified source vertex and
      -- returns the destination vertex of the next edge.
      -- Exception NO_EDGE raised if the outdegree of the specified
      -- vertex is 0.
      -- Exception NO_VERTEX raised if either the source vertex is not in
      --          the queue
      TEMP_V : NEXT_VERTICE;
   begin
      TEMP_V : FIND_VERTEX (IN_GRAPH.SOURCE_LIST, SOURCE);
      if TEMP_V.LAST_LIST = null then
        TEMP_V.LAST_LIST := TEMP_V.FIRST_EDGE;
        if TEMP_V.LAST_LIST = null then
          raise NO_EDGE;
        end if;
      else
        TEMP_V.LAST_LIST := TEMP_V.LAST_LIST.NEXT_SOURCE;
        if TEMP_V.LAST_LIST = null then
          TEMP_V.LAST_LIST := TEMP_V.FIRST_EDGE;
        end if;
      end if;
      return TEMP_V.LAST_LIST.DESTINATION;
   exception
      when NO_VERTEX => raise NO_VERTEX;
   end NEXT_DESTINATION_VERTEX;
   k. function VERTEX_IN_DEGREE (DESTINATION : VERTEX_TYPE;
                              IN_GRAPH : GRAPH ) return natural is
      -- Returns the number of edges in a graph with a specified
      -- destination vertex.
      -- Exception NO_VERTEX raised if the destination vertex
      --          is not in the vertex queue
   begin
      return FIND_VERTEX (IN_GRAPH.DESTINATION_LIST, DESTINATION).DEGREE;
   exception
      when NO_VERTEX => raise NO_VERTEX;
   end VERTEX_IN_DEGREE;
10.3.1 function EDGE_WEIGHT (SOURCE, DESTINATION : VERTEX;
                              IN_GRAPH : GRAPH ) return WEIGHT_TYPE is
      -- Returns the edge weight of an edge with source vertex SOURCE and
      -- destination vertex DESTINATION
      -- Exception NO_EDGE raised if edge has zero weight
   begin
      if IN_GRAPH.GRAPH(SOURCE, DESTINATION) = ZERO_WEIGHT then
        raise NO_EDGE;
      else
        return IN_GRAPH.GRAPH(SOURCE,DESTINATION);
      end if;
   end EDGE_WEIGHT;
10.4.1. b. procedure add_TRANSITION ( STATE_AT : in    positive;
```

```
                          SYMBOL    : in     ALPHABET;
                          STATE_TO : in     positive;
                          TO_GRAPH : in out TRANSITION_GRAPH) is
      -- Sets the transition of the state STATE_AT with SYMBOL to STATE_TO
      -- Exception NO_STATE raised if STATE_AT or STATE_TO does not
      --          reference a valid state
   begin
      if STATE_AT > NUMBER_STATES or STATE_TO > NUMBER_STATES then
        raise NO_STATE;
      else
         TO_GRAPH.GRAPH(STATE_AT, SYMBOL) := STATE_TO;
      end if;
   end ADD_TRANSITION;
 c. procedure SET_FINAL_SET (STATE    : in     positive;
                            IS_FINAL : in     boolean;
                            IN_GRAPH : in out TRANSITION_GRAPH) is
      -- Marks or unmarks a given STATE as a final state.
      -- Exception NO_STATE raised if STATE does not
      -- reference a valid state
   begin
      if STATE > NUMBER_STATES then
        raise NO_STATE;
      else
         IN_GRAPH.FINAL(STATE) := IS_FINAL;
      end if;
   end SET_FINAL_SET;
```

10.4.3 Let vertex 1 = even number a's and b's

2 = even a's, odd b's

3 = odd a's, even b's

4 = odd a's, odd b's

5 = death state

Final set = {3}

Use the transition table

	a	b
1	3	2
2	4	1
3	1	4
4	2	3
5	5	5

Chapter 11

11.1.1 a. ```generic```
```
        type ITEM_TYPE is private;
        type INDEX is (<>);
        type VECTOR is array (INDEX) of ITEM_TYPE;
        with function "<" (LEFT, RIGHT : ITEM_TYPE) return boolean;
```

```
        procedure BUBBLE_SORT (V : in out VECTOR);
        procedure BUBBLE_SORT (V : in out VECTOR) is
          TEMP_ITEM ; ITEM_TYPE;
        begin
          for OUTER in V'first .. INDEX'pred(V'last) loop
            for INNER in INDEX'succ(V'first) .. V'last loop
              if V(INNER) < V(INDEX'pred(INNER)) then
                TEMP_ITEM := V(INNER);
                V(INNER) := V(INDEX'pred(INNER));
                V(INDEX'PRED(INNER)) := TEMP_ITEM;
              end if;
            end loop;
          end loop;
        end BUBBLE_SORT;
```

11.3.1
```
        procedure LIST_INSERTION_SORT (LIST_TO_SORT : in out LIST) is
        TEMP : LIST := LIST_TO_SORT;

        procedure ADD_INORDER (NODE_TO_PLACE : in     LIST;
                               LIST_TO_SORT  : in out LIST) is
          -- Recursive procedure to add node to list in order
        begin
          if LIST_TO_SORT = null then
            LIST_TO_SORT := NODE_TO_PLACE;
          elsif NODE_TO_PLACE.ITEM <= LIST_TO_SORT.ITEM then
            NODE_TO_PLACE.NEXT := LIST_TO_SORT;
            LIST_TO_SORT := NODE_TO_PLACE;
          else
            ADD_INORDER (NODE_TO_PLACE, LIST_TO_SORT.NEXT);
          end if;
        end ADD_INORDER;

        begin
          LIST_TO_SORT := null;
          -- peel off nodes until list is empty
          loop
            exit when TEMP = null;
            -- get next node
            TEMP_NODE := TEMP;
            TEMP_NODE.NEXT := null;
            TEMP := TEMP.NEXT;
            -- Insert TEMP_NODE into LIST_TO_SORT
            ADD_INORDER (TEMP_NODE, LIST_TO_SORT);
          end loop;
        end LIST_INSERTION_SORT;
```

Chapter 12

12.1.1 b.
```
        procedure DELETE (T   : in out TABLE);
                          KEY : in     KEY_TYPE) is
          -- Deletes a given KEY-data pair already in the table T. The
```

```
-- KEY field must match the supplied KEY.
-- Exception TABLE_NOT_DEFINED raised if SIZE of T undefined,
--          which occurs when T = null.
-- Exception KEY_IS_NOT_FOUND raised if no key-data pair with
--          the specific KEY is in the table T.
begin
  if T = null then
    raise TABLE_NOT_DEFINED;
  else
    for I in 1..T.LAST_USED loop
      if KEY = T.LIST(I).KEY then
        T.LIST_LAST := 0;
        T.LAST_USED := T.LAST_USED - 1;
        -- Shift key-data pairs into used slice
        if I <= T.LAST_USED then
          T.LIST (I..T.LAST_USED) := T.LIST(I+1..T.LAST_USED+1);
        end if;
        return;
      end if;
    end loop;
    raise KEY_IS_NOT_FOUND;
  end if;
end DELETE;
```

c.
```
procedure LIST_NEXT_KEY_DATA (T    : in out TABLE;
                              KEY  :    out KEY_TYPE;
                              DATA :    out DATA_TYPE) is
-- Returns the next key-data pair in the table. Repeated calls
-- will eventually return all key-data pairs before any pair is
-- listed again.
-- Exception TABLE_NOT_DEFINED raised if SIZE of T undefined,
--          which occurs when T = null.
-- Exception TABLE_EMPTY raised if no key-data pairs are in the
--          to be listed.
begin
  if T = null then
    raise TABLE_NOT_DEFINED;
  elsif T.LAST_USED = 0 then
    raise TABLE_EMPTY;
  else
    T.LIST_LAST := T.LIST_LAST + 1;
    if T.LIST_LAST > T.LAST_USED then
      T.LIST_LAST := 1;
    end if;
    KEY := T.LIST(T.LIST_LAST).KEY;
    DATA := T.LIST(T.LIST_LAST).DATA;
  end if;
end LIST_NEXT_KEY_DATA;
```

g.
```
function KEY_IN_TABLE (T   : TABLE;
                       KEY : KEY_TYPE) return boolean is
-- Returns true if the supplied KEY corresponds to the KEY of
```

```
          -- any key-data pair in the table.
          -- Exception TABLE_NOT_DEFINED raised if SIZE of T undefined,
          --          which occurs when T = null.
       begin
         if T = null then
           raise TABLE_NOT_DEFINED;
         else
           for I in 1..T.LAST_USED loop
             if KEY = T.LIST(I).KEY then
               return true;
             end if;
           end loop;
           return false;
         end if;
       end KEY_IN_TABLE;
```

12.1.2 b.
```
       procedure DELETE (T    : in out TABLE);
                         KEY : in     KEY_TYPE) is
          -- Deletes a given key-data pair already in the table T. The
          -- KEY field must match the supplied KEY.
          -- Exception TABLE_NOT_DEFINED raised if SIZE of T undefined,
          --          which occurs when T = null.
          -- Exception KEY_IS_NOT_FOUND raised if no key-data pair with
          --          the specific KEY is in the table T.
          LEFT : natural := 1;
          RIGHT : natural := T.LAST_USED;
          MIDDLE : natural := (LEFT + RIGHT)/2;
       begin
         if T = null then
           raise TABLE_NOT_DEFINED;
         elsif T.LAST_USED = 0 then
           --Table is empty, nothing to delete
           raise KEY_IS_NOT_FOUND;
         else
           --Do a binary search for the correct position
           while LEFT <= RIGHT loop
             If KEY = T.LIST(MIDDLE).KEY then
               T.LIST_LAST := 0;
               T.LAST_USED := T.LAST_USED - 1;
               T.LIST(MIDDLE..T.LAST_USED) :=
                      T.LIST(MIDDLE+1..T.LAST_USED+1);
               return;
             else
               if KEY < T.LIST(MIDDLE).KEY then
                 RIGHT := MIDDLE - 1;
               else
                 LEFT := MIDDLE + 1;
               end if;
               MIDDLE := (LEFT + RIGHT)/2;
             end if;
           end loop;
```

```
          raise KEY_IS_NOT_FOUND;
       end if;
   end DELETE;
h. procedure INSERT (T    : in out TABLE;
                      KEY  : in     KEY_TYPE;
                      DATA : in     DATA_TYPE) is
    -- Inserts a key-data pair (KEY, Data) into a table T.
    -- Entries with duplicate keys are not allowed.
    -- Exception TABLE_NOT_DEFINED raised if SIZE of T undefined,
    --          which occurs when T = null.
    -- Exception TABLE_FULL raised if no space is available
    -- Exception KEY_IS_IN_TABLE raised if a key-data pair with a
    --          given specific KEY is already in the table
    LEFT   : natural := 1;
    RIGHT  : natural := T.LAST_USED;
    MIDDLE : natural := (LEFT + RIGHT)/2;
   begin
    if T = null then
      raise TABLE_NOT_DEFINED;
    elsif T.LAST_USED = T.SIZE then
      --Table is full, no room left
      raise TABLE_FULL;
    elsif T.LAST_USED = 0 then
      --Empty table, first pair goes in position 1
      T.LAST_USED := 1;
      T.LIST_LAST := 0;
      T.LIST(1) := (KEY, DATA);
    else
      --Do a binary serach for the correct position
      while LEFT <= RIGHT loop
        If KEY = T.LIST(MIDDLE).KEY then
          raise KEY_IS_IN_TABLE;
        else
          if KEY < T.LIST(MIDDLE).KEY then
            RIGHT := MIDDLE - 1;
          else
            LEFT := MIDDLE + 1;
          end if;
          MIDDLE := (LEFT + RIGHT + 1)/2;
        end if;
      end loop;
      --Insert pair at position MIDDLE
      T.LIST_LAST := 0;
      T.LAST_USED := T.LAST_USED + 1;
      if MIDDLE < T.LAST_USED then
        T.LIST (MIDDLE+1..T.LAST_USED) :=
                T.LIST(MIDDLE..T.LAST_USED-1);
        T.LIST(MIDDLE) := (KEY, DATA);
      end if;
```

```
          end if;
        end INSERT;
12.3.1 a. procedure UPDATE ( T     : in out TABLE);
                          KEY  : in     KEY_TYPE;
                          DATA : in     DATA_TYPE) is
        -- Replaces the data field for a given KEY-data pair that is
        -- already in the table with a new data value. The KEY must
        -- match the supplied KEY.
        -- Exception TABLE_NOT_DEFINED raised if SIZE of T undefined,
        --          which occurs when T = null.
        -- Exception KEY_IS_NOT_FOUND raised if no key-data pair with
        --          the specific KEY is in the table T.
        INDEX : natural;
      begin
        if T = null then
          raise TABLE_NOT_DEFINED;
        elsif not KEY_IN_TABLE (T, KEY) then
          raise KEY_IS_NOT_FOUND;
        else
          INDEX := 1 + (HASH(KEY) rem T.SIZE);
          for COUNT in 1..T.SIZE loop
            if T.LIST(INDEX).STATUS = IN_USE and then
              T.LIST(INDEX).KEY = KEY then
              T.LIST(INDEX).DATA := DATA;
              T.LIST_LAST := T.SIZE;
              exit;
            else
              --Collision resolution uses prime probing
              INDEX := 1 + ((INDEX + 12) rem T.SIZE);
            end if;
          end loop;
        end if;
      end UPDATE;
    f. procedure INSERT (T     : in out TABLE;
                        KEY    : in     KEY_TYPE;
                        DATA   : in     DATA_TYPE) is
      -- Inserts a KEY-data pair (KEY, Data) into a table T.
      -- Entries with duplicate keys are not allowed.
      -- Exception TABLE_NOT_DEFINED raised if SIZE of T undefined,
      --          which occurs when T = null.
      -- Exception TABLE_FULL raised if no space is available
      -- Exception KEY_IS_IN_TABLE raised if a key-data pair with a
      --          given specific KEY is already in the table
      INDEX         : natural;
    begin
      if T = null then
        raise TABLE_NOT_DEFINED;
      elsif T.COUNT = T.SIZE then
        raise TABLE_FULL;
```

```
          elsif KEY_IN_TABLE(T, KEY) then
            raise KEY_IS_IN_TABLE;
          else
            INDEX : 1 + (HASH(KEY) rem T.SIZE);
            --Collision resolution, search for empty table location
            loop
              exit when T.LIST(INDEX).STATUS /= IN_USE;
              INDEX := 1 + (INDEX + 12) rem T.SIZE;
            end loop;
            T.LIST(INDEX) := (IN_USE, KEY, DATA);
            T.COUNT := T.COUNT + 1;
            T.LIST_LAST := T.SIZE;
          end if;
        end INSERT;
12.3.3  function "=" (LEFT, RIGHT : TABLE) return boolean is
          -- Returns true the same key-data pairs are in each table
          -- exception TABLE_NOT_DEFINED raised if either table not defined
          TEMP_TABLE : TABLE;
          TEMP_KEY   : KEY_TYPE;
          TEMP_DATA  : DATA_TYPE;
        begin
          if LEFT = null or RIGHT = null then
            raise TABLE_NOT_DEFINED;
          elsif COUNT(LEFT) /= COUNT(RIGHT) then
            -- Tables cannot be equal if one has more in it
            return false;
          else
            CREATE (TEMP_TABLE, positive(TABLE_SIZE(RIGHT)));
            COPY (RIGHT, TEMP_TABLE);
            for INDEX in 1..COUNT(LEFT) loop
              -- For every key-data pair in RIGHT, ..
              LIST_NEXT_KEY_DATA (TEMP_TABLE, TEMP_KEY, TEMP_DATA);
              -- Return false if key not in LEFT ..
              if not KEY_IN_TABLE(LEFT, TEMP_KEY) then
                return false;
              elsif TEMP_DATA /= GET_DATA_FOR_KEY (LEFT, TEMP_KEY) then
                -- or return false if data doesn't match key
                return false;
              end if;
            end loop;
            return true;
          end if;
        end "=";
12.4.1 a. procedure UPDATE (T    : in out TABLE;
                            KEY  : in     KEY_TYPE;
                            DATA : in     DATA_TYPE) is
          -- Replaces the data field for a given key-data pair that is
          -- already in the table with a new data value. The KEY must
          -- match the supplied KEY.
          -- Exception TABLE_NOT_DEFINED raised if SIZE of T undefined,
```

```
--              which occurs when T = null.
-- Exception KEY_IS_NOT_FOUND raised if no key-data pair with
--              the specific KEY is in the table T.
INDEX : natural;
TEMP_ELEMENT : NEXT_ELEMENT;
begin
  if T = null then
    raise TABLE_NOT_DEFINED;
  else
    INDEX := 1 + (HASH(KEY) rem T.SIZE);
    TEMP_ELEMENT := T.LIST(INDEX);
    -- Search the bucket for the key
    loop
      if TEMP_ELEMENT = null then
        raise KEY_IS_NOT_FOUND;
      elsif TEMP_ELEMENT.KEY = KEY then
        -- key-data pair found, update data component and return
        TEMP_ELEMENT.DATA := DATA;
        T.LIST_LAST_BUCKET := 0;
        T.LIST_LAST_ELEMENT := null;
        return;
      else
        TEMP_ELEMENT := TEMP_ELEMENT.NEXT;
      end if;
    end loop;
  end if;
end UPDATE;
```

e.
```
function KEY_IN_TABLE (T   : TABLE;
                       KEY : KEY_TYPE) return boolean is
-- Returns true if the supplied KEY corresponds to the KEY of
-- any key-data pair in the table.
-- Exception TABLE_NOT_DEFINED raised if SIZE of T undefined,
--              which occurs when T = null.
TEMP_ELEMENT : NEXT_ELEMENT;
begin
  if T = null then
    raise TABLE_NOT_DEFINED;
  else
    --Find the bucket the key should be in
    TEMP_ELEMENT := T.LIST ( 1 + (HASH(KEY) rem T.SIZE));
    --Search the bucket sequentially
    loop
      if TEMP_ELEMENT = null then
        return false;
      elsif TEMP_ELEMENT.KEY = KEY then
        return true;
      else
        TEMP_ELEMENT := TEMP_ELEMENT.NEXT;
      end if;
    end loop;
```

```
        end if;
      end KEY_IN_TABLE;
  i. procedure LIST_NEXT_KEY_DATA ( T     : in out TABLE;
                                    KEY   :    out KEY_TYPE;
                                    DATA  :    out DATA_TYPE) is
      -- Returns the next key-data pair in the table. Repeated calls
      -- will eventually return all key-data pairs before any pair is
      -- listed again.
      -- Exception TABLE_NOT_DEFINED raised if SIZE of T undefined,
      --            which occurs when T = null.
      -- Exception TABLE_EMPTY raised if no key-data pairs are in the
      --            to be listed.
    begin
      if T = null then
        raise TABLE_NOT_DEFINED;
      elsif T.COUNT = 0 then
        raise TABLE_EMPTY;
      else
        -- Remember, T.LIST_LAST_ELEMENT references the last listed,
        -- not the next to be listed.
        if T.LIST_LAST_ELEMENT /= null then
          -- Get next element in the bucket
          T.LIST_LAST_ELEMENT := T.LIST_LAST_ELEMENT.NEXT;
        end if;
        if T.LIST_LAST_ELEMENT /= null then
          -- next key-data pair in bucket defined
          KEY := T.LIST_LAST_ELEMENT.KEY;
          DATA := T.LIST_LAST_ELEMENT.DATA;
        else
          -- End of bucket reached, find next nonempty bucket and
          -- return first key-data pair in bucket
          for COUNT in 1..T.SIZE loop
            T.LIST_LAST_BUCKET := 1 + (T.LIST_LAST_BUCKET rem T.SIZE);
            T.LIST_LAST_ELEMENT := T.LIST(T.LIST_LAST_BUCKET);
            if T.LIST_LAST_ELEMENT /= null then
              KEY := T.LIST_LAST_ELEMENT.KEY;
              DATA := T.LIST_LAST_ELEMENT.DATA;
              T.LIST_LAST_ELEMENT := T.LIST_LAST_ELEMENT.NEXT;
              return;
            end if;
          end loop;
        end if;
      end if;
    end LIST_NEXT_KEY_DATA;
```

Chapter 13

```
13.2.1 b. procedure APPEND (FROM   : in       STRING;
                            TO     : in       SUBSTRING;
                            TARGET : in out STRING) is
         -- Converts the substring ONTO to a string and then adjoins
```

```
      -- a copy of the string FROM onto its end and returns the
      -- combined string as TARGET.
      -- Exception OVERFLOW raised if there is insufficient space
    begin
      if FROM.LENGTH + TO'length > TARGET.SIZE then
        raise OVERFLOW;
      else
        TARGET.LIST(1..TO'length) := TO(1..TO'length);
        TARGET.LIST(TO'length+1..TO'length+FROM.LENGTH) :=
              FROM.LIST(1..FROM.LENGTH);
        TARGET.length := FROM.length + TO'length;
      end if;
    end APPEND;
d. procedure DELETE (FROM     : in out STRING;
                     START_AT : in     positive;
                     END_AT   : in     positive) is
      -- Deletes slice FROM(START_AT..END_AT) from FROM
      -- exception POSITION_ERROR raised if START_AT or
                   END_AT greater than LENGTH
  begin
    if START_AT > FROM.LENGTH or END_AT > FROM.LENGTH then
      raise POSITION_ERROR;
    else
      FROM.LENGTH := FROM.LENGTH - (END_AT - START_AT + 1);
      FROM.LIST(START_AT..FROM.LENGTH) :=
        FROM.LIST(END_AT+1..FROM.LENGTH+END_AT-START_AT + 1);
    end if;
  end DELETE;
i. function LESS ( LEFT  : STRING;
                   RIGHT : STRING ) return boolean is
    -- Returns true if the string LEFT is less than the string
    -- RIGHT when using the standard lexicographic orderings
    MIN : natural := LEFT.LENGTH;
  begin
    --Adjust minimum length if necessary
    if MIN < RIGHT.LENGTH then
      MIN := RIGHT.LENGTH;
    end if;
    -- Check item by item using lexicographic ordering with respect to
    -- ITEM_TYPE
    for INDEX in natural range 1..MIN loop
      if LEFT.LIST(INDEX) < RIGHT.LIST(INDEX) then
        return true;
      elsif RIGHT.LIST(INDEX) < LEFT.LIST(INDEX) then
        return false;
      end if;
    end loop;
    -- ITEMS are equal in range 1..MIN, check to see if RIGHT is longer
    return MIN = LEFT.LENGTH AND MIN /= RIGHT.LENGTH;
  end LESS;
```

13.3.1 c.
```
procedure INSERT (FROM    : in    STRING;
                  INTO    : in out STRING;
                  POSITION : in    positive) is
  -- Inserts a copy of the string FROM at a given position
  -- in the string INTO.
  -- Exception OVERFLOW raised if there is insufficient
  --          memory to store the result
  -- Exception POSITION_ERROR raised if POSITION > LENGTH
  TEMP1, TEMP2 : NEXT_NODE;
begin
  if POSITION > INTO.LENGTH then
    raise POSITION_ERROR;
  else
    -- Copy from position to end of string into temp2
    TEMP1 := LOCATE_NODE(INTO, POSITION-1);
    TEMP2 := TEMP1.NEXT;
    -- Copy entire string from to into starting at position
    COPY_TEMP (FROM.FIRST, TEMP1.NEXT);
    -- Put rest of into stored in temp2 back onto into
    TEMP1 := LOCATE_NODE(INTO, FROM.LENGTH+POSITION-1);
    TEMP1.NEXT := TEMP2;
    --Adjust length
    INTO.LENGTH := INTO.LENGTH + FROM.LENGTH;
  end if;
exception
  when OVERFLOW => raise OVERFLOW;
end INSERT;


procedure INSERT ( FROM    : in    SUBSTRING;
                   INTO    : in out STRING;
                   POSITION : in    positive) is
  -- Copies and converts the substring FROM into a string and then
  -- inserts it into INTO at a specified point.
  -- Exception OVERFLOW raised if there is insufficient
  --          memory to store the result
  -- Exception POSITION_ERROR raised if POSITION > LENGTH
  TEMP_STRING : STRING;
begin
  if POSITION > INTO.LENGTH then
    raise POSITION_ERROR;
  else
    -- Convert substring FROM to a string and use string INSERT
    COPY (FROM, TEMP_STRING);
    INSERT (TEMP_STRING, INTO, POSITION);
  end if;
exception
  when OVERFLOW => raise OVERFLOW;
end INSERT;
```

```
         procedure INSERT (FROM      : in      ITEM_TYPE;
                           INTO      : in out STRING;
                           POSITION  : in      positive) is
            -- Inserts an object of ITEM_TYPE into a string at a given point.
            -- Exception OVERFLOW raised if there is insufficient
            --           memory to store the result
            -- Exception POSITION_ERROR raised if POSITION > LENGTH
            TEMP_STRING : STRING;
         begin
            if POSITION > INTO.LENGTH then
               raise POSITION_ERROR;
            elsif POSITION = 1 then
               INTO.FIRST := new STRING_NODE'(FROM, INTO.FIRST);
               INTO.LENGTH := INTO.LENGTH + 1;
            else
               TEMP_STRING := (1, new STRING_NODE'(FROM, null));
               INSERT (TEMP_STRING, INTO, POSITION);
            end if;
         exception
            when storage error => raise OVERFLOW;
            when OVERFLOW => raise OVERFLOW;
         end INSERT;
```

d.
```
         procedure DELETE (FROM      : in out STRING;
                           START_AT : in      positive;
                           END_AT    : in      positive) is
            -- Deletes all items in a given string starting at position
            -- START_AT through and including position END_AT.
            -- Exception POSITION_ERROR raised if START_AT or END_AT > LENGTH
            --           or if START_AT > END_AT.
            TEMP : NEXT_NODE := FROM.FIRST;
            TEMP_FROM, TEMP_FROM_END : NEXT_NODE;
         begin
            if END_AT > FROM.LENGTH or
                 START_AT > FROM.LENGTH or
                 START_AT > END_AT then
               raise POSITION_ERROR;
            elsif START_AT = 1 then
               for I in START_AT..END_AT loop
                  TEMP := TEMP.NEXT;
               end loop;
               FROM.FIRST := TEMP;
               FROM.LENGTH := FROM.LENGTH - END_AT;
            else
               for I in 1..START_AT-2 loop
                  TEMP := TEMP.NEXT;
               end loop;
               -- TEMP points to START_AT, delete as required
               TEMP_FROM := TEMP.NEXT;
```

```
      for I in START_AT..END_AT loop
        TEMP_FROM := TEMP_FROM.NEXT;
      end loop;
      TEMP.NEXT := TEMP_FROM;
      FROM.LENGTH := FROM.LENGTH + END_AT - START_AT - 1;
    end if;
  end DELETE;
i. function LESS (LEFT  : STRING;
                  RIGHT : STRING ) return boolean is
    -- Returns true if the string LEFT is less than the string
    -- RIGHT when using the standard lexicographic orderings
    MIN : natural := LEFT.LENGTH;
    TEMP_L : NEXT_NODE := LEFT.FIRST;
    TEMP_R : NEXT_NODE := RIGHT.FIRST;
  begin
    if TEMP_L = null AND TEMP_R = null then
      return false;
    elsif TEMP_L = null then
      return true;
    else
      -- Make sure the minimum length correctly defined
      if MIN < RIGHT.LENGTH then
        MIN := RIGHT.LENGTH;
      end if;
      -- Compare ITEM by ITEM based on lexicographic order
      for I in natural range 1..MIN loop
        if TEMP_L.ITEM < TEMP_R.ITEM then
          return true;
        elsif TEMP_R.ITEM < TEMP_L.ITEM then
          return false;
        else
          TEMP_L := TEMP_L.NEXT;
          TEMP_R := TEMP_R.NEXT;
        end if;
      end loop;
      -- What if first min characters equal?
      if MIN = LEFT.LENGTH AND MIN /= RIGHT.LENGTH then
        return true;
      else
        return false;
      end if;
    end if;
  end LESS;

  function LESS ( LEFT  : SUBSTRING;
                  RIGHT : STRING ) return boolean is
    -- Returns true if the substring LEFT is less than the string
    -- RIGHT when using the standard lexicographic orderings
    -- Exception OVERFLOW raised if there is insufficient
    --          memory to store the result
```

```
    TEMP_STRING : STRING;
begin
  -- Convert substring LEFT to a string and use string LESS
  COPY_TEMP(LEFT, TEMP_STRING.FIRST);
  TEMP_STRING.LENGTH := LEFT'length;
  return LESS (TEMP_STRING, RIGHT);
exception
  when OVERFLOW => raise OVERFLOW;
end LESS;


function LESS ( LEFT  : STRING;
                RIGHT : SUBSTRING ) return boolean is
  -- Returns true if the string LEFT is less than the substring
  -- RIGHT when using the standard lexicographic orderings
  -- Exception OVERFLOW raised if there is insufficient
  --          memory to store the result
  TEMP_STRING : STRING;
begin
  -- Convert substring RIGHT to a string and use string LESS
  COPY_TEMP(RIGHT, TEMP_STRING.FIRST);
  TEMP_STRING.LENGTH := RIGHT'LENGTH;
  return LESS(LEFT, TEMP_STRING);
exception
  when OVERFLOW => raise OVERFLOW;
end LESS;
```

Chapter 14

14.2.1 b.
```
function RINGS_EQUAL (R1, R2 : RING ) return boolean is
  -- Returns true for two rings of the same length when the
  -- rings are equal item are item when the comparison starts
  -- at the top of both rings, and the same item is marked
  -- with reference to the top of both rings.
  TEMP_R1 : NEXT_NODE := R1.TOP;
  TEMP_R2 : NEXT_NODE := R2.TOP;
begin
  if R1.LENGTH /= R1.LENGTH then
    return false;
  else
    for I in 1.R1.LENGTH loop
      --Check if same node marked
        if (TEMP_R1 = R1.MARK) xor (TEMP_R2 = R2.MARK) then
          return false;
        end if;
        --Check if contents of nodes equal
        if TEMP_R1.ITEM /= TEMP_R2.ITEM then
          return false;
        end if;
        -- Get next successor node from both RINGS
        TEMP_R1 := TEMP_R1.NEXT_CW;
```

```
                    TEMP_R2 := TEMP_R2.NEXT_CW;
                 end loop;
                 return true;
              end if;
           end RINGS_EQUAL;
```

14.2.2 a.
```
        procedure ADD_ITEM (R    : in out RING;
                            ITEM : in      ITEM_ TYPE) is
           -- Adds an item to the ring at the top position. The added
           -- item becomes the new top item, the added item's successor is
           -- the old top item and the added item's predecessor is the
           -- predecessor of the old top item. If the ring was empty
           -- before the item was added, MARK is set to TOP, otherwise the
           -- value of mark is not affected.
           -- Exception OVERFLOW raised if there is no space to add an item
           TEMP : NEXT_NODE;
        begin
           if R.TOP = null then
             --Ring empty
             R.TOP := new RING_NODE' (ITEM, null);
             R.TOP.NEXT_CW := R.TOP;
             R.MARK := R.TOP;
             R.LENGTH := 1;
           else
             -- Ring not empty
             R.TOP := new RING_NODE'(ITEM, R.TOP.NEXT_CW);
             -- Make last node point to top
             TEMP := R.TOP.NEXT_CW;
             for COUNT in 1..R.LENGTH loop
                TEMP := TEMP.NEXT_CW;
             end loop;
             TEMP.NEXT_CW := R.TOP;
             R.LENGTH := R.LENGTH + 1;
           end if;
        exception
           when storage error =>
           raise OVERFLOW;
        end ADD_ITEM;
```

b.
```
        procedure POP ( R : in out RING ) is
           -- Deletes the item referenced by TOP. The new TOP item
           -- is the successor item of the previous TOP. The marked
           -- item is unaffected by the deletion unless the marked
           -- item is also deleted. In this case new marked item is the
           -- new TOP item. TOP and MARK are null if the ring is empty.
           -- Exception EMPTY_RING raised if the ring is empty.
           TEMP : NEXT_NODE;
        begin
           if R.LENGTH = 0 then
             raise EMPTY_RING;
           elsif R.LENGTH = 1 then
             R := (null, null, 0);
```

```
          elsif R.MARK = R.TOP then
            R.MARK := R.TOP.NEXT_CW;
          end if;
          R.TOP := R.TOP.NEXT_CW;
          R.LENGTH := R.LENGTH - 1;
          -- make last node point to TOP
          TEMP := R.TOP;
          for COUNT in 1..R.LENGTH loop
            TEMP := TEMP.NEXT_CW;
          end loop;
          TEMP.NEXT_CW := R.TOP;
        end if;
      end POP;
```

e.
```
      procedure ROTATE_RING (R   : in out RING;
                             WAY : in      DIRECTION ) is
      -- Sets TOP to be the current TOP's successor if CLOCKWISE is
      -- specified or to the current TOP's predecessor if
      -- COUNTERCLOCKWISE direction is specified. MARK is not
      -- affected
      -- Exception EMPTY_RING raised if the ring is empty.
      begin
        if R.TOP = null then
          raise EMPTY_RING;
        elsif WAY = CLOCKWISE then
          R.TOP := R.TOP.NEXT_CW;
        else
          --must go all the way around because you can't back up
          for COUNT in 1..R.LENGTH-1 loop
            R.TOP := R.TOP.NEXT_CW;
          end loop;
        end if;
      end ROTATE_RING;
```

14.3.1 a.
```
      procedure POP ( R : in out RING ) is
      -- Deletes the item referenced by TOP. The new TOP item
      -- is the successor item of the previous TOP. The marked
      -- item is unaffected by the deletion unless the marked
      -- item is also deleted. In this case new marked item is the
      -- new TOP item. TOP and MARK are null if the ring is empty.
      -- Exception EMPTY_RING raised if the ring is empty.
      begin
        if R.TOP_USED = 0 then
          raise EMPTY_RING;
        else
          -- Shift to delete ITEM at TOP
          R.ITEM_ARRAY (R.TOP..R.TOP_USED-1) :=
                  R.ITEM_ARRAY (R.TOP+1..R.TOP_USED);
          -- If MARK'd item shifted, adjust MARK
          if R.MARK >= R.TOP then
            R.MARK := R.MARK - 1;
          end if;
```

```
            R.TOP_USED := R.TOP_USED - 1;
            -- If the ring is empty, adjust TOP and MARK
            if T.TOP_USED = 0 then
              R.TOP := 0;
              R.MARK := 0;
            end if;
          end if;
        end POP;
```

Chapter 15

15.1.1 a.
```
      function "+" (LEFT, RIGHT : VECTOR) return VECTOR is
        -- Returns a vector whose components are the sum of the
        -- corresponding components of LEFT and RIGHT.
        -- Exception INDEX_ERROR raised if LEFT'range or RIGHT'range are
        --            not both of the form 1..N
        ANSWER : VECTOR (LEFT'RANGE);
      begin
        if LEFT'first /= 1 or else RIGHT'first /= 1
                    or else LEFT'last /= RIGHT'last then
          raise INDEX_ERROR;
        else
          for INDEX in LEFT'range loop
            ANSWER(INDEX) := LEFT(INDEX) + RIGHT(INDEX);
          end loop;
          return ANSWER;
        end if;
      end "+";
```
c.
```
      function "*" (SCALAR : float; M : MATRIX) return MATRIX is
        -- Returns a matrix whose components are a constant multiple of the
        -- corresponding components of M.
        -- Exception INDEX_ERROR raised if M'range(1) or M'range(2) are not
        --            of the form 1..N
        ANSWER : MATRIX (M'range(1), M'range(2));
      begin
        if M'first(1) /= 1 or else M'first(2) /= 1 then
          -- Note both M'last(1) and M'last(2) are both positive
          raise INDEX_ERROR;
        else
          for ROW_INDEX in M'range(1) loop
            for COL_INDEX in M'range(2) loop
              ANSWER (ROW_INDEX, COL_INDEX) :=
                          SCALAR * M(ROW_INDEX, COL_INDEX);
            end loop;
          end loop;
          return ANSWER;
        end if;
      end "*";
```
e.
```
      function "+" (LEFT, RIGHT : MATRIX) return MATRIX is
        -- Returns a matrix whose components are the sum of the
```

```
            -- corresponding components of LEFT and RIGHT.
            -- Exception INDEX_ERROR raised if LEFT'range(1) or LEFT'range(2)
            --          or RIGHT'range(1) or RIGHT'range(2) is not of the form
            --          or LEFT'last(1) does not equal Right'last(1)
            --          or LEFT'last(2) does not equal Right'last(2).
            ANSWER : MATRIX (LEFT'range(1), LEFT'range (2));
        begin
            if LEFT'first(1) /= 1 or else LEFT'first(2) /= 1 or else
              RIGHT'first(1) /= 1 or else RIGHT'first(2) /= 1 or else
              LEFT'last(1) /= RIGHT'last(1) or else
              LEFT'last(2) /= RIGHT'last(2) then
              raise INDEX_ERROR;
            else
              for ROW_INDEX in LEFT'range(1) loop
                for COL_INDEX in RIGHT'range(2) loop
                  ANSWER (ROW_INDEX,COL_INDEX) := LEFT (ROW_INDEX, COL_INDEX) +
                                                  RIGHT(ROW_INDEX, COL_INDEX);
                end loop;
              end loop;
              return ANSWER;
            end if;
        end "+";
```

15.2.1 a.
```
        function "*" (SCALAR : float; V : VECTOR) return VECTOR is
            -- Returns a vector whose components are a constant multiple of the
            -- corresponding components of V
            -- Exception INDEX_ERROR raised if V'range not of the form 1..N
            ANSWER : VECTOR (V'range);
        begin
            if V'first /= 1 then
              -- Since V'last is positive, it need not be checked.
              raise INDEX_ERROR;
            else
              for INDEX in V'range loop
                ANSWER (INDEX) := SCALAR * V(INDEX);
              end loop;
              return ANSWER;
            end if;
        end "*";
```

c.
```
        function "*" (LEFT, RIGHT : VECTOR) return float is
            -- Returns the dot product of two vectors LEFT and RIGHT.
            -- Exception INDEX_ERROR raised if LEFT'range or RIGHT'range are
            --          both not of the form 1..N
            ANSWER : float := 0.0;
        begin
            if LEFT'first /= 1 or else RIGHT'first /= 1
                    or else LEFT'last /= RIGHT'last then
              raise INDEX_ERROR;
            else
              for INDEX in LEFT'range loop
                ANSWER := ANSWER + LEFT(INDEX) * RIGHT(INDEX);
```

```
           end loop;
            return ANSWER;
          end if;
       end "*";
o.   procedure ADD_SCALAR_MUL_COL1_TO_COL2
                        ( M          : in out MATRIX;
                          SCALAR     : in float;
                          COL1, COL2 : in positive) is
     -- Multiplies every component in col1 by a constant and adds
     -- the result to the corresponding component in col2. No
     -- component in COL! is modified.
     -- Exception INDEX_ERROR is raised if M'range(1) is not of the form
     --          1..N or if COL1 and COL2 not in M'range(2).
     begin
       if M'first(1) /= 1 or else M'first(2) /= 1 or else
         COL1 > M'last(2) or else COL2 > M'last(2) then
         raise INDEX_ERROR;
       else
         for INDEX in M'range(1) loop
           M(INDEX,COL2) := M(INDEX,COL2) + SCALAR * M(INDEX,COL1);
         end loop;
       end if;
     end ADD_SCALAR_MUL_COL1_TO_COL2;
r.   procedure MAX_MATRIX_VAL_AND_LOC ( M        : in      MATRIX;
                                        MAX      :    out float;
                                        ROW, COL :    out positive) is
     TEMP_MAX : float := -float'LARGE;
     TEMP_ROW : positive := 1;
     TEMP_COL : positive := 1;
     begin
       if M'first(1) /= 1 or else M'first(2) /= 1 then
         raise INDEX_ERROR;
       else
         for ROW_INDEX in M'range(1) loop
           for COL_INDEX in M'range(2) loop
             if TEMP_MAX < M(ROW_INDEX, COL_INDEX) then
               TEMP_MAX  := M(ROW_INDEX, COL_INDEX);
               TEMP_ROW  : ROW_INDEX;
                TEMP_COL := COL_INDEX;
             end if;
           end loop;
         end loop;
       MAX := TEMP_MAX;
       ROW := TEMP_ROW;
       COL := TEMP_COL;
       end if;
     end MAX_MATRIX_VAL_AND_LOC;
t.  procedure MAX_MATRIX_COL_VAL_AND_LOC ( M        :  in MATRIX;
                                           MAX      :     out float;
                                           COL      :  in     positive;
```

```
                                    ROW      :   out positive) is
          TEMP_MAX : float := -float'LARGE;
          TEMP_ROW : positive := 1;
     begin
        if M'first(1) /= 1 or else M'first(2) /= 1 then
           raise INDEX_ERROR;
        else
           for INDEX in M'range(1) loop
              if TEMP_MAX < M(INDEX,COL) then
                 TEMP_MAX := M(INDEX,COL);
                 TEMP_ROW := INDEX;
              end if;
           end loop;
           MAX := TEMP_MAX;
           ROW := TEMP_ROW;
        end if;
     end MAX_MATRIX_COL_VAL_AND_LOC;
```

Chapter 16

16.3.1 c.
```
     function "*" (LEFT, RIGHT : VECTOR) return ITEM_TYPE is
        -- Returns the dot or vector product of two vectors. The dot
        -- product is the sum of products of components with the same
        -- index.
        ANSWER      : ITEM_TYPE :=ZERO_ITEM;
        NEXT_LEFT   : VECTOR    :=LEFT;
        NEXT_RIGHT  : VECTOR    := RIGHT;
     begin
        while (NEXT_LEFT /= null) and (NEXT_RIGHT /= null) loop
           if NEXT_LEFT.INDEX = NEXT_RIGHT.INDEX then
              ANSWER := ANSWER + LEFT.VALUE * RIGHT.VALUE;
              NEXT_LEFT := NEXT_LEFT.NEXT;
              NEXT_RIGHT := NEXT_RIGHT.NEXT;
           elsif NEXT_LEFT.INDEX < NEXT_RIGHT.INDEX then
              NEXT_LEFT := NEXT_LEFT.NEXT;
           else
              NEXT_RIGHT := NEXT_RIGHT.NEXT;
           end if;
        end loop;
        return ANSWER;
     end "*";
```
f.
```
     function "*" (M : MATRIX; V : VECTOR) return VECTOR is
        -- Returns a vector equal to M*V
        -- Exception OVERFLOW raised if there is not enough memory to
        --          complete this operation
        ANSWER : VECTOR;
        TEMP_M_ROW : NEXT_NODE;
        TEMP_V     : VECTOR;
        TEMP_VALUE : ITEM_TYPE;
     begin
```

```
          for M_ROW_INDEX in positive range 1..MAXIMUM_INDEX loop
            TEMP_M_ROW := M.ROW_LIST (M_ROW_INDEX);
            TEMP_V     := V;
            while TEMP_M_ROW /= null and TEMP_V /= null loop
              if TEMP_M_ROW.COL = TEMP_V.INDEX then
                TEMP_VALUE := TEMP_VALUE + TEMP_M_ROW.VALUE * TEMP_V.VALUE;
                TEMP_M_ROW := TEMP_M_ROW.NEXT_COL;
                TEMP_V := TEMP_V.NEXT;
              elsif TEMP_M_ROW.COL < TEMP_V.INDEX then
                TEMP_M_ROW := TEMP_M_ROW.NEXT_COL;
              else
                TEMP_V := TEMP_V.NEXT;
              end if;
            end loop;
            if TEMP_VALUE /= ZERO_ITEM then
              ADD_VECTOR_ELEMENT (ANSWER, TEMP_VALUE, M_ROW_INDEX);
            end if;
          end loop;
          return ANSWER;
        exception
          when OVERFLOW => raise OVERFLOW;
        end "*";
```

g.
```
   procedure CLEAR_VECTOR ( V : in out VECTOR) is
      -- Returns a sparse vector with no VECTOR_NODEs
   begin
      v := null;
   end CLEAR_VECTOR;
```

i.
```
   function GET_VECTOR_ELEMENT(V : VECTOR; INDEX : positive)
                         return ITEM_TYPE is
      -- Returns the value of V(INDEX) if it is in V or ZERO_ITEM
      -- otherwise
      -- Exception INDEX_ERROR raised if INDEX > MAXIMUM_INDEX
      TEMP_V : VECTOR := V;
   begin
      if INDEX > MAXIMUM_INDEX then
        raise INDEX_ERROR;
      else
        while TEMP_V /= null loop
          if TEMP_V.INDEX = INDEX then
            return TEMP_V.VALUE;
          elsif INDEX < TEMP_V.INDEX then
            return ZERO_ITEM;
          else
            TEMP_V := TEMP_V.NEXT;
          end if;
        end loop;
        return ZERO_ITEM;
      end if;
   end GET_VECTOR_ELEMENT;
```

Index

A

Abstract data type (ADT), 2, 104–105, 562–66
    ADTs in this Book, 569–71
    balking queue ADT, 171–76
    binary tree ADT, 205–16
    binary search tree ADT, 216–57
    complex ADT, 53, 55, 67
    deque ADT, 170–71
    digraph ADT, 319–78
    encapsulation, 70–72
    graph ADT, 319–78 (*See also* Digraph ADT,
        Breadth first search, Depth first search,
        Transition graph ADT)
    list ADT, 107–18
        validation program 579–84
    matrix Vector Operations ADT, 515–61
    priority queue ADT, 176–83
    queue ADT, 104, 153–201
    rational number ADT, 73
    ring ADT, 492–514
    search tables ADT, 401–48
    set ADT, 301–18
    stack ADT, 119, 121–51
    strings ADT, 444–91
    trees ADT, 202–300
    transition graph ADT, 351–55
    weighted graph ADT, 347–50
Access, 26–50
    .all, 28
    declaration of, 26
        with discriminant, 28
    dynamic, 31–33
    exceptions, 43–45
    incomplete type definition, 33
    new operator, 27
    null, 27
Ada;
    access types, 26–50
    array, 11, 14
        attributes, 15
        constrained, 11
        unconstrained, 11
    attributes, 15
    exception, 20–23, 43–50
    generic packages (*See* generics, packages)
    generic subroutines, 56–63
    operators (*See also* type)
        mod, 6
        new, 27

storage_error, 43
        rem, 6
        exponentation, 7
        overloaded, 9, 105, 140
        precedence, 9
    parameters
        mode
    private types, 66–70
    record types, 18–19
ADD_CHILD_TO_ROOT operation;
    tree, 210, 211
ADD_TRANSION operation;
    transition graph, 353
ADD_EDGE operation;
    graph, 324, 326, 336
    weighted digraph, 347
ADD_ELEMENT operation;
    set, 303, 305, 307
ADD_ITEM operation;
    ring, 494, 495, 502
ADD_ITEM_TO_HEAD operation;
    list, 108, 109, 115
ADD_ITEM_TO_REAR operation;
    list, 108, 109, 115
ADD_SUBTREE_TO_ROOT operation;
    tree, 210, 211
ADD_TO_Q operation;
    priority balking queue, 182
    priority queue, 180, 288
ADD_VERTEX operation;
    graph, 334, 337
ADT (*See* Abstract Data Type)
Algorithm, 2
    binary search, 408
    Boyer Moore pattern matching, 468–69
    breadth first maze search, 371–74
    brute force pattern matching, 464
    bubble sort, 380–82
    Caesar cipher, 477–78
    combination, 575–76
    COMPUTE_PATH_GRAPH, 328
    depth first maze search, 357
    depth first search, 139
    Dijkstra's algorithm, 349–50
    Euclid's algorithm, 73
    evaluation postfix expression 148
    exchange sort, 380–82
    expression evaluation, 149
    factorial, 82, 136–37
    Fibbonacci, 90, 95

GREATER operation;
  string, 448, 450, 456

H

Hashing;
  cluster, 412
  collision resolution, 410, 412
    double hashing, 413
    linear probing, 412
    prime probing, 413, 416
    quadratic probling, 413
  functions, 410–13
    folding, 411–12
    mid-square, 411
    requirements for, 410–11
    string, 410
  synonyms, 410
HEAD_OF_LIST operation;
  list, 108, 109, 115
Heap sort, 389–92
Height balanced tree, 232–33
High precision integer operations;
  using list ADT, 140–42
  using ring ADT, 505–8
  using priority balking queue ADT, 186
  using string ADT, 472–75

I

INFIX notation, 140
Information hiding, 105
Inorder traversal;
  bounded tree, 253
  bounded trie 279–81
  unbounded tree, 137, 218, 220, 253
INSERT operation;
  array based search table, 403, 405
  b-tree, 259–60
  closed hash table 403, 414
  open hash table, 403, 420
  string, 447, 450, 455
  tree, 218, 220, 241–43, 253
  trie, 279–80
Instantiation, (See also generic) 65, 114
Internal sorts (See Sort)
INTERSECTION operation;
  set, 302, 303, 305, 308

Iterator, 155 (*See also* NEXT_DESTINATION
  VERTEX, NEXT_SOURCE_VERTEX,
  NEXT_ELEMENT, NEXT_INORDER,
  NEXT_POSTORDER, NEXT_PRE-
  ORDER, NEXT_Q_OBJECT, NEXT
  STATE, LIST_NEXT_KEY_DATA,
  Traversal)

J

Jacobi Method, 532–33

K

KEY_AT_POSITION_ON_Q operator;
  balking queue, 174
  priority balking queue, 182
KEY_IN_B_TREE operation;
  b-tree, 259–60
KEY_IN_TABLE operation;
  array based search table, 404, 405
  closed hash table 404, 415
  open hash table, 404, 420
KEY_IN_TREE operation;
  tree, 218, 220, 253
KEY_IN_TRIE operation;
  trie, 279, 281
KEY_POSITION_ON_Q operation;
  balking queue, 173
  priority balking queue, 182

L

Leaf, 200 (*See also* tree)
LENGTH operation;
  balking queue, 174
  deque, 171, 510
  list, 108, 109, 115
  priority balking queue, 182
  priority queue, 180, 288
  queue, 154, 157, 164
  ring, 494, 496, 502
  string, 448, 450, 456
LESS operation;
  string, 448, 450, 456
Level of a node, 202–3 (*See also* node)
Lexiographic tree (*See* ADT, Trie; Trie)